Ike and Winston

Also by Jonathan W. Jordan

American Warlords: How Roosevelt's High Command Led America to Victory in World War II

Brothers, Rivals, Victors: Eisenhower, Patton, Bradley, and the Partnership That Drove the Allied Conquest in Europe

Lone Star Navy: Texas, the Fight for the Gulf of Mexico, and the Shaping of the American West

AS COAUTHOR

The War Queens: Extraordinary Women Who Ruled the Battlefield

AS EDITOR

To the People of Texas, an Appeal: In Vindication of His Conduct of the Navy by Commodore Edwin Ward Moore

Ike and Winston

WORLD WAR, COLD WAR, AND AN EXTRAORDINARY FRIENDSHIP

JONATHAN W. JORDAN

DUTTON

DUTTON

An imprint of Penguin Random House LLC
1745 Broadway, New York, NY 10019
penguinrandomhouse.com

Interior art: UK Lion © designer1088 / Shutterstock
Maps by David Lindroth Inc.

LIBRARY OF CONGRESS CATALOGING-IN-PUBLICATION DATA

has been applied for.

ISBN 9780593473139 (hardcover)
ISBN 9780593473146 (ebook)

Printed in the United States of America
3rd Printing

The authorized representative in the EU for product safety and compliance is Penguin Random House Ireland, Morrison Chambers, 32 Nassau Street, Dublin D02 YH68, Ireland, https://eu-contact.penguin.ie.

To Galina

CONTENTS

PART THREE: WATERLOO SUNSET

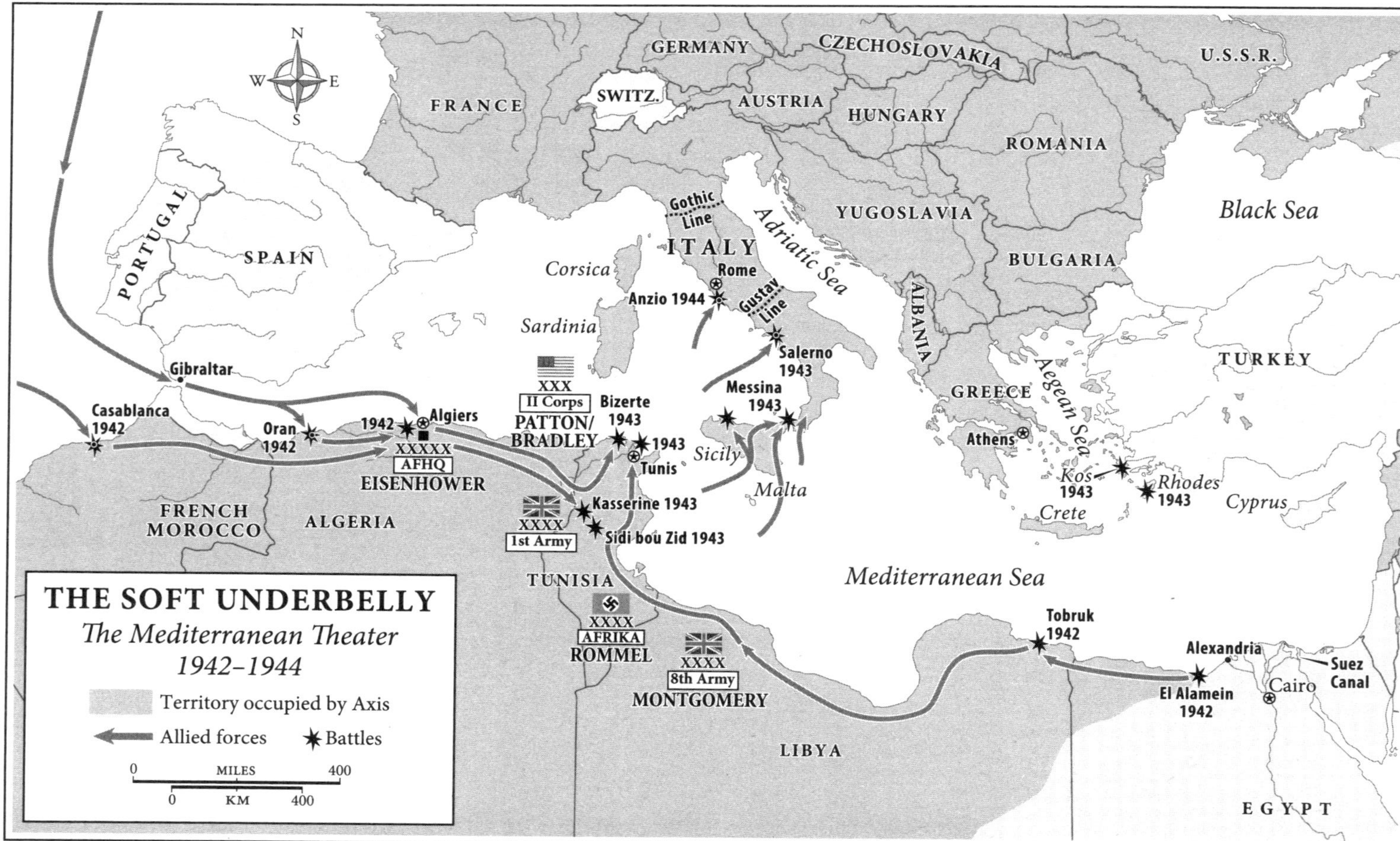

THE SOFT UNDERBELLY
The Mediterranean Theater
1942–1944
Territory occupied by Axis
Allied forces
Battles
0 MILES 400
0 KM 400
N
W
E
S
FRANCE
GERMANY
SWITZ.
AUSTRIA
CZECHOSLOVAKIA
HUNGARY
ROMANIA
U.S.S.R.
Black Sea
YUGOSLAVIA
BULGARIA
ALBANIA
GREECE
TURKEY
Aegean Sea
Adriatic Sea
PORTUGAL
SPAIN
Corsica
Sardinia
Gothic Line
ITALY
Rome
Anzio 1944
Gustav Line
Salerno 1943
Messina 1943
Sicily
Malta
Athens
Kos 1943
Rhodes 1943
Crete
Cyprus
Gibraltar
Casablanca 1942
Oran 1942
1942
Algiers
XXXXX
AFHQ
EISENHOWER
XXX
II Corps
PATTON/
BRADLEY
Bizerte 1943
1943
Tunis
Kasserine 1943
Sidi bou Zid 1943
XXXX
1st Army
FRENCH MOROCCO
ALGERIA
TUNISIA
XXXX
AFRIKA
ROMMEL
XXXX
8th Army
MONTGOMERY
LIBYA
Mediterranean Sea
Tobruk 1942
Alexandria
El Alamein 1942
Cairo
Suez Canal
EGYPT

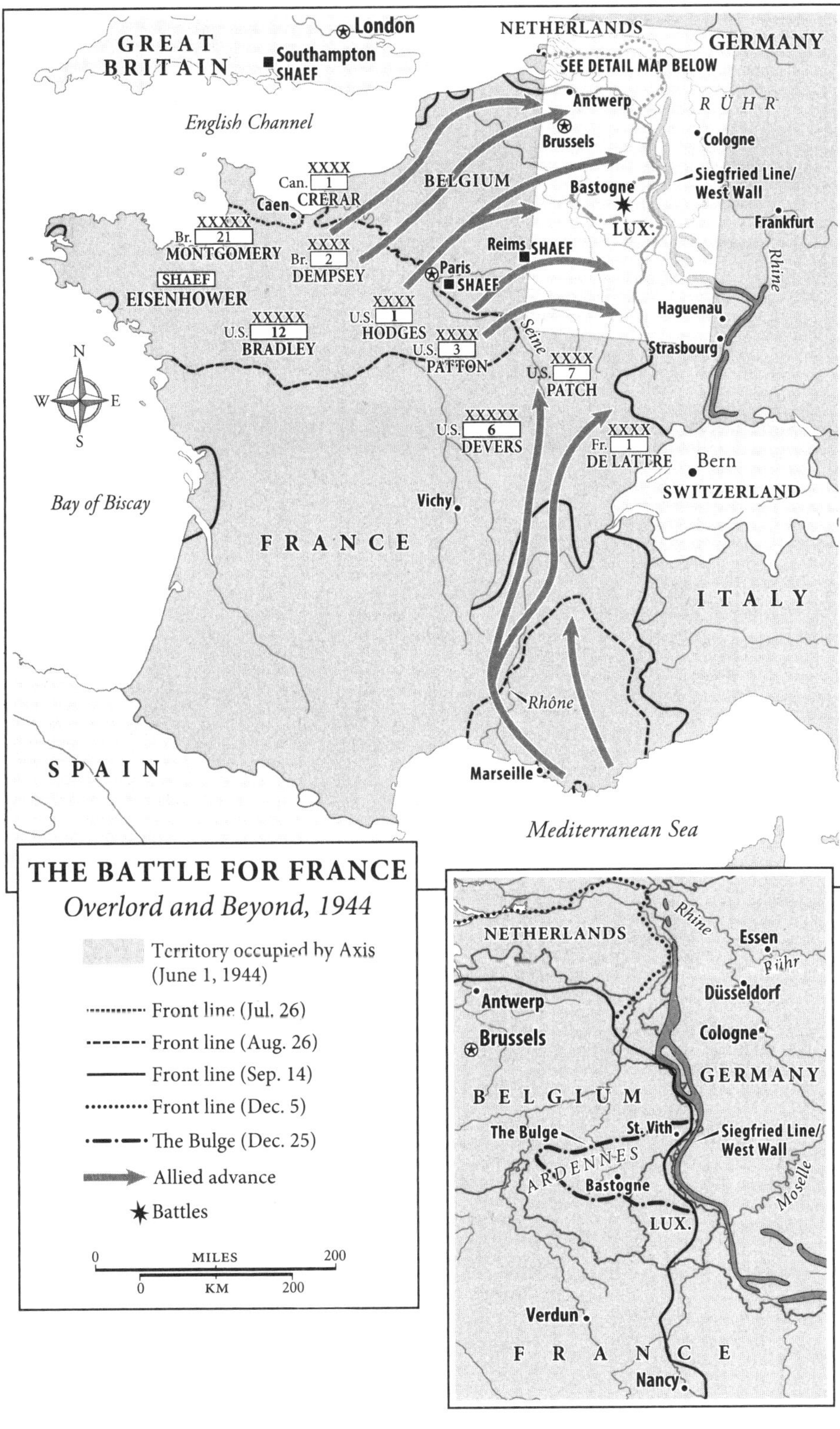

THE BATTLE FOR FRANCE
Overlord and Beyond, 1944
Territory occupied by Axis (June 1, 1944)
Front line (Jul. 26)
Front line (Aug. 26)
Front line (Sep. 14)
Front line (Dec. 5)
The Bulge (Dec. 25)
Allied advance
Battles
0 MILES 200
0 KM 200
GREAT BRITAIN
London
Southampton SHAEF
English Channel
NETHERLANDS
GERMANY
SEE DETAIL MAP BELOW
Antwerp
RÜHR
Brussels
Cologne
BELGIUM
Siegfried Line/ West Wall
Bastogne
LUX.
Frankfurt
Rhine
Caen
XXXX Can. 1 CRERAR
XXXXX Br. 21 MONTGOMERY
XXXX Br. 2 DEMPSEY
SHAEF EISENHOWER
Reims SHAEF
Paris
SHAEF
XXXXX U.S. 12 BRADLEY
XXXX U.S. 1 HODGES
XXXX U.S. 3 PATTON
Seine
XXXX U.S. 7 PATCH
Haguenau
Strasbourg
XXXXX U.S. 6 DEVERS
XXXX Fr. 1 DE LATTRE
Bern
SWITZERLAND
N
W
E
S
Bay of Biscay
Vichy
FRANCE
ITALY
Rhône
SPAIN
Marseille
Mediterranean Sea
NETHERLANDS
Rhine
Essen
Rühr
Düsseldorf
Antwerp
Brussels
Cologne
GERMANY
BELGIUM
The Bulge
St. Vith
Siegfried Line/ West Wall
ARDENNES
Bastogne
Moselle
LUX.
Verdun
FRANCE
Nancy

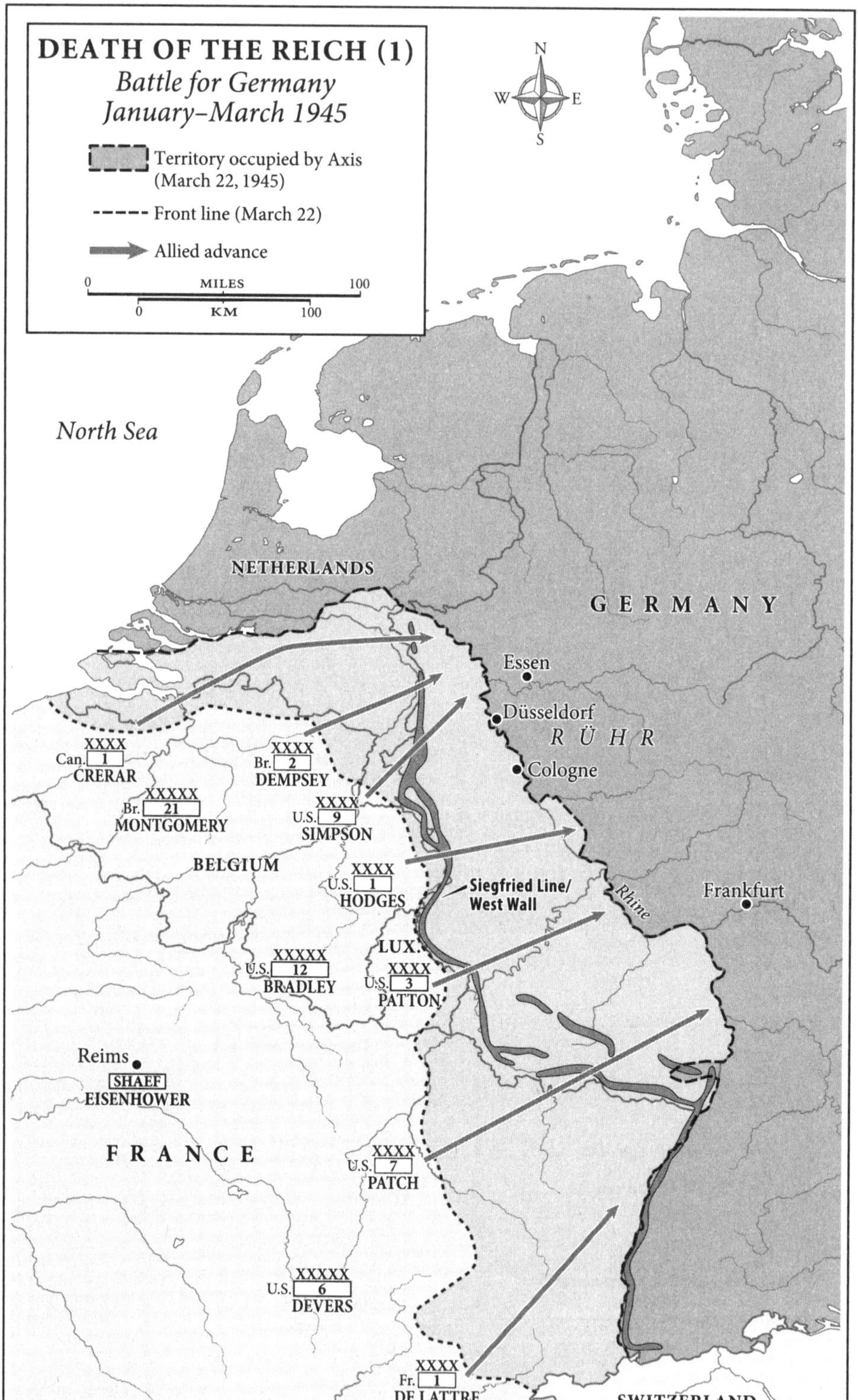

DEATH OF THE REICH (1)
Battle for Germany
January–March 1945
Territory occupied by Axis (March 22, 1945)
Front line (March 22)
Allied advance
0 MILES 100
0 KM 100
N
S
E
W
North Sea
NETHERLANDS
GERMANY
Essen
Düsseldorf
RÜHR
Cologne
Frankfurt
Rhine
Siegfried Line/ West Wall
BELGIUM
LUX.
FRANCE
SWITZERLAND
Reims
SHAEF
EISENHOWER
XXXX Can. 1 CRERAR
XXXXX Br. 21 MONTGOMERY
XXXX Br. 2 DEMPSEY
XXXX U.S. 9 SIMPSON
XXXX U.S. 1 HODGES
XXXXX U.S. 12 BRADLEY
XXXX U.S. 3 PATTON
XXXX U.S. 7 PATCH
XXXXX U.S. 6 DEVERS
XXXX Fr. 1 DE LATTRE

DEATH OF THE REICH (2)
Battle for Germany
March–April 1945
Front line (March 22)
Front line (April 5)
Allied advance
0 MILES 100
0 KM 100
DENMARK
North Sea
N
W
E
S
NETHERLANDS
GERMANY
XXXX
Br. 2
DEMPSEY
XXXX
U.S. 9
SIMPSON
XXXX
CAN. 1
CRERAR
Essen
Düsseldorf
RÜHR
Cologne
XXXX
U.S. 1
HODGES
XXXXX
Br. 21
MONTGOMERY
XXXX
U.S. 15
GEROW
XXXX
U.S. 3
PATTON
BELGIUM
XXXXX
U.S. 12
BRADLEY
Frankfurt
Rhine
XXXX
U.S. 7
PATCH
LUX.
Reims
SHAEF
EISENHOWER
XXXXX
U.S. 6
DEVERS
XXXX
Fr. 1
DE LATTRE
FRANCE
SWITZERLAND

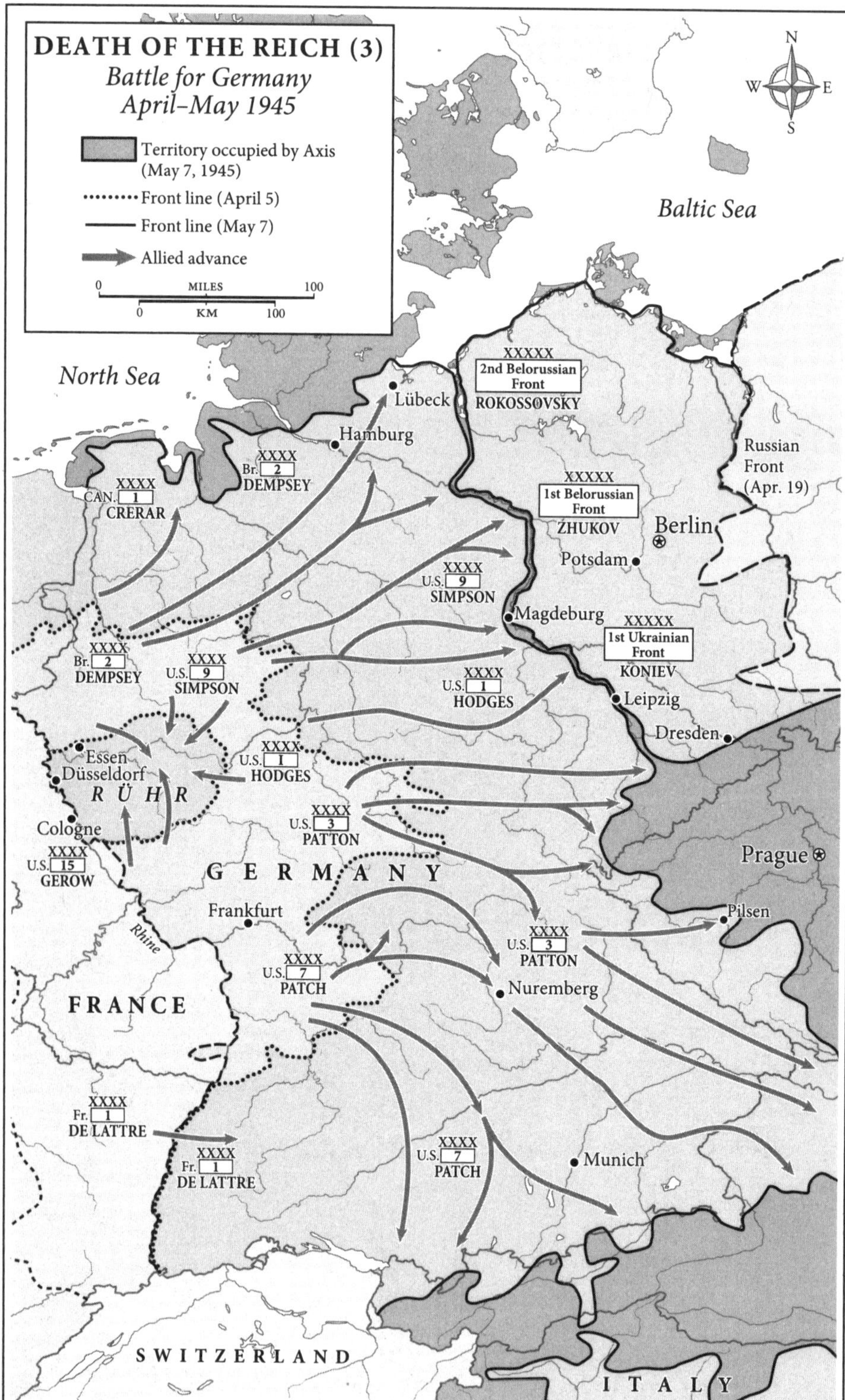

DEATH OF THE REICH (3)
Battle for Germany
April–May 1945
Territory occupied by Axis (May 7, 1945)
Front line (April 5)
Front line (May 7)
Allied advance
0 MILES 100
0 KM 100
N
W
E
S
Baltic Sea
North Sea
Lübeck
Hamburg
XXXXX 2nd Belorussian Front ROKOSSOVSKY
XXXXX 1st Belorussian Front ZHUKOV
XXXXX 1st Ukrainian Front KONIEV
Russian Front (Apr. 19)
Berlin
Potsdam
Magdeburg
Leipzig
Dresden
Prague
Pilsen
XXXX Br. 2 DEMPSEY
XXXX CAN. 1 CRERAR
XXXX U.S. 9 SIMPSON
XXXX U.S. 1 HODGES
XXXX U.S. 3 PATTON
XXXX U.S. 15 GEROW
XXXX U.S. 7 PATCH
XXXX Fr. 1 DE LATTRE
Essen
Düsseldorf
RÜHR
Cologne
GERMANY
Frankfurt
Rhine
Nuremberg
Munich
FRANCE
SWITZERLAND
ITALY

THE IRON CURTAIN
Iron Curtain
Austrian Occupation
0 MILES 400
0 METERS 400
N
W
E
S
FINLAND
NORWAY
SWEDEN
North Sea
Baltic Sea
Moscow
DENMARK
UNITED KINGDOM
SOVIET UNION
NETH.
Berlin
POLAND
EAST GERMANY
Warsaw
BELG.
Prague
LUX.
WEST GERMANY
CZECHOSLOVAKIA
FRANCE
SWITZ.
AUSTRIA
Budapest
HUNGARY
ROMANIA
Belgrade
Bucharest
Black Sea
SPAIN
YUGOSLAVIA
BULGARIA
Sofia
Tiranë
ITALY
ALB.
TURKEY
Mediterranean Sea
GREECE

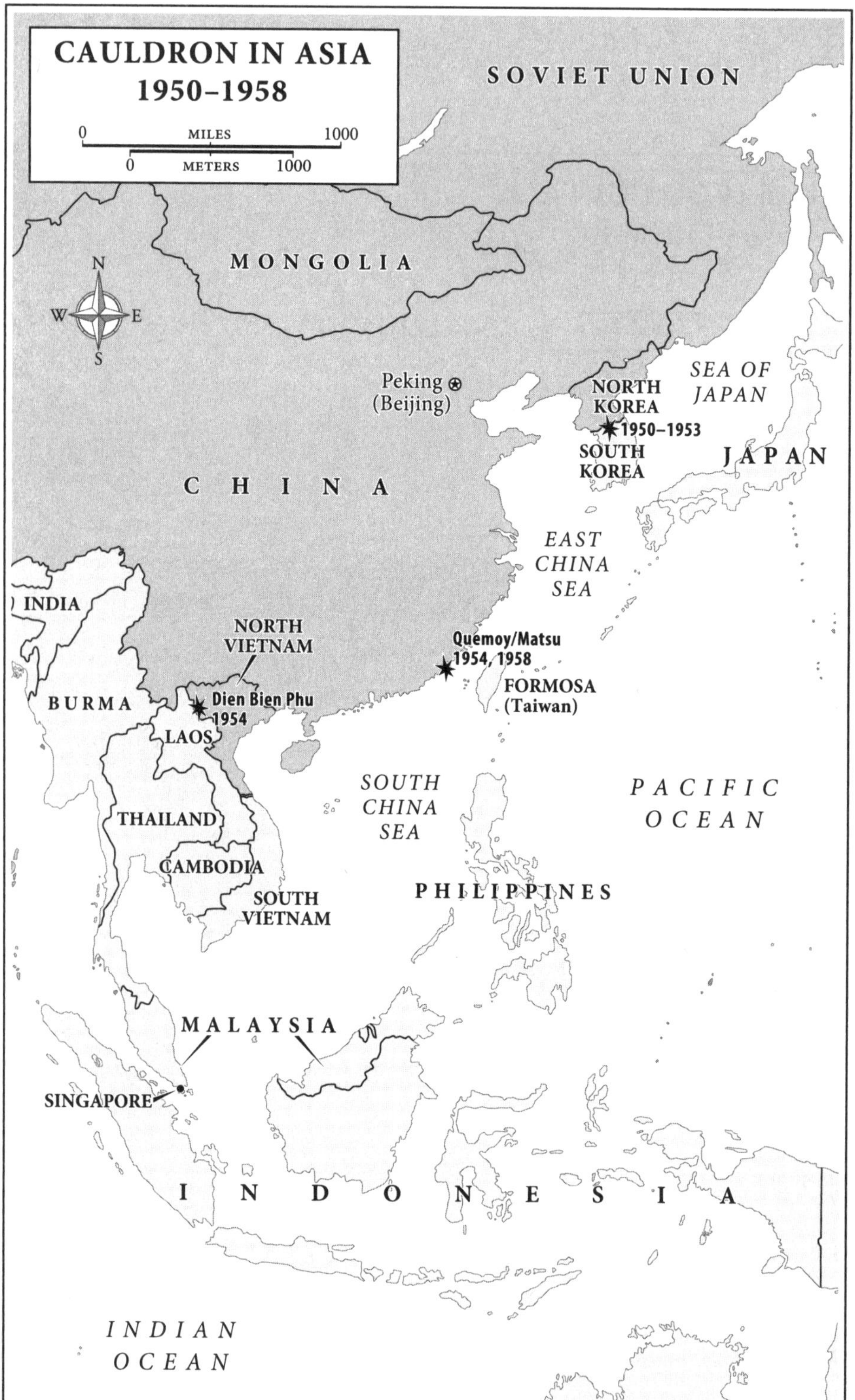
CAULDRON IN ASIA
1950–1958
0 MILES 1000
0 METERS 1000
SOVIET UNION
MONGOLIA
N
W
E
S
Peking
(Beijing)
NORTH
KOREA
1950–1953
SOUTH
KOREA
SEA OF
JAPAN
JAPAN
CHINA
EAST
CHINA
SEA
INDIA
NORTH
VIETNAM
Quemoy/Matsu
1954, 1958
FORMOSA
(Taiwan)
BURMA
Dien Bien Phu
1954
LAOS
SOUTH
CHINA
SEA
PACIFIC
OCEAN
THAILAND
CAMBODIA
SOUTH
VIETNAM
PHILIPPINES
MALAYSIA
SINGAPORE
INDONESIA
INDIAN
OCEAN

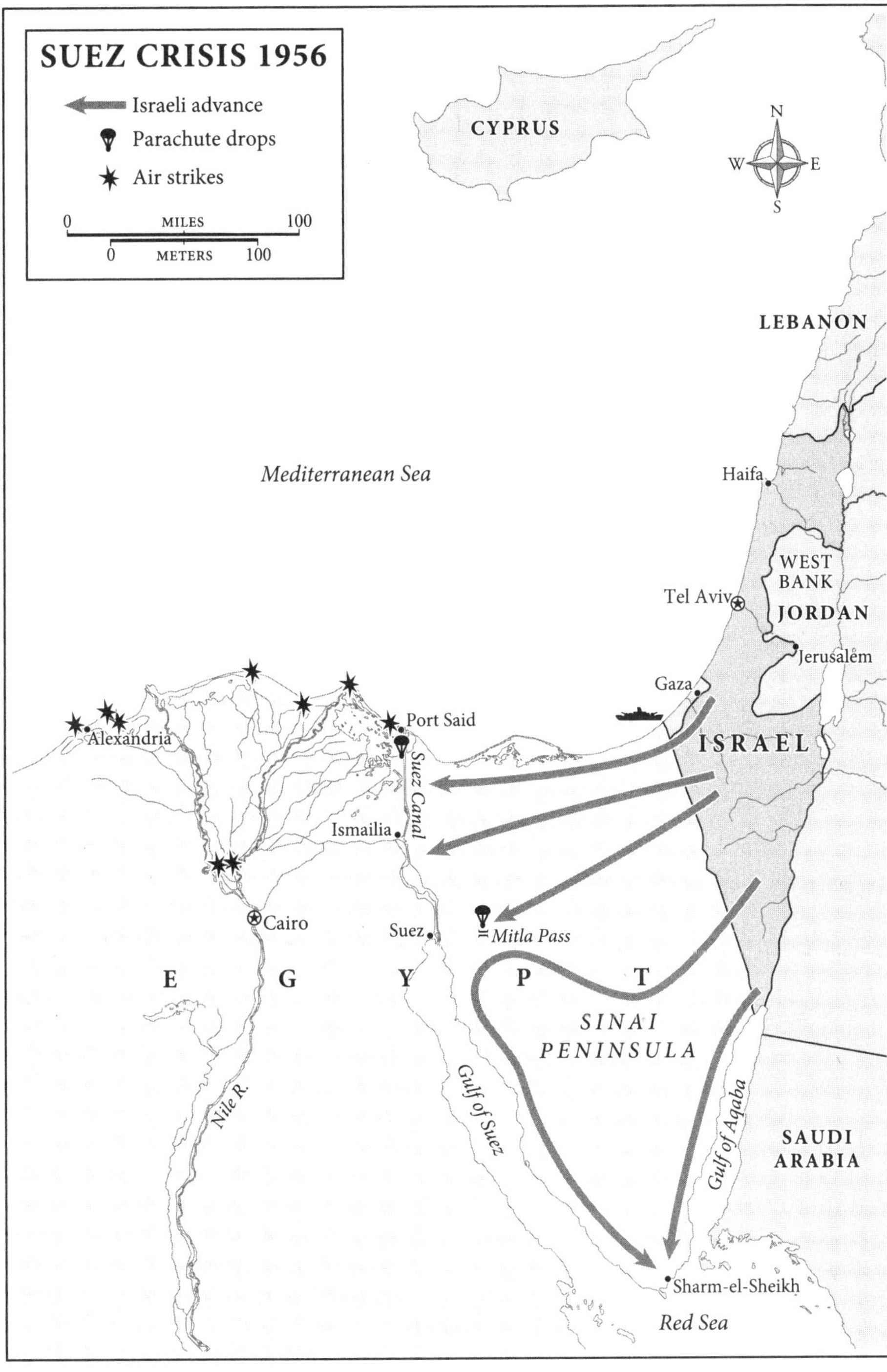

SUEZ CRISIS 1956
Israeli advance
Parachute drops
Air strikes
0
MILES
100
0
METERS
100
CYPRUS
N
W
E
S
LEBANON
Mediterranean Sea
Haifa
WEST
BANK
Tel Aviv
JORDAN
Jerusalem
Gaza
Port Said
Alexandria
ISRAEL
Suez Canal
Ismailia
Cairo
Suez
Mitla Pass
E G Y P T
SINAI
PENINSULA
Nile R.
Gulf of Suez
Gulf of Aqaba
SAUDI
ARABIA
Sharm-el-Sheikh
Red Sea

INTRODUCTION

TWO SUPERPOWERS. Two friends. Different visions.

Winston Leonard Spencer Churchill, born in the baroque splendor of Blenheim Palace, won his spurs fighting for Queen Victoria. In those swashbuckling years of Kipling and Rule Britannia, a young Dwight David Eisenhower, son of a poor Kansas pacifist, was learning to play stickball on the wrong side of Abilene's train tracks.

When Churchill's books filled shelves and his words rang through Parliament, "Ike" Eisenhower was fistfighting bullies and throwing fastballs. As First Lord of the Admiralty, Churchill laid plans for an invasion of Turkey, while Ike, a mediocre West Point cadet, crammed for exams. Churchill shaped the course of the Great War; Ike missed it.

By the time they shook hands, Churchill was a legend—a Teddy Roosevelt, Leonidas, and Green Hornet rolled into one. Eisenhower was a balding, middle-aged desk officer writing papers for men who mattered. Talented, but with no honest reason to think his story would be remembered, much less retold.

Through three years of war they marched together, each man stepping to a different cadence. Eisenhower found his rhythm quickly. He climbed onto the stage after the disasters of 1940 and 1941. He never had to beg an ally for weapons or break news of defeat to his countrymen.

From North Africa to Sicily, to Italy, to France, to the heart of the Third Reich, his armies conquered and his legend grew. "Divine Destiny," his friend George Patton called him in moments of envy. Divine or not, destiny seemed to back him.

For Churchill, the road to Berlin was pitted with potholes and broken axles. The fall of France, the evacuation of Dunkirk, the Blitz. Singapore, Tobruk, Dieppe, buzz bombs, a bridge too far—Churchill fought off everything three dictators could throw at him. Head down, shoulders back, he bulled his way forward, wincing but never flinching. Clinging to an abiding faith that if the English-speaking people stood together, the world would turn out all right.

As the Nazi empire cracked and crumbled, Churchill and Eisenhower argued, sweated, and gave the struggle everything they had. And in the glint of daylight lying between battles and planning conferences, a friendship took root.

Seven years after Hitler's death, Churchill climbed the mountain again. In the dawn of thermonuclear terror, he found himself leading Britain down another rocky path. The Empire's great dominions had broken away, tumbling into the chaos of self-rule. Britannia, still powerful, still proud, scrambled to find its footing in a world of missiles, ideologies, and a cold war poised to become hot. Through his Indian summer premiership, Churchill would shepherd his beloved nation as it slid down the mountain's reverse slope, digging his heels into the scree to arrest its slide.

Across the ocean, Eisenhower's path, like America's, led upward. The grinning face over the slogan "I Like Ike" rode a tide driven by the almighty dollar, amber waves of grain, the hydrogen bomb, and an abiding faith in American exceptionalism. Emerging from isolation, the United States took its place as the free world's paladin.

The American advance collided with an English retreat, leaving two old friends to navigate an uneasy power exchange. Eisenhower, the cold-blooded realist, contemplated nuclear holocaust while Churchill struggled to pull his friend from the brink. Churchill, a romantic at heart, gripped fraying imperial ties as Eisenhower urged him to embrace a postcolonial world. And after Churchill retired, the genial general would take a sledgehammer to what remained of the British Empire—leaving his old comrade to help pick up the shards of a once special relationship.

The glue binding one of history's most pivotal friendships was an extraordinary personal rapport, leavened with shared values and shared hardships. Ike relished Churchill's company because he saw a great man—a diamond with visible flaws, to be sure, but a diamond so large, so lustrous, that even with blemishes it outshone everything in the box.

Churchill could have had his pick of friendships, but he wanted Ike's. In the beginning, he courted Ike for what Ike offered Britain. The Kansan held the trust of men like Franklin Roosevelt and George C. Marshall. This influence gave Ike the power to destroy or create—and Ike had the gambler's nerve to use that power. London needed a friend like that.

But over time, the relationship became more than transactional. By war's end, Churchill valued Ike's friendship simply because he liked Ike. He liked him for who he was, not just for what he could do for Britain.

Through thirteen years of power and command, war clouds would gather and fade, tyrants would rise and fall, and the *ancien régime* would give way to a new and dangerous order. Through arguments over Berlin and bombers, summits and Stalin, détente and de Gaulle, they struggled to keep their friendship alive while serving countries with starkly different visions of what the world should be.

Could any friendship survive these blows? Would the chain break when duty pulled them in different directions? Could Eisenhower, the junior man, learn to lead without leaving his mentor and friend behind?

These were questions two men who knew each other as "Ike" and "Winston" would spend their years in power answering.

PROLOGUE

Forty Thousand Dead Frenchmen

APRIL 1944
20 GROSVENOR SQUARE
LONDON

When Ike closed his eyes, he could see the invasion's opening minutes. Thousands of ships bobbing off Normandy's coast—some beached, others waiting to belly up to blood-streaked sand. Swarms of men crawling over pockmarked dunes, fighting, running, dying to make room for the second and third waves. By D-day's end, the dagger's tip would be lodged in the ribs of Hitler's Fortress Europe.

Yet the glass was dark, and Ike couldn't see far enough to know what the third or fourth or fifth day would bring. He only knew this: Desperate fighting lay ahead as Rommel threw everything he had at them. For seventy-two hours, the lives of men he had ordered onto Normandy's beaches would hang in the balance.

The future of Europe had clotted into a brutal calculus of motion and mass. The Germans had fifty-one divisions in the west, and dozens more lurking beyond the Rhine. If Hitler could fling more than twelve mobile divisions against Ike's struggling invaders, they might be pushed into the sea.

Stopping those panzers before they reached the beach was the key to victory. Nothing else mattered.

Cigarette between his fingers, Ike sat back and stared at a map, his blue eyes locking on the spiderweb of French railroad lines. The Germans required a hundred trains a day to supply their armies in France—and more to bring in reinforcements. If the western allies could hurl every bomber at those rail centers in the weeks leading up to the invasion, they might slice those steel arteries. Rommel's reinforcements would be frozen as the Allies poured men and machines onto French soil. Cut off from help, the German defenders would die where they stood.

There was one problem: the political bosses in London. Bombing French rail yards meant bombing the Frenchmen who worked them. It meant obliterating wives and children living nearby or caught in the crossfire of short drops and near misses. No politician wanted his name under a front-page headline next to a picture of dead French children.

Ike had to win over His Majesty's Government to get those bombers flying. And to do that, there was one man he had to persuade.

So on a cloudy April afternoon, in his neatly pressed uniform, Dwight Eisenhower pulled up a chair and faced the prime minister of the United Kingdom, Winston Spencer Churchill.[1]

The Englishman read Ike's proposal with a mix of sympathy and horror. Hardwired for war, Churchill knew Ike's "Transportation Plan" was a decent tactical idea, one that probably would improve the invasion's prospects. But he saw a problem General Eisenhower overlooked.

The American was peering through the narrow lens of a soldier—a lens Churchill had worn many years ago, when he chased glory fighting for Queen Victoria. But in the decades since, he had mastered the black arts of journalism, politics, literature, history, and oratory. As a writer, he looked backward; as a leader, he faced the future. He had to imagine the war's aftershocks in ways the general did not.

He saw a river of blood as Lancaster and Fortress bombers rained death on Paris, Le Mans, Rouen, and three dozen other cities on Eisenhower's target list. Home Security had prepared an estimate predicting as many as 160,000 civilian casualties—with perhaps a quarter of that number killed. Forty thousand men, women, and children tossed into graves just to halt Hitler's trains for a few days.

Rarely in doubt, Churchill found himself struggling for the answer: Accept the deaths of innocents—or the deaths of liberators? Whose blood would minimize the body count?

Neither he nor Ike could foresee how the scales would balance. He knew one thing for certain, though. After war's end, after the Americans packed up and left, accounts would be settled. British responsibility for the deaths of French sons and daughters would be weighed from Brittany to Alsace. Churchill feared rekindling the ancient Gallic hatred toward England, a centuries-old flame that, reignited, could burn long after the bombers rusted in their boneyards.[2]

When the British War Cabinet had met to discuss the Transportation Plan, Churchill slouched in his chair, a puckered lower lip announcing his displeasure. A dying cigar jutted from his fist as he grilled the plan's senior advocate, Air Chief Marshal Sir Charles Portal. Why, he demanded, did an amphibious invasion require the sacrifice of forty thousand French civilians—weeks before the first Allied soldier landed?

The pipe-smoking Portal replied with clinical precision: Bombing rail stations offered the best way to isolate the landing beaches from German reinforcements. It would give the invading troops a better chance of establishing a foothold in Normandy. It would save the lives of men who would save the lives of a continent. It was a question of tolerating civilian deaths now to avoid intolerable military deaths later.[3]

Unsettled, Churchill left the meeting and dictated a letter for Eisenhower's eyes only.

> My dear General,
>
> The Cabinet today took a rather grave and on the whole adverse view of the proposal to bomb so many French railway centres, in view of the fact that scores of thousands of French civilians, men, women, and children, would lose their lives or be injured. Considering that they are our friends, this might be held to be an act of very great severity, bringing much hatred on the Allied Air Forces.[4]

As D-day drew near, Ike bent under war's weight. He worked sixteen-hour days, sucked down four packs of Chesterfields from dawn to dusk, and left blue clouds of "Goddamns" and "sonofabitches" in conference rooms and offices whenever he found something SNAFU'd, which was usually several times a day. In two months, a million men would set off on history's most complex amphibious invasion, and Ike's staff still hadn't ironed out hundreds of problems with de Gaulle and shipping, and airborne and logistics, and his damned landing ships and port capacity and who the hell knew what other screwups he'd find when the next memo landed on his desk.

In this maelstrom he turned over Churchill's letter. Ike liked and admired the old warhorse. For two years, Churchill had been a good-hearted comrade over a glass of whiskey or at the dinner table. In drawing room or conference room, Winston blended sentimentality, energy, eloquence, and vision.

But the spring of 1944 was no time for sentimentality or eloquence. It was a time for violence. Ike had been ordered to win the war, not craft the peace. He needed those bombers, and damned if he'd launch the Overlord invasion without them. If Churchill and the military chiefs wouldn't give him what he needed to win, he'd ask to be relieved of command and sent home.[5]

Desperate to keep those panzers off his men's backs, he pleaded his case to Churchill:

> My dear Prime Minister,
>
> I and my military advisors have become convinced that the bombing of these centers will increase our chances for success in the critical battle, and unless this could be proved to be an erroneous conclusion, I do not see how we can fail to proceed with the program. . . .
>
> The French People are now slaves. Only a successful Overlord can free them. No one has a greater stake in the success of that operation than have the French. . . . It would be sheer folly to abstain from doing anything that can increase in any measure our chances for success in Overlord.[6]

Winston liked Ike, and he understood the logic that had forced the Kansan to advocate such a ruthless tactic. At April's end, a frowning Churchill cautioned the War Cabinet, "General Eisenhower has an onerous responsibility, and care should be taken not to add to his burdens unnecessarily. Very great consequences might follow from interference with his plan on political grounds." But, he added, he had "not fully realized that our use of air power before Overlord would assume so cruel and remorseless a form. It was clear that great slaughter would inevitably result from the air attacks."[7]

In his heart, Winston Churchill was a romantic—an ancient cherub whose imagination and vision wove threads of hope and cruelty through the Empire's far-flung machine. His conscience told him he must do everything humanly possible to pare the butcher's bill, even if it meant risking the lives of soldiers on the beach. Even if it meant going over the head of his American friend and writing to President Roosevelt.

It was no longer a question of military tactics. It was a political problem that would shape Europe's future. That made it England's problem. *His* problem. And America's.

Roosevelt had sided with Churchill against the American generals before, and Winston hoped the president would order Ike to change his plans. If FDR backed Eisenhower's judgment, thousands of civilians would die. If he heeded Winston's warning, Ike's soldiers would face the German panzers.

He called for a stenographer.

"Prime Minister to President Roosevelt," he began.[8]

Ike and Winston

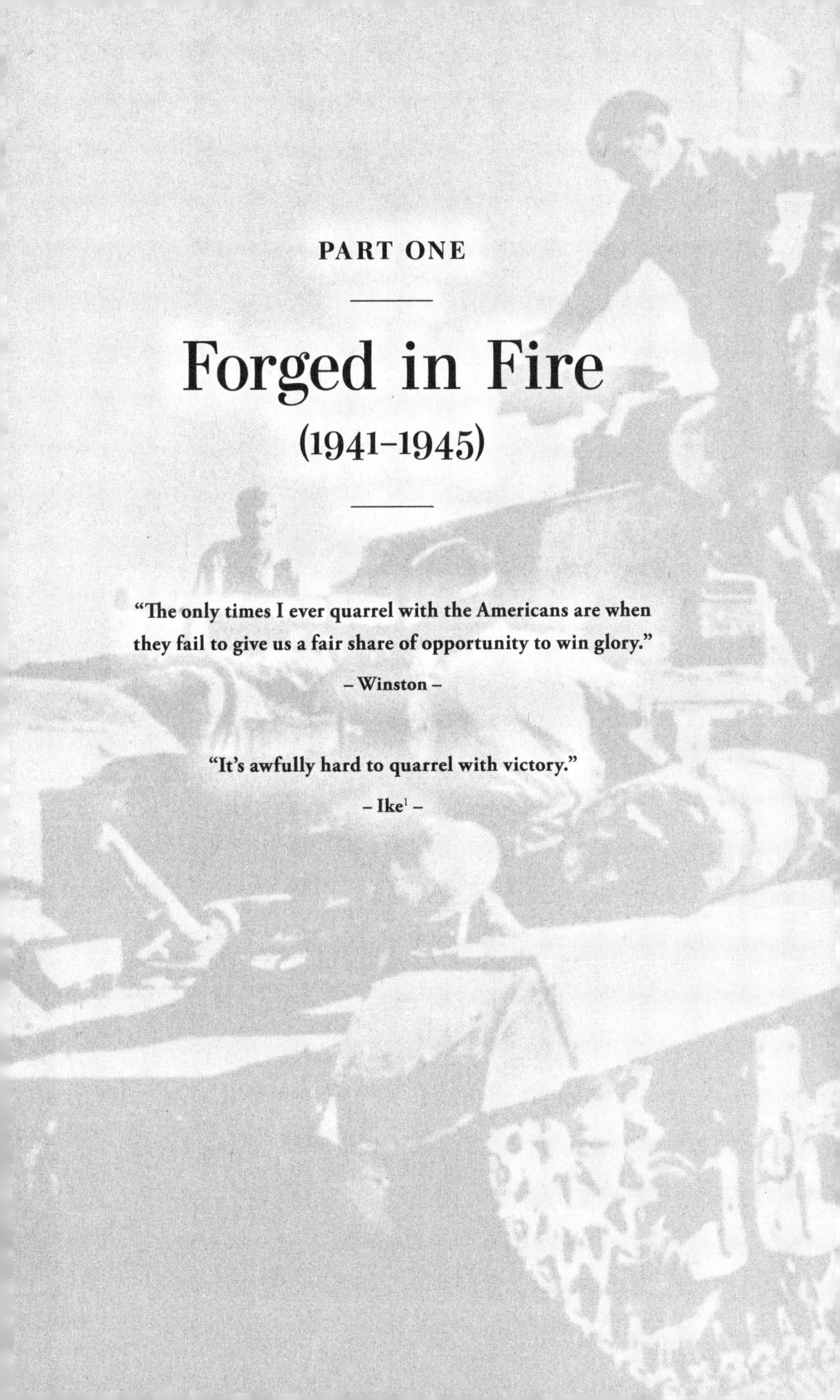

PART ONE

Forged in Fire

(1941–1945)

"The only times I ever quarrel with the Americans are when they fail to give us a fair share of opportunity to win glory."

– Winston –

"It's awfully hard to quarrel with victory."

– Ike[1] –

Operation Crusader

ONE

Winston Hours

IKE WASN'T SUPPOSED TO SAVE EUROPE. He was supposed to save MacArthur.

When the Chief summoned him to Washington five days after Pearl Harbor, he went in as the expert on the Philippines. He had sweated out that steamy outpost under General Douglas MacArthur for four frustrating years, and he knew the commonwealth's defenses better than any man stateside.

On the wrong side of 50, Dwight Eisenhower was a brigadier with no brigade. A staff officer pushing paper and sweating details. His command post was a government-issued desk and a wooden swivel chair in the old Munitions Building. His troops consisted of a few office workers and assistants.

It wasn't what he had signed up for. Ike longed for a real command, a field posting where he could sleep beneath the stars, feel the weight of a rifle in his hands, and fight battles, the way real soldiers do.

But the Army had other ideas. Too smart to put in front of a bullet, Ike had been kept stateside by the War Department during the First World War. For the next twenty years he'd been shuttled from one desk to another, where his job was to organize and plan. All the paperwork, none of the thrill.[1]

Now, in his cramped Washington office, Ike's mornings piled up, each a hangover from the night before. He ate little, slept less, and propped himself up with bad coffee and rationed cigarettes. His eyes hurt from squinting at memos and tables. He made calls, dictated reports, argued, cursed, and checked on the progress of progress until late into the night. The next day he'd get up, head buzzing, and roll a new boulder up the mountain.[2]

He had served just ten days of his sentence when an assistant to the secretary of war rang him up. The secretary, Henry L. Stimson, had just received a call from an aide to British Prime Minister Winston Churchill. The prime minister, in Washington for meetings with President Roosevelt, said he wanted to discuss the Philippines. Stimson asked Ike to accompany him to the White House in case details of air and ground forces came up.

With a "Yes, sir," Ike hung up his phone and barked orders. His staff yanked the latest information on the Philippines—garrison strength, reinforcements, supplies, convoys en route, bombers, the whole nine yards. Ike absorbed the data, rolled up a map of the archipelago, cinched his necktie, and prepared to meet the most famous man in the western world.

The famous man had trundled aboard HMS *Duke of York* eleven days earlier. Peacoat buttoned tight against December's gale, he saluted the ship's officers, bade goodbye to his daughter Mary, and paced the decks as his steel castle plowed the Atlantic.[3]

Walking the *Duke*'s passageways, he weighed the relative might of the two allies Pearl Harbor had thrown together. Before the war, Britain's arms had embraced the globe. From England, ships flying the Union Jack could sail to Gibraltar, Britain's rock guarding the Mediterranean's entrance. Gibraltar led to Malta, Britain's fortress in the central Mediterranean, and Malta led to the Suez Canal, Britain's door to the

Indian Ocean. From the Suez, troops, trade, and travelers could sail east to India, Britain's crown jewel, or press on to Burma or the island fortress of Singapore. Singapore led to Hong Kong, Britain's colonial gateway to China, and Hong Kong led to the Pacific Ocean, the Atlantic's Falkland Islands, and Britain's Caribbean possessions.

America's dominions were built on dollars, not weapons or ideology. A nation of shopkeepers: Great Power in wealth, naive in outlook, embarrassingly short of arms and men. For all her coiled-spring potential, the United States lacked the breadth of view, the international connections, and the raw power Britain possessed before the war.

But Churchill knew one thing all too well: *Before the war was a long time ago.*

The British landing party descended on the White House on the night of December 22, two weeks after Japan's attack. Aides, valets, and bodyguards fanned out through the mansion's guest quarters to ensure the "old man's" requirements were met. Accommodating White House butlers took directions from the invaders, moving furnishings around the Rose Room to quarter the prime minister and his affable manservant, Frank Sawyers. Other aides were directed to the Monroe Room, where they set up wall-sized maps of the war's theaters, each festooned with pushpins representing armies, ships, convoys, airfields, and enemy locations. They labored upstairs as their master worked the ground floor.[4]

Churchill entered a room the way a battleship enters a harbor. His eyes would traverse the space as he moved toward his berth, head lowered, jaw forward. He had one speed and no brake. In an armchair, anchoring the head of a table, or sitting up in bed, he would fire salvos of wit, insight, and earthy elegance at anyone within range.

He was impishly charming when it suited him, and good news would jolt him into a burst of optimism and energy. His blue eyes would light as a broad, "I never had a doubt" smile creased his jowls. Bad news could turn him dark in an instant. His bald head would snap forward, brows tightened, cigar jutting from his jaw as he shot the messenger or sank into lamentation.

Clare Boothe Luce, wife of *Time* magazine founder Henry Luce, called Churchill "the one Englishman Shakespeare didn't invent." His trademarks—heavy drinking and Havana cigars—were a source of endless fascination to the American public, and FDR asked his wife, Eleanor, to ensure White House stocks held plenty of champagne, brandy, and whiskey. When word of Churchill's arrival spread through newspaper and radio reports, thousands of cigars began pouring into the White House mail room from across the country—none of them, for security reasons, ending up in the PM's maw.[5*]

"Churchill is a trying guest," Roosevelt's secretary Bill Hassett told his diary. "Drinks like a fish and smokes like a chimney, irregular routine, works nights, sleeps days, turns the clock upside down." Mike Reilly, head of the president's Secret Service detachment, was more generous. "He ate, and thoroughly enjoyed, more food than any two men or three diplomats," recalled Reilly. "He consumed brandy and scotch with a grace and enthusiasm that left us all open-mouthed in awe."[6]

His long-suffering retainers were used to their master's circadian rhythms. At London's 10 Downing Street, the prime minister's residence and office complex, his day usually began at eight. Rousing himself, he would bark for his morning reading: overnight military dispatches, Enigma-code intelligence, early editions of the morning papers. After reading in silence over breakfast in bed, he would shave and bathe before getting back into bed for dictation to one of three secretaries, who turned out drafts on a custom-made silent Remington typewriter.[7]

As he dictated, the cigar-wielding Merlin crafted spells that shaped

* Britain's Secret Service, somewhat more tolerant than their White House counterparts, tested donated stogies by having Lord Rothschild smoke one cigar per box.

humanity's thought. His "Fight on the Beaches" speech stiffened the resolve of millions to resist Nazism. His "Give Us the Tools" speech tugged at American heartstrings to pass the Lend-Lease Act and aid Britain in its fight. His "The Few" peroration made Spitfire pilots global icons.

The word-weaver was oblivious as he sat at his loom. "One morning, the Prime Minister wanted to dictate while he was in his bath," recalled secretary Patrick Kinna. "He kept submerging in the bath and then when he 'surfaced' he would dictate a few more words or sentences. Eventually he got out of the bath when his devoted valet, Sawyers, draped an enormous bath-towel around him. He walked into his adjoining bedroom, followed by me, notebook in hand, and continued to dictate while pacing up and down the enormous room. Eventually the towel fell to the ground but, quite unconcerned, he continued pacing the room, dictating all the time."[8]

By noon, his morning's dictation finished, Churchill would see official visitors over lunch. He would work in the Cabinet Room until early evening, then retire to his bedroom and lie down in bed, naked but for a black satin blindfold. He would fall asleep the moment his head hit the pillow—a special pillow his entourage carried when he traveled—and after an hour he would bathe, dress again, and be ready for dinner, a film, and business meetings often beginning at ten and carrying on until two or three in the morning.[9]

Then he would turn in for what was left of the night. He left a standing order never to awaken him for any news, no matter how disastrous, unless the news was an invasion of England. He would sleep until eight, then wake up, ready to parry whatever blows the night had brought him.[10]

By taking naps, rotating secretaries, and turning the clock upside down, Churchill squeezed two workdays into one. But time compression took its toll on his inner circle. He could be a hanging judge of crimes ranging from misdemeanors, such as whistling in the hallway, to felonies like typographic errors. His valets, who performed everything from tying his shoelaces to squeezing his artist's paint from tubes, rarely lasted more than a year. "He could be terrifying," remembered secretary Grace Hamblin. "His anger was absolutely petrifying to a young woman who had never been shouted at before."[11]

In a lifetime of statesmanship, Churchill believed personal talks among leaders could do more to break down barriers and solve problems than nearly anything else. Statesmen, he would say, were at their best when working things out "jaw to jaw."

For three weeks, he made the most of his time with the president. At nights, Eleanor Roosevelt would peek in on her husband and the prime minister as they talked through midnight hours about war, politics, and the postwar world—a nocturnal duet the president dubbed the "Winston Hours." Some nights Eleanor would open the door, make a not-so-subtle hint about the next day's workload, then give up in frustration and go to bed, letting Churchill and FDR carry on.

"They looked like two little boys playing soldier," she told her son James. "They seemed to be having a wonderful time. Too wonderful, in fact."[12]

FDR got into the habit of wheeling himself into the Rose Room unannounced to discuss whatever was on his mind. Once, he rolled in as the prime minister emerged from his bath, naked but for a towel. "He is the only head of state I have ever received in the nude," Churchill later chuckled.[13]

More often, Churchill traipsed around the White House in his "siren suit," a blue overalls set he could pull on and zip up for a dash to the bomb shelter when Klaxons wailed. As a London driver later recalled, "The best way I can describe it is to say that it was very similar to a baby's one-piece sleeping suit. He liked it because he could thrust his stubby legs into it, pull it up, push his arms into the sleeves—and zip, he was dressed."[14]

Because of his close and cultivated relationship with FDR, Churchill was not averse to bypassing senior American military advisors and pressing arguments on the commander in chief over cocktails. So on December 23, the day after Japanese troops landed in the Philippines, the prime minister sent word to the U.S. secretary of war that he would like to discuss the Philippines. He needed some information for an upcoming talk with the president.[15]

The morning before Christmas, Churchill strolled down the hall to the Monroe Room to study the war's big picture. In siren suit and monogrammed slippers, he had just returned to his bedroom when Secretary Henry Stimson arrived with a military aide in tow.

The aide, a tall, balding brigadier general with an affable smile, was unfamiliar to Churchill. His name didn't matter, and if Winston heard it, he quickly forgot it. The brigadier was one of a thousand faceless generals who flit in and out of a warlord's life. They salute, answer a question, salute, then fade into the anonymity from whence they came, never to be heard from again.

Nodding the Americans in, he turned to the important man, Stimson. He wanted to know it all: military concentrations along key islands, bomber strength, airfields, Japanese landing beaches, Allied reinforcements. He was especially interested in a division of U.S. reinforcements being shipped from America to bolster MacArthur's force.

Stimson described the locations of American and Japanese forces, the course of the campaign, and the probable last stand of the defenders on the island of Corregidor. The prime minister posed a few follow-up questions about those reinforcements. His curiosity slaked, he asked Stimson to linger a few moments.

Taking the cue, Stimson dismissed the general, who quietly rolled up his maps and slipped out while the two statesmen talked.[16*]

Eisenhower knew damned well who Winston Churchill was. Everyone knew who he was. The man had fought Indians in India and dervishes in Sudan. He had escaped from a Boer prison camp, written world-famous books, railed against the Nazis back when it was unfashionable, and shook his fist at Hitler when France fell. His arrival in Washington had set off a media circus, and he kicked off his stay with an address to a joint session of Congress. Because when Winston Churchill spoke, important people listened.[17]

Ike didn't rate an invitation to meet with the big chiefs, but he did sit in on meetings once or twice as a seen-but-not-heard observer. "The Prime Minister stood above all others in imagination, fire and boldness just as he did in rank and power," he wrote years later. "His preeminence in discussion was not achieved by dictatorial methods; he seemed to love the debates engendered by differences in convictions. He was friendly; indeed, it was sometimes difficult to remember that he was not really 'one of the boys.'"[18]

Until the boys found out what he was up to. The second floor of the Munitions Building shook the next day when General Marshall received a call from a British secretary asking the military chiefs to discuss a new request: the diversion of an American division of reinforcements from the Philippines to Britain's Singapore. Agreed to, Stimson was told, by the president and prime minister.

Marshall stomped into Stimson's office, where the two men worked themselves into a froth. Trained soldiers and transport ships were pre-

* In his memoirs, Winston didn't recall this meeting with Eisenhower. But he had also forgotten that in 1917 he had met a young assistant secretary of the United States Navy named Franklin Delano Roosevelt.

cious commodities, and the War Department was sending them to rescue the Philippines garrison, not succor the British Empire. While Eisenhower was moving heaven and earth to get a convoy to the far side of the world, over drinks and casual banter Churchill had talked the president into scrapping their carefully laid plans.

Enraged that Roosevelt would divert reinforcements while MacArthur's men were fighting for their lives, Stimson rang up Harry Hopkins, FDR's closest advisor. He threatened to resign if Roosevelt changed agreed military plans. Grasping the problem, Hopkins walked into Roosevelt's upstairs study and dumped the ruckus in the two leaders' laps.

Looking like boys with their hands caught in a cookie jar, Churchill and FDR denied reaching any agreements about diverting Army reinforcements. Knowing it was a lie—or at best, a politician's truth—Stimson and Marshall let the matter drop.[19]

His business concluded, on January 14 Churchill left Washington a happy man. During their time together, FDR had assured Churchill the bulk of American might would be turned against Nazi Germany before finishing off Japan. American industry would supply and reinforce the British Isles, and the U.S. Navy would give top priority to protecting Atlantic supply convoys.

Having extracted most of what he wanted, Churchill's only major concession had been the creation of an Anglo-American "Combined Chiefs of Staff" to direct commanders in each theater of war. It was foreign to the British way of doing things, and the Combined Chiefs would formally meet in Washington, not London. But that structure didn't bother Churchill, since Britain controlled four of the eight positions, and Britain, for the moment, held a near monopoly on frontline troops and combat experience.[20]

Returning home, Churchill told King George that Britain and the United States were now "married." When a British officer suggested that the PM should be more tactful when speaking to the Americans, Churchill, a "wicked leer in his eye," shot back, "That is the way we talked to her while we were wooing her. Now that she is in the harem, we talk to her quite differently!"[21]

As the Allied dreadnought sailed into 1942, Winston filled its command bridge with British officers. The guns were American, the steel was American, and the engines were American. But the hand on the rudder belonged to Winston Churchill, and he intended to keep it there.

TWO

London's Best Friend

PAIN, IN WAR, CANNOT BE MINIMIZED. It shape-shifts, and it can be transferred from one community to another. But war's nature demands suffering, or it is not really war but something else. And for five horrid months, Britain suffered.

"We have had an almost unbroken series of military misfortunes," Churchill lamented two months after returning from America. "We were driven out of Cyrenaica, and have now only partly re-established ourselves there. We were driven out of Greece and Crete. . . . Hong Kong has fallen; the Malay Peninsula and the possessions of the brave Dutch in the East Indies have been overrun. Singapore has been the scene of the greatest disaster to British arms which our history records. The Allied squadrons in the Netherlands East Indies have been virtually destroyed in the action off Java. Burma is invaded; Rangoon has fallen; very hard fighting is proceeding in Upper Burma. Australia is threatened; India is threatened."[1]

And this was just the picture in Asia, the Mediterranean, and the Pacific. For Europe, there was nothing to say. Hitler's talons stretched from the gates of Moscow to the English Channel—and across the Channel, the Luftwaffe flew to rain explosives on London, Liverpool, Coventry, and England's other great cities.

But Churchill's Sheffield-steel optimism, scratched and dented, refused to break. "Just now I am having a very rough time, but we must remember how much better things are than a year ago, when we were all alone," he told his old friend, South Africa's prime minister Jan Smuts. When a staffer brought him news of a fresh Japanese advance, he muttered, "We must just KBO." Keep Buggering On.[2]

For the Americans, *what* and *when* proved easier than *where.* Talks in Washington had ended with no fixed plans for an invasion, but in their last big meetings before breaking up, Roosevelt, Churchill, and the military chiefs kicked around the possibility of Operation "Super-Gymnast," an Anglo-American descent upon French Northwest Africa, possibly in May of 1942.

The American brass were dead set against North Africa. Among other things, an invasion there violated the principle of concentrating forces against the main enemy. And when they last checked, the main enemy was Germany. The German Army, German transportation, and German war production were centered in Germany. The war would end in Berlin, not Tunisia, and the fastest way to get to Berlin was through northwestern France. *That* was the approach the Allies should take.

At Marshall's direction, Eisenhower drafted a memo to the Allied high command advocating an American alternative: Operation "Roundup," an invasion of northwestern France in the spring of 1943. He also outlined a preliminary operation, dubbed "Bolero," a yearlong buildup of U.S. forces in the British Isles to man the Roundup invasion. A third contingency, called "Sledgehammer," was a no-huddle emergency leap across the Channel, to be used only if the Soviet Union looked on the verge of collapse. While Sledgehammer would do little or nothing to threaten Germany, it might save Stalin's army by pulling German divisions off the Russian Front. And unlike Roundup, Sledgehammer could be ready by August 1942.

Ike knew the British would balk at a direct attack against Germany. Beaten by the Germans on land, strangled by U-boats at sea, they viewed Roundup and Sledgehammer as a lamb's walk into the lion's den. To push London, Ike suggested an ultimatum: If the British wouldn't agree to invade France, America would instead launch its first big offensive against Japan in the Pacific. The suggestion would scare the hell out of Churchill and the Brits and bring them back to reality.[3]

In an underground war room smelling of tobacco and anxiety, Winston and his military chiefs shook their heads as they examined Sledgehammer. A landing in the fall of 1942 was a fool's errand. Hitler was too strong. The Allies had too few ships, too few troops, and too little air cover. The Luftwaffe would have a field day. It was a sacrifice play, using Britain's sons as the sacrifice.

Instead, Churchill wanted something bold and useful, something that could be launched in 1942. Something achievable. Something to keep America's eye from wandering off to the bloody Pacific.

An invasion of Norway? North Africa? Either might work.[4]

Churchill knew Roosevelt, too, was anxious to launch a blow against Hitler in 1942. The American public was howling for revenge against Japan, and FDR was struggling to keep voters focused on Hitler as Public Enemy No. 1. He wanted American soldiers shooting at German soldiers that year, and he didn't particularly care where they pulled the triggers.

To settle the question, Churchill would need another jaw-to-jaw meeting with FDR. In June he crossed the ocean, and after talks at the White House, the two leaders retreated to Roosevelt's home in Hyde Park, New York. By the banks of the idyllic Hudson River, Churchill laid the facts bare: An invasion of France was impossible in 1942. If they wanted something done in 1942, that something could only be done in Africa.[5]

The afternoon of June 22 found Churchill and FDR back at the White House. Winston winced over Britain's latest humiliation in North Africa, the surrender of the garrison holding Tobruk, but he had no time to wallow in pain or pity. In the shadow of disaster, he met with two American officers: Major General Mark Wayne Clark and a two-star he might have met during his Christmas visit, Dwight D. Eisenhower.

Roundup, possibly in 1943, was the topic of the hour. Clark and Eisenhower had been summoned to answer a few questions about the landings, and for eight minutes they outlined the coming American buildup in England. As they described the plan, Winston took the measure of the two men.

Questions answered, the errand complete, Ike and Clark saluted and left for Boling Field. They had a plane to catch.[6]

Ike had spent the winter and spring drawing up invasion plans for Europe, and on June 8 he brought General Marshall a draft order creating an American European Theater of Operations. Its commander would wield authority over all U.S. ground and air forces. That man would train and organize an army, then serve as either theater commander or Marshall's chief of staff when the Chief moved to Europe to command the actual invasion.[7]

Reporting to Marshall's office, Eisenhower handed his draft order and asked Marshall to consider it carefully. He said it would be a critical document in the American organization in England.

The Chief nodded, grunting, "I certainly do want to read it. You may be the man who executes it. If that's the case, when can you leave?"

Ike left the office elated. He had been given an extraordinary compliment by the Army's top soldier. Of course, it was probably a mirage.

In the Army, there were always "maybes," and most of them never amounted to a damned thing. But three days later, Ike's life changed when he received written orders to go to London. He would set up a command post to lay the foundation for the invasion of Europe. His head spinning, Ike told his diary, "The C/S says I'm the guy. . . . Now we really go to work."[8]

He arrived in London on June 24 and checked into a suite at Claridge's. The upscale hotel lay a stone's throw from his new headquarters: 20 Grosvenor Square, a large brick office building in London's posh Mayfair district. Ike wasn't impressed by his hotel accommodations; he told his driver it looked like a fancy funeral parlor, and christened his bedroom color scheme "whorehouse pink." But for now, Claridge's, and London, was home.[9]

Ike, Clark, and Brigadier General Al Gruenther, Ike's deputy chief of staff, worked double shifts at Grosvenor Square, solving a myriad of invasion problems: housing, training space, supplies, shipping, personnel, and other things commanders have been doing for millennia.

One problem transcended everything else: How do you meld armies of two different nations into one seamless force? The war, being an *Allied* cause, meant Brits and Yanks would have to learn to work together, without fighting one another like siblings on a cross-country car ride.

One of Ike's signature qualities was his ability to conform to the style and thinking of his patron. Whether riding horseback with General Fox Conner in Panama, writing the orthodox answer on his Leavenworth exams, or preparing orders for General Marshall, Ike had an uncanny ability to appear wholeheartedly submissive to the boss.

With two bosses, one of whom ran the United Kingdom, Ike threw himself into adapting to his station. Even the most critical of his British colleagues would admit he was likable and broad-minded, with a genius for fostering a cooperative spirit. In time, he would even adopt British words like "tiffin" (lunch), "petrol" (gas), and "lorry" (truck)—to the sullen displeasure of his Anglophobic brothers like George Patton and Omar Bradley.

The job required Ike to eliminate national prejudices among hundreds of thousands of soldiers, sailors, and airmen. But how does one order a change of attitude among men he will never meet? He could crack down on the staff and senior generals who reported to him, but no matter how many cusswords, orders, and threats he slung around, his voice didn't carry far. It would take a hell of a lot more than just sending out an order.

He had spent his early years in uniform coaching football, and that experience taught Ike the value of teamwork, motivation, and training. The teachings of gridiron coaches like West Point's Ernest Graves were as ingrained in him as the maxims of Napoleon or Clausewitz. To Ike, the Allies would win the war only if Brits and Yanks acted like a team.[10]

He started with the American side. Believing education to be the best way to fight prejudices, he ordered his staff to create cultural programs for U.S. soldiers and airmen about their hosts. Americans arriving in England were given booklets explaining British customs, currency, and laws. Ike even asked the U.S. commander in Northern Ireland to encourage his enlisted men to put some of their monthly pay into war bonds or savings, so the better-paid GIs wouldn't arouse hard feelings with lavish off-duty spending in pubs, theaters, and restaurants.[11]

Through outreach like this, Ike was fast becoming Britain's best American friend. But prejudices went back to 1776, and Americans and Britons came together, he recalled, like "a bulldog meeting a tomcat."

Eisenhower "had his problems with British-American relations and just had to be pretty damn tough about it," one staffer recalled. "Officers from both sides who couldn't cooperate were fired and shipped out of there in a hurry. So, you cooperated or else, which caused some murmurs and harsh words."[12]

An "or else" came up in one conversation between Ike and Lieutenant

General Hastings "Pug" Ismay, Churchill's senior military advisor. Ismay, a middle-aged Edwardian with the kindly face of a Midlands rector, told Ike of a recent incident in a local pub. An American officer, getting drunk, vowed that "his troops would show the British how to fight."

Hearing the story, Ike's face flushed. "I'll make the son-of-a-bitch swim back to America," he snarled. He meant it, too.

Pug's eyebrows arched. He had expected Ike to give the man a reprimand, not dismiss him and send him home. He told Ike he wouldn't have mentioned the incident if he had known he would react so violently.

Ike waved him off. Cooperation required candor, he said. "If we are not going to be frank with each other, however delicate the topic, we will never win this war."[13]

Not that Ike's dealings with the cousins were always pleasant. The British Army, it turned out, had almost as many sonsofbitches as the U.S. Army had. In late May, Marshall had sent Ike and Clark on a fact-finding trip to Britain, where one of his stops was a British training camp in southeastern England. The camp was commanded by a short, wiry lieutenant general named Bernard Law Montgomery, who was giving a lecture on how to fight a war to an audience of American officers. Seated in the audience, Ike and Clark listened intently.

"I have been directed to take time from my busy life to brief you gentlemen," Montgomery said, with the air of a schoolmaster interrupted in the midst of grown-up work.

As Monty began his discourse, Clark remembered, Ike quietly fished out a pack of cigarettes and lit up. Before he could get decently into his Camel, Monty's nose crinkled and he abruptly stopped.

"Who is smoking?" he demanded.

Ike's face reddened. "I am, sir."

"Stop it," Montgomery ordered. "I don't allow it."

Ike grinned sheepishly at Clark as he stubbed out his smoke. The air cleared, Monty resumed his lecture.

On the ride back to Claridge's, Ike's driver, Kay Summersby, heard the nouns "son-of-a-bitch" and "Montgomery" combined in several sentences. Ike was "furious—really steaming mad," she remembered. "It was my first exposure to the Eisenhower temper. His face was flaming red, and the veins in his forehead looked like worms."[14]

Dealing with bulldogs and tomcats was just one of Ike's unending chores. Now that he was America's man in London, his job description included diplomat, politician, and public relations ringmaster. He was plowing new fields where knowledge of weapons and tactics—things he had gone to West Point to learn—meant nothing.

It was frustrating seeing his dreams of field command slip away. "In a place like this," he groused to his wife, Mamie, the commanding general "must be a bit of diplomat-lawyer-promotor-salesman-social hound liar (at least to get out of social affairs)-mountebank-actor-Simon Legree-humanitarian-orator and incidentally (sometimes I think most damnably incidentally) a soldier!"[15]

Though an extrovert by nature—and in demand among London's upper crust—Ike learned to refuse social invitations that weren't mission-critical to the job. Kay Summersby recalled Ike "getting into the car after one reception grumbling, 'I don't think my blood pressure can take it if one more silly woman calls me "My deeaah general." I'm nobody's goddamned "deeaah general," and I'm not fighting this war over teacups.'"

He wouldn't fight the war over teacups, but he learned some work could only be done over highball glasses. Prime Minister Churchill was the exception to Ike's ban on lunch and dinner invitations. Meetings with the PM were mandatory working sessions—even if the work was discussed across china plates and brandy snifters.

"There were countless meetings with the Prime Minister for war-gaming sessions in which the P.M. and the General went over and over all possible eventualities like two chess players with the world at stake," Summersby remembered. "Usually these sessions would be held after dinner at 10 Downing Street or in the bombproof underground shelter off St. James's Park."[16]

Ike was becoming Churchill's American aide-de-camp: a man he could summon at any time, day or night, to answer questions—and, more important, listen to his ideas for winning the war. And winning the peace.

General Marshall had three simple rules for slotting men into high command: Find the best man for the job. Give him what he needed. Hold him accountable for the results.

Ike knew the rules. Now he was staring down the barrel of Rule Three.

The job was immense, and to live up to Marshall's expectations he'd pushed himself to the breaking point. Night after night, he'd wake up and find his brain playing merry-go-round with the next day's problems, struggling with decisions no one else could make. Unable to shut his mind off, he'd sit by the window, staring into the dark until the alarm clock jolted him back to duty: shave, get dressed, put one foot in front of the other. Just like yesterday, just like tomorrow and the tomorrow after that.

He would fight the war, one problem at a time, until Hitler gave up or his own body did. And that one could go either way. He wasn't Superman; he was more like John Henry, and the song told how that turned out. Summersby saw it plain: "He was losing weight, and the wrinkles on his face were suddenly much too deep for a man of fifty-two."[17]

Ike spent most of his days projecting cheer and optimism to those around him, but he was prone to blow his stack when he encountered stupidity, inefficiency, laziness, or officers who put career over country. He'd pound his desk and fire howitzer blasts in a voice that carried down the hallways. He chewed out staffers and threatened all kinds of holy hell. "The terrible-tempered Mr. Bang," a war correspondent called him. After one outburst, an associate later remarked, "Could you compute the amount of adrenaline expended in those thirty seconds? I don't know why long since he hasn't had a killer of a heart attack."

Ike's barracks vocabulary came close to matching that of his old friend George Patton, but only in quantity. While Patton's swearing ran the octaves like Debussy on a Steinway, Ike's curses were flat, simple, and Midwestern. "Damns," "Goddamns," "hells," and "sonofabitches" were his meat-and-potatoes fare. He avoided the scatological or sexual. "He loved to swear," recalled wartime secretary Sue Jehl. "He would say, 'Goddamn it to hell' and that sort of thing, yes, sure, but none of the four-letter words."

"With Eisenhower, I never heard anything, a real obscenity. No dirty stories," a speechwriter agreed years later. "He just didn't talk that way. Cuss, he'd blow up and he'd get mad, he'd use barracks language and that kind of thing, but no real vulgarity, never."[18]

Ike worked hard to control his outbursts, believing rage a mark of personal weakness. Self-control was part of the Puritan ethos he had grown up with in a wood-framed house where the Bible was the family's guiding light. Years later, he would later tell an aide how his mother, a wise, God-fearing pacifist with an unerring moral compass, had taught him to master his temper.

The aide thought to himself, "She did a lousy job."[19]

To keep his spirit from burning out, Ike asked the Navy Department to loan him an old friend, Lieutenant Commander Harry Butcher. A former CBS executive who looked exactly like a CBS executive, Butch was a golfing buddy whose job as Ike's naval aide had nothing to do with the Navy. Officially, he was an aide and press relations advisor. Unofficially, he was Ike's lifeline.

"I've got to have someone I can relax with," Ike explained. "I get back from the office to my quarters and I just want to curl up in a corner like a sick dog, but Butcher won't let me. Butcher's job is simple. It is to keep me sane."[20]

For the war's duration, Butcher would be Ike's court jester and bon vivant—or as *bon* as one could be in wartime London. He golfed with Ike, joked, played ping-pong or bridge whenever Ike needed a break. He invented new ways for Ike to relax in his few off hours, like horseback riding or plinking in the backyard with a .22 pistol. At Ike's request, he kept a diary of Ike's daily life, which he locked in a safe after each day's entries.[21]

In quarters, Ike's Army family took care of his domestic needs. His home staff included a devoted valet, Corporal John Moaney; his mess sergeant, a former Waldorf-Astoria cook named Marty Snyder; and his orderly, Sergeant Mickey McKeogh, once a bellhop at New York's Plaza Hotel. When Ike moved into a suite at the less pretentious Dorchester Hotel, Mickey, Marty, Moaney, and a few other enlisted men rounded out his inner circle.[22]

Then there was Kay Summersby. An Irish lass who had been a fashion model before the war, Kay proved her worth as one of the most capable drivers in London's Motor Transport Corps motor pool. If Ike needed to get through blacked-out, bombed-out streets at night, he wanted Kay behind the wheel. In time, Kay would become more than just a driver. Witty, well-mannered, and a fine bridge partner, like Butcher, she was utterly devoted to Ike.[23]

By July, Churchill was overdue to follow up with the generals running the American show in England. On the fourth, he asked Ike and Clark to join him for dinner and an overnight visit to Chequers.

Chequers, the country residence of Britain's prime minister, sits about forty miles from London's center. The Tudor brick mansion, dating from the 16th century, doubles as a museum to Britannia's glories: Napoleon's ivory-inlaid table, Lord Nelson's watch, Queen Elizabeth's signet ring, a death mask of Oliver Cromwell, and a large collection of portraits adorning rooms, walls, and shelves. The mansion, which could have jumped off the pages of a Jane Austen novel, was the setting for Ike's first real glimpse into Winston Churchill.[24*]

What struck Ike was his roundness: round pate, round cheeks, round shoulders, and soft, full hands that always seemed to be moving. The comforting scent of tobacco, rich and stale, followed him like a bodyguard. Half a head shorter than Ike, Winston never gave the impression of looking up. Below pale blue eyes, his face could slide without warning from boyish triumph to intense disappointment. He could vary his voice to the precise point he was jamming home to his listener. He was an actor who carried his stage with him.

As the sun dipped low, dinner that night segued into an amusing Charles Laughton film shown in the mansion's long, paneled hallway. When the projector's last spool flickered out, the "Winston Hours" commenced.

Churchill held forth on the plums to be picked in North Africa, and as they talked, Ike noticed how the prime minister's mood matched the news. Throughout the evening, discreet servants would bring him secret dispatches from around the world. When the news was good, Ike told his diary, "The conversation would glow for the next thirty minutes or so. Conversely, a pessimistic report would get him in the dumps."[25]

While he liked what he saw, Ike wasn't blind to Churchill's agenda. "It is plain to see that the Prime Minister strongly favors an operation this year in northwest Africa," he told his diary the next day. "He is

* Ike had been to Chequers once before, for a dinner party, but at the time he had been the low man in the group. Neither he nor Churchill left a record of this dinner.

quite averse to attempting anything on western Europe between Norway and the Brest peninsula. He believes it would be slaughter because we are not strong enough, either in air, on the ground, or with the landing craft to make the operation a success and stay on the Continent this year."[26]

Having hammered his African theme, at half past two Churchill paroled his guests for an abbreviated night's sleep. Ike retired to a guest room dominated by an enormous carved-oak four-poster bed and an imposing portrait of Oliver Cromwell. Changing for bed, he found a surprise in his wardrobe: Mickey McKeogh had forgotten to pack his pajamas, so Churchill's butler had thoughtfully left one of the PM's nightgowns for Ike. Grumbling a few choice words about Mickey, Ike slipped on Winston's ill-fitting gown and drifted off to sleep.

He woke up a few hours later with a sense of being strangled. Gasping for breath, he realized Winston's short nightshirt had crept up around his neck and bunched around his throat like a noose.

He would laugh it off later, a nervous Mickey recalled. But "when he woke up with that big nightgown choking him and realized why he was in that spot, all he wanted to do was to get his hands on Mickey McKeogh," Mickey remembered. "He has awfully big hands, too."[27]

With Churchillian hangovers and five hours of sleep, Ike and Clark went downstairs and scarfed down a breakfast of ham and eggs. They left. It would be some time before Winston was up, and Ike had work piling up at the office.[28]

The Allied high command stood deadlocked. The U.S. Joint Chiefs—the Army's chief of staff, General Marshall; the Navy's chief, Admiral Ernest J. King; and the Army Air Forces head, General Henry "Hap" Arnold—wanted to wait until 1943, then launch a knockout blow through northwestern France. The British insisted on an invasion of North Africa in 1942 and violently opposed Operation Sledgehammer at any time. To break the impasse, in July FDR sent Harry Hopkins, Marshall, King, and Arnold to London with instructions to come back with a plan for 1942 everyone agreed on.

At Grosvenor Square, Ike and his staff worked eighteen-hour days churning out the maps, tables, and figures Marshall needed to argue for Sledgehammer and Roundup. But eighteen-hour days and reams of paper couldn't give Marshall the one thing he wanted most: a reasonable guarantee of success in France in 1942. The odds of staying on the Continent, Ike admitted privately, were only about one in five. Had it been a poker match, he would have folded and waited for another hand.[29]

British arguments hit the Americans like a poleax. The Germans could throw thirty divisions at the invaders without pulling a single man off the Russian Front, they said. The Luftwaffe owned the skies over France, and any landing force would be bottled up and decimated from the air. The best the Allies could hope for would be a second miracle of Dunkirk. And a miracle evacuation, as Churchill had pointed out, was no victory.[30]

Charge after charge, the Americans couldn't break the British square. With their ally dead set against Sledgehammer, and FDR demanding action against Germany in 1942, Ike's bosses had no choice but to back down. On the evening of July 22, they agreed to invade Northwest Africa under a new code name: Torch.

Churchill had gotten his way again. He knew the Americans could not act alone, and he correctly gauged Roosevelt's desire for action against Germany in 1942. As he would tell Soviet ambassador Ivan Maisky, "Basically, I am Commander-in-Chief here. I can't always carry out what I want, but I can always prevent that which I don't want."[31]

Ike was all scowl the next morning as he munched his breakfast. Strategically, it was all wrong; Northwest Africa was the suburbs, when they needed to get downtown. Torch would swallow enough men and machines to kill the Roundup invasion of Europe until the fall of 1943, at the earliest. Maybe even the spring of 1944.[32]

"I hardly know where to start," he told Butcher. When the chronicles of the war were written, he said, July 22, 1942, could well go down as the "blackest day in history."[33]

But the decision was made, and the road to Berlin now ran through the African desert.

The next order of business was selecting the invasion's commander. To assure the Americans he had no intention of denuding Bolero and Roundup, Churchill suggested appointing Marshall as supreme commander for the cross-Channel expedition, with the newly appointed Lieutenant General Eisenhower to double as Marshall's Roundup deputy and head planner for Torch.[34]

Marshall had plenty on his plate without taking on Torch. He was running a massive Army infrastructure stateside and had troops scattered across the globe. He was fighting Admiral King over the Battle of the Atlantic, the British over strategy in Europe, and MacArthur over the road to Tokyo. He was the keeper of secrets, from decryption of Japanese codes to a newfangled bomb project, and his domestic responsibilities included Congress, the budget, the press, and the White House. He didn't have time to run an invasion.

Eisenhower, Marshall declared, would command Torch. Ike would also plan Bolero and Roundup. Marshall squared the setup with Roosevelt, who cabled Churchill on August 6 formally designating Eisenhower as acting commander for Torch.[35]

For the second time in three months, Marshall had tapped Ike to be "the Guy." Ike would spend the summer in London hammering out the invasion's details, and the British prime minister would watch him as he hammered.

That meant a lot of face time. "At his request, I fell into the habit of meeting with the Prime Minister twice each week," Ike remembered. "On Tuesdays we would have luncheon at 10 Downing Street. . . . On Friday nights I would have dinner with him at his country house, Chequers, and this would sometimes be prolonged into an overnight stay."

Ike liked the PM more with every meeting. He understood what Churchill meant to a people who had sacrificed sons on three continents and four oceans. "An inspirational leader, he seemed to typify Britain's courage and perseverance in adversity and its conservatism in success," Ike would later write.

Through days and nights of long conversations, he watched a master communicator who rarely ceded the stage. "He could become intensely oratorical, even in discussion with a single person, but at the same time his intensity of purpose made his delivery seem natural and appropriate. He used humor and pathos with equal facility, and drew on everything from Greek classics to Donald Duck for quotation, cliché, and forceful slang to support his position."[36]

Sitting at his desk in 10 Downing, Churchill scanned his schedule for October 1942. He would need a lot more than Donald Duck or Homer for his next big meeting. Having subdued the Americans, he now had to sell the North African gamble to a ruthless dictator his wife had nicknamed "the Ogre." When Churchill broke the news of no second front in Europe that year, he knew the Ogre would be furious.

And there was not enough whisky in the world—or vodka—to make that talk go down easy.

THREE

The Ogre's Den

I do not like the job I have to do.
I cannot think my views will go down well.
Can I convince them of our settled view,
Will Stalin use Caucasian oaths and yell?
Or can I bind him with my midnight spell?
I'm really feeling rather in a stew.
It's not so hot a thing to have to sell,
No Second Front in 1942.

—Winston, "Ballad of the Second Front,"
composed on his flight to Moscow[1]

As Ike honed invasion plans, Churchill flew to Moscow for a jaw-to-jaw session with Josef Stalin. In the beating heart of communism, he would tell the dictator the West would not invade Europe that fall—a mission his wife, Clementine, called a "visit to the Ogre in his Den."

The Ogre had oiled his machine with the blood of millions long before Hitler's rise. Yet for all his years in power, Stalin remained an enigma even to his closest lieutenants. Charming when he wished to be, he spoke softly, puffing his briar pipe like a Georgian grandfather sitting by his hearth. His broad face was framed by a tobacco-infused mustache and thick, gray-flecked hair. Only his eyes—amber, quick, intense—hinted at the darkness lurking behind pipe and mustache.

Brilliant, calculating, paranoid, and insensible to human suffering,

Stalin had built an empire on forced labor and mass executions. To the seminarian who had renounced God, communism was a spiritual struggle against the sins of private ownership and inequality. As high priest of Marx and Lenin, he demanded devotion to the Party unto death—and put many lieutenants and their families to that test.

The visit was an eye-opener for Churchill. One night over caviar and vodka, he casually asked Stalin what his most anxious moment in power had been. Not Hitler's invasion, Stalin replied. It had been the collectivization of agriculture in the early 1930s. That had been a disaster as harvests failed and food grew scarce in the cities. To forestall riots, he sent commissars to seize food from millions of Ukrainian and Russian peasant farmers, called kulaks. Those who tried to hide food for their families were shot on the spot. Those who didn't starved to death.

"What happened to the kulaks?" Churchill asked.

Stalin shrugged. "Oh, they went away."

Man-made famine, summary executions, a shrug of the shoulders. No matter how badly Churchill needed the Ogre to help him, he could never forget who the red tsar was: a diabolical engineer pulling levers on a machine that ate men, women, and children.[2]

When Winston broke the news that there would be no invasion of Europe in 1942, Stalin took it stoically at first. But the implications sank in overnight, and the next day he stomped back in a fury and lit into the prime minister like he was muscling a Leningrad party boss.

Stunned at Stalin's behavior, Winston left the meeting steaming mad. His bodyguard recalled, "Churchill had his first row with Joe and was banging down the corridors of the Kremlin looking neither to right nor left. He struck a match on the Kremlin wall and still walking, lighted a cigar, puffing angrily."[3]

Archibald Clark Kerr, Britain's ambassador, begged Churchill to remember that Stalin wasn't the sort of gentleman he was used to dealing with. Stalin's class "came straight from the plow or the lathe. They were rough and inexperienced," he said.

"But that man insulted me," Winston protested. "I represent a great country, and I am not submissive by nature." The ambassador persisted: Britain must not to break with the Soviet Union over rough language from "a peasant who didn't know any better."[4]

Through four days of bitter arguments, overnight banquets, vodka toasts, and an impromptu dinner at Stalin's apartment, the two men groped for common ground. Stalin was an old Bolshevik, which was reason enough for Churchill to hate him. Churchill was an old capitalist, which was reason enough for Stalin to hate him. But Stalin's forces were locked in a death struggle with Hitler's Sixth Army around Stalingrad, and the Red Army had bled the Germans more than all other nations combined. Churchill wanted to bleed Germany from the south and from the air—and in time, perhaps, from the west. That was reason enough to put aside their hatred.

Unable to exile, shoot, or bully Churchill, Stalin swallowed what he despised. The Americans and English would go to North Africa, and there was nothing he could do about it. Stalin asked for more American equipment and pushed for a front in Europe as soon as possible, and the meetings ended on an outwardly cordial note.[5]

"It was my duty to go," Churchill told the War Cabinet when he returned to London. "Now they know the worst, and having made their protest are entirely friendly; this is in spite of the fact that this is their most anxious and agonizing time. Moreover M. Stalin is entirely convinced of the great advantages of Torch and I do trust that is being driven forward with superhuman energy on both sides of the ocean."[6]

That superhuman energy would come from General Eisenhower. And General Eisenhower had better deliver.

Ike's dawn-to-midnight weeks reading acres of studies, tables, and reports—days facing an unending conveyor belt of problems—were beginning to show. Wrinkles settled into his face. His blood pressure shot up like a flak shell and his temper boiled over with distressing regularity. He desperately needed a refuge, and Harry Butcher found him one.

Telegraph Cottage, a Tudor-style cottage south of London, was as "picturesque as an English Christmas card," Kay Summersby recalled. Quiet, secluded, and surrounded by a private garden, the haven became to Ike what Chequers was to Churchill. "Our cottage is a god-send," he wrote Mamie. "Butch says I'm human again!"[7*]

To give Ike separation from the war, life at Telegraph Cottage was stripped of military airs. He'd lounge around in old uniform pants, an old shirt, and straw slippers he'd picked up in Manila. Neckties were off-limits. "He didn't want no saluting or nothing like that," recalled his orderly, John Moaney. "He just wanted to come home, just like he was living regular life."[8]

When he could steal a weekend retreat, Ike would spend hours thinking of anything but the war. He would clear his head with golf, bridge with Butch and Kay, ping-pong, or baseball. Evenings began with a "sundown highball" served up by Mickey; scotch was his drink, twelve-year Chivas Regal his brand whenever he could get it. Some nights he would catch a film the morale officers didn't need for the enlisted men. He loved Abbott and Costello comedies and light Bing Crosby flicks. "He never liked war pictures because they were full of nonsense, and he didn't like tear jerkers or pictures with too much love in them," recalled Mickey. Sitting up in bed, Ike devoured western nov-

* Unbeknownst to Ike and Butch, Telegraph Cottage was located about half a mile from a decoy station used to lure German bombers away from London.

els, "with a lot of shooting in them," Mickey remembered. "It was sort of funny, considering the amount of shooting we were getting."[9]

A home-cooked meal was a welcome break from the cabbage and bully beef of British messes. Kay Summersby remembered, "One afternoon I overheard him mutter to General Clark that 'this must be the fartingist war in history.'" She recalled, "Almost every base they visited served them boiled cabbage or brussels sprouts, and the result often kept the generals rolling down the car windows."[10]

Cooking was a way Ike relaxed. Since Mamie wasn't much in the kitchen, he had prepared a lot of family meals. To Ike, it wasn't work. He enjoyed mixing, frying, and grilling as an art form and mental break from the pressures of the world. When a woman once asked Ike why he liked to cook so much, he explained, "When I'm finished with it, I know I'm finished with it, and I know if it's good or bad."

He also acquired a four-legged aide. "You can't talk war to a dog," he told Mamie. "I'd like to have someone or something to talk to, occasionally, that doesn't know what the word means!" When Kay and Ernest "Tex" Lee, Ike's adjutant, found two promising candidates—black Scotties—Ike picked the younger, rowdier of the pups. He named the dog Telek, after his getaway home, and Mickey, dubbed "Master of the Hound," took charge of dog-walking and cleanup duty.[11]

Weekends at Telegraph Cottage revitalized Ike, but weekends were never a sure thing. Some Saturdays would find him at Chequers with Winston, talking into the wee hours. Others would pull him out of town, to inspect training camps or meet with air or naval commanders. Sunday mornings at seven thirty, often as not, would find Kay pulling up the car to the cottage, where a frowning Ike, his mind far away, would be deep into his second or third coffee.[12]

Near the end of August, Ike received a one-star gift from Washington: Brigadier General Walter Bedell Smith.

"Bedell," or "Beetle," as they called him, was a high school dropout who had taken his oath as a private in the Indiana National Guard. He had clawed his way up to general through brains, hard work, and sound political sense. Trusted by Marshall, respected by the Joint Chiefs, Beetle was the whip-cracker every boss needs to get things done.[13]

For the next three years, Beetle would serve Ike as gatekeeper, ringmaster, ambassador, and Lord High Executioner. Sharp-eyed and sharp-tongued, he drove the staff mercilessly and played the heavy when Ike had to tell someone to go to hell. As Beetle told Kay Summersby, "Someone around the top has to be an absolute s.o.b., and Ike's not in a position to do it all the time. So that's my job."

S.O.B. He relished the role. Beetle had "all the sentiment of an S.S. general," Kay remembered. He would humiliate or fire a subordinate without a second thought. "He was just naturally mean," one staffer remarked.[14]

Mean, but what a difference a top-flight chief of staff could make. Beetle rapidly absorbed the invasion's essentials, learned the players, and took the wheel. He demanded, and got, smooth coordination among the logistics, intelligence, operations, and personnel chiefs on Ike's staff. Devoted to Ike, he ensured the orders of the Boss were carried out. As Ike told a friend, "I wish I had a dozen like him. If I did, I would simply buy a fishing-rod and write home every week about my wonderful accomplishments in winning the war."[15]

With Beetle, Clark, Gruenther, and the home and office crews lined up, Ike had assembled the core of a machine that would plan history's most complex invasion. But the machine needed raw materials, and that would require heavy-duty help from the man who ran Britain's side of the war.

That meant more time with Churchill.

On August 25, Winston summoned Ike and Clark to 10 Downing Street for a dinner debate that crept past midnight. Table talk centered on Torch, a subject of heated argument between the American and British brass.

Churchill, like his generals, wanted to land as far east as possible, close to Tunisia. Field Marshal Erwin Rommel's German-Italian army depended on Tunisian and Libyan ports for its ammunition, food, supplies, and reinforcements. Without those ports, Rommel's army wouldn't last a month. So it made tactical sense to land the Torch troops in east Algeria, shortening the distance to the coastal prizes.

But supply vulnerabilities worked both ways. Allied lines would stretch clear across Northwest Africa below Spain, a country led by General Francisco Franco, who was friendly to Hitler. The American Chiefs worried about these long arteries and wanted to keep some dry powder in case Franco joined Hitler and pounced. Hedging their bets, they insisted on a separate landing on Africa's Atlantic coast, in French Morocco at the port city of Casablanca.[16]

The British were thinking bold tactics; the Americans were thinking safe logistics. Ike was caught in the middle. Churchill wanted to sell Ike on the British point of view, and what better way to make his case than over soup, wine, dinner, and champagne?

When debating a point, Churchill didn't use a bludgeon, or a rapier, but a bludgeon of rapiers. Ike remembered it well. "When he got into a discussion about anything, he never just commented. He would give a little bit of an oration," Ike recalled. "Sometimes it almost silenced you. And he could use anything. He used pathos. I've seen tears run over his chin, you know, right down from the eyes when he'd talk."[17]

Winston could hold forth on everything from popular culture to theology, cutting-edge science, poetry, painting, or bricklaying with remarkable insight. And he did it with the face of an expressive little boy. But mirth could turn to anger in a snap. When displeased, Winston's brows would knit as his lower lip poked out. Britain's Ambassador Clark Kerr remarked on his "ability to transform his face from the rosiest, happiest, the most laughing, dimpled and mischievous baby's bottom into the face of an angry and outraged bullfrog."[18]

While Winston's trademarks were cigars and alcohol, Ike quickly figured out that both were more show than real. The prime minister extended one glass of sherry over an entire evening, he told Harry Butcher. Churchill "smoked" a long cigar, but mostly played with it, letting it burn out in his manicured fingers as he talked, ostentatiously relighting it several times throughout the night. "Ike had the impression that the PM rather relishes his reputation as a heavy smoker and drinker, but is actually much more moderate than rumor would indicate."[19]

Servants, liquor, and cigars were Winston's way of dominating a room. Though he genuinely loved fine Cubans, brandy, and Pol Roger champagne, they were stage props for the lectures he delivered night after night to friends, ministers, and, occasionally, his own undecided mind. Essential elements of the Churchill experience, they were placed, and paced, to leave an impression on visitors as much as for the master's enjoyment.[20]

Ike was used to theatrics. It was the same show MacArthur had performed in his office in the Philippines. The big difference between the two thespians was that Winston was empathetic enough to step into another man's shoes. At least, he tried. MacArthur couldn't. The general was often poorly informed on subjects outside military affairs, but never in doubt.

The conclave ended, and after shuffling back to his hotel suite with Clark at half past one in the morning, a bleary-eyed Ike told Harry Butcher that the prime minister, angry with his generals for disagreeing with him on the invasion's sites and date, "showed his temper by fighting his soup. . . . Since the PM is short and blockily built, his chin isn't very much above the soup plate. He crouched over the plate, almost had his nose in the soup, wielded the spoon rapidly. The soup disappeared to the accompaniment of loud gurglings."

Clark added that Churchill was oblivious to his surroundings when engrossed in a discussion. At one point he accidentally pushed a highball glass off a side table, "but went on talking, not even glancing around to see where the glass and contents had fallen."

"During the evening," Clark continued, Winston "asked a servant to bring him his change of socks—he took off his shoes, the socks he was wearing, put on the other pair, and replaced his shoes, without the slightest embarrassment." Escorting his guests to the door, he stood in the doorway, and like a cat, he "put his back to its edge, vigorously rubbed his shoulder blades against it."[21]

Friendly though not yet friends, Ike and Winston enjoyed each other's company. Both were self-driven and largely self-educated. Both were devoted to their wives, and both had lost young children in 1921: Ike's older son, Ikky, who died of scarlet fever, and Winston's daughter Marigold, who succumbed to sepsis.

Neither man had broken academic records in school. Winston had scraped through Harrow and Sandhurst. Ike stood middle of the pack at West Point. "You can't tell when people begin to mature," Ike concluded years later. "The parallel is between his rather mediocre academic record and when he got a profession to think about. Then he did better." Ike was also late to bloom. He didn't come into his own until his early mentors, George Patton and Fox Conner, lit an intellectual fire that carried him to higher levels of thought.[22]

At times, Winston's practical experience in the saddle allowed him to see things that Ike, who still worked in theories, could not. At Chequers one evening, Ike suggested that London and Washington announce large-scale American participation in Operation "Lightfoot," Montgomery's long-awaited offensive in the Libyan desert. The announcement would be a deception to draw Nazi attention away from the Torch landing to the west and hopefully keep Rommel pinned down in Libya.

Winston said Ike was too optimistic. Desert fighting, he pointed out, would be in close quarters. British soldiers would be killed or captured, and Rommel would know who was facing him. He wouldn't find any American divisions on his front, so the deception would be worthless. No sense wasting credibility when it wouldn't accomplish anything.

Ike thought it over. Having no answer, he quietly let the idea drop.[23]

On September 8, Churchill summoned Ike and Clark to 10 Downing for another dinner. Anxious as ever to commit American troops, his first question was when the invasion would take place.

"November 8—sixty days from today," Ike answered.

Winston scowled. He was hoping for an earlier November landing, a headline to help Roosevelt with his congressional midterm elections, set for November 3.

When Ike told him part of the delay was the need to finish training American soldiers, Winston suggested that British soldiers could fill out his ranks and land on the beaches wearing American uniforms. He would be "proud to have 'em wear 'em."

Ike shut down the idea. He pointed out—as Winston did earlier—that "the sham would soon be discovered and would undermine confidence in the whole American operation." Winston agreed and dropped the point.

Churchill sulked over the timing, but he knew he would have to live with it. Fine-tuning the invasion's D-day was Ike's job. If Ike said he had to wait until November 8, then Winston had to take the answer Ike gave him. He would even support Ike's judgment when speaking to Roosevelt.[24]

Winston had more to sulk about when Ike administered a second dose of reality. On September 21, Winston chaired a Monday morning meeting with Ike, Clark, Beetle, and the British Chiefs. The top agenda item was the invasion of France, and Winston asked how many

Americans would be deployed to the United Kingdom for the Roundup operation.

Around 150,000 ground troops, Ike said. They might have a grand total of 400,000 American men and women, including air forces.

Winston's face went blank. He looked like he had been slapped.

Not nearly enough, he protested. A force of 400,000 Americans, "including air forces," meant at least 100,000 mechanics, clerks, cooks, quartermasters, truck drivers, dentists, and veterinarians who would never shoulder a rifle. Hitler had thirty-odd veteran German divisions in the west.

When he recovered, Winston said he had not been aware of the "very considerable falling off" of the Bolero forces, "nor that 'Round-up' had so far receded in the minds of the American Chiefs of Staff."[25]

But Roundup hadn't receded; it had been starved. More than 100,000 fighting troops would land at Casablanca, Oran, and Algiers during the first wave of Operation Torch. Far more men—and ships, planes, fuel, and ammunition—would be needed for the follow-up drive to capture Rommel's supply ports at Tunis and Bizerte on the Tunisian coast. Since January, Ike and Marshall had complained that an invasion of Africa would drain so many men and machines from the Bolero buildup in England that Roundup wouldn't be possible in early 1943. After the Torch invasion, there wouldn't be much of anything left to send to France.[26]

Ike respectfully reminded Churchill the Americans had opposed Torch for exactly the reason they now faced. Winston pressed the issue, probing for some way to salvage a French landing in '43. But after two hours arguing the point, he came up empty-handed.

At the meeting's conclusion, Churchill asked Ike to say nothing to Marshall until he could prepare a written memorandum laying out the British case. After leaving the meeting, Ike did exactly what Churchill asked him not to do: He sent Marshall a cable for his "personal information only."

"The arguments and considerations you advanced time and again between January and July 24th apparently made little impression upon the Former Naval Person at that time, since he expresses himself now as very much astonished to find out that Torch practically eliminates any opportunity for a 1943 Roundup," Ike wrote. "These matters now have to be met face to face, and with an obviously disturbing effect upon the Former Naval Person."

In his zeal to get America committed to Africa in 1942, the Former Naval Person hadn't focused on long-range consequences. "The serious implication," Ike told Marshall, "is that either the original Torch decision was made without a clear realization of all its possible adverse consequences upon the military situation of the Allies and upon projects that are considered as of primary importance in the successful prosecution of the war, or that these considerations were ignored in the anxiety to influence the Torch decision."[27]

As November opened, troopships weighed anchor and began steaming toward Africa's coast. Soon, Ike and his staff would be sweating out opening night in a damp cave on Gibraltar, surrounded by shark-infested waters. "Every man there was as nervous as an expectant father," Kay Summersby wrote. A friend told her she looked "as nervous as a pregnant nun."[28]

Though a cold-blooded calculator, Ike wasn't about to thumb his nose at Fate. For luck, he kept a little zippered pouch of coins from the Allied nations in his pocket. He sometimes rubbed them, like a rosary, squeezing out the last ounce of fortune. "I don't know whether the General really believed they would, but he evidently thought there was no harm in finding out," recalled Mickey McKeogh. "I suppose he thought, they wouldn't anyway bring him *bad* luck."

Whether Ike prayed to his mother's God during those tense days, no one knew. Fiercely private about his religion, he wasn't telling. He played the hand as best he could, and assumed the Lord would give him a decent set of cards.[29]

Arriving at Gibraltar, Ike tipped his garrison cap to local superstition. "Ike had heard that anyone visiting the Rock should see the monkeys because they are supposed to bring good luck," wrote Harry Butcher. Ike and Butch piled into a Ford staff car and rode around looking for the little critters. "Found the monkeys," Butch reported. "Ike patted one on the head—not wanting to miss any opportunity for good luck."[30]

He'd need that luck. His men were about to hit the beaches, and Ike had no clue whether French soldiers stationed in Morocco, Algeria, and Tunisia would shoot them or join them. As he told Marshall, "We are standing, of course, on the brink and must take the jump—whether the bottom contains a nice feather bed or a pile of brickbats!"[31]

FOUR

"A Damned Good Assassin"

WINSTON WAS "HARD TO HOLD DURING YOUR TRIP," Beetle cabled Ike. "He called me and everyone else at ten-minute intervals during the last hour."

Ike's flight to the Rock of Gibraltar had begun at Hurn Aerodrome for what should have been a short trip across Spain. But his Flying Fortress bomber, whose nose was decorated with a red-horned gremlin waving Churchill's "V for Victory" sign, gave French and Spanish airspace a wide berth to avoid Messerschmitt and Focke-Wulf fighters prowling the French coast.

For several hours, no one heard from Ike's Fortress. Winston grew anxious. He had known other men who took off, never to reach their destinations; the Duke of Kent and General Gott had died in separate plane crashes just three months earlier. So his eyes grew wide when a sober-looking Pug Ismay and Beetle Smith walked in with news of General Eisenhower.

"Don't tell me he has drowned," said Winston.

Beetle assured him that Ike had arrived in good order. A little late, but fine.

Winston's face brightened. "I never had the slightest idea that it would be otherwise," he said.[1]

Feather bed or brickbats? It depended on the French mood, and the French mood was unpredictable, even to the French.

The Vichy government had over 100,000 troops in North Africa—regular, colonial, and Foreign Legion. Their reaction to the landings could spell victory or defeat. Ike needed to find a French leader with the clout to persuade French forces to march with the Allies, not shoot them. But in French politics, he was a ferryman in a fog.

To educate Ike on the French mindset, Roosevelt had sent him the State Department's expert on France, a career diplomat named Robert Murphy. He arrived in London in an Army uniform, under the assumed name "Lieutenant Colonel McGowan." (As Marshall explained, "Nobody ever pays attention to a lieutenant colonel.")[2]

Murphy told Ike the French were divided. The Vichy government, nominally led by Marshal Philippe Pétain, and the Free French resistance, under General Charles de Gaulle, had been at each other's throats since the fall of Paris.

De Gaulle, a six-foot, five-inch soldier from Lille, was an outlaw in the eyes of official France. That meant the French Army wouldn't listen to him. The Allies needed someone inside the Vichy government the army would salute.

Pétain's military number two, Admiral François Darlan, led the French Navy, nominally commanded the army, and wielded enormous political influence in Paris. Darlan was an anti-Semite and collaborator with the Nazis, but he was also a rank opportunist who might jump ship if he saw the SS *Fascism* taking on water. And as Winston told Admiral Andrew Cunningham, "Kiss Darlan's stern if you have to, but get the French Navy."[3]

The problem: Darlan's stern was out of reach.

Murphy had another idea. General Henri Giraud had been captured when France fell, but he escaped from a German prison and was living under the protection of the French underground. With a wide reputation as a French patriot and war hero, Giraud might be the one man to persuade the French defenders to lay down their arms and join the Allies.[4]

Murphy sold Ike on Giraud, and Ike sent a British submarine to the French coast to fetch him. But when Giraud arrived at the Rock, he spent four hours telling Ike the only role he would accept would be Allied commander in chief. Anything else, he explained, would be beneath his dignity.

Ike politely told him it was impossible. The Allies would appoint him leader of French North Africa and commander of its armed forces, but the Allied command structure was fixed by the governments of the United States and Great Britain—governments that were supplying all the troops, equipment, and money. Ike pleaded with Giraud to take the lesser post.

It didn't work. As Clark told Butcher, "The old General declined in seven languages, each meaning 'Prestige.'" Giraud would sit out the invasion rather than take a position of subservience to America and Britain. If the Allies wouldn't yield, Achilles would let the Greeks take Troy without his help.[5]

Ike couldn't believe Giraud would put prestige over the liberation of his homeland. But *le général* wouldn't budge, and Ike had an invasion to get back to. Giraud and his Gallic pride would sit on the Rock as Ike's troops hit the beaches. If the Allies managed to stay ashore, then Giraud would probably come back, résumé in hand, asking for another job interview. But by then, the war would have moved on, and so would Ike.

On November 8, the ships hit the shore. More than four hundred landing and supply craft crashed onto Africa's beaches near Casablanca, Oran, and Algiers, grinding their bows into sand and disgorging 116,000 soldiers and equipment.

At first, the news was good. American and British forces quickly overran the Algerian capital. French defenders at Oran put up a fight at the city's harbor, but by the invasion's second day, the Allies gained the upper hand.

To the west, Patton encountered fierce resistance as his force fought its way into Casablanca. French regulars, colonial troops, Foreign Legionnaires, even the battleship *Jean Bart* fought like leopards. While the weight of Allied air support, combined with Patton's armored reinforcements, made the outcome inevitable, every hour Frenchmen and Americans died. Until the two sides reached a ceasefire, Ike couldn't turn all his guns against Tunisia.[6]

When news of the fall of Algiers reached Gibraltar, General Giraud realized he had missed the boat. He told Ike he was ready to talk, but by then, another option had fallen into Ike's lap: Admiral Darlan.

Darlan had been in Algiers visiting his polio-stricken son when the city was surrounded and Darlan was captured. French Army commanders in Africa looked to him for orders, and that meant Ike had to deal with Darlan. Recalling Winston's dictum—"Kiss Darlan's stern if you have to"—Ike sent General Clark to Algiers to negotiate a ceasefire. Darlan's price for telling French troops to stand down was political leadership of French North Africa.

Ike had two Frenchmen to juggle, and he was desperate to put them both to work. But Giraud didn't trust Darlan, who had collaborated with the Nazis. Darlan and most French officers thought of Giraud as a traitor. Darlan was reluctant to defy the Vichy government, and Giraud was powerless to order French soldiers to stop fighting.

"Now Ike has one hell of a headache," Butcher remarked.[7]

In a conference room in Algiers's St. George Hotel, Admiral Darlan pulled out a white handkerchief. He mopped his balding brow as General Clark harangued him into throwing in with the Allies. Alternately pleading and threatening, like a cop working a suspect for a confession, Clark wrung a compromise from the two French rivals: Darlan would serve as governor of French North Africa and admiral in chief. Giraud would command French ground troops. Most important, Darlan would immediately order the French Army to stop resisting.

Ike climbed into a Flying Fortress and flew to Algiers to ratify the deal. Meeting with the French leaders in the hotel's *Salon des Ambassadeurs,* he shook hands all around and told them the arrangement was acceptable. Apologizing for his haste, he left the conference and flew back to Gibraltar on the bomber that brought him.

Darlan signed an order directing all French forces in Africa to cease fire. Radio Algiers announced that Darlan had reached an arrangement with the Allies, and the battle for Morocco and Algeria ended.[8]

Swaths of the British and American publics reacted with outrage when they read the news of Ike's pact. Ike hadn't considered Darlan's unsavory image in Britain and the United States as a Nazi collaborator—or the hell his bosses might catch by elevating a Vichy official.

"Darlan was commonly regarded as a 'stinking skunk,'" Butcher explained. The admiral had cozied up to the Nazis, enforced antisemitic laws, and been photographed with Hermann Göring and other Nazi bigwigs. In London, in the Commons and in the press, Liberal and Labour MPs raged over General Eisenhower's decision to dump the Allies into bed with a fascist. American journalists like Edward R. Murrow took up the cry, and the firestorm began to singe Roosevelt and Churchill.[9]

Ike was floored to think his political leaders couldn't grasp the military logic. Ideals meant nothing until the enemy was defeated, and he had just conquered Morocco and Algeria with a handshake. "I think that the authorities in London and Washington continue to suffer a bit from a delusion as to the extent of our military control over this country," he wrote in exasperation to Beetle. "It will be a long time before we can get up on our high horse and tell everybody in the world to go to the devil!"

Ike once said that since the beginning of time, there were two subjects amateurs claimed to know better than professionals: military strategy and prostitution. Now the amateurs were telling him how to run the war. As the mob's howl grew, he sent cables to London and Washington explaining the advantages flowing from the Darlan Deal. He hoped Churchill and Roosevelt would understand. "I do not repeat not expect any encouragement and hurrahs from the rear, but I regret that I must use so much of my own time to keep explaining these matters," he told Beetle.

Still fuming the next day, he sent Beetle another message, referring to Churchill by his code name, "Agent": "My whole interest now is Tunisia. When I can make the Allies a present of that place the Agent can kick me in the pants and put in a politician here who is as big a crook as the chief local skunk."[10]

Darlan, Ike's chief local skunk, harbored no illusions about what the Allied leaders thought of him. From the St. George Hotel, Ike forwarded to Churchill a letter from Darlan. The admiral vowed to work for French unity and said he would support the Allies. But announcements from Washington calling him a "temporary expedient" left him, he said, feeling like "a lemon which the Americans will drop after it is crushed."[11]

Ike was feeling the squeeze himself. He was in a position where military decisions were fraught with political consequences he hadn't been trained to deal with. Frustrated, in early December he wrote to his West Point roommate, "High command, particularly Allied Command, in war carries with it a lot of things that were never included in our textbooks, in the Leavenworth course, or even in the War College investigations. I think sometimes that I am a cross between a one-time soldier, a pseudo-statesman, a jack-legged politician and a crooked diplomat. I walk a soapy tight-rope in a rain storm with a blazing furnace on one side and a pack of ravenous tigers on the other."[12]

He'd stumbled, badly, but he tried to take the matter philosophically. "From what I hear has been appearing in the newspapers, you are learning that it is easy enough for a man to be a newspaper hero one day and a bum the next," he wrote his son John. "The answer is that just as one must not let his head get swelled too much by a bit of acclaim, he must not be too upset and irritated when the pack turns on him."[13]

War, even when waged for good ends, pits one evil against another. That is the bargain with the devil within. On occasion, one also has to bargain with the devil without.

Winston had sipped vodka with the Bolshevik dictator, so he knew what that felt like. Sometimes the devil appears as a fuming, sulfuric Mephistopheles, and sometimes he appears as a mustachioed Georgian with a briar pipe. Sometimes he takes the form of a dumpy Frenchman mopping a sweaty brow.

Winston liked Ike, and when the Darlan furor rose, he didn't want to throw him to the wolves. But Winston had British interests and his own career to look out for, and if Westminster's wolves bayed too loudly for Ike's carcass, Winston wasn't going to become a side dish. Friendship had its limits.

To lower the temperature, he stood before Parliament in secret session. He told the Commons that under the circumstances, General Eisenhower had made the best possible decision, one that saved lives on both sides. Even if the Darlan Deal was "not quite right," he cautioned, "I should have been very reluctant to hamper or to impede his action when so many lives and such vitally important issues hung in the balance."

He reminded the members that Britain was waging a coalition war.

"In war it is not always possible to have everything go exactly as one likes. In working with Allies, it sometimes happens that they develop opinions of their own," he said. Since 1776, for instance, "We have not been in the position of being able to decide the policy of the United States."[14]

The uproar subsided, but Winston worried. Ike was out of his depth in politics—especially French politics. So he decided to send his own man into Ike's camp. Someone who would help steer Ike down a path compatible with the Empire's interests.

Harold Macmillan, a debonaire glad-hander with a bristling mustache and ingratiating smile, had been a Conservative Party MP since the twenties and parliamentary undersecretary of state for colonies. Scion of the Macmillan publishing family, he had achieved modest recognition in England in the thirties by writing a book on economic reform titled *The Middle Way.*

Recommending him to Roosevelt, Winston stressed Macmillan's half-American parentage, much like his own: "He is animated by the friendliest feelings towards the United States, and his mother hails from Kentucky," he told FDR. He put Macmillan on a plane for Algiers, and before long the diplomat was setting up his cobbler's bench at Ike's headquarters in the St. George Hotel.[15]

On Christmas Eve 1942, the Darlan episode ended with a bang. While Ike was at the front, a young French radical managed to walk up to Darlan at his office building. Screaming something unintelligible, he whipped out a small-caliber automatic pistol and sent two bullets into Darlan's face and chest.

By the time Darlan was carried to the hospital, he was dead. The assassin was tried on Christmas Day and executed the next morning, closing the chapter as fast as it had opened. A big public relations problem was solved with a flash of gunfire and two lead slugs. With a sigh of relief, everyone could move on from the regrettable Darlan episode. Everyone except Darlan, of course.

Ike returned to Algiers when he heard the news. During the all-night ride back, he reflected on Darlan's death. It extinguished one problem, but no doubt created many more. General Giraud would become the French face of the Allied faction tasked with uniting Frenchmen under the Allied banner. De Gaulle would lead the radical Free French sect. The two lanky French generals—each tall enough to look the other in the eye—groped warily for a workable partnership.[16]

Through late fall, Ike hustled his armies east as the African weather pushed back. But mud, rain, an overstretched logistics chain, and lack of air cover turned his dash to the Tunisian ports into a crawl. In the last month of 1942, the unforgiving minute became more unforgiving with each minute.

Hitler's Mediterranean commander was Luftwaffe General Albert Kesselring, a bald, toothy Bavarian whose optimism and grin bore a resemblance to a certain general from Kansas. "Smiling Al," as he was known, was a defensive virtuoso fully alive to the danger of the Allies seizing the ports of Tunis and Bizerte. By early December, Smiling Al airlifted 31,000 men into Tunisia, enough to defend the ports and the airfields that protected them. Stukas, Heinkels, and Messerschmitts, the scourge of Europe, owned the Tunisian skies, and those raptors tore into Ike's foot soldiers as they tried to inch forward.

As German resistance stiffened along Tunisia's Dorsal Mountains, Ike realized it would be late January, maybe February, before he could mount a fresh offensive. He kept a brave face to the public, but after two months of fighting, his spirit was burning down like a Chesterfield. He had a hard time keeping cool around his staff, and typists and section chiefs winced beneath airbursts of profanity. A worried Harry Butcher told his diary, "Ike should stop saying at the lunch table: 'Ch-ee-r-i-s-t, anyone who wants the job of Allied Commander-in-Chief can have it.' Not because he isn't right, but because it may spread the wrong kind of stories of his ability to take it."[17]

Winston was having a hard time taking it, too. Christmas came and went, leaving him glowering over the lump of coal labeled "North Africa" that Herr Santa left in his stocking.

"I am far from happy," he complained to General Harold Alexander, British Middle East theater commander. "Eisenhower is reconciling himself to a two months delay, due allegedly to rainy weather, before making a main offensive against Tunis and Bizerta." The pause would give Smiling Al time to fortify his position east of the Dorsal Mountains, making the conquest that much harder.[18]

"It seems to me," Churchill wrote Ike, "that it is wise to keep the enemy bleeding and burning up his strength, even if we sustain equal losses. Thus a larger animal crushes the life out of a weaker and never gives him the chance to gather strength for a spring."[19]

But animal metaphors didn't change the picture on the ground, and for two weeks the maps didn't budge. On the last day of the year, Winston sent Ike his candid view. "I am deeply concerned about the unfavourable turn in Tunisia, and our staffs take an even more serious view," he warned. "Nothing matters now but the battle in the Tunisian Tip."

Ike wanted the Tunisian Tip as badly as Winston did. Probably more, since getting it was his only job. "I assure you that our troops have been pushed eastward as rapidly as the capacity of our communications and the availability of units would permit," he replied. He thanked Winston for standing with him, adding, "I assure you again of my confidence in the staunchness of your support."[20]

How long would that support remain staunch? Winston had been behind Ike so far, but Ike knew the prime minister, like FDR, would abandon him if he didn't get his armies moving east. The Darlan Deal had been strike one. Failing to rush Tunis and Bizerte was a second strike. Letting Rommel hang around North Africa until summer would be a third.

There were many eyes on Ike's back, and soon those eyes would be a lot closer. At the end of December, Ike learned that Churchill, FDR, and the rest of the Allied high command would converge on Casablanca for a mid-January strategy meeting. The big questions—which nations to invade, which allies to arm, and the sequence of operations—would dominate the conference.

But they wouldn't just look forward. They would also look at the mistakes they had made—who had made them, and more importantly, who would take the blame for them. At Casablanca, Ike's performance in North Africa, and his future, would be on trial.

FIVE

Neck in a Noose

In spit-polished boots and pressed khakis, Major General George Patton welcomed the Allied high command to Anfa, an upscale suburb of Casablanca that would be their home for the next ten days. As Ike's proconsul in Morocco, the cavalryman would play host to visiting VIPs—and their bosses, the VGDIPs—who would plot grand strategy for 1943.

Patton, the Army's social lion, rose to the occasion with the geniality of a Virginia hotelier. Fine weather and an abundance of Army-stocked eggs, oranges, and liquor got the conference off to a comfortable start. "Conditions most agreeable," Churchill telegraphed Deputy Prime Minister Clement Attlee. "I wish I could say the same of the problems."[1]

Like many American officers, Ike's friend Patton quietly harbored strong anti-British prejudices. "The British are pulling hell out of our leg and no one knows it," he complained to his diary the week before the conference began. Churchill, he added, "speaks the worst French I have ever heard, his eyes run, and he is not at all impressive." The French commanding general, Patton added, "said he would much rather play with US as [Churchill] wanted the whole world run his way."[2]

Time and fine liquor softened Patton's edges, but didn't change his basic view. The Englishman "strikes me as cunning rather than brilliant but with great tenacity," he wrote in a mixed review after one cocktail hour. "He did not drink excessively and smoked my last three good cigars."[3]

Awash in Army provisions and Patton's cigars, the commanders argued over strategy, material limitations, and politics. Winston and the British Chiefs wanted a landing in Sicily as soon as Ike cleared the Germans out of Tunisia. Marshall pressed for his long-deferred Roundup invasion. FDR, as usual, sat on his throne as judge while Churchill and Marshall argued their cases.

The prime minister and his chiefs considered Roundup a fantasy for 1943. The Allies lacked enough trained men. They lacked enough ships, and if they had the ships, they would lack the crews to man them. Far better to start with Sicily, which could be conquered with smaller forces. From there, they could jump over the Strait of Messina to the Italian mainland. And Sicily, they pointed out, would unlock the Mediterranean to Allied shipping and give them air bases from which to hammer Southern Europe. Those carrots interested Admiral King and Marshall's air chief, General Arnold.[4]

Outflanked again by the British negotiators, the U.S. Joint Chiefs agreed to move against Sicily. If Italy looked ripe for surrender, they would also consider attacking the Italian mainland. Someone—most likely Ike—would make that decision down the road on Italy, and Churchill was happy to take the win over Sicily now and have a discussion about Rome later. With Ike sequestered far from Washington.

Ike's friends in the War Department were bitter over the decision to push deeper into the Mediterranean rather than pivot back to France. "We came, we listened, and we were conquered," groused a senior staffer. Again, Churchill had his way. The Allies would wade deeper into the Mediterranean.[5]

The next question was what to do with Eisenhower.

Ike refused to fly on any bomber in combat shape. He wouldn't pull a plane out of the effort against Hitler, even if it meant riding a broken-down nag halfway across Africa. On January 15, that decision might have cost him his life when his decrepit Flying Fortress lurched and listed as two engines quit and a propeller shaft snapped. But the plane held a bone-rattling course just long enough to limp into Casablanca in one piece, after Ike and Harry Butcher strapped on parachutes and prepared to make an unscheduled jump into the Algerian desert.[6]

Relieved to have his feet on solid ground, Ike dusted himself off and lunched with General Marshall and Admiral King. He then went to Villa No. 2, FDR's quarters, to confer with the president and Harry Hopkins.[7]

During a long talk with Ike, Roosevelt's thoughts meandered over the French Empire. The French had lost control of Indochina and their other colonial possessions, and FDR wondered whether the United States would have to take over for France in some of those far-off places after the war.

Ike listened, silent. American intervention in the jungles of Vietnam was the furthest thing from anyone's mind, and he only opened his mouth to describe the North African campaign. When the president asked him for an end date for the conquest, Ike evaded the question as long as he could. But FDR, nodding, smiling, friendly as always, pressed Ike like a prosecutor cross-examining a witness.

When would Ike drive the Germans out of Africa?

Ike thought, then blurted out his best guess.

"May 15."

May 15. There, he had done it.

Ike had just committed himself to defeating a quarter million German troops led by Germany's famed Desert Fox in four months.

And if he didn't deliver, his role in the war would be over.[8]

As Ike shuffled back to his villa, he knew he was on thin ice. He stayed up until 1:30 in the morning talking to his friend George Patton about which way the wind was blowing. Afterward, Patton told his diary, "He thinks his thread is about to be cut."[9]

On the flight back to Algiers, Ike and Butcher compared notes. "The absence of clear-cut words of thanks from the President or the Prime Minister showed they had their noses to the political winds, and weren't going to be caught holding the bag for a general who had made an unpopular decision and hadn't yet got Tunisia," Butcher told his diary. "I told him his neck is in a noose, and he knows it."[10]

Some men lay down their lives for their country, while others lay down their careers. Ceremonies for the former might include an Arlington color guard, three rifle volleys, and a folded flag for the widow. Ceremonies for the latter might include a barstool, several double whiskies, and a volley of tears. For Ike, the Grim Bartender was pouring his glass and asking if he wanted a double. He needed a breakthrough, and soon.

While Churchill and FDR let Ike stand in the noose, they didn't pull the trapdoor lever. Not yet.

Something had to be done to get Tunisia back on schedule, so they rewrote the organization chart to include someone with more battle scars. Eisenhower would remain "Supreme Commander," nominally in charge of all air, sea, land, and supply forces, while General Harold Alexander would act as ground commander of a new headquarters called the Eighteenth Army Group. "Alex," a decorated veteran of the First World War, commander in India and Burma, and the last senior officer to evacuate at Dunkirk, would oversee ground operations of the two wings converging on the Tunisian coast: Montgomery's Eighth British

Army, driving west from Libya, and Ike's Torch forces, moving across the Maghreb from Algeria.

The move reflected British lack of confidence in Ike as a battle general. The British Army's chief of staff, General Sir Alan Brooke, later explained the arrangement: "We were pushing Eisenhower up into the stratosphere and rarefied atmosphere of a Supreme Commander, where he would be free to devote his time to the political and inter-allied problems, whilst we inserted under him one of our own commanders to deal with the military situations." As Winston told Clementine, Alex would hold "the real direction and planning of the main operation."[11]

Back in London, Winston couldn't make up his mind about Eisenhower. "I do not know whether he is a good general or not," he told the War Cabinet. "But I am bound to say that I have noticed that good generals usually do not have such good powers of expression as he has."[12]

Whether or not Ike was a good general would be an open question until he delivered North Africa to the Allies. Winston didn't yet know. But he knew the Germans had plenty of good generals. Men like Rommel and Kesselring. Ike was about to learn this the hard way.

SIX

"Taps"

February opened with a cable from Cairo. Churchill would visit Algiers on his way back to London. He had detoured to Turkey for talks with its aging president, then stopped in Cairo and Tripoli to meet with British commanders. On his way back to London, he would stop at Ike's headquarters and spend the day at Admiral Cunningham's villa. "I hope that the Admiral will be able to give our party bath and breakfast and that it will be agreeable to you if I lunch with you in a small circle," Winston wrote.[1]

Bath, breakfast, and lunch. A simple request. But a visit from Churchill was never simple. Holding aside the food and liquor needed to accommodate Winston's flying circus, security was the big thorn in Ike's side. The Germans were bombing Algiers harbor like it was London's East End, and a message from Washington warned that Nazi spies were lurking around the city, waiting for a shot at the British PM. Playing host to Winston put "quite a mental burden on us," as Ike told Marshall.[2]

Burden or not, Churchill was coming. On February 5, *Commando*, his converted B-24 bomber, waddled to the runway's end at Maison Blanche Airfield outside Algiers. Ike and his senior staffers saluted the PM as he hopped down the bomber's short belly ladder, and Ike quickly hustled Winston into his armored Cadillac, its windows smeared with mud to foil assassins.

Ike, Brooke noted, seemed nervous. For this trip, he even packed a revolver, a rare concession for a man who didn't pretend to live in a combat zone. Security was tight; six weeks after Darlan's assassination, Ike wasn't taking any chances.[3]

Winston loved the cloak-and-dagger drama. Ensconced at Admiral Cunningham's villa next door to Ike's, he savored a hot bath, soft bed, bedside radio, and the African sunshine. He enjoyed a luncheon thrown by Ike for the prime minister, de Gaulle, Giraud, Brooke, and Cunningham. He spent lunch chatting amiably with the French generals, who met his butchered French with smiles, puzzled looks, and patience. ("He is not the least bit self-conscious about his French, and it is just as you have heard, only worse," his secretary Elizabeth Layton wrote her parents.)[4]

"We had many long talks and some concrete accomplishments resulted," Ike wrote Marshall after Churchill and he ate dinner together. Knowing the pressure Ike was under, Winston agreed to send him another infantry division, and told Ike that the following week he would announce the incorporation of Montgomery's Eighth British Army into Ike's command.[5]

Friendly but still not yet friends, 90 percent of their relationship was transactional. Winston needed an American sympathetic to Britain and the Mediterranean strategy. Ike was a good asset for Britain to have. Ike, for his part, needed a big voice to protect him, and there was no bigger voice than Winston Churchill's.

But it helped that the two men genuinely enjoyed each other's company.

Winston was scheduled to leave for Gibraltar that night, but his plans changed when *Commando* sprung an engine magneto, grounding the ship. When Beetle told Ike his guest would be overstaying his reservation, "Ike hit the ceiling."[6]

"Safe in London, the PM was worth an army," he griped. "In Algiers he was a target and therefore a heavy responsibility." The War Department message about assassins was no joke; every minute Winston remained in Africa added to Ike's worries.[7]

To throw off would-be lion hunters, Beetle announced that the prime minister was leaving Algiers, and ordered a column of staff cars and escorts to make the thirty-mile drive to Maison Blanche. Butcher and Royal Navy Commander Tommy Thompson, Churchill's aide, rode in Ike's armored Cadillac, with Butch playing the part of the assassin's target. Ernest "Tex" Lee, Ike's adjutant, rode along in an armored scout car studded with two Browning machine guns.

As the caravan rolled out, a burst of gunfire sliced through the engine noise. Thompson jumped, but Butch assured him that Tex was just test-firing his Browning to make sure it wouldn't jam when they were on the road. Butch hoped his story was true as they rode to the airfield.

When they returned from the decoy run, it was apparent that Tex hadn't been testing anything. Someone had been careless with the weapon, and Tex's negligent discharge had sent live rounds in the direction of Ike's villa.

Tex sheepishly admitted that Ike's house had been "chipped" in the incident. But when Butcher checked, he found more than chips: Three bullets had lodged in the villa's wall.

"Of course it was just a casual thing," he concluded. "There wasn't a soul inside the house except the Allied C-in-C, the Chief of the Imperial General Staff, and the Prime Minister of the Empire on which the sun never sets." Ike and Winston had escaped death by staff.[8]

To everyone's relief, the next night the PM motored to the airport and boarded a repaired *Commando*. After seeing him off, Ike turned in, grateful for a good night's sleep.[9]

The path to Tunis and Bizerte wound along Africa's Mediterranean coast, threaded through the Dorsal Mountains, and angled over Tunisia's bleached hills to the ports dotting the Gulf of Tunis. Across this barren land, Ike's Allied force moved cautiously: British First Army on the left, a Franco-American corps in the center, and the thinly stretched American II Corps on the right.

Beyond the Eastern Dorsals, the enemy waited. Fifth Panzer Army, under General Hans-Jürgen von Arnim, guarded the port cities like Cerberus while Rommel's Italian-German Panzer Army conducted a fighting retreat from Libya as Montgomery's Eighth Army pushed from the east. As Monty advanced, Ike worried that Rommel, squeezed between Eighth Army and the Torch forces, might lash out against the vulnerable Americans in the middle. Maybe von Arnim would try to break the back of his British wing. Maybe both enemies would hit him simultaneously.

He was right to be worried. On the morning of February 14, von Arnim's panzers struck Ike's line at the crossroads town of Sidi bou Zid. By noon, nearly fifty Sherman tanks were burning. Within days, Rommel's *Afrika Korps* was barreling through Kasserine Pass toward American supply dumps and airfields. The American II Corps crumbled, retreating in chaos.

Through days of disaster, Ike kept a stiff upper lip, writing to Marshall of the "magnificent spirit displayed everywhere by the American enlisted men." But he was putting lipstick on a pig. Two days into the attack, Ike learned he might have lost as many as 5,000 men, along with hundreds of tanks, artillery pieces, trucks, and half-tracks. By the battle's fifth day, the picture was clearer: The Americans had lost 112 Shermans, hundreds of other vehicles, and their forward airfield.

Ike was stunned. Right after receiving his fourth star, he had been caught with a sucker punch. "It's the worst walloping we have taken in this fight, and perhaps the stiffest setback of our ground forces in the war," Butch wrote.

"Headquarters had all of the cheer of an empty funeral parlor," Kay Summersby agreed. Reeling from a week of disasters, Ike shuffled back to his villa and sat at a piano, head hung, plinking out "Taps" on its ivory keys.

"I don't think I ever saw him lower than he was that night," remembered Mickey McKeogh.

Not all bad things come to an end, but this one did. After ten miserable days, the Kasserine nightmare petered out. Lack of petrol and ammunition—the Achilles' heel of any mobile force—slowed and finally halted Rommel's advance. Ike's line had held, and his men resumed their bloody march to the sea.[10]

The debacle highlighted the inexperience of American GIs, and Ike knew the British were watching them closely. General Alexander's first impression of the American troops he commanded was of an inexperienced force that talked big but didn't know how to fight a skilled enemy.

After the Darlan Deal, the December stall, the tepid welcome at Casablanca, and now Kasserine, Ike sensed his job might become another war casualty. Picturing cables buzzing between London and Washington, he wrote his son John to lay some tough groundwork.

"It is possible that a necessity might arise for my relief and consequent demotion," he told Johnny. "It will not break my heart and it should not cause you any mental anguish. . . . Modern war is a very complicated business and governments are forced to treat individuals as pawns."[11]

To stay on the board, the pawn would need help from a king. Or a prime minister.

"I was sure the Kasserine battle would turn out all right in the end," Winston charitably wrote Ike after he learned the outcome. But when the news hit London circles, British leaders shook their heads. Eisenhower's green Americans had proven weak and incompetent when up against hardened Axis veterans.[12]

"It looks as if the US Forces have had a serious defeat last week, which will not help them in French eyes, and as if we shall have to do all the fighting there," King George wrote Churchill. General Alexander, who visited the American lines, told Winston, "I am frankly shocked at the whole situation as I found it."[13]

But Churchill, an optimist at heart, didn't see a broken force. He saw an army learning its craft through inevitable mistakes. For a while, the British Army had had its troubles, too. With mentoring and a little patience, the slow horses would pick up the pace.

"They are brave but not seasoned troops, who will not hesitate to learn from defeat, and who will improve themselves by suffering," he wrote King George. But he added, "It may be that the enemy is wasting strength on a false assumption that we are all as green as the Americans."

Privately, Winston was glad the thrashing had been taken under Ike's watch. "What a providential thing it was that I perpetually pressed for General Eisenhower to take the Command," he told the king. "The defeat of the American Corps, if it had been under a British general, would have given our enemies in the United States a good chance to blaspheme."[14]

In public, Churchill stood by Eisenhower. Privately, he harbored doubts. On February 13, as von Arnim's panzers were gunning their engines, he received a cable from Eisenhower's headquarters informing him that the landings in Sicily, code-named Operation Husky, would be delayed until July. The general wanted more ships and more troops on the scene before hitting the island.[15]

Churchill exploded when he read the news. Ike was waiting for perfection when the moment called for bold strokes. With momentum swinging to the Allied side, this was no time to wait. He had grudgingly put up with Montgomery's "down to the last shoelace" approach before Alamein. He wouldn't wait for Ike to do the same before Sicily.

"A delay of three months in the very midst of the campaigning season between the finish in Tunisia and the beginning of Husky would be a very serious disaster for the Allied cause," he wrote Ike. To pressure Ike from the White House side, he fired off a cable to Harry Hopkins: "I think it is an awful thing that in April, May and June, not a single American or British soldier will be killing a single German or Italian soldier while the Russians are chasing 185 divisions around."[16]

Through March and April, Ike stood his ground. Landing craft, amphibious training, and shipping timetables made an early date impossible. Unlike Torch, the Husky landings would be met by Italians and Germans holding defensible country. He warned the Combined Chiefs that if the landing force were met by more than two German divisions, he could not guarantee success.[17]

Winston was dumbfounded when he read Ike's assessment. *Two German divisions??* That was all Hitler needed to scare off the combined might of Britain and America? Two divisions? Where on earth could they invade and not find more than two German divisions awaiting them—Tanzania?

He shook his head. "What Stalin would think of this, when he has 185 German divisions on his front, I cannot imagine."

Perhaps, he thought, Ike was losing his nerve. He had been under heavy strain for more than a year. Men burned out under stress. Was Ike the right man for the invasions of Sicily, Italy, perhaps France?

Winston didn't know. He told the British Chiefs that operations "must either be entrusted to someone who believes in them, or abandoned." Ike's timidity in the face of a few German divisions, he added, "would make us the laughing-stock of the world. Especially this is true when, side by side with it, we are urged to attack the French coast across the scour of the Channel."[18]

Ike's stock, wallowing in a bear market, ticked up in early May as his troops closed in on Tunis and Bizerte. The Germans surrendered the ports on May 9, and by May 13 the last of von Arnim's men laid down their arms. Ike had promised FDR he'd liberate North Africa by May 15, and he made it with two days to spare.[19]

Unaware how shaky Churchill's faith had become, on May 10 Ike wrote Winston, thanking him for "the unwavering support you have given me. My feelings in this regard are all the deeper because of the circumstances that from the standpoint of your Government I am a foreign commander."

He added a personal note. "Long ago you clearly proved your right to a place on the all-time list of the greatest of national war leaders; I hope you will permit me to say that history will cite your actions during this phase of the North African campaign as additional evidence entitling you to this distinction. Personally and officially I thank you from the bottom of my heart."[20]

To Winston, Ike was a middleweight fighter who had taken some hard blows, been knocked around, even took a knee for a moment. But in the eighth round, he got back on his feet and laid von Arnim on the mat. It was an ugly knockout, but a knockout.

How many more bouts did Ike have in him? Winston didn't know. Other men before Ike had burned out, grown overconfident, died, or run out of luck.

He would find out soon enough. Ike was stepping into the ring for his next big fight: the battle for Mussolini's island.

SEVEN

Finito Benito

One of Churchill's staffers grumbled, "He is difficult enough when things are going badly, more difficult when nothing is happening, and quite unmanageable when all is going well."[1]

Truth was, Winston was never really manageable. Even on his sickbed, battling life-threatening pneumonia that winter, doctors and nurses couldn't control their patient. As one nurse wrote a friend, "One thing that might amuse you is his fluid intake chart. It goes something like this: Champagne 10 oz; Brandy 2 oz; Orange juice 8 oz; whisky and soda 8 oz."[2]

With fruits of conquest falling in Tunisia, Winston's appetite for victory swelled. He thought of the doors Sicily would open—Italy, Slovenia, the Aegean, even Austria. How long, he wondered, would it take to knock Mussolini out of the war?

Winston and FDR had agreed that Eisenhower would recommend the next steps in the Mediterranean, and during a visit to Washington in May, Winston made plans to visit Ike's headquarters again. His goal, he told South African premier Jan Smuts, was "to convince Eisenhower and others that nothing less than Rome could satisfy the requirements of this year's campaign."[3]

Winston knew lobbying Ike would lay himself open to charges of strong-arming, and he had no intention of letting the U.S. Chiefs doubt his fair play. To give the Americans a sporting chance, he asked Roosevelt to send General Marshall with him to Algiers. The U.S. Chiefs could have their representative—Ike's boss—at Winston's elbow as he made the Empire's pitch.[4]

On a balmy Friday in May, Ike stood at attention on the tarmac at Maison Blanche Airfield. The drone of engines swelled as Winston's new VIP plane, a converted Lancaster bomber christened *Ascalon*, dropped its flaps and rolled to a graceful stop. From the flying apartment emerged a beaming Winston, trailed by General Marshall, Brooke, Pug Ismay, and the usual supporting cast.

Winston clambered into Ike's Cadillac, and the two men caught up as they rode to Ike's villa. They carried the conversation onto Ike's front porch as Cunningham, Marshall, Foreign Secretary Anthony Eden, and the rest filtered in. Then they turned to the subject of Winston's visit.[5]

While Ike had bitterly opposed the Mediterranean strategy the previous summer, he had since warmed to the old man's views. Before they could invade France, he realized, the Allies had needed the blooding Torch gave them. Commanders needed time to learn how to land and supply troops on a beach. Troops needed more experience with a hardened enemy. Both nations needed more time to build landing craft and warplanes and tanks if they were going to crack Fortress Europe. *"Per aspera ad astra,"* as the Roman saying went. Or for Ike, through the desert to Berlin.[6]

The next night found Winston inviting himself to Ike's villa for another impromptu talk. Though Ike knew the late-night session would leave him worn out the next day, he was all smiles as Winston launched into another strategy pitch.

After Sicily, Winston insisted, the Italian mainland must be the next target. Knocking Mussolini out of the contest, and establishing a foothold in central Europe, would land a body blow against Hitler. Winston had no doubt they could do it. As Butcher recalled, "The PM said that he confidently looked forward to having Christmas dinner with Ike in Rome."

Winston kept up his pace, leaving no rhetorical shell unfired. After one in the morning, his rounds spent, his limbers emptied, he left Ike's quarters. It was a short night for Winston, another long one for an early riser like Ike.[7]

A week into his visit, Winston was confident Ike would follow the British line of thought. Their personal rapport bloomed, and they enjoyed some lighthearted banter. As they discussed Pantelleria, a stepping-stone island Ike wanted to capture before taking Sicily, Winston said there couldn't be more than 3,000 Italians defending the place. Ike was sure there were far more, but Winston stuck to his number. He offered Ike a wager of one centime for every soldier captured above 3,000, and Ike, calculating the worth of a franc, took the bet.[8]

Winston also asked Ike if he could go along with the fleet to watch the Pantelleria invasion. Ike politely refused on grounds that it would hazard an unnecessary risk to an irreplaceable man. Winston accepted Ike's decision—though he later pouted when he found out that Ike and Cunningham intended to watch the landings from a Royal Navy cruiser.[9*]

After Ike sent waves of bombers to pound the small island, Pantelleria surrendered, yielding 11,121 prisoners. Learning of the island's fall, Winston cabled Ike to remind him of their bet. "Many congratulations. How does our centime account stand? I hope to have to pay you a lot."[10]

---

* In his memoirs, Ike wrote, "Two years later he reminded me that I had been very unfair to him on that occasion, especially as he had a personal financial stake in the enterprise."

"I think the entire settlement came to about $1.60," Ike remembered. He wrote Winston, "I am carefully saving the sixty-five francs with which you purchased the surplus Italians out of Pantelleria in the hope that with it I may one day buy you a nice drink of Italian brandy."[11]

Friendly exchanges didn't win battles, but they revealed a shared sense of humor. In one note, Winston suggested that Ike stop using the old British terms "aerodrome" and "aeroplane" in official communications and substitute the more familiar "airfield" and "aircraft." "Aircraft" and "airfield," Winston suggested, are "good English and good American." Like himself. Perhaps, he added, even "airport" could be used where an airfield received overseas flights.

"I am delighted to trade 'airport' for 'aircraft' and 'airfield,' thus getting two good English words for one of doubtful ancestry," Ike replied.

"Good," wrote Winston, "but what about these bastards: aeroplane, aerodrome, airplane and airdrome. Can we not scupper the lot?"

Ike smiled as he read. "All bastards mentioned in your message have been adequately scuppered in accordance with your suggestion," he promised.[12]

As June gave way to July, the engine again churned to life. More than a thousand oceangoing ships and 149,000 men were ready to sail from Africa to Sicily. The argonauts would land on Sicily's eastern half and fight their way to the port of Messina, the island's bottleneck and link with the Italian mainland. Take Messina, and Sicily's defenders would run out of food and bullets. Like their comrades in Tunisia, they would surrender or die.[13]

For this operation, Ike would see several familiar faces. Beetle Smith ran Allied Forces Headquarters (AFHQ) in Algiers. General Harold Alexander commanded Fifteenth Army Group from Tunis. Beneath Alexander, George Patton would command the Seventh U.S. Army, Air

Marshal Arthur Tedder the Allied air forces, and Admiral Andrew Cunningham the Allied fleet.

But the show's star—the general who would lead the Commonwealth troops into Messina—was the man who had driven Rommel from Libya: General Bernard Montgomery.

"Monty," the son of an Irish bishop, was a product of St. Paul's School and the Royal Military College at Sandhurst. Twice shot in the First World War, he had made his name in 1940 leading a division in France, then shepherding his troops to Dunkirk and safely home. In England, he had trained a home guard of 100,000 troops until the summer of '42, when Winston sent him to Cairo to lead the British Eighth Army.

A short man with a towering ego, Monty had little sense of subordination and none for diplomacy. He regularly crossed lines of decorum or tact—not out of defiance, but because he was blissfully free of the shackles of self-awareness. He ruthlessly sacked officers who didn't meet his high personal and professional standards, and lectured others in a supremely condescending manner. And as Ike had learned, he bit the head off any officer crass enough to smoke in his presence.

In battle, Monty wasn't nimble. He liked his lines fortified, his tanks massed, and his ammunition piled sky-high before launching his attack. If he wasn't ready, he wouldn't move—and would ignore cables from superiors urging him to get on his bicycle and pedal. Winston liked to say he prodded field commanders "like a great blue-bottle buzzing fly over a huge cowpat," but even Winston couldn't push Monty when he wasn't ready to go.

When he did launch a blow, however, it landed like a wrecking ball. In North Africa, his offensive at El Alamein had shattered Rommel's lines and forced him into permanent retreat. In nine days, Monty pushed *Panzerarmee Afrika* back to Tobruk with the loss of 60,000 men. After driving the Desert Fox into Tunisia, Monty cracked his fortified line and crushed the defenders between his wing and Ike's. Ike's army was the anvil, but Monty's was the sledgehammer.

The world took notice. The Oscar-winning documentary film *Desert Victory*, released the month after Ike's Kasserine debacle, made Bernard Montgomery a household name. It transformed the image of Britain's soldiers from cannon fodder into conquerors. By Husky's launch, the Hero of El Alamein was, after the king and prime minister, the most famous Briton in the world.[14]

On the morning of July 10, Ike sat in "the Wake," the signals hub on Malta where the first reports of the Sicily invasion would drop. He rubbed his lucky coins and watched the air fleet fly overhead on its way to the Sicilian coast.[15]

As hours dragged, then raced, the tension broke with hourly reports from Montgomery's Eighth Army laying out the precise location of British and Canadian units. From George Patton's Seventh Army, there was an ominous silence. Somewhere on Sicily's southern coast, Patton and his men were fighting, but Ike didn't know where.

For twenty years, Patton had been one of Ike's closest Army friends. They had trained tankers together after the First World War. They had lived next door to each other, sharing family dinners, sipping drinks on their porches, and watching their children play together. Patton had introduced Ike to senior men who advanced his career and opened doors, and he had loaned Ike his class notes from the Leavenworth general staff school when Ike studied there. Before the war, Ike had begged Patton for a regimental command in his tank division, and Patton tried to oblige him.

Famously quotable, Patton was prone to shoot his mouth off when he should have kept it shut. Now, on Husky's D-day, he kept it shut when he should have been talking. Ike had aircraft, supplies, and men waiting to support Seventh Army, but damned if he knew where to send them.

Two days later, under an early-morning sky, Ike boarded a Royal Navy destroyer to rendezvous with Patton's command ship off the Sicilian coast. Flashing a toothy grin, Patton saluted Ike as he came aboard. In a command cabin, he showed Ike his army's progress as generals, admirals, and aides looked on. Seventh Army had fought off counterattacks by the elite Hermann Göring and Livorno Divisions, and were pushing beyond Gela into open country. They had every right to be proud of their progress thus far.

"When [Ike] breaks into a smile, his face lights up," remembered Lucius Clay, Ike's friend from the Philippines. "When it's not in a smile, it's a pretty stern, rugged-looking countenance." Ike's stern face told everyone in the room all they needed to know.[16]

Drawing himself to full height, Ike blew his stack on his old friend. Seventh Army's reports had been terrible. Montgomery was keeping headquarters fully informed, and Patton had told him damn near nothing for a full day. Ike had paratroopers, supplies, tanks, and planes waiting to move onto the island. How the hell was he supposed to support Patton if the Germans knew where his men were, but headquarters didn't?

"Ike stepped on him hard," Butch wrote afterward. Admirals and generals stood frozen, staring at Ike, then at Patton, not making eye contact.

George took the thrashing like a West Point plebe. As soon as Ike paused, he turned to his chief of staff and ordered him to send headquarters four daily reports—causing Ike to chew Patton's ass again, this time for being too quick to reply. Dammit, George had to think before opening his mouth.

Word spread quickly. "He must have given Patton hell, because George was much upset," wrote Major General John Lucas, who saw a red-faced Patton right after the incident. As Ike's old friend and onetime patron, Patton thought he deserved better.[17]

Ike never explained why he lit into Patton. But George learned the hard way that being Ike's friend didn't make a damned bit of difference when Ike found performance lacking. To Ike, duty was the North Star. Safety, career, family, religion, friendship—especially friendship—meant nothing when the mission's success hung in the balance. If duty required Ike to wring the neck of a pal he owed a lot to, or relieve him, or bust him down to his permanent rank and send him home depressed and bitter, he'd do it without blinking. That cold, impersonal reality was what he and Patton and every other officer signed up for when they took the oath.

For the next two weeks, Patton's men ground their way through Sicily's hills and ravines. The fighting was relentless and bitter, but on July 22, Sherman tanks rolled into Palermo, the island's capital. Wheeling his men east, Patton drove his GIs to their limits until they reached the capstone city of Messina. They made it there first, beating Montgomery to the prize and completing the conquest of Sicily.

The political shock waves rocked Rome. Afraid of turning his kingdom into a battlefield, King Victor Emmanuel III ousted fascist dictator Benito Mussolini and named Marshal Pietro Badoglio prime minister. With Mussolini under house arrest, Badoglio opened secret discussions for an armistice.

Il Duce's fall shouldn't have come as much of a surprise. Dictators don't often get to retire, and Italy's strongman was bound to go sooner or later. But the timing, on the heels of Patton's capture of Palermo, caught the Allies unprepared. Like North Africa, they had to neutralize Italy and get Allied armies north of Rome before Hitler and Kesselring could pour German divisions down the Italian boot.

FDR and Churchill agreed that the king and Marshal Badoglio were Eisenhower's correct points of contact for a negotiated armistice. But it would be a military pause only, without political implications. Roosevelt told Churchill, "In no event should our officers in the field fix any general terms without your approval and mine." Churchill heartily agreed.[18]

Ike's chance to grab Rome without a fight slipped away as he waited for instructions from the home governments. "Ike regretted existence of rapid communications," wrote Butcher. "If we were still in the day of sailing ships, he thought he could deal more quickly and advantageously with the Italians than is possible when he has to communicate to both Washington and London and wait for the two capitals to concur or direct."[19]

Frustration ran in both directions. Winston was furious over a propaganda broadcast from Ike's headquarters, in which AFHQ announced that the Allies had paused the bombing of Italy to give the Italians a chance to unite for peace. Calling for political changes in Italy, Winston complained to Harry Hopkins, amounted to meddling where generals didn't belong.

"Serious embarrassment is caused here by proclamations from AFHQ having it seems the authority of Eisenhower behind them," he wrote. Admitting that low-level propaganda didn't need to be managed from London and Washington, he insisted, "Broadly speaking, it is surely right that the generals should do the fighting and the politicians the talking."[20]

Winston's complaint wound its way through a maze of Foreign Office channels to Harold Macmillan, who passed it to Ike. Ike couldn't fathom what Winston found so offensive. The announcement had been approved by a Board of Political Warfare—on which both Macmillan and Murphy sat—as well as by Ike's British chief of staff, General John "Jock" Whiteley. He had done everything by the book and resented Winston calling him out to his boss.

"It is the first time within my knowledge that the PM has complained to the President of Ike's operation," a worried Butch told his diary. "Heretofore, the PM had registered any bellyaches direct with Ike. Something is irritating the old boy."[21]

In frustration, Ike drafted his own complaint to General Marshall. Realizing that criticizing the British prime minister would escalate the dispute, he didn't fire it off. "This he would let cool until after lunch and then take another look at it," Butch told his diary. "We had played a game of ping-pong to clear the mental processes." After the game, Ike took a fresh look and toned down the letter.[22]

As Ike told Marshall, the home governments had to give him latitude to seize small, time-sensitive opportunities. "I do not see how war can be conducted successfully if every act of the Allied Commander in Chief must be referred back to the home government for advance approval," he wrote. "I have been quick to acknowledge that in all my prior operations, including the difficult days of last February, the Prime Minister stood like a rock in supporting everything that we found necessary to do and this in the face of reverses and discouragements. In this instance, I personally think he has telegraphed to the President without a full knowledge of the facts."[23]

Two weeks later, Winston learned Macmillan had given Ike a copy of his complaint. A little embarrassed, he sent Ike a letter for his eyes only. "My personal and secret telegram to Mr. Hopkins was not written for your eye and was couched in unceremonious style," he admitted. But Ike had to be careful. "I hope you will realise that I am liable to be cross-examined in the House on the exact wording of every declaration to the Italian people that carries or purports to carry your high authority. . . . Therefore, I hope you will consider my difficulties as well as your own."[24]

For all Ike's frustrations, by October he could feel a quiet satisfaction. North Africa was behind him. Sicily, too, and now southern Italy. His forces had driven Rommel out of Tunisia, zipped up the Mediterranean from Gibraltar to the Suez Canal, established a bomber base in Italy, and sucked Hitler's armies into the Italian boot, keeping them out of the Red Army's fight. And out of France.

Plenty of struggles lay ahead, of course. His landing on the Italian mainland—Operation Avalanche—had nearly been defeated by heavy German counterattacks. More ominously, the Italian front hardened south of Rome, as Hitler's man in the Mediterranean, Smiling Al Kesselring, was putting up a bitter fight along the strongly fortified Gustav Line.

But the war's momentum had shifted. Ike could begin thinking of Rome and northern Italy—and from there, wherever the Combined Chiefs told him to go. Little by little, the liberator's sword was digging deeper into the Third Reich's vitals.[25]

Winston, too, could look back with satisfaction on a year managing the alliance with America. In Washington, he had persuaded FDR to overrule his military chiefs, abandon Sledgehammer, and go for North Africa. At Casablanca, he had convinced the Americans to defer Roundup for the year and jump onto Sicily. In Algiers, he had gotten Ike to move from Sicily to Italy. Winston's willingness to travel far and wide to make his case, jaw to jaw, was paying handsome dividends.

The Americans had been deferential, even generous. "No people respond more spontaneously to fair play," he once told Clement Attlee. "If you treat Americans well, they always want to treat you better." With luck, thought Winston, before the year was out, he would guide the Alliance into the Aegean and the Balkans.[26]

Through it all, Winston had stood by his right-hand American. But that summer he saw something disquieting forming on the horizon. Ike was finding his voice. And he was learning to use that voice to say no.

EIGHT

Land of the Cyclops

"All I am asking for is the capture of Rhodes and the other islands of the Dodecanese," Winston pleaded. His voice carried that mix of supplication and command that came naturally when his heart was set and he would use every weapon in his arsenal to get it.

The Dodecanese Islands, lying in the Aegean Sea near the Turkish coast, called to Winston like sirens to Odysseus. Their capture might induce Turkey to throw in with the Allies. It would open a new front near the Balkans. It would redeem Britain's loss of Rhodes the previous month. And it would eliminate German soldiers who would otherwise be thrown into the battle for Italy.

It mattered not that Turkey had been the "Sick Man of Europe" since Churchill's youth, nor that Turkey would require a massive influx of modern weaponry to be worth a toss as a fighting ally. Nor did it bother him that critics would accuse him of trying to erase the memory of the Gallipoli invasion—his pet project of 1915, which ended in slaughter for 32,000 British, Australian, and New Zealand troops. To Winston, the Aegean was worth it.

When Italy surrendered in September 1943, the Germans took Rhodes by storm. British forces briefly occupied the nearby island of

Kos, but a month later, German troops ejected them, capturing nearly 1,400 British troops at a cost of fifteen dead. That angered Winston. The Germans followed Kos with a paratroop assault on Leros, where the outnumbered attackers captured or killed another 3,800 British troops and bagged another 5,000 Italians. That also angered Winston.

Hackles raised, he turned to Ike.

Ike ordered bombers to hammer German positions on the islands. But courtesy had its limits: He wouldn't devote scarce divisions or landing craft to Rhodes, Kos, or any other volcanic speck in the Aegean. He needed them in Italy, where bigger fish were frying.[1]

Accepting military logic, the British Chiefs sided with Ike. Winston wouldn't hear of it. He wanted the Allies to carry the war to the land of cyclops and minotaur, regardless of what Ike, Brooke, or anyone else told him.

"He is extraordinarily obstinate," General Brooke complained to a staffer. "He is like a child that has set its mind on some forbidden toy. It is no good explaining that it will cut his fingers or burn him. The more you explain, the more fixed he becomes."[2]

Winston ignored all protests. He insisted that control of the Aegean would help Ike's Italian struggles by diverting German troops away from Italy. The capture of Sicily had knocked Italy out of the war; Rhodes might even induce Turkey, Hungary, and Romania to join the Allies.

Beyond strategy, there was gratitude. Winston was Ike's sponsor and mentor. He had backed Ike after the Darlan and Kasserine debacles and had built him up in letters to Roosevelt and speeches to Parliament. It was bad grace for Ike not to return a small fraction of the favor.

"I thought he owed me much," grumbled Winston.[3]

"On questions of broad—and I mean really broad—strategy, I think there is no judgment in the world I respect more than I do Winston's," Ike would later write. "I still cannot agree with him in many of his ideas about the tactical uses of troops and, sometimes, with his calculations as to great results that would have resulted from minor adventures."[4]

Rhodes and Kos were two of those minor adventures, but Ike gave Winston's obsession a fair hearing. "My staff and I studied the problem with the greatest possible sympathy," he remembered. "We came to the conclusion that aside from some temporary air support there was nothing we could give."

Winston didn't want sympathy; he wanted landing craft and troops. So he tried again. At his insistence, Ike held an all-hands meeting with the British commander of the Middle Eastern Theater, General Henry "Jumbo" Wilson and their top commanders. When Ike, Wilson, and their lieutenants gathered to discuss the Aegean, Ike put his foot down.

He didn't need to. "It was the simplest, most unargumentative of any similar conference I attended during the war," he later recalled. Every officer agreed with Ike's conclusions, even though there would be a shrill, dissenting voice in London. "All of us knew that the decision would be a bitter one for the Prime Minister to accept."[5]

After the meeting, Ike wrote his official bosses, the Combined Chiefs of Staff, and laid down the facts of life. "We must therefore choose between Rhodes and Rome," he concluded. "To us it is clear that we must concentrate on the Italian campaign." If the Combined Chiefs ordered him to pivot to the Aegean, he would do it. Otherwise, he wouldn't budge.[6]

Winston found himself alone. Brooke, the Joint Planning Staff, the American Chiefs, and Secretary Stimson all lined up behind Ike. When FDR told Churchill he wouldn't force Eisenhower to do it, Winston conceded defeat. Grudgingly, as always.[7]

"The difficulty is not winning the war," he muttered to one secretary. "It is in persuading people to let you win it—persuading fools." He said he felt "almost like chucking it in."

The bitter pill stuck in his throat for a long time. He blamed Ike, a man who owed him much, for thwarting him. As he would later write,

"The painful episodes of Rhodes and Leros . . . constitute, happily on a small scale, the most acute difference I ever had with General Eisenhower."[8]

Ike knew Winston would sulk over the Aegean, and felt he owed him an explanation. "It is personally distressing to me to advise against a project in which you believe so earnestly," he wrote, "but I feel I would not be performing my duty if I should recommend otherwise."[9]

Winston wouldn't let it go. Years later, when his war memoirs were coming out in print, he told Ike, "The only point about which I was unhappy at the time was your inability to give me the help I needed to take Rhodes in the autumn of 1943. I still hold to the view I took then."[10]

Ike had the ability to help Winston take Rhodes; he just didn't want to. His job was to win battles and conquer continents. Ike measured strategy the way he calculated bridge bids: without passion, without considering political prizes to be won, or friendships to be lost.

Winston saw something else. Something cold behind Ike's reassuring tone and steady grin. A disturbing pattern was emerging—a pattern he would see again as Operation Overlord took center stage.

NINE

"The Devil Is on My Side"

CHURCHILL HAD CALLED THE TORCH LANDINGS the "end of the beginning." But the end of the beginning was not the same as the beginning of the end. A year after Torch, the beginning of the end was still a long way off—and 1944 promised to be bloodier than '43.

To sketch out the tragedy's next act, FDR and Churchill agreed to meet with Stalin in Tehran. They had many things to discuss, chief among them Operation "Overlord," the new name for the Roundup invasion of northwest France. Overlord's commander would be selected, and the Big Three would fix the timing of the invasion.

General Marshall, as everyone knew, would command the operation. Marshall had been the plan's staunchest advocate, and he held the trust of both Allied governments. The British would pick one of their own to replace Eisenhower in the Mediterranean, and Ike would go back to Washington to take Marshall's seat among the Joint Chiefs. That was the scuttlebutt, at least. It was FDR's decision, and he hadn't announced it yet.

Before flying to Tehran, Winston and his military chiefs stopped at Malta to see Ike. They spent a day discussing the problems of capturing

Rome and future operations in Italy, then dined together at the ancient palace of the Knights of Malta.

The evening's highlight was Winston's presentation of the ribbon of the Africa Star to Ike and General Alexander, an award personally approved by the king. Because everyone was terribly busy, the ceremony was short and simple. One guest remarked that centuries earlier, in this same castle, the award would have been accompanied by days of jousting tournaments, feasts, and processions.

Suffering from a cold, Winston was in a foul mood. Still peevish over the Aegean, he suspected the Americans wanted to shortchange the soon-to-be British theater. To Brooke and Tedder, he grumbled that if the Americans wouldn't play fair in the Mediterranean, Britain wouldn't play nicely with Overlord, and that evening, he circled back to one of his favorite themes: Germany's "soft underbelly."[1]

Ike, nursing a cold of his own, listened but did not interject. "I could not escape a feeling that Mr. Churchill's views were unconsciously colored by two considerations," he later wrote. "The first of them was his concern as a political leader for the future of the Balkans." In other words, a world where the Red Army overran Eastern and Central Europe.

"The other," said Ike, "was an inner compulsion to vindicate his strategical concepts of World War I, in which he had been the principal exponent of the Gallipoli campaign." Ike didn't voice that thought, of course, and admitted he had no proof of Winston's motives. But the ghost of the Dardanelles would explain Winston's obsession with the Mediterranean.[2]

But Ike misjudged his comrade. Winston wasn't refighting Gallipoli. He wanted a theater to garner laurels for British arms without having to share them with the Americans. America would provide over half the troops in France, and in 1943 it would produce nearly as many airplanes as Britain, Germany, and the Soviet Union combined. The West's pup had grown into a wolf—and before long, it might replace Britain as the pack's alpha. The Mediterranean theater was Britain's refuge.

Winston had watched this disturbing trend for more than a year.

The previous spring, he had briefed King George on an upcoming conference of Commonwealth prime ministers and leaders. Churchill's purpose, the king told his diary, was to "discuss the question of putting up a united British Commonwealth and Empire front to show the world and USA that we are one unity. The Americans are always saying they are going to lead the post-war world."[3]

The need for parity drove Winston to protect British-led theaters, even if it meant advocating schemes like the Dodecanese or a thrust around the Alps. "He hated having to give up the position of the dominant partner which we had held at the start," Brooke concluded. "As a result, he became inclined at times to put up strategic proposals which he knew were unsound purely to spite the Americans."[4]

Winston had promised Overlord to General Brooke earlier that year. But the Americans, who would supply most of the troops, had insisted on a U.S. commander.

Winston didn't want to bow to American pressure again, but the Americans were beginning to realize how powerful they were becoming, and he reluctantly told Brooke command of the invasion of Europe would go to an American.

Brooke was hurt by the way Winston casually mentioned it, as if he were telling Brooke he had left his spectacles in his other suit. But though he did not let on, Winston felt awful. He told Ike that "it had been most embarrassing to him to have to tell Brooke of the change because he appreciated and sympathized with the anguished disappointment that Brooke was thus compelled to suffer."[5]

In return for appointing Marshall as Overlord's overlord, the Americans agreed to put a Briton in charge of the Med for the "soft underbelly" attack. Ike, a third wheel, would have to go home, and on Malta Winston broke the news.

"I am sure you will realize, my dear general, that we are quite happy with you," Winston said. "But it would obviously be unfair to us to be foreclosed from both major commands in Europe."[6]

Outwardly, Ike said the only thing he could say: He would cheerfully carry out any orders his superiors issued. Inwardly, he took it hard. "Going home" was the exile he doled out to officers for crimes like insulting British colleagues or violating security rules. He'd demoted those sinners down to their permanent ranks and banished them to the States—"on an unescorted ship," he liked to say.

Now it was his turn. He'd keep his four-star rank, he'd become chief of staff, and his ship would probably have an escort. But he'd still be going home. Thinking of the political swamp he'd be wading into, he muttered to Butcher, "I'll be carried up to Arlington Cemetery within six months."[7]

Well, the decision hadn't been announced, not yet. Overlord's command was a call only the president could make, and as FDR boarded his ship to cross the ocean, he hadn't made it. Ike's plot in Arlington would have to wait.[8]

In Tehran, Stalin and FDR crushed Winston's hopes for a big Italian offensive. At the first meeting of the Big Three leaders, Stalin pounced on Winston, shutting down talk of alternative fronts and pushing hard for a spring invasion of France. Joining the chorus, Roosevelt suggested a diversionary landing in southern France, code-named "Anvil," to draw German forces away from Normandy before the main landing took place. In Italy, the western Allies would push beyond Rome, but not as far as the Alps. Britain's Mediterranean theater would be relegated to a sideshow.[9]

Against the two giants, a frustrated Winston made no headway. FDR, for all his vision, couldn't see what Russia would look like once Hitler was defeated—or how Europe's center of gravity would shift to Moscow. One diplomat recalled Winston's lament: "There I sat with the great Russian bear on one side of me, with paws outstretched, and on the other side the great American buffalo, and between the two sat the poor little English donkey who was the only one . . . who knew the right way home."[10]

Adding insult to injury, Roosevelt, whom Winston considered a friend, tried currying favor with Stalin by cracking jokes at Winston's expense. Quips about Winston being "cranky" or getting up on the wrong side of bed—and belittling references to his "John Bull" mentality—elicited polite smiles from Stalin that FDR interpreted as a personal connection. Truth was, jokes and insults didn't move Stalin's stone heart an inch. Stalin lacked the wiring to respond to personal feelings. But Winston felt them, and Roosevelt's remarks cut him deeply.

"It's a rather tragic thing, of Roosevelt's changing the objects of his affection," Ike's son John Eisenhower put it decades later. "He was insulting toward Churchill in his courting of Stalin, and then Roosevelt and Stalin actually ganged up to force Churchill's hands as to the timing of the Channel, the cross-Channel attack. So Churchill in his zeal for unity between the Anglo-Americans was not only frustrated but rejected."[11]

Winston's daughter Mary agreed: "My father I think was very hurt by the, as it were, drawing away of Roosevelt from him and Roosevelt concentrating his considerable magnetic charm and personality on his relationship with Stalin."[12]

The four-day conference included military meetings, diplomatic meetings, Big Three meetings, and, of course, exhausting banquets, where liquor flowed and tables groaned beneath platters of fish, meat, and sides. Winston and Stalin neither trusted nor liked each other, but the two men got along cordially and engaged in some friendly banter.

"I believe that God is on our side," Winston quipped at one dinner. "At least I have done my best to make Him a faithful ally."

Stalin grinned, his dark eyes twinkling. "The Devil is on my side," he replied. "Everyone knows that the Devil is a Communist—and God, no doubt, is a good Conservative."[13]

What about Overlord's commander? The question still hung in the air.

It stumped Roosevelt as he sifted the implications of sending Marshall to Europe. Harry Hopkins, FDR's confidant, said the president thought Marshall was the only man who could "stand up to Churchill." The Chief would be invaluable to Overlord, but he seemed irreplaceable at home. *Time* magazine's "Man of the Year" for 1943 held the trust of Congress, the press, the public, and the British high command. And Marshall wasn't a political threat to Roosevelt, as MacArthur might be; like most Army officers, Marshall didn't vote and he avoided partisan politics.

Unsure what to do, Roosevelt promised Churchill and Stalin he would name a commander within a few days after the conference ended. He had to think some more.[14]

As the meetings in Tehran wound down, Churchill brooded on the world after the war. The victors would eye each other warily as Stalin's missionaries preached their gospel across Europe. Stalin himself, drunk on victory, would only be held in check by western strength, not by Roosevelt's glad-handing or manufactured displays of disunity. Salvation lay in the democracies standing together.

"Until he came here, the PM could not bring himself to believe that, face to face with Stalin, the democracies would take different courses," Winston's physician, Lord Moran, recalled. "Now he sees he cannot rely on the President's support. What matters more, he realizes that the Russians see this too."[15*]

* Dr. Charles Wilson, later Lord Moran, was Churchill's close companion for many years, and Churchill's sentiments expressed in Moran's memoirs can generally be taken at face value. Historians have, however, questioned many of Moran's exact quotes.

From Pearl Harbor to the surrender of Italy, Winston had bent the Americans to his will. But the tide was turning. Ike hadn't budged on Rhodes, and Marshall was about to take charge of an operation that, Churchill feared, would crush the German Army but leave much of Europe occupied by the Red Army. Poland, Czechoslovakia, and their neighbors might simply be trading one boot heel for another.

Before leaving Tehran, Winston spent an evening at the old British legation building, a fading two-story beauty that, like Winston, had been built during Queen Victoria's reign. Sipping whisky one night with Lord Moran, he saw with frightening clarity a catastrophe in the making.

He did not know what the spark would be. Perhaps Poland, perhaps Turkey. Perhaps some damned island in the Pacific. But Winston couldn't shake the vision of a *diabolus ex machina* crawling from the war's ashes.

Roused from his reverie, he sprang from his seat and stood over Moran.

"I believe man might destroy man and wipe out civilization," Moran recalled him saying. "Europe would be desolate, and I may be held responsible."

Moran said nothing as Winston looked away.

"Why do I plague my mind with these things? I never used to worry about anything."

His face grew dark.

"Stupendous issues are unfolding before our eyes, and we are only specks of dust that have settled in the night on the map of the world."

Another pause.

"Do you think my strength will last out the war?" he asked. "I fancy sometimes that I am nearly spent."

His doctor had no answers, of course, and Winston didn't expect any.

Having voiced his fears, Winston went to bed.[16]

TEN

Eisenhowerplatz and 10 Downing

"One never knew when Winston Churchill would pop in," remembered Kay Summersby. "Sometimes his visits were scheduled, and other times he just appeared—like a little boy who could not stay away from the action."[1]

The little boy would pop in on Ike after the Tehran meetings, but first he had to see Roosevelt in Cairo. They needed to discuss next moves in the wake of their Big Three decisions, and one of those moves was the selection of Overlord's commander.

The obvious choice had always been Marshall, but Marshall was the one nearly irreplaceable man in Roosevelt's military structure. The Pennsylvanian could win over Republican congressmen and the anti–New Deal press in a way FDR couldn't. Roosevelt wasn't sure he wanted to part with him.

There was also the question of working with Churchill. Overlord's commander would spend a lot of time in London, and that meant close contact with the prime minister. Churchill had butted heads with Marshall many times, first over Marshall's demand for a Combined Chiefs' command structure, then over operations in North Africa and the Aegean. When Churchill waxed rhapsodic over the Dodecanese—"Muskets must flame!" he told Marshall—the general replied with unusual bluntness: "Not one American is going to die on that goddamned beach."[2*]

"It seems pretty clear that Winston will refuse absolutely to let Marshall take over," FDR told his son Elliott. "It's not that he's argued too often with the P.M. on military matters," he explained; "it's just that he's won too often." Maybe Ike would be an easier sell.[3]

During a break in their Cairo meetings, Winston and FDR piled into a car and rode over to see the Pyramids. They asked the Sphinx if she had any advice to offer. She didn't, but as their limousine rumbled up to the lion's stone paw, Roosevelt casually remarked that he had decided on Overlord's commanding general. He couldn't spare George Marshall, he said. He wanted Eisenhower in London.

Winston was delighted. "I said it was for him to decide," Winston later wrote, "but that we had also the warmest regard for General Eisenhower, and would trust our fortunes to his direction with hearty good will."[4]

Wrapping up an exhausting eight days of meetings in Cairo, Winston popped into Ike's headquarters in Amilcar, a suburb of Tunis, for a short visit. The short visit would stretch into a two-week, life-threatening ordeal.

After a nine-hour flight, a bureaucratic screwup diverted *Ascalon* to the wrong airfield, forty miles from where Ike and his entourage were waiting. In the cold night air, Winston sat beside the runway on a suitcase as the flight crew figured out where they were supposed to go. Destination corrected, Winston and the party climbed aboard and straggled into Ike's headquarters compound.

The next day Winston's chest became heavy, his breathing labored.

* Ike would later write of Marshall and Churchill, "During the entire war I never heard an instance, even when debate between the two became vigorous, when there was an iota of damage to decorum. They were far too big for that." There was a lot Ike didn't hear about these two men he idolized.

Pneumonia set in, and this time it wasn't bluffing. Winston's temperature spiked, he could barely move, and his 69-year-old body trembled with heart fibrillations. Brooke and Moran called in specialists, nurses, and medical equipment to keep Winston breathing. Moran dosed his patient with everything he had to keep Winston's heart working as his body fought the infection.

A nervous Ike could do nothing but stay out of the way. As doctors conferred, the RAF flew Clementine from London to see her husband, possibly for the last time. Western leaders, including Ike, braced for the worst.[5]

But Winston had the lungs of a lion, and after several touch-and-go days, his stubborn body crawled back. Bucking medical advice, on Christmas Eve he met with Ike and his staff to discuss Operation "Shingle," the upcoming Allied landings at Anzio, near Rome.

Scheduled for mid-January, Shingle was intertwined with the Anvil landings on the French Riviera and the main Overlord landings, because all three invasions drew from the same scarce pool of landing ships. Balance among the three was important to the Allies, especially England, and Winston was not about to let the Americans make those decisions without him.

Defying his doctors, Winston convened a Christmas Day conference with Ike, Wilson, and the West's senior theater commanders. He told the assembled brass he wanted Shingle to have enough troops, ships, and air support to drive to Rome and beyond. Ike, the Med's lame-duck commander, agreed, reasoning that every soldier defending Italy was one less man defending Normandy.

Between meetings, Winston hosted a Christmas luncheon for Ike and the theater's top commanders. It was the first meal he had taken out of bed since falling ill, and his only nod to doctors' orders was to remain in something approximating his bedclothes. In a silk robe adorned with blue and gold dragons, he looked, thought Harold Macmillan, "like a figure in a Russian ballet."

"The PM is remarkably well," Winston's secretary wrote his wife. "The doctors are quite unable to control him and cigars etc. have now returned."[6]

Two weeks into the new year found Ike back in London. He had spent a fortnight in Washington, meeting with Marshall and Roosevelt, and squeezed in an all too brief reunion with Mamie and his son, West Point Cadet John Eisenhower.

He was happy to see his wife and son, but even as he and Mamie embraced, Ike's mind was far away. Nervous and distracted by a job gnawing at him, he wrapped up his meetings, gave Mamie a goodbye kiss, and boarded a Skymaster for England.[7]

The morning after Ike checked into his London hotel, a staff car brought him to his old office in Grosvenor Square, the complex Butcher had nicknamed "Eisenhowerplatz." A thick January fog enveloped London that morning, the kind of disorienting mist Jack the Ripper, or possibly Montgomery, might jump out of. Visibility was so bad, two enlisted men had to walk ahead of Ike's car, shepherding it the sixteen blocks from hotel to office. His guides got lost between the street curb and the front door and disappeared into the fog.[8]

Ike would disappear into his own fog, and he wouldn't emerge until Berlin lay in ruins.

While Ike was Overlord's showrunner, his top lieutenants would be British. Air Chief Marshal Arthur Tedder would serve as his deputy, Admiral Bertram Ramsay would run naval operations, Air Marshal Trafford Leigh-Mallory would command Overlord's air arm, and either Alexander or Montgomery would take charge on the ground.

Winston knew Ike wanted Alex as his ground commander. They had gotten along well in the Mediterranean, while Monty rubbed the

Americans—and many Britishers—the wrong way. But Brooke backed Montgomery, and the War Cabinet settled on the hero of El Alamein, mostly for public relations reasons. If British casualties proved heavy during Overlord, the politicians would take less heat if they had chosen Britain's most successful, famous commander. Winston went along, so Monty it would be.[9]

In early March, a heavily guarded cluster of buildings in London's Bushy Park, code-named "Widewing," opened for business. Widewing would serve as main headquarters for SHAEF—Supreme Headquarters, Allied Expeditionary Force—Eisenhower's command post for all military, logistical, and civil affairs functions.[10*]

The Widewing campus—a huddle of sandbag-lined block buildings, Nissen huts, mess, and communications hub—was draped in camouflage netting and hemmed by an eight-foot wall. White-helmeted MPs, nicknamed "Ike's snowballs," guarded the entrances, but they could not keep out the damp English chill that penetrated coats and numbed toes and fingers as the SHAEF crew labored to bring Overlord to life.[11]

Ike ran his headquarters on a seven-day week. He was in the office by eight and left after six or seven, if he was lucky. Mornings ran on American coffee breaks at eleven; evenings paused for British tea at five. Unless he had lunch with the PM, Ike ate in his office or at the main dining hall, dubbed the Yankee Doodle Room. If he didn't have guests, he'd scarf down a soup and sandwich at a corner table and get back to his office to absorb the next salvo of problems.[12]

On a few treasured weekends, he would retreat to Telegraph Cottage, where he and his inner circle picked up where they'd left off in November of '42. Kay resumed her place as Ike's secretary, chauffeuse, and confidante. Marty Snyder kept the kitchen stocked, while Mickey McKeogh, John Moaney, and the rest kept Ike's personal life running smoothly. Butch, who moonlighted as SHAEF's public relations consul-

* Cynical GIs insisted SHAEF actually stood for "Should Have Army Experience First."

tant, resumed his post as Chief Diversion Officer, filling Ike's scarce off hours with ping-pong, target shooting, bridge, golf, jokes—anything to keep the Boss's mind from burning out under pressure.[13]

As SHAEF grew, so did Ike's household. Before long, his entourage included a waiter, a tailor, and another cook. Pushing personal privilege, Ike asked Winston to allow Telek and his mate, Caacie, still in Tunisia, an exemption from six months of kennel quarantine when they returned to England. Unfortunately for Ike and the dogs, they'd have to complete their six-month sentence with no time off for good behavior. Some rules even a prime minister cannot bend.[14]

While Telek and Caacie were doing time, Ike's household acquired a black cat named Shaef, courtesy of Air Marshal Tedder's wife. Over the next year and a half, Shaef would contribute to the war effort by lounging on headquarters furniture and hissing at Ike's dogs.[15]

As Kay Summersby would later write, "The only thing Ike really deplored about the P.M. was his habit of staying up until all hours. By nature Ike was an early-to-bed, early-to-rise man; the P.M. was the opposite."[16]

Thinking of those late nights before Torch, Ike set hard stops on routine meetings with Winston. "If you want a night conference, if it is called after 9:30, you will have to do it without me," he told him. "I get up early, I have to work with my staff all day, and I just cannot carry on the way you do."[17]

Winston bowed to Ike's need for regular sleep, and late-night invitations trailed off. His meddling did not. "Mr. Churchill had fresh ideas every day on how to conduct the invasion and insisted on imparting them to Ike himself," Kay remembered. "He often telephoned after midnight to discuss a new brainstorm. Ike could not simply tell the P.M., 'That idea stinks.' He had to point out to him exactly why such and such an idea would not work or would not be politic. This took lot of time and an awful lot of patience."[18]

Through winter and spring, Ike and Winston fell into a steady rhythm of Tuesday lunches at 10 Downing Street and Friday dinners at either 10 Downing or Chequers. Winston unabashedly used his access to Ike—and their growing friendship—to persuade, cajole, and argue his way into SHAEF policy.

"I admired and liked him," Ike later wrote. "He knew this perfectly well and never hesitated to use that knowledge in his effort to swing me to his own line of thought in any argument. Yet in spite of his strength of purpose, in those instances where we found convictions in direct opposition, he never once lost his friendly attitude toward me."[19]

Winston appreciated Ike's commitment to Allied harmony, a Herculean job given the scale of the U.S. invasion of Great Britain. Grateful as they were for the help, Britishers took exception to the worst habits of their American occupiers—especially the wanton destruction of property during training exercises, public drunkenness, pub brawls, dangerously fast trucks and jeeps, race discrimination, and the gaze-diverting appearance of soiled condoms left in parks and alleys, evidence of off-duty activities with English women. These indignities, more glaring with every abandoned rubber and beer bottle, tested the patience of even the most British of British hosts.

"General Eisenhower's supreme ability to make Anglo-American relations a fact rather than table talk is going to require a lot of exercising here," wrote C. D. Jackson, SHAEF's Psychological Warfare Board deputy. "There is not a single square inch of London on which an American is not standing, and add to this the fact that, if he is standing after dark, he is standing unsteadily; I think that there is plenty of trouble brewing."[20]

To keep trouble from bubbling out of the pot, Ike and Winston tackled local problems like a pair of city councilmen. Winston, for instance, quickly responded to American complaints about high rents charged to U.S. officers. "There is no reason why the Americans should not pay a fair and equitable price for accommodation, which they are quite willing to do, but I do not think extortion or profiteering should be allowed," he complained to his deputy, Labour's Clement Attlee.[21]

In return, Winston went to Ike to address English grievances. Foreign Secretary Anthony Eden brought local complaints about reckless driving to Winston's attention and suggested he make a statement on the subject to Parliament. Winston disagreed. There was no need to bring all of SW1 into a problem he and Eisenhower could handle quietly, he said. He trusted Ike's sense of fair play. "The remedy for the reckless driving which is causing so much trouble is a conversation between me and Eisenhower," he replied to Eden. "I should greatly prefer to let Eisenhower put his screw on and see what happens."[22]

Sometimes the problems went beyond nuisance. At one point, Ike needed English ports to accept forty additional ships loaded with invasion munitions. But the overloaded ports were already slated for ships carrying food for a hungry British public. Turning food ships back would mean the loss of a half million tons for a people whose rations were meager. But when Ike raised the subject, Winston told Ike he would get the ports cleared for the Overlord shipments. In return, he and Eden asked for Ike's help in getting Roosevelt to make up for the loss after D-day. A grateful Ike asked Marshall to secure the president's approval, so everyone could have what they needed.[23]

As host country, Britain naturally gave more than it got, and nowhere did this become more tense than with Ike's request that Britain cut off all communications and travel with the outside world, starting shortly before D-day. Diplomats, especially from France and Commonwealth nations, were furious. They inundated Eden's Foreign Office with protests.

Churchill and Eden told Ike they could give him a temporary

communications ban, but they needed to lift the blackout shortly after D-day. Ike pushed back. SHAEF had coordinated a massive head fake by designating Patton to lead a fictitious army group based near Dover. Radio traffic, dummy planes, and tents gave the impression of a large invasion force to the north, to get Hitler thinking the main blow would land around Calais, and that Normandy was a diversionary feint. But if travel and communications resumed, it wouldn't be long before the Germans figured out the real target. Hitler would be free to send his tanks down to Normandy's beaches—spelling death for many men and jeopardizing the mission.

Ike tried to hold the line. He wanted the communications ban to stay, not just to D-day, but more than a week or so afterward. The longer he could hold those panzers around Calais, the better his men's chances of survival. "It is my own point of view and the opinion of all my principal subordinates that the lifting of the ban will indicate to the enemy that our major effort has at last been launched." He couldn't agree to a fixed date to lift the travel and communications ban.

This time, Winston wouldn't budge. The ban had to be rescinded after D-day. "You probably have no idea of the enormous inconvenience and friction which this system has caused," he said. Moreover, an editor from the *Chicago Tribune* had been allowed to enter and leave the United Kingdom during the diplomatic ban. "I must confess that I had not realized that unofficial Americans would be free to come and go between here and the United States during all the time we are putting this ban on all Embassies," he protested. He would not agree to anything longer than seven days after D-day.

In the end, Ike left the choice to Winston. "I quite realize that this ban was imposed voluntarily and unilaterally by the British Government and no matter what decision you find it necessary to make I will accept it in good part," he said. He would trust Winston to make the correct decision.[24]

When Winston needed to crack the whip at home, sometimes Ike filled in as the whip. One of the most complex projects of the invasion was the construction of two artificial harbors to feed the invasion force. A major port had always been vital to supply the massive armies landing on D-day, and since the Germans held the nearest ports, the Allies would build their own. They would sink old ships and enormous concrete blocks in the shallows near the invasion beaches to create a breakwater against the Channel's choppy waves. With the seas calmed, the Royal Navy would ferry in prefabricated floating piers, code-named "Mulberry," big enough for cargo ships to off-load everything from trucks to toilets.

It was a massive engineering and naval feat, and it put a tremendous strain on Britain's engineers and labor force. Winston needed more men for the job, but his War Cabinet ministers simply couldn't reallocate scarce talent from other projects. They had scraped clean the bottom of the barrel.

That's where Ike came in.

Before a Cabinet meeting, Winston asked Ike to come to his office. He told Ike he would need Ike to appear before the ministers and offer a few U.S. Engineer regiments to help get the Mulberries finished on time.

"Of course," said Ike. "They will be available tomorrow."

"Oh, no, general," Winston said, a hint of a grin pushing his jowls. "I just want you to *offer* them, not *send* them."

That evening, when Cabinet discussion turned to Mulberry, Winston asked the ministers for more engineers to move the harbor project. As expected, each pleaded poverty.

Winston turned to Ike. In a worried voice, he asked Ike how the shortage would affect the invasion.

"This was my cue," remembered Ike. "I said that we had to have the artificial harbors. If they could not be ready unless we speeded up production by using more manpower, I would volunteer a number of efficient U.S. engineers for British use." Those men were on important training missions, he said, but the harbors were so vital, he would pull fighting men out of training to get the work finished.

"This was exactly what the prime minister wanted," Ike recalled. With an embarrassed look, Churchill turned to his ministers.

"It seems that our commander-in-chief is the only one present who can produce a constructive idea," he said. "We thank him for his generous offer, especially because its acceptance would interfere with his necessary military program."

Then his look turned to one of accusation.

"But gentlemen, are we to admit that the British Government is so helpless, so unimaginative, so lacking in determination, that it cannot, except by calling upon our allies, carry out a simple duty that it took upon its own shoulders?"

He let the thought sink in.

"I cannot believe that we are so stripped of resources that we cannot fulfill our pledges, made in good faith to our partner in this great enterprise. I want each person here to make another survey of the capacity of his organization and I expect to meet with you here tomorrow, where we shall produce a solution to this problem, which I refuse to admit is unsolvable."

The next day Winston called Ike. Everything was on track. "He said I had given him the ammunition he needed and now I could count, without fail, on the readiness of the artificial harbors."[25]

Part of what made Ike and Winston click was their social makeup. Though raised worlds apart, they shared similar impulses. When she first met Ike in the spring of '42, Kay Summersby had been struck by the Kansan's authenticity. He could chat with an English baron or an Iowa private in the same down-to-earth tone he'd use with an Abilene neighbor. "He had an unassuming curiosity that I can only describe as charming," Kay remembered. "If he didn't know something, he asked questions. There was no pretense at the godlike knowledge many generals seem to believe their rank demands."[26]

Winston, too, enjoyed flouting upper-crust conventions. "He always acted on impulse socially, without thought of his dignity—the same characteristic which so many persons found attractive in General Eisenhower," Kay noted. Except when addressing the king—whom he revered as the personification of empire—Winston would say and do whatever he thought best, regardless of whom he was addressing.[27]

Between the press of war and politics, they found lowbrow moments to relax together. One afternoon, Ike invited Winston, his daughter Sarah, Monty, and Tedder over to Telegraph Cottage for a hot dog luncheon on the lawn. Ike's mess sergeant remembered Ike and Winston spearing wieners in a boiler with a skewer. Winston, used to washing down caviar with champagne, declared them "a delicacy fit for a king."[28]*

Ike and Winston were, at heart, two social artists who admired each other's work, actors who recognized talent when they saw it. In conversation, Ike was a fine bourbon served from a plain glass bottle. Its unbranded simplicity concealed a brow-raising complexity and ninety-proof fire. Winston was a Pol Roger champagne, bubbly and delightful to the senses. Words fizzed and popped as they poured out, overwhelming the palate with dry, flavorful bursts. Each was different, but appealing in his own way, and they spoke each other's language.

Winston had another, more practical reason for keeping Ike close: Britain's once reliable trump card—Winston's friendship with FDR—wasn't working the way it used to. When Roosevelt had the energy to direct his lieutenants, Winston could go to the president and steer plans

* They were, for King George VI had enjoyed hot dogs with Roosevelt at a picnic at Hyde Park five years earlier.

for Torch, Sicily, and Italy. But FDR was fading. His energy came in flurries, not sustained waves. He took longer to recover from colds and relied increasingly on advisors like Marshall, Harry Hopkins, or Admiral King.

Lately it was their voices Winston heard when he read FDR's secret cables. "I cannot believe any of these telegrams come from the President," he muttered to Eden in early 1944. "They are merely put before him when he is fatigued and pushed upon us by those who are pulling him about." Ike was Winston's back channel to the men pulling the president's strings.[29]

So Winston would show Ike friendship, even deference. Kay, who frequently drove Ike to Number 10, noted that Winston walked Ike out to his car when they were done—a courtesy he showed few others.[30]

Friendship wouldn't fix everything, of course. Facts have a way of showing up, and the facts of Overlord wouldn't budge. In the spring, that meant coming to blows over Anvil.

When he first saw the three-division Overlord plan, Ike concluded the operation needed considerably more strength. But by February, it was obvious that there weren't enough ships and landing craft—"lift" in British parlance—to carry out simultaneously a five-division Overlord and a two-division Anvil while pushing British-led forces to Rome and beyond. The Shingle invasion at Anzio had turned into a blood-soaked stalemate, and Hitler's *soldaten* were putting up a savage fight along the Gustav Line south of Rome. If it came down to a bigger Overlord or Anvil, Ike would reluctantly cut Anvil.[31]

To Winston and the British Chiefs, the solution flashed in bright, unmistakable letters: Anvil must go. Allocating Anvil's ships and soldiers to Italy would let the Allies reap the rewards of Anzio by pushing into northern Italy. An Italian job would also support Overlord by drawing German troops down into the boot. It might even allow Allied armies to push past the Po River into the Alps—where they would meet the Russians and keep Middle Europe out of Stalin's clutches.[32]

But the American Joint Chiefs wouldn't budge. Anvil, they argued, would open the French port of Marseille and allow reinforcements to pour into southern France. It would give French soldiers a role in the liberation of their country. And at Tehran, Roosevelt had assured Stalin they would add Anvil to the lineup. Having disappointed the dictator so many times, FDR wasn't going to walk back his promise.

The Washington brass ordered Ike to hammer the Anvil line in London. In conferences, Ike put on the Joint Chiefs hat and argued the American case to the British Chiefs and the prime minister—the toughest audience of the war.

"The fact that he represents the U.S. Chiefs of Staff in dealing with the British Chiefs throws a tremendous weight on his shoulders," Butcher told his diary. "It makes him the recipient of all the arguments and pressures which the British, particularly the Prime Minister, may wish to advance."[33]

On February 22, Ike met with the British Chiefs to thrash out priorities for Overlord and the Mediterranean. He agreed to keep landing ships in Italy for an extra month to give the Rome campaign more sustained muscle. He also agreed to push Overlord's D-day from May to June, giving U.S. shipyards an extra month to crank out sorely needed landing craft—most especially the big, straight-to-the-beach ships known as "landing ship, tanks," or "LSTs."[34]

Jumbo Wilson, Ike's successor in the Mediterranean, wouldn't compromise. He told the British Chiefs he couldn't let go of any ships or troops until Rome was captured—and with the fighting around Anzio in a stalemate, that would take time. The British Chiefs of Staff agreed and dug in their heels.

Ike believed a big push in Italy would pin down more German

troops than a May or June Anvil would. Inwardly, he also believed Anvil was impractical. But Roosevelt had promised Stalin, and the president wouldn't welch on his promise.[35]

"Ike is in the middle," wrote Butch. "He feels as if the American Chiefs think he is trying to press for the British view and, at the same time, senses that the British think he is wrangling for the American view."[36]

After weeks of hard bargaining, Ike sold Winston on a compromise. Anvil would be deferred until mid-July. The delay would give General Alexander, the British ground commander in Italy, additional time and resources to bust out of Anzio and capture Rome. Jumbo and Alex would return the landing ships and peel off some of Alex's troops to launch Anvil. That would still leave a slight shortage for Overlord, but the numbers were close enough that Ike felt they could scrape up the ships to do the job.[37]

The American Chiefs, weighing Ike's opinion, agreed. They also accepted Ike's recommendation to delay Overlord from May to early June.[38]

Accepting Ike's compromise, Winston backed down on Anvil—for the moment. He would return to the theme, but with Ike's help, he had protected the Mediterranean from the Washington interlopers.

He and Ike had other problems to work out, questions that would test their moral strength. The darkest of these was the slaughter of Frenchwomen and children. It wouldn't go away, and by April 1944 the decision was coming at them like a bullet.

ELEVEN

"Are We Beasts?"

CHEQUERS AT NIGHT. The long hall went quiet as the film projector flickered to life. Winston, surrounded by dinner guests, slumped in his chair as smoke, fire, and debris filled the silver screen. Allied bombers had returned from a raid over Germany, and the newsreel showed the ancient cities of Charlemagne, and their inhabitants, torn to pieces.

In theaters, British audiences cheered as they watched German cities pulverized. But in the darkened hall, a look of pain spread across Winston's face as plumes rose and city blocks collapsed.

"Are we beasts?" he asked, sitting up. "Are we taking this too far?"[1]

Perhaps they were. Perhaps they had all become beasts. Because Ike wanted to bomb Frenchmen, too.

Ike spent February in a Byzantine wrestling match with Allied air commanders. The tournament prize this time: temporary command of the strategic bomber fleet.

The big four-engine bombers—Flying Fortresses, Lancasters, and Liberators—were property of British Bomber Command and U.S. Strategic Air Forces. Their job was to smash targets vital to Germany's ability to wage war: oil refineries, steel plants, Krupp cannon works, ball bearing factories. Things the Wehrmacht couldn't live without.

During the critical early stages of Overlord, Ike wanted the heavies—and their smaller, two-engine siblings—to knock out German bunkers, supply dumps, and troop concentrations along the Normandy coast. Those target priorities had to be set by SHAEF, so Ike needed the heavyweights under his command, at least until his foot soldiers were firmly ashore.

The bomber barons balked. Their planes were built to win the war, not smash little pillboxes on Normandy's beaches. They might occasionally permit bomber groups to hit local Overlord targets, but they weren't going to hand over their crown jewels to Ike.[2]

Ike, a veteran of bureaucratic infighting, didn't flinch. He wouldn't put himself at the mercy of air lords who might yank his flying carpet when he needed it most. Lack of air support had nearly cost him the invasion of Italy, and damned if he'd let that happen again. If the Combined Chiefs didn't give him temporary command of the strategic air forces, he'd ask to be relieved and go home.

"Listen, Arthur," he told his deputy, Air Marshal Tedder, "I am tired of dealing with a lot of prima donnas. By God, you tell that bunch that if they can't get together and stop quarreling like children, I will tell the Prime Minister to get someone else to run his damned war—I'll quit!"[3]

Entering the fray, Winston spoke to Ike over dinner. The problem was the barons didn't trust Ike's air commander, Air Marshal Trafford Leigh-Mallory, he explained. Leigh-Mallory had grown up commanding fighters, not bombers, and strategic bombers are as different from fighter planes as a howitzer is from a pistol. No one thought Leigh-Mallory capable of running a bomber show, and they weren't going to give him their heavies.

A frustrated Ike told Winston he would have preferred having Arthur Tedder as his air commander. The pipe-smoking Scotsman was smart and diplomatic, and he had risen through the bomber ranks. But the British had appointed him as SHAEF's Deputy Supreme Commander, a job slightly less defined than the American vice president's. Having sidelined Tedder, whom the bomber marshals trusted, the British had given Overlord's air command to Leigh-Mallory—whom they didn't.

Winston refused to shove Leigh-Mallory down Bomber Command's throat. "The Prime Minister was quite violent in his objections," Ike told Marshall, and at the end of the night, Winston was still leaning against Leigh-Mallory and Ike. Ike played for time, telling him he'd send a detailed plan that would allay Bomber Command's fears.

"He seemed very impatient," Ike wrote Tedder the next morning. "I hope you can push conferences and planning so that we can have an answer quickly. Otherwise the P.M. will be in this thing with both feet."[4]

After painstaking arguments, Winston, Ike, and the bomber chiefs hammered out a compromise: During the run-up to D-day and for a short time after, strategic bombers would temporarily fall under Ike's command. Eisenhower would exercise his authority through Tedder, who would be, in Winston's words, the "aviation lobe of Ike's brain." Tedder would draw up Ike's orders and give them to Leigh-Mallory, who would do exactly what he was told. The bomber barons wouldn't have to trust Leigh-Mallory; they would trust Tedder. Once the Overlord forces were firmly established on the Continent, the bombers would revert to Bomber Command, which would send them back to do what they did best: wreaking biblical destruction on German cities.[5]

It was a head-spinning mix of bureaucratic gymnastics and wordsmithing, but Ike won the round. He had his bombers. His next fight was over where he could use them.

Ike's planners knew time would favor the Overlord invaders—if they survived the first three days. But those seventy-two hours would be a knife fight in a phone booth. Field Marshals Gerd von Rundstedt and Erwin Rommel would rush divisions from Germany to hit the waterlogged Allied soldiers as they struggled off the beach, and SHAEF soothsayers calculated that if Rommel could get thirteen mobile divisions into the fray during Overlord's first three days, the Allies might find themselves pushed back into the sea.[6]

So Ike had to stop thirteen divisions.

Unsheathing Occam's machete, he found the answer in the railways. Bomb the rail yards in France, Belgium, and the Netherlands, and Rommel would get no reinforcements. Germans defending the beach would find themselves stranded and alone. With the rail hubs destroyed, Hitler would be forced to send his men in long, exposed road convoys, where the inevitable traffic jams would make them sitting ducks for Leigh-Mallory's Hurricanes, Thunderbolts, and Mustangs. Championed by Ike's deputy, Air Marshal Arthur Tedder, the bombing campaign became known as the "Transportation Plan."

By the end of March, the bomber commanders and chief of the RAF, Sir Charles Portal, gave the Transportation Plan the nod. But RAF approval was just the military side of the equation. Ike still had to sell the plan to Winston and the British War Cabinet. And those politicians were a hell of an audience.[7]

When Ike and Tedder circulated a list of seventy-three rail targets, Britain's Ministry of Home Security raised the alarm. Civilian casualties, it warned, could reach 80,000 to 160,000, with perhaps a fourth of that number killed. Politically, those numbers stank like a three-day-old battlefield, so the War Cabinet, including Churchill, objected.[8]

"Considering that [the French] are all our friends, this might be held an act of very great severity, bringing much hatred on the Allied Air Forces," Winston explained in a letter to Ike. It was a close call, he conceded, for "the argument for concentration on these particular targets is very nicely balanced on military grounds." But Winston wouldn't back Ike's sledgehammer approach, even after Ike agreed to warn civilians in advance. SHAEF would have to find some other way to isolate the battlefield.[9]

The fight over the Transportation Plan pitted Winston the romantic against Ike the realist. Ike's thoughts ran only to military victory—an equation in which death and destruction were two inputs. Terrible inputs, to be sure. But if the inputs were managed correctly, the outputs would be peace and freedom.

In this case, one of those inputs was the destruction of French civil railways. Yes, French women would die. Children, too. But women and children were dying from Crimea to Amsterdam every day the war dragged on. The question wasn't whether innocent people would die, but whether the deaths of these particular innocents would hasten the war's end.

Ike thought they would.

Probably. But he wouldn't know until after the line was crossed.

Winston saw it differently. As a soldier, Ike's horizon ended with a military armistice. Winston's stretched beyond surrender, beyond Hitler's death, into the postwar peace. He believed even the Second World War did not command a ceaseless drumroll of carnage—at least, not against friends. So on the night of April 3, he called Tedder, Brooke, and Portal into the Map Room for another discussion about bombers.

"At 10.30 had to attend one of those awful meetings of the PM," Brooke told his diary the next day. "He is opposed to Tedder's plan to use them on the railways because he does not think that the results to be achieved will be much and secondly owing to casualties amongst French civilians which must result from it."

Winston expounded on these themes until after midnight. He said he would discuss the matter further with Ike, but for now, there would be no bombing of any targets where high French casualties were likely.[10]

As Winston pushed off a final decision, new casualty estimates softened the blow. It turned out those shocking early death numbers had rested on shaky assumptions. For instance, not every French citizen would be unwise enough to loiter at the rail yards after being warned they would be bombed. The 160,000 number Home Security had calculated also included everyone who was even slightly injured, so the number could have been high by a factor of ten. Perhaps the horrors were not so great as Winston had feared.[11]

Though relieved to see the butcher's bill lower than expected, Winston remained unconvinced. He feared that "even if the casualties were not so great as was estimated, they might well be sufficient to cause an unhealable breach between France and Great Britain & USA." While he permitted small-scale strikes on outlying rail yards, he ordered Tedder to keep a close eye on French losses and report them to Downing Street.[12]

Ike squirmed as politicians dithered. With seven weeks until D-day, the sands were running out. In late March, he and Winston had spent two days crisscrossing the English countryside in *Bayonet*, Ike's VIP railcar, watching soldiers training for the coming invasion. Those young men would be fighting for their lives come June, and Ike owed them their best possible chance of getting off the beaches alive. "I protested bitterly at allowing details of a few targets to interfere with the operation of a whole plan," he told his diary.[13]

By mid-April, Tedder and Portal offered Winston a sliver of hope: French casualties had consistently been lighter than expected, and the number of trains sidelined or stranded on tracks was growing.

Still, Winston hesitated. Five weeks before D-day, he called the brass back to the Map Room. He told them Ike's bombing plan would "build up a volume of dull hatred in France which would affect our relations with that country for many years to come." Bombing a friendly city in the heat of battle was one thing; dropping bombs out of a peaceful spring sky was another. He said he might overlook this hatred if he felt the gains were clear—but they weren't.[14]

The politicians held one view, the military men another. At a War Cabinet meeting on April 27, the foreign secretary, paymaster general, lord president, and Winston lined up against Ike, Tedder, Leigh-Mallory, and the British Chiefs of Staff. After a lengthy discussion, the political leaders drew a line: Ike's Transportation Plan should be revised to prohibit attacks where total French casualties would likely exceed 150 civilians.[15]

Winston called Ike into the Map Room to explain it face to face. After the war, he said, the Allies must be able to say they tried their best to spare French lives. Forgoing a military advantage where French deaths would be excessive would show the French the Allies had done everything they could.

Ike was dumbfounded. They needed the Transportation Plan to protect Overlord's prospects—and Winston was siding with the paymaster general and the foreign secretary over every military expert?

It was a hell of a way to run a war.

When Ike got back to his office, he fumed to Tedder. The Allies had bombed submarine bases in Brittany and arms factories in Belgium. They had dropped 400 tons of bombs on the Renault motor works near Paris. Those raids killed a hell of a lot of French and Belgians. No one gave a damn when they bombed German military hubs and motor pools in occupied France—even though many of them had been located in town squares filled with civilians going to market. Those civilians had been blown apart, too. You couldn't help it; there was no way a wave of bombers flying at 20,000 feet, dodging flak, could take out a rail yard and guarantee fewer than 150 casualties.[16]

Time was slipping. Ike wrote Winston another letter, telling him bluntly that limiting the Transportation Plan to casualties of 150 per raid would emasculate the plan. If Overlord's success were truly paramount, if American and British and Canadian soldiers were going to pay with their lives on D-day, then the French would have to contribute to the bill. He wasn't backing down.[17]

He met with Winston on Friday, April 28, and reiterated that "military necessity dictates bombing of transportation areas." Winston repeated the War Cabinet's "grave concern" over French deaths, and the meeting ended with Ike telling Winston the final decision had to be made by the Combined Chiefs. If the Chiefs told him to forgo an operation that might aid Overlord's success, he would naturally follow orders. But in Ike's view, they would be making a terrible mistake.[18]

Ike met Winston for lunch three days later. Ike said he was meeting with his air experts down to the third level below his position. He had promised the technicians immunity from retaliation by their bosses if they would give him their honest, unvarnished opinions. He told Winston he'd get back to him as soon as he had heard from the experts.[19]

Again Winston convened the War Cabinet. He summarized the arguments for and against, then told the ministers General Eisenhower believed that limiting casualties to 150 civilians would jeopardize the operation. Ike bore a heavy burden for Overlord's success, he said, and he asked the politicians not to make Ike's job more difficult.

But Winston added that he hadn't fully realized how cruel the plan would be. French noncombatants would be slaughtered, and after the war, when Russia swallowed up Eastern Europe, the western Allies would have to stand together. Would they stand together in the shadow of British bombers over Paris?[20]

The meeting ended with no firm decision. Clement Attlee, the opposition leader, doubted the plan's necessity and said he was convinced "there was a grave danger that it would spoil our political future in Europe." Oliver Lyttelton, minister of war production, agreed. Anthony Eden was less convinced, but his Foreign Office worried about the German propaganda line: While Russian armies were fighting Germans on the battlefield, British and Americans were killing Frenchwomen from the air.

Desperate to hold the casualty ceiling, Winston turned to Tedder. When the Transportation Plan was done, would it end up killing fewer than ten thousand civilians?

Tedder said he did not know. He hoped so, but he could not say for certain.[21]

After weeks of handwringing, Winston laid out his objections in a letter to Roosevelt. He warned the president that the bombings "may easily bring about a great revulsion in French feeling toward their approaching United States and British liberators. They may leave a legacy of hate behind them."[22]

Roosevelt responded with the sang-froid of a leader far from the blast zone. While he agreed that every means of assuaging French bitterness should be pursued, he concluded, "I am not prepared to impose from this distance any restriction on military action by the responsible commanders that in their opinion might militate against the success of 'Overlord' or cause additional loss of life to our Allied forces of invasion."[23]

With those words, the argument ended. Winston had stood on principle, but Ike would have his way. In British eyes, the burden of the slaughter would rest with Ike and Roosevelt. In French eyes, they would all share the blame.

May skies offered that beautiful, clear flying weather wing commanders love. Waves of bombers overswept French and Belgian rail yards, raining death from above. Their victims were ordinary folk whose only crime had been to fall under the Nazi jackboot and show up for work. Winston anxiously watched the death count rise like a steady, irresistible tide.

"You are piling up an awful load of hatred," he wrote Tedder. To Eden, he muttered, "Terrible things are being done."[24]

Terrible things, and the invasion hadn't even been launched. As that hour drew near, more terrible decisions lay ahead.

TWELVE

"We Will Go Down Together"

Six weeks before Overlord, a strange request landed on Winston's desk. General Montgomery asked the prime minister to arrange a special Church of England service to "hallow" the armed forces of the Crown. He suggested King George wear his coronation regalia for the ceremony. With scepter, orb, and ermine fur, the king would offer a benediction and declare a national day of prayer to beseech the blessings of the Almighty upon British forces in their upcoming crusade.

Winston rolled his eyes. Ike was keeping his nose to the grindstone, not in the Book of Common Prayer. SHAEF staffers were devoting every waking second to the approaching battle. The run-up to D-day was no time for a dressed-up Passion play in which Monty would assume the role of Messiah.

Barking for a secretary, he dictated his answer to his secretary of state for war:

> I am of the opinion that the Army Council should instruct General Montgomery to bring to an end his public tours and civic receptions. We are getting very near the great battle, and a bad effect will be produced if it is thought that the General immediately re-

> sponsible is spending his time at demonstrations which are more appropriate after the victory than before. Let not him that girdeth on his harness boast himself as he putteth it off. . . . If anything were to go seriously wrong and it were found that something had been neglected, the General would come in for heavy criticism.[1]

Monty didn't get his pulpit—but he did get a stage. On April 7, he stood before a packed house in the assembly room of his alma mater, St. Paul's School in West London. Top Allied military commanders had gathered to hear him give everyone the big picture of Operation Neptune, the D-day landing phase, and the Overlord campaign that would take them to Paris.

Ike took his seat amid a sea of admirals, air marshals, generals, naval captains, colonels, and aides. No cigarettes or pipes glowed, per Monty's strict standing rules, and a curtain of silence descended as Monty began to speak.

Striding like a colossus over an enormous map of Normandy, he sketched the operation in bold, grand strokes. He held forth with confidence and clarity for ninety minutes before handing the floor to Admiral Bertram Ramsay, commander of naval operations, and Air Marshal Leigh-Mallory, Ike's tactical air commander.[2]

Other generals and admirals filled in details throughout the morning and early afternoon. During a break, General Montgomery announced that the prime minister would be joining them after teatime. "Monty added that, as the Prime Minister would undoubtedly arrive with a large cigar, smoking would be allowed after tea," remembered one spectator. The audience chuckled over Monty's obvious displeasure.

As cigarette smoke hung in the air, Winston addressed the room. In his lispy growl, he spoke of the need for utter confidence. The Allies were throwing two armies against two German brigades on the beach. They would be supported by an immense naval armada and would hold complete mastery of the skies. "He said he had not been convinced in 1942, or in 1943, that this operation was feasible. He was not expressing an opinion on its feasibility now," recalled Major General Sir John Kennedy. "But he had hardened very much on *this*: that the time was now *ripe*."

Churchill said the right words, but the fight was missing. "He was in a very weepy condition, looking old and lacking a great deal of his usual vitality," Brooke told his diary. Kennedy agreed: "There was the usual wonderful flow of fine phrases, but no fire in the delivery. I thought he was going to burst into tears as he stepped down to sit beside Eisenhower and Monty."[3]

He tried never to show it, but in unguarded moments Winston let his pessimism slip. Even around Ike.

"My God, I can give you some of the words of the Prime Minister during those early months of 1944," Ike told an interviewer later. "'My dear general, when I contemplate the beaches choked with the flower of British and American youths, and with the tides running red with their blood,' he said, 'I must say I have my doubts.'"[4]

Ike understood. At least, he tried to. "You must remember," he explained, "the British had visions of their experience in World War I of getting on the ground fighting in France, and you had Vimy Ridge, and Passchendaele, and all of those other terrible battles where you would lose a couple of hundred thousand men and not gain a foot, or at least not gain any mileage. So I think it was only natural that he would be cautious about authorizing or giving his blessing to an operation where that could happen."[5]

Under the weight of days, Winston's resolve and resignation battled each other. Ike told Harry Butcher that at the end of a private lunch, Winston had become emotional when they parted.

"I am in this thing with you to the end," he said, his eyes shiny, voice thick. "If it fails, we will go down together."[6]

As D-day drew near, a restless energy filled 10 Downing Street. Pacing like an expectant father outside a delivery room, Winston fixated on the idea of watching the Neptune landings from the bridge of a Royal Navy warship.

He considered it his right. Drake, Nelson, Jellicoe: England's legendary commanders had watched war's panorama unfold from the quarterdeck of a fighting ship. Why shouldn't he? As prime minister and head of the Ministry of Defence, he felt he should be allowed to see the fruits of his labors. He even joked to his private secretary, Jock Colville, "What fun it would be to get there before Monty."[7]

At the end of a meeting of senior commanders, Winston pulled Admiral Ramsay aside and quietly asked permission to watch the invasion from a ship. Any ship. Remembering how Ike had scotched his request to watch the Pantelleria landings a year earlier, and worried about the king's reaction, he asked Ramsay to say nothing to Admiral Cunningham.[8]

The next day, Ramsay answered. The cruiser HMS *Belfast* would be ready for him on D-minus-1. But he added, "You told me not to mention this plan to the First Sea Lord and I have not done so, but you will appreciate that, as Supreme Commander, it was essential that General Eisenhower should know of what was in the air, and I must tell you that he is very averse to your going. You mean so much to the Nation at this stage of the war that I venture to suggest that any risk to your life, even though it may be small, should not be undertaken unnecessarily."[9]

"I think that you are just too valuable to the whole Allied cause, and I don't believe you should run the risk of running into a mine," Ike pleaded with Winston.

Winston bristled. "I think that the First Minister of His Majesty ought to go along to see an event such as this, and I think I should go," he said.

"Well, I'll tell you this, you'll never do it with my consent."

Winston thought a moment before replying. "You have no authority whatsoever on the administrative side of His Majesty's forces."

"No, I don't," Ike admitted.

"Then of course I can ship along in one of the ships as a member of the crew and you can do nothing about it."

"No, I can't do anything about this," said Ike. "Except that I'd worry. And I think it's rather unfair to give me another burden on a day like this."[10]

Winston said nothing, and Ike assumed the matter was settled. But Winston wasn't done. He pressed the Admiralty to let him board a warship, notwithstanding Ike's objections. His back up, he was determined to go until the king stepped in. It took His Majesty's personal intervention to stop Winston from riding a cruiser to the French coast on D-day.[11]

In early June, Kay chauffeured Ike to his forward headquarters in Portsmouth, a campus near England's southern coast code-named "Sharpener." In a woods under camouflage netting sat Ike's "circus wagon," a trailer with bed, washroom, personal gear, and a stack of western novels, courtesy of Mickey McKeogh. Two other trailers housed Kay and another secretary, while Butcher, British aide James Gault, and the rest of Ike's Army family slept in field tents pitched beneath maples and oaks.

Inside his circus wagon, Ike's body reeled from the crushing weight. As decisions crashed at him on all sides, his blood pressure spiked, his ears were ringing, and his left eye developed an infection. When not preparing for the greatest amphibious invasion in history, Ike fought with insomnia to steal a few hours' sleep. Insomnia usually won.[12]

Portsmouth, wrote Butcher, soon became "the favorite calling spot for the Prime Minister and his old crony, Field Marshal Smuts."

Churchill's mood was as foul as the English weather as D-day, June 5, drew close. After the king barred him from watching the Overlord invasion, Winston, more than a little petulant, tried to ground Ike, too. "Winston was pouring the heat on Ike to prevent him from going across on D-Day, saying Ike is too valuable, must be handy for emergency decisions, et cetera," Butch told his diary.

Ike was tempted to do what he told Winston he could not. But that would be unfair to the poor warship captain who had more important jobs to do than play water taxi to the Supreme Commander. So with the same reluctance Winston had shown—but with less fuss—Ike decided to stay put when the curtain rose.[13]

In the opening hours of June 4, Ike postponed the next day's invasion for at least twenty-four hours. The weather over Portsmouth was mild, but Ike's chief meteorologist had informed him that a rare confluence of storms was about to hit the French coast. Minimum conditions for the invasion—high clouds, low waves, mild winds, high visibility—were out of the question on June 5 and quite possibly for the rest of the week. Ike would check in with him that evening to see whether there was any hope for June 6. After the seventh, tide and moon conditions for the invasion wouldn't be right until the end of the month. Surprise would be lost, and morale would slump as men waited in cramped marshaling camps for another shot.

During the lull, Winston's entourage returned to Sharpener. "Filled their gas tanks and diminished our supply of Scotch, there being some ten or more parched mouths to moisten," grumbled Butcher.[14]

Rain slashed and wind whistled in the early hours of June 5 as the Atlantic gale the weathermen warned of shook Portsmouth. In the night's gloom, staff cars converged on Southwick House, disgorging somber-faced marshals, generals, and admirals who had come to learn whether Ike would launch the invasion on the following morning.

Into Southwick's library stepped RAF Group Captain James Stagg, Ike's chief meteorologist. Stagg and his teams had spent months chasing storm fronts across maps from Canada to the French coast. Several hours earlier, the lanky Scotsman had given the commanders a provisional forecast. Now, in Southwick's library, he would deliver the final verdict.

The men fell silent as all eyes turned toward Stagg. Against a backdrop of rattling windows, he offered some rare good news: A depression over the Atlantic would suck bad weather out to sea long enough to give them a short break. On June 6, they could expect twelve hours, maybe more, before another Atlantic cyclone rolled in. The supreme commander could wait for better conditions . . . or he could gamble on a precarious half day.

Millions of lives hinged on Eisenhower's next words.

He sat in silence for perhaps half a minute, weighing the odds of success, the price of failure. The risks of waiting.

"I thought it was just the best of a bad bargain," he would later say. "We hoped that with this break we could do it. It would still be a chancy thing."

After a moment, he looked up. "OK, we'll go."[15]

Commanders dashed off to send coded messages that would launch a thousand ships, and Ike sat in the library, a lonely spectator to a battle he had set in motion.*

He'd bet it all on one play. No folds, no mulligans, no second chances. Ike could rub his lucky coins all he wanted, but if wind or waves turned against them, if the little boats floundered, it would be over before it started. The invasion would end with bloated corpses drifting on the

* The dozen or so men with Ike that morning later gave different versions of Ike's exact words. "O.K., we'll go," comes from Eisenhower's 1964 interview with Walter Cronkite in the room where he made the decision. But Ike admitted he did not recall his exact words, and he never disputed any of the various versions.

English Channel's tide. As he later told an assistant, "Assume the weather had gone against me. I would have been a worse murderer than Xerxes."[16]

He walked from Southwick House, forcing thoughts of buyer's remorse from his mind. "I don't see any point in changing after having once made up your mind," he had written John that spring. In Ike's world, most decisions, when made with the best available information, should be seen through. Second-guessing usually didn't produce better results.[17]

But on the inside, he wasn't as stoic as he seemed. He recalled the long ride back from the 101st Airborne's field, where he had watched the "Screaming Eagles" climb onto C-47s for their drop into France. "I was really tired, alone in the back of the car," he remembered. "I tried to lie down in the big old car but all I could feel was just tension. All I wanted was news, news, and I just couldn't think of anything else so there was nothing to do."[18]

Pulling out a scrap of paper, Ike penned an announcement to be released in the event the landings failed. He would tell the world the Allied soldiers, airmen, and sailors had done everything duty could demand. "If any blame or fault attaches to the attempt," he wrote, "it is mine alone."[19]

The short exercise gave his mind something to think about—something to blot out, for five minutes, the maddening tick-tick-tick of the clock. Accepting responsibility for failure was part of the job, the third law of the Marshall Rules. As he quipped years later, "If it did fail, I was going into oblivion anyway, so I might as well take full responsibility."[20]

For all Winston's worries about Overlord, the day before the landings found him near euphoric. "PM very worked up about 'Overlord' and really in about a hysterical state," Admiral Cunningham told his diary.

"He really is an incorrigible optimist." Brooke agreed: "I found him over optimistic as regards prospects of the cross Channel operation and tried to damp him down."[21]

Under the surface, the optimist held few illusions about the price they would pay. After dinner with Clementine in the underground Annexe, he and Clemmie wandered into the Map Room, where an enormous chart of the French coast beckoned from a wall. Pushpins placed by meticulous staffers showed waves of men crossing the Channel. Men about to be pitched into a life-or-death struggle.

Maps like this one stripped away any pretense of control. Winston, Ike, the senior commanders—they were all spectators. The fight now belonged to men who did the hard work: paratroopers and boat captains. Quartermasters, beachmasters, bombardiers. Men with Enfields and Garands and BARs and bangalore torpedoes. Men on the ground who would fight and die to roll the stone from the crypt.

Like Ike curled up in the back of a Cadillac, Winston was anxious and brittle. Before Clemmie went to bed, he turned to her, his blue eyes rimmed with sadness.

"Do you realize that by the time you wake up in the morning twenty thousand men may have been killed?"[22]

He shuffled off for a fitful night's rest. As he slept, Map Room staffers moved their pushpins up to Normandy's coast.

THIRTEEN

Monty's Bicycle

D-DAY'S DAWN BROKE with Ike lying in bed, flipping through a dog-eared western, a cigarette hanging from his lips. Butcher poked his head in to report that casualties from the airborne drops had been lower than expected. Too worn to react, Ike just nodded.

Messages began streaming into "the Wake," SHAEF Advance Headquarters in Portsmouth, but Ike knew the real story wouldn't take shape for several hours. Mickey brought in breakfast, but Ike barely touched it. Looking like hell warmed over, he sipped fruit juice and coffee.[1]

"It was the soberest day we ever had," Mickey recalled years later. "There just didn't seem to be anything more to say, and the little things that came up to laugh at most days didn't come up. Nobody made any of the silly little jokes we usually make. . . . We just waited."[2]

As hours ticked by, the picture twisted into focus. General Omar Bradley's Americans were hitting stiff resistance at Omaha Beach, and the air bombardment hadn't been as effective as advertised. But the naval guns had smashed beach defenses and men were ashore. Rangers scaled the cliffs, beachmasters were working overtime, paratroops had a toehold farther in, and foot soldiers were clawing their way from sand to grass. After two years of planning, arguing, and waiting, they had cracked Fortress Europe.[3]

As American, British, and Canadian troops joined beachheads over the next week, a breath of fresh air swept into Ike's world. His son Johnny had graduated from West Point on D-Day, and the War Department gave Second Lieutenant John S. D. Eisenhower a two-week leave to visit his father in London.

Delighted to see his son in uniform, Ike kept him close at hand. He was proud that John was following in his footsteps, and peppered his letters with fatherly advice. But for Ike, parental affection—like friendship—had its limits. "He loved John very much," recalled Kay. "He was proud of him, but he was also critical. Sometimes I thought he was supercritical."

Love was one thing, duty another, and Ike was careful not to mix the two. Johnny had better remember his place in the chain of command, because Ike sure as hell would. "There isn't an officer in this theater who doesn't rank above you and below me," Ike curtly reminded him once. He didn't have to remind him again.[4]

Though the single gold bar on his shoulder entitled Lieutenant Eisenhower to no special treatment, Ike had someone he wanted him to meet. On a gray, rainswept day, the pair rode through a thunderstorm to Whitehall to visit the Ministry of Defence. When Ike and John splashed up to the door, Winston greeted them with a scowl. Not for them, but at whoever was running God's Ministry of Weather.

"This is the worst weather I have ever seen in my life," he barked. "They have no right to give us weather like this!"

John wasn't sure who "they" were, but it was clear Winston felt that God owed the Allies a lot more than He was doling out. Years later, John reflected on the contrast between the two men. Churchill "seemed to feel that the Almighty had an obligation—a personal obligation—to render all necessary assistance to their accomplishments." Ike, on the other hand, "appeared to view any situation with the cold, calculating attitude of a professional, confident as he was throughout his life that the Almighty would provide him with a decent set of cards. He never wavered in his faith that he would win, but he appeared not to share the metaphysical feeling that God owed him anything specific, such as good weather on a given day."

As they chatted, Winston softened. For John's benefit, he gave them a short tour of the military nerve center. Their visit complete, Winston ushered Ike and son to the door, and the two officers sloshed back through the rain to their waiting car.[5]

The Allies were supposed to take the city of Caen on D-Day and march to Paris in ninety days. German reinforcements had been held at bay—the result of the Transportation Plan, an effective ruse near Calais, and Hitler's flawed intuition—but a month in, the Allies were nowhere close. Monty still hadn't captured Caen, Bradley was bottled up on the Cotentin Peninsula, and they damned sure hadn't reached the open country beyond the beachhead.

It wasn't just the weather holding them back. Ike's men faced panzers to the north and a maze of hedgerows to the south. German mortars, machine-gun nests, and 88-millimeter cannon bristled from tree lines and ditches.

On July 8, Ike rode over to Chequers to see Winston. Sitting up in bed, the prime minister grilled him for an hour and a half over the stagnant battle for France. Ike assured him Monty was bleeding the Germans along the line; sooner or later, their thin crust would have to crack.

Winston frowned. He didn't like the "or later" part. Neither did Ike.

Back at headquarters, Ike stared at his maps. The grease pencil lines weren't moving, and that meant long-term trouble. Without a larger bridgehead, Ike couldn't activate Patton's Third Army for a flanking sweep through central France. Without more real estate, he also couldn't bring in divisions of Canadians and Brits waiting in England.

SHAEF staffers, British and American, quietly complained about Montgomery's failure to punch through. In their eyes, Monty sauntered about his headquarters in beret, corduroy pants, and sweater like a bohemian painter on holiday, assuring anxious superiors everything was going to plan. For now, though, Monty wouldn't be rushed, and he refused to move without overwhelming superiority.[6]

But overwhelming superiority was a luxury the Allies didn't always have. Sometimes you go to war with what you've got, not what you wish you have.

On July 12, Montgomery delivered his long-awaited plan, Operation "Goodwood." He would use waves of heavy bombers to blast a hole in the German line near Caen, then rush three armored divisions from Second British Army through the hole, forcing the Germans to fall back. The German front, he promised, would "burst into flames."[7]

Ike latched onto Monty's assurance and went into cheerleader mode. "I am confident it will reap a harvest from all the sowing you have been doing during the past weeks," he wrote Montgomery. "I am looking forward to the happy chore of telling about your accomplishments as soon as we have put this one over. I hope you will forgive me if I grow a bit exuberant."[8]

Ike's exuberance vanished as Goodwood belly flopped in the pool's shallow end. Bombs fell, tanks rolled, and Hitler burned irreplaceable reserves, but Monty still couldn't crack the carapace. Three days into the operation, he halted it.

Ike's staffers blew gaskets when Monty stopped. Tedder wanted him fired. Others, British and American, joined the chorus. They were fed up with Monty's "down to the last shoelace" approach, and soon office gossip swirled over Monty's impending exit.[9]

Forgetting his "burst into flames" promises, Montgomery reimagined Goodwood's objective. Ike's team, he said, didn't understand the operation. Goodwood was never intended as a breakthrough. It was a "battle for position" to open land around Caen and pin the Germans so Bradley could break out to the south. In Monty's mind, Goodwood was another success for Monty.[10]

Ike was "blue as indigo," wrote Butcher. With Goodwood, the Allies had dropped 7,000 tons of bombs to take seven miles and 2,500 prisoners—while losing five hundred tanks and 4,000 men in the process. How long, he wondered, could they afford to drop a thousand tons of bombs to gain a mile?

Ike didn't know, but he knew they wouldn't get to Berlin at that rate.[11]

Elsewhere, the Allies were on the march. In White Russia, the Red Army was swallowing an entire German Army group. In Italy, Alexander was forcing Kesselring back to the Gothic Line. In the Pacific, Admiral Nimitz announced landings on Guam.

And on the mighty European front, Ike had a strip of beach and a wrecked port.

He was desperate for a breakthrough. "Ike is like a blind dog in a meat house—he can smell it but he can't find it," quipped Butcher. Stress mounted, his blood pressure shot up, and his chain of Lucky Strikes burned down faster than Monty's alibis. Thinking of Major General Theodore Roosevelt Jr., who had just died of a heart attack, Butch started worrying that Ike might go out the same way: "What a blow if he should pull a Teddy Roosevelt."[12]

Ike remarked to Winston on Monty's lack of results. He had given Monty every bomber, Sherman tank, and Long Tom the Allies could muster, but Montgomery had become the West's 150-pound mastiff:

terrifying in a fight, but immovable when he sat down. And now he was sitting down. Ike said he "wanted Monty to get on his bicycle and start riding."[13*]

It looked like Winston might have lost patience, too. In the dawn hours of July 25, Butcher roused Ike from his sleep to take a call from the prime minister. Churchill wanted to discuss General Montgomery, and judging from Ike's reaction, Butch inferred, "The P.M. also after Monty's scalp."

Butch misread the room, however. In a half-hour conversation, Winston told Ike he was impressed by the way Monty had gathered his strength for another big push. A breakthrough no doubt hovered on the horizon, and he was "supremely happy" with Monty's preparations.

Ike grumbled to Butch, "Monty obviously had sold Winston a 'bill of goods.'" He couldn't ask Winston to fire Monty, and immediately ordered Butch to get Beetle Smith on the phone—"Get him out of the meeting if he's in it." He warned Beetle not to hint at "the subject we have been discussing."

Beetle said he understood. Winston's support for Monty was decisive. For now, "the subject we have been discussing" would be dropped.[14]

As Ike and Winston shouldered a stalemate, Omar Bradley, Ike's West Point classmate, offered a plan to break into the open country between Brittany and Paris. Dubbed Operation "Cobra," it was a twist on Monty's Goodwood theme. A thundercloud of bombers—heavies, mediums, and fighter-bombers—would blast a four-mile hole in the German line at the city of Saint-Lô. Brad's infantry would rush through the hole and hold open its shoulders. Then three full tank divisions, plus the Big Red

* In Ernest Hemingway's 1950 novel, *Across the River and Into the Trees,* his protagonist orders a martini known as the "Montgomery," fifteen parts gin to one part vermouth. The drink was a reference to Monty's reputation for attacking only once he held a 15-to-1 advantage over his opponent.

One in motorized transports, would pour through the hole, fan out, and drive into open country down the Cotentin Peninsula.

This time, it worked. Cobra ripped the liver out of the German line, and Bradley's attack captured enough ground to activate Patton's Third Army on the southern flank. Patton didn't waste any time; like a wolf unchained, his army tore through Brittany and the Loire Valley, scattering Germans before them. Day after day, thousands of enemy prisoners shuffled into detention camps as the Allies closed in on Paris.[15]

Victory seemed imminent, the road to Berlin clear. But as Sherman tanks raced to the Seine, seeds of discord, sown in the rush, took root. And they sprouted faster than Ike or Winston realized.

FOURTEEN

Rind of an Orange

While Ike was prodding Montgomery, Winston worked to shut down Washington's pet project: Operation Anvil.

The landing on the southern French coast would begin as a two-division assault, but Winston knew it would grow into an entire army group, sucking troops, planes, and supplies from Italy. He wanted that muscle and steel driving up the Italian boot to the Po River. From the Po, Alexander's armies could sideslip the Alps through Slovenia's Ljubljana Gap and knife into Austria's heart. But the American Chiefs—General Marshall, Admiral King, and Marshall's air chief, General Henry "Hap" Arnold—seemed deaf to the possibilities a bold thrust in Italy offered, and insisted on going forward with Anvil.[1]

The relegation of Italy to a backwater elevated the American-run theater in France to center stage, and Winston didn't like it one bit. Darlan had lamented over being squeezed like a lemon and thrown away. With Anvil, the Italian theater would be tossed aside the same way. It would certify the British Empire's status as a second-class ally, fit for a second-class theater.

In early July, six weeks before the scheduled landing, Winston dictated a draft letter to FDR. He didn't hold back. "The whole campaign in Italy is being ruined, and ruined for what?" he smoldered. "No one ever contemplated that everything that was hopeful in the Mediterranean would be flung on one side, like the rind of an orange, in order that some minor benefice might come to help the theater of your command."[2]

Intemperate language to use with the president of the United States. Impolitic, even. But Winston had to set it down on paper before he could clear his mind. Having gotten it off his chest, he tossed the draft like the rind of an orange and began a new one.

He told Roosevelt the Anvil decision was, "in my humble and respectful opinion, the first major strategic and political error for which we two have to be responsible." He reminded FDR of Ike's arguments against Anvil early in the year. Leaving no stone unturned, he appealed to Roosevelt's well-known Gallophobia, adding, "It would no doubt make sure of De Gaulle having his talons pretty deeply dug into France."

Tugging at heartstrings, he ended his message on a sentimental note: "It is with the greatest sorrow that I write to you in this sense. . . . I send you every personal good wish. However we may differ on the conduct of the war, my personal gratitude to you for your kindness to me and for all you have done for the cause of freedom will never be diminished."[3]

Winston figured there was little chance Roosevelt would change his mind, with the U.S. Joint Chiefs against him, but he wasn't finished. Despite the conciliatory words that closed his letter, Winston Churchill was not a man to suffer in silence. He was merely resting his mount for another gallop.

"I hope you realize that an intense impression must be made upon the Americans that we have been ill-treated and are furious," he wrote Pug Ismay, his chief military advisor. "Do not let any smoothings or smirchings cover up this fact. After a little, we shall get together again; but if we take everything lying down, there will be no end to what will be put upon us."

He added, "The Arnold-King-Marshall combination is one of the stupidest strategic teams ever seen. They are good fellows and there is no need to tell them this."[4]

Having lost this round to Washington's congress of the blind, he set his sights on another good fellow. One with more sympathy to England than Arnold or King or Marshall.

For two years, Winston had honed Eisenhower like a blade. In England, in the Mediterranean, then in France, he had stood behind Ike and touted his military authority to Parliament, the Cabinet, and the American high command. He had mentored the political neophyte, taught him how to play the coalition game, and helped make Eisenhower a household name in England and America.

Ike had learned quickly. Perhaps too quickly. His elevation meant Winston could no longer dictate the way he used to. Through their differences over Darlan, the Aegean, and the Transportation Plan, Ike had learned to say no. And Winston had learned he had to persuade Ike, the way a father does when his son grows into a headstrong man whose obedience he can no longer compel.

Now Ike wanted the south of France. He envisioned a mass of armies stretching from the Swiss border to the North Sea. Numbers were on the Allied side, and Ike intended to use the power of four great nations to grind the Wehrmacht into dust. That required Operation Anvil, recently rechristened "Dragoon."

Winston went to Ike and pulled out all the stops to cancel Dragoon. Driven by a fear of irrelevance, he gave his most forceful performance. "I have never seen him so obviously stirred, upset, and even despondent," Ike wrote Marshall afterward. At one point Winston emoted, "If [Dragoon] should happen, I should have to go to His Majesty and lay down the mantle of my high office."[5]

No rhetorical weapon was off-limits. "Oh, God, he'd wipe tears around! God, he could pathos!" remembered Ike. "But he was hell in an argument, I'll tell you that."

Ike listened, but didn't bend. A thrust through the Ljubljana Gap was sheer fantasy. He recalled telling Winston, "You don't like to talk about logistics when you're in favor of a plan. You're saying, 'just sweep right through,' but do you see anything soft about the Alps and about the country across Yugoslavia? Do you see anything particularly attractive by a line of communications that has to, at least, go by land up [Italy], unless, either in the Adriatic or in Genoa, something like that, there was a strike there? What do you feel is so attractive, militarily?"

Winston argued his point like a barrister in a murder case, but both knew Ike was right.

"Look, I wasn't being insubordinate to the man," Ike said later. "I loved the man and he knew it. He wasn't above using that knowledge, too."[6]

As August dawned, Winston tried another approach. He informed his chiefs that Ike had agreed to cancel the Dragoon landings and redirect the operation to Brittany, on the French Atlantic coast. Landing in western France would require less from Alexander's Italian front, leaving Alex enough force to drive beyond the Po. On August 4, without invoking Ike by name, Winston wrote to FDR alluding to "opinion here" that the operation should be mounted around Brest, not Marseille, and he directed the British Chiefs to ask their U.S. counterparts to divert Dragoon resources to Brittany.[7]

"I have telegraphed to the President backing up your suggestion about switching 'Dragoon' directly into the Brest Peninsula to reinforce your Armies," he cabled Ike. "Why should we bash in the back door when we have the latch key of the front door?"[8]

The bit in his teeth, Winston dashed off letters to his senior commanders, ordering them to get ready to invade Brittany. He arranged a meeting with Monty to discuss the pivot and sent a "personal warning order" to Jumbo Wilson, telling him, "We feel strongly that far the best strategy is to switch Dragoon or at least as much as possible of 'Dragoon' to ports in Brittany."[9]

As he explained to Admiral Cunningham, "There are plums to be picked in the Brest Peninsula." When Cunningham pointed out that Ike hadn't asked for any naval operations off Brittany, Winston snorted, "It is not the least use telling me that General Eisenhower has not asked for anything. He is very busy with the land battle and knows very little about the sea."[10]

Ike was horrified to learn what Winston was telling the president. He never said Dragoon should be canceled. He had only considered Brittany a contingency plan *if* and *when* conditions were ripe. And conditions were definitely *not* ripe.[11]

"I learn that the Prime Minister has sent a message to the President relating to 'Dragoon,'" he wrote Marshall the day after Winston's letters went out. "It is possible that the Prime Minister may have misconstrued or misunderstood my stated opinion on these matters but I have never wavered for a moment." He insisted, "I will not repeat not under any conditions agree at this moment to a cancellation of 'Dragoon.'"[12]

The same day, Winston and his military chiefs crossed the Channel to visit Ike at Shellburst, his forward headquarters in Normandy. In a French orchard, he and his entourage lunched with Ike, Butch, Kay, and some office staff.

As they ate, Ike's dog Telek trotted up to Winston, tail wagging. Unable to resist those begging eyes, Winston gave the Scottie a bit of food. Then Caacie, Telek's mate, appeared. Winston fed her a scrap, too. Then Shaef, the black kitten, approached the pack. Wary of the dogs, back arching, Shaef stood off both Scotties, then sprang onto the table, near Winston's elbow.

The guests were appalled, but Winston smiled. "The Prime Minister said that he was the cat's friend and immediately asked for a saucer and some milk, which he fed Shaef right on the table in front of him," one of Ike's secretaries told her diary. "The kitten was not a bit abashed by the illustrious company before which he fed and begged for more by nosing around the pitcher, so the P.M. poured him another saucer and then a third. We decided that perhaps it would be better to get the kitten off the table before any untoward accident occurred."[13]

After lunch, the two leaders returned to Dragoon and Brest. Ike used to joke that Winston would say, "All I want is compliance with my wishes, after reasonable discussion." Now Winston wanted a reasonable discussion of Brittany.[14]

"Ike said no, continued saying no all afternoon, and ended saying no in every form of the English language at his command," wrote Butcher, who watched the debate go back and forth like a tennis match.[15]

"To my surprise," Admiral Cunningham told his diary, "found Eisenhower dead against it and had never sent a message putting it forward." The admiral added, "It was very apparent that the PM knowingly or not had misled the [British Chiefs] and bounced them into sending their telegram to the United States [Chiefs]."[16]

The next day, the British mission in Washington relayed the bad news to Winston: Dragoon wasn't going anywhere. The British envoy added that their only shot at killing it was to unequivocally tell the Joint Chiefs that Eisenhower backed the switch from the Riviera to Brest.[17]

They couldn't say that, of course. The British Chiefs sheepishly told their Washington counterparts, "We were under the impression that General Eisenhower favoured the switch, and indeed that he had telegraphed to Washington recommending it. We now learn that he did not send any telegram, and that he is in fact opposed to any interference with 'Dragoon' as planned."[18]

That ended the discussion. With Washington's help, Ike had won another round.

"The PM was still a bit pouty over Anvil," Butcher wrote after Ike met with Winston on August 9, six days before the scheduled landings. Winston, Ike said, "was bemoaning the future of Alexander's campaign in Italy. He saw the Italian front drying up just when such fine opportunity presented itself to enter Jugoslavia."[19]

Ike understood the truth behind Winston's fury. It wasn't about a strategic flanking movement. It wasn't even about the Balkans or Austria. It was about the future of the British Empire.

"As usual the Prime Minister pursued the argument up to the very moment of execution," Ike later wrote. "Although I never heard him say so, I felt the Prime Minister's real concern was possibly of a political rather than a military nature. I told him that if this were his reason for advocating the campaign into the Balkans, he should go instantly to the President and lay the facts, as well as his own conclusions, on the table. I well understood that strategy can be affected by political considerations."

But on purely military matters, Ike wouldn't bend, and that frustrated Winston. "This was very contrary to Churchill's way of thinking how things should be, for him to be arguing with a general," John Eisenhower reflected years later. "He bullied his own generals. But not only arguing with a general, but hearing 'no' from him."[20]

Butcher wrote that Ike and Pug Ismay "both love the Prime, as they frequently speak of him, and their comment about him is like that of two admiring sons discussing a cantankerous yet adorable father." It hurt Ike that Winston was so upset over Dragoon, and two days after their clash, he sent Winston a personal letter.[21]

"To say that I was disturbed by our conference on Wednesday does not nearly express the depth of my distress over your interpretation of the recent decision affecting the Mediterranean Theater," he wrote. "During all these months I have leaned on you often, and have always looked to you with complete confidence when I felt the need of additional support. This adds a sentimental to my very practical reasons for hoping, most earnestly, that in spite of disappointment, we will all adhere tenaciously to the concepts of control brought forth by the President and yourself two and one half years ago."[22]

Their arguments were a barometer of the shifting partnership between America and Great Britain. "I must say his obvious reactions to latest decisions in the Mediterranean disturb me greatly," Ike wrote Marshall. "He seems to feel that United States is taking the attitude of a big, strong and dominating partner rather than attempting to understand the viewpoint that he represents. . . . I have never seen him so obviously stirred, upset, and even despondent."[23]

Winston had his flaws, and Ike saw them with clarity. Emotion could cloud his judgment. But Ike also revered what Winston stood for. He kept coming back to Winston's value to the Anglo-American alliance. Churchill wasn't just a leader; he was the embodiment of the will of democracies to resist tyranny, dictatorship, and aggression. Winston didn't just represent the British Empire. He stood for the individual whose freedom was under attack from tyrants.

"He thought Churchill's misjudgments were very, very minor compared to his overall worth as a symbol and as a means of getting the British nation, keeping it right in line behind the war effort," John Eisenhower concluded. "I think that Dad looked at Churchill as a whole rather than as a strategist, and as a whole I think he thought he was irreplaceable."[24]

Winston hated losing, whether at the racetrack or on the battlefield. At the bezique table, he often sulked when the cards ran against him. "He was an ardent player," bodyguard Edmund Murray remembered. "And he would cheat—there's no doubt about it—he would cheat. . . . Churchill didn't want to lose."[25]

He lost this round. August 12 found him on a naval barge in the Mediterranean, returning to Naples from a visit to Yugoslavia's Marshal Josep Tito. From the ship's rail, he spied a troop convoy heading to the Riviera for the Dragoon landings. As the vessels passed, soldiers on the other ships recognized Winston. Soon thousands crowded the decks to cheer "Winnie" as he flashed his "V for Victory" sign across the water.

He gave the men a politician's smile, concealing his feelings for the venture. "They did not know that if I had had my way they would be sailing in a different direction," he admitted.[26]

Three days later, Winston stood on the deck of the destroyer HMS *Kimberley* to watch the Dragoon landings. The invasion, under U.S. Lieutenant General Alexander Patch, went smoothly, for most of the Germans who could have opposed them were off in the north fighting Ike, Monty, and Bradley. A frustrated Winston wrote to Clemmie, "Eisenhower's operations have been a diversion for this landing instead of the other way round." With a hint of spite, he predicted that Ike "will take Paris before General Patch takes Marseilles."[27]

Dragoon had ruined his plans—and hamstrung Britain's future battle record. Alexander's great drive through the Alps had been knocked arse over tip by inviting a new mouth to feed: an entire army group in southern France, two full armies under U.S. Lieutenant General Jacob Devers.

Until Dragoon, he told Jock Colville, the great struggle against Hitler "has been like a bull-fight: Torch, Husky, etc. were like the preliminaries—the Picadors, the banderillas etc. Then came Overlord, the Matador coming at the crucial moment to make the kill waiting till the bull's head was down and his strength weakened. But 'Dragoon,' the landing in the South of France, has been a pure waste; it has not helped Eisenhower at all and, by weakening Alexander's armies, had enabled the Germans to withdraw troops from Italy to Northern France."[28]

As Ike's armies closed in on Paris, Winston couldn't resist taking a jab. "You have certainly among other things effected a very important diversion from our attack at 'Dragoon,'" he wrote Ike.[29]

Ike ignored the barb. He had Marseille, he had northern France, and he took Winston's surly capitulation in good humor.

"I am delighted to note in your latest telegram to me that you have personally and legally adopted the Dragoon," he wrote back. "I am sure that he will grow fat and prosperous under your watchfulness."[30]

Ike had won, but it had been exhausting. Winston had fought him every step of the way.

"When I think of all the mental anguish I went through in order to preserve that operation," Ike wrote Marshall, "I don't know whether to sit down and laugh or cry."[31]

FIFTEEN

"He's After My Job"

As Ike's armies surged across France in late August, another battle brewed. This one couldn't be won, only managed. And in this eruption, Winston, still sore over Dragoon, would hold the wild card.

Come first of September, Ike would take personal control of the land war. As Allied ground commander, he would issue direct orders to three army groups. On the north end of the Allied line, Montgomery's Twenty-First Army Group commanded the Second British and First Canadian Armies. In the center, Omar Bradley led Twelfth Army Group, with the First and Third U.S. Armies. To the south, Jacob Devers commanded Sixth Army Group, which included the Seventh U.S. and First French Armies. Montgomery, Bradley, and Devers, commanding two armies apiece, would be equals under Eisenhower.

To the British man on the street, Monty was being kicked downstairs. From Allied ground commander to also-ran, as they saw it. Fleet Street newspapers, sensitive to their readers' pride, cried foul over Monty's "demotion" and blamed American lack of appreciation for British sacrifices. The cry was taken up in Parliament, and that wasn't good for either Ike or Winston.[1]

Ike tried to calm the storm with a press conference. Two days before the changeover, he praised Monty's skill at chewing up panzers. He said Hitler had lost his best troops fighting Montgomery's men around Caen, and the British had much to be proud of. But, he explained, the front was now so broad the Allies needed another army group. Bradley's assignment to Twelfth Army Group, he stressed, was no reflection on Montgomery. It was military necessity.[2]

Winston appreciated Ike's fair play. Ike consistently lavished praise on Commonwealth troops and framed each leap forward as an "Allied" victory. But Winston didn't see Bradley as Monty's equal, and he wasn't about to let the American lieutenant general get any ideas to the contrary. So he arranged for Montgomery's promotion to field marshal—a five-star rank—effective September 1. That gave Monty a two-star advantage over Bradley and a one-star edge over Ike on the day Ike took over. It would not change the chain of command, but it was a sop to national pride.

"I considered this step necessary from the point of view of the British nation with whom Montgomery's name is a household word," Winston explained to Ike shortly before the promotion was announced. But he reassured Ike, "It, of course, makes no difference in the military relations prevailing between Montgomery and other high-ranking American officers."[3]

Ike didn't mind. He had spent two years commanding men who outranked him. He was the supreme commander in Western Europe, and Monty's promotion didn't change who saluted whom.

"Thank you very much for sending me the message about Montgomery's promotion," he wrote Winston the day Monty received his field marshal's baton. The notice "enabled me to send my congratulations promptly."[4]

The week of Montgomery's promotion saw British tanks sweeping up the Channel coast. On September 1, Monty's Canadians captured

Dieppe; from there they overran German V-2 rocket sites. On the third, British troops liberated Brussels and the Americans and Free French entered Lyon. The next day British tanks rolled into the strategic port of Antwerp, and by week's end, the exiled Belgian government was moving back into its old palaces.[5]

But in war good fortune, like good weather, rarely lingers. On September 9, Montgomery reported the Germans "holding strongly" at the ports of Dunkirk, Calais, and Boulogne. His troops had captured Antwerp, but its sea entrances at the Scheldt Estuary remained in German hands; until Monty cleared the Scheldt, the port would be useless and Ike's armies would be short of the supplies they needed to advance. South of Monty, the Americans were running perilously low on fuel. The sprint of August became September's crawl.[6]

With supplies running low everywhere, Montgomery spent August and September hectoring Ike for the lion's share of ammunition and gas trucked in from Normandy's beaches.

"Montgomery feels that if his Army Group is given practically all of the maintenance available to both Americans and British, his 21st Army Group could rush right on to Berlin," Butcher told his diary. "This, however, would mean immobilization of all other divisions, as their transport and supplies would go largely to Montgomery."

That didn't make sense to Ike. The Germans were experts at shifting defenders up and down the map. A long, narrow advance by Montgomery into northern Germany would leave his group open to dangerous counterattacks along his right flank. With Bradley's tanks frozen in place for want of fuel, Montgomery would face Hitler's wolf pack alone.

Monty was playing to an inside straight—an inside straight flush, really—and Ike wouldn't back those odds. "This damn business of having your own flank, an exposed flank, clear across a continent, or across a whole country was a little bit thick," Ike told an interviewer afterward. He wrote to Pug Ismay, "We were unanimous in our convictions that this scheme was impractical—in fact, slightly hair-brained."[7]

Better, Ike thought, to do what Grant had done to Lee in the Civil War: hit the enemy everywhere, overstretch his resources, deny him breathing space to regroup. Ike needed a posse, not the Lone Ranger, and his team would push east *together*. No single force would take the glory—or extreme risk—of a dash to Berlin. A broad front advance would mean moving slowly and deliberately, but it wouldn't put Monty's neck on a chopping block and offer Hitler a free swing of the axe.[8]

While he wouldn't budge from his "broad front" strategy, Ike did give Montgomery the lion's share of his two most precious commodities: artillery ammunition and POL—quartermaster jargon for "petroleum, oil, and lubricants." He also allocated Monty a full airborne corps to seize a bridgehead over the Lower Rhine in Holland, and tilted truck and air transport toward the British side of his line.[9]

This, of course, meant mouths down the line went unfed. Patton's Third Army ground to a halt as rations, ammo, and POL dried up, and Ike's favoritism infuriated his old friends. "Monty does what he pleases and Ike says yes sir," Patton fumed to his diary. Bradley, Patton added, "feels that Ike won't go against Monty. . . . Bradley was madder than I have ever seen him and wondered aloud what a 'Supreme Commander amounted to'—nothing."

Bradley's press relations head, journalist Ralph Ingersoll, spoke for many in Brad's headquarters: "The key to [Eisenhower's] selection was the approval of Winston Churchill and the British Government. They selected Eisenhower by the simple process of being in a position to veto the selection of any man who they felt might not be sympathetic to their point of view. Eisenhower was sympathetic and he got the job."[10]

As with the British tempest, Ike let the American storm blow past. He had bigger problems than carping from his friends or Monty's supporters. He was the Boss, and Monty, Patton, and Bradley would follow his orders. They didn't have to like it. They just had to obey.

But the Allied governments didn't have to obey. As his bosses, they wouldn't take his strategy on faith forever. They wanted a payoff soon.

"A bullfighter can never see the work of art that he is making," Ernest Hemingway once wrote. "He has no chance to correct it as a painter or writer has. He cannot hear it as a musician can. He can only feel it and hear the crowd's reaction to it."[11]

The same holds true for battle captains. Once Ike made a move, the board changed and he couldn't take it back. He couldn't know how his decisions would play out—how they would look to his superiors, to the enemy, or to history. In the moment of decision, when skeptics raised their voices, Ike couldn't tell them with mathematical certainty that he was making the right call. He had to cling to faith in his judgment—and his luck.

But the audience was out there, and critics were taking notes. His art would be splashed across situation maps, after-action reports, and neatly arranged crosses in green fields. In families with missing sons, in books of later generations filled with praise or scorn.

The size of the front brought up another dicey question: Who would run the land battle? As Supreme Commander, Ike issued orders to all ground, air, naval, logistical, and civil affairs forces. Since his background was in army operations, he let the admirals, air marshals, and civil affairs heads do their jobs more or less independently. For the land battle, he wore the hat of Allied ground commander and directed the army group commanders.

Montgomery agreed that Ike should remain "supreme commander," a lofty chairman of the board. But he fervently believed the Allies needed one warlord whose sole job was to run the land war. A man of high rank, brilliance, clarity of thought, and unmatched accomplishment. And since late August, he had been offering Ike a helpful suggestion: Since Ike plainly could not devote enough time to the land battle, he should let someone else take over the burden of ground command.[12]

A joke making the rounds said that when King George VI congratulated General Harold Alexander on his army group's victory in North Africa, the general wore an anxious look.

The king remarked, "You look worried."

"I am, sire," replied Alex. "I think Monty is after my job."

"What a relief," said the king. "I thought he was after mine."[13]

Now he was after Ike's.

Ike considered Monty's demand for control over strategy and American armies. The mental process took roughly no minutes and zero seconds. Ike wasn't about to give the egotistical field marshal command of American armies. For one thing, the American generals—including Marshall—would raise holy hell. They blamed Monty for letting a lot of Germans escape from a trap at Falaise in August, and his messianic complex made him an intolerable choice. For another, as soon as he became "Allied Ground Commander," Monty's first assault would be directed against Ike's broad front strategy.

No, Monty was exactly where Ike wanted him. He'd give Monty's armies the bulk of SHAEF's fuel and ammo, and he'd order Brad to support the British attack against Germany's industrial heart, the Ruhr region. But he wouldn't let Montgomery run the land show from Switzerland to the North Sea. Ike could swallow a lot, but he was boss as long as the Combined Chiefs said he was boss. If Montgomery insisted on rewriting the Allied command chart, one of them would have to go, and the Combined Chiefs would have to choose who went home.

Monty, who held a perfect battle record against self-doubts, refused to drop the subject. Ike finally had enough, and on October 13 he threatened to make it a him-or-me issue for the Combined Chiefs. He wrote Monty, "If you, as the senior Commander in this Theater of one of the great Allies, feel that my conceptions and directions are such as to endanger the success of operations, it is our duty to refer the matter to higher authority for any action they may choose to take, however drastic."[14]

"However drastic." Ike didn't bark much, but he had a hell of a bite. Seeing fangs instead of the usual smile, Monty backed down—for now.

But Monty knew he was right. Ike couldn't competently handle the ground war on his own. He would take up the subject with Field Marshal Brooke and the PM when the timing was right.

Winston missed this round of the Eisenhower-Montgomery drama, for he had bigger things on his mind. Greece was in revolt, the Red Army was trampling through Eastern Europe, and the future of Central Europe was an open question.

Those boiling kettles lay east of Berlin. Stalin's front.

That meant going back to the Ogre's Den.

SIXTEEN

Ursa Major

NEVER FORGET THAT BOLSHEVIKS ARE CROCODILES," Winston warned Eden. But, he supposed, some crocodiles could be charmed. Or at least nudged in the right direction.[1]

Winston was walking a tightrope strung between a Moscow Leninist and a Washington Wilsonian. He had spent part of September meeting with Roosevelt in Quebec, and now he needed to see Stalin in Moscow.

The Quebec meetings revealed how differently America and Britain saw the world. To Roosevelt, Churchill's worldview smacked of Old Europe realpolitik—of spheres of influence and gunboat diplomacy, of power plays of Bismarck, Talleyrand, and Napoleon. The world America was fighting to change. FDR believed in consultation and collective action. Best, he felt, to let the Big Three solve international problems together. Better yet, a United Nations Organization.[2]

Churchill told his ambassador in Washington, "There is no question of spheres of influence." But FDR's rule against spheres of influence created practical problems. Crises flared up fast, often with little warning, and someone had to be ready to fight the fire. When a communist-backed mutiny arose among Greek soldiers, Winston put down the revolt before it could spread. When Egypt's King Farouk sacked his prime minister, Winston's troops maintained law and order in Cairo. If every decision required a globe-spanning telegram debate, events would spin out of control before the Big Three could react.[3]

There was certainly no shortage of crises. Hitler's Hungarian ally was suing for peace, the Balkans were seething with revolt, French communists threatened de Gaulle's provisional government in Paris, and Greek communists and Greek monarchists were killing one another.[4]

Worst, as always, was Poland. When the Red Army approached Warsaw, the Polish Underground rose against their Nazi oppressors, anticipating quick help from Soviet tanks parked just over the Vistula River. But as partisans battled SS troops in Warsaw's streets, the Red Army sat still, watching through binoculars as Germans slaughtered the rebels. The Warsaw "adventure," Stalin claimed, was the "work of criminals."

Churchill was appalled. How could Stalin betray Poles fighting Hitler, their common enemy?[5]

Perhaps he should have known better. The war in Europe began with Stalin and Hitler carving up Poland. Why should Stalin treat the Poles decently now?

From 1917 until Hitler's rise, Winston had done everything in his power to strangle Bolshevism in its cradle. He clamored for guns and men and money to support the Whites in the Russian Civil War. He had written and cried out against communism and fought socialist movements at home. Germany's invasion of Russia created an interlude in the struggle, nothing more. Now, with Hitler's defeat on the horizon, the dreads he'd frozen were beginning to thaw.

"Winston never talks of Hitler these days," Lord Moran wrote. "He is always harping on the dangers of Communism. He dreams of the Red Army spreading like a cancer from one country to the other. It has become an obsession, and he seems to think of little else."[6]

Yet Churchill, as Brooke had said, was an incorrigible optimist. He had engaged with Stalin in Moscow and Tehran with good results.

Building on the success of these talks, he hoped to make the postwar world a little more stable, a little more predictable—and thus a little safer—with another jaw-to-jaw session at the Kremlin.[7]

"Eden and I are off to Ursus Major," he wrote his friend Jan Smuts, and on October 7, he climbed aboard *Ascalon* for a voyage to see the Big Bear in his den. But unlike his previous trip, this one, code-named "Tolstoy," wouldn't center on battles or second fronts or supply convoys. For this voyage, he and Stalin would talk of the world after the war.[8]

Churchill landed in Moscow on October 9 and stopped at the suburban dacha of the Soviet foreign minister, Vyacheslav Molotov, to freshen up. By ten o'clock, he was sitting before Stalin.

He opened their talks suggesting they start with the most tiresome problem: Poland. As in 1939, it was half occupied by Germany, half by the Soviet Union—and its government-in-exile was split. The nationalist London Poles and the communist Lublin Poles hated one another. Moscow backed one, London the other. Neither faction could find common ground.

"At present," Winston groused, "each had a game cock in his hand."

Stalin was noncommittal. "It is difficult to do without cocks," he said. "They give the morning signal."[9]

Pausing the Polish question, Churchill moved to a survey of Eastern Europe. He proposed that among the powers, Moscow should have the "first say" on affairs in Romania. It lay on Ukraine's border, and Russia had a natural interest in her tranquility. Greece, on the other hand, was crucial to Britain. England had sacrificed men fighting the Germans there, reflecting British interests in Mediterranean shipping.

Stalin nodded. He acknowledged Britain's sacrifice and agreed Britain should have first say in Greece. He would handle Romania.

Churchill then pulled out a list of nations with rough estimates of what he considered to be the appropriate interests of West and East. Admitting that the Americans would be shocked to see how crudely he had put the matter, he passed the "naughty document," as he called it, across the table to Stalin. It read:

Roumania	
Russia	*90%*
The others	*10%*
Greece	
Great Britain (in accord with USA)	*90%*
Russia	*10%*
Yugoslavia	*50-50%*
Hungary	*50-50%*
Bulgaria	
Russia	*75%*
The others	*25%*

Stalin examined the list carefully. The percentages, though simplistic, were a sensible way to define the influence West and East would hold after the war.

Besides, it was a long way from a slip of paper to real power, and Stalin had a nose for sniffing out power. On paper, he could afford to support Winston. He picked up a blue pencil and made a large check mark on the list, then slid it back.

The two men looked at each other.

"Might it not be thought rather cynical if it seemed we had disposed of these issues, so fateful to millions of people, in such an offhand manner?" Churchill said at last. "Let us burn the paper."

"No, you keep it," said Stalin.[10]

Over ten days of talks, Winston began to see Stalin differently. At a human level, he believed he could work with the Ogre, at least for now. "I have had very nice talks with the Old Bear," he wrote Clemmie midway through his trip. "I like him the more I see him. Now they respect us here & I am sure they wish to work with us."[11]

He left Moscow on October 19 to plunge back into problems at home. As a farewell gift, Stalin gave Winston a pair of beautiful vases: For Clementine, a vase showing a steersman piloting a riverboat. For Winston, one with a scene ironically titled "Hunter with bow against bear."[12]

Back in London, Winston consulted his naughty document. It wasn't theory anymore; it was policy. When a British envoy in Bucharest protested unilateral action taken in Romania by the Soviet government, Winston told Foreign Secretary Anthony Eden that their emissary "evidently does not understand that we have only a 10 percent interest in Roumania and are little more than spectators."[13]

Three days later, trouble erupted in Greece. British diplomats in Athens worried about the Soviet reaction to a crackdown that the Greek prime minister, Georgios Papandreou, was planning against Greek communists. Winston didn't hesitate. His understanding with Stalin gave Britain latitude, and he intended to use it.

"Having paid the price we have to Russia for freedom of action in Greece, we should not hesitate to use troops to support the Royal Hellenic Government," he wrote Eden. When Stalin didn't retaliate, he sent Eden an I-told-you-so letter: "Remember the percentages we wrote out on paper. I think we have had pretty good treatment from Stalin in Greece, much better in fact than we have had from the Americans."[14]

Pretty good treatment—for now. But how long would Stalin's word hold? Long enough, he hoped.

Half a continent would hope so, too, as the Red Army steamrolled toward Europe's heartland.

SEVENTEEN

Undesirable Gossip

A cold and bitter rain lashed the French countryside as Winston crossed the Channel to see Ike. They hadn't talked since before the Quebec conference with Roosevelt, and in early November, Winston wanted to know how Ike planned to conquer Germany.

At Ike's advance headquarters at Reims, the general went over a map of the front as he described his strategy to Winston and Brooke. The Ruhr River region was his immediate target, for it was Germany's industrial heart. Steel, coal, Krupp cannon, Rheinmetall 88s—the machines that kept the Wehrmacht alive were produced there. Monty would lead the attack from the north. Bradley would support him with two armies and push a third army, Patton's, to the Rhine farther south. Devers's Sixth Army Group, which had fought its way through the Vosges Mountains, would cover the Rhine closer to the Swiss border, around Colmar and Strasbourg. Along this broad front, the Allied armies would cross the Rhine and steamroll into Germany.

As usual, Brooke was unimpressed. Montgomery might have been Ike's biggest critic, but the field marshal ran a close second—and as a member of the Combined Chiefs of Staff, he was one of Ike's bosses.

Brooke got much of his information from Montgomery, and what he saw at Ike's headquarters confirmed his low opinion of Ike's generalship. "No one running the land battle," he complained to his diary. "Eisenhower, though supposed to be doing so, is detached and by himself with his lady chauffeur on the golf links at Rheims—entirely detached from the war and taking practically no part in the running of the war! . . . Personally I think he is incapable of running the war even if he tries."

Ike's association with Kay, whom he had promoted from driver to social secretary, had raised eyebrows the year before. Winston had recalled that Ike flew into a "horrible bad temper" at a high-level dinner because his "lady chauffeur" had not been invited. The attractive Irish lass now sat next to Churchill at the head of the luncheon table wearing the gold bars of a U.S. Women's Army Corps second lieutenant. "In doing so Ike produced a lot of undesirable gossip that did him no good," Brooke wrote.[1]

After Winston and Brooke returned to London, Montgomery fed the fire. He sent Brooke a fresh diatribe bemoaning the "strategic reverse" the Allies had suffered ever since Ike took over the ground war. Monty needed more of everything in his northern sector so he could take the Ruhr, and complained that Ike, a simple-minded egalitarian, insisted on giving every army enough to attack everywhere along the front. Eisenhower was violating one of war's cardinal rules by spreading Allied forces so thin they weren't strong enough to be useful at any given point. The Allies, said Monty, needed a "full blooded thrust" as only he could achieve. North of the Ruhr.

After meeting with Ike on November 28, Monty followed up with a letter to Ike confirming that the two men had agreed Ike's broad front plan had "failed." Monty also confirmed that they had agreed the Allies had suffered a "strategic reverse."

"We now require a new plan," Monty said. "And this time we *must not fail.* The need to get the German war finished early is vital, in view of other factors. The new plan *must not fail.*"[2]

Ike was spitting nails as he read Monty's letter. The sonofabitch loved the word "failure," didn't he? The word must've had a beautiful ring to Monty's ears when he lobbed it at someone else. And in follow-up letters, he twisted the knife, repeating the noun as if it were a firstborn son who'd made his daddy proud.

Ike sure as hell didn't know how liberating France and reaching the German frontier by Thanksgiving was a "strategic reverse," much less a "failure." True, the Allies weren't in Berlin, but it wasn't because Monty lacked the title of ground commander, or because Ike shortchanged his armies. It was because the Allies had run out of gas and ammunition—shortages Monty might have averted if he'd captured the sea approaches to Antwerp back in October, as Ike had ordered him to do.

Monty's grand plan made no sense, either. His own staff had told SHAEF planners that Twenty-First Army Group couldn't support more than twenty-five divisions for a drive north of the Ruhr. Taking Monty's advice meant leaving tens of thousands of rifle-toting GIs sitting in camps to the south and rear, waiting their turn in line while Monty's spearheads were getting outflanked by the Hun.[3]

Then there was his tone. Always the same, cocksure and condescending. His outpouring of wisdom to lesser mortals. He only needed a toga, laurel wreath, and scroll. And maybe a chalice, for the hemlock.

After a while, Ike's temper cooled. Taking a deep breath, he wrote a tactful response. He pointed out that the situation was not so different from late July, when the Allies had been bogged down along a strip of beach near Caen for almost two months—a time when Montgomery was ground commander. That stall wasn't a failure or a strategic reverse. It was just war's ragtime tempo. "I beg of you not to continue to look upon the past performances of this great fighting force as a failure because we have not achieved all that we could have hoped," he asked.[4]

Monty quieted down for the moment, but Brooke was another matter. Echoing Monty's lamentations, Brooke met with Winston at month's end and told the prime minister the Allies had suffered their "first strategic reverse" since D-Day, thanks to Ike's broad front strategy. Ike's approach, he said, was "sheer madness." He told Winston, "We must take the control out of Eisenhower's hands, and the best plan [is] to repeat what we did in Tunisia when we brought in Alex as a deputy to Eisenhower to command the land forces for him."[5]

Brooke complained about Eisenhower like there was an OBE in it for him, but Winston didn't think the Allies needed another general running the ground war. Not yet, at least. "[The prime minister] made some queer statements during our discussion!" Brooke vented to his diary. "One was that he did not want anybody between Ike and the Army Groups as Ike was a good fellow who was amenable and whom he could influence!" Brooke responded: "I could see little use in having an amenable Supreme Commander if he was totally unfit to win the war."[6]

Amenable or not, the Allied slowdown worried Churchill. Patton's dash through the Loire Valley, Monty's Channel sprint, the capture of Paris and Brussels and Antwerp—those victories were distant memories. Ahead lay slugging matches over fortified cities and dense forests that would cost time, treasure, and much blood.

Yet Winston saw something Brooke and Monty didn't. Ike, in London, was easier to deal with than the increasingly frail FDR—or, worse, the American Joint Chiefs. "I have the greatest regard for Eisenhower and am sure we must back him up," he confided to Jan Smuts. "You must remember that our Armies are only about one-half the size of the American and will soon be little more than one-third." Ike was becoming Winston's replacement card for FDR.[7]

Still, the situation on the ground worried him, and in early December he took up the matter with Roosevelt. "The fact remains that we have definitely failed to achieve the strategic objective," he wrote, echoing Monty's words. He stopped short of asking FDR to order Ike to give Monty or Alexander full control of the ground war, but suggested that the Allies must force the Rhine "on the shortest road to Berlin." In other words, Monty's strategy.[8]

Ike felt a surge of anger when he learned Winston had gone over his head on military strategy. "For one of the few times in their long, close association General Eisenhower was irked at his friend Churchill," John Eisenhower wrote later. "Now with things going almost exactly as he had predicted, Eisenhower found himself harassed by outside pressure to change his plan radically."[9]

He needed help, and General Marshall—as protective of Ike as Brooke was critical—leapt to Ike's defense. He shut down all talk of a change at the top and drafted a reply for the president's signature.

As he read Marshall's draft, FDR wrestled with a problem one of his predecessors had struggled with. In the Civil War, the North, with its larger manpower and industrial base, had been unable to put down the rebellion until Lincoln found a general who was willing to "face the arithmetic." Ulysses Grant knew the South couldn't replace men and guns at the rate the North could. Fight enough battles, win or lose, and Johnny Reb would be ruined.

Like Grant, Ike could face the arithmetic. More than three-quarters of the world opposed Germany and her shrinking circle of confederates. Though lacking in parry-and-lunge finesse, Ike's approach was the surest route to victory. Slugging matches around Metz, the Scheldt, and Hürtgen Forest were hard to watch, but they chewed up soldiers the Third Reich couldn't afford to lose. Sooner or later, Hitler would break.

So FDR came down on Ike's side. "General Eisenhower estimated that on the Western Front Line he is inflicting losses in excess of the enemy's capability to form new units," he wrote Churchill. "I still cannot see clearly just when, but soon a decisive break in our favor is bound to come." In typical Roosevelt fashion, he suggested they let the military picture play out a little longer and not rush into decision.[10]

Winston wavered, Ike's allies rallied, the Eisenhower magic worked again. Despite Monty and Brooke, despite even Churchill, Ike had escaped, emerging from the icy river, straitjacket and handcuffs gone, the crowd applauding from the bridge. He would direct the Allies in the final battle for Germany.

For now, at least. With Hitler's tanks revving their engines in the dark forests of the Ardennes, Winston's faith in Ike would face a new and brutal test.

EIGHTEEN

Cleansing the Temple

In the Ardennes Forest, a quarter-million *soldaten* waited in the cold. In tanks, in armored cars, huddled in tree lines along the few passable roads, their breath rose in puffs of smoke as they pulled on helmets and checked their weapons.

On December 16, they stormed out of the snow-flecked woods and slammed into Bradley's center line in Luxembourg and Belgium. Tiger and Panther tanks smashed roadblocks and rushed picturesque crossroads towns like St. Vith, Malmedy, and Houffalize. The Fifth and Sixth Panzer Armies—Hitler's best in the west—tore a hole in the belly of First U.S. Army. Driving toward the Meuse River, they forced the overstretched VIII Corps into headlong retreat, creating an enormous bulge in the lines crossing Allied war maps and threatening to split Ike's forces in two.

Ike had looked forward to fresh victories in 1945. Now he was facing a possible disaster. If Hitler's tanks crossed the Meuse, the enemy would be in his rear and the road to Antwerp would lie open. Hitler was staking everything on a last, desperate chance to force the Allies into a negotiated peace, and in the first hours of the attack, his bet looked pretty good.

Bradley had overstretched First Army at the Ardennes, assuring Ike there was nothing in his center the Germans could capture that would get them beyond the Meuse River. And if Mother Nature gave Ike no more than average weather, Allied airpower would blow to hell any German brave enough, or dumb enough, to show his face on a road.[1]

But Mother Nature had been stingy lately. Clouds hung low and snow fell hard, so panzers rolled west without having to look skyward. German spearheads cut Bradley's telephone lines, and communications between Bradley and his two northern armies—the First and Ninth—were all but gone. In the north, Brad was virtually blind, and without his guidance, First Army's commander, Lieutenant General Courtney Hodges, floundered in the storm's eye. That left Brad with only Patton's Third Army to the south.

Watching from the far north, Montgomery did his part for the Allied cause by sending frequent messages informing Brooke that Ike's situation was "not repeat not good." "Not good" wasn't as melodious as "definite failure," of course, but it gave Monty another chance to savor Ike's distress, put on his beret, and get ready to save the day.[2]

"It is absolutely impossible in an Allied force to shift command of any unit from one nationality to another during a period of crisis," Ike had once written Marshall. "This should be accomplished, if considered necessary, during periods of inactivity but not repeat not while the going is tough."[3]

The going was tough. American riflemen fought heroically from Spa to Bastogne, but their commanders, Bradley and Hodges, seemed lost in war's fog. First Army headquarters broke camp and retreated, leaving behind working phones and top secret situation maps. Supply dumps went up in flames as stories of SS massacres, enemy paratroopers, saboteurs, and assassins spread as far back as Ike's main headquarters at Versailles.

On the night of December 19, two senior British officers on Ike's staff, "Jock" Whiteley and Kenneth Strong, talked over the situation. The Germans were moving fast, snipping phone lines as they advanced, cutting off Bradley's ability to direct the fight. Strong and Whiteley figured Bradley hadn't been in effective communication with his two northern armies for two days.[4]

In the early hours of December 20, Whiteley and Strong woke up Beetle Smith with an emergency recommendation. Strong outlined the darkening picture, and Whiteley recommended transferring command of everything north of the Ardennes to Montgomery—the First and Ninth U.S. Armies.

It would be a hell of a thing to do. Taking armies away from Bradley, even temporarily, would cause a riot at Twelfth Army Group, even if Montgomery had been an American team player. And Monty was neither a team player nor American. Beetle knew Ike wouldn't like rocking the boat in a crisis.

Beetle first picked up the phone and called Bradley. He laid out the facts with a trial balloon: He suggested that giving Monty command north of the bulge would help control the battle better.[5]

Bradley said he felt it was an overreaction. He was working on routing phone wires west of the Meuse to fix the problem. And transferring U.S. troops to a British commander wouldn't play well with the American public.

Smith then asked, "Would the arrangement make sense if Montgomery were an American?"

Bradley paused. "Bedell, in that case, it would be hard for me to object. Certainly, if Monty were an American commander, I would agree with you entirely."[6]

Beetle hung up and turned the idea over in his head. At the end of his morning briefing to Ike, he recommended moving Bradley's First and Ninth Armies to Montgomery's command.

Ike knew what had to be done. He had preached the gospel of

Anglo-American unity, and now he would put sermon into practice. Even if it meant slapping the face of his oldest Army friend.[7]

He picked up the phone and delivered the news. Bradley, furious and hurt, protested bitterly, but Ike didn't give a damn about Brad's feelings when lives were on the line. After letting Bradley vent, he cut off further discussion: "Well, Brad, those are my orders."[8]

Monty burst into First U.S. Army headquarters like "Christ come to cleanse the temple," one staffer put it. He wasted no time: He shored up defensive lines and shuffled a British force behind the Meuse to block a German crossing. As at Kasserine, the German offensive fizzled out before its spearheads reached their strategic goals, but the damage was done. Ike was sitting with a huge bulge digging into his long line of armies. Bad American tradecraft, thought Monty, no surprises there.[9]

Squirming down in Verdun, Bradley thrashed wildly for something to flatten the Bulge, erase the shame, and restore his command. He pitched Montgomery on a combined counterattack by Patton's Third Army and Hodges's First to snip off the Bulge. The Germans were overstretched, he argued; the Allies had a golden opportunity to turn a setback into victory.

But Montgomery ran the show north of the Bulge, and Montgomery wasn't going anywhere. He said the Americans should admit they had been beaten. He told a red-faced Bradley he must face facts: Hitler had inflicted a "proper defeat" on the Allies, and the sooner the Americans admitted it, the better.[10]

Monty sang the same dirge to Ike. The U.S. Army had taken "severe losses," he said, and it was "useless to pretend that we were going to turn this failure into a great victory." The Germans were getting ready for another big attack, and Monty would wait for the German attack, absorb it, and counterattack only after the Germans had run dry.[11]

Monty's ego, condescending manner, and love affair with the word "failure" poured gasoline on the fire. But Ike's job wasn't to lay blame or score personality points. It was to fix a problem and win the damn war. He would swallow his pride and let Monty have his way. Again.

As Ike struggled to hold his lieutenants together, Winston watched the drama from London. He had been sanguine during the battle's first three days, telling Cunningham he was glad the Germans had come out to fight. But after reading a cable from Monty warning of disaster along the American front, he realized the gravity of Hitler's attack.[12]

To help rally American support, he telephoned Ike and told him he would raise the age limit of drafted infantrymen to 38 and would call for volunteers from the Home Guard to go to the Continent. In a public statement on December 22, he asked Parliament to conscript another quarter million men. As he told Ike, "I am putting this out as a mark of our confidence in you."[13]

Inside, however, that confidence was wavering. He wrote Jan Smuts, "We have suffered a disaster comparable to that of Gough's Fifth Army in the last war. . . . Eisenhower's functions appear to be more like those of a great administrator of our vast war machine in the West, with the Chiefs of Staffs planning in their home offices. In practice, if not in theory, there seems to me to be a defect or hiatus in our arrangements at the front, which now, more than ever, calls for a real field Commander-in-Chief."[14]

A commander like Field Marshal Montgomery.

Yet Winston stayed out of Ike's thin hair for most of the battle, thanks to a timely uprising by Greek communists. Responding to the latest Balkan crisis, Winston upended the holiday plans of his inner circle by sailing to Athens on Christmas Eve. He spent the next several days brokering peace among Greek monarchists, moderates, and communists, and didn't have time to critique Eisenhower's performance.[15]

Aboard HMS *Ajax* off the Greek coast, Winston received a cable from Monty reporting that Fifth Panzer Army was still attacking the American line. "The American divisions are all weak and below establishment," Monty reported. But the next day's message was brighter. Christmas, he said, had been a "very good day." The weather broke, and Allied artillery and air smashed German attempts to renew the attack. Two days later, he cabled Winston that Fifth Panzer Army had been forced to give up its lunge toward Namur. For the Allied armies, the hour of danger had passed.[16]

"Montgomery, Alan Brooke and Churchill came at us like sharks at a shipwreck," remembered Bradley, still bitter decades later. "Montgomery was the first to scent blood and attack. He led the pack."[17]

The pack grew. British officials and commentators began clamoring for Montgomery's elevation to Allied ground commander. The British Chiefs had drafted a paper lambasting Ike for failing to put all his chips on Monty back in September. By insisting that all Allied armies reach the Rhine before penetrating Germany, they argued, Ike had set them on a slow, dangerous, war-lengthening path.[18]

By December 29, Montgomery sent Ike a "Top Secret" and "Personal" message demanding control over Bradley's army group. "We have had one very definite failure" because he didn't have control over Brad's armies, he said. He required this control "only because I am so anxious not to have another failure."[19]

Monty's December letter was one "failure" too many. Passing the limit of his patience, a furious Ike threw down his trump card. He drafted a letter to the Combined Chiefs asking them to choose between his strategy and Monty's. If they chose Ike's, they would have to relieve Monty.

Word of the draft letter got back to Monty. In a rare surprise attack of self-awareness, he realized he had overplayed his hand. He folded his cards with an apology for his latest "failure" letter. If Ike had his mind made up, Monty would loyally follow his commander's orders.

"Very distressed that my letter may have upset you and I would ask you to tear it up," he wrote in a letter on the year's last day. He signed the letter, "Your very devoted subordinate, Monty."[20]

It was a rare concession for Bernard Montgomery to make to his commander, and Ike was relieved to have snuffed out a fire before the smoke reached the Combined Chiefs, 10 Downing, or the White House.

But he had barely shaken off Monty when a new storm rolled in—one from a tall, angry man neither Churchill nor Roosevelt could control.

Winston and FDR at a White House press conference in December 1941.

ZUMA Press, Inc./Alamy

Ike's driver and secretary, Kay Summersby, seen here with Ike in Africa in 1942. Kay would remain close to Ike until the war's end. *Eisenhower Library*

Winston meets with Stalin in 1942. Stalin would not be smiling when Winston told him the Allies would not invade Europe in 1942.
Office of War Information Photograph (public domain)

Ike shares a laugh with Lt. Gen. George S. Patton Jr. in Africa in March 1943. *Eisenhower Library*

BELOW: Winston unveils his vision for the Mediterranean campaign at Ike's headquarters in Algiers, June 1943 (*foreground l–r:* Foreign Secretary Anthony Eden, Gen. Alan Brooke, Air Marshal Arthur Tedder, Adm. Andrew B. Cunningham, Gen. Harold Alexander, Gen. George C. Marshall, Ike, Gen. Bernard Montgomery). *Eisenhower Library*

Winston visits Ike's command post in North Africa in 1943.
Eisenhower Library

Winston is back on his feet after a near-death bout of pneumonia at Ike's headquarters in Tunisia. Here he is with Ike at a Christmas 1943 luncheon.
Eisenhower Library

Ike, Winston, and Lt. Gen. Omar Bradley try out the U.S. Army's new M-1 carbine in 1944. *Eisenhower Library*

Winston and Ike inspect members of the 101st Airborne Division prior to D-Day. *Eisenhower Library*

Ike and Winston discuss French liberation with Charles de Gaulle shortly before D-Day. *Eisenhower Library*

Winston visits Ike at his trailer in November 1944. *Eisenhower Library*

Ike had his hands full keeping relations civil between British Field Marshal Bernard "Monty" Montgomery and Ike's West Point classmate Lt. Gen. Omar Bradley. *Eisenhower Library*

Ike congratulates Patton on his relief of Bastogne as Bradley looks on. *Eisenhower Library*

Winston meets Ike to discuss the final battle for Germany. *Eisenhower Library*

By 1945, Ike was wearying of press trouble his old friend George Patton was causing the War Department. *Eisenhower Library*

Churchill delivers his "Iron Curtain" speech. To his right sits President Truman.
Popperfoto/Getty

BELOW: Ike, Army chief of staff, shares an enjoyable moment with Winston in Williamsburg, Virginia, shortly after Winston's "Iron Curtain" speech.
Everett Collection Historical/Alamy

Winston, Monty, and Ike share a laugh at a 1951 dinner celebrating Monty's victory at El Alamein. Ike was serving as NATO's commanding general and would leave the next year to run for president. *Keystone-France/Getty*

Winston and Ike catch up with Bernard Baruch shortly before Eisenhower's inauguration in January 1953. *Smith Archive/Alamy*

Kremlin leaders stand watch—over one another—at Stalin's funeral in March 1953 (*l–r:* Molotov, Voroshilov, Beria, Malenkov; and Bulganin, Khrushchev, Kaganovich, Mikoyan). *Smith Archive/Alamy*

French premier Joseph Laniel meets with Ike and Winston on Bermuda in December 1953, when Winston made another pitch for a peace meeting with the Soviet leaders. *Walter Carone/Getty*

Mamie and Ike host Winston on his last visit to the White House as prime minister (*behind them l–r:* Anthony Eden, Secretary of State John Foster Dulles, and Vice President Richard Nixon). *Universal History Archive/Getty*

Prime Minister Anthony Eden addresses the nation on the Suez Crisis in August 1956. *PA Images/Alamy*

Soviet leaders display missiles at a military parade in Red Square in 1956. *Bettmann/Getty*

Mamie and Ike inspect Winston's brushwork during a 1958 American tour of Churchill's paintings. *Glasshouse Images/Alamy*

Ike and Winston share a friendly moment with a dying John Foster Dulles. Above Dulles sits a portrait of Winston, painted by Ike during his presidency. *Eisenhower Library*

Mamie and Ike escort Winston to his ride after his last stay at the White House.

Eisenhower Library

Winston and Ike at a 1959 dinner in London hosted by Prime Minister Harold Macmillan. *Paul Slade/Getty*

NINETEEN

"A Wise and Proper Thing"

IKE SCOWLED AS HE LOOKED SOUTH. Near the German border, Hitler's Nineteenth Army was holding the French town of Colmar, not far from Strasbourg. Jacob Devers's Sixth Army Group had them hemmed in, and the rest of the line had moved east.

Devers hoped the defenders would run out of supplies and give up, but he couldn't promise Ike anything. The ring around the Colmar pocket was thin and the Germans were desperate. He and Ike worried they might try to break out and stab First French Army in its spine.

Enemy code decrypts weren't reassuring. Reports showed German tanks streaming toward Haguenau and Strasbourg. Operation "Nordwind," as the Germans dubbed it, sounded like a major effort aimed at Seventh Army. After the Ardennes, Ike couldn't take any threat lightly.[1]

He spent a cold New Year's Day hearing about panzers rolling toward Strasbourg. SS chief Heinrich Himmler, one of the worst of the Nazi bastards, was personally commanding the attack. If they drove a wedge in Ike's line like the one at the Bulge, Devers's two armies could find themselves outflanked. Or worse.

The next day, the Germans were squeezing Strasbourg from north and south. As the noose tightened, Devers told Ike the writing was on the wall: Strasbourg was as good as lost. Agreeing, Ike ordered Devers to give ground and withdraw to a defensible line on the slopes of the Vosges Mountains. Better to lose a city than an army.[2]

There was one problem: The French wouldn't accept Ike's verdict. The day Devers reported the probable loss of Strasbourg, French General Alphonse Juin stormed into Ike's headquarters with a letter from Charles de Gaulle vehemently protesting Ike's order to abandon Strasbourg. Its citizens had hung American and French flags from their windows as Allied tanks rolled through the city, and now they faced massacres at the hands of vengeful SS troops if the Germans returned.

To de Gaulle and his followers, Strasbourg was sacred ground—stolen by Bismarck, then by Hitler. The city had become a rallying cry; its abandonment would be a political calamity for de Gaulle's fledgling provisional government. De Gaulle warned Ike that if he didn't countermand his withdrawal order, the French government would pull First French Army out of the Allied fold and fight on its own.[3]

Ike boiled. De Gaulle was talking mutiny during a pitched battle. Tactical withdrawals were never optional; they were forced on an army to stave off defeat. Ike had vowed never to shortcut military objectives to please political leaders, and he damned sure wouldn't do it now. If military reality left a few scars on de Gaulle's government, then *c'est la guerre*. It's how wars work.[4]

Winston couldn't let that happen. Britain would have to live with France after the war, and he had to prevent a break between de Gaulle and the Americans. So when Ike and de Gaulle locked horns over Strasbourg, he flew to Ike's headquarters at Versailles to make sure things didn't go off the rails.[5]

He and Ike hadn't been talking long when de Gaulle stormed into Ike's office. His face was dark, his voice loud and sharp. Towering over

Ike and Winston, he declared that Strasbourg would be held at all costs. The French people would not stand by and watch French soil surrendered without a fight.

He handed Ike a letter to First French Army's commander, General Jean de Lattre de Tassigny: First Army would defend Strasbourg to the last bullet, no matter what orders the Supreme Allied Commander might issue.

Ike had no intention of giving in to this histrionic Frenchman, and he held the cards to win. He could shut off all food, fuel, and ammunition to First French Army, freezing them in their tracks. If de Gaulle wanted to play hardball, Ike was ready.

But as de Gaulle spoke, Ike began to see where the dominoes would fall. If the Americans pulled out of Strasbourg, the French public would be furious, both at the Allies and at de Gaulle. De Gaulle's fragile hold in Paris might shatter in a wave of anti-Allied indignation. Whether that convulsion ended with French withdrawal from the Allied military coalition or a wholesale political collapse didn't much matter. The Allies would lose an army, and Ike's long supply lines would stretch through an angry, unstable populace. Ike didn't want that any more than de Gaulle did.

Winston could have stepped in and handed Ike the answer. But he watched, uncharacteristically silent, to see whether Ike would look beyond his operations maps. In this round, Ike couldn't think like a soldier. He had to think like a statesman.

Groping for a compromise, Ike settled on an order he could justify on military grounds. Reasoning backward, he concluded that French stability was a vital military interest, because Allied supply lines ran across France. To avoid chaos in his rear, he would order Devers to make a reasonable effort to hold Strasbourg. Sixth Army Group would hold the city "firmly," though not necessarily to the last man.

De Gaulle considered the proposal, then nodded. If the Allies held firm, Strasbourg would survive. Ike called Devers and gave the order.

Winston exhaled. It had taken hours of arguing, but Ike had found the answer.

"You have done the wise and proper thing," he told Ike afterward. "A break with General de Gaulle would have been bad."

It was late, and watching de Gaulle rant could wear out even Winston. He was ready to retire to Ike's VIP guest quarters. "Could we have a whisky and soda before we go to bed?" he asked.[6]

Wise, perhaps. But proper? Ike wasn't sure. He was blurring lines between politics and military judgment, rationalizing one to fit the other. It wasn't the kind of decision soldiers are supposed to make.

He was defensive as he dictated his report to Marshall. "I originally looked at the matter as a conflict between military and political considerations and felt completely justified in handling the matter on a purely military basis," he said. "However, when I found that execution of the original plan would have such grave consequences in France that all my lines of communication and my vast rear areas might become badly involved through loss of service troops and through unrest, it was clearly a military necessity to prevent this."[7]

Like the Darlan Deal, Ike's military decision left political ripples. But he was learning to thread needles, and somehow he had found a way to satisfy de Gaulle, Churchill, Marshall, and Devers. As 1945 opened, he was getting better at balancing the needs of the statesman and the rifleman.

But no sooner had he defused the Strasbourg bomb than he turned around and saw an old one ticking again.

TWENTY

Applause and Applesauce

British papers fell on Ike like a pack of wolves. Fleet Street editors blamed him for the Bulge, for the slow grind east, for cutting Monty out of command. Coming on the heels of appalling losses in the Ardennes and the scare at Strasbourg, Ike looked battered and vulnerable.

In early January, the Battle of the Bulge still raged around Bastogne and Houffalize, and the public wanted answers. If Ike didn't have the answers, they wanted to hear from Monty.

"I think the less one says about this battle, the better, for I fancy that whatever I do will almost certainly be resented," Monty would later write. But saying less wasn't his style. Like MacArthur, Montgomery was a brilliant battle captain whose ego insisted he was brilliant at everything else. So Monty decided to use his public relations skills to help Ike.[1]

For all his carping about failures and strategic reverses, Bernard Montgomery believed the Allies were on a path to victory. It was not the path he would have chosen, but there they were. In his letter he had promised Ike his full support, and he intended to keep his word. He had saved the Americans in the Ardennes, and now he would save Ike with a snappy talk to the British press.

To make sure he said nothing offensive, Monty sent Winston a letter outlining the points he would make. He promised, "I shall stress the great friendship between myself and Ike."

Winston approved wholeheartedly. The Americans, especially Ike, needed a show of support from their ally, and Monty was just the man to give it. "I think what you propose would be invaluable," he wrote back. "Thank you very much."[2]

On January 7, Monty, resplendent in paratrooper field jacket and double-crested maroon beret, stepped before a bouquet of microphones. The room fell silent, cigarettes were stubbed out, and in crisp tones, Monty laid out the Battle of the Bulge as seen from the top.

"The whole allied team rallied to meet the danger; national considerations were thrown overboard; General Eisenhower placed me in command of the whole northern front," he told them. "The first thing I did was busy myself in getting the battle area tidy—getting it sorted out." Under his generalship, the Allies had "seen off" the enemy as they had at El Alamein in 1942. "You have thus the picture of British troops fighting on both sides of American forces who have suffered a hard blow."

He made glowing references to several American units. He talked of his friend General Eisenhower and his command of two magnificent U.S. Armies before triumphantly concluding that the Battle of the Bulge "has been most interesting; I think possibly one of the most interesting and tricky battles I have ever handled."[3]

It wasn't what Monty said; it was the way he said it. The voice. The confidence. The reference to Alamein. While he paid high tributes to the

American soldier, he came across like an officious school headmaster who had helped his little boys out of a mud puddle they'd fallen into. In his account, the Battle of the Bulge was mostly a story of himself, of beleaguered Americans who snapped back under his command—and of Ike, whom he had pulled from the jaws of defeat.

British papers hailed Monty as the hero of the Bulge. "MONTGOMERY FORESAW ATTACK" blared a headline in the *Daily Mail*. "ACTED 'ON OWN' TO SAVE THE DAY." The *Daily Telegraph*, unclear on how permanent Monty's command of First and Ninth Armies was, emoted, "MONTGOMERY'S NEW COMMAND HAILED IN U.S., CHOICE MADE ON MERIT."[4]

Across the ocean, the reaction was different. The *New York Daily News* headline read: "APPLAUSE TO MONTGOMERY; APPLESAUCE TO THE YANKS." Monty had taken credit that thousands of GIs, living and dead, deserved.

German propagandists, sensing an opening, put out a fake BBC report and sent it through Radio Arnhem on a wavelength used by Allied soldiers. The report made it sound like Field Marshal Montgomery had claimed all credit for stopping the Germans. Stolen valor.[5]

Omar Bradley wasn't a man who lost his temper often, but he blew his stack when he learned of the press conference. Monty's statements, he claimed later, "did more to undermine Anglo-American unity than anything I can remember." He issued his own press statement, stressing that Montgomery's command of American forces was a *temporary* expedient. The *Daily Mail* called out Brad's statement under the headline "A SLUR ON MONTY." Aghast that Monty might lose control over the American forces, it editorialized, "The British people would view with dismay the relegation of this great soldier to the somewhat meagre share of the front which he held before Rundstedt's breakthrough."[6]

The Anglo-American relations Ike had worked so hard to stitch together were unraveling. He couldn't fire the British hero. All he could do was contain the shrapnel. In his memoirs, he wrote, "This incident caused me more distress and worry than did any similar one of the war."[7]

He hoped Winston would pitch in on this one. He told Marshall that publicity about Monty's command "is still rankling in Bradley's mind, and I must say that I cannot blame him much. As soon as the Prime Minister comes back, I am going to enlist his help to see whether such things cannot be avoided in the future."[8]

Winston cringed when he heard the story. Montgomery was such a polarizing figure, probably nothing he could have said would have sat well against bruised American egos. But Monty had taken a bad situation and made it immeasurably worse. "He made such a cock-a-doodle about it all that the Americans said that their troops would never again be put under an English general," Winston grumbled to Lord Moran.[9]

Calling for a secretary, he minuted his reaction to his military chiefs:

> Personally I thought his speech most unfortunate. It had a patronizing tone and completely overlooked the fact that the United States have lost perhaps 80,000 men and we but 2,000 or 3,000. Through no fault of ours we have been very little engaged in this battle, which has been a great American struggle with glory as well as disaster. Eisenhower told me that the anger of his Generals was such that he would hardly dare to order any of them to serve under Montgomery. This of course may cool down, but it also may seriously complicate his being given the leadership of the northern thrust.[10]

Ike and Winston worked to mend fences as best they could. Ike gave Bradley a medal for outstanding leadership. Winston, while not rebuking Monty, cautioned the House of Commons, "Care must be taken in telling our proud tale not to claim for the British Army an undue share of what is undoubtedly the greatest American battle of the war and will, I believe, be regarded as an ever-famous American victory."[11]

Winston would leave Ike to smooth things out between the British and American military camps. That was Ike's particular specialty. Winston's specialty was dealing with Roosevelt and Stalin. And before long, he would see them on the far side of the world.

TWENTY-ONE

The Riviera of Hades

"No more let us falter! From Malta to Yalta!"

Winston had been pushing for another Big Three meeting since the fall. It had been a year since Tehran, and he and Roosevelt needed to look Stalin in the eye. There were questions to be settled: Germany's future, borders in Central and Eastern Europe, the war with Japan. Much was uncertain. Much could be misinterpreted.

Getting the leaders together was no easy thing. Stalin wouldn't fly, and he wouldn't leave Soviet soil. Roosevelt was ailing, and it took a great deal of persuasion to get the president to meet Stalin on his home turf. But by the end of 1944, the giants agreed to convene outside Yalta, a Crimean resort on the Black Sea.

Crimea had been the scene of bitter fighting the year before. Fifty thousand German and Soviet corpses lay rotting across the peninsula, and most of the region was in ruins. Winston loathed the prospect of slogging to a cold, damp battlefield in winter. "The Riviera of Hades," he called it. "If we had spent ten years on research, we could not have found a worse place in the world."

But he added that he could survive if he brought an "adequate" supply of whisky—a vaguely defined but formidable unit of measure. So, on January 29, he lifted off in *Paralos*, his American-built VIP Skymaster, for another round with the Ogre.[1]

As *Paralos* winged its way east, Winston envisioned the world he, Stalin, and Roosevelt would shape. The victors would be staring at one another like lions over a freshly killed gazelle, so it was critical they see eye to eye. "The only hope for the world is the agreement of the Great Powers," he told Anthony Eden. "If they quarrel, our children are undone."[2]

While settling in at Yalta, Winston realized the strongest cards lay in the weakest hands. Roosevelt's mind was as quick as ever, but his frame was crumbling. His stare lingered. Hollow eyes peered over a slack jaw. He needed bed rest between meals and struggled to keep up with the circus of diplomats, field marshals, ministers, and translators. At the conference table, he husbanded his strength for two things: enlisting Stalin's help against Japan and establishing a United Nations Organization. The rest was mostly up to Churchill.[3]

Personal relations among the Big Three remained cordial. They smiled and chatted through luncheons, conferences, and dinners peppered with endless vodka and wine toasts. Unlike FDR, Winston rose to the occasion. "PM seems well, though drinking buckets of Caucasian champagne which would undermine the health of any ordinary man," one of Eden's diplomats wrote his wife.[4]

At one dinner, Winston raised his glass. "It is no exaggeration or compliment of a florid kind when I say that we regard Marshal Stalin's life as most precious to the hopes and hearts of all of us," he declaimed.

But he knew better than to trust the fleeting glow of triumph. "Do not let us underestimate the difficulties. Nations, comrades in arms, have in the past drifted apart within five or ten years of war," he warned. "We now have a chance of avoiding the errors of previous generations and of making a sure peace."[5]

He did his best. Before it was over, Stalin had agreed to Poland's "free and unfettered election on the basis of universal suffrage and secret ballot." Moscow would declare war on Japan within three months of Germany's defeat and support a United Nations Organization. In return, the Soviet Union would get half the roughly $20 billion in reparations Germany would pay, its navy would receive a major anchorage in the Pacific, and the western Allies would hand over all Soviet nationals in their custody for sorting out by the NKVD.[6]

Though pleased with their formal agreements, Winston left Yalta with a sense of unease. The only bond of the victors was a common hatred of Nazism, and that bond would dissolve before the year was out. As he told his secretary Elizabeth Nel, "What shall we do when an iron curtain comes down between us and only occasionally raises to allow a face—and not a very pleasant face at that—to peer through it?"[7]

Winston returned to London basking in praise over Yalta. The *Times* gave the conference a glowing page-one review, and even Clement Attlee, the opposition leader, tipped his hat.[8]

Not everyone was effusive, however. A wing of Winston's Conservative Party, stirred by the London Poles, accused the PM of failure: failing to fight for Poland's old borders, failing to safeguard the rights of noncommunists in the new Polish government, failing to get a better guarantee of free elections. Britain had declared war in 1939 to help Poland throw off Nazi chains; after Yalta, they might have simply exchanged them for communist shackles, riveted by the Red Army.

Winston stood defiant. The new borders were fair, he insisted. They were dictated by geopolitical circumstances, not intimidation. In a speech to Parliament, he thundered, "I repudiate and repulse any suggestion that we are making a questionable compromise or yielding to force or fear."[9]

But he *had* yielded to force, and he knew it. The Poles knew it, too. Most of all, Stalin knew it.

In private, Winston harbored doubts that Stalin would keep his promises. Had he been played, the way Hitler played Chamberlain seven years before? Had Yalta become the new Munich?

He brooded over the world to come, a time when Germany lay prostrate and the Red Army was drunk on victory. "What will lie between the white snows of Russia and the white cliffs of Dover?" he asked his doctor, Lord Moran.

He foresaw a day when the western Allies would need to take a hard stand. At the very least, they must be ready for the moment—even if the moment demanded more blood. As he told secretary Jock Colville, "I have not the slightest intention of being cheated over Poland, not even if we go to the edge of war with Russia."[10]

Yet the British Empire could go only as far as the United States would dare—and FDR, physically spent from his journey, had no stomach for a fight. All Winston could do was send a sick old man cheerful missives about a brighter day to come: "Our friendship is the rock on which I build for the future of the world so long as I am one of the builders."[11]

But one of the builders was dying—and Eisenhower was drawing a line across his war maps that cut straight through Winston's hopes. The bonds of the brotherhood would face a new test when Ike fired off his next round of orders.

TWENTY-TWO

Lovers' Quarrels

"WHY SHOULD WE TAKE BERLIN FOR THE RUSSIANS?" Omar Bradley asked Ike in his Missouri twang. "I estimate it will cost us 100,000 casualties, and I don't like sacrificing American lives solely for the sake of the Russians."[1]

Neither did Ike.

Berlin was the war's big prize, of course. The road home ran through it, and every GI and Tommy was waiting to hear it had fallen. So was every politician. But Ike wasn't after Berlin. He was after the German Army.

The *Heer* wasn't polishing their medals under the Brandenburg Gate. The bulk of Hitler's western forces was falling back to Germany's center and south. SHAEF's Intel wizards were picking up rumors of a guerrilla resistance movement being formed in the mountains of Bavaria, birthplace of national socialism, and Ike wasn't about to let Hitler's fanatics set up their Alamo in the Alps.

Besides, thought Ike, even if Berlin made military sense, the politicians had already sliced up the map. They had agreed to give Stalin eastern Germany and half of Berlin when the shooting stopped. Damned if Ike wanted to tell some mother in Iowa her boy died capturing a city everyone knew we'd hand over to the Russians.

To Ike, an attack through the center and south made more sense than grinding it out in Berlin's streets. If Stalin wanted to go there and pull the rattlesnake out of the mailbox, he could do it. He probably would. But Ike wouldn't. Not without orders.[2]

He was staring at a different problem, the kind a rifleman would understand. Two trigger-prone armies, one heading east, the other west, had been blasting everything in front of them for three years. In a world of "shoot first, ask questions never," a friendly-fire war was certain to break out unless Ike drew a line so unmistakable a buck private from Arkansas, or Siberia, would know to stop shooting when he reached it.

To fix that border, on March 28 Ike sent the Red Army's boss a letter outlining his strategy. Speaking as one military commander to another, he told Stalin that after capturing the Ruhr, "my next task will be to divide the enemy's remaining forces by joining hands with your forces." He would drive south of Berlin, sending two of Bradley's armies toward Magdeburg and Leipzig, keeping just west of the Elbe River. Patton and Patch would stretch farther south, toward Munich and through Bavaria. Ike asked Stalin where Marshals Zhukov, Konev, and Rokossovsky would be, so the two clamps of the vice could link up for Germany's final destruction without risking friendly-fire incidents.[3]

Then he wrote Monty. Bradley would take center stage for the war's finale. Ninth U.S. Army would go back to Brad's command, and in a reversal of their usual roles, Twenty-First Army Group would guard the American left flank as Bradley drove south and east. Ike would let Monty sweep the north German ports and secure Denmark, but that was it.[4]

For months, Winston had been watching the warning flares rise above the horizon. Stalin was playing hardball with the London Poles, communists were fomenting unrest throughout Eastern Europe, and Foreign Minister Vyacheslav Molotov—the blunt instrument Lenin had nicknamed "Iron-Ass"—was accusing the Allies of negotiating a separate peace with Hitler. The temperature in the Kremlin was getting frigid, and power politics was coming back in vogue. It would be hard to pry the Red Army out of any territory it held when the guns fell silent, so the Allies had best sweep up what they could before Germany surrendered.[5]

When Ike's message about halting at the Elbe reached 10 Downing Street, it hit like a buzz bomb. Winston picked up the green scrambler phone and rang up SHAEF Forward for an explanation. Summoned to the phone, Ike promised to send the prime minister a detailed written reply. Hanging up, he began dictating a letter.

He told Winston he would send Bradley through Germany's center, cutting the enemy's remnants in two and capturing Germany's last big industrial region. Monty would protect Brad's left flank, Devers his right. When Bradley was finished, Monty would sweep the north German coast through Denmark, while Devers would drive through Nuremburg toward Austria. The one place missing from Ike's letter was Berlin.[6]

Clemenceau once remarked, "War is too important to be left to the generals." To Winston, Ike's letter was proof. His textbook approach might have earned him a passing grade at West Point, but in 1945, every military move was fraught with political implications. Having survived Darlan, the Transportation Plan, and Strasbourg, Ike should know that by now.[7]

Berlin was not some farming village. It was the beating heart of the beast, and its capture would ripple through the postwar era. Through history. Hitler's destruction was assured, but *who* destroyed him mattered—and Ike still had time to alter history's course.

The next day, Winston sent his reply:

> Why should we not cross the Elbe and advance as far eastward as possible? This has an important political bearing, as the Russian armies of the South seem certain to enter Vienna and overrun Aus-

> tria. If we deliberately leave Berlin to them, even if it should be in our grasp, the double event may strengthen their conviction, already apparent, that they have done everything.

Stinging over Montgomery's humiliating new role—handmaiden for Omar Bradley—Winston also suggested that Ike let Monty keep the Ninth Army and capture Berlin. "This would not be in any way inconsistent with the great central thrust which you are now so rightly developing as a result of the brilliant operations of your Armies south of the Ruhr," he wrote. "It only shifts the weight of one army to the northern flank and this avoids the relegation of His Majesty's forces to an unexpectedly restricted sphere."[8]

To Ike, none of that mattered. The Soviets had lost over twenty million citizens and slaughtered the large majority of Hitler's troops. If, in their conquest, the Allies had slogged through blood, the Russians had drowned in it. They would damn sure think they had "done everything," regardless of whether Monty waltzed into Berlin at the war's tail end.

The military path was straight and narrow. Ike's judgment told him the most efficient way to finish off the enemy was to drive through the center. If the Combined Chiefs wanted to change his orders and make him take Berlin, he'd take Berlin. If not, he was moving against Leipzig and Bavaria.[9]

As for Winston's comment about Monty being relegated to a backwater—that one stung. Ike had bent over backward to give His Majesty's forces the lead in Sicily, Goodwood, the drive to the Rhine, and the Ruhr. He had taken heat from close friends for being too "pro-British" and for starving Brad, Hodges, Patton, and Patch so Monty could carry the Union Jack into Germany. Now Winston was accusing him of being unfair to his British friends.

Ike sent Winston a cable marked "Personal." After explaining his military reasoning, he added,

> I am disturbed, if not hurt, that you should suggest any thought on my part to "relegate His Majesty's forces to an unexpectedly restricted sphere." Nothing is further from my mind and I think my record over two and a half years conduct commanding the Allied forces should eliminate any such idea.[10]

Winston groaned as he read Ike's reply. The Kansan wasn't backing down, and the U.S. Chiefs would support him. Again. Affairs had reached an alarming state when an American theater general could refuse an emphatic suggestion from the First Minister of the British Empire.

Once upon a time, Winston could have bent Ike to his will. That time was long past. Always respectful, always friendly, Ike had refused to go along in the Aegean, with French railway bombings, now Berlin. For two years, Winston had outmaneuvered Roosevelt, the War Cabinet, the Combined Chiefs, the British Chiefs, and the Labour Party. But he couldn't seem to best this bridge-playing general from Abilene.

How did Ike do it? He was not devious, or especially clever, in any political sense. He didn't have to be. He just said no.

In London, the British Chiefs worked themselves into a window-rattling furor over Ike's letter to Stalin. Writing to the Soviet dictator was a matter of statecraft, and generals don't engage in statecraft. Brooke, Portal, and Cunningham wanted the Combined Chiefs to censure Ike over the misdemeanor, and they brought the matter to the prime minister's attention.

Winston knew better. Despite his frustrations over Berlin, Ike had become too powerful for a schoolboy scolding. Winston had mentored him into an Achilles—or a Foch—and the British Chiefs would have to swallow the bitter with the sweet. Winston could spar with Ike in private, but he urged his chiefs not to cross swords with the Americans over Ike's letter.[11]

Winston would continue to shield Ike from British criticism. When rumors hit Washington that the British Chiefs were sharpening their knives for Ike, he cleared the air with a letter to Roosevelt: "I wish to place on record the complete confidence felt by His Majesty's Government in General Eisenhower, our pleasure that our Armies are serving under his command and our admiration of the great and shining qualities of character and personality which he has proved himself to possess in all difficulties of handling an Allied command."[12]

But there was still Berlin to deal with. Much as he liked Ike, he lobbied the president to overrule Ike's Berlin decision.

"The Russian Armies will no doubt overrun all Austria and enter Vienna," he told Roosevelt. "If they also take Berlin, will not their impression that they have been the overwhelming contributor to our common victory be unduly imprinted in their minds, and may this not lead them into a mood which will raise grave and formidable difficulties in the future?" He drove his point home: "I therefore consider that from a political standpoint we should march as far east into Germany as possible and that should Berlin be in our grasp we should certainly take it."[13]

The decision lay in Roosevelt's lap. As with the Transportation Plan and Torch, FDR would have the final say.

His appeal filed with Roosevelt, Winston considered a personal matter: Ike's hurt feelings over his "relegation of His Majesty's forces" remark. The accusation of unfair play against British friends evidently stuck in Ike's craw.

Normally Winston would not bat an eye—or even notice—an insult or disappointment to a general. But Ike was different. He was too important an ally to lose, even over an issue like Berlin, and Winston wasn't about to strain their personal relations. Calling for a secretary, he dictated a smoothing-over letter to Ike:

> It would be a grief to me if anything in my last disturbed or still more pained you. I only meant that the effect of the 21st Army Group arriving on the Elbe so spread out that it would be condemned to take a static role would be a good deal less than what we hoped for, namely, to enter Berlin side by side with our American comrades.

He reiterated his desire to see Allied soldiers far beyond the Elbe before the shooting stopped. "I am, however, all the more impressed with the importance of entering Poland, which may well be open to us," he concluded. "I deem it highly important that we should shake hands with the Russians as far to the East as possible."[14]

Winston's letter of support to FDR meant a lot to Ike. He was grateful, and he told Winston so:

> I feel a deep sense of humility in reading the glowing personal tribute to my services that you dispatched to the President. The generosity of your language is equaled only by my continued determination that every action of mine shall be governed by the single purpose of winning this campaign at the earliest possible moment. In doing so I shall likewise devote myself toward sustaining among the forces of the United States and Great Britain those feelings of mutual respect and unification that have been the mainspring of effectiveness in this command.[15]

Grateful though he was, he wouldn't budge on Berlin. On April 6, he wrote Montgomery with crisp clarity: "I am quite ready to admit that it has political and psychological significance, but of far greater importance will be the location of the remaining German forces in relation to Berlin. It is on them that I am going to concentrate my attention. Naturally, if I get an opportunity to capture Berlin cheaply, I will take it."[16]

Since he knew Berlin couldn't be taken cheaply, that ended the discussion for Ike. He wouldn't sponsor any "death or glory" charge to the Brandenburg Gate.*

On April 5, the ailing president weighed in on Ike's side, cutting off all further discussion. With Roosevelt's decision to back Ike, Winston ran up the white flag—or something that resembled one from a distance.

"My personal relations with General Eisenhower are of the most friendly character," he wrote FDR. "I regard the matter as closed, and to prove my sincerity I will use one of my very few Latin quotations: *amantium irae amoris integratio est.*"[17]†

That sincerity was skin-deep. The Americans were shoving their cousins off center stage, and Winston's frustration simmered below the surface. "The only times I ever quarrel with the Americans are when they fail to give us a fair share of opportunity to win glory," he wrote Clementine. "Undoubtedly I feel much pain when I see our armies so much smaller than theirs. It has always been my wish to keep equal, but how can you do that against so mighty a nation and a population nearly three times your own?"[18]

Amoris or not, Winston would never get over Ike's decision. Years later, he would tell an American friend, "I tried my best to persuade Ike to take Berlin and to move as far east as possible, because I knew the Russians would make trouble in the end. But Eisenhower thought only

---

* The Red Army suffered more than 360,000 casualties taking Berlin, three times Omar Bradley's estimate and more than a third of all U.S. Army casualties suffered in the entirety of World War II.

† "Lover's quarrels always go with true love," according to FDR's staff. Winston more colorfully translated it to secretary Marian Holmes as "The wrath of lovers hots up their love."

of the military position. I couldn't get him or the others to consider the political problems, which were as plain as day."[19]

"I do not quite understand why the Prime Minister has been so determined to intermingle political and military considerations," Ike said in frustration. But they had come through the worst of it, and the end was in sight.[20]

Ike and Winston knew how to separate friendship from their official disagreements, no matter how fundamental those disagreements might be. Winston could happily break bread with Labour opponents working to unseat him, while Ike almost never let policy disagreements curdle into personal resentment. As Ike explained their connection: "Churchill and I were close friends, and had a good deal of respect for each other. We argued a lot, but there was never anything personal involved."[21]

It helped, of course, that Ike usually came out on top. Since the fall of '43, in most disputes he'd had nothing to complain about. As John Eisenhower once remarked on his father, "He's very good-natured at home as long as everything goes his way."

Years later, Ike told a staffer that on military questions, the arguments "didn't really matter, because I was the boss." And to Winston's distress, the boss was about to lay down some hard rules in Central Europe.[22]

TWENTY-THREE

Kattegat & Bohemia

Sitting at a banquet table with Stalin and Winston the previous October, a bootlicker referred to Stalin, Churchill, and FDR as the Holy Trinity. "If that is so," quipped Stalin, "Churchill must be the Holy Ghost. He flies around so much."[1]

But by April 1945, the Holy Ghost was flying on fumes. He had poured his soul into the struggle against Hitler, and behind the defiance, the speeches, the cigars, and "V for Victory," after the exhausting fight, he feared he had nothing left for the world to come.

Omens that Stalin wouldn't honor his agreements accumulated like kindling. Molotov reneged on his promise to let western Poles participate in the provisional government. The Lublin communists refused to allow western observers to monitor elections. Fifteen London Polish leaders in talks with the Lublin faction disappeared. And Poland was just the beginning.[2]

If the enemy of my enemy is my friend, what happens to my friend when the enemy is gone? The red tsar seemed bent on forcing communism on Europe, and the war-torn states west of the Elbe lacked the men, tanks, and aircraft to stop him. Perhaps the will, too.

Only the United States, with eleven million men under arms, wielded enough power to hold the red tide. With its shipyards and factories, its mines and farms, America had built a vast military-industrial machine capable of sustaining two unlimited wars on opposite sides of the planet—a feat unparalleled in history.

To protect Europe's future, Winston was certain of one thing: Ike's armies must seize the high ground. They must drive beyond the Elbe. After shaking hands with the Red Army as far east as possible, Ike's men should remain there until the president and the prime minister decided when and where to withdraw them. Even a few days east of the Elbe would send Moscow a message of strength. And if Stalin understood anything, it was strength.

"Surely Eisenhower's columns should advance so as to salute the Russians as far east as possible," Winston told Pug Ismay on April 7. "There cannot be such a hurry about withdrawing from a place we have gained that the few days necessary for consulting the Governments in Washington and London cannot be found."[3]

One of those governments didn't have a few days. The twelfth of April found Winston immersed in another day of imperial business: Cabinet at noon, Question Time in Parliament, another round with the Cabinet, photographs with Dominion representatives, evening nap, and dinner with an old friend, financier Bernard Baruch. It was the life of a wartime prime minister—ceaseless, urgent, all-consuming.[4]

At midnight he was at his station, working into dawn's early light. Though he was superstitious about Friday the 13th, it started as an ordinary day until the news reached London: Franklin Delano Roosevelt had died at his cabin in Warm Springs, Georgia.[5]

Winston's bodyguard, Walter Thompson, watched Winston's reaction: "For a long time, Winston Churchill just walked about his room, talking of Roosevelt—weeping, reminiscing, smiling, going over the days, the years; recalling conversations, wishing he had done this, wondering what had been meant when Roosevelt said this or that," Thompson remembered. "I realized Winston could not stop talking—here in the middle of the night—because he could not bear the agony."[6]

"I feel deeply for Winston," MP Harold Nicolson told his diary the next day. "This afternoon it was evident from his manner that it was a real body-blow."[7]

Through wet eyes, Winston called for a secretary and dictated condolence letters to Eleanor Roosevelt, Harry Hopkins, and the new president, Harry Truman. "He was sitting there and somehow his face looked utterly crumpled and his figure looked crumpled and he seemed almost to have paled," remembered Elizabeth Nel, one of his secretaries. "When he dictated his voice was quite unlike his usual. It was sort of gentle and quiet."[8]

Whatever he might build with Truman could never approach the intimacy of his bond with FDR. Since forging the Atlantic Charter in the dark days of '41, they had lived together, worked side by side, shared the humiliations of Pearl Harbor and Tobruk, savored the victories of Italy and Overlord. FDR had been his friend, his fellow visionary, and, at times, his only ally against narrow-minded military chiefs. Now Ike would have to shoulder some of that delicate role. And April's end found Winston taking a hard look at Eisenhower's battle lines.

"Call from P.M.," Kay Summersby wrote in her office diary on May 4. "He is much disturbed over the fact that the Russians are landing in Denmark."[9]

Of course the PM was disturbed about the Russians. Everyone was disturbed about the Russians. Ike wasn't blind to politics, and while he wouldn't rush his men into the Soviet occupation zone, he wasn't going to let Red Army troops, commissars, agitators, and secret police spread like typhus through the Allied zone.

At the end of March, he had ordered Montgomery to dash across the Elbe to the German port of Lübeck, on the eastern shoulder of the

Danish peninsula. Reaching that port ahead of the Russians would slam shut Denmark's front door.[10]

But Montgomery moved like molasses in January. Ike stressed the importance of getting to Lübeck first, and in mid-April, he even offered Monty an American army corps and rail transport to get there. Yet by April 27, the Elbe was behind them, and Lübeck still lay ahead.

Ike didn't want Copenhagen sharing the fate of Warsaw, Bucharest, and Belgrade. "The Prime Minister is finally waking up to one danger that I have been warning him about for some weeks, namely, the possibility that the Russians can reach Lübeck and the neck of the Danish Peninsula ahead of us," he wrote Marshall. "I have done everything humanly possible to support Montgomery and to urge him to an early attack across the Elbe to Lübeck."[11]

"Early" wasn't in Monty's vocabulary, but on May 3, his spearhead finally reached Lübeck, cutting off the roads to Denmark just ahead of the Red Army. An American corps moved up to Copenhagen, and German commanders surrendered their forces in northern Germany and Denmark. By hours, Denmark escaped Soviet occupation. The northern end of the Allied line was fixed.[12]

Looking south, Winston squirmed as he wondered where Ike's drive would end. His spearheads could reach Prague, even Vienna, and Winston wanted American flags planted in both of those capitals. It might cost Patton or Patch a few hundred soldiers to get there, but what were a few hundred men in a war that had swallowed millions? Besides, what sane German would toss away his life resisting the Americans when his cause was plainly lost and the Red Army was rolling in from the east?

On April 24, he spoke to Ike about Bohemia. To Winston's disappointment, Ike politely but firmly told him Prague was not his next milestone. Two or three German divisions barred the way, and he would have to change settled plans to amass enough men to take the city by storm. He would move Patton as far as Pilsen and Karlsbad, but he wouldn't commit to anything farther east.

Winston was frustrated. Like Lübeck, Prague was a breakwater against the communist tide. The Allies hadn't formally decided on end lines in Czechoslovakia, nor occupation zones in Austria. That made Prague fair game for both sides. It burned Winston that Ike wouldn't order Patton to rush the Czech capital.

At April's end, Winston went over Ike's head with an appeal to President Truman. Eisenhower, he said, should seize any opportunity to push deep into Bohemia. "There can be little doubt that the liberation of Prague and as much as possible of the territory of Western Czechoslovakia by your forces might make the whole difference to the post-war situation in Czechoslovakia and might well influence that in nearby countries," he wrote. "I think the highly important political consideration mentioned above should be brought to his attention."[13]

But the new president deeply respected Stimson and Marshall, and Stimson and Marshall respected Eisenhower. Truman let Ike decide.

Again, Ike wouldn't commit to Prague. His orders were to defeat the German Army, not take cities like bridge tricks. As with Berlin, he simply said, "I shall not attempt any move which I deem militarily unwise."[14]

Winston couldn't force Ike to move, but he wouldn't give up without making one last attempt. He told Ike he hoped his plan "does not inhibit you to advance to Prague if you have the troops and do not meet the Russians earlier. I thought you did not mean to tie yourself down if you had the troops and the country was empty." Knowing it was becoming a sensitive question, he ended his letter by saying, "Don't bother to reply by wire but tell me when we next have a talk."[15]

Truman's support for Ike ended all discussion of Prague, just as Roosevelt's had ended talk of Berlin. Ike had won the argument—though Winston believed the future would prove him right. Years later, Winston drafted, then deleted a line in a letter to FDR's war mobilization director, James Byrnes: "My recollection is that I did my utmost to persuade General Eisenhower to let his two armoured divisions roll into Prague, as they could so easily have done in a few hours. In this also great disasters have followed and no one can measure what will happen in the future."[16]

But Ike's was not the Man on Horseback style Winston idolized in the Duke of Marlborough, Napoleon, and Wellington. "Churchill later speculated that if MacArthur had been the Supreme Commander in Europe, America would not have sat back and watched Eastern Europe succumb to Soviet domination," Richard Nixon reflected years later. "Eisenhower was not Churchill's kind of general."[17]

As the Third Reich listed and took on water, the rats scampered off—only to find death waiting for them. On April 23, Hermann Göring, accused of treason by Hitler, was placed under house arrest. Five days later, Mussolini and his mistress met their end on the shores of Lake Como, gunned down by Italian partisans, their bodies taken to Milan and strung up by the heels from the roof of an Esso gas station. On the last day of April, Hitler and Eva Braun committed suicide in a Berlin bunker as Russian shells pounded the crumbling capital. Goebbels and his wife had their six children sedated with morphine and dispatched with cyanide; shortly afterward, the parents followed their children. Heinrich Himmler attempted a surrender through Swedish intermediaries, then went into hiding before being captured. He, too, bit down on a cyanide capsule.

On May 1 German radio broke the news of Hitler's death. The propagandists had one last lie to tell. The leader of the twelve-year-old Thousand Year Reich, they said, died "fighting with his last breath against Bolshevism."[18]

On May 5, German Admiral Hans-Georg von Friedeburg traveled to SHAEF headquarters at Reims to negotiate the surrender of German forces. His instructions, from Hitler's successor, were to surrender to the western Allies while fighting the Soviets in the east—conditions unacceptable to the Allies.

To Ike, unconditional surrender wasn't just policy. Germany's leaders had to know they were undeniably, emphatically, thoroughly beaten on the field of battle. No stab-in-the-back myths this time. "Ike wants to seal the Allied victory so completely that no one in Germany, civilian, soldier, airman, or sailor, will fail to appreciate the fact that the 'super-race' has had the hell beaten out of it," wrote Harry Butcher. "He doesn't want our kids left to an inheritance of World War III."[19]

William Faulkner once said a man is the sum of his misfortunes. So it is with countries. In the Belle Epoque, Germany was a beautiful woman, with Bach and Goethe and Bierstadt and Planck adorning the mosaic of a strong, exquisite face. But war, depression, and more war had carved scars into her cheeks and forehead. When she emerged from the collapsed mine and crawled back to the table, the Valkyrie of 1913 was a broken, dust-covered crone. Pitied by few, loved by none.

Meanwhile, the hammer and sickle had swept across Eastern Europe, and its dictator was moving against the center. Ike had shut out Stalin from the Kattegat Strait on the North Sea to western Bohemia in the south. But in Winston's eyes, Ike was allowing too much of Central Europe to fall into Stalin's gauntlets in the name of fair play.

"I fear terrible things have happened during the Russian advance through Germany to the Elbe," he wrote to Anthony Eden. "The territories under Russian control would include the Baltic Provinces, all of Germany to the occupational line, all Czechoslovakia, a large part of Austria, the whole of Yugoslavia, Hungary, Roumania, Bulgaria, until Greece in her present tottering condition is reached. It would include all the great capitals of middle Europe including Berlin, Vienna, Budapest, Belgrade, Bucharest and Sofia."[20]

Victory should have been cane-sugar sweet. "It is astonishing one is not in a more buoyant frame of mind in public matters," he wrote Clementine on May 4. "During the last three days we have heard of the death of Mussolini and Hitler; Alexander has taken a million prisoners of war; Montgomery took 500,000 additional yesterday and far more than a million today; all north-west Germany, Holland and Denmark are to be surrendered early tomorrow morning. . . . [W]e are all occupied here with preparations for Victory-Europe Day."[21]

At three in the morning of May 7, Pug Ismay awoke to the sound of his phone ringing. When he picked it up, the operator told him General Eisenhower was on the line.

Because Winston's standing orders prohibited interrupting his sleep unless Germans were invading British soil, Pug intercepted the prime minister's overnight military calls. "These nocturnal calls had never brought good news, and I was afraid that something had gone wrong," Ismay would write. He put the handset to his ear.

"Is that you, Pug?" A friendly Kansas voice came across the line.

"Yes, Ike, what has happened?"

"They have signed on the dotted line. It's all over."[22]

Winston awoke the next morning to find his Map Room manager, Captain Richard Pim, standing over him, armed with a message from Ike. Ike's official cable, directed to the Combined Chiefs, simply read, "The mission of this Allied force was fulfilled at 0241 local time, May 7th, 1945."

A broad, childlike smile spread across Winston's face.

"For five years," he told Pim, "you've brought me bad news, sometimes worse than others. Now you've redeemed yourself."[23]

TWENTY-FOUR

"I Am Now a Londoner"

"When this war is over, I am going to find the deepest hole there is in the United States, crawl in and pull it in after me," Ike had written an old friend.[1]

But war has a way of changing men and changing dreams, and the aspiring hermit wouldn't find his hole anytime soon. No longer shielded by a phalanx of wartime press censors, Ike had to adjust to his celebrity status. With war's end, Ike's hole became a fishbowl, starting with his first real night on the town.

A week after the German surrender, Ike and a small group flew to London for a day of unwinding. The flight was delightful, with Ike and Kay pairing to sweep Bradley and an aide at bridge, winning 100 francs before they landed. Not much money, but enough to start the day off right. Then they stopped for lunch at Telegraph Cottage, and by the time they reached the champagne buffet at Bradley's suite at the Dorchester, they were in a mood to celebrate.

Accompanied by his son John, Kay, and Kay's mother, Ike took in *Perchance to Dream*, a West End musical. When the show's star announced Ike's presence during intermission, the audience applauded. When, at the end, the curtain fell and the lights came up, the crowd again turned to Ike's box and cheered.

Ike stood, and the ovation became a roar. With a smile, he thanked cast and audience for a wonderful evening. He added, "I wonder if you people realize what it means to me to be back here among friends, among people whose language I can almost speak." The crowd loved it.

The night wasn't over. Outside, a swarm of well-wishers thronged Ike's car as it inched from Piccadilly Circus to Leicester Square. Eventually, Ike's party reached Ciro's nightclub, where the evening continued with dining, drinking, and laughing. Ike stepped out on the dance floor and swept a beaming Kay for several rounds under the chandeliers as the band played on.

"That night was the one time in his entire war career when I ever saw General Eisenhower completely relaxed, thoroughly enjoying himself, without a care or wrinkle or worry," Kay remembered. His eyes lit up and he smiled from ear to ear as the club orchestra played "For He's a Jolly Good Fellow" and "One Dozen Roses," a tune he often ran on the phonograph player for Mamie.[2]

Over lunch the next day, Winston floated the idea of a formal ceremony in Ike's honor. Ike urged him to downplay celebrating his role as supreme commander. The real work had been done by millions, he said, so he hoped they would not overglorify the man at the top. He suggested they arrange something simple.[3]

But Winston wasn't thinking of simple. He was thinking of a moment in history, an inflection point in the Anglo-American brotherhood. In their hour of joint triumph, it was a time for the world to witness the emotional bond between two great empires—a bond sealed with shared language, shared sacrifices, and shared dreams.

In mid-May, he told Ike he would receive London's "Freedom of the City," an honor steeped in medieval tradition. London's Lord Mayor would confer the status of "Citizen of London" at the imposing Guildhall, after which Ike would deliver an acceptance speech to London's civic and political elite.

For several days, Ike pondered what he would say. He felt a kinship with Britain, a bond forged by more than just the pressures of war. He felt it keenly when ordinary English folk smiled at him and he smiled back. They were his neighbors, fellow citizens he might meet on the street back home. "On your soil, I do not feel particularly a foreigner or a stranger," he had told a class of British Army cadets graduating from Sandhurst the spring before D-Day.

Now he was given a chance to put into words what Britain meant to him.

How could he thank a people who had supported him with their blood, sweat, treasure, and cheers through three years of war? At his new headquarters near Frankfurt, he sketched out ideas in pencil on a yellow pad. Notes became typed drafts, with Ike jamming scribbles into margins for secretaries to decipher and retype. At night, he marked up fresh drafts in bed, paragraph by paragraph, repeating phrases in his head until sleep took him.[4]

On June 12, Ike flashed the "V for Victory" sign from a horse-drawn landau as crowds lined London's Fleet Street. Men, women, and children from all walks of life cheered as the horses clip-clopped toward their destination: the Guildhall.

Winston, in top hat and tails, greeted Ike at the building's grand entrance. A sexton with a 600-year-old ceremonial mace escorted Ike to his seat. With Kay and company sitting proudly in the audience, Ike received a jewel-encrusted scimitar as a token of London's thanks, while the Lord Mayor conferred London citizenship on the man from Abilene, Kansas.[5]

When his moment came, Ike rose to the lectern, hands behind his back, ramrod straight, his dress uniform impeccable. No notes, just a message. Clearing his throat, he spoke not of kings or conquerors, but of the common man.

"To preserve his freedom of worship, his equality before law, his liberty to speak and act as he sees fit, subject only to provisions that he trespass not upon similar rights of others, a Londoner will fight. So will a citizen of Abilene," he said. "When we consider these things, then the valley of the Thames draws closer to the farms of Kansas and the plains of Texas. To my mind it is clear that when two peoples will face the tragedies of war to defend the same spiritual values, the same treasured rights, then in the deepest sense those two are truly related. So even as I proclaim my undying Americanism, I am bold enough and exceedingly proud to claim the basis of kinship to you of London."

He dismissed skeptics who claimed the English-speaking cousins could never work together in tight quarters. "I hope you believe we proved the doubters wrong," said Ike. "Moreover, I hold that we proved this point not only for war—we proved it can always be done by our two peoples, provided only that both show the same good will, the same forbearance, the same objective attitude that the British and Americans so amply demonstrated in nearly three years of bitter campaigning."[6]

The audience listened, spellbound by this idealistic American. "There were tears rolling down the cheeks of many of these English who prided themselves on their reserve," Kay remembered. "It was as though he spoke without thought, as though he spoke to one person instead of an audience. It was more of a private soliloquy, an outpouring of the heart."[7]

His speech finished, the party moved to the nearby Mansion House for the reception. Below its street-side balcony, a sea of shopkeepers, sailors, housewives, and newsboys gathered from every walk of life. They cheered and waved to Europe's liberator as he appeared on the second-floor balcony.

London might have been Winston's city, but today it was Ike's show. Winston watched with unfeigned pleasure as his friend basked in the crowd's affection. With a grin and a wave, Ike leaned into a microphone and treated the crowd to the Eisenhower touch.

"Whether or not you know it, I am now a Londoner myself," he began. "I've got just as much right to be down in that crowd yelling as you have."

The crowd laughed and cheered.

"To every Londoner that has ever taken one of my soldiers into his home, I say you'll always have my profound gratitude. To everyone who has smilingly directed one of my men to the Albert Hall, or to Marble Arch, I owe thanks also," he continued. "You have done something in cementing bonds that must always remain between your country and mine."

With a polite farewell, he turned on his heel and was gone. Winston, doffing his hat, stepped forward to the microphone, eyes glistening with the pride of a father for a son.

"You have just seen and listened to the words of a great commander," he said.

Another cheer from the crowds.

"A man . . . who has shown a capacity for making great nations march together more truly united than they ever have before." He followed Ike inside.[8]

Indoors, among London's upper crust, it was Winston's turn to speak from the heart. "I have had an opportunity of seeing at close quarters General Ike, for that is what I call him, in action. I have seen him all sorts of times," he began. "I have had personal acquaintance with him now for three years. It is not much, but three years of this sort may seem five-and-twenty. I feel we have here a great creative, constructive and combining genius, one from our sister nation across the ocean, one who will never speak evil but will always cherish his contact with the British people."[9]

"Through the battle, through defeat, moving yet and never stopping," Walt Whitman wrote in his ode to the American pioneer. Winston, a product of the Old World, loved and admired the spirit of the New that Ike

personified. He warmed to Ike's words of solidarity because he romanticized the ideal of two brothers reunited—and because on those ideals he looked to build Britain's future.

If he were given the chance, that is. In a democracy, the people get their say every now and then, and that time was approaching. In a month, Winston had voters to face.

TWENTY-FIVE

Order of the Boot

"When the war of the giants is over, the wars of the pygmies will begin."

—Winston[1]

I FEAR THAT A VERY GREAT EVIL MAY COME UPON THE WORLD," Winston told Anthony Eden. "The Russians are drunk with victory and there is no length they may not go."[2]

History flowed through Winston's veins like whisky, art, and politics. Great tides of human progress flashed through his mind like a sixth sense. "Demons seem to whisper things to him," his old friend Violet Bonham Carter once said.[3]

Now the demons were whispering.

"The destruction of German military power had brought with it a fundamental change in the relations between Communist Russia and the Western democracies," he would later write. "They had lost their common enemy, which was almost their sole bond of union. Henceforward Russian imperialism and the Communist creed saw and set no bounds to their progress and ultimate dominion."[4]

At Yalta, Churchill and Roosevelt had tried to forge a working partnership with Stalin in Eastern Europe. The parties had agreed to "free and unfettered elections" in Poland, but the fetters were brought out, and they were being clamped on Polish limbs. Warsaw's provisional government had become a shadow box of puppets, which didn't bode well for the Baltics, Czechoslovakia, Austria, or any other place the Red Army planted its boots. Using a metaphor he had been toying with, Winston wrote Truman, "An iron curtain is drawn down upon their front."[5]

He pressed for another Big Three meeting, and Stalin agreed to meet with Truman and Churchill in Berlin, or what was left of it. Winston anxiously looked forward to the next round of talks, for what they might do and what they might prevent. The summit wouldn't be just another diplomatic congress. It would be a meeting of train conductors to stop a collision.

On July 16, as British votes were being counted in the national election, Winston flew to Potsdam, an unshattered suburb of Berlin where the conference would take place. His entourage set up shop in a residence dubbed "10 Downing Street, Potsdam," and Winston met the freshman president of the United States.[6]

The two western leaders found they were well matched. Both preferred plain speech over FDR's tendency to dissemble. Both valued Christian principles—Winston for its secular inspiration and individuality, Truman for its innate spiritual worth. Winston called Christ's Sermon on the Mount "the last word in ethics," while Truman told radio listeners, "I do not believe there is one problem in this country or in the world today which could not be settled if approached through the teaching of the Sermon on the Mount."[7]

Stalin believed in a different holy trinity: Marx, Lenin, and the Party. He had sacrificed millions to his vision of a proletarian utopia, a paradise demanding submission to centralized authority. Centralization requires mass compulsion, and mass compulsion sometimes requires—make that *always* requires—the fist of repression.

With two fundamentally opposing worldviews and no pressure to defeat Germany, the Potsdam delegates ran into brick walls. Their leaders made good progress on easy subjects, like the impending Soviet entry into the war against Japan. But national boundaries, Poland, elections, and much else defied resolution—and Winston's distractions with the election at home didn't help.

As diplomats shuffled among conference rooms at Cecilienhof Palace, a light flashed in the New Mexico desert. The Americans had split the atom and exploded a bomb with the power of 21,000 tons of TNT. The Allies now controlled a weapon of unprecedented destructiveness. A weapon that could end wars—or start new ones.

While the official report from Major General Leslie Groves recapitulated the facts—bomb yield, blast area, cloud height—it was an eyewitness account of his deputy, Brigadier General Thomas Farrell, that came across in language guaranteed to arrest Winston's focus:

"The effects could well be called unprecedented, magnificent, beautiful, stupendous and terrifying," Farrell wrote. "It was that beauty the great poets dream about but describe most poorly and inadequately. Thirty seconds after the explosion came, first, the air blast pressing hard against the people and things, to be followed almost immediately by the strong, sustained, awesome roar which warned of doomsday and made us feel that we puny things were blasphemous to dare tamper with the forces heretofore reserved to the Almighty."[8]

Winston understood the impact of raw power on politics. Weapons technology—the Maxim gun of his youth, the dreadnought battleship of his early adulthood, the tank, the strategic bomber—was the spear's tip of empire. The "final argument of kings," as the Sun King once called it.

Now it might be the final argument of humanity.

Along with thinkers like Truman, Henry Stimson, and Robert Oppenheimer, the project's lead scientist, Winston pondered the impact of this biblical force. "What was gunpowder?" he asked Stimson. "Trivial. What was electricity? Meaningless. This atomic bomb is the Second Coming in Wrath."[9]

Like a converted disciple, Winston gushed to Brooke over the new balance of power and told the field marshal how he would use it with Stalin. The jaded Brooke felt Winston had gone off on a wild debouch over a single test.

"I was completely shattered by the PM's outlook!" he told his diary. "Now[, Churchill said,] we had a new value which redressed our position (pushing his chin out and scowling), now we could say if you insist on doing this or that, well we can just blot out Moscow, then Stalingrad, then Kiev, then Kulbyshev, Karhov . . . Sebastopol etc., etc. . . . I *shudder* to feel that he is allowing half baked results of one experiment to warp the whole of his diplomatic perspective!"[10]

Warped or clairvoyant, Winston pressed on at Potsdam as the Big Three and their retainers discussed Japan, postwar finance, and the future. They made some inroads, but none of the thorny issues were resolved by July 25, when Winston and his coalition deputy, Labour Party leader Clement Attlee, flew to London to learn the election results.[11]

Democracies have their moods. Dynamic and human, they get bored when left unchallenged. They fidget for the fresh and the new, even if new isn't always best, or wise.

The curtain was rising on Act Two, but the set design was entirely different. The Britain of 1945 bore little resemblance to the Britain of the Blitz. The war had drained the United Kingdom of a quarter of her wealth, and the Empire owed more than three billion pounds to its creditors, mostly to the United States government. At home, heavy industry lacked workers, markets, and investment capital, while four million homes needed rebuilding.

The Few of 1940, to whom Britain owed so much, were now the

many of 1945. And the many were demanding much from their government. Attlee's Labour Party promised national health care, subsidized industry, full employment, and pension protection. Churchill's Conservatives offered tight budgets and outward strength against a communist nation Britons had called their ally for four blood-soaked years.

Large crowds turned out for Winston at campaign stops in Edinburgh, Leeds, and Glasgow. But cheering wasn't the same as voting, and Labour was riding the crest of a wave demanding a social welfare state.[12]

To the public, Winston Churchill was a war relic. Like Nelson's HMS *Victory*, he was admired and respected, but much of the modern world had passed him by. His most memorable speeches—"We Will Fight on the Beaches," "Their Finest Hour," "Give Us the Tools," and the rest—were battle cries. Winston the defiant, Winston the war leader, Winston the conqueror. *That* was the Winston the British voter knew.[13]

With Europe's war over, the public saw no dragons to slay. Where, exactly, did that leave a paladin?

After Roosevelt's reelection in 1944, Winston had wired FDR, "I always said that a great people could be trusted to stand by the pilot who weathered the storm." Now the world would learn whether the great people of the United Kingdom would stand by their pilot.[14]

Back in London, Winston settled himself into a chair in the Map Room to watch the election results. He claimed to have no idea of the outcome, though he privately told Truman's secretary of state the gambling books favored a Tory win. His choice of clothing for the night—the zippered suit he wore when air-raid sirens wailed—underscored his connection to Britain's darkest hours.[15]

Captain Pim pinned results to a screen as they were wired in by voting districts. After thirty minutes, returns told of a Tory rout. Across the map, Conservative stalwarts went down like Stukas over Biggin Hill. Brendan Bracken lost in North Paddington. Duncan Sandys was trounced in Norwood. Harold Macmillan crashed in Stockton. Labour had roared back from the wilderness to capture a majority of 146 seats, outpolling Tories by two million votes.[16]

Sarah Churchill remembered how her father refused to let the hurt show. "His natural humour reasserted itself, superficially anyhow," she recalled. Clementine saw the election as a chance for Winston to rest after the strain of war. When she suggested that the loss could be a blessing in disguise, he quipped, "At the moment it seems quite effectively disguised."[17]

His humor masked a deep wound. "It's no use, Charles, presenting I'm not hard hit," he confessed to his physician, Lord Moran. "I can't school myself to do nothing for the rest of my life. It would have been better to have been killed in an aeroplane, or to have died like Roosevelt."[18]

The next day, Winston rode to Buckingham Palace and tendered his resignation to King George.

"It was a very sad meeting," the king told his diary. He offered Winston the high honor of the Order of the Garter, prompting Winston to demur with the reported quip, "Why should I accept the Order of the Garter from His Majesty when the people have just given me the Order of the Boot?"[19]

He rode over to the Annexe to offer a benediction to the staffers who had served him through five years of war, loss, triumph, and sorrow. He thanked his Map Room crew, and as he began his move out of Number 10, the man adrift paid a last visit to Chequers.

In the guest book, he wrote one word: "FINIS."[20]

INTERREGNUM

The Rising Son

"How the great democracies triumphed, and so were able to resume the follies which had so nearly cost them their life."

– Winston, *Triumph and Tragedy* –

Eisenhower accepts the Republican presidential nomination.

Getty Images

TWENTY-SIX

Return of the Native

It was the biggest, loudest, New Yorkest parade anyone could remember. Beaming from the back of a Cadillac convertible, Ike waved to four million spectators lining thirty-seven miles of streets from LaGuardia Airport to Central Park, to City Hall and back through Times Square. Homemade confetti floated down from Gotham's skyscrapers and crowds cheered from curbs and balconies. Despite pleas from the New York Telephone Company not to shred phone books to make streamers, New York's sanitation commissioner reported that his department cleaned up 77 tons of paper left on the parade route.[1]

Two months from the war's end, Ike brought star power to the Big Apple. He knew how to play to a crowd—whether the crowd was sitting in the House of Representatives chamber, cheering from London's streets, or checking weapons for a jump into Normandy. As the *New York Times* remarked, "Through many a New Yorker's mind that day ran the thought: 'There goes the next President of the United States.'"[2]

It wasn't just *Times* editors speculating. Washington insiders from both parties saw Ike as their potential White House standard-bearer. "He's done a whale of a job," Harry Truman told his wife, Bess. If Ike wanted the presidency, he said, "I'd turn it over to him now if I could." At Potsdam, Truman told Ike he would give him anything he wanted, which "definitely and specifically includes the presidency in 1948."[3]

Ike soaked up the hoopla with a thin but genuine veneer of humility. He was doing his duty, fulfilling a role like millions of others in uniform. With an endearing, aw-shucks expression, Ike, like Superman's Clark Kent, seemed to have extraordinary powers cloaked in a humble, everyman identity.

How would he use those powers now that the war was won? That was a question both parties were anxiously asking as Ike left on a goodwill visit to the heart of communism.

August found him standing in the shadow of the Kremlin, perched on a reviewing stand beneath Moscow's brooding skies. Across Red Square, center stage of Stalinist might, the cream of Soviet athleticism paraded by on that bright summer day.

In May Ike had raised eyebrows by suggesting a trip to the Soviet capital. The Combined Chiefs initially shot down the idea, but they reconsidered when Soviet diplomats extended an official invitation three months later. Ike cleared it with his bosses and promptly accepted, taking his son John among his entourage.[4]

The Bolsheviks carried a lot of pungent baggage, and Ike knew most Americans distrusted them. But they had fought valiantly and sacrificed millions fighting Hitler, a fact America couldn't ignore. Ike also respected and liked the Red Army's top commander, Soviet Marshal Georgi Zhukov. In Berlin, he and Zhukov had honored each other with medals—the Legion of Merit for Zhukov; for Ike, the Order of Victory, a dazzling platinum star smothered in diamonds and rubies.[5]

The camaraderie of Ike's Guildhall speech fueled his hopes for a lasting friendship with the Soviets. The world's future plainly depended on it. The victors, whose armies wielded unprecedented might, had to learn to work together.

Ike felt they could. He likened the Soviets to the British in the early stages of the war: Yanks and Brits had been wary of one another at first, but as bulldog and tomcat got to know each other, suspicion had thawed into wholehearted friendship.

"The more contact we have with the Russians, the more they will understand us and the greater will be the cooperation," he told Butcher. "It should be possible to work with Russia if we will follow the same pattern of friendly cooperation that has resulted in the great record of Allied unity." There was no Hitler to fight, but in peace, he said, "the motive for cooperation is the betterment of the lot in the life of the common man."[6]

Under the watchful eye of the Kremlin's clock tower, Ike smiled from the reviewing stand as the Sports Day parade went by. A kaleidoscope of athletes marched, cartwheeled, cycled, and danced across Red Square's timeworn cobblestones. Crammed with him on the stand over Lenin's Tomb, Politburo *shishki* jockeyed to get close to Stalin. Khrushchev flashed a gap-toothed grin. Molotov applauded cyclists and runners. Beria scanned platoons of female athletes, his gaze lingering on the prettiest and youngest, while a dough-faced Malenkov waved to gymnasts high-stepping across the square. As the Soviet anthem thundered from loudspeakers, Ike stood at attention, his stiff soldier's salute revealing no sense of rivalry or distrust. When Ike smiled at the crowd and draped his arm around Zhukov's shoulders, a roar went up. Even the Russians liked Ike.[7]

Moscow had rolled out its reddest of carpets, and Ike, who had never shaken hands with a tyrant, ate it up. To reporters, he described Stalin as a "benign and fatherly" figure and urged the United States and Russia to work together in a spirit of amity. As he told journalists, "I see nothing in the future that would prevent Russia and the United States from being the closest possible friends."[8]

He still had much to learn.

After several days touring Russia, Ike flew back to Frankfurt to oversee the military occupation of Germany. He wouldn't be in charge much longer; the War Department had ordered him to pass the reins to Lieutenant General Lucius Clay, a brilliant Georgian he knew and trusted from his Philippines days. Ike was going back to Washington to replace General Marshall as Army Chief of Staff.[9]

As he pondered the return home, he began pruning his inner circle. First to go was the flamboyant Patton, whose battlefield brilliance had been eclipsed by a reckless mouth. Pressed by reporters on his tepid implementation of Allied denazification policies, Patton, in his glib way, dismissed ex-Nazis as former members of a political party, much like Democrats and Republicans back home.

Ike and Patton owed each other their careers. Patton had mentored and befriended Ike right after the First World War. In the Second, Ike had covered for George when he had gotten himself in hot water for slapping two enlisted men in Sicily and making headline-grabbing comments in England. Ike's personal affection for Patton was genuine, but his official support was based on the cavalryman's ability to move fast and hit the enemy hard. When the guns fell silent, George had nothing to offset his PR liabilities. His only currency was battlefield victories, and after V-E Day, that market crashed.

Being soft on ex-Nazis was bad enough; comparing them to Democrats and Republicans created an uproar Ike couldn't ignore. Distraught but determined, he relieved his old friend from command of his beloved Third Army and exiled him to a paper headquarters.

"General Eisenhower came in looking as though he hadn't slept a wink," Kay Summersby wrote. "I knew at once he had decided to take action against his old friend. He had aged ten years in reaching the decision, which was inevitable in the light of Patton's past mistakes and the universal furor over this one."

Hurt beyond words and feeling betrayed, Patton blamed Ike's political ambitions. "Ike wants to be president so much you can taste it," he spat to diplomat Robert Murphy. "How can we expect any backbone in a man who wants to be President?" the general wrote his wife, Beatrice. "Ike is bitten with the presidential bee. . . . He will never be president!"[10]

Kay went next. The girl from Skibbereen had given Ike the companionship and affection he needed through the anxious days of Torch and Husky, Avalanche, Overlord, and the Bulge. Bridge partner, hostess, secretary, driver, and confidante, Kay had brought sunlight into Ike's world of death and destruction. But photos and news stories of Ike dancing with his Irish beauty at Ciro's, or sunbathing with her on the French Riviera, couldn't sit well with Mamie—or Truman and Marshall. It was the stuff of career-destroying scandals.[11]

Kay dreamed of a future with Ike, and as Ike prepared to leave for Washington, she made plans to follow him. She would apply for U.S. citizenship, and hoped to work for him at the Pentagon. But Ike knew his relationship with Mamie and her family, his reputation—everything he'd worked for—would be ruined if Kay turned up in his American life. So when the roster of Ike's official family accompanying him to Washington was finalized, Kay's name wasn't on it.[12]

Ike told his hatchet man, Beetle Smith, to break the news to Kay. He had General Clay give her a job—in Germany—and penned a sterile goodbye letter. In a cordial, safe tone underscored with finality, he wished her well and suggested she stop by if she were ever in town.

Then he made sure Kay would never see him again.[13*]

* After the war, Ike handled Kay's presence gingerly, careful not to enrage her and even more careful to steer clear of her. She brought Telek to Ike's Pentagon office once in 1947, and the two corresponded infrequently until late 1952. But he pushed back on allowing her to meet him at Columbia University, when Kay and Ike (and Mamie) lived in New York City. As Kay was writing her first memoir, ultimately titled *Eisenhower Was My Boss*, Ike wrote a letter to her literary agent objecting to the original title—"Eisenhower's 'Girl Friday.'" He suggested a jargon-laced title that would ensure no one would read it: "A WAC in SHAEF." Kay's controversial second memoir, *Past Forgetting*, in which she described a wartime love affair with Ike, was released in 1975—after her and Ike's death, but during Mamie's lifetime. John Eisenhower concluded his father had "overestimated Kay's loyalty to him."

TWENTY-SEVEN

The Missouri Wilderness

THE STREETS OF LONDON blurred with celebration over Japan's surrender. After five blood-soaked years, the war was finally over. Ordinary people could get on with their lives, without the extraordinary fears they'd carried around since 1939: being bombed, drafted, captured, or dying in some far-off, malaria-infested hellhole.

Among the faces in London's crowded city center, Winston's wore a scowl. Clement Attlee and his Labour Party were being showered with credit for Japan's surrender, even though Attlee had barely moved into 10 Downing Street when the Americans dropped the atomic bomb. Attlee inherited the moment—and the glory.

Winston groused to his secretary Elizabeth Nel, "Not a single decision has been taken since I left office which could allow them to say that victory over Japan was their work."

Nel tried to look on the bright side. "Aren't you glad you can have a rest now?" she asked.

"No," he said. "I wanted . . . I wanted . . ."

His voice faltered, trailing into silence.

"I knew what he was going to say," Nel said later. "He had wanted to be given a chance to build the peace because people had always called him a warmonger and said that he was only good in war."[1]

"It is difficult indeed for me to use any form of address to you other than 'Prime Minister,'" Ike wrote Winston in August. "Though I live to be a hundred I shall always think of you in that capacity and with that title."

He knew the blow had been hard. In sympathy, he offered Winston the use of an Army R&R villa on the French Riviera for a vacation. "Nothing could give me greater pleasure than to make available to you any facility at any time that could possibly add to your recreation and enjoyment," he wrote. "There is no one living to whom I have a greater desire to show, in some concrete way, the depth of my admiration and affection."[2]

Ike's orders to the Pentagon hadn't given him time to say goodbye in person. "I am sure you understand that I would never have deliberately separated my official connection with the European Theater without paying a final call on you," he explained in a letter from Washington. "I hope that circumstances will yet permit me to come back to your wonderful country sometime during the next few months and, if that should eventuate, that I may have the honor of calling upon you personally."[3]

A month into his Pentagon post, an aide dropped on Ike's desk a news clipping that made his stomach turn. *The Saturday Evening Post* announced the publication of excerpts from Commander Harry Butcher's forthcoming book, *My Three Years with Eisenhower*, an edited version of Butcher's secret diary as Ike's naval aide. The *Post* promised its readers an insider's account of the Allied high command in Europe. In other words, Ike's personal life.[4]*

Ike's pulse quickened as he read the teaser. His mind flashed over three years of wartime frustrations. His worries. His mistakes. His

* Mamie grumbled that she could write a book titled "My Three Years Without Eisenhower."

profane outbursts and wisecracks, some directed at senior British colleagues. Some directed at Winston.

During the war, he could have shut down the story. Hell, the diary had been stamped "Top Secret" and kept in a locked safe. But back then he'd had a lot on his mind besides Butcher, or a diary, or a future tell-all book. The war's end had seemed so far away.

Now neither Butch nor Simon & Schuster saluted Ike. The five-star general was powerless to stop his ex-aide and golfing buddy from making a buck off his relationship with the liberator of Europe.

At least Ike could sound off about how he felt. "My feeling is that you were admitted into a circle where every individual had a right to believe that the matters discussed were to remain secret," he wrote Butch. "I or any other participant in the discussion had every right to believe that the matter died at the instant it was born. There is no possibility of my giving you any line of demarcation but you know how repugnant it would be to me ever to appear in a position of having violated good faith."[5]

He sent Winston a frantic warning. "The publication of all of this stuff is as much of an astonishment to me as it can be to anyone else," he wrote. "The whole thing gives me that sense of uneasiness that is bound to follow when a man suddenly finds a member of his own household ready to lay before the public gaze every instance of his irritations, his foibles, and the habits of his daily life."[6]

Ike scrambled to limit the shrapnel blast. Just before Christmas 1945, he sat down with Butcher and went over the manuscript. One passage, from August of '42, recalled a juvenile dig at Winston. *"We had soup,"* it went. *"Ike undertook to demonstrate how the Prime Minister eats his soup—if 'eats' is the word. Being short and blockily built, the P.M.'s chin isn't very much above the soup plate. He crouches over the plate, almost has his nose in the soup, wields the spoon rapidly. The soup disappears to the accompaniment of loud and raucous gurglings. While showing me how it was done, Ike almost choked."*[7]

Ike almost choked as he read this. He told Butcher he took "earnest exception" to the paragraph, and ordered him to cut it. Butcher revised it—but only slightly—to delete the reference to Ike's mimicry. The final version read, "Since the PM is short and blockily built, his chin isn't very much above the soup plate. He crouched over the plate, almost had his nose in the soup, and wielded the spoon rapidly. The soup disappeared to the accompaniment of loud gurglings." The edited entry didn't say *Ike* lampooned Churchill's eating habits, but readers could connect the dots.[8]

Winston read the *Post*'s excerpts while vacationing in Miami. "I must say I think you have been ill-used by your confidential aide," he wrote Ike, referring to a passage about Ike suppressing a yawn during a late-night conference. "I really do feel very sorry to have kept you up so late on various occasions," he said. "It is a fault I have. . . . It is rather late at my age to reform, but I will try my best."[9]

"Your comments on the 'Diary' echo my sentiments," a red-faced Ike replied. "I assure you that I never complained about staying up late. I didn't do it often and certainly I always came away from one of those conferences with a feeling that all of us had gotten some measure of rededication to our common task."[10]

There wasn't much else he could say. Before long, *My Three Years with Eisenhower* would hit bookshelves and Book-of-the-Month Club mailboxes. Ike would wince, but Butcher's book gave America a closer look that raised Ike's image profile. He became more approachable, more three-dimensional, than the smiling figure Americans had known from black-and-white newsreels.

A month later, Winston would be back in the papers, too.

March 1946 found Winston playing cards with Harry Truman aboard the presidential train, the *Ferdinand Magellan*, bound for Fulton,

Missouri. In Truman's home state, Winston would accept an honorary degree from Westminster College. He would repay the honor by delivering a major speech on the importance of the Anglo-American relationship to world peace.

That peace faced a new peril. Hitler had been dead nearly a year, yet the Red Army still had nearly three million soldiers in Eastern Europe. Sooner or later, Stalin would also have an atomic bomb. Holding back that tide stood a flimsy barricade of small European states picking themselves out of war's wreckage. And America.

As *Magellan* clacked along the tracks toward Jefferson City, Truman's secretary of state gave the president an oral synopsis of Winston's speech. Truman said he had no objections. "He told me he thought it was admirable, and would do nothing but good, though it would make a stir," Winston reported to Clement Attlee.[11]

Draped in academic regalia, Winston sauntered up to the lectern in Westminster College's auditorium. Tossing his floppy tam onto a chair with a flick of the wrist, he launched into his favorite subject, the fraternal association of the English-speaking peoples. "This means a special relationship between the British Commonwealth and Empire and the United States of America," he declared. On that special relationship sat the hopes of millions of Europeans for peace and freedom.

A shadow clouded his face as he turned to the globe's far side. In the low growl that had once vowed Britain would fight on the beaches, he warned the world:

> From Stettin in the Baltic to Trieste in the Adriatic, an iron curtain has descended across the Continent. Behind that line lie all the capitals of the ancient states of Central and Eastern Europe; Warsaw, Berlin, Prague, Vienna, Budapest, Belgrade, Bucharest and

> Sofia, all these famous cities and the populations around them lie in what I must call the Soviet sphere. . . .

"From what I have seen of our Russian friends and allies during the war, I am convinced that there is nothing they admire so much as strength, and there is nothing for which they have less respect than for weakness, especially military weakness," he continued. Peace demanded strength. It demanded Anglo-American unity.[12]

He had titled his address "The Sinews of Peace," a nod to Cicero, but everyone remembered it as the "Iron Curtain" speech. Reaction was swift. In America, author-activist Pearl S. Buck branded the speech a "catastrophe" that steered America in "a dangerous way." The *Chicago Sun* accused him of calling for "world domination, through arms, by the United States and the British Empire." From Eleanor Roosevelt to Dean Acheson, liberals said Winston had gone off the rails, baiting a reasonable Josef Stalin and launching a cold war against the East. Truman, taken aback, ran for cover, denying any advance knowledge of what Churchill was going to say.[13]

In England, more than a hundred Socialist Party MPs signed a motion censuring Winston for warmongering. Playwright George Bernard Shaw left a vegetarian luncheon early to fire off a quote to the press: Winston's Anglo-American dream, he said, was "nothing short of a declaration of war on Russia." While the *Times* of London gave the speech a neutral shrug, the *Daily Herald*, a Labour Party organ, denounced Winston's belief that the world could be saved through a "special relationship." Weathering the storm in London, Anthony Eden quietly counseled Winston against "further polemics with Stalin."[14]

Stalin, who had built his career on polemics, responded with a bitter interview to *Pravda*. "Mr. Churchill is now in the position of a warmonger," he declared. "In this respect Mr. Churchill and his friends bear a striking resemblance to Hitler and his friends."[15]

None of this sturm und drang ruffled Winston. Playwrights and liberals could have their say. He wanted to get the public talking. He knew what Stalin meant to the free world, and he wouldn't allow that world to lapse into the somnolence of the 1930s. His wilderness years railing against the Nazis had taught him that when he was right, he must never give in to the whims of public opinion. After all, what good was a prophet who only told people what they knew—or what they wanted to hear?[16]

Three days after his Iron Curtain speech, Winston sat with Ike on a VIP train to Richmond. In the Virginia capital, he doubled down on his Anglo-American unity theme in an address to state legislators. "Peace will not be preserved by pious sentiments expressed in terms of platitudes or by official grimaces and diplomatic correctitude," he told his audience. "Among the English-speaking peoples, there must be the union of hearts based upon conviction and common ideals. That is what I offer. That is what I seek."[17]

The next day the party traveled to Colonial Williamsburg, where an 18th-century coach awaited Ike and Winston for a horse-drawn tour of Virginia's old capital. Newsmen snapped pictures of the iconic pair as they piled into the carriage. As flashbulbs flashed and colonial-garbed trumpeters fired off horns, the horses spooked. Heads rearing, the mounts bucked in their harnesses, threatening to upend the coach as frock-coated footmen frantically pulled on their reins.

For an alarming moment, the picture of Winston flung to the cobblestone street flew through Ike's mind. His friend Patton had died of injuries from a low-speed car accident four months earlier, and Ike would have been horrified to see Winston survive Hitler's Blitz, only to be done in by an American horse.

The mounts settled down, and Winston pretended to ignore the fracas. "His calmness was colossal," Ike remembered afterward. "He just lit his cigar. . . . He wasn't bothered in the least, though I was really worried."

The Victorian cavalryman didn't blame the horses. "The fault lay with the newspaper photographers and their awful flash bulbs, which were detonating all over the place," Winston explained to reporters. "You cannot thrust those fiendish twentieth-century contraptions into the face of a twelfth-century animal and not expect the animal to be slightly unnerved."[18]

He didn't add that other fiendish 20th-century contraptions were beginning to unnerve him.

At Ike's request, Winston repeated his Anglo-American theme in a talk to senior Pentagon officers. Introducing Winston, Ike said, "I was very happy when . . . Mr. Churchill consented to come today in order to renew World War contacts he made with many of us, and, in addition, to come a little closer to some of us that were affected by his decisions, but who did not have that privilege of his close association."[19]

With a smile, Winston spoke of the wartime partnership. "The prevailing feature of our work together was the intimacy of association," he said. "Language is a great bridge. There are many, many ideas we have in common and also practice. But there was a spirit of loyalty, of goodwill, of comradeship which has never been seen in all the history of war."[20]

They parted with warm hearts as Winston left for speaking engagements at Columbia University and New York's Waldorf-Astoria. At a dinner party thrown by *Time*'s Henry Luce, his fondness for Ike was evident to Luce's guests.

"General Eisenhower, whom he unfailingly addressed as 'Ike,' is obviously a great favorite of his," said one. "He seemed to enjoy immersing himself in the memory of Ike's friendship, as a swimmer floats pleasurably in warm water." When someone remarked that Ike seemed nostalgic for their wartime days, Winston replied, "Ah, so Ike, too, would like to have the sound and panoply of war again."

Pausing, he added, "War is the greatest of all stimulants." For a moment, he drifted back, remembering the intoxicating feel of war's energy, the focus it stirred—the exhilaration, he once wrote, of being shot at without result.

He knew perfectly well statesmen do not have the luxury of indulging such feelings during business hours. But in New York he was on his own time, and as a private citizen, he could relive the thrill of battles past the way he savored a fine brandy or robust cigar.[21]

Ike wasn't savoring much of anything these days. His work was piling up like it was 1942, and official duties as Army Chief of Staff left him little time for reveries. And when he had off-hours time, he was spending it with new friends. Rich, powerful friends.

TWENTY-EIGHT

Popularity: "Enormous"

At 57, Ike was riding a carousel with the wealthy, famous, and influential. Parades, speeches, and awards catapulted him into that elite circle of men other elite men want to know. A cadre of businessmen and political insiders, nicknamed "the Gang," coalesced around the general, and in time they would become his sounding board, kitchen cabinet, and devoted friends.

The Gang's hub was Bill Robinson, a *New York Herald Tribune* exec whom Ike had known during the war. Its elder statesman, Robert Woodruff, was president of The Coca-Cola Company. Other Gang members included Ellis "Slats" Slater, a liquor distribution mogul; Alton "Pete" Jones, head of the petroleum juggernaut Cities Service Company; George E. Allen, a Truman confidant and former chairman of the Democratic National Committee; and investment banker Cliff Roberts, founder of Georgia's Augusta National Golf Club.[1]

The Gang's members were Ike's 101st Airborne: ready to drop whatever they were doing, hop on a corporate plane, and fly to New York for a dinner party, to Denver for eighteen holes at Cherry Hills, or to Washington for a stag dinner fueled with steaks, drinks, thoughtful discussion, and mostly clean jokes.

The Gang also introduced Ike to Augusta, Georgia, home to golf's annual Masters Tournament. The sleepy town on the Savannah River became one of Ike's favorite retreats, what Warm Springs, four hours distant, had been to FDR. With its tall yellow pines and quiet pace of life, Augusta offered Ike the peace and privacy Telegraph Cottage had given him in England.

By 1948, commentators were talking up Ike as presidential material. In an era when one could become famous simply for being the best at an important job, Gallup polls crowned General Eisenhower the most respected man in America. An avalanche of letters begging him to run rolled into his Pentagon office. EISENHOWER FOR PRESIDENT buttons began popping up on lapels of both Democrats and Republicans, and men like Marty Snyder, his mess sergeant in France, lobbied local Democratic bosses to get behind a "Draft Ike" movement.[2]

Voters gravitated to Ike's quick smile and first-name persona. Even better, his lack of discernible political views made him all things to all voters. As the *New York Times* summed up his public image:

> *Political leanings:* probably liberal Republican like his family, somewhat tempered by military conservatism.
>
> *Record:* victor in one of the greatest military campaigns in history; acknowledged master of diplomacy in ironing out disputes among Allied military and political leaders and in dealing with Congress.
>
> *Liabilities:* political inexperience; America's traditional distrust of the military in civilian government posts; bad precedent of the corrupt administration of the Civil War hero, U. S. Grant.
>
> *Popularity:* enormous.[3]

As the summer of '48 blazed on, Ike issued more than a dozen statements denying he'd run for the presidency. But the more he denied it, the more the public wanted him.[4]

Wrestling with temptation, in June he wrote Winston about the "terrific personal struggle through which I have gone during the last twelve months." He didn't want to run, he said, but he believed no man could set limits on how he would serve his country. Problem was, any denial with conditions sounded like a "Maybe, if you ask nice enough."[5]

Winston replied two weeks later. "About the Presidency, my feeling is that you were right not to intervene on this occasion," he said. "If you had stood as a Democrat, it would have looked like going to the rescue of a party which has so long held office and is now in difficulties. On the other hand if you had stood as a Republican it would have been hard on the party whose President you served."

He added: "Luckily there is plenty of time."[6]

As Pentagon business settled into a routine, Ike grew restless. He needed something he could sink his teeth into, something to engage his fidgeting, searching mind. So he plunged into a new project: writing his version of World War II.

Setting aside distractions, he attacked his manuscript like it was the Torch invasion. From six in the morning to eleven at night, he dictated, reread old reports and letters, and scratched edits in the margins of typewritten drafts. Aides fact-checked chapters while three secretaries typed dictated passages and worked in his nearly indecipherable hand edits. Ike called the manuscript, completed in mid-April, *Crusade in Europe*.[7]

Like its author, *Crusade in Europe* was straightforward. No fluff, no gossip, no humble-brags. While Winston's writings sound dictated by a master orator, Ike's were planned and executed with parade-ground precision. He focused on strategy, steering clear of personality or controversy. In Ike's telling, the Allies march to Berlin—or toward the general vicinity of Berlin—in a spirit of candor, camaraderie, and dedication to a common cause. While he alluded to differences of opinion—the Anvil landings being their "longest-sustained argument"—Ike painted a mural of shared purpose that brushed aside their disagreements.*

In Ike's view, one man embodied the wartime spirit more than any other. "One of my real pleasures," he wrote Winston, "was to pay the tributes I honestly feel toward many brilliant and even great men with whom I was privileged to work. Among these, none will ever rank higher than yourself."[8]

Crusade in Europe became a runaway bestseller. Ike earned a staggering $635,000 in royalties, enough to allow him and Mamie to buy a farm near Pennsylvania's Gettysburg battlefield. While Ike couldn't compete with Winston in either quantity or eloquence, *Crusade* reminded the American public of the humble human spirit that drove the liberation of North Africa and Europe—and the steady hand of the man who led it.[9]

As Ike plowed through chapter rewrites, life threw him another curveball. Not a bad one, like Kasserine or the Bulge, just something different. During the war, his younger brother Milton had been president of Kansas State University. The notion of life as an academic attracted Ike, who had grown up with a love of history and an appreciation of the opportunities a college degree offered. Though he figured a quiet, rural

* As a man who took the Middle Way, Ike avoided the extravagant language Winston reveled in. "He was death on superlatives," remembered one of Ike's cabinet undersecretaries. "He had arrived at this rule while working with General MacArthur, who was always tossing off such statements as 'Never before in history has an operation of such magnitude, etc.'" Years later, when speechwriter Robert Kieve drafted a statement referring to a Boy Scouts initiative as a "noble" endeavor, Ike's secretary sent back a note: "The President wants you to know that the word 'noble' is one that should never really be attached to any enterprise whose scope is smaller than that of the Normandy landings."

college would be his best fit, he received an offer from one of the most urbane Ivy League institutions in America: New York's Columbia University.

Ike would later joke that the trustees meant to give the job to Milton, and when they discovered they had offered it to the wrong Eisenhower, they were too embarrassed to say anything. But they meant it, and after talking it over with Mamie, Ike informed the secretary of defense that he would be retiring from active service to take Columbia's helm.[10]

On May 2, 1948, Omar Bradley, Ike's friend and successor as chief of staff, showed up at the door of Quarters One to escort Ike and Mamie to their car. A detachment of troops from the 3rd Infantry Regiment stood at attention as commands rang out. Hands clapped rifles, a color guard stood at attention. At the end of the line sat a spit-and-polished Cadillac convertible waiting to take him away.

Ike, in uniform, his old SHAEF patch on his shoulder, walked out the door with Mamie at his side. An Army band played "Ruffles and Flourishes," and an infantryman handed Mamie a bouquet of yellow roses.

Walking to the car, Ike strode like a man on a mission—even if he wasn't sure he understood the mission. He and Mamie climbed in, the doors shut, and off they rode to a strange world of skyscrapers and intellectuals.[11]

TWENTY-NINE

Red Dawn

"THE BLOOD WENT TO THEIR HEADS," said Winston.

In 1948, enemies were stirring behind the Kremlin's walls. Soviet priests talked of revolution, broken chains, and a worker's paradise, while behind the slogans their leaders forged a cruel and violent empire that glared west. "They had the Balkans. They had Poland. They were victorious everywhere. . . . It looked as if the whole world was sliding their way."[1]

What was Britain's way? For centuries, its destiny had been to grow rich from trade and stabilize Europe's balance of power. England had fought Philip of Spain, the Sun King, Napoleon, the Kaiser, and Hitler to keep the wolf from eating the flock. Now Russia was the new wolf, and Britain would rise to defend the new flock.[2]

A Soviet-backed coup in Czechoslovakia in February offered Winston a chance to repay Stalin's *Pravda* slanders: "Stalin has perpetrated exactly the same act of aggression in 1948 as Hitler did when he marched into Prague in 1939, nine years ago," he told a Welsh audience. "This is all set forth before our eyes as plainly as Hitler told us about his plans in his book *Mein Kampf.* I hope that the Western nations, particularly our own country and the United States, will not fall into the same kind of deadly trap twice over."[3]

Winston's answer? Peace through overwhelming force. Atomic blackmail. Lewis Douglas, the U.S. ambassador in London, reported in early 1948: "He believes that now is the time, promptly, to tell the Soviet that if they do not retire from Berlin and abandon Eastern Germany, withdrawing to the Polish frontier, we will raze their cities. It is further his view that we cannot appease, conciliate, or provoke the Soviet; that the only vocabulary they understand is the vocabulary of force."[4]

"We ought to bring matters to a head and make a final settlement," Winston insisted. "The Western nations will be far more likely to reach a lasting settlement, without bloodshed, if they make demands while they have the atomic bomb and before the Russian Communists have got it too."[5]

To hold back the Soviets, he concluded, one must convince them that "you are not restrained by any moral consideration if the case arose from using that force with complete material ruthlessness. And that is the greatest chance of peace, the surest road to peace."[6]

In principle, Winston abhorred weapons of mass destruction. But he accepted reality and wasn't unalterably opposed to using them when they could avoid greater bloodshed from conventional wars like the last one. He had argued this point during the war when the British Chiefs raised the question of using chlorine and mustard gas. "I would not use it unless it could be shown either that (a) it was life or death for us, or (b) that it would shorten the war by a year," he wrote a month after D-Day. As for ethical objections, "It is absurd to consider morality on this topic when everybody used it in the last war without a word of complaint from the moralists or the Church. On the other hand, in the last war the bombing of open cities was regarded as forbidden. Now everybody does it as a matter of course. It is simply a question of fashion as she does between long and short skirts for women. . . . I want the matter studied in cold blood by sensible people and not by that particular set of psalm-singing uninformed defeatists which one runs across."[7]

While Winston squirmed from the political sidelines, Stalin's physicists were hard at work. In August 1949, they achieved their first breakthrough by splitting the atom. The test bomb, code-named "First Lightning," broke the West's easy hold on power. It shattered the illusion that atomic weapons were democracy's risk-free trump card. Now the spear pointed in both directions.

When the news reached London, something in Winston ruptured. The prospect of all-out atomic war, with mushroom clouds blooming across Europe, took root in his fertile mind. The next war might not turn on battles, but on one terrible swift blow. A blow that might end a hundred centuries of human progress.

"Do you think that the atomic bomb means that the architect of the universe has gotten tired of writing his non-stop scenario?" he once asked playwright George Bernard Shaw. "There was a lot to be said for his stopping with the panda. The release of the bomb seems to be his next turning-point."[8]

To Winston, human progress—scientific, political, economic, even religious—had been shaped by competition among peoples climaxing in war. Like a light beam tugged by the gravity of a distant star, the human race bent toward war until each war, like a dying star, burned itself out. From the chaos and dust, a chastened humanity resumed its course, in time seeking the attractions of a new star, turning the endless wheel of progress, prosperity, destruction, and renewal.

But what if the next star consumed everything? What if the cataclysm exceeded humanity's ability to adapt? The next great crisis could be the last. Faced with extinction, it was up to every statesman to ensure nuclear-armed nations never fought each other, no matter how glittering the temptation of the moment.

Winston believed this. He was certain Truman believed it, too. The question was whether the Soviet leaders believed it. And whether American leadership would push the world away from the abyss—or toward it.

He wouldn't wait for Washington to make the first move. With an atomic rivalry emerging, what was once unthinkable to Winston became inevitable: a negotiated settlement with the Bolsheviks.

"The idea appeals to me of a supreme effort to bridge the gulf between the two worlds, so that each can live their life, if not in friendship, at least without the hatreds of the Cold War," he told an Edinburgh audience. "It is not easy to see how things could be worsened by a parley at the summit, if such a thing were possible."[9]

His phrase "at the summit" coined a new diplomatic term. Another talk, jaw to jaw, among men at the top: It held the promise of an extended peace, a respite in which the world could spend more time building than destroying.

Of course, to be effective, negotiations must be backed by strength. "Appeasement from weakness and fear is alike futile and fatal," he told Parliament. "Appeasement from strength is magnanimous and noble and might be the surest and perhaps the only path to world peace."

So, for the moment, Winston rejected calls for a pledge of no first use of atomic weapons. Such a promise, he quipped, meant "you must never fire until you have been shot dead. That seems to me undoubtedly a silly thing to say and a still more imprudent position to adopt. Moreover, such a resolve would undoubtedly bring war nearer."[10]

When Winston spoke, the public politely listened. But his words meant little when he was out of power. To British voters, global security took a back seat to domestic reforms. They wanted cheap bread, free doctors, and a pension that paid the bills. Attlee's Labour government offered them that.

To pay for their social vision, Attlee and his ministers slashed the military budget and hauled down the Union Jack from colonies across the globe. The Crown granted India and Pakistan independence in 1947, followed by Ceylon and Burma. In the Middle East, the Transjordan became an independent kingdom. In a divided Palestine, Britain folded its tent and brought its troops home, leaving Arabs and Jews to fight over a land both called home.

And that was all right with voters. Britannia's children had grown weary of empire's burdens, of wars against natives, of faraway names in which pounds and pence disappeared. They set aside the conquests of Marlborough and Queen Anne, George and Victoria, Clive and Wolfe, as if they were an old saber hanging on a smoking room wall. Empire had become an awkward motif in brittle volumes of Rudyard Kipling and T. E. Lawrence. An ideal that stoked no pride, stirred no hearts. An ideal kept alive in the memory of old men like Winston.[11]

"It is with deep grief I watch the clattering down of the British Empire with all its glories," he lamented to the House the year India and Pakistan broke away. "Many have defended Britain against her foes. None can defend her against herself."[12]

Across the ocean, ties between Washington and London frayed and twisted. American politicians distanced themselves from Europe. Congress passed a law forbidding its government from sharing atomic secrets with anyone—including Britain, the Bomb's coinventor. Isolation again seemed more than just a moody moment.

Adding to the relationship's troubles, one of Britain's best friends had just taken a comfortable job in New York City. Shedding his five-star uniform for a gray business suit, Winston saw Ike lulling himself to sleep in an academic monastery, throwing fundraisers and chairing committees while Moscow grew strong and restive.

Would Eisenhower shake off the dust of books and awaken in time to help stop the peril? The answer would depend on whether Columbia liked Ike. And whether Ike liked Columbia.

THIRTY

Taking the Black

"YOU CAN IMAGINE HOW LOST I FEEL," Ike wrote his brother Earl the day after he left Quarters One. "Everything is strange and, entirely aside from learning new methods of work, I have to learn to know new faces and the job to which each face is attached."[1]

If SHAEF had a polar opposite, Columbia might have been it. No snap to attention, no tight salutes, no rush to get everything done yesterday. Most of all, no clarity in the command chain. A university president, Ike quickly learned, lacked those godlike powers of a general over subordinates. He would have to *persuade* deans, administrators, and the tweed-jacket-and-briar-pipe crowd to move Columbia forward—whatever "forward" meant.

Before the war, when General Marshall took over as Army chief of staff, he streamlined the organization chart and delegated major details to subordinates. That left him free to concentrate on big-picture issues, like Congress, mobilization, and strategy. At Columbia, Ike tried Marshall's approach. From his luxurious office at Columbia's Low Memorial Library building, he surrounded himself with sharp minds, assigned large responsibilities to department chairs, and relied on military aides like Majors Robert Schulz and Craig Cannon to screen out unnecessary meetings and paperwork.[2]

What worked at the Pentagon didn't translate to a freethinking institution. "Let's put it this way," said Dr. Grayson Kirk, Columbia's provost. "He brought to the university his military staff approach to problems, and this approach did not work very well in a university." Ike kept his distance from the enlisted ranks—professors and lecturers—and deans grew frustrated with Schulz and Cannon, who routinely denied meeting requests with the president.[3]

It didn't help that Ike began moonlighting as senior advisor to the secretary of defense and the Joint Chiefs. Five-star generals don't fully retire, and Ike's duties required him to pick up the phone whenever Washington called.

Washington called often. The month he and Mamie settled into their brick mansion in New York's Morningside Heights, Stalin closed the autobahn to West Berlin, pitching Europe into its first big Cold War crisis. The following spring, changes at the top hit the Defense Department when a new secretary stepped in to replace James Forrestal, who had suffered a nervous breakdown from the strain of mediating a bitter rivalry between admirals and generals. Before long, a distraught Forrestal would take his last step from a sixteenth-floor hospital window.[4]

Ike spent March of 1949 working over budget problems with the same crowd that had driven Forrestal to suicide. He shuttled between Washington and Morningside Heights with robotic discipline, keeping spinning plates from crashing, but after eight years of command, his body was wearing out. He'd weathered the Depression, MacArthur, the Philippines, and World War II, but as a chain smoker at 58, he was losing his ability to bounce back.

"He had a temper, and criticism of his motives and so forth wasn't something that he'd take lightly," remembered Craig Cannon. "I didn't want to see him having a heart attack trying to blow his stack."[5]

It wasn't his heart; it was his gut. After a luncheon in March, he doubled over from pain in his abdomen. His driver rushed him to the Statler Hotel, where his physician, Major General Howard Snyder, diagnosed him with severe gastroenteritis. He needed treatment and rest. Truman had the presidential plane *Independence* whisk Ike to a naval hospital in Key West so he could recuperate. "For days, my head was not off the pillow," Ike remembered.[6]

Exiled to South Florida, he missed a dinner thrown by *Time*'s Henry Luce for a visiting Winston Churchill, who was staying in New York as a house guest of financier Bernard Baruch. Ike had Major Schulz send a note of regret, telling Winston he was sorry to miss a chance for another "full and frank discussion" with him. "Our reactions today as we look Eastward cannot be too greatly different," he added.

Winston cabled Ike the next day. "I deeply regret we have not been able to meet and still more the cause," he wrote. "I do hope you will take care not to attempt too much. Bernie says you have been subjecting yourself to very hard strain. We need you so much in the future."[7]

In Florida's balm, Ike recovered quickly. Ten days later, he was well enough to get a half hour's practice at his golf swing. He took a month off in Augusta, where he improved his putt, but he couldn't change the long-term prognosis. His health was sliding, and to preserve what was left of it, Dr. Snyder gave him the blunt truth: He must give up smoking.[8]

Ike had been addicted to cigarettes since his cadet days. His usual ration was two packs a day, but in times of stress, he'd burn through four. He knew it would be nearly impossible to cut back gradually; the smell of tobacco was too enticing, too comforting, and under severe pressure, a pack would become two, or three, or four. So he took the plunge and quit cold turkey.[9]

Clare Boothe Luce, a former Republican congresswoman and wife of Henry Luce, remembered stopping by Ike's office not long afterward. Clare had known Ike in Europe, and she glanced around his desk for a cigarette. Not seeing his usual Chesterfields, she asked, "Aren't you smoking?"

"No, I quit," he said. "I had a little heart trouble, a little warning from my doctor, and so I quit."

"Why, Ike, how did you ever do it?"

With a trace of pride, he answered, "I simply gave myself the order."[10]

As Ike cut out cigarettes, he found he needed to keep his hands busy and mind clear. In the agonizing days before Overlord, he'd been struck by the serenity Arthur Tedder and Harold Alexander drew from oil painting. They seemed to find peace in the sweep of brush over canvas, of colors and creation. Of no time limits and freedom of imagination. Ike had wanted that feeling, too.

In a tense weekend at Telegraph Cottage, he had tried sketching a big pine tree in the yard. After several earnest attempts, he scrawled "Baloney" under the drawing and threw it out. But the desire lingered, and Mamie noticed.

On Valentine's Day, the anniversary of their engagement, she bought him paints, brushes, and a canvas. He began by copying a portrait of Mamie done by artist Thomas Stephens. The result didn't look much like her. Ike called it "weird and wonderful to behold," which was about the most charitable thing one could say about it. Mamie told a reporter, "I just don't know the word for it"—adding quickly that Ike was a wonderful cook.[11]

It didn't matter. For Ike, it wasn't about making a picture to hang on a wall. It was the joy of creating.

"I have had a lot of fun since I took up, in my somewhat miserable way, your hobby of painting," he wrote Winston. "I have no instruction, have no talent and certainly no justification for covering nice white canvas with the kind of daubs that seem constantly to spring from my brushes. Nevertheless, I like it tremendously."[12]

Clare Luce, who knew them both, later wrote, "Eisenhower, like Churchill, is an energetic painter. He attacks the canvas, daubing rapidly, even recklessly, and gazing at his work with his brow bunched and reddened when he is dissatisfied with it."

The difference lay in their perspective. Winston saw everything he touched through the lens of history. Every act of creation—on dictated page, on stretched canvas—was a legacy in the making, a work to be studied, perhaps admired, long after his death.

Ike saw everything as a mission with a D-day and a V-day. Attack, accomplish, move on. Pleasure came from the process, and when he finished a work, he would often tell his orderly, Sergeant John Moaney, to trash it.

"In a way," Luce concluded, "it was like a round of golf—when it was done, it was done with."

Though she added, "Perhaps the comparison is not a good one, however, for Eisenhower took his golf far more seriously than he ever took his painting."[13]

While Ike gave Columbia the old college try, he had too many outside interests to devote himself to fundraising or stroking the egos of pretentious dons. The world beyond Morningside Heights was calling.

Storm clouds were gathering over Europe. The Berlin Crisis, the coup in Prague, the continued occupation of Austria, communist meddling in the Balkans and the Middle East—the signs were flashing to anyone paying attention: Stalin was bullying his way westward. From his dark-paneled office, Ike worried that Western Europe might yield to Moscow's fist rather than risk becoming the Poland of World War III. He wasn't alone.

In April 1949, Western European leaders signed a defensive pact with the U.S. and Canada establishing the North Atlantic Treaty Organization. The treaty created a multinational military structure charged with keeping the Red Army east of the Elbe. Its core was a pledge of mutual defense: An attack against any member would be considered an attack on all.[14]

As with most treaties, the devil danced in the details. Who would command? How many soldiers, and how much money, would each nation contribute? Whose weapons would fill NATO's arsenals? By year's end, treaty organizers were hardly beyond where they started. Words flooded the air, but words don't stop armies.

At Tehran in 1943, Stalin had said that until Overlord's commander was appointed, Overlord could not be considered a serious operation. NATO was the same. It had no commander and no headquarters. It was a paper theory in need of someone with universal credibility to persuade nations like Belgium and Italy to contribute to the common defense. It needed someone from the United States to demonstrate American commitment. And it needed someone who had proven himself in Europe.

That someone had turned down an offer from President Truman to run for the White House as a Democrat, and Truman knew that someone was receiving similar offers from Republicans. Perhaps, thought Truman, Ike could organize NATO's armies with the same magic he had worked during World War II. It would demonstrate America's commitment to European security—and it would keep Ike away from Republican snollygosters who were trying to lure a decent man into opposition politics.

What would it take to get Ike back in uniform?

THIRTY-ONE

Supreme Commander (Again)

IN THE SUMMER OF 1950, while Ike was giving fundraising speeches to Columbia alumni, North Korean tanks and troops crossed the 38th Parallel and stormed into South Korea. In three days, the Korean People's Army captured the southern capital of Seoul. In a month, the KPA overran nearly the entire peninsula, forcing the hard-pressed defenders, bloodied and outgunned, back to a scrap of land around the port city of Pusan.

Kim Il Sung had launched the attack, but the world saw Stalin's fingerprints all over the murder weapon. The equipment was Soviet: Names like Antonov, Katyusha, and Tupolev appeared on crates, planes, and artillery pieces filling Kim's weapons depots and hangars. The invasion put the world on notice: Stalin's ambitions were no longer confined to rhetoric and agitation. He was backing them with fire and steel.

Delegates to the North Atlantic Council—NATO's toothless political organization—could no longer avert their gaze. They agreed to create a field army under a supreme commander charged with Europe's defense. By consensus, that commander would be an American.[1]

As talk of General Eisenhower's possible appointment made the rounds late in the year, Winston was drafting the sixth volume of his World War II memoirs. He had reached the point in his narrative where the two men butted heads over Ike's refusal to capture Berlin and Prague. Since Hitler's death, the same Stalin whom Ike had spoken so highly of had blockaded Berlin, launched a coup in Czechoslovakia, occupied eastern Austria, supported Mao's revolution in China, and backed North Korea's invasion of its neighbor. Winston hoped Ike had learned from his mistakes.[2]

Winston sent Ike a copy of *The Hinge of Fate*, the newly published fourth volume of his war memoirs. Ike was delighted to relive the Anglo-American alliance, the North African campaign, and the Casablanca Conference. "In these passages more than history is involved," Ike wrote in his thank-you letter. "There are valuable hints on human behavior, and there are lessons for the future."[3]

Ike was about to put some of those lessons into action.

At a meeting of the North Atlantic Council on December 18, foreign ministers gathered to vote on a Canadian motion to appoint General Eisenhower "Supreme Allied Commander in Europe," or "SACEUR." Introducing the motion, Canada's foreign minister added a touch of charm to the proceedings. "In Canada," he said, "we showed our appreciation to him the only way we could think of big enough, that is, we gave him a mountain."*

One by one, ministers rose to shower praise on America's boy wonder. Norway's foreign minister spoke of the "joy" that would greet Ike's posting. The Dutch minister said Ike would "restore confidence" throughout Western Europe, while Count Sforza said the appointment would make an "excellent impression" on the Italian people. Around the room they went—Belgium, Luxembourg, Portugal, Denmark, Britain, and France—delivering paeans with diplomatic flourish. When the

* Mount Eisenhower, in Banff National Park, reverted to its original name, Castle Mountain, in 1979.

speeches died down, the council asked President Truman to assign General of the Army Dwight D. Eisenhower. Truman obliged.[4]

Ike saw the NATO job as a call to duty he couldn't refuse. Mamie thought he could and should. They were living the good life in a 10,000-square-foot New York mansion. She was supervising renovations of their Gettysburg farm and watching their two young grandchildren grow up. She felt that after thirty years of Army life, they had earned every luxury they now enjoyed. She didn't want their life, on a green path to retirement, turned upside down.[5]

But it turned, and on January 6, 1951, Truman saw Ike off at Washington National Airport. As cameras rolled, Ike, looking fit in his Eisenhower jacket, said in his press voice, "Mr. President, I devoutly pray that the mission on which I am leaving this morning will result in nothing but peace, security, and tranquility for our various nations of the Western alliance."

Truman nodded. In his flat, direct tone, he said, "I agree with you, general, and I'm sure that's going to be the result."[6]

Arriving in France, Mamie made the transition from New York brick to French baroque. She picked out a mansion at Marnes-la-Coquette—Emperor Napoleon III's former home—and the Eisenhowers moved into the Trianon Palace Hotel while contractors and designers fixed up their residence with a stocked trout pond, manicured landscaping, and furniture that Marie Antoinette would have endorsed.

"I could have anything I wanted out of any musée," Mamie recalled with delight. "We had a tapestry that was priceless in the dining room. We had an Aubusson rug on the drawing room floor. We had Napoleon's bed from Fontainebleau. They gave me entrée to anything I wanted." With status, the trappings of wealth, and a VIP plane to take her and her friends wherever they wished, Mamie accepted her destiny.[7]

While he lived in baroque splendor, Ike "had an impossible job," recalled John Eisenhower. "He was sitting there facing 175 Russian divisions, and he didn't have the forces to fight their way out of a paper bag."[8]

Part of Ike's job was cheerleading to an audience of war-weary, cash-strapped governments. He spent his first month in a valley of dry bones, visiting capitals and hearing lamentations of government ministers. "Norway is short of manpower," he told his diary. "Italy has excess productive capacity in vehicles & planes—many others have none at all! France & Germany (the key powers of the region) are on opposite sides in many problems because of French hatred for the Boche as well as the fear of a restored western Germany. Each nation watches its neighbor to see that the neighbor's contribution to the common security is at least equal to the first nation's ratio—and none is ever so convinced!"[9]

"He had the type of relationship where he had to stimulate and inspire a somewhat apathetic civilization in Europe," recalled General Alfred Gruenther, Ike's NATO chief of staff. "He had to be a Billy Sunday to arouse people. He had to be a military genius, to plan what they were going to do, and he had to be able to get some type of uniting of the peoples of Europe."[10]

It was hard work, but by spring, Ike's winter seeds began to sprout. *Time* told its readers, "Never in recent history has Europe experienced such a lifting of heart as it got from Ike's inspiring presence and his skillful, patient incubation of the North Atlantic Treaty Organization. In December 1950, NATO seemed just another paper plan doomed to failure. By April 1951 it was a psychological reality: Europeans began to believe that Europe could and would be defended."[11]

On July 3, Ike, Mamie, their son John, and John's wife, Barbara, traveled to London's Grosvenor House, where Ike would deliver a dinner speech to the English-Speaking Union. The event was a grand affair, with Prime Minister Clement Attlee, Foreign Secretary Herbert Morrison, and Winston Churchill in attendance at the head table.

Winston nodded along as Ike preached Anglo-American amity. "The bond that joins us—stronger than blood lines, than common tongue and common law—is the fundamental conviction that man was created to be free, that he can be trusted with freedom, that governments have as a primary function the protection of this freedom," he emoted.

A key to protecting this freedom was an economically and politically united Continent, a concept Winston had recently supported. "European leaders, seeking a sound and wise solution, are spurred by the vision of a man at this table—a man of inspiring courage in dark hours, of wise counsel in grave decisions," he said. "Winston Churchill's plea for a United Europe can bear such greatness of fruit that it may well be remembered as the most notable achievement of a career marked by achievement."[12]

As Ike spoke, Winston smiled at the general tone he expected to hear. But at 76, he was nearly deaf and could follow little of what Ike said. He took Ike's delivery on faith until he could get a copy of the speech two days later. Reading the text, he was electrified by Ike's call for unity and strength.[13]

"This is one of the greatest speeches that has been made by an American for many years," he wrote Lord Woolton. "It seems to me that it expresses the policy of our Party, and I trust of our country, in the most complete and perfect form." He went even further: "I wish that several millions of copies shall be printed, and that it shall become apparent that this is *our* policy, purpose and plan."[14]

Enthused by Ike's commitment to their common defense, Winston wrote to congratulate him. "I am sure this is one of the greatest speeches delivered by any American in my lifetime—which is a long one—and that it carries with it on strong wings the hope of the salvation of the world from its present perils and confusions."

Peering into the future, he predicted, "I believe that events in the next two years are going to be our servants and we their masters."[15]

"Any praise from the master speech maker was heady stuff," Ike admitted. He sent a "Dear Winston" letter, thanking him for his kind words. "It would be quite impossible for me to tell you how flattered I was by the nice things you had to say about my talk," he wrote. "While I have no great hope that the timorous leadership of Europe will, under the spell of Eisenhower eloquence, suddenly begin with head up and chest out to march sturdily forward, along the rocky road to unification, yet the making of the talk did me the personal good of putting into public words something that I believe very deeply."[16]

Reflecting on the exchange years later, John Eisenhower recalled, "From my viewpoint, that moment illustrated a dramatic change in the relations between Ike and Churchill, that Churchill had now recognized Ike as a statesman, not a mere soldier."[17]

Part of Ike's genius was that he could befriend genius without being seduced by genius. He revered Winston's genius on the big questions. Without Winston's dogged opposition to Hitler, or his willingness to court Stalin, Nazi Germany might be the master of Europe.

Then there were Anvil, the Balkans, and the Dodecanese. That last one turned up in *Closing the Ring*, the fifth volume of Winston's war memoirs. "I noticed that he is still rather bitter about the decision not to commit additional forces to the Rhodes, Leros and Cos adventure in late '43," Ike wrote Pug after reading it—not knowing that Winston had also called Ike "obdurate" and "unreasonable" in earlier drafts of the book.

"In spite of all my admiration for his judgment in these affairs (to say nothing of my personal affection for a character in whom I found so much to admire and like), I still cannot agree with him in many of his ideas about the tactical uses of troops and, sometimes, with his calculations as to great results that would have resulted from minor adventures."[18]

In Ike's eyes, Winston still had plenty to offer as symbol, voice, and big thinker. But whether he would be more would depend on the path he took as old age pursued him. In September 1951, Ike asked Harold Macmillan the question on everyone's mind: Would Winston run for the premiership again?

Macmillan, like everyone else in Britain, had no answer.[19]

As the world wondered, a secretary laid a letter before Winston. On 10 Downing Street letterhead, it read:

> My dear Churchill,
>
> I have decided to have a General Election in October. I am announcing it tonight after the nine o'clock news.
>
> Yours sincerely,
> C. R. Attlee[20]

THIRTY-TWO

Prime Minister (Again)

By 1951, British voters were feeling buyer's remorse. Attlee's Labour government had ushered in a welfare state that promised care and comfort, but service came with a price tag: High taxes. Scarce household goods. A 30 percent devaluation of the British pound, wreaking havoc on pocketbooks and national pride. Britain even groaned under wartime food rationing, a ghost that Germany, defeated in two world wars, had exorcised a year earlier. That stung.[1]

Elections in 1950 had reduced Labour's majority in Parliament to a razor-thin five seats. Hoping to bolster his majority, in September 1951, Attlee called a snap election for October. This time Winston, Eden, Macmillan, and other Tory leaders were ready. They rolled out a campaign theme that played to the country's mood: "Britain Strong and Free" resonated with voters tired of food lines, taxes, and the slow-motion collapse of empire.[2]

Armed with cigars, homburg, and bow tie, Winston showed voters he was still up to the job of prime minister. "He has used these days to give a demonstration of energy and vitality," Macmillan wrote after a day at Winston's side. "He has voted in every division; made a series of brilliant little speeches; shown all his qualities of humour and sarcasm, and crowned it all by a remarkable breakfast (at 7.30 a.m.) of eggs, bacon, sausages and coffee, followed by a large whisky and soda and a huge cigar. The latter feat commanded general admiration."[3]

Attlee's sloganeers painted Winston as an old warmonger. "Vote for Churchill and reach for your rifle; vote Labour and reach old age," blared Labourites. The *Daily Mirror* asked its readers, "Whose finger on the trigger?" over a photo of the cigar-wielding Englishman with a menacing grin. Churchill would drag Britain back to the trenches.[4]

Winston assured voters he was no war lover. "I do not believe that a Third World War is inevitable," he told an audience. "It will not be a British finger that will pull the trigger of a Third World War. It may be a Russian finger, or an American finger, or a United Nations Organization finger, but it cannot be a British finger." In a BBC radio broadcast, he stressed, "I do not hold that we should rearm in order to fight. I hold that we should rearm in order to parley."[5]

The public believed him, and after six years in the wilderness, the Tories came roaring back. Conservatives reaped a clean majority, 321 seats to Labour's 295. A short visit to Buckingham Palace, and the racehorse was back.

On his first day on the quarterdeck, Winston plunged into a frenzied round of appointments. As in World War II, he strapped on the Ministry of Defence like it was an old sidearm, while Anthony Eden reclaimed his place as Foreign Secretary. Harold Macmillan headed Housing, and R. A. "Rab" Butler, a dependable domestic minister, took hold of the Exchequer's purse strings.[6]

Having never held power in peacetime, Winston found domestic policies as uninspiring as Ike found university fundraising. He paid attention to home-front issues dominating the *Times* and *Daily Mirror*, of course, but apart from a housing initiative and a push to end food rationing, he left much of the bricks-and-butter business to Rab Butler and Harold Macmillan. He and Eden tended to global statesmanship.

London needed statesmanship, for by 1952 the British Empire was stretched like a prisoner on history's rack. In Malaya, nearly 100,000 British, colonial, and police forces were bogged down in a nationalist uprising that cost the Crown fifty million pounds a year. In Korea, Red China was playing with matches that could turn a local fire into a global blaze—with the British colony of Hong Kong on the burn line. In Kenya, an anti-colonial rebellion was about to bubble over, while the Middle East, center of world oil production, gave Winston no end of worry.[7]

Egypt was the immediate migraine. The Suez Canal was Britain's crown jewel. Protected by 80,000 soldiers, the waterway anchored Britain's lifeline to its eastern possessions. It was also a magnet for Egyptian rage. The sight of khaki-clad Tommies marching over sands pharaohs once ruled stung Egyptian pride. Cairo's leaders whipped up crowds by railing against London, and those crowds produced fedayeen guerrillas who wouldn't hesitate to murder an unwary soldier who strayed into the wrong bazaar or alley.[8]

Winston called the Egyptian unrest "the bastard child of the Iranian situation," for Iran was another house of horrors. Its villain: a Tehran lawyer named Mohammad Mosaddeq. Tall, bald, and with the grace of a startled flamingo, Mosaddeq had studied law in Paris and Switzerland. Considered pro-western in his early years, he rose to political prominence as a die-hard nationalist. He and his supporters wanted King George out of Iran's affairs, and in April 1951 he was elected Iran's prime minister on a wave of national pride. Before Winston's Tories took power, he signed legislation nationalizing the Anglo-Iranian Oil Company.[9]

The Anglo-Iranian Oil Company was to Iranians what the Suez Canal was to Egyptians: a symbol and tool of a detested colonial power. The AIOC generated obscene profits for London and cast breadcrumbs to the nation whose oil it drilled, pumped, and carried away. Iranians, from street vendors to palace insiders, viewed the corporation as highway robbery on a national scale. They wanted the British parasite gone.

To Britain, the AIOC wasn't just a symbol of imperial might; it was the Empire's lifeblood. The company pumped 6 percent of the world's crude and more than 80 percent of the Royal Navy's fuel. That was about the same proportion of oil that another island empire, Japan, had imported from the United States in 1940. And Japan hadn't hesitated to go to war for that 80 percent.[10]

Closer to home, Winston's gaze turned to Europe. Stalin's hordes loomed just beyond the Elbe River, and the grand idea to stop them was a European Defense Community. The EDC would field an army comprised of units of every western European nation and controlled by a European body—a NATO without America or Canada. The structure would graft West Germany's economic and military potential onto Western Europe without threatening its neighbors.

But the French, who had proposed the EDC, began having second thoughts. With memories of jackboots stomping beneath the Arc de Triomphe, leaders in Paris opposed West German rearmament, freezing efforts to create an all-European army.[11]

Winston had reservations about British participation in the EDC. Like his attitude toward the Church of England, he preferred to play the role of buttress, not pillar—he supported it from the outside. He was skeptical of integrating British forces into a Continental army and felt England's most important relationships lay off the Continent. As he put it, "Our first object is the unity and consolidation of the British Commonwealth and what is left of the former British Empire. Our second, the 'fraternal association' of the English-speaking world; and third, United Europe, to which we are a separate closely and specially related ally and friend."[12]

Britain wasn't just a hub of a diplomatic Venn diagram; it was still an independent world power. The nation had clawed its way back from war's ruin and now boasted the world's third-largest economy. It manufactured more than 8 percent of the world's output and produced a quarter of the world's exports. Jewels had been plucked from the imperial crown over the last seven years, but London still ruled thirty-five colonies and a population of seventy-four million.[13]

While Britain could not complete with America in raw power, it had assets America lacked. Its network of intelligence sources, cutting-edge aerospace technology, and long experience in diplomacy were the keys to British relevance as the curtain rose on Winston's second premiership.

To help manage the Crown's march into an uncertain world, Winston would rely on his right-hand man and heir apparent, Foreign Secretary Anthony Eden.

Eden was the model of a modern British diplomat. Tall, handsome, and impeccably dressed, he radiated sophistication and intelligence. Educated at Eton, he spoke fluent German and French. He had studied Farsi and Arabic at Oxford. He had won the Military Cross in the First World War, where he fought at the bloody battles of the Somme, Messines Ridge, and Passchendaele. But he would make his mark as a statesman, not an officer.[14]

As fascism's shadow spread across Europe in the 1930s, Eden's star rose. Before he turned 38, the Foreign Office dispatched him on assignments to meet Stalin and Hitler. Appointed Foreign Secretary in 1935, he resigned from Neville Chamberlain's cabinet to protest Chamberlain's appeasement of Mussolini. His act of sacrifice put him firmly in Churchill's anti-fascist camp, so when Churchill moved into 10 Downing in 1940, he tapped Eden to be his foreign minister and, informally, his political successor.

For all his brilliance, a cloud hung over Eden. Now in his mid-50s, he suffered from jaundice and relied on pills and morphine injections to stifle abdominal pain. Whenever frustrated with work, which was often, he would retreat to his residence and sulk among his 18th-century furniture and exquisite art collection. He so often lamented to the prime minister's staff, "Tell Winston I am at the end of my tether," staffers simply abbreviated the message to: "The Foreign Secretary's at the E of his T again."

In 1944, while he and Winston were visiting Moscow, a diary entry reflected Eden's state of mind:

> *A pretty trying day. After work at Embassy went to lunch at our conference building. Terrible and interminable ceremony with many speeches lasting until 4 p.m. or later. No chance to eat anything and had to drink in desperation. These things are only bearable at night.*[15]

Also unbearable was his long wait to succeed Winston Churchill as prime minister. As Churchill's successor, he had languished for twelve years in a shadow as immovable as the Elizabeth Clock Tower. Driven by his ambitions and those of his wife—Winston's niece, Clarissa Spencer-Churchill—he endured the water torture of waiting for Winston to announce a retirement that, like the horizon, seemed always in the distance.

Retirement was not on Winston's playbill. As his friend Brendan Bracken told Lord Beaverbrook a few years earlier, Winston was "determined to continue to lead the Tory Party until he becomes Prime Minister on earth or Minister of Defence in Heaven."

Now, with Churchill gripping the reins tighter than ever, Anthony Eden again found himself dangling at the E of his T.[16]

Shortly after Winston's election, Ike invited him to visit the new SACEUR headquarters in Rocquencourt, a modern office complex a dozen miles west of Paris. Delighted to renew ties with his wartime comrade, Winston arranged a trip in mid-December.

Ike, wearing his old SHAEF insignia on his left shoulder, ushered him into his office for a private conversation before calling in senior staffers to meet "my old friend."[17]

To those who hadn't known the lion in his prime, the 77-year-old Englishman personified a defiant Britain. A feeling of near reverence pervaded the room as he spoke. "Our feeling was that he was still the same grand old man that had brought Britain, and, I think, the whole western alliance through the war," recalled Andrew Goodpaster, one of Ike's NATO staffers.[18]

Ike knew better. After Winston returned to London, he told his diary, "Frankly, I believe that, subconsciously, my great friend is trying to re-live the days of his greatest glory. . . . He has taken upon his own shoulders, as he did in World War II, the dual position of Prime Minister and of Defense Minister. . . .

"My regretful opinion," he concluded, "is that the Prime Minister no longer absorbs new ideas; exhortation and appeals to emotions and sentiment still have some effect upon him—exposition does not."[19]

Still, when Winston spoke, men followed. He wielded magic, even if he had to husband his energy and pick his moments. "His voice can, at particular moments, still boom out with authority and appeal over great sections of Europe," Ike wrote Defense Secretary Robert Lovett. "Consequently, we must do our best to have him 'booming' on the things that we see as necessary to the security and tranquility of us all."[20]

The meeting at Ike's headquarters sparked intense political speculation. The day before Winston arrived, Ray Daniell of the *New York Times* told readers, "Both American and European history may be profoundly affected by tomorrow's meeting of Prime Minister Churchill with General of the Army Dwight D. Eisenhower in Paris. Upon its outcome may well depend the decision General Eisenhower must make whether the grand design for the unification of Western Europe can best be accomplished by his remaining as Supreme Commander of the North Atlantic Treaty forces or by laying down his command to seek the Presidency of the United States."[21]

No, thought Winston, Ike wouldn't throw his garrison cap into the ring. At heart, he was a soldier, not a politician. He had made that clear to Winston many times during the war; their biggest fights were because Ike wanted to *avoid* politics. Even now, he said, it would take enormous pressure to pull Ike into the 1952 election. "Ike has not only to be wooed but raped," he told Lord Moran.[22]

But there were plenty of suitors lining up to woo him, filling his ears, appealing to his love of country. How long could any man resist the siren's song? The call of duty might be seduction enough.

THIRTY-THREE

The Seduction of a Soldier

AFTER TWENTY YEARS WANDERING IN THE POLITICAL DESERT, Republicans weren't looking for another humiliation. The numbers spoke for themselves: The country was 47 percent Democrat, 27 percent Republican, 22 percent independent. That meant the conservative frontrunner, Ohio's Senator Robert Taft, would get flattened by Harry Truman or any other garden-variety Democrat. Four more years as the butt of political jokes.

The GOP needed a fresh face—someone dazzling—and General Eisenhower had it in spades. His steel blue eyes, flashing over the kind of smile advertising companies pay big bucks for, had stared down Hitler and won. Add his NATO résumé, middle-America humility, and gift for public speaking, and you couldn't build a more appealing candidate.[1]

On domestic issues, Ike's politics were murky. That would be a big plus in the general election, but it wouldn't help him with the primaries. "We had a hell of a time proving he was a Republican," remembered Thomas Stephens, Ike's appointments secretary. "We had to get letters that he'd written to people where he'd say . . . something that might dovetail with what was in the Republican plank." Beetle Smith, now Truman's CIA chief, told Harold Macmillan the man they had worked for during the war "was temperamentally more in sympathy with Democrats." That gave him appeal to moderates in both parties.[2]

Ike kept them guessing. During a big NATO conference in Rome, Theodore Achilles, a State Department diplomat, popped into the general's office just before lunch to find him wearing a Cheshire cat grin.

"What's pleasing you?" asked Achilles.

The grin widened. "I've just turned down forty thousand dollars for one word."

"What was it?"

"Well, there was a fellow from *McCall's* in here this morning, who offered me forty thousand dollars for a yes or no answer to the question, 'Are you a Republican?'"[3]

Ike's eyes twinkled. He didn't need the money. He enjoyed the game.

In October 1951, a pack of U.S. business leaders, encouraged by General Lucius Clay, visited Ike in Paris. They urged him to run on the Republican ticket as an alternative to Taft's anti-NATO isolationism. Ike listened politely, nodded sympathetically, but gave them nothing they could hold him to.

The next month, Ike took a short trip to the States, where he met with President Truman. Rumors immediately swirled that over a private lunch, Truman had told Ike he would bow out of the next race if Ike would run as a Democrat. Both men denied it, and Ike publicly refused the crown.

"I will not be a participant in any movement that attempts to secure for me a nomination because I believe that the Presidency is something that should never be sought," he told his diary.

Then the caveat: "I believe, of course, that it could never be refused. . . . I merely admit that, as of now, I would consider the nomination of which they speak, if accomplished without any direct or indirect assistance or connivance on my part, to place upon me a transcendent duty."[4]

What, exactly, was "transcendent duty"?

Ike told himself that if he were drafted, he would be answering the call of the nation. The office would seek him, not the other way around. He would be a devoted servant of the Republic, not a snake-oil huckster kissing babies, eating state fair corn dogs, and mouthing stump speeches on a whistle-stop tour.

Of course, Ike was fooling himself. He could play the reluctant warrior, but his closest friends knew better. George Patton had made several snide remarks about Ike's presidential ambition at the war's end, and in early 1951 Ike had squelched talk of a Sherman denial.* He wouldn't stop anyone from nominating him. He wanted the job. He was just too proud to beg for it.

In Washington they saw the cracks. Republican Senator Henry Cabot Lodge Jr. of Massachusetts organized an Eisenhower for President committee. Powerful senators, governors, and business leaders quickly climbed aboard the train, and by January, they only needed the driver.[5]

On January 7, 1952, Ike said no again. But this time, he left the door open. "Of course, there is no question of the right of American citizens to organize in pursuit of their common convictions," he conceded. "I realize that Senator Lodge and his associates are exercising this right in an attempt to place before me next July a duty that would transcend my present responsibility. In the absence, however, of a clear-cut call to political duty I shall continue to devote my full attention to and energies to the performance of the vital task to which I am assigned."[6]

There it was again. That curious word, *transcend*. And "next July"—the month of the Republican National Convention.

* In 1884, General William Tecumseh Sherman refused appeals to run for president on the Republican ticket. "I will not accept if nominated and will not serve if elected," he declared. Sherman's statement is considered the gold standard for a candidate's refusal to run.

Ike's non-denial threw open the door of a "Draft Eisenhower" movement. He wasn't driving the train, but he had stepped aboard and was inspecting the engine cab with more than idle curiosity.

In February, the curtain rose on the opening night of "Draft Eisenhower" at New York's Madison Square Garden. Fifteen thousand citizens braved a Manhattan downpour for a star-studded "Serenade to Ike" rally. Appearances by Clark Gable and Jackie Cooper punctuated musical performances by Ethel Merman, Richard Rodgers, and Irving Berlin. Crowds filled buckets with silver dollars, funding a campaign Ike hadn't launched, and extended chants of "I Like Ike!" swept the auditorium.[7]

A month later, Ike watched from Rocquencourt as the nation's first big primary week kicked off. With the enthusiastic backing of New Hampshire Governor Sherman Adams, Ike swept the state, easily beating Senator Taft. One week later, Minnesota Republicans went to the polls. Though Ike's name wasn't on the ballot, enough supporters wrote him in to take second place behind Minnesota's favorite son, Harold Stassen. Taft had to settle for third.[8]

Two days later, Ike told reporters, "You gentlemen probably realize how astonished I was by the result of the Minnesota primary. The mounting numbers of my fellow citizens who are voting to make me the Republican nominee are forcing me to re-examine my personal position and past decisions."[9]

He hadn't formally declared himself a candidate, but he was acting like one. And that meant he was one.[10]

Before D-Day, Ike had leaned on Group Captain Stagg for the confidence to say, "O.K., we'll go." In late March, the GOP sent their own Captain Stagg.

With the face of a small-town bank manager, Herbert Brownell could have blended into any government office. But beneath his mild demeanor lay a razor-sharp mind for law and politics. The Nebraskan had steered two of Governor Thomas Dewey's presidential campaigns, each unsuccessfully, and this time he thought he'd found a winner.

On March 24, Brownell spent a long day at Rocquencourt, giving Ike a reality check. Brownell assured Ike he had done enough for his country and owed nothing more. Unless Ike had a genuine, heartfelt urge to run, he shouldn't run. He "shouldn't go in as a—'gee, I don't want to do it but I guess I gotta do it' attitude," Brownell told an interviewer later. The presidency was too immense a task for Ike to take on just because others wanted him to.[11]

Then another hard truth. Time was running out. If Ike was in, he had to come home and campaign, and soon. There were a lot more primaries besides New Hampshire and Minnesota, and Taft had a big head start. Ike would have to get back to the States in time to win over delegates before the convention in Chicago.

So Ike couldn't sit on the porch and await victory. Even for him, it was a stomach churner. "He was quite frank that he dreaded a campaign," General Clay remembered.

Feeling nervous, Ike didn't promise Brownell anything that day. "But," Brownell recalled, "I had the distinct feeling, when I left, that if he had decided in his own mind not to be a candidate, I would have known it before I left."[12]

Two weeks later, a wire service photo flashed across western papers: a grinning Ike waving from his car window. The *New York Times* headline that day blared: "EISENHOWER PLANS TO LEAVE THE ARMY IF NAMED BY G.O.P."[13]

THIRTY-FOUR

A General on Campaign

Before Ike and Mamie returned to the States, Winston gave them a send-off at 10 Downing Street. The evening's guest list was a tapestry of old comrades: the Alexanders, the Brookes, the Portals, the Edens, Jumbo Wilson, Clement Attlee. Men who had sweated bullets over Torch and D-Day and the Blitz, the Rhine, the Ruhr, and Berlin. The brothers in the room where the decisions were made.[1]

The evening was warm, the dinner suffused with old stories and drinks, laughter and memories. "The atmosphere could not have been more cordial," Jock Colville told his diary. Ike, now 61, looked vigorous as he faced a future promising more stress from more directions. He fed off the energy of his British friends, and over dinner he emphasized his devotion to the Anglo-American brotherhood. Colville reported, "When Ike left he said that if he were elected he would pay just one visit outside the USA—to the UK—in order to show our special relationship."[2]

For Ike, the evening was a gulp of cool air before leaping into the furnace. "If I had been given a wish how I would spend my last night in England before saying farewell, I could not have had it fulfilled in all respects so completely as I did at your dinner party," he wrote Winston. "It was indeed a privilege to be present at such a distinguished gathering of old and trusted friends with you at their head."[3]

Hanging up his uniform for a second time, Ike stepped onto the stage to clinch the GOP nomination. For his running mate, the convention nominated Richard Nixon, a sharp junior senator brimming with California energy. For the general election, Eisenhower and Nixon squared off against Illinois Governor Adlai Stevenson, a smooth-talking liberal, and Senator John Sparkman, a Deep South segregationist.

"Ike and Dick" made a potent team. Nixon's West Coast youth balanced Ike's gravitas and East Coast connections. Nixon had made a name for himself rooting out communists in the Alger Hiss spy case, so his selection would assure the Republican right of the ticket's dedication to fighting Reds at home and abroad.[4]

"In the '52 campaign, the Republicans were able to use the slogan 'Communism, Korea and Corruption,'" remembered *Time*'s editor Henry Luce. In Ike's stump speeches, he focused on the first two while he let Dick bang the corruption gong as the ticket's attack dog.

Ike promised to fight communism with the passion he brought to the war against Hitler. Reds from Moscow to Pyongyang were "preparing this whole great mass of people so that they may surpass our own productive capacity," he warned an American Legion crowd. "They are preparing those people psychologically and materially for whatever decision the Kremlin makes—even global war."[5]

His centerpiece pledge was to end the Korean War, a festering wound in America's otherwise bucolic life. By 1952, more than 300,000 Americans were marooned half a world away, fighting in obscure places like Panmunjom, the Punchbowl, and Heartbreak Ridge. Two years of seesaw fighting had taken a heavy toll: more than 124,000 dead, wounded, or missing.[6]

With Korea, Ike held the political high ground, for he had been nowhere near the mess when it started. He moved to Columbia two years before North Korea attacked, and had been in Europe leading NATO as the war ground to a stalemate. Sharing no blame for the war, he climbed the polls with a promise to end it.

In October, Ike dramatically raised the stakes by vowing to visit Korea after the election. He would look over the terrain and see for himself how best to end the war. The image of the Liberator of Europe finishing a war bungled by smaller men electrified a war-weary public. Shortly after his announcement, Adlai Stevenson announced that he, too, would go to Korea. But Ike had stolen the moment, and voters have a nose for sniffing out cheap political theater: The picture of an effete liberal egghead splattering battlefield mud on his expensive shoes was ludicrous.[7]

The campaign trail was grueling, but it wasn't all high-pressure. At one stop, Ike shared a lighthearted moment with reporters over unsolicited advice from the British prime minister. He said Winston once "gave me unshirted hell" for giving a speech from memory rather than reading carefully prepared remarks.

"He said never trust your memory in anything like that with people following every word you say to see if you repeated exactly what was written," Ike recalled. Winston would read from notes and drop them, a page at a time, behind the lectern, leaving a pile of paper sheets at his feet when he finished. He also told Ike not to be afraid to wear reading glasses when he spoke—"big, round spectacles which you can take off and shake in their face. And if you have notes don't try to hide them. Shake them in their face, too."

Winston was used to an unruly, heckling crowd of opposition MPs, but that wasn't Ike's style. He didn't like baiting audiences. "There's a dignity about a crowd of people that cannot be insulted," he explained. "I have to give them everything I've got."

It was the difference between a milk creamer from Abilene and an aristocrat born in Blenheim Palace: One led with humility, the other by force of will.[8]

Press conferences were Ike's weakness, for his off-the-cuff charm didn't always translate onto paper. He tended to ramble, exposing a tortured approach to the English language.

"Ike had a kind of nonstop delivery which took very little account of syntax and established grammatical forms," one reporter recalled. Ike's son John admitted, "His mind was going so much faster than his tongue could. . . . Sometimes it would require a little bit of deciphering to figure out—to follow a sentence."[9]

Ike was aware of his quirks. "Look, this speech we're about to give, for God's sake, don't let me give it extemporaneously," he once told a handler. "I have a capacity for starting a sentence on something that's happened in my backyard and before I put a period on the sentence I'm talking about the Normandy landings."[10]

A gentle breeze rustled pine needles lining Augusta National's fairway as Ike lined up his shot. Taking a break in the hurricane's eye, he wound up, swung his club, and sent the ball flying.

Before he could leave the green, an Atomic Energy Commission official scurried up with a folder stamped TOP SECRET. Taking a cart to the clubhouse, Ike paged through a summary of "Ivy Mike," the code name for a nuclear weapon test over a Central Pacific atoll.

Mike was no ordinary atom bomb. Harnessing the power of the stars, the Mike device used a Nagasaki-type explosion to generate enough heat to melt hydrogen atoms. When the nuclei fused together, they shed some of their mass, which became energy. Explosive energy.

How much energy? Well, Einstein said it would be equal to the lost mass times the square of the speed of light, which is a higher number than most people care to count to. But enough energy, in this case, to vaporize a Pacific island.

The energy of seven hundred Hiroshima bombs exploding at once.

Enough energy to make Winston Churchill remark, "We are now as far from the age of the atomic bomb as the atomic bomb itself from the bow and arrow."[11]

And that was just the beginning. Explosive force and heat aside, Mike threw off enough radiation to ruin photoreconnaissance aircraft equipment miles away. It could destroy human cells with gamma radiation far beyond the blast area. And the explosive yield could be increased exponentially simply by adding more fuel. Like a fragment of a star brought down to earth.

Frowning as he read the report, Ike pondered what an explosion of ten million tons of TNT looked like.

More important, why? Prometheus stole fire from the gods, but fire is useful. What possible good could come from a fusion bomb? He wondered aloud what possessed humans to build "enough destructive power to destroy everything."[12]

But the why didn't matter much now. Megatons had replaced kilotons. At great expense and trouble, mankind had pried open the coffin lid. Inside the box lay an invitation—an invitation every future president would read.

With a heavy heart, he went back to his clubs. In the time it took him to get from first tee to the 18th hole, the world had changed its course. Again.

As Americans descended into election frenzy, Winston watched the show with professional detachment. Though his working relationships had been with key Democrats, he had no particular worries. "Once the American election is over," he wrote Clementine, "we may be able to make real headway. Either Ike or the Democrats would be all right."[13]

To the public, he maintained a strict neutrality and muted anti-American criticism. A year before, he had redacted complaints about Ike in *Closing the Ring*, the fifth volume of his war memoirs. But he secretly hoped it would be Stevenson, not Eisenhower, who won the White House. The Illinois governor was cut from the comfortable old liberal cloth of FDR and Harry Truman. Stevenson had opposed loyalty oaths and fought red-baiters like Senator Joe McCarthy. He had even testified as a character witness for Soviet spy Alger Hiss—a move that marked him as either a courageous idealist or a political fool—and seemed receptive to negotiating with Moscow, rather than coming at Stalin with clenched fists.[14]

To the British public, candidate Ike was a riddle wrapped in an enigma. The average Briton liked him, but no one knew what he really stood for besides Europe's defense. London's political left painted him as a puppet of right-wingers like Taft and McCarthy. *The People*, a far-left rag, shrieked, "Ike will be forced by the screams of the Right to go in and 'finish it all with all we've got.' That means bombs on China—even atom bombs—and certainly what is now a minor skirmish would be turned into a world war."[15]

Winston didn't share the left's hysteria, but he watched his friend's ascension with mixed feelings. They had fought shoulder to shoulder against Hitler, sharing maps and whisky for three years. Winston even kept an I LIKE IKE pin stuffed in his pocket, sometimes flashing it to American visitors whose discretion he could trust. As he told Jock Colville, "If Eisenhower were elected President, he would have another shot at making peace by means of a meeting of the Big Three. For that alone it would perhaps be worth remaining in office."[16]

On the other hand, Ike was surrounding himself with bankers, lawyers, and corporate executives unused to pulling the levers of power. Men skilled at moving money, not armies. Fledgling hawks, Chinese Nationalists, and McCarthyites. It was hard enough for Ike to walk the tightrope of diplomacy alone; carrying a gaggle of shouters on his back would make his job far harder.[17]

After a weekend at Chartwell, Churchill's estate in the Kent countryside, Jock Colville confided in his diary, "Should Eisenhower be elected President of the U.S.A. in November—an event thought to be decreasingly probable—there will be further trouble on this score, because W. has several times revealed to me his hopes of a joint approach to Stalin."[18]

Colville didn't read the electoral room. Ike's ability to connect with the everyday hopes of the middle class, his sense of moderation and balance, and his reputation as America's greatest soldier told voters he could be trusted. As citizens lined up at the polls on November 4, 1952, Ike motored to Columbia's Morningside Drive mansion to paint and talk with friends as news flowed in.

By nightfall, the picture was clear: Republicans swept for the first time since 1928. Ike took nearly every state outside the Old Confederacy—including Illinois, Stevenson's home—and won the popular election by nearly seven million votes.

"For your own private ear, I am greatly disturbed," Winston grumbled to Colville. "I think this makes war more probable."[19]

PART TWO

Red Lightning

(1953–1955)

"He was friendly, but he never smiled: a change from the Ike of war days."

– Jock Colville, on Ike[1] –

"[Eisenhower] told me that Churchill was one of the most difficult people he had to deal with because he became so emotionally involved in whatever he was doing."

– Richard Nixon[2] –

Ivy Mike test

U.S. Government

THIRTY-FIVE

Dinner at Bernie's

As 1952 rolled to a Times Square end, Ike's staff sifted résumés, dossiers, and reference letters in a makeshift transition center in New York's Commodore Hotel. Awash in cigarette butts and coffee, they hunted for high-level nominations President-elect Eisenhower would approve or reject.

One post loomed above the rest: Secretary of State, the man who would define America's relationship with friends and foes. Ike had to get that one right. And he figured he did.

John Foster Dulles surveyed a sinful world through a jaundiced eye. Six feet tall, straight as a church pulpit, the son of a Presbyterian minister blended moral certainty with a Princeton brain and Sorbonne savoir faire. After the First World War, the Wall Street lawyer had attended the Paris Peace Conference as the American delegation's legal counsel. After World War II, Harry Truman tapped him to negotiate for the State Department. Dulles brokered the San Francisco Peace Treaty, ending World War II in Asia, and was midwife to the U.S.-Japanese Security Treaty and ANZUS alliance with Australia and New Zealand.[1]

If Ike's smile could warm a room, Dulles sucked in frost. Formal and self-righteous, he preached the Ten Commandments of anti-communism and saw America as the world's Moses. "Dulles felt that he had something of a God-ordained mission to carry out his beliefs in foreign policy," mused one career diplomat. Ike's speechwriter Emmet Hughes complained of his "fondness for embellishing his political statements—usually rendered with the cold finality of judicial decisions—with moralistic flourishes more appropriate to church councils than to international conferences."[2]

In secular councils, Dulles spoke slowly and deliberately, groping for the exact word to fit his precise idea. He would halt midsentence, mouth gaping, as listeners waited for verbs and modifiers to line up and slow-march like a New Orleans funeral procession. Listening to Dulles in conference, Ike would tap a pencil on a notepad or thigh, nodding, waiting, saying nothing. To Ike, Dulles's thoughts were worth waiting for.[3]

The British had their own history with Dulles. In 1951, he had promised Attlee's government the U.S. wouldn't pressure Japan to recognize Formosa's Nationalist government. But behind the scenes, Dulles arranged a secret agreement with Tokyo to do exactly that. Neither Winston nor Eden had forgotten or forgiven Dulles's double-dealing, and Ike's selection appalled them both.[4]

"You have no idea, you couldn't have any idea, how much he was mistrusted by Winston Churchill," Ike's ambassador to London later told an interviewer. "Churchill's own mistrust of Dulles permeated the whole Cabinet."[5]

But it was Ike's call, and Winston kept his worries to himself. Without much sincerity, he wrote Dulles, "I send you my sincere congratulations on the great office to which you are to be appointed."

He would keep Dulles at arm's length, wary of every move. "It was sort of a cat and dog watching each other," Ike admitted years later.[6]

Out of the gate, Dulles ruffled feathers in London over the seemingly simple decision to replace U.S. Ambassador Walter Gifford with Winthrop Aldrich.[7]

After nearly three years in London, the popular Gifford wanted to come home. Aldrich seemed the perfect replacement. The Chase Bank president had known Churchill since 1924, and Aldrich had been awarded an honorary Knight Grand Cross of the British Empire by King George VI for his work on behalf of the British War Relief Society.[8]

But Aldrich had loose lips and lots of friends, and on the first of December, a leak about his appointment made its way into the *New York Times.* An unhappy Dulles immediately called Gifford to give him the news, then hastily informed Her Majesty's Government so the Foreign Office wouldn't learn of the posting from the papers.[9]

In his rush to get ahead of the leak, Dulles didn't have time to ask Eden for HMG's consent. He simply informed London—a jarring breach of protocol that angered Eden. Gifford later told Ike the appointment sparked "a feeling on the part of the British, at that time, that the new administration intended to be pretty rough with them and with our other allies."

Ike understood the bruised egos in Westminster. He told his diary, "They are, of course, very sensitive indeed and are watchful for every affront to their dignity and rights. Beyond this, they feel that they should have something of a special position with us because of our close partnership during World War II."

Ike mused on that one. As an officer in Europe, he had been a key player in the partnership. He believed passionately in Anglo-American amity. But his thinking had evolved since D-Day. America really had two relationships with Britain. As he told his diary,

> *It is quite clear that unless the English-speaking peoples of the world can live relatively close together and can set something of a model for the necessary cooperation among free peoples, then we are truly in for desperate trouble. However, no such special relationship can be maintained or even suggested publicly. In public relationship all nations are*

sovereign and equal. This means that on the personal and informal basis we must find a way of agreeing with our British friends on broad objectives and purposes. Thereafter, each must pursue its own detailed methods of achieving these purposes. Some hurt feelings will occasionally be inevitable—but as long as our hearts are in the right places and both sides are reasonably intelligent, we should be able to work for the common aim of a free and secure world based upon common sense among nations and decent respect for each other.[10]

A freshman president leading the West. Winston didn't need a history book to tell him how that might play out. At Potsdam in 1945, Truman had been an understudy abruptly shoved into the leading role. His inexperience left the wrong impression on Stalin, who pushed the envelope in Berlin and Korea—two crises that had dragged the world to the brink of Number III.

Now America had another freshman. Who knew what Ike and Dulles would do—not out of naivete, but from a knee-jerk foreign policy that lashed out against Moscow and Peking. If America fancied itself Gary Cooper in *High Noon*, the world would slide toward war. Roosevelt had been too trusting, Truman too inflexible. Winston feared Ike would be too quick to draw his gun.[11]

To keep those six-shooters holstered, Winston wanted a sit-down with Ike. He was still kicking himself for missing his chance to meet Truman at FDR's funeral, and with Ike's inauguration day on the calendar, he wanted time with his old friend before January 20. "He was very keen to see President Eisenhower, he looked forward to a very close relationship—the old wartime relationship," remembered Sir Roger Makins, Britain's newly appointed ambassador to Washington.

Ike's trip to Korea ruled out most of December, so Winston decided to visit early in the new year. Signing a cable to Ike with his wartime alias, "Colonel Warden," he proposed meeting in New York in January, possibly as an impromptu stop on Winston's upcoming trip to Jamaica. Unofficial, of course. Just two old friends catching up. Two old friends who happened to lead the free world.

Ike knew some people believed Winston would manipulate him into doing Britain's bidding, and he damn sure wasn't going to create any Svengali stories before his presidency began. To keep the meeting low-key, he agreed to a quiet gathering at the home of their mutual friend, Wall Street financier Bernard Baruch. At Bernie's Upper East Side apartment, they could talk unofficially over a couple of evenings.

"I cannot imagine anything but good coming out of an informal meeting between the two of us," Ike wrote. "This would not be so satisfactory as a longer and more leisurely visit over our respective easels, yet it would be, from my viewpoint, far better than no meeting at all."[12]

Ike asked Baruch to play dinner host for a night or two. He added, "We would like of course to make our meeting appear as natural and casual—in other words 'unplanned'—as possible."[13]

On a cold January morning, the majestic silhouette of the *Queen Mary* slipped through the mists of New York Harbor. In the liner's elegant Verandah Grill, Winston met with fifty-odd newsmen for a few short remarks. He wielded his Havana like a conductor's baton as he downplayed the significance of their talk. "There is nothing extraordinary in our meeting," he assured reporters. "I suppose General Eisenhower and I have met at least a hundred times to deal with business of one kind and another—some quite important business."[14]

With a gruff smile, he flashed his iconic "V for Victory" sign, clambered into a limousine, and rode over to Baruch's apartment. He settled in for a pleasant chat with Bernie, and at five minutes after five, President-elect Dwight D. Eisenhower stepped through the door.

It was Ike, but not the Ike Winston remembered. His garrison cap had widened into a gray homburg. The Eisenhower jacket had lengthened into a double-breasted suit from William Goldman & Sons. His russet Type II shoes had become shiny black wing tips, and from his cuff, a gold Rolex peeped out.[15]

But his signature grin was still there, and it brought back memories of shared struggles and triumphs.

"You're looking much better than when I last saw you, Mr. Prime Minister," Ike said as he, Winston, and Baruch sat for a short photo session. As jockeying cameramen snapped the reunion, Ike remarked, "The one thing I have so far learned in this damned game of yours is that you have just got to have a sense of humor."[16]

With the cameramen ushered out, Winston led the night's discussion while Ike sat attentively, contributing but respectful. They talked about politics, people they remembered, life during wartime—things old friends do when they pick up in the middle of a conversation interrupted months earlier. The subjects ranged far and wide, but Winston always brought them around to his theme of Anglo-American unity.

"A protoplasm is sexless, then it divides into two sexes, which, in due course, unite again in a different way to their common benefit and gratification," Winston quipped with an impish grin. "This should also be the story of England and America."[17]

Ike accepted the metaphor—to a point. His empathy, better developed than Winston's, told him what marching lockstep would look like to smaller nations: a coalition of great powers bent on enforcing the colonial status quo. The two countries would always be friends, but in public, the U.S. must treat Britain with the same dignity and deference it gave every other sovereign nation. No less, but no more.[18]

Winston was polite, but he saw Anglo-American relations as unique. The bond was no Cold War convenience. It was sacred: a brotherhood of a common tongue, forged by shared history and shared values. It was nothing like their relationships with, say, Sweden or Swaziland, and there was no use pretending otherwise.

Entranced by the dream of renewing the old wartime comradeship, after Ike left, Winston wrote Anthony Eden of his "most friendly and intimate talks" with Ike. Ike had suggested a formal visit, perhaps in late February, and was sympathetic to Britain's position on the Mid East and Europe. The president was even open to closer cooperation on atomic weapons, a working relationship abruptly cut off during Truman's term. "My own feeling is that we might easily get a supply [of atomic weapons] from the United States," Winston wrote Eden.

But, he admitted, "These are not his words but my impressions."[19]

The next evening found Ike and Winston back at Bernie's. Over cordials, talk turned to Stalin. Because Candidate Eisenhower had vilified the dictator on the trail, Winston was floored when President-elect Eisenhower seemed willing to consider a summit meeting with the dictator. That night, Winston reported to Eden and Rab Butler that Ike "thought of making it plain in his inauguration speech that he would go to, say, Stockholm to meet him, if Stalin were willing."

Colville relayed the conversation to the Foreign Office's Evelyn Shuckburgh. "Ike asked if Winston saw any objection to his meeting Stalin alone. Winston said, 'I would have objected strongly during the war when our contribution in forces was about equal. Now I don't mind. But don't be in a hurry.'"

Winston was in a hurry, but he didn't want Ike doing anything precipitous, whether that meant escalating the Korean War or striking out for a premature summit with Stalin. Going slowly, avoiding early mistakes, seemed the sensible path for a political novice.

Winston advised Ike to keep his inauguration speech general. "Wait till he could survey the whole scene at leisure, and have all official information, before taking plunges. There was no battle going on, and as a General he could afford to wait for full reconnaissance reports," Winston recounted to Eden. After all, said Winston, "The election was over; he had four years' certain power. Why be in too great a hurry?"[20]

Winston left Baruch's dinner table with a spring in his step, buoyed by the energy of two days with Ike. The incoming president had deferred to Winston's age, experience, and eloquence, and now he was talking about a superpower summit and atomic weapons cooperation. Winston had high hopes of guiding his protégé down the right path, just like in the days of World War Two.[21]

"Winston is trying to relive the days of World War Two," Ike told his diary, his impressions spooling out in neat lines. "In those days he had the enjoyable feeling that he and our President were sitting on some rather Olympian platform with respect to the rest of the world, and directing world affairs from that point of vantage. Even if this picture were an accurate one of those days, it would have no application to the present. But it was only partially true, even then."

Ike subscribed to the "good fences make good neighbors" rule, and he wouldn't hold star chamber meetings with Winston to decide the fates of small nations. Britain and America shared fundamental ideals—individual freedom, democratic government, market economies—but Ike wasn't going to let America get mixed up in Britain's now unfashionable colonial mindset. Former colonies should be allowed to make their way in the world without the heavy hand of imperialism, whether that hand held the Union Jack or the hammer and sickle.[22]

Winston acknowledged fence lines, but he didn't like them. Sometimes things needed fixing by leaders who knew better. As Ike told his diary:

> *Winston does not by any means propose to resort to power politics and to disregard legitimate aspirations among weaker peoples. But he does*

take the rather old-fashioned, paternalistic approach that since we, with our experience and power, will be required to support and carry the heavy burdens of decent international plans, as well as aid infant nations towards self-dependence, other nations should recognize the wisdom of our suggestions, and follow them.

The old, paternalist approach might have been the only approach Winston knew—another indication the sun had set on his best years. "Much as I hold Winston in my personal affection and much as I admire him for his past accomplishments and leadership, I wish that he would turn over leadership of the British Conservative Party to younger men," Ike wrote. "He could perform a very great function by coming forward with his inspiring voice only when critical circumstances so demanded."

But Ike knew Winston too well to expect him to shuffle off quietly. "I am very much afraid that he will never voluntarily adopt this kind of semi-active role," Ike told his diary the following month. Just before Winston's election, Ike had suggested his friend take the mantle of PM for a short time, then turn it over to a younger leader.

"Not at all! Not at all!" Ike remembered Winston saying. "My greatest opportunities for service may still be before me. Why should I step down when I can have a hand in helping British progress?"

To Ike, one hallmark of a great leader is the wisdom and grace to ride into the sunset when time erodes his usefulness. A leader should never subject his people to undue risk that he will die in office with no succession plan, like Roosevelt, or govern as a bedridden, befuddled shell, like Woodrow Wilson.

"Again I am reminded of how hard it is for older men to retire and accept the inevitable verdict of passing years," Ike wrote. "I have watched this over my life, and I continue to pray that I, in my turn, will not fall victim to the same human failing."

The prayer felt like a promise to himself. Out of uniform, with no one to salute, the choices were his.

"So here I am," he concluded. "The reason for reciting the record to date is that if I do finally succumb to the same kind of thing that now seems to rule my great friend Winston, I will at least have a record that for a period I had somewhat better sense."[23]

When Ike left that night, Winston struggled to grasp the changes in his friend. The brigadier he'd known during the war—the salutes, the technical analysis, the obsession with leaving politics to political leaders—was gone. Now he was the one making the big decisions.

"There was a difference between General Eisenhower as Supreme Commander under Allied orders, who had no political control, and General Eisenhower as president of the United States," reflected Ambassador Makins. "I think both the Prime Minister and Anthony Eden never really quite made that distinction."[24]

After Ike left Bernie's, Winston dined with Baruch, New York Governor Tom Dewey, and Foster Dulles. Winston's mood quickly soured when Dulles pulled back on Ike's suggestion of an official visit to Washington in February. "He explained that the American public thought that W could cast a spell on all American statesmen," Jock Colville told his diary.

Dulles was probably right, but being right didn't satisfy Winston. After Dulles left, Winston worked himself into a burst of anger. He "said some very harsh things about the Republican Party in general and Dulles in particular," Colville wrote. Winston would describe Dulles as a "dull, unimaginative, uncomprehending, insensitive man; so clumsy," lamenting, "I hope he will disappear."[25]

Dulles was an easy lightning rod when Winston could not bring himself to blame Ike. But he realized the lawyer had outsized influence on the novice president. In a fit of pique, he complained to Colville that Ike had become a "real man of limited stature" and wondered whether the Americans had the skill to avoid war with Stalin.

His faith in his friend began to waver as Ike and Mamie moved their belongings into the White House.[26]

THIRTY-SIX

75 Percent Cold-Blooded

"One of Dad's problems was, besides not liking politicians, that he didn't know the players," said John Eisenhower. "He knew the players in the Army, but in the political arena he had to take people's word on personnel."[1]

Politicians played by different rules. They didn't read Clausewitz, they ducked blame, and their mistakes didn't haunt them through neatly lined casualty reports. They took risks with other people's lives and money and hoped they were right—or, if not right, that they would be long gone by the time the bill came due.

It was a hell of a way to run a country, and Ike wanted a team that would solve problems the way SHAEF solved them in Europe. So he borrowed George Marshall's rules: Pick the best men you can get. Give them the broad strategy. Let them do their jobs. Hold them accountable for results.

Dulles was an early choice, but in the bowels of CIA headquarters, Ike found an extra Dulles. This one would run another important arm of his foreign policy.

Allen Dulles had followed his older brother from Princeton to the law firm of Sullivan & Cromwell. As counsel to the U.S. delegation to the League of Nations in the 1930s, the pipe-puffing Ivy Leaguer had met Hitler and Mussolini. During World War II, he moved from diplomat to spook and had been one of Wild Bill Donovan's OSS cowboys. Under Harry Truman, he worked for Beetle Smith as the number two man at the CIA.

By elevating Allen Dulles to Director of Central Intelligence, Ike expected the Dulles brothers to forge close ties between State and Intelligence. Budget conscious and averse to hot wars, he had a big role in mind for the CIA—within the larger framework Foster would set. State would write the melody; the CIA would carry the subtle harmony.[2]

Other cabinet picks were a mixed bag. Charles Wilson, Ike's new secretary of defense, was a silver-haired executive from General Motors. Loud and proud, "Engine Charlie" knew how to defend things like profits and stock options, but he nearly sank his nomination by refusing demands that he divest his $2 million trove of GM stock. As he told stunned senators in his confirmation hearings, "I thought what was good for the country was good for General Motors, and vice-versa." It might have been the most American answer the senators ever heard.[3]

In the West Wing, a few key players ran the inner machine. Sherman Adams, the New Hampshire governor who helped launch Ike's campaign, would run the White House as chief of staff. His blunt, negative style earned him the nickname "Abominable No-Man." James Hagerty, a former *New York Times* reporter with a perpetual growl, signed on as Ike's press secretary. Ann Whitman, a tireless secretary who had worked for Radio Free Europe, took Kay Summersby's role at SHAEF—though, being dutifully if not happily married to a United Fruit Company spokesman, Ann didn't carry the baggage Kay had lugged around Europe.[4]

Ike's military aides, like Colonels Andrew Goodpaster, Robert Schulz, and Craig Cannon—and later, his son John—kept notes, compiled analyses, and handled correspondence on national security matters. They also kept minutes of the National Security Council, a group comprised of the Joint Chiefs, the secretaries of state, defense, and treasury, the CIA director, the vice president, and other key foreign policy advisors.

While Harry Truman had more or less ignored the council, Ike used the NSC as a key strategy-defining body. It met every Thursday morning in the Cabinet Room, rain or shine, and during his presidency Ike personally chaired 319 of its 343 meetings. The NSC would set big Cold War goals the way SHAEF set military strategy in World War II.

Then there was Beetle Smith, Ike's right-hand man in the Mediterranean and Europe. Sharp, tough, and mean when he had to be. Ike had leaned on him like a crutch. "If I should write any memoirs," he wrote in 1943, "I should certainly have to devote a full chapter to the debt I owe to Smith." *Crusade in Europe* didn't give Beetle a full chapter, but Ike praised him throughout for his brilliant management in two great theaters of war.

After the war, Beetle had served with distinction as U.S. ambassador to Moscow, then ran the CIA—two posts where distrust and ruthlessness were cardinal virtues. During the 1952 campaign, Ike had told a CIA briefer he had a big job in mind for his old chief of staff if he were elected, and with Ike's election, Beetle saw the finish line: Army Chief of Staff, Marshall's old job. Perhaps even White House chief of staff.[5]

Then life kicked him in the ass. Beetle was a holdover from the Truman crowd, and Joe McCarthy's dogs would howl if he became Ike's gatekeeper. Beetle's health was also precarious—stomach surgery reduced him to 135 pounds—and Ike didn't like the optics of two Army generals running the White House.

While Ike often remarked on the debt he owed Beetle, he never felt obliged to repay it. Ignoring Beetle's desire for promotion to the Army's head, he moved Beetle over to State to work as undersecretary to Foster Dulles. The consolation prize.

Beetle took the job, but it stung. He considered Foster Dulles a sonofabitch. He had once chewed out the younger Dulles, and now he would be saying "Yes, Mr. Secretary" to the older one.*

Beetle had labored for years as Ike's hatchet man, consigliere, and manager. He had gone to bat for Ike in London, in Algiers and Malta, and in Washington. He had been a key link in a chain of Fate that pulled Ike from a cramped office in London to the Oval Office at the White House. He felt he deserved better.[6]

Ike disappointed Beetle the same way he tossed aside Kay Summersby, George Patton, and anyone else who'd outlived their usefulness. Subordinates were tools to be used, then put back in the box or discarded when no longer needed. You don't give loyalty to tools; you use them. Beetle would stick around another eighteen months as undersecretary of state, but he never forgave Ike for welching on the old debt.

"I remember poor old Bedell Smith, who had to carry out a lot of tough decisions for Eisenhower," Richard Nixon recalled years later. "In his later years he started to drink a lot, probably to try and forget the things he had to do in his early years. He was at my house one night and he started to cry and he said, 'All my life I've just been Ike's prat boy, doing his dirty work.'"[7]

Nixon sympathized. During the '52 campaign, when Nixon got into a tight spot over a campaign finance question, Ike was ready to drop him from the ticket. If Nixon hadn't pulled off the biggest comeback since Lazarus—a televised speech that cleared him in the public mind—Ike would have tossed him like a used Kleenex. Or like Patton.

---

* In 1947, Foster Dulles, a senior partner at the New York law firm of Sullivan & Cromwell, headed a delegation to Moscow, where Beetle was serving as ambassador. Over drinks, delegation and embassy staffers mused about what jobs their Soviet counterparts would hold if they had been born capitalists instead of communists. When they turned to Andrei Vishinsky, Stalin's notorious prosecutor for the Show Trials of the 1930s—trials leading to the executions of thousands of innocent victims—Beetle remarked, "There's no doubt about it. He would have been a senior partner at Sullivan & Cromwell."

To Ike, personal feelings didn't count when the job was on the line. Everything was measured in risks and benefits, in probabilities and costs. In public usefulness. Cards close to his vest, Ike would play out his presidency as half smiling grandfather, half cold-blooded calculator.

"Make that 75 percent cold-blooded," John later admitted.[8]

Ike projected the folksy image of a Midwestern grandfather, but after fifteen years at the center of power, living in châteaus and dining and golfing with powerful men, his tastes ran higher than corn and hominy. He enjoyed French cuisine and classical music—though after calling Stevenson an "egghead," he downplayed the foie gras and Bach, telling an assistant his favorite song was "Ragtime Cowboy Joe."

Like Winston, he could lose himself in poetry. In a lull just before D-Day, he recited Kipling's poem "If" to his headquarters family and opined that the greatest poem ever written, for meter and line, was Thomas Gray's meditation "Elegy Written in a Country Churchyard." Not exactly Pennsylvania barroom talk.

He cussed over roaring motorcades and police escorts, but secretly he enjoyed the pomp. He preferred the company of royalty and business titans; his secretary once said he liked seeing his old Abilene schoolmates "for ten minutes."

"While he had the externals of modesty," remarked Robert Murphy, Ike's advisor from Algiers, "I thought at times he was a bit spoiled."[9]

Spoiled or not, the Boss set the rules. As with Winston, sometimes those rules were arbitrary. Whistling didn't bother him—it was Winston's pet peeve—but Ike hated being interrupted while reading an important memo or working on a speech. Protocol experts who nagged him over Byzantine rules also got on his nerves. He disliked modern or abstract art, women who cried, men who were afraid of him, and politicians who stood too close to him, slapped his back, or acted physically familiar.

Then there were crows. He loathed blackbirds hanging around his Gettysburg farm. Once on his front porch, while discussing designs for a new fifty-star American flag with aides and artists, he saw a murder of crows gathering near his garden. Ike attempted his own murder with a porch shotgun, startling his secretary and flag designers as he blasted away at the squawking intruders.[10]

Most of all, he demanded diversions. From golf to painting, he channeled social, physical, and artistic passions to take his mind off what he called the "eternal pound, pound, pound" of duty. Regular diversions had kept him sane during the war. "When doing anything, golf, bridge, conversation, it's evident he has an ability to completely lose himself in whatever happens to be the thing of the moment," Slats Slater explained. "That's what enables him to get so much done. . . . To lose himself completely frees his mind of his concerns."[11]

He was a gracious winner but a bad loser. Competitive from childhood, he hated losing, whether at ping-pong, bridge, warfare, or politics. He wouldn't cheat at cards, but damned if he didn't take liberties on the golf links when adding up his score or improving his ball's lie.[12]

Structure, smiles, hierarchy. Flashes of ruthlessness, diversions, idiosyncrasies. Those were the castle walls of Ike's world.

Where did this leave Mamie? Castellana of the fort. But the demands of running the world's most famous household pushed her limits. Like Winston, she carried out many of her official duties from her bed, such as coordinating dinners or autographing photos. "Mamie is far from a strong, robust person," Slater concluded. "If she didn't spend these mornings and even days in bed she wouldn't be able to carry on for so long."[13]

Mamie's strength was her fierce devotion to her husband's health and happiness—an unheralded asset he relied on more as the presidency's weight bore down on his soul. Mamie provided Ike the emotional support and physical care he needed. Outside her self-imposed mandate, Mamie was no Eleanor Roosevelt or Clementine Churchill. She kept to her lane and stayed out of official business. As she later told an interviewer, "In all of the eight years that Ike was president, I don't think I ever went to his office over three times."[14]

THIRTY-SEVEN

Sparks Jumping Around a Fuse

When Ike set foot in that office, Job One was ending the Korean War.

Visiting the battlefront in December, he had weighed the advice of the UN commander in Korea, General Mark Clark. Clark, Ike's North African deputy and West Point schoolmate, offered a victory plan Montgomery would have loved: a decisive battle with massive reinforcements, allied troops from Formosa, overwhelming air and sea attacks. They would hit the Reds hard from all sides and drive them back behind the Yalu River.

Ike didn't buy Clark's big-budget solution. A fresh campaign above the 38th Parallel wouldn't bring peace. It would bring escalation. A bigger bonfire and more coffins.

Sitting before the National Security Council, Ike didn't talk decisive battle. He talked about what voters had elected him to do: end the war. Campaigns against an enemy with more lives to squander wasn't what they had in mind. Ike's team didn't have to make Kim sign surrender papers; they had to bring peace and get the troops home.

A big conventional push was out of the question, he told his advisors. Aside from the political and human cost, the country couldn't afford to dump billions of dollars into a furnace. National debt might buy America a battlefield victory, but the nation's grandchildren, their economy hobbled by massive federal debt, would struggle to pay for it.[1]

To Ike, fiscal responsibility was a matter of national survival, and expensive wars weren't a sustainable model. A massive tax-and-spend binge—or, worse still, unbridled deficit spending—was like a marooned man drinking salt water. The first sip demands more sips until sips become gulps. The blood thickens, organs shut down, and the man dies. As Ike had put it, "Bankruptcy and loss of freedom due to our own stupidity would, in the long run, be almost as bad as would be loss of freedom to the aggressor."[2]

What about atomic weapons? Could a single bomb, or a small volley of bombs, do the work of 200,000 soldiers?

Ike asked his advisors to consider that. Perhaps atomic weapons could be used against the communist sanctuary in the Kaesong region. Perhaps that would end the war.[3]

Militarily, the atom bomb was no magic bullet. Chinese and North Korean troops were deeply dug in, and recent tests in the Ivy series showed that entrenched troops could survive a near miss from a tactical atomic shell or bomb. And, in case anyone had forgotten, the Russians had their own bombs. Seoul lay 460 miles from Vladivostok's airfields. If Stalin decided to jump in, crowded U.S. naval and air bases offered far better targets than forests and creek ravines in North Korea.

Splitting atoms also risked splitting allies. Foster Dulles argued that Soviet propagandists had persuaded much of the world that nuclear devices belonged in a "special category" of weapons. Other nations simply wouldn't tolerate their first use.

Ike knew all this. The Bomb was one of the worst cards in the deck. But it was in the deck, and by damn, he wanted the option studied. He said he hated being handcuffed by Soviet propagandists—or European screamers, whom the U.S. taxpayer was paying billions to protect. If

America's allies raised hell about atom bombs, they could draft their own troops and send them to Korea. But the stalemate had to end.[4]

"Somehow or other, the taboo which surrounds the use of atomic weapons would have to be destroyed," he concluded. In the end, it might be cheaper to dislodge the communists with atomic weapons than a big-budget battle that would send thousands of Americans home in boxes. If an atomic strategy were executed quickly and ended the war, America's allies would go along—and the world would scratch another dangerous flash point off the map.[5]

As they debated Korea, another flash point began to spark. On Formosa, the Pacific Rim island the locals called Taiwan, Chiang Kai-shek's Nationalist forces were preparing to attack the Chinese mainland. That rattled everyone—including Winston, who knew the British colony of Hong Kong would be on the front line of any Sino-Western war.[6]

In his maiden address to Congress, Ike had announced that he would pull the U.S. Seventh Fleet out of the Formosa Strait, the hundred-mile-wide ribbon of water separating Taiwan from mainland China. The fleet's presence there had ensured that neither country would attack the other. But to Ike, the Navy risked getting caught in the crossfire between Chiang and Mao.

To many Britons, it sounded like the United States was clearing a path for Chiang's troops to invade Red China. London's *Daily Express* ran the story under the headline "IKE MOVE ALARMS BRITAIN," while the *Sunday Pictorial* led with a scathing column headlined in inch-tall letters, "THINK AGAIN, IKE."[7]

Whitehall ministers grew anxious. What, they asked, was the U.S. planning? And why didn't Ike or Dulles give Her Majesty's Government the courtesy of advance warning?[8]

Ike wrote Winston to assure him the fleet's withdrawal merely meant the U.S. Navy was out of the business of protecting China. Mao's minions were killing Americans in Korea, and America looked stupid playing peacekeeper in the Formosa Strait. "We intend nothing aggressive," he told Winston on the second of February. "We are just tired of being dupes."[9]

The outcry in London simmered down, but seeds of doubt lingered. "My dear Ike—if I may so venture," Winston replied. "I was glad to get your letter of February 2, and to feel that our private correspondence will continue apart from the regular official communications."

Winston felt America and Britain would work together harmoniously, but that meant letting London backstage sometimes. He added, "What I do hope is that where joint action affecting our common destiny is desired, you will let us know beforehand so that we can give our opinion and advice in time to have them considered. Now that you are in the saddle and can deal with long term policies, this ought to be possible."[10]

One facet of their common destiny was, of course, coexistence with Russia. As it stood, the Cold War was likely to drag on for years, and unless Winston could bring Stalin and Ike to the table, the frost would outlast his premiership. Though he had urged Ike to go slow when they met at Bernie's, Winston saw a three-power summit as the only real solution. On March 2, he told the Commons he would be "quite ready at any time to meet President Eisenhower and Marshal Stalin."[11]

Winston wasn't the only one running out of time. At week's end, on the far side of the globe, the soaring strains of the Soviet national anthem on Radio Moscow gave way to the deep, melodic voice of Russian news anchor Yuri Levitan:

On March 5 at 9:50 p.m., Josef Vissarionovich Stalin, Secretary of the Central Committee of the Communist Party and Chairman of the Council of Ministers, died after a serious illness. The heart of the collaborator and follower of the genius of Lenin's work, the wise leader and teacher of the Communist Party and of the Soviet people, stopped beating.[12]

THIRTY-EIGHT

"It Would Be a Pity If a Sudden Frost Nipped Spring in the Bud"

The Ogre was dead. A relief, thought Winston. An opportunity. As he looked east to Moscow, Winston saw the rod of tyranny, not the gospel of Marx and Engels. In the workers' paradise, no worker was safe, not even Stalin's lieutenants. Especially Stalin's lieutenants. His disciples lived in daily dread of Black Marias pulling up to their flats; the heavy knock on the door at 2 a.m.; of the night the red tsar, perhaps on a whim, perhaps drunk, would pick up a pencil and add their names to Beria's lists. The henchmen who sent millions to their deaths might have become the Ogre's next victims had the Ogre lived another month.

So when TASS broke the news of Stalin's death, Winston glimpsed a heavy stone door rolling open. He could not shake the feeling that behind the door, men who'd survived purges, war, and more purges were interested in peace, not conquest. The trick was getting them to admit it.

And getting Ike to admit it.

He called for a secretary and wrote his friend. "The path of duty is clear," he said. "We must not cast away a single hope, however slender, so long as we believe there is good faith and goodwill."

But whose goodwill? Winston had foreseen a power struggle after Stalin's demise. Which henchman would come out on top? Molotov? Malenkov? Beria? Some troika of survivors?

That, he couldn't foresee. Yet hope's petals spread even as the tyrant's corpse lay in the Soviet House of Unions.[1]

To Winston, power was a living force, at its best and most effective when wielded by great statesmen to shape the world for the better. Those rare glowworms of history were, like himself, flesh-and-blood men who nurtured dreams and sought better lives for their people. Men who, he hoped, wished to be remembered kindly by history. They could bequeath that legacy by building an era of peaceful coexistence—but the rivals must talk.

He raised the subject with Ike a week after Stalin's death. "I remember our talk at Bernie's when you told me I was welcome to meet Stalin if I thought fit, and that you intended to offer to do so," he wrote. "Now there is no more Stalin I wonder if this makes any difference."

He nudged Ike. "I have a feeling that we might both of us together or separately be called to account if no attempt was made to turn over a leaf so that a new page would be started with something more coherent on it than a series of casual and dangerous incidents at the many points of contact between the two divisions of the world."[2]

As if on cue, the new Soviet premier, Georgi Malenkov, delivered his first speech to the Supreme Soviet. In a sharp break from Stalin's invectives, he urged rapprochement. "There is not one disputed or undecided question that cannot be decided by peaceful means on the basis of mutual understanding," he told the assembly.[3]

Western papers called it a "peace offensive," and not long afterward, Winston instructed his ambassador to broach a few test issues with Moscow: the Anglo-Soviet Fisheries Agreement of 1930, exchange rates, legal cases over individual British subjects, and the like. Small stuff. "Talks on them may give us further indication of the depth of the Soviet purpose," he explained to Ike.[4]

Having knocked on the door, he waited for Ike's answer.

The first news that Stalin was ill had sent Ike's advisors scrambling. C. D. Jackson, his special assistant for international affairs, saw an opening for a propaganda campaign. Foster Dulles cautioned against poking a wounded bear. Allen Dulles theorized that Stalin's successors, desperate to project strength, might be harder to deal with than Stalin had been. Nixon pointed out that with Stalin gone, Congress might assume peace was at hand and might slash the military budget.[5]

"Might." "Maybe." "Caution." The air was thick with theories and caveats, but no one had a plan.

Ike had expected a blueprint would have been in someone's files for a long time, but he realized his men had been caught flat-footed. His frustration boiled over during a Cabinet meeting two days after Moscow's announcement, where old Mr. Bang from his war days turned up. "Ever since 1946," he thundered, "all the so-called experts have been yapping about what would happen when Stalin dies and what we as a nation should do about it. Well, he's dead. . . . We have no plan. We are not even sure what difference his death makes. It's—well, it's criminal, that's all I can say."[6*]

The bitter truth was that caution was the only path for now. Pirouetting on Stalin's grave, or urging Soviet masses to throw off their shackles, would enrage the new regime. But an olive branch, Foster Dulles argued, was also premature. Any illusion of peace would hamstring ef-

* Psychological Strategy Board records show contingency plans for Stalin's death going back to August 1952 under the code names "Cancellation" and "Midrib," though these plans didn't go anywhere. One penetrating analysis from November 1952, the apparent result of expert study and redrafting, concluded with a high level of confidence: "Stalin must die sometime."

forts to unite Western Europe behind a European Defense Community—which, in the long run, was Europe's best defense against Moscow. So Dulles squelched suggestions of a summit proposal.

Dulles had another reason for opposing top-level talks. Any dance had to be choreographed by the professionals. There were too many ways a leader could end up stepping on his partner's foot, slipping on the floor, or gliding to the wrong tempo. A conclave of foreign ministers would be needed to start the process. Preliminary agreements should be reached, momentum built, protocol details ironed out. Once everything was locked down, the leaders could come together, smile, shake hands, and sign on the dotted line as flashbulbs popped. Ike shouldn't take the risk of a busted summit when he had Dulles and a corps of diplomats to lay the groundwork. "You know, fellows, God didn't come to earth," Dulles like to say. "He sent his Son."[7]

Ike didn't need Dulles to lead a summit. He was the first president since Thomas Jefferson to personally know foreign leaders from a life lived abroad. He'd told Churchill no over bombers and Berlin. He'd haggled with de Gaulle, fixed a stop line with Stalin, and negotiated the surrenders of Italy and Germany. Press secretary Jim Hagerty remembered, "There were many times when I was in the office with Mr. Dulles and Mr. Eisenhower, when there was a question, let's say, with the British. And the president would say, 'Well, hell, Foster, don't send a cable. I'll call Winston.' And he'd pick up the phone and get Winston Churchill."[8]

Yet Ike was wary. A high-stakes summit could give the Soviets an opportunity to grandstand, nitpick, and make America regret offering the hand of friendship. Foster was right. If the Soviets wanted dialogue, they'd have to earn it. The Kremlin could pull the Red Army out of Austria or force North Korea to sign a peace treaty. It could make progress on German reunification, or cut its military expenditures. But it had to do *something* to show Ike he wasn't negotiating with the Dillinger Gang.[9]

He let Winston in on his thinking. "I tend to doubt the wisdom of a formal multilateral meeting since this would give our opponent the same kind of opportunity he has so often had to use such a meeting simultaneously to balk every reasonable effort of ourselves and to make of the whole occurrence another propaganda mill for the Soviet," he wrote the week after Stalin's death.[10]

Instead of climbing to the summit, Ike would go to ground level.

For some time, Ike had been thinking of something bigger than a summit. Something fundamental, visionary. A speech proposing a rise in the world's standard of living—a world in which no nation would spend more than a tenth of its income on weapons. A world in which nuclear weapons were limited by a UN-enforced treaty.[11]

For decades, Ike had lived with the problem of guns and butter. His old infantry regiment had put down labor unrest at a California factory that could assemble passenger planes or P-51 Mustangs. Shipyards in New England could build oil tankers or destroyers. Ford's Willow Run plant had churned out B-24 bombers, not delivery trucks or passenger cars. The garrison state consumed society's wealth; the merchant state created it.

Since Korea, Ike felt that America had tilted too far toward the garrison state. It was pulling able-bodied men from the workforce, stuffing them into uniforms, paying them with taxpayer money, and training them to guard forts and march around camps. Soldier inflation, with too many draftees chasing too few conflicts. America couldn't afford a bloated army of "bottle washers and table waiters," as he called them.[12]

The Soviet people faced a similar problem. Every Five-Year Plan the Kremlin rolled out promised a better standard of living, only to flop. Ike felt a proposal to give Russians, Americans, and everyone in between better lives might appeal to the masses. It might create a momentum for peace that promises from politicians couldn't. At the very least, it would force Soviet leaders to show the world whether they were serious about making the world safer.[13]

Standing before an Oval Office window one day, Ike heard the roar of a jet fighter cutting though the sky. Speechwriter Emmet Hughes remembered Ike's words: "As I looked at it," Ike said, "I thought to myself, 'The money from that plane, I wonder just how much good it could do in this world if instead of putting that damn thing up in the sky we could build hospitals with it, or something of that kind.'"

His thoughts tightened into focus. "It occurred to me right now that the one thing we haven't done with the Soviets right now, and that we might do with them now on this occasion of Stalin's passing and somebody else's coming onto the scene, is let them know that we would like to reduce our armaments and with them to do some good for the world with the money that we save. . . .

"Just *one* thing matters," he concluded: "What have we got to offer the world? What are we ready to do, to improve the chances of peace?"[14]

This time, Ike wouldn't give the thousandth indictment of communist oppression. He wouldn't talk about truces and treaties. He wanted a speech changing the narrative from the ground up. A talk addressing "the common man's yearning for food, shelter, and a decent standard of living."[15]

"Here is what I would like to say," he told Hughes. "The jet plane that roars over your head costs three-quarters of a million dollars. That is more money than a man earning ten thousand dollars a year is going to make in his lifetime. What world can afford this sort of thing for long?"[16]

Advisors pushed back, but his mind was made up. When C. D. Jackson suggested that Kremlin leaders weren't going to be moved by bourgeois talk of schools and hospitals, Ike's face took on that pink tinge that signaled Mr. Bang might be dropping in for a visit.

"Dammit," he snapped, "I remember in that one four-hour session

I had with Stalin, damn near all he talked about was the essential things his people needed—homes and food and technical help. When he talked about seven people to a room in Moscow living quarters, he seemed to me just as anxious as you or I would be in looking at an American slum problem. Hell, these boys *have* to think in material terms. It's all they believe in."[17]

Hughes cautioned Ike about a recent hard-line statement from Dulles threatening Chinese communists. A peace-themed speech from Ike would undercut Dulles's tough talk. It would make the administration look like it hadn't made up its mind about the Reds.[18]

His cheeks reddening, Ike shot back, "If these very sophisticated gentlemen in the State Department, or Dulles and all his advisors, really don't mean they can talk peace seriously, then I'm in the wrong pew. If it's war we should be talking about—I know the people to discuss this with, and they're not in the State Department!"[19]

After reading an early draft of Ike's speech, Winston, contrary to his usual boldness, urged postponement. He had second thoughts about putting the new regime on the defensive too soon. Moscow had been sending encouraging signals. It was softening its rhetoric and hinting at resolving the German question. Even Lavrenti Beria, Stalin's Himmler, was posing as a people's liberator, rolling back some of the purges he personally engineered.

Perhaps the Cold War was thawing. Perhaps Ike should see which way the winds were blowing first. "The apparent change of Soviet mood is so new and so indefinite and its causes so obscure that there could not be much risk in letting things develop," Winston advised.[20]

Ike was tempted to hold fire. But he felt the weight of the moment. The death of the red tsar was a watershed event, and he wanted to meet the event with the right message.[21]

He assured Winston he wouldn't be too strident in his demands for advance concessions on Korea or Austria. "I have a considerable sympathy with your point that we must be careful to avoid anything that would make the Russians retreat into their shell, if they are, in fact, sincere in extending certain feelers for peace," he wrote. "I shall consequently soften the parts concerning Korea, and change certain other expressions so that there can be no misinterpretation of our position to be fully and completely receptive to any peace proposals, while at the same time never letting down our guard."[22]

Winston worried that Ike's insistence on "never letting down our guard" would overshadow his receptiveness to peace. He pressed his point to Ike in a follow-up letter:

> It would be a pity if a sudden frost nipped spring in the bud, or if this could be alleged, even if there was no real spring. I do not attempt to predict what the Soviet change of attitude and policy, and it seems to me of mood, means. It might mean an awful lot. Would it not be well to combine the re-assertions of your and our inflexible resolves with some balancing expression of hope and that we have entered a new era. A new hope has, I feel, been created in the unhappy, bewildered world. It ought to be possible to proclaim our unflinching determination to resist Communist tyranny and aggression and at the same time, though separately, to declare how glad we should be if we found there was a real change of heart and not let it be said that we had closed the door upon it.[23]

Ike reassured Winston his speech wouldn't be provocative. "I agree with the tenor of your comments and shall certainly strive to make my talk one that will not freeze the tender buds of sprouting decency, if indeed they are really coming out," he wrote.[24]

To Winston, that wasn't a ringing endorsement. Ike was striking out on his own, leading the world down a path that might crush the fragile sprouts underfoot.

But it was the best he could get from his friend. For now, at least. He would keep trying.

"Members of the American Society of Newspaper Editors, and guests, I have the honor of presenting to you the President of the United States."

The Presidential Ballroom of the Statler Hotel awoke with applause as eyes turned to the lectern.

Hours before his speech, Ike had felt a stabbing pain in his abdomen. As he flew from Augusta to Washington aboard *Columbine II*, he lay curled up in the big plane's bunk, bathed in sweat. Suffering from another bout of gastroenteritis, he was still damp when the *Atlanta Journal*'s editor introduced him. He walked stiffly to the podium, beads welling on his forehead.[25]

Unsteadily, he began. His voice was stilted. He gripped the podium so tightly his knuckles turned white. As he went through the large-font text, he dropped sentences from his script, then whole paragraphs. Letters danced before his eyes, and he had no recollection of what he said toward the end of his speech.[26]

But he forced just enough words past his lips to tell the world what he hoped for.

"Every gun that is made, every warship launched, every rocket fired signifies, in the final sense, a theft from those who hunger and are not fed, those who are cold and not clothed," he declared.

> The cost of one modern heavy bomber is this: A modern brick school in more than 30 cities. It is two electric power plants, each serving a town of 60,000 population. . . . We pay for a single fighter plane with a half million bushels of wheat. We pay for a single destroyer with new homes that could have housed more than 8,000 people. . . . This is not a way of life at all, in any true sense. Under the cloud of threatening war, it is humanity hanging from a cross of iron.

He proposed talks aimed at reducing global armaments, agreed limits on raw materials for military use, international control of atomic energy, numerical limits on nuclear weapons, and a UN mechanism to enforce this new approach. The resulting savings would benefit civilians in all walks of life. "The monuments of this new kind of war would be these: Roads and schools, hospitals and homes, food and health."

To start down this path, he said, the Soviet leaders would have to show their peaceful intentions through concrete action—a treaty to guarantee Austrian independence or pressure on North Korea and China to end their war. If the Kremlin would demonstrate its commitment to easing tensions, the West would work with Russia as partners in peace.[27]

As applause filled the ballroom, Ike stepped from the lectern and left, clammy and glistening. He had willed himself through the pain and said what he had to say.

Out of sight, he slumped onto a sofa, doubled over, eyelids shut, until the pain passed.[28]

THIRTY-NINE

Winston Strikes Back

"I SHOULD LIKE TO KNOW WHAT YOU THINK should be the next step," Winston wrote six days later. "I'm sure there will, however, be a strong movement here for a meeting between the Heads of States and Governments. How do you stand about this?"

Ike's speech had opened the door to a thaw, but Winston wanted a flame, not a thaw. An East-West summit, his diplomatic Holy Grail, glistened on the horizon, and only Ike could help him reach it. Like the Churchill of 1944 nagging Roosevelt to come to Yalta, the Churchill of 1953 begged Ike to engage—somewhere, anywhere.

Months earlier, at Baruch's Manhattan apartment, Ike had floated Stockholm as a possible venue. Winston reminded Ike and pressed him to act. If he wouldn't, Winston might have to go at it alone. Politely but firmly, he warned, "If nothing can be arranged, I shall have to seriously consider a personal contact. You told me in New York you would have no objection to this. I should be grateful if you would let me know how these things are shaping in your mind."[1]

To Ike, the rendezvous at Bernie's seemed so long ago. "The situation has changed considerably since we talked in New York and I believe we should watch developments for a while longer," he wrote Winston. "We have so far seen no concrete Soviet actions which would indicate their willingness to perform in connection with larger issues. In the circumstances we would risk raising hopes of progress toward an accommodation which would be unjustified."

Ike had looked for the signs, but he and Winston saw the world differently. Churchill saw governments as extensions of men—their courage, their cowardice, their wisdom, follies, and perfidy. Ike saw governments as machines with human parts. When a part wore out, it was replaced and the engine chugged away as before—whether the replacement part was an army private or a head of state.

Over a quarter century, Stalin had built a machine, created in his image, after his likeness. In the early years following Lenin's death, the machine had been Stalin's to shape. But over thousands of executions, *ukazes*, show trials, and wars, the apparatus had taken on a life of its own. Stalin's acolytes inherited the machine, and as they pulled its levers, each Politburo member would feel the eyes of the others on his back. To survive, each man must show he was as strong and resolute, as devoted to the Communist Party as the mighty Stalin had been. So Ike feared any summit proposal would be answered with high-handed conditions unacceptable to the West. Propaganda campaigns, not serious efforts at peace.

Ike still held one trump card: time. He could retreat to his easel or golf greens and let the Kremlin stew as pressure for peaceful coexistence mounted. As Winston had suggested at Bernie's, no need to move quickly. So he doused Winston's summit flame.

He knew he couldn't order Winston to stay put in London. The old lion probably wouldn't fly to Moscow on impulse—probably. But Ike couldn't be sure. He was worried enough to write Winston, "If you should find it necessary for some special and local reason to seek a personal contact, we would hope for as much advance notice as you could possibly give us."[2]

Just as Ike feared, Soviet skepticism emerged in the days following his "Chance for Peace" speech. *Pravda* lauded Ike's general desire for peace, but complained his suggestions were too general, his olive branch too conditional. *Izvestia* vilified Dulles over a follow-up speech emphasizing that Ike's words of peace would be backed by growing strength. And while Molotov announced that the Soviets were willing to join a five-power summit, he remained silent on Austria, Germany, Korea, or any of Ike's prerequisites.[3]

As the cities on the Potomac and Moskva drifted farther apart, Winston's summit dream floated aimlessly in the gulf that lay between. But dreams, like the man himself, had a way of persisting.

Checked but not checkmated, Winston wouldn't let the game end there. If Ike didn't lead, he would. A month after Ike's speech, he sent Ike a draft message to Molotov suggesting he could fly to Moscow for an informal meeting with Malenkov. Nothing binding, just a friendly exchange between Churchill and Malenkov over vodka, caviar, and state secrets.

"I have a feeling that it might be helpful if our intercourse proceeded with the help of friendly acquaintance and goodwill instead of impersonal diplomacy and propaganda," Winston told Ike. "I do not see how this could make things worse."[4]

Ike felt no strong objections as he read the letter, and he drafted a reply for Dulles to review. In his draft, he wrote, "Foster and I foresee no special harm to our country's interests though your carrying out the intention suggested in your cable."[5]

Dulles did foresee special harm. No matter what disclaimers Winston might offer, leaders from Moscow to Madrid would see western leaders kowtowing to Moscow, and everyone would think Winston was going with Ike's blessing. The alternative impression would be worse: that Britain, swept away by rapprochement, was breaking with America.

After marking up Ike's draft, Dulles sent it back to Ike. It went to London with a very different tone than the one Ike drafted.

"Foster and I have considered it deeply since you sought my views and I must say we advise against it," the message began. "You will pardon me, I know, if I express a bit of astonishment that you think it appropriate to recommend Moscow to Molotov as a suitable meeting place. Uncle Joe used to plead ill health as an excuse for refusing to leave territory under the Russian flag or controlled by the Kremlin. That excuse no longer applies and while I do not for a minute suggest that progress toward peace should be balked by mere matters of protocol, I do have a suspicion that anything the Kremlin could misinterpret as weakness or over-eagerness on our part would militate against success in negotiation."[6]

Red-faced, Winston set down the letter with a growl. It was the bite of a protégé daring to lecture his mentor.

Peace was too important a prize to lose to Ike, Malenkov, or anyone else. The one man who had stood between Hitler and conquest in 1940 was now the one man who could persuade enemies to build an era of peaceful coexistence. Winston would not give way on this.

He summoned a secretary and dictated an equally determined reply. "According to my experience of these people in the War we should gain more good will on the spot by going as guests of the Soviets than we should lose by appearing to court them," he wrote. "I am very anxious to know these men and talk to them as I think I can frankly and on the dead level. . . . I find it difficult to believe that we shall gain anything by an attitude of pure negation and your message to me certainly does not show much hope."[7]

Winston blamed the president's men—especially Dulles, who wanted everything worked out before letting Ike off the leash. Whenever Winston beckoned down a path to peace, Dulles, as a matter of

Newtonian physics, pulled Ike in an equal and opposite direction. Ike was, Churchill thought, "a nice man, but a fool" for letting men like Dulles erect barricades on the summit road.[8]

What would Winston do? For the moment, no one could rein him in at home, for the foreign secretary was laid up on the other side of the ocean. Feverish and jaundiced since the previous summer, Anthony Eden had gone under a London surgeon's knife for what should have been a routine gallbladder removal. But his doctor had botched the operation, requiring a second surgery to repair the damage. When Eden's condition didn't improve, he flew to Boston for a third operation. His recovery kept him bedridden for three months.

While Eden was lying in a hospital bed, Winston—recently knighted as "Sir Winston"—took over the job of foreign minister, adding to his broader responsibilities as head of Her Majesty's Government. The weight of the free world rested on his broad shoulders. Again.[9]

Winston's frustration with America—and with Ike—bubbled to the surface as he spoke to the House of Commons on May 11. In a much-anticipated response to Ike's "Chance for Peace" speech, Winston surveyed the world situation. He laid some of the blame for the Cold War on hot war decisions made by the American leadership—meaning one general in particular.

"If our advice had been taken by the United States after the armistice with Germany, the Western allies would not have withdrawn from the front line which their armies had reached to the agreed occupation lines unless and until agreement had been reached with Soviet Russia on the many points of difference about the occupation of enemy territories," he asserted. "Our view was not accepted, and a wide area of Germany was handed over to Soviet occupation."

American naivete had emboldened Stalin, setting the stage for eight years of crisis and tragedy. Now, Churchill said, Stalin's death had handed East and West a golden opportunity to settle their sharpest disagreements. A summit meeting would be the first step toward a world free of nuclear terror. It only needed someone to make the first move.

"It would, I think, be a mistake to assume that nothing can be settled with Soviet Russia unless or until everything is settled," Winston emoted. "It would be a mistake to try to map things out too much in detail and expect that grave, fundamental issues which divide the Communist and non-Communist parts of the world could be settled at a stroke by a single comprehensive agreement. Piecemeal solutions of individual problems should not be disdained or improvidently put aside."

He called for statecraft, not stagecraft. "I believe that a conference on the highest level should take place between the leading Powers without delay," he said in his peroration. "If there is not at the summit of the nations the will to win the greatest prize and the greatest honour ever offered to mankind, doom-laden responsibility will fall upon those who now possess the power to decide. At the worst, the participants in the meeting would have established more intimate contacts. At the best, we might have a generation of peace."[10]

"Churchill did not disappoint his listeners," Ambassador Aldrich cabled Dulles after the speech. "In delivery, tone, and content, it was, perhaps, Churchill's greatest performance since the war, and he touched whole range of emotions of British people."

London's *Times* hailed the address as "magnificent in its broad survey and penetrating in its analysis." The Labour-leaning *Daily Herald* gave its qualified approval, and even the communist *Daily Worker* called it the "most pacific and hopeful speech delivered by a British prime minister in recent years." Three-quarters of Britain's public favored a top-level meeting of East and West, and as the cry rose, American papers began to take up the call.

Though Ike had sent Winston a draft of his "Chance for Peace" speech before delivering it, Winston hadn't reciprocated. He knew what Ike and Dulles would say when he called for a parlay with Malenkov, and this time he didn't need or want their advice.

"For the first time in a major address on foreign affairs, Churchill did not mention [the] Anglo-American alliance or the necessity [of] solidarity with United States," observed Aldrich. "While the speech was characteristic of the Churchillian temperament, it also reflects serious British misgivings about the present state of Anglo-American relations."[11]

Winston was forcing Ike's hand.

His call swept the American public, too. A Gallup poll showed 78 percent of Americans supported a summit meeting, mirroring the British reaction. Unwilling to be backed into a Yalta, or worse, Ike tapped the brakes at his next press conference. "I have no objection whatsoever to Sir Winston's proposal," he told reporters. "But I would like, before I would commit this government to participation, something that would be an earnest of good faith all around." Until the Kremlin gave tangible proof of its desire for peace, he wouldn't budge.[12]

Ike's refusal laid bare a rift. "We and the Americans are now in total disagreement," Harold Macmillan told his diary. "The President is very naïve and inexperienced; Dulles is ignorant and stupid; some of the old Republicans are hopelessly reactionary—but we have got to get along with them. Malenkov has made a breach in the Anglo-American front such as Stalin never succeeded in doing."[13]

America held the hydrogen bomb and many of the world's purse strings, but Britain was still formidable. It fielded troops and boasted bases, intelligence assets, and diplomatic connections all around the world. Britain had exploded its own atomic bomb, punching its ticket to the

Atomic Club and, Winston hoped, giving it some influence over American strategy. A young, energetic monarch sat on the throne—Queen Elizabeth II had succeeded her late father—and the Queen's formal coronation that year showcased the kingdom's grandeur and might.

Winston was winning over public opinion on both sides of the Atlantic, marshaling masses for peace the way he had once rallied them to war. He was forcing Ike to the table. If he could get Ike alone in a room, any room, he knew he could close the deal.

FORTY

Borrowed Time

IKE HAD NEARLY KILLED THE SUMMIT, but Winston's speech started its heart beating again. People were talking. The wind was shifting. Eisenhower, Churchill, and Malenkov: The idea didn't seem so preposterous. But if it were going to happen, Winston would need to talk to Ike directly. Persuade him, face to face, jaw to jaw.

An opportunity arose in mid-May, when French Prime Minister René Mayer suggested he meet with Eisenhower and Churchill. Ike rang up Winston on the transatlantic phone line, and the two men discussed a conclave with Mayer—the would-be fourth in any "Big Four" summit—during the second half of June.[1*]

On their call, Ike spent most of his time "shouting at the top of his lungs [on] account of Churchill's deafness and suggesting Churchill put somebody else on, which Sir Winston would not do," remembered C. D. Jackson. Ike suggested a three-way meeting on Presque Isle, Maine, but Winston said he could not hear Ike over the telephone line. Oblivious to Maine, he launched into a pitch for a meeting on British-controlled Bermuda.

* In 1953, the fourth power was France, as the U.S. would not formally recognize the People's Republic of China until 1979.

A frustrated Ike gave in. Winston could hear that part. After the call, Ike groused to his security assistant Robert Cutler, "Winston pleads increasing deafness when you want to talk about something he's opposed to, but he's sharp as a tack when he mentions something which he likes."[2]

To Ike, the Bermuda meeting was a goodwill gesture between America and two of its closest friends. It would also mend fences with gaping holes, for Ike had told the NSC that relations with Britain had grown worse in the past few weeks than at any time since the end of the war.[3]

But he still wouldn't commit to seeing Malenkov. As he wrote Winston, "I have conveyed to Mayer our understanding, that this proposed meeting is not in any way tied to Four Power talks with the Soviet Union or to be considered as preliminary thereto." He suggested that he, Mayer, and Winston bring their wives along. The presence of Mamie, Clemmie, and Denise Mayer would make the conclave look more like a social event among colleagues rather than a policy-driven parlay.[4]

For Winston, it wasn't promising. He hoped for a private tête-à-tête with Ike, and somehow found himself in an awkward ménage à three. But it was a start, something he could build on.

"Clemmie is looking forward greatly to coming," he wrote back, exaggerating more than a little. "My present idea is that we should all three stay in the Mid-Ocean Golf Club." He added, "I do not (repeat not) play golf any more, so I shall bring my paint-box."[5]

Given Ike's widely known addiction to golf, press secretary Jim Hagerty counseled Ike to meet somewhere else: "No golf club and no battleship," he advised. Ike told Winston while a round or two was "personally appealing," since they were world leaders discussing serious issues, staying at a hotel rather than a golf club might play better in American papers.[6]

Winston assured him the location would be all right. It wasn't really called a golf club, anyway. "The official name is Mid-Ocean Club," he explained. "I put 'Golf' in it to attract you."[7]

The French threw a wrench into the meeting when their government du jour collapsed in June. Winston saw the Parisian chaos as a golden opportunity to seclude himself with Ike, and suggested the two go ahead with the meeting.

Ike said he wanted to give the new French government a little time to get on its feet. He was all right with rescheduling. Winston, unwilling to be deflected, said that keeping the rendezvous date would encourage Paris to get its government in order *tout de suite.* "These recurring delays are very painful to me and very bad for world affairs," he wrote. "You and I have quite a lot of things which concern us both on which our public agreement would be helpful all round."[8]

As he pushed for a meeting in Bermuda, Winston's body had other plans. During a state dinner for the Italian prime minister, Winston held his audience captive with a delightful speech about Caesar, his legions, and Winston's amity for the Italian people. After regaling his companions, the meal wound down and guests began getting up.

After rising to join the men in the drawing room, Winston took a few steps, then slumped into a chair. He managed to half stand, but his legs refused. He sank back down.

His son-in-law Christopher Soames calmly crossed the room to see Winston as Winston's daughter Mary, from a distance, watched with alarm.

One side of Winston's mouth sagged. His speech slurred. He sounded like a tired, old drunk, except he wasn't tired or drunk.

In a stage voice, Christopher told Mary that Winston was tuckered out.

"We must get him to bed, then," she said, nodding agreeably.

Lowering his voice when she came close, Christopher added, "We must get the waiters away first; he can't walk."

A "spasm of the small artery," Lord Moran called it. Doctorspeak for a stroke. That Winston could shuffle with a limp the next day—that he had any feeling in his left leg—was nothing short of a miracle.[9]

The Queen's first minister wasn't satisfied with limping. Certain he could run the British Empire through force of will, he refused to let Moran talk him out of governing. The next day he presided over the Cabinet meeting. He looked subdued and pale, but from his usual spot, he chaired a policy meeting addressing Korea, colonial welfare, an uprising in East Berlin, army pay, and a new commercial television channel. Sometimes nodding or nonchalantly waving when words failed him, he managed to pull off the illusion of a man in command.

Cabinet members were fooled. His doctors were not. They saw a man breaking down. Question Hour was out of the question—and a formal meeting with Ike utterly impossible.

For a while, the man who had bent FDR to his will, stared down Hitler, and held his own with Stalin thought he could outfox his own body. But as his condition deteriorated, his symptoms became undeniable. Paralysis worsened, disabling his left leg and arm, and his inner circle kept his condition secret from all but the Queen and a few trusted lieutenants. Britain's leader, they said, was suffering from "overstrain," but the truth was darker: The British Empire was rudderless.[10]

"The shock of seeing a great oak tree felled is as close as I can get to describing what I felt," Winston's daughter Sarah wrote. Recovering at Chartwell, Winston talked as if life's promises were over.

"I feel, Charles, I could do something that no one else could do. I was at the peak of my opportunities, exchanging friendly messages with Malenkov," he told Moran. "I have stretched out a hand to grasp the paw of the Russian bear. Great things seemed within my grasp. Not perhaps world peace, but world easement. I feel I could have changed the bias of the world. America is very powerful, but very clumsy. . . . I could have made her more sensible."[11]

He had so much more to say, so much to do. He refused to remain bedridden. He would fight his infirmity in the bedroom. He would fight it at the conference table. He would fight it at his writing desk. He would never surrender.[12]

But neither could he see Ike. Not now.

He called for a secretary. He had some explaining to do.

"You will see from the attached medical report the reasons why I cannot come to Bermuda. I am as bad as the French," he wrote.[13]

Ike sent back an immediate reply. "I am deeply distressed to learn that your physicians have advised you to lighten your duties at this time," he said. "I look upon this only as a temporary deferment of our meeting," he assured Winston, adding, "Your health is of great concern to all the world and you must, therefore, bow to the advice of your physicians."[14]

As he recovered, Winston followed up with a longer explanation.

"My dear Ike," he wrote, "I am so sorry to be the cause of upsetting so many plans. I had a sudden stroke which as it developed completely paralysed my left side and affected my speech. I therefore had no choice as I could not walk with you along the Guard of Honour of the Welch Regiment complete with their beautiful white goat, whose salute you would I am sure have acknowledged."

He took pains to point out that he overcame a major stroke before. "Four years ago, in 1949, I had another similar attack," he wrote. "I kept this secret and have managed to work through two General Elections and a lot of other business since then. I am not without hope of pursuing my theme a little longer."[15]

Through a summer of convalescence, Winston kept a light schedule. Obeying his doctors, he let them take his temperature, he swallowed their pills, he answered their questions, he complained to Moran. He relaxed over pages of *Jane Eyre*, *Phineas Finn*, and *Candide*. He ate and he rested.[16]

The man with the constitution of a Spanish bull would not stay down long, however. His mental energy pushed its way to the surface as he began seeing a small circle of visitors privy to his condition. "My first impressions were of astonishment that a man who had suffered such a calamity could show such gaiety and courage," Harold Macmillan wrote after Winston's second week of recovery. "During dinner, and until he went to bed, just after 11 p.m., his talk seemed much the same as usual." His discourses ranged from death's "velvet sleep" to the Conservative Party's future, to Buddhism and Christianity, to Pol Roger champagne, to "a wine, a woman and a horse; and many other topics."[17]

Winston also busied himself finishing his sixth volume of war memoirs. Mindful of American sensitivities, he wrote Ike that in editing *Triumph and Tragedy*, he had "taken great pains to ensure that it contains nothing which might imply that there was in those days any controversy or lack of confidence between us."[18]

Colleagues in the Foreign Office, and old curmudgeons like Brooke, felt Winston was bending too far backward to edit his memoirs—a monument of history—to suit his American friends. Winston waved them off. Because he was the prime minister, his friendships were, in a sense, the Crown's property. "If I am going to die," he told Moran, "I can say what I like and take the view that I believe to be right. But if I live and am still Prime Minister, then I must not say things which will anger Ike."[19]

Of course, his private thoughts were a different story. When Field Marshal Montgomery popped in for a visit, he and Winston mulled over five great mistakes the Americans had made that prolonged the war. Two of them—the broad front and the failure to take Berlin, Prague, and Vienna—fell squarely on Ike's shoulders. Winston would wallpaper over his disagreements with Ike, but he would never forget them.[20]

At 78, Winston had outgrown the young firebrand who had tried to strangle Bolshevism in its cradle. Nuclear weapons had torn up that playbook. War was no longer a continuation of politics; it was a question of human survival. Winston felt he alone had the credibility on both sides of the Iron Curtain to broker an understanding that would pull humanity from the cliff. He intended to cash in that goodwill. But he needed to know if the Russians would go with him.[21]

Winston clicked the safe's dial, straining to hear the tumblers drop. Hope flickered on July 10, when *Pravda* announced that Lavrenti Beria, one of four men poised to succeed Stalin, had been dismissed for "anti-Party and anti-State activities." Beria, the head of Stalin's secret police for much of the Great Terror, had personally tortured prisoners and signed death warrants for hundreds of thousands of men and women. Children, too, for the Georgian was a predator whose bodyguards regularly abducted teenage girls—often gymnasts or ballerinas, sometimes just the young and attractive he noticed on a Moscow street. Those unfortunates he had raped, terrorized into silence, and occasionally had murdered. Now another ogre was gone.[22*]

Winston spoke wistfully to his physician, Lord Moran, about the prospect of a summit that summer. How he would have handled the Russians.

"I would have met them more than halfway," he said. "We would have promised them that no more atomic bombs would be made, no

* Beria would die on his knees that December, begging for his life until a bullet through his head silenced him.

more research into their manufacture. Those already made would be locked away. They would have had at their disposal much of the money now spent on armaments to provide better conditions for the Russian people."[23]

He doubted Ike was alive to the rumblings beneath Red Square. "The Americans are behaving like fools. Dulles particularly," he fumed in a draft message to Lord Salisbury. "They want to make enemies of Russia and to stir up her satellite states. That can only lead to war."[24]

Winston pushed, but Ike didn't budge—and Winston grew more sullen the longer Ike and his men held out. "I am disappointed with events in America," he told Moran. "They've bitched things up."[25]

To Winston, the world turned on an axis of human interplay. His epic speeches, the Atlantic Conference, the Tehran and Yalta summits, even his "naughty document" had done more to move the world than ten thousand memos from ten thousand diplomats. As Stalin had pointed out in Tehran, the Big Three leaders didn't need their ministers telling them what to do. A meeting among Ike, Malenkov, and Winston might move the world past its dark age of nuclear terror before it was too late.[26]

From his bed, he made another feeble push. They could go informal, jaw to jaw, no strict agenda. "I thought that you and I might have formed our own impression of Malenkov, who had never seen anybody outside Russia," he told Ike. "I am very sorry I was not able to make this appeal to you personally as I had hoped."[27]

The next day Winston's doctor found his patient seething to Clemmie and Christopher Soames over the American State Department's influence. "Apparently Ike is like a king; he can't deal with detail," Winston groused to Moran. "There was no nonsense of that sort about Franklin Roosevelt." He added, "Of course, Dulles is at the bottom of this."[28]

He could only shake his head. The inmates were running the

asylum, and the most dangerous of them was the secretary of state. "Dulles lied when he said Ike did not want to do detail," Winston told Moran. "When I saw him six months ago it was Ike himself who suggested a conference at Stockholm."

"Is Ike really fitted for his present job?" asked Moran.

"Well, in the war he had a very genuine gift for friendship and for keeping the peace," said Winston, echoing Monty and Brooke. "But I decided in the States six months ago that he was really a brigadier."[29]

Not long afterward, he wondered whether the brigadier's election had been a good thing for the world.

"Perhaps, after all," he said, "we should have been better off with Stevenson and the Democrats."[30]

In late July, Jock Colville told his diary his master was "still wrapped up with the possibility of bringing something off with the Russians and with the idea of meeting Malenkov face to face. Very disappointed in Eisenhower, whom he thinks both weak and stupid. Bitterly regrets that the Democrats were not returned at the last Presidential Election."[31]

Clementine explained her husband's predicament to Lord Moran: "He is talking now of going to America to see Ike. But Ike does not want to see him; he was delighted when Bermuda was scratched," she said. "If Winston was at his best, then he might be able to fix up something with the President in the course of the next two years, but as it is, Ike is waiting to see which way the cat jumps, and whether Winston will retire. Moreover, Charles, Ike does not like his countrymen saying that the Prime Minister of Britain is making up the President's mind."

What could he do? "K.B.O.," he had once said. Through deafness, stroke, and the fragility of old age, Winston pushed on the only way he knew. Moran, who had spent the afternoon with him at Chequers, told his diary,

He leant towards me. "You realize, Charles, I'm playing a big hand—the easement of the world, perhaps peace over the world. . . . If it came off, and there was disarmament," he lisped in his excitement, "production might be doubled and we might be able to give to the working man what he has never had—leisure. A four-day week, and then three days' run. I had my teeth in it. I have become so valuable that they would allow me to do it my own way."

As he spoke the words, tears began to run down his cheeks. For several moments, the weeping prophet found himself speechless.[32]

To Ike, summits weren't the catchall solutions Winston imagined. At home, they could be political cyanide. "Yalta" had become the vilest insult that could be hurled at an American statesman, the way "Munich" was to British politicians. With a vocal Republican right wing championed by Red-hunting blowhards like Wisconsin's Senator Joe McCarthy, Ike couldn't afford to look as if he had been duped into another Yalta.

And what if the leaders climbed the mountain only to find they couldn't reach an agreement? A presidential overseas trip was a traveling circus—250 to 300 people, including White House staff, Secret Service, Signal Corps, and the press, all packed off for a show. High profile meant high hopes, even if diplomacy with Molotov was like negotiating with an armored car. If nothing could be settled, each side would blame the other. Tensions would rise, and a busted summit might leave everyone worse off than if they'd stayed home.[33]

Ike also had to consider how a summit would impact a homegrown European defense force. Momentum for a European Defense Community army—or, failing that, for a stronger NATO—would lose steam if a summit's mirage gave cash-strapped parliaments an excuse to pinch francs and lira. In June, for example, the Luxembourg prime minister had told General Matthew Ridgway, "Churchill's recently extended hand of friendship to the Soviets constitutes a serious weakening influence" on a united EDC army.[34]

Finally, the man at the top wasn't always the best one to negotiate complex agreements. The State Department had professionals for that. As Ike told his Cabinet, "This idea of the President of the United States going personally abroad to negotiate—it's just damn stupid. Every time a President has been abroad to get into the details of these things, he's lost his shirt."[35]

Ike liked his shirt, so he tried to explain his hesitation to Winston. "I have a feeling that it is dangerous to talk generalities to the Russians unless and until their proposals for Germany and Austria show that we can depend on them," he wrote. "I do not like talking informally with those who only wish to entrap and embarrass us. I would prefer, at any rate in the first instance, to leave the initial approach to the Foreign Ministers."[36]

As with the campaign against Germany, the western allies needed to be methodical, not extemporaneous. A diplomatic variation of his old broad front approach. He hadn't let Monty rush to Berlin, and he wouldn't let Winston gallop off to the peace table. Ike would get there when the time was right, and not a minute sooner.

Fighting Hitler, defeating the Nazis—it wasn't enough. Winston wanted to leave a legacy of peace. He wanted the old libels of warmongering blotted out. He wanted the world to see him as something more than a vampire killer.

He came close. In October 1953, his private secretary, Anthony Montague Browne, gave him some electrifying news: Winston had been awarded the Nobel Prize.

The Nobel Peace Prize was the honor he most craved—the highest certification of his work in the cause of a better world. He'd been nominated twice before, but each time he had lost to an American.

"When he heard he'd got the Nobel Prize he was thrilled," wrote Montague Browne.

Then he told Winston the category he had won for.

"When he heard it was for literature his face fell." That year's Peace Prize went to another American, General George Marshall, for championing the European Recovery Plan. The Marshall Plan, they called it.[37]

The prize was real, but the category was wrong. The Nobel Prize for Literature was a consolation prize that offered little consolation. Winston was an actor who had been typecast as an action hero and would never get a different role, no matter how many times he auditioned.

But he sensed the mood shifting, felt the pulse of peace quickening. The people were ready to step back from the brink. Perhaps the Russian leaders were, too. Eventually Ike would be, too.

Russia was the great challenge Winston and Ike faced, but not the only one. That turbulent year, the two men had other business to take care of. Quiet work. The kind no one talked about.

FORTY-ONE

The Peacock Throne

As the Cold War pulled Ike and Winston apart over a summit, it brought them together in Iran.

In Britain's 1951 election campaign, Winston had blasted Labour's flaccid response to Middle Eastern troublemakers. Topping the list was Mohammad Mosaddeq, Iran's first democratically elected prime minister. Mosaddeq had nationalized the Anglo-Iranian Oil Company, and since then, he had amassed near-dictatorial powers.[1]

To Britain, nationalization of the AIOC had been a kick in the bollocks. For over forty years, the company had been one of the Empire's crown jewels. It had kept British factories and the Royal Navy awash in cheap and abundant oil, and its colossal refinery at Abadan represented Britain's single-largest overseas investment. When Mosaddeq seized the refinery, London papers and MPs frothed over what they called outright theft. Attlee's government slapped a boycott on Iranian oil, but Mosaddeq refused to compromise.

As the din grew at home, Britain's Secret Intelligence Service, MI6, began laying groundwork for Operation Boot, a black bag scheme to send Mosaddeq packing. In late November 1952, Anthony Eden's Foreign Office proposed an Anglo-American effort to oust the prime minister. In the shadows, MI6 began lobbying Allen Dulles for help.

Knowing the American attitude toward colonialism, they baited their request as an effort to keep communism out of the Middle East. The Americans bit.

By the spring of '53, Mosaddeq seemed vulnerable. His National Front coalition, united chiefly by opposition to the British, began to fracture. Clerics and bazaar merchants who had backed him split off, leaving Tudeh Party communists as his largest support bloc. The Majlis, Iran's parliament, careened into deadlock, and shouting matches and fistfights broke out in its chambers. Threatened with a no-confidence vote, Mosaddeq dissolved parliament. He then rigged a referendum on his government that alienated Iranian liberals as well as religious and secular conservatives.[2]

By August 1953, Mosaddeq was peering over a ledge. All he needed was a push.

Not all communists arrive in tanks. Some seep in quietly, through universities and radio stations, in cadre cells and protest marches. They wave banners demanding "Land Reform" or "Workers' Rights." And in the early 1950s, those Soviet calling cards began turning up in countries like Guatemala, Egypt, and French Indochina. And Iran.

At an NSC meeting in March 1953, Allen Dulles described the threat: Mosaddeq's coalition was in slow-motion collapse. If he were assassinated or forced out, Iranian communists would rush into the power vacuum. If Iran fell to the Reds, communism would spread to other Mid-East nations, putting 60 percent of the world's oil reserves in the communist camp.

Ike wasn't about to let that happen.

The stakes were high, but for the moment, Ike wasn't sure what to do. The almighty dollar didn't promise results, for Ike probably couldn't buy off Mosaddeq with a fat foreign assistance loan. Even if he could, if the winds shifted in downtown Tehran, any deal with Mosaddeq wouldn't be worth the parchment it was printed on. America could try buying out Britain's AIOC claims and put a friendly face on the dispute, but Washington would simply be stepping into London's mud-splattered shoes. That led nowhere.

One thing was certain: He wouldn't send in troops. Iran and the USSR shared a thousand-mile border, and they had a treaty of friendship dating back to 1921. The Politburo wouldn't sit quietly while the 82nd Airborne dropped into Tehran; the Red Army would move into northern Iran, risking World War III.

Ike muttered that he wished he could read about pro-American mobs rioting, waving American flags instead of the hammer and sickle. C. D. Jackson, Ike's chief propagandist, jumped on the point; if the president wanted mobs, American agents could get them.[3]

Hired agitators raised the question of a covert option. Black bag jobs were cheaper than armed confrontation or economic incentives and—if done right—were more effective than bent-knee diplomatic pleading. Quick, deniable, and cheap.

But risky.

When the meeting ended, Ike let that subject hang in the air.

Ike's America had built its case on democratic ideals, and he was reluctant to yank the rug from under a democratic government. In June he rejected Winston's suggestion to topple South Korea's President Syngman Rhee. Rhee had incensed Washington and London by sabotaging negotiations to end the Korean War, prompting a frustrated Winston to write Ike, "The following is only a thought of my own. Syngman Rhee arrested or dismissed from office."[4]

Ike would have loved to knock Rhee off his perch. Peace in Korea was as important to Ike as settling scores in Iran was to Winston. As Ike joked to his advisors, "We can all relax and start understanding the British in Iran a little better. Now [in Rhee] we have *our* Mosaddeq."[5]

But Winston was playing by Old World rules—rules of an empire that, like Winston, didn't keep up with the times. Ike, a New World man, was supposed to play a clean game. In his America, even superpowers had to respect the will of indigenous peoples. Or, at least, appear to.

So he declined to overthrow Rhee. British Ambassador Roger Makins conveyed Ike's sentiments to Winston. The president, he said, "sympathized with your desire but emphatically felt that any change must come or appear to come from within. He felt strongly that the Western Powers who had intervened in Korea to uphold freedom and democracy must not be seen to be setting up a puppet government."[6]

Appearance was the important thing; not being caught cheating was different from not cheating. In war, Ike was willing to play by dirty rules. But if you throw a spitball, you'd better not get caught. America's national interest required the *appearance* of living up to its ideals.

That didn't mean he'd let the communists control the world's oil supply, of course—and in Iran, Mosaddeq didn't seem capable of stopping them. In a world where good and evil were graded on a sliding scale, the verdict ran against Mosaddeq. To Winston, he was a thief; to Ike, he was weak. So, by the summer of '53, they wanted the same thing: Mosaddeq gone.

Late in Truman's tenure, Beetle Smith's CIA began sketching out Operation TP Ajax, a plan to overthrow Iran's elected government. Drafted with help from MI6, Ajax was a contingency plan. No presidential approval yet, but Allen Dulles kept it on the front burner, simmering until Ike gave the nod.

When Ike authorized the CIA to lay the groundwork, the pace quickened. CIA and MI6 split the budget like a dinner tab, and on July 1 the CIA's chief of covert operations, Kermit Roosevelt, received word that Prime Minister Churchill had given the operation his blessing. Ten days later, Ike gave Ajax the green light. Kermit's men went to work.

The CIA funneled money to Iranian agents supporting Fazlollah Zahedi, a right-wing ex-general whom the agency tapped as the next prime minister. For a fortnight, hidden assets planted inflammatory stories about Mosaddeq, bribed officials, whipped up fury among religious conservatives, and delivered false-flag bomb threats in the name of the Tudeh Party.[7]

The cabal's weak link was the Shah of Iran, Mohammad Reza Pahlavi. A spineless man in his early 30s, the Shah had shrunk from challenging Mosaddeq. He refused to move, despite general assurances of American support. He even resisted an intense lobbying campaign by his twin sister, Princess Ashraf. A glamorous expat who lived on the French Riviera, the princess didn't shrink from getting her manicured hands dirty.

A direct American effort by Major General H. Norman Schwarzkopf nudged the Shah closer, but still he wavered. It took personal assurances of U.S. backing from Kermit Roosevelt to push the reluctant king to order Mosaddeq's dismissal.[8*]

Most black bag jobs don't go according to plan, but this one went off the rails quicker than most. Just before midnight on Saturday, August 15, two truckloads of rebels led by an Iranian colonel pulled up to Mosaddeq's home and surrounded it. But word of the plan had leaked, and the rebels quickly found themselves surrounded by a battalion of loyalists.

Stirred but not shaken, Mosaddeq rallied his supporters as the army and police secured key positions around Tehran. Tudeh Party organizers paid neighborhood bosses to funnel angry, chanting crowds of Mosaddeq supporters into the streets. Mosaddeq's mob converged on the royal palace, forcing the Shah to flee to the safety of British-friendly Baghdad.

* Kermit Roosevelt was Theodore Roosevelt's grandson. General Schwarzkopf's son, "Stormin' Norman" Schwarzkopf, would lead a less covert Middle East operation in 1991.

The plotters' nerves failed, and key army officers went into hiding. General Zahedi moved from safe house to safe house, staying one step ahead of government forces.

For Mosaddeq, the fire was out. The rebellion had been crushed, and he told his supporters to return to their homes. Army units marched back to barracks, and Radio Tehran proudly announced the coup's death.[9]

"The move failed," Beetle wrote Ike in disgust. "We now have to take a whole new look at the Iranian situation and probably have to snuggle up to Mosadeq if we're going to save anything there."[10]

Kermit Roosevelt wasn't ready to snuggle. Mosaddeq had doused the fire, but the embers were still hot. CIA agents pushed harder, paying demonstrators to take to the streets and planting false news stories about Mosaddeq seizing dictatorial power. Tehran buzzed with rumors: looting mobs, Tudeh bombs, fear of dictatorship—or a communist takeover.

Roosevelt's follow-on push breathed new life into the coup. It reached a tipping point in the early-morning hours of August 19, when rent-a-mob thugs flooded Tehran's bazaars and the city center. Emboldened royalist military units kicked in the doors at Radio Tehran and fired on Mosaddeq supporters. An officer seized the microphone and broadcast the royal decree removing Mosaddeq while General Zahedi arrived at the head of a column of Sherman tanks.

Zahedi's men sent a tank shell flying through Mosaddeq's home, bringing Mosaddeq's reign to an abrupt and undignified end. The toppled prime minister was arrested, Ike noted with satisfaction, "in pajamas." The Shah returned to his throne, greeted by his new prime minister, General Zahedi. Iran's cancer was in remission, and America had a staunch ally in the Middle East.[11]

"I listened to [the] detailed report, and it seemed more like a dime novel than an historical fact," Ike told his diary in amazement.

Of course, Operation Ajax could never see the light of day. "The things we did were 'covert,'" he wrote. "If knowledge of them became public, we would not only be embarrassed in that region, but our chances to do anything of like nature in the future would almost totally disappear."[12*]

Across the Atlantic, Winston sat up in bed, propped by pillows as he enjoyed the coup's story. For over two hours, Kermit Roosevelt walked the length of the Ajax roller coaster while Winston listened, asked questions, and sometimes dozed off.

When Kermit finished, Winston's face broke into a grin. "Young man, if I had been but a few years younger, I would have loved nothing better than to have served under your command in this great venture."[13]

While Winston relished a good spy story and was happy to see Mosaddeq gone, this one gave him heartburn. Americans were scooping up the benefits of decades of British groundwork in Persia. Winston had authorized Operation Boot to reclaim the AIOC for Britain. Then Ike and Dulles stepped in, demanding assurances from HMG that Britain would be "flexible" on the oil question when the new Iranian government took power and contracts were renegotiated.

Britain salvaged a portion of her economic pipeline, but it was hardly the triumph Winston hoped for. The AIOC, now renamed British Petroleum, signed a contract with the National Iranian Oil Com-

---

* For Ike's lifetime and a decade after his death, the White House and the CIA considered Operation Ajax a smashing success. Moscow hadn't penetrated Iran, and a potential war over oil fields had been averted. But, as U.S. Ambassador Loy Henderson prophetically wrote the day after Mosaddeq's fall, "Zahedi's Government like all governments of Iran eventually will become unpopular and at that time the US might be blamed for its existence." Over the next two decades, the Shah consolidated his power and ruled a brutal police state, where shiny American-built F-14 fighter jets stood on runways against a landscape of homelessness and poverty in Tehran's streets. These conditions erupted into the Iranian Revolution of 1979, and official Iranian hatred of America burned well into the 21st century.

pany. And it wouldn't be only the Crown cashing in. Ike's friends at Big Oil received Iranian contracts, too, and suddenly BP was just another bloated western oil company in a crowded market.[14]

America was elbowing its way into Britain's old markets, and not just in places like Iran. To Winston, that didn't bode well as the nuclear race took a horrifying turn in another desert.

FORTY-TWO

Counting Cards

"TRII . . . DVAH . . . ODIN . . ."

The flash reflected off goggles of Soviet scientists. Miles distant, a hellish cloud rose over the Kazakh steppe. The ground rumbled as physicists and engineers stared into the apocalypse.

"The earth trembled beneath us, and our faces were struck, like the lash of a whip, by the dull, strong sound of the rolling explosion," remembered one observer. "Day was replaced by night. Thousands of tons of dust were lifted into the air. The huge mass moved slowly over the horizon."

Less than a year behind the United States, the USSR took its first step into the thermonuclear age.[1]

The weapon Andrei Sakharov's team detonated yielded a relatively low blast—only about twenty-seven times the size of the Hiroshima bomb. RDS-6, as it was code-named, was a boosted fission bomb, rather than a true thermonuclear fusion device. But it was a giant leap in Soviet destructive power. A one megaton monster, sixty times the size of Hiroshima's "Little Boy," lay within reach.

Sakharov's team would receive medals, dachas, cars, and other perks—a firing squad or gulag sentence would have been failure's reward—and the Soviet Air Force began its calculus of annihilation:

bomber size, payload capacity, number of nuclear-capable planes. Distance to the great cities of Europe and America.

Sakharov reflected on what it is like to witness a nuclear test. "When you see all of this yourself, something in you changes," he wrote. "When you see the burned birds who are writhing on the scorched steppe, when you see how the shock wave blows away buildings like houses of cards, when you feel the reek of splintered bricks, when you sense melted glass . . . all of this triggers an irrational yet very strong emotional impact. How not to start thinking of one's responsibility?"[2]

Like Sakharov, Ike was thinking of his own responsibility.

He knew the Soviets would be relentless in forging a nuclear arsenal. Their engineers were developing ever-longer ranges for a small but growing stockpile of ballistic missiles. Their factories were riveting new jet bombers—Ilyushin-28 "Beagles"—and converting them to carry atomic death.

To deter them, the United States must be ready to strike back, instantly and savagely. But what would massive retaliation gain? If the seal were broken, the horsemen loosed, hundreds of millions would perish within a few hours, their homes and bodies turned to ash, their futures, and their children's futures, wiped forever from the earth. Survivors on both sides, stumbling through radioactive rubble, ordered about by the few living soldiers, would envy the dead. Under those conditions, how could either side claim victory?[3]

During the Rhine campaign, Winston had told Omar Bradley, "There will come a day when we walk into a cabinet room, break the glass over a switch, dial to the nation to be bombed and push a button to declare war." Science had at last caught up. In the late 1940s, East and West had been gunfighters at the O.K. Corral, hands hovering over holsters, waiting for the signal to draw. Now they were two engineers standing on a mountain of dynamite, each holding the detonator's switch.[4]

Truman's grand strategy had been containment. Soldiers, tanks, ships, and planes strung like barbed wire around the globe. But the fence had gaps. America couldn't match the Soviets rifle for rifle. Like Rome at its bloated peak, Washington lacked the wealth and manpower to hold everything, everywhere, all at once. Whatever America spent would never be enough. The cost of a world police force would send the nation down the road of a garrison state, followed by four different horsemen: debt default, hyperinflation, economic controls, and, eventually, tyranny.[5]

To Ike, nuclear war was almost unimaginable. But the price of a conventional arsenal—a castle built on battalions, fleets, and air bases—looked nearly as grim. Speaking to Defense Secretary Charlie Wilson, he didn't mince words: "Any person who doesn't clearly understand that national security and national solvency are mutually dependent, and that permanent maintenance of a crushing weight of military power would eventually produce dictatorship, should not be entrusted with any kind of responsibility in our country."[6]

If ruin lay at the end of both roads, would global nuclear war really be the lesser of the evils? Could debt collapse be averted through a short, decisive blitz launched before Russia acquired atomic plenty? Thinking the unthinkable, Ike told Dulles, "The cost [of conventional superiority] would either drive us to war—or into some form of dictatorial government. In such circumstances, we would be forced to consider whether or not our duty to future generations did not require us to initiate war at the most propitious moment."[7]

Through the summer of 1953, Ike pondered that duty. He ordered a thorough "down to the bolts" study of American strategy accounting for the nation's economic, diplomatic, and military limitations. The result was the "New Look," its nickname a nod to popular fashion trends of designer Christian Dior. Under the New Look, America would keep its conventional military budget small while remaining poised for massive nuclear retaliation. On the ground, America would contain communism through covert operations, diplomacy, and economic measures.[8*]

In Normandy, Ike had used airpower to replace foot soldiers. With the New Look, atomic weapons would replace draftees: a thousand nuclear-tipped bombers instead of four million soldiers. Those millions not drafted into the Army would remain civilians, hold jobs, provide for their families, pay taxes, and contribute to a better society.[9]

The New Look only worked if it deterred war. And to deter war, Ike had to be ready to order those bombers up. He had to be ready to murder millions. More important, the Russians had to believe he'd do it.

Continent-destroying bombs. A willingness to use them. Two implacable foes pushing each other on the fringes. Could humanity thread extinction's needle?

With the end drawing so near, Winston believed he knew the answer.

* According to Ike, it was the gruff Admiral Arthur Radford, chairman of the Joint Chiefs of Staff, who referred to the emerging strategy as the "New Look." The old sailor was more evidently couture conscious than one might have guessed.

FORTY-THREE

A Goat, a Six-Shooter, and Atom Bombs

"We are confronted with a deadlock," wrote Winston. "Why not let us try Bermuda again?"[1]

Ike read the letter with a sense of inevitability. If they met in Bermuda, Winston would bring up a summit like a broken record.

Ike saw no point in high-level talks. The Kremlin hadn't moved an inch on any of his European proposals, like pulling out of Austria or discussing German unification. And the Soviets had refused an offer for a foreign ministers meeting. Why try to achieve grand goals when the little ones fizzled out?[2]

Winston's physical stamina was another question. Admiral Arthur Radford, the new chairman of the Joint Chiefs, had met with Churchill in London and described him in less than heroic terms. He was fragile. Hard of hearing. Difficulty concentrating. Capable of holding one big idea of a peace conference. Not the wingman you'd want when negotiating with hardened Kremlin bandits.

But the old man could still surprise. At Margate Winter Gardens, in a fifty-minute oration calling for peace talks, Winston had shown that, despite strokes and advancing age, the old lion could still roar. "I still think that the leading men of the various nations ought to be able to meet together," he declared to a spellbound audience. "Let us try to see whether there is not something better for us than tearing and blasting each other to pieces."[3]

Voters on both sides of the Atlantic loved it. In London, the *Times* declared the Margate speech "a personal triumph in a very special way. The cheers that were raised at the end have been echoed throughout the land." Winston's stock was suddenly rising. Beetle told Ike that 70 percent of the public favored a meeting between Ike and Winston—and Winston had asked for one so many times, they couldn't decently refuse him much longer.[4]

With a sigh, Ike put Bermuda back on the calendar. They would meet in early December. As before, they would invite the French prime minister and his foreign secretary for a three-power discussion. Winston would get his powwow.

But he cautioned Winston not to tell the press they would discuss an East-West summit. The Reds had recently sent western governments a long, snotty diatribe pushing back on Germany and Austria, and Ike was in no mood to placate their poison-pen scribes. "It would be necessary of course to avoid creating a false impression that our purpose in meeting is to issue another invitation to the Soviets," he wrote. "There is nothing to be gained by showing too much concern over their intransigence and bad deportment."[5]

Blowing past all caveats, Winston was jubilant.

"I put out my paw to Ike, and it was fixed up at once," he told Lord Moran. Bermuda was more than a political engagement. The beacon of hope was flaming bright on the horizon. There was still time to arrange a summit with Moscow's leaders before their time together ran out. He only needed to get Ike in a room where the spell could work.[6]

As he prepared to leave England, Winston found himself back in the public eye for his writing. In November, his publisher released *Triumph and Tragedy*, the sixth and final volume of his World War II memoirs. He had drafted it before November 1952, but wanted a chance to make final edits after he knew the election's outcome.

Though Winston and Monty had once spent an afternoon at Chequers ruminating over five "capital mistakes" the Americans made during the war—two of which were Eisenhower's—Winston permitted no public criticism of Ike. He even scrapped a paragraph explaining the meaning of the book's title. Describing Patton's advance toward Prague, he had written:

> Our troops could, and in my opinion, should have liberated it, but in fact were restrained from doing so by the direct intervention of the highest American authorities. Berlin, Prague, and Vienna were needlessly yielded to the Soviets. Here may be discerned the Tragedy in our hour of Triumph.

Winston's self-censorship appalled his private secretary, Anthony Montague Browne. "The published version was mild," he wrote. "A pity, I thought. History is history, and you don't do much good by failing to illuminate the grosser errors. To which the reply is, of course, that you don't do much good by offending the new US President either."[7*]

Winston arrived in Bermuda on December 2 aboard *Canopus*, a majestic Boeing VIP Stratocruiser. Stepping off the plane and into the sun, he

* In a 1957 press conference, Mrs. May Craig of the *Portland* (Maine) *Press Herald* asked Ike, "Do you see any major thing that you think the Allies could have done differently?" Ike replied, "Oh, well, yes, of course. All the time." But, he added, "it's awfully hard to quarrel, Mrs. Craig, with victory."

reviewed a spit-and-polish detachment of the Royal Welch Fusiliers, who stood at attention with their celebrated mascot, a huge white Kashmiri goat named Gwilym.

"All well. Goat splendid," Winston reported to Clemmie.[8]

Ike wouldn't arrive until Friday, December 4, so after the usual local welcome, Winston settled down to a quiet dinner with Moran, Colville, and a few trusted friends. Over their meal, Moran probed Winston about the Soviet threat.

"Does Russia want war?" he asked.

"I believe it is not in her interest to make war," said Winston. "When I meet Malenkov we can build for peace."

"Then who is making difficulties?"

"Ike," snapped Winston. "He doesn't think any good can come from talks with the Russians. But it will pay him to come along with us. I shall do what I can to persuade him. I might stay longer here than I meant, at any rate, if I could persuade Ike to stay too. He is the key man in this business."

He paused, his thoughts turning to Washington. Another visit there might be worth arranging.

"I could manage it," he said, though he didn't seem convinced.

"I don't feel old, though I have some of the disabilities of old age. . . . This old carcass of mine is a bloody nuisance."[9]

As Ike flew to Bermuda, Winston hoped the carcass had one more fight left.

Ike stepped down *Columbine*'s stairway sporting a small bandage on his left hand, testament to an Old West lesson gone wrong. Shortly before leaving Washington, he had fetched a six-shooter from his collection and was showing Mamie how gunfighters rapid-fired their Peacemakers by fanning the hammer. The move—which always seemed to work in the movies—ended with the hammer's spur biting the heel of Ike's hand, spilling blood and cusswords across the family quarters.[10]

Winston met Ike at the airport. Though they greeted each other as friends, some in the British delegation sensed something was wrong. "Ike struck me as more ceremonial, withdrawn, royal, than last year," diplomat Evelyn Shuckburgh told his diary. "He greeted the PM and was then marched smartly off to inspect the guard, leaving the old man trotting behind, neglected and pathetic."[11]

Unwinding from the flight, Ike warmed up. During the limousine ride to the Mid Ocean Club, the recovering cowboy and the old lion exchanged gossip and shared memories. Talk was light, the kind longtime friends use to anchor their relationship. They carried their conversation into the sitting room of Ike's suite, where they talked for the better part of an hour.

"It was a genuine sense of friendship," remembered Robert Bowie, Ike's planning director. "They didn't think of each other as president and prime minister so much as old colleagues, on account of their wartime experience. . . . The mood was not one of playing your cards close to your chest, but sort of easy give and take."[12]

To the outside world, they honored formalities. Winston, said Jim Hagerty, "addressed the president in public or when anyone else was around (including myself or other members of the president's staff or his own staff) as 'Mr. President,'" while Ike addressed his old friend as "Sir Winston." But when they were alone, or with their families, it was Ike and Winston—or even "Winnie," when the mood was right.[13]

Ike's advisors urged him not to let his feelings for Winston blunt America's dominance. As C. D. Jackson told Bobby Cutler, "Out of Bermuda must emerge tripartite unity, but at the apex of the triangle there must be the U.S. in the person of President Eisenhower. This role should not be sacrificed because of the very human feeling of decency and generosity towards an opinionated old gentleman who is still sufficiently sharp and selfish to grab every advantage with bland assurances of unwavering esteem."[14]

Ambassador Aldrich agreed. He had warned Dulles, "It must always be borne in mind, however, that [Churchill] is imaginative, unpredictable, firm in the belief of his own genius, and apparently determined to attempt one last crowning act on [the] world stage."[15]

The two leaders shuffled down the hall to Winston's suite for a private lunch with Eden and Dulles. The scene was familiar: a stream-of-conscious talk going round the world, stopping here and there, marking major issues they would take up in detail later.

"Once again, Winston and I were working together, each of us with heavy responsibilities and both engaged in a common effort to resolve momentous problems," Ike later wrote. "Although the years had aged the Prime Minister, adding in the process a new weapon to his defensive armament—a partial deafness which he seemed able at times to turn on and off to suit his purposes—time had not dulled his mind or tongue."[16]

Nor had it dulled the limits duty imposed on friendship.

Ike's pressing question was what to do if North Korea resumed the war. Peace in Korea had been the centerpiece of his presidential campaign, and an armistice signed at Panmunjom that summer delivered on that promise—but just barely. No peace treaty had been signed, and it looked like Kim Il Sung, goaded by Peking and Moscow, might break the truce and renew fighting.

To Ike, Korea wasn't a spot on a map. It was a test of the West's resolve. His resolve. He had staked his personal credibility on ending the war, and he wasn't going to let a poor man's Stalin invade a U.S. ally. If Pyongyang deliberately broke the truce, he said, the United States would feel free to use atomic weapons against military targets.

Winston didn't argue. If war resumed, he said he would be able to tell Parliament that he had been consulted in advance and had agreed America should have freedom of action.[17]

Leaving Korea, their conversation wandered to other places. When they came to emerging countries Queen Victoria once ruled, Ike banged FDR's old drum: He didn't want any perception that America and Britain were "ganging up" against outsiders—especially former colonies. Collaboration should be done in private meetings and through secret communiqués. To the outside world, they must conduct themselves as independent sovereigns, not coconspirators.

To Winston, world peace was best assured by "ganging up" against mutual threats. Alliances, bold, formal, and emphatic, were vital. If America and Russia had ganged up with Britain and France in 1938, for instance, the world might not have endured six years of carnage.[18]

They took a break. Winston relaxed on the beach, climbing the dunes with assistance for an hour's swim and sunbathing. Lying on the sand, he reflected on the difficulty of channeling the American force. He looked, Colville wrote, "like King Canute defying the incoming tide."[19]

At five o'clock, the "Big Three" leaders—Ike, Winston, and an ailing French premier, Joseph Laniel—strode into the hotel's main conference room to commence formal talks.[20]

The opening session promised nothing and delivered. Without warning, the parties were plunged into darkness when a fuse blew out, killing the lights and forcing servants to hustle in oil lamps and candles.

Bathed in a monastic glow, Winston proposed that Ike chair the meetings. When Ike agreed, Winston asked, "not as a sign of personal indulgence but rather as an indication of the informal nature of the talks, if he might have permission to smoke."

Ike grinned. Winston without a cigar was unthinkable, so in his first ruling as chairman, Ike ruled that all participants were free to light up.[21]

Getting down to business, Ike outlined a draft speech he would give to the United Nations General Assembly on his return from Bermuda. He would urge the UN to create a pool of uranium, contributed by the great powers, to fuel energy, medical, agricultural, and industrial projects. Each measure of uranium contributed would reduce the amount available for weapons.[22]

Next came the Soviet Union. When it was Winston's turn to speak, he rose from his chair. Bathed in candlelight, he turned to his recurring theme.

"Is there a new Soviet look?" he asked. The Russians might have given up their pretensions of world domination because of two key developments since Potsdam: American rearmament for the Korean War and the failure of the communist utopia to materialize. Russia might be more temperate than she had been in Stalin's days. Winston said he would "not be in too much of a hurry to believe that nothing but evil emanates from this mighty branch of the human family."[23]

Ike saw plenty of evil. When Winston finished speaking, he rose and gave what Colville described as "a short, very violent statement, in the coarsest terms" about the Soviet leadership.

Comparing the Soviet Union to a tarted-up street whore, he said, "If we understood that under this dress was the same old girl, if we understood that despite bath, perfume or lace, it was still the same old girl, on that basis then we might explore all that Sir Winston had said. . . . Perhaps we could pull the old girl off the main street and put her on a back alley."

He emphasized that "he did not wish to approach this problem on the basis that there had been any change in the Soviet policy of destroying the Capitalist free world by all means, by force, by deceit or lies. This was their long-term purpose. From their writings it was clear there had been no change since Lenin."

Ike's crude rebuke, wrote Colville, elicited "pained looks all round." Diplomat Evelyn Shuckburgh told his diary that Ike "came down like a ton of bricks, very rude I thought and vulgar."

As Winston looked on, crestfallen, Ike adjourned the meeting.

"To end on a note of dignity," wrote Colville, "Eden asked when the next meeting should be."

Eden's question hung in the air like a balloon until Ike popped it.

"I don't know," he muttered. "Mine is with a whiskey and soda."[24]

The next morning, Ike, Winston, and their nuclear advisors—Lewis Strauss and Lord Cherwell—sat down to discuss coordination of weapons. Admiral Strauss's notes have Ike saying, "Atomic weapons were now coming to be regarded as a proper part of conventional armament and that he thought this a sound concept." With bureaucratic finality, Strauss's notes conclude, "Sir Winston concurred."*

Sir Winston did not concur. Since his private meeting with Ike the day before, he had considered the connections between Korea, atomic escalation, Russia, and London. The Kremlin had a vested interest in backing North Korea and China, and Russia had the hydrogen bomb. Russia also had bombers that might not reach America, but they could reach London, Liverpool, Birmingham, and any other major city on the British Isles. And with U.S. bombers based in East Anglia, England would be the bull's-eye of any Soviet strike. One good hit and life on the island would go up in smoke. Winston wasn't ready to sacrifice London to defend Seoul.

Winston's thinking had come a long way from the showdown days of Potsdam, Fulton, and Czechoslovakia. If the Soviet atomic bomb did not make war a two-way street, a Soviet H-bomb most certainly did. The inevitability of world-destroying arsenals aimed at each other had convinced him the risks of escalation were too great for each side to nudge

* Because the subject of discussion was atomic weapons and the French had none, Prime Minister Laniel was not invited. Falling ill about the time he arrived, Laniel would skip much of the conference, his place taken by his foreign minister, Georges Bidault.

the other to the brink. The Cold War was a dark, sometimes frightening affair, but a cold war offered one priceless advantage: It wasn't a hot war.[25]

Summoning the emotions of Anvil and the Aegean, he told Ike he feared dropping atomic bombs "would bring on the third world war and the consequent bombing of London." He pleaded with his friend; he could not bear to think of "the destruction of all we hold dear: ourselves, our families and our treasures. Even if some of us temporarily survive in some deep cellar under mounds of flaming and contaminated rubble, there will be nothing to do but take a pill to end it all."[26]

The ghastly imagery slid off Ike's shoulders. With the confidence of a poker player holding three kings, he assured Winston the Soviets would never attack London over Chinese military targets along the Yalu River. No one was talking about bombing Peking or Shanghai—just air bases and troop concentrations feeding Pyongyang's war. That's all.[27]

That's all? thought Winston. That might be enough. War, as he knew from painful experience, does not follow mathematical rules. Millions were not supposed to die over an archduke's murder. Millions weren't supposed to die over an oil embargo with Japan. Millions had perished from miscalculations of generals, kings, and statesmen who claimed to know precisely what the enemy would do. Statesmen don't live on a chessboard; they work in a world of chaos. And chaos draws closest when one of them breaks a taboo.

"British thinking—apparently both governmental and personal thinking—still looks upon the possible use of the atom bomb as the initiating of a completely new kind of war," Ike told his diary the next morning. "This feeling unquestionably arises out of the fact that up until this time the British have had no atom bombs and because of their experience in World War II, they see themselves as the initial, and possibly principal, target of a Soviet bomb offensive. They apparently cling to the hope (fatuous to us) that if we avoid the first use of the atom bomb in any war, that the Soviets might likewise abstain."

Ike saw it differently. "Our thinking, on the other hand, has come a long ways past this kind of conjecture and hope," he wrote. "We have come to the conclusion that the atom bomb has to be treated as another weapon in the arsenal."

He told Colville, "Whereas Winston looked on the atomic weapon as something entirely new and terrible, he looked upon it as just the latest improvement in military weapons." Colville added that Ike "implied that there was in fact no distinction between 'conventional weapons' and atomic weapons: all weapons in due course become conventional weapons."[28]

When Ike looked at his friend, he saw a man past his prime. A cavalier in an atomic age.

"Winston is a curious mixture of belligerence and caution, sometimes amounting to almost hysterical fear," Ike concluded. "When he really wants to do something, he pooh-poohs and belittles every word or hint of risks involved. On the other hand, if he is in opposition to an argument—as for example, the thought that we would count on using the atomic bomb to repel massive aggression in Korea—he can rake up and expound on every possible adverse effect on Russian intentions and reaction, and on public opinion throughout the world."[29]

He had become an old light bulb flickering as filaments burned thin. As Ike told his old friend Swede Hazlett, "At times Winston seemed to be his old and hearty self, full of vim and determination. At others he seemed almost to wander in his mind." But he noted, like deafness, Winston's apparent senility "seemed to come over him only when the subject under discussion or the argument presented was distasteful to him."[30]

On much they disagreed. But they were friends and war comrades, and while they weren't exactly David and Jonathan anymore, neither had lost faith in the other's better angels. "Things are very easy between us," Winston told Moran after eleven hours of private talks with Ike. "I think he trusts me."

Over dinner with Pug and Moran, Ike said much the same thing. "No one has treated me so well as Winston Churchill," he agreed. "He knows I love him; sometimes he takes advantage of that."[31]

Afternoons followed a familiar pattern: drinks, cigars, conversation. Ike's appointments secretary recalled ushering in Winston for an afternoon session in Ike's sitting room. They talked and talked, and when their talk and Winston's Havanas were spent, the old man shuffled back to his room, a half-full highball glass sitting by his chair.

"You know," remarked Ike after Winston left, "I have never actually seen that man finish a drink. I've seen him get it down to a certain point and have it refilled, but come to think of it, I've never seen him finish a drink."[32]

After three days of talks, Ike had to leave for New York to give his "Atoms for Peace" speech before the UN General Assembly. They hadn't accomplished much in Bermuda. The issues were deeply felt and complex.

Before heading to the airport, Ike jotted a personal note to Winston, thanking him for his hospitality. He apologized, obliquely, for his occasional outbursts and reiterated his devotion. "While my disposition has not always been equal to the pressures of some of the lectures, I think that I came through my first international conference—in a political role—in fairly good shape," he wrote. "Give my love to Clemmie and all your nice family."[33]

Before boarding *Columbine*, Ike joined Winston for a final review of the honor guard from the Royal Welch Fusiliers. Ike walked past stiff lines of soldiers, nodding as he approached the Kashmiri mascot, Gwilym. Stopping, Ike asked the goat if he wanted a cigarette. The goat ignored him.

Landing in New York that afternoon, an aide handed Ike a message from Winston, wired through Britain's UN delegation: "In explanation of the Goat's refusal to accept the cigarette you offered him this morning, I think I ought to point out that he was aware that smoking on parade is strictly forbidden."

"The Goat's soldierly deportment puts me to shame," Ike wrote back. "You would suppose that after some forty years in the Army, I would not have embarrassed him so sadly."[34]

Their banter glossed over hard reality. Winston returned from his biggest summit since Potsdam empty-handed. Ike had agreed to a foreign ministers conference, but for a summit, he demanded conditions the communists weren't likely to agree to. America and Britain couldn't agree on the Middle East, the Far East, and, for now, talks with the Kremlin.

Unwilling to blame Ike completely, Winston's frustration found its target in Ike's Iago. "I am bewildered. It seems that everything is left to Dulles," he snarled to Moran. "It appears that the president is no more than a ventriloquist's doll."

After a moment of sullen silence, Winston resumed. "This fellow preaches like a Methodist Minister, and his bloody text is always the same: That nothing but evil can come out of meeting with Malenkov."

Another silence.

"Dulles is a terrible handicap."

His voice rising, tears of frustration welling, he half shouted, "Ten years ago I could have dealt with him. Even as it is, I have not been defeated by this bastard. I have been humiliated by my own decay."[35]

FORTY-FOUR

Twilight's Last Gleaming

TARGET 001 WAS MOSCOW. Strategic Air Command's orders placed top priority on wiping out Soviet aircraft in and around Russia's capital. SAC war planners sketched out a decapitation scenario that would turn a city of five million souls into a pile of radioactive rubble and human ash. As an operations analyst remembered, planners were told, "Level Moscow if you can."

As arsenals grew, so did SAC's appetite for destruction. Leningrad, with 3.2 million residents, lay in its crosshairs. So did Kyev, Minsk, Gorky, Vladimir, and twelve hundred other targets behind the Iron Curtain. During the war, SAC's commander, General Curtis LeMay, had incinerated a quarter million Japanese civilians without blinking. He wasn't blinking now.

In Pentagon war rooms, Defense Department analysts estimated that a single coordinated nuclear strike against the Soviet Union would kill around sixty million people. In the 118 major cities targeted for destruction, around 75 to 84 percent of the population would perish. In an afternoon, an American president could put numbers on the board Hitler, Stalin, and Mao couldn't touch.[1]

But an extinction-level stockpile of H-bombs was no longer relevant, except to deter someone else from using his extinction-level stockpile. As long as everyone knew that if *anyone* launched, *everyone* dies, then missiles, bombers, and submarines might keep the peace. Ike's settled conclusion: "We believe that the power of modern weapons makes war not only perilous—but preposterous—and the only way to win World War III is to prevent it."[2]

As New Year's revelers opened 1954 with champagne, kisses, and "Auld Lang Syne," Ike could look back on his first year with quiet satisfaction. He had ended the fighting in Korea. American aid kept Viet Minh rebels at bay in Indochina. Communists had been shut out of Iran, and America was seen, mostly, as an honest broker in the Middle East. Stalin was dead, the economy was healthy, and his administration had weathered the year with few domestic stumbles, none of them fatal.

But a fresh field of land mines lay ahead in the new year, and the presidency didn't forgive mistakes. Jim Hagerty recalled a crack a friend made about the difference between the corporate world and the White House: If a corporate manager screws up, he might lose the Italian-American spaghetti account. If the White House screws up, it might lose Italy.[3]

Nowhere was the tightrope more frayed than over the nuclear chasm. Delivery systems on both sides of the Curtain were growing. Missiles flew higher and farther. Atomic weapons could be delivered by howitzer or jeep. The globe-spanning B-52 bomber would be rolling off assembly lines, and the Soviets were not far behind with their "Bear" and "Beagle" bombers.

"As of now, the world is racing toward catastrophe," Ike had told his diary after Bermuda. "Something must be done to put a brake on this moment."[4]

How do you put the brakes on a runaway train? Ike didn't know, but he had to try. In February, he wrote Winston a deeply personal letter about the world's future. "I am sure that when history looks back upon us of today it will not long remember any one of this era who was merely a distinguished war leader," he said. "It will remember and salute those people who succeeded, out of the greatness of their understanding and the skill of their leadership, in establishing ties among the independent nations of the world that will throw back the Russian threat and allow civilization, as we have known it, to continue its progress."

Ike wasn't just speaking of political ideology, of capitalism or communism, of Adam Smith and Karl Marx. To him, the divide went deeper—the ancient battle between good and evil. "It is only when one allows his mind to contemplate momentarily such a disaster for the world and attempts to picture an atheistic materialism in complete domination of all human life, that he fully appreciates how necessary it is to seek renewed faith and strength from his God, and sharpen up his sword for the struggle that cannot possibly be escaped."

Ike closed his letter with a somber reflection: "Destiny has given priceless opportunity to some of this epoch. You are one of them. Perhaps I am also one of the company on whom this great responsibility has fallen."[5]

"*Sharpen up his sword for the struggle that cannot possibly be escaped*"?

Winston didn't know what to make of Ike's letter.

He and Ike had been frank with each other, but this was an intimate and disturbing glimpse into a soul contemplating the apocalypse. Winston hoped it was nothing more than Ike's stream-of-consciousness musing—not the warning of a man girding for a war the world wouldn't survive.

Since it was sent as a personal message, he didn't circulate the letter through official channels—the Foreign Office, the Cabinet, and the like. But he did give a copy to Clementine and asked for her thoughts.

"I think Eisenhower looks to you for help," she concluded after reading the letter twice. A personal meeting, she suggested, might help clear the air. "But if only America were not so unsympathetic & indeed unhelpful to us."[6]

Winston talked over the letter with Eden. "It may be that he is indulging in a general and informal 'thinking aloud' and that its implications are not serious," the secretary suggested.

But when a president opens his mouth, his words matter. And Ike's phrasing—"sharpen up his sword for the struggle that cannot possibly be escaped"—worried Eden.

"Taken by themselves, these words could mean that the President thinks that a war with the Soviet Union cannot be escaped and that we should build up our armaments with that end in view," he said. At a minimum, he suggested, Winston should nudge Ike back from the cliff with a suggestion that he must have been speaking of a spiritual struggle, not a military one.[7]

Ike had second thoughts, too. A week later, he sent a follow-up note, softening the tone. His previous letter had been "only an item in a friendly exchange of ideas which has extended now over a period of a dozen years. I think that possibly I was merely testing my thoughts against yours to determine whether we are as basically in agreement as we think we are."[8]

They were not. Winston's thoughts of the Bomb—and his and Ike's responsibility for containing it—had crystallized enough to write Ike a long, emotional letter on the subject.

"My dear Friend," he began,

> You can imagine what my thoughts are about London. I am told that several million people would certainly be obliterated by four or five of the latest H bombs. In a few more years these could be delivered by rocket without even hazarding the life of a pilot. New York and your other great cities have immeasurable perils too,

> though distance is a valuable advantage at least as long as pilots are used. . . .
>
> [H]uman minds recoil from the realization of such facts. The people, including the well-informed, can only gape and console themselves with the reflection that death comes to all anyhow, sometime. This merciful numbness cannot be enjoyed by the few men upon whom supreme responsibility falls. They have to drive their minds forward into these hideous and deadly spheres of thought. All the things that are happening now put together, added to all the material things that have ever happened, are scarcely more important to the human race. I consider that you and, if my strength lasts, I cannot flinch from the mental exertion involved.
>
> I wondered, pondering on your letter, whether this was the background which had forced you to express yourself with such intense earnestness. I understand of course that, in speaking of the faith that must inspire us in the struggle against atheistic materialism, you are referring to the spiritual struggle and, that like me, you still believe that War is not inevitable. I am glad to think that in your spirit, as in mine, resolve to find a way out of this agony of peril transcends all else.

Returning to the drum he had banged since Stalin's death, he added, "Of course I recur to my earlier proposal of a personal meeting between Three. Men have to settle with men, no matter how vast, and in part beyond their comprehension, the business in hand may be. I can even imagine that a few simple words, spoken in the awe which may at once oppress and inspire the speakers, might lift this nuclear monster from our world."[9]

Ike agreed—to a point. "I have pondered over your letter. You are quite right in your estimate of my grave concern at the steady increase in methods of mass destruction," he admitted. "Whether or not the specific possibilities of devastation that you mention are indeed demonstrated capabilities, the prospects are truly appalling. Ways of lessening, or, if possible, eliminating the danger must be found."

But he still wasn't ready to gamble on a Big Three summit. The time wasn't right. Winston would have to wait.[10]

Death closes all: but something ere the end,
Some work of noble note, may yet be done.

Winston had become Tennyson's Ulysses—the old man in a hurry, as his father had once derided Gladstone. Ike was in no hurry. He had three more years in power. Seven, perhaps. Winston didn't have time to wait for Ike. His time was running out.[11]

First his hearing, now his stamina. Since his stroke, he had taken Moran's Benzedrine, Drinamyl, and Edrisal pills to boost his concentration through long Cabinet meetings and important speeches. Without his magic "Morans," he could be tiresome and unfocused.

Cracks were showing, and the press noticed. The left-wing *Daily Mirror* led the pack with a scathing editorial called "Twilight of a Giant." "The exposure of the myth of Winston as a post-war leader is now complete," the editors declared. "Old and tired, he mouthed comfortless words in the twilight of his career. His battles are past."

The column ended with a sad verdict: "This is the Giant in Decay."[12]

Decaying, but still a giant. He wasn't finished yet. The old man in a hurry would finish one last crusade. New revelations over the size of American H-bomb tests intensified his obsession with a parlay at the summit.

"I shall not relinquish office until I meet Malenkov," he told his daughter Diana and her husband, Duncan Sandys, on April 8. "Ike said once that he would like to meet Malenkov in Stockholm. I could join the Russians there."

He felt he alone could bridge the Cold War's frozen abyss. "At my age, with death at my shoulder, the Kremlin cannot speak of jealousy," he told Moran. "They know I have nothing to gain. I would pop over to America first, to make it all right with them. I know them well, they would not think I was up to dirty work."

Would the Americans object? Moran asked.

Winston's eyes twinkled.

"The Americans know I am the greatest anti-Communist of all time," he said. "Besides, they would see I was going in any case."[13]

FORTY-FIVE

Good for the Gander

Casino Royale, Ian Fleming's first James Bond novel, hit British bookstore shelves as Winston was pressing Ike to see Malenkov. Across 213 pages, Fleming's brooding MI6 spy dueled Soviet agents with British savoir faire and American cash. The novel was overlooked in the United States at the time of its release, but to UK readers, 007 became something more than a spy: He personified a rugged, sophisticated Britain that could still play the Great Game with the best of them.

But the buy-in at this baccarat table was steep—and nowhere more so than in Egypt. There, 80,000 soldiers manned the Suez Canal Zone at a cost of nearly fifty million pounds a year. Despite this heavy outlay, the ground game was turning against London. Cairo's prime minister, Colonel Gamal Nasser, had built his power base on Arab pan-nationalism, antisemitism, and anti-colonialism. Stirring the pot, Nasser encouraged hotheaded fedayeen to snipe and bomb the Canal garrison and murder unwary Tommies who strayed beyond their barbed wire. Outside Egypt's borders, Nasser worked to weaken Britain's chief regional allies, Jordan's King Hussein and Iraq's King Faisal II.

Winston stared at the dilemma. Pull out of Suez, and he could stop the bleeding, save fifty million pounds a year, and remove a thorn from the side of Anglo-American relations. But quitting Egypt would mean surrendering a jewel of the Empire—a betrayal of the Victorian ideals he had labored to uphold. And losing Suez might trigger a domino-like collapse of Her Majesty's influence in Iraq, Libya, Jordan, and the Arabian Peninsula.

Winston and Eden tried to meet Nasser halfway. They opened negotiations to pull Britain's combat troops out, leaving behind only technicians to run the Canal's locks and equipment. To save face, the technicians would wear British Army uniforms, and London would officially maintain the Canal Zone as a military base. And in the event of war, the British wanted the right to return and defend the Canal. But the practical reality was that the British Army would be out of Egypt.

Nasser wouldn't compromise on anything. He kept up his guerrilla and propaganda attacks, knowing the British public would grow weary and demand a retreat soon enough—as it had in India and Pakistan, in Burma and Libya, in Palestine and Malta. Time had been on Egypt's side for four thousand years, and time would favor Egypt again. Nasser would fight London and ask for support from other powers—including Eisenhower's United States.[1]

Ike wasn't worried about the Canal. He was worried about communism. Marxism's appeal to much of the world lay in its promise to break the chains of Old World oppression—chains forged by colonial powers like Britain and France. To keep the Reds from exploiting populist rage, America needed to show support for independence movements and self-rule. In public, anyway.[2]

Ike knew how much of the world saw Britain. The British Empire was the undeveloped world's bully—or, at best, an overbearing father keeping his grown children down on the farm. France was doing the same to her colonies in North Africa and Indochina, and she was paying a heavy price. As Ike had complained to Averell Harriman, "Our side deals primarily with the classes that have been exploiting their own people since time immemorial."[3]

When Winston appealed to Ike to join the Canal negotiations on Britain's side, Ike refused. That didn't go over well with Winston.

"When I tell him this kind of 'ganging up' has certain positive disadvantages . . . he merely grows confident to the point of aggressiveness," Ike told his diary. "He gives me a lecture on the might, the power, the majesty of the two great nations of the United States and the United Kingdom marching before these little trembling dictators and announcing our decision—which of course is always based upon justice, reason and consideration, to say nothing for a very deep concern for all humanity."

Ike reread his entry, then softened the blow. "This particular sentence I do not mean to be as sarcastic as it may sound—to give Winston his due, I think there is a very great deal of good sense in the various stands that he wants us jointly to take with respect to these several problems. However, the method of the 'joint ultimatum' is, in my opinion, self-defeating."[4]

With negotiations in Cairo stalled, it was up to Foster Dulles to find the right mix of carrots and sticks. As always, one of those carrots was economic aid, and his men at Foggy Bottom began looking for funds to dangle in front of Nasser.

His thinking didn't sit well with his closest ally. Hearing rumblings of dollars for Nasser, Winston reached for his pen. "I am very much worried at the idea of the grant of American economic aid to Egypt at a time when our differences with them are so acute," he wrote Ike. "It would, I am sure, have a grave effect in this country on Anglo-American relations."[5]

Ike wrote back an "eyes only" letter laying out his reality. "There are in parts of this country many people who believe the United States has treated the Arab countries shabbily and, because parts of the Arab holdings are vital to the Western World, this segment of our citizenry asserts that we should work to improve our relationships with the Arab countries. But this Government has always refused to do this at the cost of anything we believed detrimental to the Anglo-American best interests."[6]

Winston wasn't satisfied. "It is always difficult to explain the internal politics of one country to another and I have not succeeded this time," he replied. Britons were outraged that America would tilt against its best friend to help a small-time dictator. From 10 Downing he would continue to support American objectives as best he could, but he warned, "It will, however, make it more difficult for Anthony and me to help you in the Far East if we have to do it in the face, not only of Socialist opinion, but of general indignation throughout the country."

Having dangled a Far East carrot before Ike, Winston said he hoped America would stand with Britain in the Near East. "No doubt the Egyptian issue seems petty to you in comparison with the other great questions, including China, confronting us both," he continued. But Egypt was important to the United Kingdom. "50,000 British graves lie in Egypt and the approaches," he reminded Ike. "Our being on opposite sides in the Mediterranean will gird on every enemy we have in common throughout the world."[7]

As Ike and Winston squared off over Egypt from their sterile offices, French soldiers hacked out graves in a crossroads town in northern Vietnam.

For eighty years, France had ruled Indochina, the fertile corner of Southeast Asia ethnically divided into Vietnam, Cambodia, and Laos. Shortly after World War II, a nationalist rebellion broke out near Vietnam's border with China. The rebel leader, a socialist known as Ho Chi Minh, soon controlled the country's northern region around Hanoi. The war teetered for seven grueling years as Ho's communist-backed Viet Minh launched hit-and-run attacks against the French Army.

Then, in early 1954, the French commander conceived a daring plan to destroy the Viet Minh by setting a trap for himself. General Henri Navarre moved a 16,000-man force into a remote northwestern valley hamlet called Dien Bien Phu. The town was far from French reinforcements and dominated communist supply roads. Navarre calculated that the enemy would come out to fight. Once in the open, the natives would break against a wall of French élan and western technology.[8]

Or maybe they wouldn't. On March 13, Navarre's men faced a rude awakening when artillery shells began raining from the hills surrounding their camp. Vietnamese General Vo Nguyen Giap had ringed the valley with heavy guns and pounded the French defenders like they were the Russians at Austerlitz. French soldiers clung to trenches and pressed themselves against sandbag walls as Soviet-made howitzers, mortars, and rocket launchers blasted them from the high ground.

The wounded screamed in half-shattered dressing stations. The unwounded prayed. Bodies piled up, and the garrison held on by its fingernails through March and April. As graves were filled, blown apart, and filled again, the French foreign ministry frantically begged President Eisenhower—the liberator of France—to rescue his comrades.

Ike watched the French stumble into disaster. He told Swede Hazlett he had begged them to ask the United Nations to legitimize an international force, as in Korea. But the "frantic desire of the French to remain a world power"—the Gallic pride he had faced in World War II—compelled them to dash in under the Tricolor. They were now chin deep in *merde* and needed Ike to pull them out.[9]

Ike was still trying to get a signed armistice in Korea, and he had no appetite for pulling troops from one battlefield and thrusting them onto another. Yet Indochina seemed different. It was symbol and linchpin. The key to all of Southeast Asia. At a news conference on April 7, he introduced the metaphor of "falling dominos." If Indochina fell to the communists, he explained, the rest of the region would follow: Japan, Formosa, the Philippines, and beyond—Burma, Thailand, Malaysia, even Australia, would be the new front line.[10]

The first domino was wobbling. How could Ike stop it from tipping?

His military advisors suggested air strikes from carriers stationed off the Gulf of Tonkin. Ike scotched the idea. He had relied heavily on airpower in Normandy, but this wasn't Normandy and the Viet Minh weren't the Wehrmacht. "Aircraft will not do the trick," he told Admiral Radford. "You put your air carrier bombers in, they bomb, and the fellows simply pull back and head into the jungle, we don't do any serious damage to them."

In canopied forests, air strikes were a high-risk, low-reward tactic. "If we go in with carrier-borne aircraft . . . we have committed the United States to military participation in that war," he explained. Since bombing would be ineffectual, "We have only two choices left. One choice is to retreat with our tail between our legs because it hasn't done any good, and it hasn't broken the siege; and the other choice is to go in since we've committed American prestige and if we retreat with our tails between our legs it will send a signal to all our allies that we're not very dependable."[11]

In Ike's mind, Vietnam was an all-or-nothing proposition. He wanted to keep the bamboo curtain north of Hanoi, but he didn't want America to get a black eye, either. He decided to go hot only under three conditions:

First, the French had to guarantee Vietnamese independence when the war ended. As Ike told Dulles, "You can't go in and win unless the people want you."

Second, the French had to share military command with the United States. He wouldn't put American boys under generals who had made such a mess of things already.

Third, the effort had to be truly international, not just America and France. "To contemplate anything else is to lay ourselves open to the charge of imperialism and colonialism—or at the very least—of paternalism," he wrote Al Gruenther. He didn't want "isms" obscuring the good he was trying to do.[12]

"Dad wasn't going to do anything unilaterally without allies involved," John Eisenhower said later. "He was sensitive about having a 'white man's war' against brown men or yellow men."[13]

It wasn't just Ike. Congressional leaders, led by Texas Senator Lyndon Johnson, would only go along with intervention if other countries joined the crusade. No coalition, no intervention. America would not—could not—go it alone.[14]

That meant Ike needed Winston's help.

Ike wrote his friend on April 4. "It is difficult to see how Thailand, Burma and Indonesia could be kept out of communist hands. This we cannot afford," he said. He asked Britain to join him in a coalition with France and other Asian nations—such as southern Vietnam, Laos and Cambodia, or Thailand, or the Philippines. Hopefully Australia and New Zealand, too. A truly international force, much like the UN command in Korea.

Ike knew it would be a hard sell. Pleading his case, he fell back on the parable of Munich. "We failed to halt Hirohito, Mussolini and Hitler by not acting in unity and in time," he wrote Winston. "That marked the beginning of many years of stark tragedy and desperate peril. May it not be that our nations have learned something from that lesson?"[15]

The reference, he hoped, would strike an irresistible chord. In 1938, Churchill and Eden had railed against the British government's Munich Agreement with Hitler, which gave the Nazis much of Czechoslovakia. Ever since, Winston had been the enemy of Munich-style appeasement, just as he had been communism's most dogged foe.

Now Ike was counting on the old firebrand to help him keep Vietnam free and democratic. If Britain didn't saddle up, *didi mau*, the French defenders would be doomed. And with them, possibly all of Southeast Asia.[16]

Ike's comparisons to Hitler and Munich were, in Winston's rolling eyes, the rhetoric of the desperate. Ho Chi Minh was no Mussolini, much less a Hitler, despite the trouble he was making for the West.

Winston valued his relationship with France, but he had little sympathy for its plight. Britain had relinquished India, the star of its imperial crown, along with many other colonies since the war's end. Having tossed those vanities on the bonfire, he wouldn't cry over France losing Indochina. As he told Lord Moran the year before, he had lived 78 years without hearing the word "Cambodia," and he did not plan to start worrying about the region now.[17]

He didn't buy Ike's vision of falling dominoes, either. Southeast Asia wasn't a line of dominoes; it was a patchwork quilt. Communism could be held back in many places. It could be held in Thailand, perhaps through an alliance that included India, Pakistan, and Burma. Or Vietnam could be divided in two—the communists getting the northern half, the capitalists the south, like in Korea.

Most of all, Winston wanted to keep Ike from provoking a second Korea—a war in which U.S. intervention would draw in China. A war with China that could escalate into a nuclear showdown with Russia.

"My dear Friend," he wrote Ike on April 7. "We discussed your proposal about Indo-China in the Cabinet this morning and are certainly giving it a great deal of thought. It is however a topic which raises many problems for us." The most London would do was consider an announcement that America and Britain would consult with other nations "with a view to possible collective defense measures." Nothing more.[18]

As Ike scrounged for allies, Winston dined at Chequers with Admiral Radford, Ike's shoot-from-the-hip military chairman. Over china plates and crystal, Radford expounded on falling dominoes and lurid tales of a communist-dominated Asia. Sympathetic but unbudging, Winston said he "regretted that the United States had not stood with them two years ago in coping with their problem in Egypt and in maintaining the security of the Suez Canal."

Taking the hint, Radford suggested the president might be more willing to help with Suez if Her Majesty's Government were more accommodating in Vietnam, where time was running out for the French defenders.

Winston knew better. And even if Churchill thought America would help him negotiate with Nasser, he wasn't going to plunge Britain into a new war in Asia. The stakes might be high in the jungles of Indochina, but the risk of escalation and global nuclear war—with Britain on the front line—was intolerable.

Fear of the Bomb had gripped Britain. The public release of film footage of the Ivy Mike tests left jaws dropping as moviegoers saw the power of the stars unleashed on a tiny Pacific atoll. "The British people would not be easily influenced by what happened in the distant jungles of Southeast Asia," Winston told Radford. "But they did know that there was a powerful American base in East Anglia and that war with China, who would invoke the Sino-Russian Pact, might mean an assault by hydrogen bombs on these islands."[19]

He returned to his big point: Don't fight communism around the fringes. Go for a summit at the center. Stress the hopelessness of war to the Kremlin. Persuade their leaders, jaw to jaw.

Ike's face darkened as he read Radford's report.

"The British are frightened," he complained to his childhood pal

Swede Hazlett. "They have a morbid obsession that any positive move on the part of the free world may bring upon us World War III. Secondly, they are desperately concerned about the safety of Hong Kong." He concluded, "I personally feel that if the Communists would take a good smacking in Indo-China, they would be more likely to leave Hong Kong severely alone for a long time."[20]

But he couldn't smack without Winston's help. And as Winston had said years before, he might not be able to direct events, but he could veto them.[21]

If the French were going under, would Ike send troops to Indochina without British support? Nixon thought he should. "To do no more than we have done would be tantamount to giving the British a veto on U.S. action in Southeast Asia," he argued at a NSC meeting on April 29.

Ike considered a world where America was the town sheriff—and where that might lead. If everything rested on Washington's shoulders, wouldn't it be better to forgo costly battles in Asia and strike at the enemy's heart? Hit Russia with everything, while there was still time?

He had advocated the direct approach against Hitler in 1942. That might be the way to go now. As the French perimeter at Dien Bien Phu shriveled, he told his advisors, "If our allies were going to fall away in any case, it might be better for the United States to leap over the smaller obstacles and hit the biggest one with all the power we had. Otherwise, we seemed to be merely playing the enemy's game—getting ourselves in brushfire wars in Burma, Afghanistan, God knows where."

Thinking it over, he concluded the stakes were too high. He wouldn't intervene. Not without allies. Winston really did hold a veto—even if his veto meant the world would be condemned to watch a slow-motion train wreck in the heart of darkness.

"To go in unilaterally in Indochina or other parts of the world which were endangered, amounted to an attempt to police the entire world,"

Ike explained. "The concept of leadership implied associates. Without allies and associates, the leader is just an adventurer like Genghis Khan."[22]

After fifty-six days of fire, mud, and gore, the Viet Minh overran the last French defenders. Northern Indochina was lost. A peace conference in Geneva ended with Vietnam, like Korea, sundered into a communist north and a democratic south. Ike and Winston hadn't seen eye to eye on either Egypt or Vietnam, and they were losing both.

And, in a way, Britain and America were losing each other.

"They want to run the world," Eden groused. "They want to replace us in Egypt, too." He told Ambassador Makins, "Americans may think the time past when they need to consider the feelings or difficulties of their allies. It is the conviction that this tendency becomes more pronounced every week that is creating mounting difficulties for anyone in this country who wants to maintain close Anglo-American relations."

Winston, the biggest advocate of those relations, held on. "Ike's friendship is very important to Britain," he reminded the secretary. It was a principle as immutable as gravity.[23]

But London had stood firm on Vietnam and discovered the Americans couldn't move without English help. When Ike backed down on Indochina, Eden realized Britain could defy Ike's America when the stakes were high enough. And sometimes, the old Empire could win.

FORTY-SIX

Family Matters

"I'VE DECIDED TO LET THE OLD MAN COME OVER FOR THIS VISIT," Ike told Jim Hagerty in June. "Winston really wants this conference, although I don't know how much good will come of it. But I decided to go along with him once again and play it more or less by ear."

Winston had been knocking at Ike's door for months, and by the summer of '54, they needed to talk. In April, Ike had suggested a meeting; after the bruises of Suez, Korea, and Indochina, he wanted to "explore why we seem to reach such drastically different answers to problems involving the same basic set of facts."[1]

At a press conference in mid-month, he downplayed the visit—as much as a return visit from Winston Churchill could be downplayed. "To make it a friendly, informal thing, I invited him to come to the White House and spend a weekend," Ike told reporters. "He is an old, old friend, as you people know. I haven't the slightest idea of exactly what we will talk about. But I will tell you, very frankly, that I doubt whether there is a subject that anyone could ask a question about this morning of any international concern that we won't talk about. We will talk about everything—I have been in these before. As you know, again I repeat, I like and admire him, and I look forward to his visit with the greatest of pleasure."

It would be basic maintenance, not damage repair, he stressed. "There is a bridge here across the Potomac, and thousands of people use it every day, and that is not news," he told the journalists. "But let the bridge fail or fall some place, and it is instantly news. Now, we are not trying to make news; we are trying to keep the bridge between America and Britain strong."[2]

Assistants and Unders and Deputies at State always got nervous when Churchill came calling. They fretted over the president's fondness for him—and where his friendship would lead America. Full of warnings and caveats, they wrote memos, shuffled papers, and briefed the president, drilling him on subjects the prime minister would raise. To Dulles and his men, these rehearsals were reminders to be on guard, a sort of mental calisthenics before the Fuller Brush salesman showed up at the door.

Ike appreciated their efforts, but he didn't need warnings. He had said no to Winston more than any other living American, and had been on his guard since 1942. "Winston has a wonderful way of turning conversations at some later time into ironclad agreements," he said. "I'll tell Winston right off that we are not here to make agreements and decisions, but if we have to, we will write them out and initial them so we both know exactly what we are talking about."

Dulles proposed an Anglo-American study group to iron out their differences over Europe, the Mid East, and Asia. Ike thought that made sense. He said he would bring it up in a way that would make the initiative seem like it came from Winston. "That's the way you have to work with Winston," he said, explaining a technique Winston often used on FDR. "You have to get him thinking it's his own idea."

The perennial sticking point would, of course, be colonialism. The British were facing international pressure to leave Cyprus, while the French were trading their old crisis in Indochina for a new one in Algeria.

Dulles complained that the British were always asking the Americans to make a distinction between bad French colonialism and good British colonialism.

Ike agreed. "The British always think their colonialism is different and better," he said. "Actually, what they want us to do is go along to help them keep their empire."[3]

The briefings finished, schedules prepared, dinner invitations sent out, by Thursday afternoon, June 24, the White House was ready, down to the last case of cognac, which arrived from the French National Association of Cognac Producers. The delivery slip was addressed to Sir Winston Churchill.[4]

Bottles on hand, Ike waited for his friend.

"The heroic figure of the stooped warrior, Sir Winston Churchill, is probably moving across the United States political scene for the last time," James Reston wrote in the *New York Times*. The stooped warrior was so indelibly etched into the American mind that Reston's readers could picture the famous silhouette: the stocky figure leaning on a gold-tipped cane. Cigar clamped between his manicured fingers. Polka-dot tie, bowler derby. He was appearing on the American stage for his hold-over engagement.[5]

Canopus touched down at National Airport on the morning of Friday, June 25. Fortified with a breakfast of champagne and caviar, Winston emerged from the plane to a greeting committee headed by Richard Nixon and Foster Dulles. Shaking hands with the dignitaries, Winston sauntered over to a jostling group of reporters to offer a few cheerful words.[6*]

* Because Ike hadn't gone to the airport to greet visiting heads of state such as the Queen of Greece and Ethiopia's Emperor Haile Selassie, his protocol team felt he could not go there to greet Winston, a mere head of government. Protocol would change with Winston's next visit.

"I have come with Anthony Eden to talk over a few family matters, and to try to make sure there are no misunderstandings," he said as cameras clicked and scribes scribbled. "The English-speaking family—or brotherhood—is rather a large one, and not entirely without a few things here and there, and if we work together, we may get along all right ourselves and do a lot to help our neighbors."[7]

Warm smiles. All positive. But he didn't tell them what he was really thinking—something he discussed with Eden on the flight: "We, the Americans and British, must go and talk to the Russians in an effort to avert war, diminish the effect of Cold War and procure a ten years' period of 'easement.'" He didn't tell them he wanted to pull Ike back from nuclear saber-rattling. Nor did he share his growing fear that Eden and Dulles, feuding over the Far East, might smash the bridge he had spent so many years building.[8]

Ike and Mamie waited on the steps of the North Portico as Winston's motorcade rolled up. The old man stepped from a convertible limousine, smiling as usual, nodding to reporters before shaking hands with Ike and Mamie.[9*]

It was Winston's first visit to the Eisenhower White House, and the hosts were in full bloom as they ushered him inside. Mamie, smiling, radiating middle-class imperium in a floral-patterned dress, offered Winston his choice of rooms. He selected his usual quarters: the Rose Room, where he and Ike had met a dozen years before. Mamie and Ike gave him a short tour of the renovated family quarters, pointing out the new decor added by the reigning mistress.[10]

Ike and Winston spent a pleasant half hour catching up. Like two

* Ike had wanted to meet Winston at the South Portico, which would look more informal and downplay expectations. Through a screwup by the social secretary, the usual North Portico reception had been arranged. When told at the last minute, Ike was angry that his orders had been overlooked but had no choice but to go along with it.

generals walking an old battlefield, they strolled to the Oval Office together, memories rushing in as Winston conjured up the ghosts of 1941.

"I remember being here in this room when I visited President Roosevelt and I had a press conference," he reflected, blue eyes alight. "The room was absolutely full. They couldn't see me; I had to stand on a chair."

Ike nodded. He had been in the West Wing in those dark days and remembered them well. Because FDR couldn't walk, he delivered press talks in the Oval Office.

But times had changed, Ike said. Nowadays he held press conferences across the street in the old State, War, and Navy Building, where they had room for a bigger crowd and television cameras.

Another way the world had changed.

He guided Winston around his office, showing him personal touches that made the space his own. His hand hovered over an ancient ibis statue given to him by Egypt's General Mohamed Naguib, Nasser's predecessor. "It was made at the beginning of the bronze age, represented the God of Wisdom and Science, and corresponded to the Greek god Hermes," he explained. Winston, who despised Naguib and Nasser and rarely spoke of Hermes, merely nodded.

Turning to a framed landscape hanging on a wall, Ike's face lit up. It was an "original Eisenhower," he said with pride.

Squinting at its hues and brushstrokes, Winston asked Ike where he had painted it. Ike described the scene: a valley in Colorado that had intrigued him with its cold, stark beauty. He couldn't quite capture the ruggedness of the Rocky Mountain winter, but he liked it just the same. Like most of his memories, nearly everything in the Oval Office was government property. This painting was his.

Winston gave a solemn nod, at last declaring the scene not "overstressed."

They talked about painting, they talked about work. Winston asked Ike whether he found it difficult to paint when the press of business interrupted.

Ike confessed he did. After dealing with a decision, or crisis, or problem, he would return to his easel with no memory of how he'd intended to color a field or a cloud bank. Colors were far more complex than he used to think of them. A sky was never just blue. Clouds were never just white. What he had once seen as a green field, he now saw as a mosaic of twenty different greens.

Winston nodded. He described statesmanship the way Ike described green. "In the last twenty-five years of peace and war, things have gotten ten or fifteen times more complicated," he said. "The problems I have now to face are much greater in numbers and complexity."[11]

After the half hour's reverie, Eden and Dulles arrived to nudge along the afternoon's agenda. The topics rolled in fast, heavy, and sometimes random: "Germany, France, Guatemala, the Hapsburg and Ottoman Empires, the Kerensky Government in Russia, African colonies, the French position in North Africa, Indochina, the Oppenheimer case, the internal problem of communism, the Boer War, World War II, the relationship of Communist China to Russia, the EDC and NATO and the Locarno Pact," the American minutes noted.

Things got prickly when talk turned to Egypt, where Britain was locked in bitter negotiations over withdrawal of troops from the Canal Zone. Eden, looking to step out of the old man's shadow, had pushed for the withdrawal over Winston's objections—one of several disagreements between Winston and his right-hand man.

Stepping over that thorn bush, Ike downplayed the importance of the Canal Zone. Winston did not. In an emotional riff, he reminded Ike that fifty thousand British graves had been dug in Egypt or its frontiers. He wanted Ike's promise not to send arms or economic aid to Cairo until Nasser reached an agreement with London. Most important, he said, "the situation must be avoided in which people would think that the United States had driven the UK out of Egypt."

Ike had no intention of getting dragged into an Anglo-Egyptian squabble, and he vaguely assured Winston of his general support. He would never help Nasser drive the UK out of Egypt, he said.

In Vietnam, the table turned. Ike wanted tangible support from Britain in Southeast Asia. Winston told Ike he was anxious to share some of the general burden. But, he cautioned, "England would never accept going to war in Indo-China. He doubted that the United States would, either." He wouldn't give Ike any more assurances than Ike had given him on Egypt.[12]

A little before three o'clock, they took a ten-minute break for a photo session in the Rose Garden. Sitting together, flanked by their foreign secretaries, Ike nodded genially as Winston flashed his trademark Cuban cigar.

As photographers dashed off to their darkrooms, Ike stood as Winston's legs battled gravity. Ike offered a hand.

"I can get up," growled Winston.

"I know you can," said Ike, smiling. In many ways, Winston needed Ike's help—but he was too proud to beg for it.[13]

By the time they moved to Ike's upstairs study, clouds had thickened. Under darkening skies, Winston returned to his old summit theme. As usual, Ike pumped the brakes—though this time, he didn't say no. He couldn't be absent from the country for too long, so he'd borrow a page from his Darlan playbook. He might come for the first day of a conference, but would leave Nixon or Dulles there to work out an agreement, then come back for the last few days to sign the agreement. As always, he needed to know a summit would be productive before he put America's prestige on the line. *Before*—not while sitting in a room with Malenkov.

Winston offered to make a personal "reconnaissance in force" to test Russian waters—waters he felt were inviting. The Soviet people, he said, were emerging from decades of struggle. They were not so different from westerners anymore. As he told Henry Cabot Lodge, "[T]he average Russian wants 'knick-knacks for his cottage.' He wants movies and bars and football. He wants the kind of fun that people have in a democracy. But they have had 50 years of the most horrible existence, what with the Czars, two world wars, and the oppression of their own rulers. It has all been dreadful beyond description." The mood in Russia must have changed for the better.[14]

As Ike warmed to a summit, he and Winston reaffirmed the principle of nuclear deterrence. A robust network of western air and missile bases would ensure no Soviet attack could take out everything before the West hit back with enough to wipe out most of Russia. That fact alone kept the Soviets in check. As Winston remarked, "What might be the doom of the world could prove to be its salvation."[15]

Outside, the wind picked up. A squall began to spit, drip, then lash Washington as the men took a short break. Jock Colville and Christopher Soames, Winston's son-in-law, were sipping highballs in the sitting room downstairs when, Jock recalled, the old man "suddenly emerged and summoned us to go up to the 'Solarium' with him to look at a great storm which was raging." Colville told his diary, "I can't imagine anybody else interrupting a meeting with the President of the United States, two Secretaries of State and two Ambassadors just for that purpose."[16]

But Winston was not anybody else. Molded by the adventures of his youth, he had a strange relationship with chaos. In the middle of a tempest—a cavalry charge, a pitched argument, a bombing raid, a storm—he came alive. The romantic in him drew energy from maelstroms, whether of God or of man. The awe of a storm, the dread of a hydrogen blast: Where others fled, his mind ran at them full tilt, exploring every corner, feeling out the dark and the light. Looking for what lay beyond.

Alone with Ike the next afternoon, Winston sipped scotch and soda that was more soda than scotch. He brushed aside differences over peripherals like Egypt and Vietnam. Like the ancient hedgehog, he returned to his one big idea.[17]

Ike listened. He began to come around. Perhaps he was warming to a Big Three summit. Not on communist territory, of course, but maybe, say, Stockholm, or the Hague. Ike thought Winston might reach out indirectly, through diplomatic channels, and he didn't object to a mild overture so long as Winston didn't give Malenkov an opening to "hit the free world in the face."

"I swear to you that I will not compromise you in the slightest," Winston assured him. He promised to sound out the Cabinet on a "reconnaissance" and give Ike an answer within forty-eight hours of his return to London.[18]

Winston left the Saturday meeting elated. After two years of groundwork, momentum was shifting. Winston was perfectly happy to be the advance man—John the Baptist setting the stage—for it would be his hand engineering the big event. As Moran told his diary, "It is his belief—and this he holds with a fierce, almost religious intensity—that he, and he alone, can save the world from a frightful war which will be the end of everything in the civilized globe that man had known and valued."[19]

The next morning dawned quiet. Ike, Dulles, and their wives went to church at National Presbyterian. Winston and Eden slept in. Later, they gathered in the Screening Room to watch a newsreel of the Queen's much-publicized world tour.

"During the movie the President kept up a running conversation with Churchill," Jim Hagerty told his diary. As the film showed scenes of Gibraltar and North Africa, a cheerful Ike pointed out places he and

Winston had been during the war. "When an arch to train elephants in Ceylon was shown, the President said, 'Winston, there must be a lot of Republicans over there.'"[20]

The lights came up, and Ike excused himself to take care of some business. Winston spoke to Dulles about the summit. As the men spoke, Winston realized that skipping church hadn't gotten him out of a fire-and-brimstone sermon.

"I pointed out to Mr. Churchill that it was extremely dangerous to have such a meeting unless it would have positive results," Dulles wrote after the meeting. "An illusion of success would be bad, and also an obvious failure would be bad and might create the impression that the only alternative was war." He also warned Winston that an exploratory mission to the Soviet capital "would not be looked upon well in this country." Meaning it wouldn't be looked upon well by Dulles.[21]

The secretary complained to Jim Hagerty afterward. "The Prime Minister was still obsessed with the idea of going to Moscow for a meeting," he said. "Of course, we are unalterably opposed to such a trip."

He added, "It may be if we do not go, Churchill will anyway."[22]

Monday morning found Winston back in the Oval Office with Ike, Dulles, and Eden. Winston strained to listen, but without his hearing aid, the voices blurred. Hagerty told his diary, "The Prime Minister didn't seem able to hear the conversation or to follow it and constantly broke in with questions that had to be explained to him by either the President or Eden in a shouting tone of voice."[23]

The two leaders agreed to meet the next morning to sign a joint press statement. Ike, who lived on farmers' hours, jested, "Winston, I will be ready to meet you anytime you want. I get up at 6:30 and will be available from seven o'clock on."

Winston smiled. "Mr. President, as you know, I have a habit of getting up a little later than that."

"10:30?" asked Ike.

"A little later than that, please."

"11:30?"

"That will be fine. That is more normal."[24]

The next morning, they concluded the visit with a bland communiqué pledging to work together to free the oppressed and slow the growth of nuclear arsenals. In deference to Winston's seniority, Ike signed his name below Winston's. Winston took Jim Hagerty aside and told him that Ike's name, as a head of state, should go first—and he made Jim promise that in the version that went to the press, Ike's name would go above his own.[25]

After Ike walked Winston to his car for one last photo opportunity, Winston rode over to the British embassy for a luncheon. He joked that if he were ever banished from England, he would come to America and run for Congress. "He would then propose two amendments to the American Constitution: (i) that at least half the members of the US Cabinet should have seats in Congress, (ii) that the President, instead of signing himself Dwight D. Eisenhower a hundred times a day, should be authorized to sign himself 'Ike.'"[26]

Shortly after leaving, Winston penned a note to Mamie, thanking her for her hospitality. "Being in the bedroom which I know so well brought back many memories and certainly this last visit to the White House, so beautifully renewed inside by you, will remain among the pleasantest and most enjoyable," he told her.[27*]

* Before leaving, Jock Colville discreetly asked Ann Whitman how much Winston and Eden should leave as tips for the White House butler staff. Ann noted to Ike that White House employees are directed to say that nothing is expected, but the Emperor of Ethiopia had left $400 in tips, and Jock

Despite Winston's limitations, Ike felt he had made progress and staved off a summit threat. Ike's charm was his armor, and like Winston, he knew how to leverage a friendship. "He said that he was one of the few people who could kid and laugh Churchill out of a position instead of talking straight or sternly to him," wrote C. D. Jackson.[28]

The friendship was genuine, but official relations between Britain and America were nearly as frosty as before. The fight over a summit had ended with no knockout and neither man backing down. Under the smiles, disagreements were laid bare, and now Eden and Dulles, who'd differed violently over Vietnam, were barely on speaking terms. Winston still despised the American secretary, supposedly referring to him as "the only case I know of a bull who carries his china closet with him."[29]

Ike and Winston were so stubborn about their commitment to friendship, they wouldn't admit the bruises hurt.

But bruises grow and blacken over time, as they were about to learn.

---

suggested $100 apiece from Winston and Eden. Ike scribbled a note that $200 for the party would be "*more than* ample."

FORTY-SEVEN

Grass Underfoot

QUEEN *ELIZABETH* WAS A FADING DAME of the Old World cruise set. The elegant ocean liner sliced through the Atlantic's chops as she carried Winston and Eden home in style. But her well-heeled passenger market had shifted from the British upper crust to a rowdier sort from farther west, and she dressed to flatter a new crowd.

"Oh, the changes that have taken place, in order to please the great dollar-producing clientele, since we last sailed on the *Queen Mary* in 1953!" Jock Colville lamented to his diary. "The Verandah Grill food, which formerly equalled or surpassed many famous French restaurants, has become Americanised and has sunk to a level of ordinariness, if not tastelessness, which bewilders and disappoints. The same applies to a lesser degree in the service and appearance of the ship's company. . . . It is a pity, and rather a humiliating pity, that the Cunard line must go to these lengths to de-Anglicise themselves."[1]

Pity or not, *QE* was following the trade winds. During the war, GIs had planted seeds of Americana from Tokyo to London, and by 1954 those flowers were in bloom. Marilyn Monroe and Marlon Brando filled silver screens, Satchmo blew his horn from vinyl records, and Coca-Cola, Marlboro cigarettes, Sugar Ray Robinson, and Mr. Potato Head were worldwide icons. The British Empire—mother of Parliament, common law, the English tongue, and the Industrial Revolution—was taking more than a few elbow jabs from her boisterous son.

In his stateroom, Winston was running out of time to play the long game. The world could not go much longer with the two sides refusing to meet jaw to jaw. As he told journalists, "We have to live with all sorts of people in this wicked world." Despite Dulles's frosty Sunday sermon, he felt the moment to play matchmaker had come.

"Ike has crossed the gulf which separates a mission to destroy Bolshevism from living side by side in peace," he told Lord Moran. "I must admit that I myself have crossed that gulf. I would like to visit Russia once more before I die."[2]

He drafted a letter to Molotov asking his view on a personal visit. If Molotov saw a path, Winston would ask the Cabinet to make an official request. The United States would not participate, but "my feeling is that the United States would make it as good for me with their public opinion as they could."[3]

He considered the letter personal, but a letter from the British prime minister to the Soviet foreign minister implicated both governments. So before he could send the letter, he had to clear a few hurdles.

The first was Anthony Eden, who was horrified when he read the draft. Dulles had been clear: Any overture would open a rift with the Americans. Talks would also discourage European countries from approving a badly needed defense force. The Cabinet would revolt. There were far too many risks, he said.

But Winston was in no mood to listen. He didn't have much time left, and he needed a summit. From his cabin, he told Jock Colville to warn Eden that if the Cabinet wouldn't let him write to Molotov, he would resign.

A shocked Colville tried to reason with him. The party's future lay with Eden, Macmillan, and other Tories who would inherit the leadership when Winston retired. A seamless transition from Churchill to Eden would lay a foundation for Conservative dominance into the

1960s. To resign in protest, Colville warned, "would split the country and the Conservative Party from top to bottom."

Winston nodded. Yes, it would, wouldn't it?

But if leaving now meant peace, resignation—even casting his party into the wilderness—would be a price worth paying.

"He was absolutely determined; nothing would shake him; he would go on alone; if his colleagues abandoned him, he would appeal to the country, who would support him," wrote Harold Macmillan when he learned what had happened. "All this from strength. It was his last passionate wish—an old man's dream—an old man's folly, perhaps, but it might save the world."

For a whole day Churchill and Eden remained on separate decks, in separate suites, refusing to meet. They argued in writing, with Colville shuttling between the statesmen like a truce messenger in no-man's-land.

After a day of fighting, Winston sent for Eden and offered a compromise: He would ask for Cabinet approval to write to Molotov, but only if he could tell the Cabinet that Eden supported him. If Eden wouldn't stand with him, he would resign, go home to Chartwell, and let the chips fall where they might.

Eden knew where the chips would fall, and he resented Winston's power play. He had waited ten years to succeed the old man. The premiership was nearly within his grasp. He had taken the transatlantic ship voyage, rather than a fast flight home, just to persuade Winston to hand Conservative Party leadership over to him that summer.

Now Winston had put him in a bind. If Eden refused to support Churchill's Moscow fantasy or threatened to resign in protest if he sent the letter, the old man would resign. He would go home and paint landscapes of the French Riviera while the Conservative Party burned. Labour would win the next election, and Eden's dream of becoming prime minister would turn to ashes. Eden would be known as the man who broke the Tory run.

"I am afraid the PM has been ruthless and unscrupulous in all this,"

Colville told his diary. "He must know that at this moment, for both internal and international reasons, Eden cannot resign."

Eden could have resigned. He could have gambled that Winston would back down. But he lacked the gambler's instinct, the force of will, to defy his mentor and play for the highest stakes.

Eden gritted his teeth and submitted. Winston could tell the Cabinet Eden approved the Molotov letter. "Under the pressure of the tremendous force of this old man's character, Eden gave way," Macmillan concluded.

With Eden out of the way, Winston cleared the telegram with Rab Butler—just Rab, not the entire Cabinet as he had promised—and fired it off to Molotov before the ship reached Southampton.[4]

Over bezique and drinks, Eden and Winston patched up their spat. Winston assured Anthony he would succeed him at 10 Downing, though he was loose about the timing.

He also repeated his long-held conviction: Britain must stay close to Ike's America. "Up to July 1944 England had a considerable say in things," Moran recorded him telling Eden. "After that, I was conscious that it was America who made the big decisions. She will make the big decisions now."

The unsettling thought hung between them. "We do not realize her immeasurable power. She could conquer Russia without any help. In a month the Kremlin would be unable to move troops. The Americans would become enraged—violent. I know them very well," he said. Britain's only course was to guide Washington, gently but steadily, down the path of peace.[5]

Molotov's reply to Winston's message arrived as he reached London. The Kremlin would welcome an overture. Winston forwarded the cable to

Ike, along with a carefully cropped summary of his letter to the Soviet minister.

Thinking of grand possibilities, Winston told the Cabinet he would be amenable to a summit meeting in some neutral venue. Perhaps Stockholm or Vienna. Wherever the Americans might agree to go.[6]

He had set talks in motion. A personal visit to Moscow, then a three-power talk to settle things. The old man had defied Ike, defied his Cabinet, even defied time. His reward lay just ahead.

"You did not let any grass grow under your feet," a red-faced Ike wrote Winston after he read Winston's letter and Molotov's response.

> When you left here, I had thought, obviously erroneously, that you were in an undecided mood about this matter, and that if you had cleared your own mind I would receive some notice if you were going to put your program into action. However, that is now past history and we must hope that the steps you have started will lead to a good result.[7]

Ike was furious. The leash had snapped, and Winston seemed hell-bent on seeing the onion domes again. "The President said Molotov's double-talk should make [Winston] suspicious, but it won't," Dulles told his secretary. "Only another stroke would keep him from going."[8]

The next day they began a long-distance exchange that stressed friendship and fundamental differences.

Winston:

> I hope you are not vexed with me for not submitting to you the text of my telegram to Molotov. I felt that as it was a private and

personal enquiry which I had not brought officially before the Cabinet I had better bear the burden myself and not involve you in any way. . . .

Much grass has already grown under our feet since my telegram to you of May 4, 1953. . . . I have of course stated several times to Parliament my desire that a top level meeting should take place and that failing that I did not exclude a personal mission of my own.[9]

Ike:

Of course I am not vexed. . . . Personal trust based on more than a dozen years of close association and valued friendship may occasionally permit room for amazement but never for suspicion. Moreover, I cannot too strongly emphasize to you my prayerful hope that your mission, if you pursue it, may be crowned with complete success. . . . No one could be happier than I to find that I have been wrong in my conclusion that the men in the Kremlin are not to be trusted.[10]

Winston:

I am very much relieved by your kind telegram which assures me that no serious differences will arise between our two governments on account of a Russian excursion or "solitary pilgrimage" by me. . . .

All this may be moonshine. The Soviets may refuse any meeting place but Moscow. In that case all would be off for the present, or they will give nothing and merely seek, quite vainly, to split Anglo-American unity. I cherish hopes not illusion and after all I am "an expendable" and very ready to be one on so great a cause.[11]

Ike:

I am certain that you must have a very deep and understandable desire to do something special and additional in your remaining period of active service that will be forever recognized as a milestone in the world's tortuous progress toward a just and lasting peace. Nothing else could provide such a fitting climax to your long and brilliant service to your sovereign, your country and the world. . . .

As you know, while I have not been able to bring myself to believe wholeheartedly in the venture, I most earnestly pray that you may develop something good out of what seems to me the bleakest of prospects. This I say not primarily because of my deep affection and respect for an old and valued friend and the satisfaction I would take in such a personal triumph of yours, but because the world so desperately needs to be strengthened in hope and faith and confidence. . . .

Having said this, I must also say that because of my utter lack of confidence in the reliability and integrity of the men in the Kremlin and my feeling that you may be disappointed in your present hopes, my mind has been turning toward an exploration of other possibilities by which you could still give to the world something inspiring before you lay down your official responsibilities. . . . I suggest to you a thoughtful speech on the subject of the rights to self-government.

Championing, not opposing, self-determination of Britain's former colonies would give the democracies a powerful weapon in the fight against communism. "In far too many areas the Kremlin is pre-empting the right to speak for the small nations of the world. We are falsely pictured as the exploiters of people, the Soviets as their champion," Ike wrote. "Colonialism is on the way out as a relationship among peoples."

He hoped Winston would make a virtue of necessity. He should see nationalism for what it was—the emerging current of history. "Should we try to dam it up completely, it would, like a mighty river, burst through the barriers and could create havoc. But again, like a river, if we are intelligent enough to make constructive use of this force, then the result, far from being disastrous, could redound greatly to our advantage, particularly in our struggle against the Kremlin's power."

Ike had the letter sealed and sent it through diplomatic pouch rather than through State Department channels. "I want no other to see it except you and me."[12]

It seemed Ike might have been right. The Kremlin proposed a European summit to discuss security issues. Its motive was obvious: A European Defense Force was nearing acceptance, and Molotov was trying to sidetrack it by dangling the prospect of a Soviet-led alternative. It was a transparent effort to keep Europe divided and weak. Even Winston knew he could not forge ahead.

With a heavy sigh, he sent Molotov a letter withdrawing his proposed visit.[13]

In a follow-up letter to Ike, he gathered his hopes and fears: "I am not looking for the means of making a dramatic exit or of finding a suitable Curtain," he said.

But he made one last try:

> It will seem astonishing to future generations—such as they may be—that with all that is at stake no attempt was made by personal parlay between the Heads of Government to create a union of consenting minds on broad and simple issues. . . . Fancy that you and Malenkov should never have met, or that he should never have been outside Russia, when all the time in both countries appalling preparations are being made for measureless mutual destruction.

> Even when the power of Britain is so much less than that of the United States, I feel, old age notwithstanding, a responsibility and resolve to use any remaining influence I may have to seek, if not for a solution at any rate for an easement.

"The interest of both sides is Survival," he emphasized. "Now, I believe, is the moment for a parlay at the summit."

He closed his letter: "Please believe me always your sincere friend, Winston S. Churchill."[14]

Winston gave way, but he would never agree. He wanted talk that could lead to agreement. Ike wanted agreement before he would talk. Winston had tried everything he knew—public oration, letters, personal talks in Bermuda and Washington, a power play to Molotov—but Ike's distrust of the Kremlin's leaders was stronger than Winston's faith in human nature.

And as the world would soon learn, Ike was prepared to battle communism with every weapon he had. The Bomb, the dollar—or cloaked daggers.

FORTY-EIGHT

Wet Work

"I WAS BROUGHT UP TO FEEL PROUD OF MUCH THAT WE HAD DONE," Winston told Ike in a reply to his letter suggesting Winston throw his support on the side of colonial independence movements. "I am a bit sceptical about universal suffrage for the Hottentots even if refined by proportional representation. The British and American Democracies were slowly and painfully forged and even they are not perfect yet. I shall certainly have to choose another topic for my swan song. I think I will stick to the old one: 'The Unity of the English-speaking peoples.' With that all will work out well."[1]

Winston had come of age during Rule Britannia, and the onetime colonial secretary liked to expound on the blessings of British influence. The original Parliament met in Westminster Palace, but its offspring gathered, debated, and voted in New Delhi, Ottawa, Cape Town, Karachi, Rangoon, Melbourne, and elsewhere, a testament to British wisdom and liberalism.

Back in 1943, while Churchill had been visiting the White House, FDR had invited Helen Reid, publisher of the *New York Herald Tribune* and an outspoken champion of Indian independence, to a luncheon with the prime minister. Halfway through the main course, Reid pointedly asked Churchill, "What are you going to do about those wretched Indians?"

With a polite smile, he replied, "Let's get one thing clear. Are we talking about the brown Indians in India, who have multiplied alarmingly under the benevolent British rule? Or are we speaking of the red Indians in America who, I understand, are almost extinct?"[2]

FDR broke out in a hearty laugh. But on colonial matters, Winston wasn't joking.

Though he wouldn't say it out loud, by 1954, America was becoming an empire. It didn't send viceroys to rule over natives, and it didn't use the dirty word "colony." But the United States was asserting spheres of influence and deploying soldiers to protect far-flung interests, just as Britain had for two centuries. America didn't like to admit it, but it was acting like an empire—and had no business telling Britain not to act like one.

"My steel struck no spark from his flint," Ike glumly wrote Al Gruenther after reading Winston's reply. Winston, he said, "is completely Victorian in this regard, even though he is absolutely right in his contention that a number of these peoples who are screaming for independence are not yet equipped to support it, and that by now laying down British responsibility in this regard, he would be merely contributing to further unrest and possibly the spread of Communism in the world."[3]

Winston's defiance had been his greatest strength when fighting Hitler. But that defiance bound him to old ways in a world evolving faster than ever.

"Philosophically, I think there is much to be said for Winston's view," Ike admitted to his diary. But, he told Winston, he "must go with the current of history on this, since it's going to happen anyway and become a rapids and—and if you don't go with it, your canoe will be wrecked."[4]

As they sparred over colonialism, the Cold War took an unexpected detour through Central America. In March 1951, Colonel Jacobo Árbenz

Guzmán, Guatemala's left-of-center president, extended a socialist-style land redistribution program. Communists hitched their wagon to Árbenz's reforms, and the fingerprints they left bore the same loops and whorls as those in Tehran. The following year Truman gave Beetle Smith's CIA approval to plan Árbenz's overthrow.

In May 1954, the tempo quickened with a CIA report that a Swedish ship carrying Czech and German weapons had docked in Guatemala. To Ike and Dulles, Eastern bloc weapons meant only one thing: communist infiltration. Left unchecked, it would spread like cancer through Central America. Ike needed a tool to fix Guatemala, and he found one in the CIA's Operations Division.[5]

Allen Dulles's appetite for black bag operations had grown since Iran, and Foster Dulles wanted communism thrown out of the hemisphere. The brothers agreed on a covert solution.

CIA propagandists began jamming government radio broadcasts, sending leaflet bombers over the capital, and broadcasting antigovernment messages from a mysterious radio transmitter called "Voice of Liberation." Conservative oligarchs, disgruntled Catholics, and the merchant class grew restive, and by the time Árbenz awoke to the storm, it was on him.

On June 15, Eisenhower gave final approval to a military coup, dubbed "Operation PB Success." He told the brothers Dulles to preserve the fiction that the United States wasn't involved. But Ike was a gambler, and he played to win. If it came down to a choice between deniability and victory, he wanted victory. He told his lieutenants, "I want all of you to be damn good and sure you succeed. . . . When you commit the flag, you commit it to win."[6]

Three days later, a ragtag company of mercenaries rolled across the Guatemalan border from Honduras in a motley parade of trucks, station wagons, and sedans. The circus was led by Colonel Carlos Castillo Armas, a right-wing enemy of Árbenz. The 170-man force, vastly outnumbered by the Guatemalan Army, crawled timidly and halted often. But President Árbenz, unwilling to risk an all-out battle against an army whose size he didn't yet know, kept his troops close to the capital as the rebels crept forward.

Overhead, a few World War II–vintage fighter-bombers began strafing the capital's Guardia de Honor barracks and the National Palace. The planes did little damage, but the explosions were loud enough to make the capital's inhabitants think something bigger was coming.

The CIA's air campaign sputtered when a fighter-bomber ran out of fuel and crash-landed over the Mexican border. Two others were knocked out by ground fire. Without an air force to buzz the capital, the curated image of an unstoppable rebel army would evaporate. And if army officers got wise to the real size of the *"Ejército de Liberación,"* they would move forward and crush the rebels.[7]

At a White House meeting, Ike agreed to replace the lost fighter-bombers through the friendly Nicaraguan government. The move was risky and might expose the American hand, but the card player who had launched six amphibious invasions didn't harbor misgivings. He had the killer instinct, and now was the time to act decisively. As he explained to Andy Goodpaster, his military aide, "If you at any time take the route of violence or support of violence—which of course is what had happened in this case—then you commit yourself to carry it through, and it's too late to have second thoughts."[8]

The next day, Guatemala's UN ambassador frantically announced that unknown forces had invaded his country. He called for a Security Council meeting to approve a UN investigation. Ike and Dulles directed their UN ambassador, Henry Cabot Lodge Jr., to urge the council to refer the matter to the Organization of American States, a toothless debating society dominated by Washington.

Britain's UN ambassador, Sir Pierson Dixon, voiced HMG's opposition to any attempt to overthrow a democratically elected government. When he learned the U.S. was behind it, he quietly told Lodge the United States was committing the same flagrant aggression Stalin had perpetrated in Korea. As a matter of principle, Britain would have to support a Security Council resolution for a UN investigation.[9]

Ike wasn't having any of it. He told Dulles that Lodge was being "too damned nice to the British on this." America would use its UN veto to "show the British that they have no right to stick their nose into matters which concern this hemisphere entirely." It wasn't like he was sending the CIA into, say, the Belgian Congo. Guatemala was only eight hundred miles from the Panama Canal, and he wouldn't give the Reds a foothold close to Texas.[10]

As ordered, Lodge warned Ambassador Dixon. The threat was unmistakable: If Britain broke with Ike over Guatemala, it would pay a price. As Dixon cabled Eden, "If we took an independent line in an area vital to the United States, they would feel entitled to take an independent line in areas vital to Great Britain, such as Egypt."[11]

While Eden and Dulles maintained a veneer of civility, they deeply disliked each other. Dulles needled "Ant'ny," as he called him, occasionally asking whether he had gotten his premiership yet. "The trouble with you, Foster," Eden dryly retorted, "is that you want World War Three." When they were late returning from one meeting, Winston muttered, "I hope they haven't quarreled and killed each other."[12]

Part of their problem lay in their communication styles. "Dulles was a lawyer and an intellectual, so he developed his thought at some length," recalled British Ambassador Roger Makins. "Eden was an intuitive man, and so he got bored listening to this long exposition and did not take it in."

A master of understatement, Eden wrapped difficult positions in layers of nuance. Sometimes his message was more about what he didn't say than what he said. As a result, key points sometimes got lost in a mosaic of nouns, verbs, and modifiers.[13]

Winston was cut from a different cloth. You didn't have to search for his point. He made it, emphatically and often, with crisp, neon clarity—a language Ike was fluent in after years studying the man.

"We differed on a great many policies with Mr. Churchill," remembered U.S. Assistant Secretary for Far Eastern Affairs Walter Robertson. "But at least in our relationships with Churchill, he would put the cards on the table. We'd put the cards on the table. He would tell you what he could do and what he couldn't do, and why he couldn't do it. He would criticize our position and we would defend it and criticize theirs, but it was always on a basis of two friends trying to meet a common viewpoint about a common problem."[14]

Eden believed the Americans were wrong to block Guatemala from having its day before the Security Council. The UN was supposed to deal with aggression against weaker states. It wasn't just a moral principle; it assured small nations they didn't need to arm themselves to the teeth for protection against bullies. Now Ike had thrust London into a dilemma: stand by America or stand by British principles.[15]

Dulles delivered the blunt message to Eden in the limousine ride to the White House during Winston's family matters visit. The U.S. would oppose a UN investigation, and Eisenhower expected Britain to follow America's lead. As Jim Hagerty put it in his diary, "The President and Dulles talked cold turkey to the Prime Minister and Eden and told them that we would use the veto against them if they insisted on putting the Guatemalan question in the Security Council."[16]

Eden looked to Winston to reset America's moral compass. Might shouldn't unmake right. Winston had influence with Ike, and he alone could bring America around.

Winston loved Anthony Eden like a son. When Anthony married his niece Clarissa, in fact, he became Winston's nephew-in-law. But sometimes Anthony lacked a sense of proportion, and this was one of those times. Winston muttered to Jock Colville, "Eden was sometimes very foolish: he would quarrel with the Americans over some petty Central American issue which did not affect Great Britain, and could forget about the downtrodden millions in Poland."[17]

In a long life spent watching moral conflicts, Winston accepted that sometimes principles, even cherished ones, must give way for the greater good. Eleven years earlier, he and Roosevelt stood mute when Stalin claimed 20,000 Poles found murdered in western Russia's Katyn Forest had been massacred by Germans. Winston knew perfectly well Stalin's NKVD had carried out the executions, and the falsehood weighed on his conscience. But Winston was at war with Hitler, and he needed Stalin more than he needed to vindicate the truth. So he ignored the truth and fought the war.

In the Cold War, some principles were outweighed by bigger ones. With hydrogen isotopes hovering over humanity, what was Guatemala? "I'd never heard of this bloody place Guatemala until I was in my seventy-ninth year," he growled. Europe was the main battleground, East Asia the flank. As one of Eden's diplomats put it, "Guatemala is not the only pebble on the beach."

So Winston would politely avert his eyes and let Ike do what he must. He told Eden to drop the matter. Ambassador Dixon would abstain from the Security Council vote, and they would let the Organization of American States bury the mess.[18]

Though incensed that the United States would overthrow a democratically elected president, Eden kept his mouth shut. Publicly, at least. "If allies are to act in concert only when their views are identical, alliances have no meaning," he rationalized to himself.[19]

But alliances were a two-way street. Winston might stick with Ike, but his successor at Number 10 had to consider Britain's future greatness. Having given in on a matter of principle, Eden now had a chit he could cash in someday. As a matter of fair play, if London wished to get tough over, say, the Suez Canal or Cyprus, Ike would have to follow London's lead.[20]

So for now, Eden said nothing.

In Guatemala, the war theater proved more theater than war. Fighter-bombers buzzed the skyline like angry wasps, dribbling incendiaries, smoke bombs, and explosives on airports and oil tank farms. Too little to cause much damage, but their job wasn't to smash. It was to scare the hell out of the capital's citizens.

The pilots had help on the ground. Voice of Liberation radio broadcast phony reports of government defeats in the field and warned of an army of thousands closing in on the capital. Bribes were slipped to local commanders, and the American embassy staff set up loudspeakers on the roof to play recordings of bomber attacks, fueling panic.

Believing the rebels numbered in the thousands—not the few hundred they really were—the Guatemalan Army refused to move. The capital's citizens lost confidence in their government, which seemed paralyzed. Bitter residents nicknamed the rebel pilots *"sulfatos,"* a laxative, for the effect they supposedly produced on President Árbenz and his ministers.[21]

As Árbenz's supporters melted away, his hardcore loyalists, among them a 26-year-old radical named Ernesto "Che" Guevara, felt powerless to resist the approaching rebel army. On June 27, eleven days into the operation, Árbenz resigned and fled into exile. A military junta headed by anti-communists took power and began ousting leftists from their posts.[22]

From Ike's perspective, it had been a messy thing, but the mission was a success. Ike had insisted, Britain had stepped aside, and Ike had gotten his way. Now, as he turned to the Far East, others would have to give way.

FORTY-NINE

Atomic Bullets

BACK IN LONDON, WINSTON TOLD THE CABINET Britain could not remain a first-tier power if she lagged in hydrogen bomb development. Peace through strength required British strength, not just American strength. And British strength required something more powerful than an atomic bomb.

"The primary aim of our policy was to prevent major war, and the possession of these weapons was now the main deterrent to a potential aggressor," the Cabinet minutes recorded. "[The prime minister] had no doubt that the best hope of preserving world peace was to make it clear to potential aggressors that they had no hope of shielding themselves from a crushing retaliatory use of atomic power."[1]

Retaliation was where he differed from Ike. Winston believed in clear boundaries: Conventional weapons deter conventional aggression, nuclear weapons nuclear aggression. A simple principle, really.

Ike's message was muddled and often contradictory. For all his love of clear lines of organization, Ike embraced nuclear ambiguity. He used hydrogen bombs the way a poker player bids while holding two pair, aces and eights. He believed the fuzzier the line, the more likely the communists would tread carefully.[2]

But along China's coast, they looked ready to call his bluff.

The wind turned bitter on the Pacific Rim in the fall of 1954. On September 3, Chinese artillery unleashed a barrage against Formosa's Quemoy and Matsu Islands, sending high-explosive shells three miles across the Formosa Strait.[3]

Formosa, the large island locals called Taiwan, was to Peking what West Berlin was to Moscow. To Chairman Mao and his premier, Chou En-lai, the anti-communist redoubt was a national insult lying just out of reach, an insult that posed a small but persistent threat to China's communist government. General MacArthur once called Formosa an "unsinkable aircraft carrier," a description that brought to mind England's role in Eisenhower's Normandy invasion.

The Nationalist-held Quemoy and Matsu Islands made tempting targets for Mao. Much closer to China than Formosa, they were hard to hold and easy to hit. But Formosa's Nationalist leader, Chiang Kai-shek, didn't plan on holding off the People's Liberation Army by himself. He counted on Ike's backing, and Chiang's 40,000 troops stationed on the islands were little more than a trip wire for American intervention.

After the loss of North Vietnam, Ike felt the West couldn't let Chiang go down like Davy Crockett at the Alamo. "The loss of Formosa would doom the Philippines and eventually the remainder of the region," he wrote to Winston, repeating his domino theme. "We are determined that it should not fall into the hands of the Communists, either through all-out attack or, as would appear to be far more likely, through harassing air attacks, threats and subversion."[4]

But Formosa was one thing. Quemoy was another. Questions loomed large as artillery shells shook the ground: Was Quemoy expendable? Would it be the next domino? Would it justify U.S. entry into war?

Would that war go nuclear?

Ike was vacationing west of Denver when the crisis erupted. He motored over to Lowry Air Force Base and held a special session of the National Security Council. The meeting room was tense as Ike and his advisors batted round the question of whether Quemoy was essential to the defense of Formosa—and whether Formosa was essential to the defense of the United States.

Three of the Joint Chiefs argued that the use of atomic weapons would be justified. A weak response, they warned, would embolden Mao. General Matthew Ridgway, Army chief of staff, dissented on political grounds: Other nations would see the use of atomic weapons as an act of unnecessary aggression. Dulles took up the familiar domino theory, Nixon voiced his usual hard line.

A frowning Ike juggled diplomacy and deterrence. "He was personally against making too many promises to hold areas around the world and then having to stay there to defend them," the NSC minutes recorded him saying. On the other hand, he said, "If we are to have a general war, he would prefer to have it with Russia, not China."

Though a hard-liner, Dulles admitted that "the British fear atomic war and would not consider the reasons for our actions to be justified." Ike said most Americans wouldn't, either. They didn't want their sons dying on a few islands no one gave a damn about before the crisis. But if America did get into war, if Ike committed the flag, he would go all out for victory—even if victory required a few atomic shocks.

He ordered the Joint Chiefs to prepare for any action, but make no move just yet. He would make his final decision when the picture crystallized.[5]

Through the winter, questions hung in the air. If China grabbed Quemoy, would Washington interpret the seizure as a prelude to a Formosa invasion? Would Ike open an atomic battle over a few unknown specks of sand? Would Malenkov?

Chekhov once said that if the audience sees a gun in Act One, it must be fired by Act Two. And Ike, Winston, Mao, and Malenkov were well into Act Two.

As the crisis stretched into the new year, Winston watched, his stomach tightening. If China invaded Formosa, that meant general war with America. And probably with Britain.

Formosa, yes. But what about the Matsus? He had seen this film before. Another archduke shot in an alley. Another Fort Sumter, a sinking of the *Maine*, a blunder in the night. Did Ike have the skill—was he big enough—to avoid a nuclear showdown?

One rash act on the Chinese coast, and England could wake up with mushroom clouds blooming over London.

In February he wrote Ike to urge restraint. "You know how hard Anthony and I have tried to keep in step with you, and how much we wish to continue to do so," he said. "But a war to keep the coastal islands for Chiang would not be defensible here."[6]

Ike responded with his usual line: kind, but unmoved. "Quite naturally," he wrote, "it distresses us whenever we find ourselves in even partial disagreement with the conclusions that you two may reach on any important subject."

China, he argued, had mistaken past restraint for weakness. "There comes a point where constantly giving in only encourages further belligerency," he said. "Further retreat becomes worse than Munich because at Munich there were at least promises on the part of the aggressor to cease expansion and to keep the peace. In this case the Chinese Communists have promised nothing."[7]

Munich.

Winston's eyes lingered on the word. He had played the Munich card with Ike. Ike had played it with him. It was a metaphor you grabbed when you had no facts to grab. Watching Ike toss it on the table, Winston didn't find it any more persuasive now than when he had played it over Egypt.

But Ike held other cards. Ten-megaton cards, and he seemed ready to play them, too. At a presidential press conference on March 16, 1955, Charles von Fremd of CBS News asked the question on everyone's mind: Would America use nuclear weapons in the Far East?

Nodding gravely, Ike said, "I see no reason why they shouldn't be used just exactly as you would use a bullet or anything else. I believe the great question about these things comes when you begin to get into those areas where you cannot make sure that you are operating merely against military targets. But with that one qualification, I would say, yes, of course they would be used."

His words hung in the air like dust after a blast.

"I have one great belief," he said. "Nobody in war or anywhere else has made a good decision if he was frightened to death. You have to look facts in the face, but you have to have the stamina to do it without just going hysterical."[8]

Two weeks later, Ike complained to Winston that Britain wasn't moving with America. "It is because of this confidence in our common intent—indeed, I hope I may say our indestructible personal friendship—that I venture to bring up an apparent difference between our two governments," he wrote.

The tone was cordial, but the message carried weight. "Although we always seem to see eye to eye with you when we contemplate any European problem, our respective attitudes toward similar problems in the Orient are frequently so dissimilar as to be almost mutually antagonistic."

He opened the old hymn book and sang the refrain. "Two decades ago we had the fatuous hope that Hitler, Mussolini and the Japanese war lords would decide, before we might become personally involved, that they had enough and would let the world live in peace. We saw the result," he said. "The Communist sweep over the world since World War II has been much faster and more relentless than the 1930 sweep of the dictators. I do believe that all of us must begin to look some of these unpleasant facts squarely in the face and meet them exactly as our Grand Alliance of the 40's met our enemies and vanquished them."[9]

"You have to look facts in the face without going hysterical," Ike had said. But how could a rational person consider using weapons that might snuff out a billion lives without going hysterical? Winston could only wonder.

Well, there wasn't much Winston could do. He could urge Ike not to unleash Grendel's mother over a meaningless island and hope for the best. As he told Eden, "I will watch the situation as a cat does a tiger."[10]

But he knew he couldn't watch forever. The clock, Winston's foe since he moved back to 10 Downing, was beginning to chime.

FIFTY

"Never Be Separated from the Americans"

By the summer of '54, Winston's battles had lost their thrill. Problems of peace lacked war's clarity, its urgency, its moral certainty.

Reminiscing over the war's dark days, he told a visitor, "In many ways I had an easier time of it. If we won a battle, we simply began preparing for the next. If we lost one, it was the same. We always knew exactly where we stood, and we had the power to act as we thought best."

He paused.

"Now everything is different. There is so much patter, patter, patter, chatter, chatter, chatter, it's a wonder anything ever gets done."[1]

Not that British voters seemed to care much about the world beyond their shores. They wanted jobs, housing, medical care, and peace. The cost of empire had become inconvenient. The workingman of Manchester, Birmingham, Liverpool, or Battersea was happy enough to shed the imperial burden if it meant lower taxes and cheap food.

It was lonely blowing on the embers of a dying fire when so many wanted the fire out. As Winston glumly remarked, "I could have defended the British Empire against anyone except the British people."[2]

Now he was running out of ways to brush off Eden's hints that he must resign. The foreign secretary had a fair point: Under British law, the next national election couldn't be pushed beyond October 1956. To give the Conservative Party its best chance of staying in power, Eden would need time to cement himself at the helm of Number 10, time for voters to see him as captain rather than first mate. He needed Winston out.[3]

There was also the question of the old man's ability to focus. The only remaining MP to have been elected during the reign of Queen Victoria, Winston had trouble concentrating and required complex papers summarized for him in a paragraph. *The Economist* lamented "mounting evidence that the flow of domestic policy is now subjected to a serious bottleneck at the Cabinet level." The *New York Times*'s London desk painted a picture of defense chiefs and ministers "waiting for a summons to the Cabinet that never comes because it is engrossed in foreign affairs or is listening to Sir Winston's views on the world at large."[4]

There were plenty of reasons to retire, but Winston defied them all. He scoffed to his doctor about the perennial objection, his health.

"Of course I know that I'm nearly eighty and that I may get another stroke any day," he groused to Lord Moran. "My heart may stop at any time, but my health is certainly no excuse for evading all these great issues, just because one doesn't know the answers. I'm not going to quit. It would be cowardice to run away."

He was no coward. If Eden wanted the job that badly, he'd have to prove he could handle it, for the job of Queen's first minister was not for the faint of heart—or body. Anthony had been out of action for months after his gallbladder debacle, and the effects of three major abdominal surgeries had left him in chronic pain.

"It is not as if I were making way for a strong young man," Winston told Moran. "Anthony seems to be very tired. I detect strain in his telegrams. Sometimes he sends three thousand words in one day—and there is nothing in them."[5]

At Dorneywood, country residence of the Foreign Minister, Eden squirmed. For a decade, he had watched and waited, like the Wise Men of the East, for a sign that Winston would go. But the star hadn't appeared.

And in 1954, no one could shove him out. To the people, Churchill was a stallion among geldings. His jowls, homburg, and cigar were the most recognizable trademarks of any man on earth. A coalition of one, he stood immovable as the Tower of London, and no Conservative would dare suggest a palace coup. Not yet, anyway.

So summer segued lazily into fall. Eden waited and Winston lingered, savoring the twilight of his reign, looking for his own sign. A sign from the west.[6]

Ike watched the approach of Winston's eightieth birthday, and on November 28 he sent an official message through State Department channels. But nothing State could draft up would be wholly adequate for their friendship, so he followed it up with another "Dear Winston" letter:

> I want to add to that deeply felt but somewhat official note, a sense of my appreciation of the privilege that has been mine to call you friend—in the truest meaning of the word—for these many years. Mamie and I join in warmest affection and admiration to you.
>
> Ike E.[7]

The friend's birthday set Ike's mind to musing on greatness. He had met most of the world's great leaders, knew a few of them well, and had at least passing acquaintance with many now gone or in retirement. So a few days after his letter to Winston, he set down some thoughts in a letter to his high school chum Swede Hazlett.

"Not long ago my old friend Winston reached the venerable age of four score," he wrote. "The occasion was made one of celebration throughout the Empire, and our own papers were filled with reminiscent accounts of his experiences and accomplishments. Some of these were, I thought, both reasonable and accurate; others extravagant. In reflecting on some of the statements made, I began in my own mind to arrange in priority of 'greatness' the people I have known."

A great man, said Ike, must be generally acknowledged as preeminent in some broad field of human endeavor, or have discharged some great responsibility that left a favorable imprint on future generations. Plato, Martin Luther, George Washington, and Napoleon had those qualities (though Napoleon had obvious defects as well, he noted). In Ike's lifetime, George C. Marshall topped Ike's list among great Americans.

Then he turned to his old friend.

> Now Churchill. Unquestionably he is a great politician and a great war leader. In addition, he has displayed many of the qualities of a great man. For my part, I think I would say that he comes nearest to fulfilling the requirements of greatness in any individual that I have met in my lifetime. I have known finer and greater characters, wiser philosophers, more understanding personalities. But they did not achieve prominence either through carrying on duties of great responsibility or through giving to the world new thoughts and ideas of such character as to bring them by popular acclaim the title of great.[8*]

* John Eisenhower recalled that when his father took a break from writing *Waging Peace*, the second volume of his presidential memoirs, he jotted down the names of the greatest men he had known,

---

Winston painted the way he lived—bold, direct, unafraid. As he told Clare Boothe Luce, "You just sit down, my dear child, and you *attack the canvas.* If you don't win the first battle, there's always another, so long as there's another piece of canvas."[9]

In political arts, his approach was the same. Sweeping strokes. Enough color, enough action, enough emotion to light up the darkest hours. The human story, dark imagery, and hope's beacon splashed across his oratory like the colors of Renoir's cafés.

Ike's political art was more utilitarian, more down-to-earth than Winston's. He spoke to the middle class; he spoke to teachers, to factory workers, grocers, and weekend golfers. Methodical and measured, Ike's style was the realism of Grant Wood's farmers and Hopper's nighthawks. He wasn't there to launch a crusade. He was there to protect and reassure.

A month after Winston's birthday, he sent Winston a personal request, one he felt he could ask because of their long friendship. Nothing to do with statecraft.

"As you know, I occasionally flatter myself by attempting to paint likenesses of friends," he wrote. "I would be tremendously intrigued by the effort to paint one of you. Would it be an intolerable burden on you to allow an artist friend of mine to visit you long enough to take a few photographs and draw a few hasty color sketches that I could use in such an attempt? The final result would, of course, not be good, but also it might not be so bad as to be unendurable."[10]

Winston would have preferred a request involving Russia, but with a shrug he told Ike he would submit to lens and pad. So Thomas

---

then chucked his list into the wastebasket. John fished it out and read the names Churchill, Marshall, de Gaulle, Foster Dulles, and Charles Portal. A few months later at dinner, John asked his father to list the five greatest men he had known in his lifetime. Ike rattled off the same names.

Stephens, a British-born artist, flew to London to photograph and sketch Winston during a busy workweek. Winston humored him, welcoming the interruption. Afterward, he wrote Ike, "I hope that the results will inspire you."

"The inspiration is guaranteed," Ike replied. "The big question mark is the result."[11]

Slowly, glacially, Winston grew comfortable with the specter of retirement, the way an old man sheds his fear of Death—and sometimes welcomes him. He reached that tipping point early in 1955 after some bitter rows with Eden. With no prospect of a Big Three summit, Winston accepted the inevitable: He would relinquish power by Easter.[12]

But his mind wasn't made up, and Anthony was becoming irksome. With an eye on the October 1956 election deadline, Eden pushed and pulled to get Winston to resign.

"The old man feels bitterly towards me, but this I cannot help," Eden told his diary. "Someone has to give a heave."[13]

The heave came from the Kremlin. In February 1955, the Soviet TASS news agency abruptly announced Malenkov's resignation as premier. He would hang on a while for the sake of optics, but he had officially been sidelined. Defense Minister Nikolai Bulganin stepped up, seconded by Communist Party First Secretary Nikita Khrushchev.

That was the end for Winston. "Until Malenkov fell, [Winston] believed that he, and he alone, could help to make the Russians see reason," wrote Lord Moran. "When Malenkov went, the bottom fell out of Winston's plans."

Winston blamed Ike for the impasse. "I might have been able to persuade the President that a meeting with Malenkov would be useful," he grumbled to Moran. But "Ike got into his 'royal' mood and said he could not leave the country."[14]

By this point, no one in Winston's inner circle would have been surprised if Winston decided to work until he died on the floor of the Commons. But at February's end, he lost hope. His reign would end before he rolled that last boulder to the summit. He told Harold Macmillan he would definitely resign on April 5 and laid plans for a formal dinner with the Queen on his last night as prime minister.[15]

Macmillan, having heard this story more than once, told his diary, "We shall really miss him if he really does go—which I doubt."[16]

He almost didn't. In March 1955, hope's topsail broke over the horizon. An aide interrupted Winston's bezique game with a cable from Washington. Ambassador Makins reported that Ike was toying with the idea of going to Paris in May to ratify West Germany's entry into NATO. With the Atlantic alliance firm, he might "lay plans for a meeting with the Soviets in a sustained effort to ease tensions and to reduce the risk of war." Ike wanted the Paris trip by May 8, the tenth anniversary of Germany's surrender.[17]

Winston's face lit up. For over two years he had chased a dream, and now Ike was willing to join him. "A meeting with the Soviets," Makins had said. And Ike wanted everything done by May 8!

Winston had not publicly announced his resignation date, so what difference would another month or two make? A mere rounding error in history's timeline.

"All bets were off," he told Colville. He would stay, and with Eisenhower, he would meet the Russians.[18]

The next day Winston broke the news to Eden. The ambassador's cable, he said, "is of prime importance. It is the first time President Eisenhower has responded to my appeals beginning May 11, 1953 and has shown willingness to visit Europe in person." He said, "This proposal of a meeting of Heads of Government which he would attend himself must be regarded as creating a new situation which will affect our personal plans and time-tables."[19]

"Our personal plans and time-tables." Eden seethed. Winston's resurrected sense of purpose couldn't have come at a worse time. With the old man in retirement, Eden could call a snap election for May, at a time when the Labour Party was tearing itself apart in one of its internal feuds. An extended stay meant forfeiting a golden opportunity to cement Conservative Party dominance for another five years.

"Chequers and Dorneywood are not on telephoning terms at the moment," Macmillan told his diary. In correspondence, the two men barked like bulldogs over a bone.[20]

Three days later the balloon burst. Fearing the old man might hang on, Eden ordered Ambassador Makins to clarify exactly what the president had in mind. Makins's follow-up report, wrote Macmillan, "made it clear that the President was *not* thinking of High Level talks with Russia. He merely thought that while he was in Europe, useful discussions could take place with a view to a note to the Russians suggesting a meeting in October. . . .

"At this word," Macmillan wrote, "Churchill made a gesture of disappointment." Winston wrote Clementine, "If it is clear that Ike will not in any circumstances take part in the near future in a top level meeting, that relieves me of my duty to continue."

He said *"If,"* still unwilling to admit that his mission was over, but he accepted Fate's verdict. He would lay down his office, as promised, on April 5. Anthony Eden would succeed him as prime minister.[21]

Winston and Ike had held the reins for a long time. Thirteen years. The world of 1942 was a faraway stranger to the world of 1955, and now it was time for the senior partner to take his bow.

Winston called for a secretary.

"My Dear Friend," he began, "I am sorry we shall never have a top-level confrontation of our would-be friend." He said he hoped their friendship would carry on beyond their official tenures.

He let go of business and turned to happier things. Oil paints on canvas. He asked about Ike's "Churchill Project."

"How are you getting on with the portrait? I hope you will show it to me when it is finished and I warn you I shall claim full rights of retaliation."[22]

Ike had to give the old man credit. After building an unmatched reputation as a war leader, he had been ready to cash in a lifetime of chips—and the future of his party—on a long shot at peace.

Musing on their years together, he began dictating a reply.

Dear Winston,

> . . . Your letter, with its implication that you are soon to withdraw from active public life, started, in my memories, a parade of critical incidents and great days that you and I experienced together, beginning at the moment we first met in Washington, December, 1941. Since reading it I have been suffering from an acute case of nostalgia. . . .
>
> In these later years, starting with my return to Europe in January of '51, I have valued beyond calculation my opportunities to meet with you, especially when those meetings were concerned with the military and diplomatic problems of the free world and our struggle against the evil conspiracy centering in the Kremlin. Because I do so highly value this long association and friendship with you, I echo your hope that the impending divergence of our lives will apply to political occasions only. Indeed, I entertain the further hope that with this greater leisure, you will more often find it possible to visit us in this country—after all, we do have a fifty percent share in your blood lines, if not in your political allegiance.

As for his "Churchill project,"

> I discovered a small black and white print portrait of you that was painted some years ago. In order to obtain some practice in the task I had set for myself, I have painted a small canvas, using this photograph as a guide. I do not know the name of the original artist, but it is a picture of you sitting in a straight-backed chair, in a paneled study, and holding a cigar in your right hand. Considering my lack of qualifications in this field, it did not turn out badly and I have had a color photograph made of it, which I am forwarding with this letter.
>
> Actually, I have not had time to complete every detail of this particular canvas because I must say that it is difficult for me to give a fairly realistic impression of the stripes in a statesman's trousers. I could wish that, at least for the day you sat for that portrait, you could have worn your wartime "zipper suit."
>
> With my affectionate regard and my most prayerful wishes for your continued good health and happiness,
>
> As ever,
> Ike[23]

Smiling, Winston dictated one of his last letters on Prime Minister letterhead. "My dear Friend," he said. "By the time you get this very inadequate reply I shall have resigned my Office as Prime Minister and relinquished my direction of British policy."

Hopeful as always, he added, "To resign is not to retire, and I am by no means sure that other opportunities may not come upon me to serve and influence those causes for which we have both of us worked so long. Of these first is Anglo-American brotherhood, and the second is the arrest of the Communist menace. They are, I believe, identical."[24]

With the transition of power, he had much to do and set aside his draft. In the chaos of the moment, he never finished the letter.

How dull it is to pause, to make an end,
To rust unburnish'd, not to shine in use!

Tennyson's ode to an aging Ulysses summed up Winston as he stood on the threshold of retirement. He didn't romanticize his place as statesman emeritus, a doddering grandfather to be taken off the shelf, handed a medal or portrait or degree, then ignored. The ringing plains of windy Troy lay far behind him, retirement's bucolic uplands ahead. His sword, so often unsheathed, would rust unburnished in its scabbard.

Of course, he took comfort in his legacy. During his lifetime, the Tower of London had not fallen to blows from the Kaiser, Hitler, or Stalin, all of whom were long gone. He had taken the worst the dictators could dish out yet remained on his feet—a broken nose and bloody lip, but standing in the ring, gloves up for another fight.

He would amass honors and encomia from around the world, though by now accolades meant little. In April, Jock Colville discreetly floated to the Queen's private secretary the idea of offering Churchill a dukedom. After checking, palace mandarins determined that new dukedoms could go only to members of the royal family. The Queen could, as a gesture of courtesy, offer one, but only with the understanding that the offer would be declined.

When Jock broached the subject, his master snorted. "First of all, what could he be duke of?" Colville recorded. "Secondly, even if he were Duke of Westerham, what would Randolph be? He could only be the Marquis of Puddleduck Lane, which was the only other possession he had apart from Chartwell, his country home. And thirdly, quite seriously, he wished to die in the House of Commons as Winston Churchill."[25]

On the eve of his resignation, the Queen and her husband, Prince Philip, paid the unprecedented honor of dining with the outgoing minister at No. 10 Downing Street. In sash and knee breeches, Winston bowed and Clementine curtsied as they shook the Queen's hand. A beaming Winston had laid out tables for fifty. Lords, ladies, and Cabinet men, with their wives and sovereign, celebrated with a night of grandeur straight out of an Evelyn Waugh novel.[26]

Finishing the condemned man's last meal, Winston bade a warm good night to his guests and shuffled off to his room. As Colville kept him company, he sat on the edge of his bed. He looked old and tired as he gazed out the window, lost in thought.

A sudden realization jolted him. He turned and glared at Colville.

"I don't believe Anthony can do it," he said.[27]

As minutes ticked down to his appointment at Buckingham Palace, Winston presided over his final Cabinet meeting. He spoke of the road ahead, his hope for a future built on the foundation they had laid in war and peace. Then came his parting advice—a rule he had followed ever since that fateful Christmas 1941, when Pearl Harbor lay in ruins and he met an obscure brigadier named Eisenhower:

"Never be separated from the Americans."[28]

The afternoon of April 6 was a pretty day by London standards, and more than a thousand well-wishers gathered outside Number 10 Downing Street to cheer a legend into retirement. At 5:10 that afternoon, he appeared in the doorway in full Churchillian regalia—black overcoat, black homburg, long cigar in one hand, walking cane in the other.

The old man's eyes glistened as he scanned the jumble of faces. From inside the residence, the off-key but recognizable notes of "For He's a Jolly Good Fellow," sung by a score of staffers, wafted into the streets.

Flashing a smile lined with nostalgia and loss, he stepped into his car. An aide carried a small cage housing the parakeet Toby, while his luggage and his poodle, Rufus, were loaded into a second car.

The limousine rolled forward. Flashbulbs snapped, the crowd roared, and Winston was gone.[29]

PART THREE

Waterloo Sunset

(1955–1965)

"He was really not only to my mind a great man;
he is certainly one of my greatest friends."

– Ike, on Winston[1] –

"There was a difference between General Eisenhower as
Supreme Commander under Allied orders, and
General Eisenhower as president of the United States.
I think both the Prime Minister and Anthony Eden never
really quite made that distinction."

– British Ambassador Roger Makins[2] –

Operation Musketeer

Imperial War Museum

FIFTY-ONE

Relief and Denudation

"IT IS A PRETTY TOUGH ASSIGNMENT to follow the greatest Englishman in history, but I feel sure that Eden will make a good job of it." So Harold Macmillan, the new foreign secretary, told his diary.[1]

One way to follow the greatest Englishman was to capture his signature cause, and Eden wasted no time. He began pushing for a summit meeting with himself, Eisenhower, Khrushchev, Bulganin, and the French premier, whoever that might be. Ike, a little surprised by the reversal—Eden had advised going slow when Winston was in charge—sent Dulles to London to talk it over with Macmillan.[2*]

The logjam broke in May, when the Soviet government agreed to withdraw its troops from eastern Austria, ending ten years of Red Army occupation. Withdrawal had been one of Ike's conditions for a summit meeting, and the two sides agreed to a Big Four conference in Geneva on July 18, three and a half months after Churchill's retirement.

Geneva would be a far cry from Winston's vision of a jaw-to-jaw parlay among a few great men. No side conversations, no naughty documents, no give-and-take over brandy and caviar. The conference would

* On Eden's newfound zeal for a summit, Winston grumbled to Macmillan, "How much more attractive a top-level meeting seems when one has reached the top."

run like a SHAEF planning session: fixed agenda; coordinated position papers; an army of experts, bureaucrats, and staffers. No room for improvisation or artistry. Peace negotiations were serious business, and serious men holding folders and briefing books would treat them as such.

"I was sorry I could not persuade Ike to test the Malenkov 'New Look' in 1953," Churchill wrote Eden the month after his retirement. But he added, "Krushev has the Army in a way that Malenkov did not, so that if there is a 'New Look' it may be more fruitful. I do not think the Russian Army wants war. There is no such thing as military glory now."[3]

No glory, just faster ways to kill. Arsenals had grown, and with them the stakes—enough to make Winston despise certain aspects of human progress. During a series of dinners with Henry and Clare Luce, he had remarked, "If I were elected dictator of the world, I should kill all the scientists and burn all the books. . . . I would make it a criminal offense for anyone to go around bothering molecules. The little atom would be left in peace forever."[4]

From his study at Chartwell, Winston labored on his long-delayed *History of the English-Speaking Peoples* with help from Ike's former speechwriter Emmet Hughes. During one visit, Hughes watched Winston struggle to accept that he was no longer at the center of the peace movement.

"Ten days before the Geneva meeting, the old man could not suppress great emotion as he contemplated the imminent conference," Hughes remembered. "He had so ardently hoped for the meeting to occur during his last months as Prime Minister, to mark a climactic initiative for peace. And now his pale blue eyes welled with tears as he looked back upon the unhappy timing of his resignation barely three months earlier. For days thereafter, I could not erase the memory of the sad face and the blinking eyes, watching history—at long last—move pitilessly past, to leave him behind to gape."[5]

Hughes wasn't the only one thinking of Winston. Before Ike boarded *Columbine* for Geneva, Ann Whitman left a note on his desk. "If I were an old man who had dreamed of and worked hard and unsuccessfully for a Summit meeting for years, I would want more than anything a message from 'my boy' as he approaches such a meeting," she said.[6]

Ike agreed: "I could not help thinking, 'What a disappointment it must have been to Winston Churchill not to have been able to represent Her Majesty's government in this critical period.'" So he dictated a note to the summit's greatest advocate:

> Dear Winston,
>
> Soon Anthony and I will be meeting with the French and the Russians at Geneva. As you know, I feel sure that the Western nations could not, with self-respect, have earlier consented to a Four Power Summit Meeting. Yet I cannot escape a feeling of sadness that the delay brought about by the persistently hostile Soviet attitude toward NATO has operated to prevent your personal attendance at the meeting.
>
> Foster and I know—as does the world—that your courage and vision will be missed at the meeting. But your long quest for peace daily inspires much that we do. . . .
>
> As I leave Washington, my thoughts are with you.
>
> Your old friend,
> Ike[7]

Winston replied with his own "Dear Friend" letter:

> It is a strange and formidable experience laying down responsibility and letting the trappings of power fall in a heap to the ground. A sense not only of psychological but of physical relaxation steals

> over one to leave a feeling of both relief and denudation. I did not know how tired I was until I stopped working. . . .
>
> I am very glad that the meeting "at the summit" is now to take place, and I will gladly do anything in my power from a distance and a private station to help it to a good result. . . . My belief is that, so long as we do not relax our unity or our vigilance, the Soviets and the Russian people will be increasingly convinced that it is in their interests to live peaceably with us.
>
> Yrs as always, W.[8]

The summit, held at Geneva's Palais des Nations, fell short of Winston's hopes. Ike, the senior leader, boldly proposed reconnaissance flights over American and Soviet airspace. An "open skies" policy, he argued, would avoid misunderstandings about the state of each other's arsenals. No surprises, no shadows, no overcoats concealing daggers. Khrushchev, knowing much of the Soviet arsenal was a bluff, refused. Ike pressed for German reunification; Khrushchev refused. Khrushchev pushed for a European security system—a ploy to weaken NATO—and Ike predictably refused.[9]

Refusals, refusals.

But at least they were talking. At least they had met, jaw to jaw. As the Parisian daily *Le Figaro* concluded, "Nothing has been settled, but nor has anything been lost."[10]

Winston had sown a seed and left Ike and Eden to tend it. The seed might not ever sprout. But the "Spirit of Geneva," a chance for peace through parlay, was Churchill's legacy and hope. And if there was one thing Winston would never surrender, it was hope.

Winston spent the balance of 1955 basking in the Mediterranean sun, painting, testing his luck in Monte Carlo, and enjoying the hospitality of Greek shipping tycoon Aristotle Onassis. From time to time, he would come home to stump for Conservative Party candidates and attend Parliament.

The MP from Woodford still could pack Westminster's green benches with a speech to the Commons. But it was getting harder to summon the energy for a good stem-winder, and Churchill appearances on the floor became rarer than pine marten sightings. At home, he walked the grounds at Chartwell, his only form of exercise. His steps were slower, his legs heavier, yet he soldiered on. "I get my exercise as pallbearer to my many friends who exercised all their lives," he quipped.[11]

He ruffled feathers with an interview to *U.S. News & World Report.* He told the reporter the Allies had erred in not capturing Berlin at the end of World War II. Then, in a speech in Hastings, he criticized Ike's "Broad Front" strategy, suggesting Monty should have been let off the leash north of the Ardennes. His statements hit a nerve with Omar Bradley, who promptly wrote Ike offering to give an interview rebutting Winston's comments.

Ike shrugged it off. By then, he was recovering from a heart attack that kept him bedridden for six weeks. He had neither the time nor inclination to play armchair general over past grudges. The present was hard enough.[12]

"It has been far too long since I have had the great privilege of hearing from you directly," Ike wrote to Winston the following spring. "I still miss the occasional letters and far too infrequent personal conversations that we had until the date of your retirement."

Ike's letter rambled over the differences between the West and East. He mentioned the Mid East as a place where America and Britain still struggled to stay aligned. He spoke of the specter of nuclear war before returning to the heart of his message: "When I started this letter, I had no other intentions than to tell you how earnestly I pray that your health continues to be good, that Clemmie is well, and that you are both finding time to enjoy your own company and that of your family."

He signed it, "With deep and abiding affection from your old friend, Ike."[13]

Winston replied two weeks later. "Our friendship has lasted through many anxious years, when we were concerned with matters that have passed, on the whole safely, into history," he wrote. "But the fact that you should write to me so fully on the still grave situation which continues to afflict the world is not only a proof of your friendship, but a compliment of the highest order."[14]

Ike was keen to continue the conversation, and in April 1956, he thanked Winston for sending him an advance copy of his forthcoming *History of the English-Speaking Peoples.*

"I immediately plunged into its reading," he wrote. "I am anxious to see whether you make of Richard III a terrible villain as does Sir Laurence Olivier in his interpretation of Shakespeare's tragedy."

Despite the usual friction between America and Britain, Ike said he admired Eden and his new foreign minister, Selwyn Lloyd. "Both Foster and I think that Anthony and Selwyn Lloyd make a splendid team," he said.[15]

He would soon learn the splendid team was walking down a dark path. Trouble was bubbling from the headwaters of the Nile River, and the world was about to find out whether Eden could match Ike's steel under pressure.

And whether the alliance Ike and Winston forged was as strong as they hoped.

FIFTY-TWO

"We Don't Need the Americans for This"

LIFE HADN'T DEALT ANTHONY EDEN A KIND HAND since Winston's curtain call. Stepping from the shadow of the most celebrated Englishman since Henry V was hard enough. Stepping into a year like 1955 was harder still. Inflation and trade deficits gnawed at the pound sterling. Factories slackened. Workers lost their jobs. Labour and Liberal leaders blasted Eden when his cash-strapped government cut milk and bread subsidies. Even his Conservative base roiled, angry over a Cabinet shake-up.[1]

At 57, Eden's silvery hair and tanned face exuded the intelligence and grace voters looked for in their leader. But beneath his skin, Eden's body was falling apart. His botched gallbladder surgery left bile seeping into his bloodstream, triggering fevers and setting off waves of pain he took opiates to dull. Ugly rumors claimed his daylight energy came from a steady diet of Benzedrine and whatever else the doctors gave him. Eden angrily denied the rumors, but the fact that he had to deny them told its own story.[2]

His years under Churchill's lash had left scars. He had weathered many crises during his fifteen-year apprenticeship, but always as lieutenant, not the ship's captain—and Captain Churchill never let him forget who ran the ship.

"I have heard Churchill speak to Anthony Eden before other foreign ministers in a way that you wouldn't speak to a busboy," senior American diplomat Walter Robertson remarked. "It wasn't that he didn't like him. He did. He was devoted to him. But he treated him almost like he was a bad boy. And Eden in my opinion had lost the power of decision."[3]

Eden's persona didn't help. He came across as vain, too polished, too driven by ambition. After the Geneva summit, one of Dulles's aides complained that during the conference, Eden had been "interested in keeping this impression of glamour as much to [his wife, Clarissa] as to the public. He was obviously taking sunbaths or a sunlamp every day, because throughout the entire conference he had a blossoming, vigorous tan." His Conservative Party rival, Rab Butler, remarked, "Anthony's father was a mad baronet and his mother a very beautiful woman. That's Anthony—half mad baronet, half beautiful woman."[4]

Now Eden was feeling the pressure of Britain's toughest job. "I think that his physical condition led to his being even more likely than he had been in the past to exaggerate the urgency of any problem with which he was faced," remarked Ambassador Aldrich. "He had a tendency to feel in every case that a crisis had arisen which required immediate action."[5]

Most of all, Eden lacked the easy friendship Winston enjoyed with FDR, Truman, and Ike. "When Mr. Churchill retired and Eden came in, we had the exact opposite relationship," remembered Walter Robertson. "When we went to a conference with Eden, and came out, we didn't try to evaluate so much as what he said, but what he meant in spite of what he said. He was the most devious foreign minister among our allies of that period."[6]

In Cairo, Gamal Nasser nurtured a grand vision: a colossal dam, irrigation, and power plant complex on the Nile River at Aswan, near the Sudanese border.

His dream promised to electrify Egypt and transform desert into farmland. But it carried a staggering price tag: $1.3 billion—about the cost of the Manhattan Project, more than the New York subway, almost ten times the cost of the Grand Coulee Dam. A loan that size would require a syndicate of lenders and hefty government backing, so the Egyptian president had to win over Washington and London.[7]

At first, Ike wanted to support the project. Funding would show the world America stood with emerging nations, even if they were led by a dictator. But in September 1955, Nasser sent shock waves by inking a $250 million weapons purchase brokered by Moscow's favorite arms dealer, Czechoslovakia. Nasser also encouraged guerrillas to attack Israel, supported anti-French rebels in Algeria, and spewed anti-western propaganda over Voice of the Arabs radio.

Nasser was a disrupter, but Dulles considered him a *nonaligned* disrupter, a sort of fire-breathing Nehru. Nonalignment made all the difference. As long as he wasn't a Soviet puppet, he could be worked with, even managed. So despite the Czech deal, Ike offered to help back the Aswan Dam loan.

While Nasser's men haggled over loan terms and conditions through early 1956, Ike and Dulles took a closer look at the project. The more they saw of it, the less they liked it. Egypt had mortgaged its future cotton harvests to buy Soviet weapons, and now it was a poor credit risk.

Benjamin Franklin once said, "Creditors have better memories than debtors." Someday America would come to collect, and when that day came, Nasser would scream, "Imperialist!" The goodwill Washington earned from extending the loan would vanish like a puddle in the desert. So when congressional leaders soured on the project, Ike and Dulles had an excuse to back off.

Breaking up was the harder question. They wanted no sudden rupture and no confrontation that might give the Soviets a fissure to exploit. They would quietly let negotiations wither as Nasser refused to accept Washington's terms for the loan. Eventually the project would die on the vine, but they could still work toward other points of agreement.

"It's just like your family," Ike told reporters. "Every difference or spat doesn't mean you're going to the divorce courts."[8]

But divorce papers were being drawn up, for by the spring of 1956, Ike and Dulles reluctantly concluded they couldn't win over Nasser. He had staked out an anti-western position, and that meant anti-American, too. At a White House meeting in late March, Dulles proposed a below-the-radar approach to destabilize Nasser without forcing him into the Soviet camp. Dulles recommended inaction rather than action: denying arms and cutting grain and oil shipments to Egypt. America would isolate Nasser by strengthening ties with moderate alternatives in the region, like Arabia's King Saud and Jordan's King Hussein.[9]

The emissaries continued to talk, but sooner or later, Dulles would have to tell Nasser that America wouldn't be its Aswan Dam banker. And Ike knew Nasser wouldn't be happy when he found out.

Knowing nothing of Washington's position, in July Egypt's ambassador, Dr. Ahmed Hussein, flew to Washington to close the Aswan Dam loan deal. He carried instructions from Nasser to drop objections to the fine print and accept all American terms.

Thinking he would emerge with a deal, Hussein was stunned when, in a private meeting, Dulles told him that the administration was no longer willing to fund the dam. Adding insult to injury, right after the meeting, the State Department announced that Egypt lacked adequate resources to make the project a success—lenderspeak for "They can't pay us back."[10]

State's announcement tarred Egyptian credit in international bond markets. As World Bank President Eugene Black later remarked, "It was just about the same as if you went to a bank and asked the bank to lend you some money, and they had a perfect right to say no, but they shouldn't put in the paper that they were saying no because your credit wasn't any good."[11]

Hussein left Washington in a rage. He snarled to a reporter, "He could have told me that they weren't going to back the Aswan Dam, but he didn't need to kick me in the ass in doing it."[12]

Hussein returned to Cairo to give Nasser the bad news. The next move was up to the dictator.

Nasser waited seven days. Then he struck.

"The Suez Canal belongs to us," he told a cheering throng in Alexandria's Al-Manshiya Square as police fanned out through Suez Canal Company offices. "The Suez Canal was built by Egyptians and 120,000 Egyptians died building it. . . . [One hundred million dollars] has been taken from us every year by the Suez Canal Company. We shall use that money for building the High Dam. We shall rely on our own strength, our own muscle, our own funds."[13]

The square exploded in celebration. For hours, Nasser and his bodyguards were trapped by a sea of singing, chanting, dancing citizens clamoring to kiss the hands and feet of "Nasser, Lord and Savior of Egypt and of the Arabs."[14]

It didn't matter that Nasser exaggerated the Canal's finances and its history. What mattered was the moment. After seven decades, Egypt was reclaiming control of its land from the West. Nasser had lit a fire in Cairo that would unite the Arab world.

Outrage washed over the British Isles. The papers exploded in fury. Harold Macmillan called Nasser an "Asiatic Mussolini," while opposition leader Hugh Gaitskell told the Commons, "It is exactly the same that we encountered from Mussolini and Hitler."

Since Kipling's day, the Suez had been a dividing line between the

British Empire's near and far. To Eden, protecting the Suez Canal Company was a matter of principle: Her Majesty's Government would never give in to force.[15]

It wasn't just prestige or principle. Suez was the artery through which 80 percent of Western Europe's oil passed. A third of the 14,666 ships using the canal the previous year had been British, and Britain owned 44 percent of the Suez Canal Company. Nasser had a tourniquet to clamp on Britain's oil and trade whenever he pleased.[16]

The confrontation became personal. It carried Anthony Eden back to his finest hour nearly twenty years before. He had resigned from Neville Chamberlain's government for kowtowing to Italy's fascist dictator; his public stand against Mussolini and Hitler had won him the respect of millions, including Winston Churchill.

Now, with his mentor in retirement and his own popularity flagging, the Suez Crisis was Eden's Churchillian moment. His chance to arrest the Empire's decline while upholding the rule of international law. His chance to show he hadn't been duped when he agreed to withdraw British troops from the Canal Zone. His chance to step into the boots of a great man.[17]

It became an obsession. Nasser was Eden's great white whale, the monster he would pursue, harpoon in hand, until the beast was no more. State Minister Anthony Nutting recalled Eden shouting over the phone, "What's all this nonsense about isolating Nasser or 'neutralizing' him, as you call it? I want him destroyed, can't you understand? I want him removed, and if you or the Foreign Office don't agree, then you'd better come to the Cabinet and explain why!"[18*]

Looking across the Atlantic, Eden felt he had every right to expect Eisenhower to stand with him. Britain had backed America with troops in Korea. Britain had remained quiet during the atomic peril of the Formosa Strait crisis. Britain had given Ike's men free rein in Guate-

* Years later, Nutting claimed Eden used the word "murdered," not "destroyed."

mala, despite Eden's misgivings. Britain lived under a nuclear shadow by hosting American bombers in East Anglia. And Ike's abiding friendship with Winston symbolized an unbreakable tie between the English-speaking nations.

So Anthony Eden would push in the chips Winston had stacked since that long-ago Christmas Eve in 1941. They were all going on one big play.[19]

Winston watched the crisis from afar in Germany, where his racehorse Le Pretendant stumbled to a dismal tenth of eleven on a Düsseldorf track. Hoping Britain would make a better showing in Egypt than his horse did in Westphalia, he wrote Clementine, "Personally, I think that France and England ought to act together with vigour, and if necessary with arms, while America watches Russia vigilantly. I do not think the Russians have any intention of being involved in a major war. We could secure our rights in the Arab world."[20]

There were places in the world governed by legal niceties, but Egypt was not one of them. "The Middle East is one of the hardest-hearted areas in the world," he told his secretary, Anthony Montague Browne. "Peace has only reigned when a major power has established firm influence and shown that it would maintain its will. Your friends must be supported with every vigour and if necessary, they must be avenged. Force, or perhaps force and bribery, are the only things that will be respected. It is very sad, but we had all better recognize it."[21]

Like Eden, Winston saw Nasser's act as an opening for London to reassert its dominance. If Ike would keep the Russian bear out of the Middle East, Britain could handle Nasser on its own.

"He's finished after this," Winston fumed to Lord Moran. "We can't have that malicious swine sitting across our communications."

"What will the Americans do?" asked Moran.

"We don't need the Americans for this."[22]

On August 5, Harold Macmillan, now Chancellor of the Exchequer, dined with Winston at Chartwell. The conversation meandered through political gossip before turning to a military plan Eden had hinted at: The British Army would land a humiliating blow against the Egyptian Army, deflating the myth of Nasser the Invincible and knocking him from power.

"Churchill got out some maps and got quite excited," Macmillan told his diary. The two men talked of Britain's options as Winston's mind ran faster than Le Pretendant. The next day, he took a nondescript car to Chequers for a private talk with Eden. On the drive, he dictated a memo that took a sober look at the risks:

> The military operation seems very serious. We have a long delay when our intensions are known. . . . The more one thinks about taking over the Canal, the less one likes it. The long causeway could be easily obstructed by a succession of mines. We should get much of the blame of stopping work, if it is to be up to the moment of our attack a smooth-running show.[23]

Instead of taking the Canal Zone from Cyprus, he suggested a bold alternative: British tank forces in Libya should drive through Alexandria, capture Cairo, and topple Nasser from the west. Field Marshal Montgomery, visiting Chartwell, had suggested exactly that. It made no sense to rely on a military setback along the Suez to cause Nasser's fall. "Our object is to knock Nasser off his perch," Monty said. "It shouldn't take too long to do that going overland from Tobruk to Cairo." Winston agreed.[24]

But Eden had no appetite for an invasion from Libya. It did not fit his narrative about protecting the Canal and upholding international law. A coup de main through Alexandria also meant dead women and children, tarnishing Britain's reputation for years. He pushed ahead with his Canal gambit, never seriously questioning his basic assumption that if Britain seized the Canal, Nasser would fall.

In mid-August, Eden wrote Winston to update him. The Great Game was afoot. "We are only at the beginning but there are some encouraging elements," he said. French leaders, battling rebels in Algeria supported by Nasser, hated Nasser as much as Eden did and were ready to move against him. "Most important of all," Eden said, "the Americans seem very firmly lined up with us on internationalization."[25]

Was Ike firmly lined up against Nasser?

He would have been glad to see the sonofabitch run out of Cairo on a rail. Nasser's anti-American rhetoric grated on his nerves, and Ike understood why Eden was ready to reach for his rifle: At a NSC meeting on August 30, Dulles opined that the British and French would be finished as top-tier powers leaders if they couldn't hold Egypt in check.[26]

But a military operation against Egypt ran into two of Ike's brick walls. First, he wouldn't do anything to give communists an entrée to the Middle East—and an invasion by Old World imperialists would certainly do that. Second, you don't invade another country out of self-interest, or misguided thoughts of "national prestige." That wasn't how the world worked anymore.

In 1950, Britain, France, and the United States had signed the Tripartite Declaration, limiting weapons sales to both sides of the Arab-Israeli struggle. They also pledged to come to the aid of any nation attacked. It was a measure to keep the peace and give hostile nations comfort that they didn't have to arm themselves to the teeth against their neighbors. Those promises meant something. Ike wouldn't suspend the rules of the road just because his friends didn't like the speed limits.

To Ike, the Suez Canal Company was nothing more than a

corporation operating on Egyptian territory, like a Ford factory turning out cars in Germany. If Nasser wanted to nationalize it, he could nationalize it—as long as he paid the British fair compensation and ran the Canal competently. Neither of those things required an invasion.[27]

Ike sent Dulles to London to discourage military action. Meeting with Eden, Dulles cautioned, "A way must be found to make Nasser disgorge. We believe, however, that force is the last method to be tried. We do not exclude it if all other means fail, but if it is used, we believe that it must be backed by world opinion."[28]

Feeling he had made his point, Dulles returned to Washington. He and Eden had talked and talked, but neither really heard what the other was saying.

"When the two met," remembered British Ambassador Roger Makins, "Anthony Eden didn't really listen too hard to Mr. Dulles' explanation, and Mr. Dulles didn't always assimilate the flashes of Sir Anthony Eden's intuition. And that undoubtedly complicated the relationship."[29]

"It was a sort of cat and mouse game," remembered Robert Bowie, State's senior policy planner. "Dulles was constantly trying to maneuver the situation so that force wouldn't have to be used and that still a satisfactory solution could have been gotten. Eden was trying to maneuver the situation in such a way that the use of force would be legitimate."[30]

"A way must be found to make Nasser disgorge," Dulles had said. That was the goal, wasn't it?

Eden and his Cabinet hawks interpreted American signals as diplomatic niceties, not hard limits. They had a dance to finish before they could use force, so London would patiently step through the quadrille. When the music stopped, Ike could say he tried, and Britain, and possibly France, would go for the kill.

Eden flashed signals to Washington that war plans were being laid.

Ike warned against it. "I am afraid, Anthony, that from this point onward our views on this situation diverge," he wrote on September 2. "The use of force would, it seems to me, vastly increase the area of jeopardy. I do not see how the economy of Western Europe can long survive the burden of prolonged military operations, as well as the denial of Near East oil."

He raised his real concern: "The peoples of the Near East and of North Africa and, to some extent, of all of Asia and all of Africa, would be consolidated against the West to a degree which, I fear, could not be overcome in a generation, and, perhaps, not even in a century."[31]

Eden pleaded with Ike, playing back the language of dominoes and Munich—metaphors Ike had used with Winston, just as Winston had used them with Ike. In the 1930s, Eden said, Hitler had moved carefully at first, creeping into the Rhineland, then annexing Austria, then seizing the Sudetenland, then invading Poland. Every time Hitler gambled and won, his addiction to conquest grew.

"The seizure of the Suez Canal, we are convinced, is the opening gambit in a planned campaign designed by Nasser to expel all Western influence and interests from Arab countries," Eden wrote. "When that moment comes Nasser can deny oil to Western Europe and we here shall all be at his mercy. . . . We have many times led Europe in its fight for freedom. It would be an ignoble end to our long history if we tamely accepted to perish by degrees."[32]

Dulles phoned Ike after reading Eden's letter. "*Ignoble end to our long history*"? All Europe at Nasser's mercy? This was Egypt, not the Third Reich. Dulles told Ike the letter was intemperate, not well thought out. That last bit about perishing by degrees seemed moralistic. Ike said it sounded like Winston's sweeping arc-of-history rhetoric.[33]

Andy Goodpaster, Ike's military aide, said the boss made it "quite clear to the British, repeatedly and personally, that he would not support them if they were to go to take up arms in this affair." But Eden, obsessed with Nasser, was drawn to the rumble of guns. He listened closely to his hawks in the Cabinet. He listened to hawks in Parliament. He listened to hawks in Paris. He wasn't listening to Ike.[34]

Eden had let the diplomatic line play out till it ran off the spool. Now he could plan military operations.

As for Washington, he told himself Ike was simply uneasy about a crisis so close to the U.S. elections, set for November 6. Ike was locked in a rematch against Adlai Stevenson and didn't want an international crisis breaking on the eve of what looked like a smooth sail to reelection.

"I fear he has a mental caveat about November 6. We cannot accept that," Eden wrote Winston on September 21. "We are struggling hard to keep a firm and united front in these critical weeks."

But he added, "Firm is even more important than united."[35]

In stacking "firm" over "united," Eden was gambling on Ike's goodwill. "In spite of what the President had said, I think the British Cabinet thought that their old relationship with the President would mean that he would stand aside at all events," recalled Ambassador Roger Makins. "That's where they made a mistake of identifying their old friend, the Commander in Chief, with the President of the United States."[36]

Ike hoped Paris and London would accept the necessity of a peaceful settlement, and for a while, it looked like the diplomats might win. On October 12, he appeared on a town hall television show called *The People Ask the President.* Flashing his trademark smile, he reported, "I have got the best announcement that I think I could possibly make to America tonight." Britain, France, and Egypt had reached agreement on principles for a peaceful resolution of their differences.

"It looks to me like here is a very great crisis behind us," he told his audience. While they were not out of the woods yet, in his heart he had "a very great prayer of thanksgiving" for the breakthrough.[37]

This time Ike was flying on hope, not hard facts. Three days later, he learned that the CIA's U-2 spy planes captured images of sixty French Mystère fighter-bombers parked on Israeli airfields—not twelve as the French had reported to the State Department. It was a clear violation of the arms limits of the Tripartite Declaration—and a cover-up, to boot.

Something was going on. British Canberra bombers were massing on Cyprus. Radio chatter between Paris, London, and Tel Aviv surged, overwhelming NSA decryption teams. Diplomatic communications went dark, and the Israeli Defense Force began mobilizing.

"From about this time on," remembered Ike, "we had the uneasy feeling that we were cut off from our allies."[38]

It could have been a scene from a Graham Greene novel. On October 22, three Israelis landed in Paris under the cover of darkness: Prime Minister David Ben-Gurion, Defense Minister Shimon Peres, and Israeli Defense Forces Chief of Staff Moshe Dayan. At a shadowy safe house in the suburb of Sèvres, they met with British Foreign Secretary Selwyn Lloyd, French ministers of defense and foreign affairs, and the French Army chief of staff.[39]

The conspirators agreed on "Operation Musketeer Revise," the British code name for an Anglo-French seizure of the Suez Canal. On October 29, Israel would launch a lightning invasion of Egypt's Sinai Peninsula, setting off a crisis that would threaten the Canal. Britain and France, donning the masks of peacekeepers, would issue an ultimatum to both Egypt and Israel: Both sides must withdraw ten miles from the Canal Zone. Israel would comply immediately, and when Egypt predictably refused, France and Britain would launch air strikes, obliterating the Egyptian Air Force.

Black bag men would then broadcast radio propaganda and planes would drop leaflets over Cairo urging the people to overthrow Nasser. A week into this psychological campaign, when the ground force was ready, British and French troops would descend on the Canal and destroy Egypt's remaining military force. With no army to protect him, Nasser would lose face and fall from power. A new government would sue for peace, the Canal would be safe, and the world would be rid of Nasser.[40]

How a few bombs and leaflets—during a Jewish invasion of Arab territory—would topple a leader recently hailed by his people as the "Savior of Egypt" was never fully explained. It was a question Eden should have been the first to ask. But he barreled ahead, stepping over questions he refused to ask and answers he refused to hear.

Because by October 1956, no one in Her Majesty's Government was prepared to say no to a prime minister bent on Nasser's overthrow.[41*]

Ike could hear the spears rattling, but he couldn't tell where they were pointed. From the bird's-eye view of a U-2 camera, Jordan looked like the target. On October 15, the CIA startled the White House with fresh intelligence: Israel was mobilizing its army.

It might be gearing up for operations against Egypt, analysists cautioned. The scale of the call-up wasn't large enough to indicate all-out war, but there was something else—an unconfirmed report that France might be planning to attack Egypt.[42]

The news made Ike sit up. Worse, when Ambassador Makins was recalled to London for a long-planned transfer to Exchequer, communications with London dropped off.

Dulles didn't think the transfer was a coincidence. "We are quite

* The most senior official to oppose force in the Suez, Defense Minister Sir Walter Monckton, resigned over the affair. To avoid a political stink, Eden removed Monckton on health grounds and shifted him to the paymaster general's office.

disturbed here over [the] fact there is apparently a deliberate British purpose of keeping us completely in the dark," he wrote U.S. Ambassador Aldrich in London. "We have had no high-level contacts on any of these matters with British Embassy for a week." Ike echoed Dulles's complaint, claiming in his memoirs, "We were in the dark about what [the British] planned to do."[43]

He wasn't completely in the dark, however. London wasn't picking up the phone, but Ike had other tools. U-2 spy planes flew fourteen missions over Israel, Egypt, the French naval anchorage at Toulon, and British bases on Cyprus and Malta. The high-altitude birds collected photographic and signals intercepts, and the CIA set top priority on analyzing their data. It painted a picture Eden wouldn't.[44]

"My brother said the State Department was taken by surprise. . . . But we had the Suez operation perfectly taped," Allen Dulles later told a reporter. "We reported that there would be a three-nation attack on Suez. And on the day before the invasion, CIA reported it was imminent."[45]

Ike and Dulles couldn't tell Eden they knew he was massing forces. If they did, they'd have to admit America was spying on her best friend. "It was necessary for the Secretary to allow it to appear that he was surprised and to act as if this were something done behind his back," explained State Department Intelligence Chief Park Armstrong. "It was a wheel within a wheel. . . . It was necessary for the leaders on both sides, with perfectly straight faces, to say things which they knew their opposite numbers knew were not true."[46]

On October 28, Ike was in the home stretch of his election campaign when Dulles called with a fresh warning. "Reference made to build-up around [Cyprus]," went Ann Whitman's notes of the call. "French profess to know nothing. British had warning, guilty conscience."[47]

Ike wasn't convinced the British were involved. Eden kept up an air of nonchalance with Ambassador Aldrich, and Foreign Secretary Selwyn

Lloyd told Aldrich negotiations with Egypt were scheduled to resume in Geneva at month's end. To Washington it looked like a French-Israeli cabal. "Dammit, the French, they're just egging the Israelis on—hoping somehow to get out of their *own* North Africa troubles," Ike sputtered to Emmet Hughes.[48]

"We didn't know what was going to be the target or the timing," Ike later told an interviewer. "The fact was that we didn't know what the British and French were going to do."[49]

That evening, the American ambassador sat across the dinner table from Foreign Secretary Lloyd. Over wine glasses and fine china, Aldrich asked Lloyd if he knew why Israel was mobilizing for war. Lloyd said he worried that the Israelis were preparing to attack Jordan. If that happened, he said, Her Majesty's Government would be treaty-bound to come to Jordan's defense and fight Israel. HMG did not wish to find itself at war with Israel, he said, but it would be the honourable thing to do.

Probing further, Aldrich asked whether Israel was preparing to attack Egypt. Lloyd, who had negotiated the Sèvres protocol to do exactly that, said he was "unwilling to believe Israelis would launch a full scale attack [against] Egypt."

And what about the French? Aldrich asked. Were they pushing Israel to fight?

Lloyd met his gaze. "He also said categorically his recent conversations with French give him no reason to believe French are stimulating such an Israeli venture," Aldrich reported.[50]

Scanning the board, Ike saw pawns and knights moving, but he couldn't figure out London's angle. All military action, by definition, creates a vacuum. If fighting broke out, whom did Eden think would fill that vacuum when the battlefield was quiet?

For now he would take Eden and Lloyd at their word. "I can't believe they would be so stupid as to invite on *themselves* all the Arab hostility to Israel," he told Hughes. "These things will have my blood pressure up to 490."[51]

As the fuse sparked and sputtered, Winston soaked up Mediterranean sun at La Pausa, a seaside mansion the Duke of Westminster had built for his mistress, fashion icon Coco Chanel. He painted, read, and edited his *History of the English-Speaking Peoples*. He smoked his cigars and dined with friends until October 20, when he suffered a stroke. He returned to London eight days later, confined to bed under doctors' orders.

From his bed, he watched events move faster. On a late October morning, Eden called Winston's private secretary, Anthony Montague Browne. He asked Montague Browne to convey a top secret message to his master.

"You are to promise not to tell anybody except Winston until this is all over," Eden said.

Britain was going to war.[52]

FIFTY-THREE

Death or Glory

ISRAELI AIR FORCE FIGHTER-BOMBERS SHRIEKED across the Sinai sky. Strike teams blasted Egyptian airfields and outposts as IDF paratroopers dropped from planes. The paras hit the ground fast and locked down a critical gap in the Sinai Peninsula's Mitla Mountains. By the afternoon of October 29, tanks and trucks emblazoned with the Star of David were west, outflanking defenders and overrunning Egyptian outposts.

Firebases fell. Roadblocks crumbled. By dawn the next morning, columns spread across the Sinai, heading toward Sharm-el-Sheikh in the south, to the Suez Canal in the west. The desert belonged to them.

"In the course of the night," Ike would remember, "the Israelis had knifed seventy-five miles into Egypt, arriving at a point only twenty-five miles east of Suez." The ancient chessboard had changed once again.[1]

The first threads of the crisis began spinning into Washington that afternoon. Ike, cutting short a campaign swing through Florida and Virginia, took *Columbine* back to the White House and convened an emergency meeting of his security advisors. He ordered U-2 flights over Egypt and Israel. Within twenty-four hours, a high-flying recon pilot named Francis Gary Powers was snapping pictures over the Sinai from 70,000 feet.[2]

At the Cabinet table that night, Allen Dulles suggested it was just a probing attack. Admiral Radford told Ike he believed the Israelis were waging a full-scale war, not a mere raid. He estimated they would be at the Suez Canal in about three days. The admiral and the CIA director agreed the Israelis would stop shooting soon, but it wasn't clear whether Britain or France would jump in.[3]

Ike wanted to trust London. As he liked to tell his staff, "It's often hard to get the British to make a clear commitment, but when they make it, you don't have to look behind it." But this time, there was no clear commitment, and Foster Dulles smelled a rat. Britain and France had conveniently massed forces in Cyprus just ahead of the Israeli strike—an odd coincidence if they hadn't known what was going to happen. "British and French intervention must be foreseen," he warned. "They appear to be ready for it, and may in fact have concerted their action with the Israelis."[4]

Ike thought that one over. London and Paris both wanted Nasser gone. But the 1950 Tripartite Declaration bound America, Britain, and France to protect any Middle Eastern nation that was the victim of aggression. Two years earlier, Eden himself had told Parliament that Britain would be duty bound to defend an Arab state if Israel attacked.[5]

Now Egypt was under attack. Would Britain and France honor their commitment? What would they do if the U.S. sent forces to protect Egypt? In a bizarre twist, if America stood by its word, it might have to oppose—even fight—its closest allies.

"The British are calculating that we must go along with them," Ike concluded. But his verdict was clear: "We recognize that much is on their side in the dispute with the Egyptians, but that nothing justifies double-crossing us." He added, "If the British get into this operation, it may open a deep rift between us."

Maybe Eden and his French counterpart, Prime Minister Guy

Mollet, figured Ike was too tied up with the election—or too worried about the pro-Israeli vote—to intervene. If so, they didn't know Eisenhower. He told his advisors he "really did not think the American people would throw him out in the midst of a situation like this, but if they did, so be it."[6]

Still reluctant to believe Eden was playing a deadly charade, Ike asked Britain to join America in defending Nasser through the UN Security Council. He summoned British Chargé d'Affaires John Coulson to the White House and told Coulson the prestige of both nations was at stake. The Tripartite powers had given their word to protect the victims of aggression, and they must redeem that promise.

The first step, he said, was the Security Council. They would get there when the doors opened with a resolution. They would act before Moscow beat them to the punch. Dulles was drafting a resolution calling for an immediate end to the fighting.[7]

A flustered Coulson didn't know how to respond. He said he had no instructions from his government. But Ike and Dulles knew someone who did.

From his New York apartment, Ike's UN ambassador, Henry Cabot Lodge Jr., rang up his British and French counterparts. He implored them to support a Security Council resolution America would introduce the next morning. It called for a ceasefire between Israel and Egypt, an immediate withdrawal of Israeli troops from the Sinai, and for "all powers" to refrain from intervening.[8]

After speaking with Britain's UN ambassador, Sir Pierson Dixon, Lodge called Dulles and told him the encounter was one of the most unpleasant of his life. "Dixon until now had always been amiable, but at this conference the mask fell off and he was virtually snarling," he reported. When Lodge spoke of honoring the Tripartite Declaration, Dixon snapped, "Don't be silly and moralistic. We have got to be practical." He told Lodge the British would veto any ceasefire resolution, whether sponsored by the United States or anyone else.[9]

Had the British really double-crossed them? Had Eden renounced their pledge without telling them?

From Dixon's reaction, the shocking answer seemed to be "Yes."

Ike sat down at his desk and drafted a letter to Anthony Eden:

> Dear Anthony,
>
> I address you in this note not only as head of Her Majesty's Government but as my long time friend who has, with me, believed in and worked for real Anglo-American understanding. . . .
>
> Last evening our Ambassador to the United Nations met with your Ambassador, Pierson Dixon, to request him to join us in presenting the case to the United Nations this morning. We were astonished to find that he was completely unsympathetic, stating frankly that his government would not agree to any action whatsoever to be taken against Israel. He further argued that the tripartite statement of May, 1950, was ancient history and without current validity. . . .
>
> [T]he possible involvement of you and the French in a general Arab war . . . seems to me to leave your government and ours in a very sad state of confusion, so far as any possibility of unified understanding and action are concerned. It is true that Egypt has not yet formally asked this government for aid. But the fact is that if the United Nations finds Israel to be an aggressor, Egypt could very well ask the Soviets for help—and then the Mid East fat would really be in the fire.

He asked for a clear presentation of British views and intentions, signing his letter, "Ike E."[10]

Ike brought the draft letter to his advisors the next morning, October 30. As they discussed America's response, he wondered aloud whether Winston's hand might be behind the Israeli scheme. The move, he reflected, "is the mid-Victorian style."[11]

A message from Eden interrupted Ike's thoughts. Egypt's attitude toward the Tripartite Declaration, Eden said, relieved Britain from those obligations. "Egypt has to a large extent brought this attack on herself by insisting that the state of war persists, by defying the Security Council and by declaring her intention to marshal the Arab States for the destruction of Israel."[12]

Had Eden known Ike better, he might have played it differently: He could have said siding with Israel was exactly what the Tripartite Declaration called for—defending a victim against aggression. Egypt had backed fedayeen raids on Israeli towns. Egypt had cut Israel's access to the Canal. Nasser insisted that a state of war existed between the two countries, and Nasser announced his intention to use violence to sweep the Jews from the Middle East. Self-defense was, at the very least, plausible.

Some in Ike's circle agreed. "If [the British] wanted to come back and say, 'Thank you very much. We certainly agree with you, and we think the Israelis are the victims,' we could agree with them or disagree," Admiral Radford later mused. "If we disagreed, nothing could be done to settle the agreement for at least three or four days. By that time, the Israelis would have cleaned up on the Egyptians." He added, "I do not think we would have been too unhappy if that had happened."[13]

But Eden didn't take that road. Instead, he tossed aside a principle America and Britain had followed for six years. He had backed Ike into a corner, leaving him with one agonizing choice: support London's play, or oppose America's best friend.

Ike seriously considered accepting Eden's move as a fait accompli.

On the afternoon of October 30, he drafted another letter to Eden. He could hardly see any good coming from alienating the entire Arab world, but he added, "I assume, however, that you have gone too far to reconsider so I must further assume that your plan is so worked out that you foresee no dreary and unending prospect stretching out ahead." He concluded, "Now we must pray that everything comes out both justly and reasonably peacefully."

He sent the draft to Dulles, who advised against sending it. At this early stage, the president was presuming too much: that the British and French would see their plan through to its conclusion; that the end would be swift and decisive; that the Soviets would not storm onto the board. Neither Ike nor Dulles knew what the conspirators would do—or what they were capable of. There were many ways this crisis could end, and Dulles saw no need to concede anything until the picture crystallized a little more. He asked Ike to hold the letter for at least a day.

Ike held off. The moment passed, and Ike never sent the letter. Had he done so, what happened next might have been different.[14]

Standing before Parliament, Eden announced that Britain was prepared to send in peacekeeping troops to occupy the Canal Zone. The key cities were Port Said in the north, Ismailia in the center, and Suez at the southern end. The 1954 troop withdrawal agreement with Egypt, which allowed Britain to return if Egypt were attacked, justified Her Majesty's Government taking action, and take action it would.

Eden told Parliament that upon learning of Israel's mobilization, he had directed his ambassador in Tel Aviv to call Golda Meir, Israel's foreign minister, to "urge restraint." He said the British and French governments had informed both Egypt and Israel they had twelve hours to agree to withdraw troops ten miles from the Canal. If they did not, "British and French forces will intervene in whatever strength may be necessary to secure compliance."[15]

Though worded as a "declaration" and addressed to both sides, it was plainly an ultimatum directed at Egypt. As agreed, Israel promised to "withdraw" to a line ten miles from the Canal Zone—permitting Israeli forces to move forward, since they were more than ten miles away.

Just as predictably, Nasser refused.[16]

In Washington, Dulles called Ike and read Eden's announcement. The ultimatum, he said, was "about as crude and brutal as anything he has ever seen."

There was no point in studying it, he said. It was virtually a declaration of war. Eden's peacekeeping charade, what was left of it, went up in smoke like Dracula in daylight.[17]

Ike tended to blow his stack when blindsided. "He always retained a gift for somehow conveying—with most eloquent wrinkling of brow and bulging of eyes—an astonishment akin to awe when forced to gaze at the spectacle of dramatic and aggressive stupidity," speechwriter Emmet Hughes remembered.[18]

Now Ike was seeing it.

As he later told Dulles, "You are not going to get a cease-fire by saying everybody please stop." But he didn't intend to fight fire with fire. Instead, he met with the man who ran his secret weapon: a kindly looking administrator with the face of a college dean.

Dr. Arthur Flemming was Ike's director of the Office of Defense Mobilization, the point man for wartime rationing and economic policy. Summoning him to the White House, Ike asked what would happen if the Egyptians blocked the Canal.

The first impact, said Flemming, would be a disruption of the western world's petroleum pipeline. America, with its Texas gushers, could manage. But Western Europe would have to make up the loss with fuel from the United States and Venezuela. Britain and France would also have to reroute tankers around Africa to get Saudi and Iranian oil flowing again. That would cost money. A lot of it.

Ike knew where Flemming was going. "Before long, they would be short of dollars to finance these operations and would be calling us for help," he concluded.

He knew what he would tell them. "Those who began this operation should be left to work out their own oil problems—to boil in their own oil, so to speak."[19]

As the twelve-hour deadline expired, the skies over Cairo split open. British and French bombers streaked down on Egyptian airfields in attack formation, and in minutes, lines of Soviet-made MiGs and Ilyushins erupted in fireballs. The attacks continued with surgical precision, and three days into the bombardment, Britain's Ministry of Defence proudly reported, "The annihilation of the Egyptian Air Force would seem to be almost complete."[20]

As black plumes curled over runways, the Royal Navy hunted its prey. Her Majesty's ships found an Egyptian frigate near the Canal's southern end and sent it to the bottom. To the north, the French battleship *Jean Bart*—the monster that had battled Patton's Torch forces—steamed toward the Canal's Mediterranean mouth, while a French cruiser shelled Egyptian positions near Gaza.

RAF planes dropped leaflets over Egyptian cities, encouraging citizens to defy Nasser. Arabic-language "black radio" broadcasts, courtesy of MI6, called on Egyptians to throw off the yoke of their leader and warned of an overwhelming invasion to come.[21]

But the British troops assembled on Cyprus were still on Cyprus. The British Chiefs, kept in the dark by Eden, had been caught short when 10 Downing gave them the green light. Britain, according to Eden, was a neutral bystander as surprised as anyone by the Israeli assault, so it couldn't very well have troops hovering off Port Said just before Israel attacked. It would take a week to move forces from Cyprus to Port Said at the Canal's north end and to the city of Ismailia in the Canal's center. That long delay would give Nasser time to react.

"They had pitifully small forces available at that time," remembered Admiral Radford, who had seen the U-2 reports. "*We* had to help them, if anybody was to help them. And if they expected our help, it was a hell of a way to get it after what we had told them."[22]

As American children made their trick-or-treat rounds on Halloween, Ike spoke to the nation from the Oval Office. In a steady voice, he spoke of the twin crises of Hungary—where Soviet tanks were crushing a popular revolt—and Suez.

America was powerless to aid the Hungarians. Budapest lay well behind the Iron Curtain, and short of starting World War III, America could do nothing to change the result. After expressing hopes that the uprising signaled a newer, brighter chapter in Europe's history, the president turned to Egypt.

Cool but focused as he stared into the camera, Ike told the nation Israel, Britain, and France had broken basic United Nations principles. "We believe these actions to have been taken in error," he said. "We do not accept the use of force as a wise or proper instrument for the settlement of international disputes."

He stressed that America wasn't consulted and wasn't complicit. The United States would maintain its friendships with the invaders, of course. It would not intervene militarily, but it would pursue a ceasefire resolution through the UN General Assembly.

"There can be no peace without law," he declared. "And there can be no law if we were to invoke one code of international conduct for those who oppose us, and another for our friends."[23]

Next morning, the National Security Council met. The Anglo-French veto of the UN Security Council resolution shifted the debate to the UN General Assembly.

Dulles stressed that America could not be seen as complicit. It had to handle this crisis by the book. The event was, said Dulles, "close to marking the death knell of Great Britain and France." If America sided with Britain and France, he warned, "Win or lose, we will share the fate of Britain and France."[24]

Had Nasser been toppled, had the fighting ended quickly, Ike would have shrugged and moved on. It would have been like Guatemala or Iran. As he told an interviewer eight years later, "We assumed that, if the three nations did attack, they would all move at one time; and it would be over in almost twenty-four hours. . . . Had they done it quickly, we would have accepted it."

But, Andy Goodpaster remembered, "We were waiting and waiting and nothing happened."[25*]

Ike treasured friendships, but he never let them get in the way of the job. In North Africa, he had written his son about how nations use men as expendable pawns. In Europe, he had busted and sent home a West Point classmate for loose talk about Overlord's invasion date. He had cut Kay Summersby from his life the way a surgeon wields a scalpel on a

* Admiral Arleigh Burke, Ike's chief of naval operations, spoke to Admiral Louis Mountbatten, First Sea Lord, during the crisis. Mountbatten said the British Chiefs had previously told the Cabinet they could be ready to invade by October's end. But the Cabinet did not authorize the Chiefs to lay the preliminary groundwork, so the military was caught short when the order finally came. "They didn't have them get started with preparations," Burke told an interviewer. "Then the dates slipped up pretty close, and then they told them to go ahead and do it. Well, they couldn't do it, because they didn't have the ships ready."

growth that might not be benign. He fired his dear friend George Patton for shooting off his mouth one too many times. He humiliated Omar Bradley during the Battle of the Bulge, banished Harry Butcher for penning his memoirs, nearly cut Dick Nixon from the ticket, and disappointed Beetle Smith, the man to whom he owed so much, by passing him over for secretary of state and Army chief of staff.[26]

Now, as he told Senate Minority Leader William Knowland, "I'm about to lose my British citizenship."[27]

At 2:30 in the morning of November 2, John Foster Dulles rose before the United Nations to introduce Resolution 997, calling for an immediate ceasefire by Britain, France, Israel, and Egypt. The resolution passed in three hours by a vote of 64 to 5. Britain, France, and Israel were decisively outvoted, mustering only the support of New Zealand and Australia. A follow-up resolution authorized the formation of a UN emergency peacekeeping force to occupy the Canal as a neutral guardian until Egypt could resume control.[28]

Britain was now an outcast in a body whose charter Eden had helped draft.

Eden was desperate for time. Time for his troops to embark from Cyprus and Malta. Time to raise the Union Jack over Port Said. Time to drive the Egyptians from the Canal Zone, time for Nasser to wobble and fall. Time to pretend Britain hadn't colluded with the Israelis.

And time was running out.

Like a plague victim battling a fever, Britain boiled from within. Opposition leader Hugh Gaitskell vowed to oppose Eden's Suez adventure. When Eden defended his government's action in Parliament, Labour MPs erupted in boos and cries of "Resign!"

"It was a deplorable scene, totally unworthy of the Mother of Parliaments," recalled Minister of State Anthony Nutting. "Labour Members booing the Prime Minister, refusing to acknowledge the Speaker's authority and rendering any kind of ordered discussion impossible."[29]

Chaos in Parliament spilled into the streets, where anti-war protests grew larger, louder, and angrier. In Trafalgar Square, 20,000 protestors chanted, "Fascist Bullies!" and "Eden Must Go!" until they were hoarse. Aneurin Bevan, the Labour Party's radical bête noire, whipped the crowd into a frenzy with fiery anti-government rhetoric. Protestors tried to take their grievances to 10 Downing Street; the mob would have reached Eden's doorstep had not 500 foot and horse-mounted bobbies charged the mass, truncheons out, arresting 27 protestors.[30]

On November 3, the cracks widened. Nutting resigned in protest, threatening Eden's standing among young Conservatives. Lord Mountbatten also submitted his resignation as First Sea Lord, protesting Eden's refusal to announce that the military bore no responsibility for war's political repercussions.[31]

The maelstrom churned, sucking Eden into the vortex. Desperate for a lifeline, he reached out to his old mentor.

Winston had been fighting his own war. The October stroke had hit him hard. It initially paralyzed his right arm, right leg, and the left side of his face, leaving him struggling to complete sentences. He clawed back, mostly, but as Eden flailed, Winston remained mute.[32]

Eden turned to the convalescing Winston to help stanch the bleeding. He asked Winston for a public statement of support. Too weak to dictate anything, Winston asked his secretary, Anthony Montague Browne, to draft a letter to the local Conservative Party boss. Winston picked at the letter and nodded it off, knowing it would be republished in the national and world press.

"The frontiers of Israel have flickered with murder and armed raids," the letter proclaimed. Egypt, in the face of British, French, Israeli, and U.S. unity, had rejected restraint. Now Her Majesty's Government was working on the world's behalf to restore peace and order to this volatile region, an area of vital interest to Britain.

As for the Americans, said Churchill, "Unfortunately, recent months have shown us that at present it is not possible to hope in this area for American co-operation on the scale and with the promptness necessary to control events." He remained confident that "our American friends will come to realize that, not for the first time, we have acted independently for the common good."[33]

When Churchill's letter hit the papers, Eden breathed a sigh of relief. "My dear Winston," he cabled, "I cannot thank you enough for your wonderful message. It has had an enormous effect, and I am sure that in the US it will have maybe an even greater influence."

"I am so glad it was a help," the ailing man wrote back.[34]

It didn't help where Eden needed help, however. As expected, Egyptians scuttled ships along the Canal. Soon fifty-two vessels were sunk between Suez and Port Said, choking off the waterway and threatening a quarter of Britain's trade. Ships carrying rubber from Malaya, wool from Australia, tea from Malawi, and manganese from India—for starters—were stranded in the Red Sea. They would have to fuel up and take the long way around Africa.[35]

Then came oil, the real choke hold. Arab nationalists sabotaged Iraq Petroleum Company pumping stations in Syria, cutting off oil shipments to the Mediterranean. As pipelines running across Syria, Lebanon, and Iraq dried up, Eden persuaded the Queen to sign an order permitting Her Majesty's Government to impose gasoline rationing if necessary.[36]

The squeeze was on.

On Monday, November 5, British paratroopers dropped over Gamil Airfield, west of the Canal near Port Said. Chutes snapped open in the wind and the soldiers hit the ground fifteen minutes ahead of the French contingent on the city's south side.[37]

Shadows lengthened over the Nile as the allied forces pushed into the city. By evening, they reached a temporary ceasefire with the local Egyptian commander. The British strike force command sent a flash message reporting the local halt to headquarters in Cyprus.

Higher-ups on Cyprus interpreted the signal liberally. The operation's ground commander, General Sir Charles Keightley, believed it meant the impending surrender of Port Said, and he radioed London an optimistic report. In London, the ceasefire grew into a virtual surrender.[38]

Back at the Commons, word reached Eden as he and Lloyd were being pilloried by opposition leaders. Eden leapt up to interrupt a grueling cross-examination of Lloyd to announce a ceasefire at Port Said. The announcement drew cheers from Conservative benches. Eden rushed back to 10 Downing to congratulate his military chiefs.

"My dear Chiefs, how grateful I am!" he said, with the tone of a reprieved death row inmate. "You have been magnificent! It's all worked out perfectly!"[39]

Except it hadn't. The jubilation died a few hours after its birth. Egyptian quartermasters unloaded crates of Czech-made rifles on the streets of Said and handed them to anyone willing to fight the invaders. Egyptian loudspeaker trucks announced that the Soviets were bombing London and Paris; World War III had begun, they claimed. As the ceasefire evaporated, Radio Cairo announced that the paratroopers had been "completely annihilated." These were lies, of course, but they kept local Egyptians fighting, which was all they had to do.[40]

Eden's knockout blow had landed like a left hook thrown by Mamie Eisenhower. "To be successful even in a narrow field, the operation had to be a *coup*," the London *Times* bemoaned. "It threatened to become a long drawn out fight." And a global crisis.[41]

Eden claimed that he had delayed the ground troop landings in hopes that the UN, the Americans, or someone would enter as a peace-keeping force. Few believed him. His delay in the landings only infuriated his French allies, who had fewer qualms about world outrage. But the French couldn't complete the mission without British help.

Eden was stranded, trying to justify a war to stop Egypt and Israel from fighting—when Egypt and Israel were no longer fighting.

As paratroops and commandos battled in the streets of Port Said, a new threat emerged half a world away. Soviet Premier Nikolai Bulganin delivered a chilling message: Moscow was prepared to escalate.[42]

"There are countries now which need not have sent a navy or air force to the coasts of Britain but could have used other means, such as rocket technique," Bulganin warned Eden and Mollet. "If rocket weapons had been used against Britain and France, they would probably have called this a barbarous action."

Bulganin reminded the West what was at stake: "War may spread to other countries and become a third world war."[43]

It might be Kremlin saber-rattling, but Ike couldn't take chances. Not with a man who had hydrogen bombs at his fingertips.

Ike had asked the Joint Chiefs to estimate what would be left after a Soviet nuclear strike. The answer was simple: virtually nothing. National government, gone. Financial markets, gone. Energy and transportation infrastructure, gone. Essentially, the end of nearly everything America had done since the colonists reached Jamestown.[44]

He called his men together and told them what worried him. With Red Army tanks blasting through central Budapest, with Bulganin threatening Armageddon, no one knew what Moscow might do. "We may be dealing here with the opening gambit of an ultimatum," he told his team.

"He said the Soviets are scared and furious, and there is nothing more dangerous than a dictatorship in this state of mind," according to Goodpaster's notes. "He referred to Hitler's last days."[45]

What would America do if Bulganin widened the war? "Massive retaliation" depended on Ike's ability to keep brushfire wars from escalating into global ones. Now the brush was blazing. If Soviet jets attacked British or French troops—troops under the flag of fellow NATO members—would that be the moment to go all out?

For the first time in Earth's history, the possibility of thermonuclear war loomed. This wouldn't be a local atomic attack on North Korean trenches or the Chinese coast. It was the real deal: SAC bombers in the air, ballistic rockets tearing through the stratosphere, Regulus missiles popping from submarines.

Ike couldn't make a mistake. He couldn't show weakness.

"We have to be positive and clear in our every word, every step," he said. "And if those fellows start something, we may have to hit them, and if necessary, with *everything* in the bucket."[46]

"Stupid, stupid, stupid," Ike muttered as he stared through a magnifying glass. A sixteen-foot mosaic of U-2 photos of the Canal carpeted the Oval Office floor. On hands and knees, he crawled over pictures of scuttled ships and broken bridges, wondering how he would clean up the mess.

"Goddamn stupid," he said, pushing himself up.[47]

He caucused with Allen Dulles, Andy Goodpaster, Undersecretary of State Herbert Hoover Jr., and mobilization chief Arthur Flemming. The war seemed ready to shift. British intelligence claimed Soviet airpower was moving into Syria, while the French feared an imminent

Russian attack. More ominously, Allen Dulles presented Ike with an intelligence report indicating that the Soviets had assured Nasser they would "do something" to help Egypt. What that meant, no one knew. But the Kremlin had a lot of options.

"Our people should be alert," Ike said at last. "If the Soviets attack the French and British directly, we would be in war." He ordered Allen Dulles to keep U-2s over Syria to see whether the Russians were really moving MiGs there. If Moscow had air forces near Damascus, then Britain or France might attack them, drawing the world into global war.[48]

The Joint Chiefs steadied themselves for the Big One. At Ike's direction, they increased the number of interceptor aircraft on high alert, ready to shoot down any Tupolev nuclear bombers crossing the Arctic toward American airspace. They dispatched the aircraft carriers *Forrestal* and *Franklin D. Roosevelt* to the Azores, deployed anti-submarine units, and put troop carrier flotillas on twelve-hour alerts.[49]

From London, Eden begged Ike to stand with his comrades. He played to Ike's sense of friendship, channeling Winston's old refrain: "The future of all of us depends on the closest Anglo-American cooperation. It has of course been a grief to me to have had to make a temporary breach into it which I cannot disguise, but I know that you are a man of big enough heart and vision to take up things again on the basis of facts."

He closed his plea: "If you cannot approve, I would like you at least to understand the terrible decisions that we have had to make. I remember nothing like them since the days when we were comrades together in the war."[50]

Ike set the message down. *"Comrades together in the war,"* Eden said. Eden might as well have made his pitch to Mount Rushmore. Nostalgia and sentiment meant nothing to Ike. The world had reached the threshold of nuclear war, and he wasn't going to let anyone, friend or foe, cross it without suffering the consequences.

He unholstered his biggest gun and aimed it at Britain.

As Musketeer capsized in the Canal, Harold Macmillan, Chancellor of the Exchequer, sounded the alarm.

Britain's currency, the pound sterling, was one of the last slabs of tenderloin on the Empire's bones. In October 1956, a quarter of the world's trade was conducted in pounds. It was the economic glue binding the "Sterling Area," a clubby group of Anglophile countries conducting trade in pounds and holding currency reserves at the Bank of England.[51]

But a reserve currency carries burdens as well as blessings. Maintaining the pound's value required the British government to assure markets that one pound was worth a fixed exchange rate, $2.80 in U.S. dollars. To support that value, the Bank of England needed to hold at least $2 billion in dollars or gold at all times. That meant Her Majesty's Government had to observe strict spending limits.

When Nasser blocked the Canal and saboteurs destroyed Syrian pipelines, crude oil prices skyrocketed. Western European countries, including Britain, scrambled to boost oil imports from the United States, Venezuela, or other countries that could ship around Africa.

Macmillan ran the numbers. The cure would be expensive. Running ships around Africa and buying western oil would cost about a half billion dollars—most of which would have to be paid in dollars to countries outside the Sterling Area, drawing down Britain's dollar reserves.

The drain began overnight. During the first two days of November, the Bank of England bled $50 million. Bean counters at the Exchequer foresaw massive losses piling up through November. The bank's executive director reported that it was hemorrhaging dollars at an unsustainable rate: By year's end, dollar and gold reserves would drop below the all-important $2 billion mark, forcing a devaluation of the pound.[52]

Eden hadn't thought about the sinews of war before launching Musketeer, and now Britain was desperate for cash.

Her Majesty's Government had options. One was a withdrawal of dollars Britain kept on deposit with the International Monetary Fund. Another was a loan from the U.S. Export-Import Bank. Another was to get America to delay a war loan payment of $175 million coming due in December. Problem was, each escape route required American help—or, at least, lack of active opposition of the Eisenhower administration.

To his horror, Eden learned Ike wouldn't play white knight until Britain pulled its troops off Egyptian soil. Ike had Treasury Secretary George Humphrey quietly block an IMF withdrawal, and he made it clear there would be no deals until Nasser had his canal back.[53]

In the Cabinet, anxiety rose like stomach reflux as Eden's hawks began buckling. The drain on dollar reserves and international pressure drove Harold Macmillan, Musketeer's number one hard-liner, to make a U-turn and demand Eden agree to a ceasefire. Macmillan's insistence, supported by Rab Butler and Lord Salisbury, swayed the rest of the Cabinet, leaving Eden isolated within his own inner circle.[54*]

Eden stared in disbelief. The United States was standing with the Soviet Union—the same dictatorship crushing Hungarian protestors under the treads of T-54 tanks.

With Ike behind him, Eden could handle Bulganin. He could handle Nasser. He could handle the run on the pound. He could handle

* French Foreign Minister Christian Pineau later told an interviewer that Prime Minister Mollet said Eden told him Ike had threatened, "If you don't get out of Port Said tomorrow, I'll cause a run on the pound and drive it down to zero." In their memoirs, neither Eden nor Ike mentioned this triple-hearsay statement. Harold Macmillan recalled that a request for an IMF refund was denied on November 6. He implied this message was the final straw that forced Eden to accept the ceasefire. Eden, in his memoirs, referred to a call from Secretary Humphrey to Rab Butler along the same lines. State Department records do not reflect any such message on that date, and historians have not found a smoking gun among Treasury records. U.S. economic threats were used *after* the British Cabinet accepted the ceasefire, to pressure Britain into withdrawing her soldiers from the Canal in accordance with the UN resolution.

slings and arrows from the UN, the press, the protestors, the Labour opposition.

Without Ike, he was lost.

He drifted through 10 Downing like a man in a forest of mirrors. For all his years in the Foreign Office, his Etonian education, his knowledge of the Middle East and command of Arabic and Farsi, Anthony Eden had not been built to carry the weight Ike and Winston shouldered. He had been pushed into war by Macmillan, Rab, his glory days fighting Mussolini, and his need to prove himself.

The price? Pethidine to stop the headaches. Barbiturates to help him sleep. Drinamyl, an amphetamine-barbiturate cocktail, to shake off last night's barbiturates. Hair of the dog, in pill form.

Since early October, he had suffered from chronic fevers, at one point reaching 106 degrees. His body was breaking, and his mind wasn't far behind.[55]

"The prime minister is no Churchill," French Foreign Minister Christian Pineau sadly concluded. "He has neither the tenacity nor the steel nerves. The test, instead of strengthening him, exhausts him. It is not yet a 'breakdown,' but we are not far from it."[56]

Like Icarus, Eden lived in the shadow of a famous man. He disregarded Winston's admonition to stick close to the Americans; he defied Ike's warnings. He had strapped on ambition's wings and stepped off the wall, eyes fixed on the sun.

Now, he was falling.

"We think A.E. has gone off his head," Selwyn Lloyd's secretary confessed to his diary. Eden's press secretary told his, "The PM is mad, literally mad."[57]

FIFTY-FOUR

The Old Man and the Sea

TUESDAY, NOVEMBER 6, DAWNED GRAY OVER LONDON. At Buckingham Palace, footmen swung open the gates. From the grand archway emerged a gold-trimmed carriage escorted by a troop of silver-clad cuirassiers on majestic black steeds. Four immaculate white horses carried Queen Elizabeth II to Westminster Palace for the ceremonial opening of Parliament.

She alighted and stepped through the Sovereign's Entrance, where attendants placed the jewel-encrusted Imperial State Crown on her head. Her train flowed behind her as she walked with measured grace into the House of Lords. The royal cypher, EIIR, gleamed on the throne where she took her seat.

Before her stood assembled lords and members, gathered together to hear the Queen's Speech.

She touched on issues she desired Parliament to address: independence of Ghana, unrest in Cyprus, reforming the House of Lords, modernizing the fishing fleet, and so on. But the first task Her Majesty charged her government with was the "prompt and just settlement of the many problems arising from the grave situation in the Middle East."[1]

Her précis complete, the Queen left Parliament and rode back to the palace. As the *New York Times* reported, "The Horse Guards had doffed their glittering helmets and the coach was back in the stables when Sir Anthony arose last evening to announce what more than one of his right-wing supporters termed 'a climb down.'"[2]

In the Commons chamber, Eden stood before a hostile Parliament, his eyes darting like a gazelle sensing a lion in tall grass. He announced that Britain would accept the UN resolutions commanding an end to the fighting. Swallowing reality and fighting to keep it down, he spoke of victory for the rule of law. He projected optimism and scratched for something good to say about his bridge too far.

The truth was plain to everyone with a newspaper. French and British troops had been on the ground for just over thirty-six hours when Eden called off the operation. Of the three allied objectives, only part of one—Port Said—was even tenuously in allied hands. Nasser controlled the waterway's southern half and had shut down the canal Britain fought to protect. Nasser controlled Egypt. Nasser threatened Israel. And from his office in Cairo, Nasser still taunted the West.[3]

Suez was more than a fiasco—it was a humiliation the world gawked at, a battle halted before it reached the decisive moment. The nursery song's Grand Old Duke of York, for all his marching up and down the hill, at least got to the top before marching down again. Eden had barely pulled his boots on before sounding retreat.

Looking like a barrister whose client had been caught with the murder weapon and needs a story to tell the jury, Eden told the MPs the stage was set to show what the UN could do. "As the dust settles," he grandly declared, the UN had an opportunity, thanks to quick British action, to become "a really effective international organization."

Eden's words hung in the chamber for a moment. Then a voice boomed from the opposition benches: "When did you think that one up??"[4]

Across the ocean, as American voters lined up at the polls, Ike picked up the transatlantic telephone.

"First of all," he told Eden, "I can't tell you how pleased we are that you found it possible to accept the cease-fire."

Eden's voice was flat. "We have certainly taken a risk, but I think it is justified."

Ike let it go. He told Eden he wanted French and British troops out as soon as the UN sent in troops. Someone had to clean up the mess, but if Eden insisted that someone had to be British, the ceasefire would fall apart.

"I hope you will be there," said Eden, scrounging for a scrap of support. "Are we all going to go out?"

"I would like to see none of the great nations in it," said Ike. "I am afraid the red boy is going to demand the lion's share. I would rather make it no troops from the Big Five."

Ike assured Eden that even a small UN force would be enough. If Egypt attacked the UN, everyone would have to line up against Nasser.

Eden said he'd think it over. He had to go back to the Commons now, and he might not come out as prime minister.

"If I survive here tonight I will call you," he said. "How are things going with you?"

Ike shrugged. "We have given our whole thought to Hungary and the Middle East. I don't give a damn how the election goes. I guess it will be all right."[5]

It was all right. Ike cruised to an easy reelection, and at 1:30 in the morning, Adlai Stevenson called him to concede defeat for a second time. Ike gave a victory speech to a cheering crowd at the Sheraton-Park Hotel, and at four in the morning, he and his staff went to bed.[6]

When Ike stepped on a friend, he wouldn't lift his boot until he got what he wanted. Eden learned that the hard way.

Britain had agreed to a ceasefire, but Her Majesty's troops still occupied Port Said. Desperate to save face, Eden tried to keep them on the Canal a little longer, tasking them with clearing ships out of the waterway. Even if an extended occupation wouldn't do much to hurt Nasser, it might soften Britain's humiliation.[7]

But Ike knew how to use power. He wanted Britain out so the Kremlin would have no excuse to go in. Britain was desperate for money and oil, and Ike had both. So until Eden agreed to remove Her Majesty's troops, Ike wouldn't lift a finger. No money, no oil.

By November 16, British cash reserves had dropped by $200 million. Projected losses were $300 million when November's final figures were tallied. With Iraqi and Saudi oil shut off, Europe was staring at an energy crisis.

Ike held the power to order his mobilization chief to ship emergency oil to Europe, and he could have pressured the Saudi king to backfill the shortage. But through mid-month he stood, immovable as the Washington Monument, while Her Majesty's Government floundered.[8]

Behind closed doors, Macmillan implored Ambassador Aldrich to recognize that Britain had two choices: withdraw and admit impotence, or renew hostilities. While the second choice would risk drawing in the Soviets and igniting World War III, he said, the first would mean that "loss of prestige and humiliation would be so great that the government must fall." And at least some in the Cabinet were willing to risk war.[9]

To Ike, a choice between crippling Britain and igniting World War III was no choice at all. On November 24, when a UN resolution condemned Britain and France for refusing to withdraw their troops from the Canal Zone, the U.S. again joined the majority against her best friend and ally.[10]

Macmillan hinted to Aldrich that the prime minister might not be healthy enough to go to Washington. Eden was a sick man, and now he was suffering from acute political asphyxiation.

On November 23, pale and spent, Eden abruptly left for Jamaica on a three-week medical leave. His office announced that doctors ordered rest and seclusion, and he and Clarissa boarded a DC-7 for the peace of Montego Bay. There they remained at GoldenEye cottage, the winter home of Eden's friend, spy novelist Ian Fleming.[11]

As Eden wallowed in warm Caribbean waters and cold self-pity, reporters and cartoonists around the world had a field day. The *Daily Mirror* asked its readers to "solve" the Suez Crisis, offering as first prize a three-week holiday in Jamaica. A cartoon in the *Pittsburgh Post-Gazette* showed a marooned Eden waiving a tattered Union Jack over Jamaica as his ship, labeled "Egyptian Cruise," sank. The *Detroit News* drew Eden in a sea captain's uniform, walking the plank, pleading with parliamentary pirates, "I can explain everything!"[12]

Five years earlier, Ernest Hemingway published a novella about a poor Cuban fisherman, down on his luck, who tries to reclaim his dignity by catching a giant marlin. But after a long, exhausting battle, he hasn't the strength left to haul the fish aboard his boat. As he drags the marlin back to shore behind his skiff, sharks tear his prize to pieces. The old man weeps as he staggers back to his shack, humiliated, empty-handed, almost broken.

Sitting at GoldenEye pondering wrecked dreams, Eden must have wondered how Ike could have turned on him. Britain had stood shoulder to shoulder with America in World War II, in Korea, and the dark alleyways of Tehran. Winston had even deferred to Ike on talks with the Kremlin—talks that might have led to a safer, more peaceful world.

Ike owed Eden. America owed Eden. But when the chips were down, Ike had turned on him. He'd sided with a lowborn demagogue against America's greatest ally. He'd sided with Kremlin gangsters he had once compared to streetwalkers.

And in doing so, he had torn the heart from the carcass of the British Empire.

FIFTY-FIVE

"Despicable Conduct"

When a bronzed and rested Eden returned from Jamaica on December 14, Tory colleagues treated him like a ghost at his own funeral.

Labourites had mounted a "no confidence" challenge, and by year's end, Eden's career was bouncing in the tumbril on its way to the guillotine. For decency's sake, the pallbearers decided Eden's health would be the official reason for his resignation, his exquisite tan notwithstanding.[1]

With Eden gone, the new man at Downing Street, Harold Macmillan, quickly moved to mop up the mess. The Cabinet agreed to pull all troops out of Suez and set a deadline of December 22 to quit Egypt for good.[2]

Once London agreed to a deadline, Ike's men at State and Treasury jumped into action. They unlocked over a billion dollars through the World and Export-Import Banks. A pleased Macmillan announced that Her Majesty's Government had financial backing for the pound, including an IMF withdrawal and likely waiver of U.S. loan payments due in December. Britain wouldn't go under.

Ike's corporate connections at Big Oil stepped up, too. They rerouted tankers and boosted crude supplies to a petrol-starved Europe, mitigating what could have been a winter disaster.[3]

Ike rescued the pound, but his price was steep: Britain's freedom to act as an independent power. America moved into the vacuum, shoring up relations with Middle Eastern moderates like Saudi Arabia and Jordan. It held its military forces in readiness to halt any signs of communist encroachment in the region, a policy soon known as the Eisenhower Doctrine. Everyone in the region knew who the real power was.[4]

Like Oedipus, the son had killed the father and taken his throne. "The British action was the last gasp of a declining power," a chastened Macmillan admitted to Foster Dulles in December. "Perhaps in two hundred years, the United States would know how we felt."[5]

From London, the *New York Times*'s Drew Middleton wrote, "The British are realistic enough to understand that the fiasco over the Suez intervention has accelerated their decline as a world power." Ambassador Aldrich was sharper: "No Englishman or Frenchman could fail to realize that their countries had been reduced to the level of third-rate powers which could not act effectively without the active support of the United States."[6]

Three-quarters of the world chuckled, as if watching an armored knight slip on a banana peel. Khrushchev gloated as T-54 tanks crushed the revolt in Budapest, and gleefully told the Egyptian ambassador, "You have cut off the British lion's tail and we have drawn his teeth. Now he can neither roar nor bite!"[7]

But neither the Kremlin nor Nasser had done the real damage. The Suez misadventure had been Eden's idea, but it was Ike's fist that smashed the lion's teeth.

The Kansan who had once stood on a London balcony waving to adoring crowds—the man who had extolled Anglo-American brotherhood at Guildhall and had been mocked by his friends for being "pro-British"—became the object of rage from Dover to Inverness. In cinemas, moviegoers hissed when Ike's face flashed in newsreels. Gas stations refused to fill cars driven by Americans, and taxis on London streets ejected passengers as soon as they heard American accents. One Air Force major was evicted from his London flat by his landlord via a letter denouncing the "despicable conduct" of the United States.[8]

"The wave of anti-American feeling in Great Britain . . . could not possibly be exaggerated," Rab Butler told Ambassador Aldrich. Aldrich warned Washington that if the UN did not reopen the Canal, Britain "would withdraw from the UN and . . . the U.S. would be asked to give up its bases in Great Britain."

The *Times* of London foresaw the rift: "A Britain united in anti-Americanism—and there is a growing danger of this—is not merely a Britain headed for disaster but also a Western world and an American Continent headed for disaster."

When a bone breaks, it is never the same. The fracture may mend, but there will always be a line bearing witness. Something in the Anglo-American relationship had broken. And after Suez, the bone wouldn't support the old weight.[9]

From Augusta National's fairway, Ike told Dulles he received a desperate message from Pug Ismay. "They have been the best of friends over the years," Dulles wrote afterward, "but [Ismay] is now adopting the European conviction that we deserted our two friends in their hour of trial."[10]

It wasn't just Ismay. Many in Ike's circle felt he should have let the allies take down Nasser. "The indignation we turned against the British and the French at that time was greatly overdone," concluded CIA's Richard Bissell. "If we had found ways to drag our feet for two or three days, the British and the French could have consolidated their hold of the Canal. . . . I think we could have preserved a reasonably righteous posture, at the same time doing less damage to our European alliance."[11]

Admiral Arleigh Burke, chief of naval operations, summed it up with his usual bluntness: "You support your friends, and you kick the hell out of your enemies," he told an interviewer. "When you have a friend, you've got to forgive him quite a bit. You can't make him over. You became friends because of certain qualities he had, and in spite of certain other qualities that he had. And you can advise him. But if he goes ahead and does it anyway, you support him, or else you are no longer friends."[12]

In time, even Dulles came to regret the episode. On his deathbed in 1959, he is said to have confessed, "Perhaps I made a mistake at Suez."[13]

As frigid air settled over London, Winston considered England's agony—and whether Ike was beyond redemption. He and Ike had once shared a close, trusting friendship. They had carried that trust into their high offices. That official trust had been broken—by Eden's duplicity and Ike's ruthlessness. To the nations they served, Suez was a right arm mangled.

Well, he thought, the official relationship was in tatters, but the friendship had survived. Perhaps one could help heal the other. He didn't know, but he was willing to use the time he had left to try.

FIFTY-SIX

Oil on Canvas

"Churchill Takes News Calmly," the *New York Times* told its readers. After hearing that his protégé had resigned as prime minister, Winston went to a movie theater to watch a showing of the classic *Gone With the Wind*.[1]

"Never be separated from the Americans," Winston had told the Cabinet before he left. Eden, first among those who should have listened, had broken Winston's cardinal rule. Now Eden was gone with the wind.

Among his close confidants, Winston didn't look like he took the news calmly. He looked sad, wounded, and embarrassed. "The Suez fiasco was a hard blow to WSC, obviously for its effect on our national destiny," remembered Anthony Montague Browne, his private secretary for the long sunset. "WSC sank into a mood of deep melancholy, the symptoms expressed mainly in a slow but progressive withdrawal of interest in public affairs."[2]

As a child, Winston had frolicked in a world of pomp and certainty. A world in which Queen Victoria reigned supreme, Britannia ruled the waves, and the Crown carried civilization's torch to primitives from Pretoria to Papua. But the Camelot of his youth had devolved, inch by inch, into a sordid, mud-splattered struggle against dollar-wielding barbarians on one side and nuclear-armed Cossacks on the other. Winston's Act III had opened at the fag-end of empire: a former superpower that, broken by war, meekly took its place as handmaid to an ex-colony it founded.

And it was Ike—wartime comrade, longtime friend—who had driven Boudica's chariot over Britain's remains.

Of course, the lion's share of blame went to the man in Number 10. Winston excoriated Eden, first for not winning over Ike, then for bungling the operation.

"I am shocked by what he did, and I'm an Anthony man," he fumed to Lord Moran. "I cannot understand why our troops were halted. To go so far and not go on was madness."[3]

Over lunch with Jock Colville in his London home at No. 28 Hyde Park Gate, Winston didn't hold back. He called the Suez operation "the most ill-conceived and ill-executed imaginable." He muttered to Montague Browne, "I would never have dared to do it without squaring it with the Americans, and once I had started, I would never have dared stop."[4]

Unable to shake his grief, the following week he replayed the nightmare with Moran. "Of course, one can't tell what one would have done, but one thing is certain," he said. "I wouldn't have done anything without consulting the Americans."[5]

Did he mean it? Had Winston been in the driver's seat, would the end have been different? Would Britannia have been spared crucifixion?

Winston was no Eden. His bond with Ike wasn't Eden's. His relationship to America wasn't Eden's. His capacity for cruelty, when necessary, wasn't Eden's. The man who had ordered the Royal Navy to sink French warships at Mers-el-Kebir, the man who stood alone against Hitler—the man who stepped aside as Ike bombed French civilians—possessed the nerve to defy the world once he committed to the Union

Jack. The child of Blenheim turned out to be a lot closer to the child of Abilene than Eden could ever be.

"If Churchill and Eisenhower had been running the thing themselves, it never would have happened," Ambassador Aldrich concluded. "Each would have known what the other wanted to do." They had cooperated on Iran and Europe's defense. They'd clashed over Vietnam, China, Egypt, and a Kremlin summit. But agree or disagree, each knew where the other man stood. Had Winston been at Number 10, it would have been true to form for him to tell Ike what he was going to do. If Ike had balked, Winston might have waited—as he did with his treasured pilgrimage to Moscow—until Ike saw the light.[6]

Yet even Winston struggled to comprehend how Ike could side with a crude dictator against his oldest and best ally. "He looked on [Ike] as a friend, as somebody who was totally impartial between Britain and America when he was commander-in-chief in the early days," Montague Browne reflected. "He was fond of him and was bitterly disappointed over Suez."[7]

Well, no use crying over spilled milk, thought Winston. America was Britain's ally, and Ike was his friend, even if he let men like Dulles pull his strings. Winston had watched Fate's pendulum swing too many times to hold a personal grudge.[8]

"After Suez," Clementine remembered, "he specifically set out to mend fences with the United States." Winston was revered in his mother's homeland, and a U.S. public opinion poll in early 1957 reported Ike the most admired man in the world, followed by Sir Winston Churchill. Perhaps, thought Sir Winston, he could spend some of that capital on bridge repairs.[9]

Even before Eden's departure, Jock Colville suggested that Winston "write a letter to Eisenhower pointing out that the enemy are not the

British but the Russians." He asked Jock to draft something he could work with, and shortly before Thanksgiving, he sent it out.

My Dear Ike,

There is not much left for me to do in this world and I have neither the wish nor the strength to involve myself in the present political stress and turmoil. But I do believe, with unfaltering conviction, that the theme of the Anglo-American alliance is more important today than at any time since the war. You and I had some part in raising it to the plane on which it has stood. . . . To let events in the Middle East come between us would be an act of folly, on which our whole civilization may founder.

His piece spoken, the old Churchillian optimism returned. "I write this letter because I know where your heart lies," he wrote. "Yours is a heavy responsibility and there is no greater believer in your capacity to bear it or true wellwisher in your task than your old friend."[10]

Ike replied that Eden had made fundamental mistakes that had compelled him to act. With communist propagandists ready to pounce on any moral slip, the western democracies had to be scrupulous about international law. Eden hadn't followed the law and had kept secrets from his ally. Lacking good-faith cooperation, Ike had to turn to the United Nations.

But he, too, felt any quarrel was transitory. They still had a common foe and a common cause. "I hope that this one may be washed off the slate as soon as possible and that we can then together adopt other means of achieving our legitimate objectives in the Middle East," Ike wrote. "Nothing saddens me more than the thought that I and my old friends of years have met a problem concerning which we do not see eye to eye. I shall never be happy until our old time closeness has been restored."[11]

Reading Ike's letter, Winston "was saddened and vexed by the unrepentant tone of the President." He forwarded a copy to Queen Elizabeth, who sent back a correct if sterile response: "I hope it means that the present feeling that this country and America are not seeing eye-to-eye will be speedily replaced by even stronger ties between us."[12]

Sitting quietly at La Capponcina, Lord Beaverbrook's sun-kissed villa on the Riviera, Winston pondered mankind's end. It wasn't hard. He had read novelist Neil Shute's *On the Beach*, a story of humanity after thermonuclear war. Shute's description of the last survivors, awaiting death in southern Australia as radioactive clouds engulfed the planet, worked its way into Winston's fertile imagination.

"I think the earth will soon be destroyed," he said at last. Offering a cosmic suggestion, he added, "If I were the Almighty, I would not recreate it, in case they destroyed Him, too, the next time."

In Moscow, Nikita Khrushchev emerged from a power struggle to become the Soviet Union's unchallenged leader. Though Winston had missed the chance to see him at the Geneva summit in 1955, he thought of sending Khrushchev a copy of Shute's book. It might give the man who held the launch codes a better perspective on the threat facing Russians, Americans, Englishmen, and everyone in between.

Asked whether he should also send a copy to his friend in Washington, Winston gave a derisive snort. "It would be a waste of money. He is so muddle-headed now."[13]

Ike wouldn't let policy, strategy, or politics ruin friendships. He met regularly for drinks with Sam Rayburn and Lyndon Johnson, the Texas

Democrats who ran Congress. He had mended fences with his old Republican opponent, Senator Taft, and now he wouldn't let Suez spoil things with the British. As English steam hissed off, a suggestion from a friend in the greeting card industry gave him an idea how to help mend the special relationship: He would tie it to America's love affair with Winston Churchill.[14]

In March 1957, Ike floated to Harold Macmillan the idea of inviting Winston to America for a traveling exhibition of his paintings. Ike had long believed in cultural and educational exchanges, and he hoped the public's embrace would help bridge the chasm that yawned over the Atlantic. Paintbrush diplomacy.

Macmillan thought the idea splendid, but he wondered about Winston's health. So Ike had his contacts discreetly reach out to Winston's daughter Sarah.

Winston had spent his life reveling in art. Over eight decades, his colors had been splashed across radio waves, newspaper pages, history books, and the hearts of people. His gallery was a library of forty-three books, his exhibition a body of speeches echoing across time and space. His museum held broken swastikas and the resolve of millions to tear down the Iron Curtain.

And now he was reduced to oil on canvas.

But when Sarah told Ike that the invitation would do her father good—"he feels left out of things," she said—Ike wrote to Winston with a formal proposal. Proud of his paintings, Winston said he was "much complimented" by Ike's suggestion. He would make thirty oils available.[15]

Ike worked behind the scenes to promote the exhibition. He penned the foreword to the collection's catalog. When several museums, including Pittsburgh's Carnegie Institute and the Cincinnati Art Museum, turned up their noses, Ike appealed to the trustees at New York's Metropolitan Museum of Art. "I truly believe that Sir Winston's exhibition will add much to our firm bonds of friendship and will prove a source of pride to the British, in addition to being highly interesting to the American public," he wrote. The Met signed on for the tour.[16]

By December 1957, Winston selected thirty-five paintings for a ten-city exhibition, opening in Kansas City the following spring.

"I know that the exhibition of your paintings would be outstandingly successful and an event that will excite and interest all Americans," Ike assured him. He added, "Mamie and I look forward to having you as our guest some time the latter part of April."[17]

Winston wrote back with cautious optimism. At his age, making plans was always a roll of the dice. Still, he hoped to be there and said he would "value the opportunity of seeing you and my other old friends."

Ike replied with delight and invited Winston to stay at the White House.[18]

The two kept up their correspondence through the early months of 1958. But before valets could prepare the Rose Suite, illness intervened. Stricken with bronchial pneumonia and a high fever, Winston regretfully told Ike he would have to remain in Europe during the art tour.[19]

"I have had a setback, which will mean that I have to take things quietly for a time," he wrote Ike. He promised to try for a visit later in the year. In the meantime, he invited Ike to choose one of his paintings to keep when the tour ended.

After careful consideration, Ike selected *Valley of the Ourika and Atlas Mountains*, a cheerful oil ablaze in color and light. Winston's rendition of the Moroccan pass brought a smile to Ike's face. On this piece of canvas, he saw serenity on a continent once scarred with the Torch landings, the Darlan Deal, Kasserine Pass, Tunis, and Bizerte.[20]

Now he had another way to remember Africa. And Winston.

The years after Suez offered plenty to keep Ike busy: desegregation in Little Rock, a sputtering economy, Sputnik, Formosa again, the space race, crisis in Lebanon, talk of a missile gap. But he regularly checked on Winston through mutual friends and hoped the old lion would feel strong enough for one more visit.

Yet the two men were in different places. During their years together in power, Ike's invitations had been the overtures Winston longed for. He had courted Ike not just for friendship, but for what America could give Britain—and the world. Ike, always warm, had kept collaboration at arm's length.

Now, with Winston's power a fading memory, Ike wanted more of Winston's company—purely for friendship. To Ike, the Englishman was a symbol and bearer of memories. Through Winston, he could relive an extraordinary past.

Above all, Winston was interesting.

In July 1958, Winston's battle with pneumonia subsided enough for him to consider a parliamentary speech on the U.S. deployment of troops in Lebanon. It was America's first major incursion into the Middle East under the Eisenhower Doctrine, and the British public would be quick to label Ike's move another Suez adventure. To keep the scar from tearing open, Macmillan asked Winston to speak to the Commons to discourage criticism of their American ally.

Winston began pulling his thoughts together, preparing notes stressing themes he had championed since 1940:

> *America & Britain* must work together,
> reach *Unity* of purpose.
> The complications which the problem presents

can be cured if, & only *if*,
they are dealt with by united forces
& common principles . . .
It wd be too easy to mock USA
We should refrain. . . .
I do not want to take points off the US
& point the finger of scorn at them
How easy to say
Look at US & compare them with us at Suez.
We were right. . . .
What is really foolish is for two nations like
England & USA
To search for points of difference
No case for picking a quarrel with USA.[21]

Yet at 83, the effort proved too much. His voice was spent, his throat hoarse from a lifetime of roaring. He didn't have it in him anymore.

"I spent an hour or two thinking over what I would say and came to the conclusion that I had nothing worth saying," he reluctantly told Macmillan. "I will turn up to support you in the Lobby. Forgive the change of plan."[22]

FIFTY-SEVEN

"After a Brief Silence, Reveille"

As the embers of empire cooled and cracked, Winston slipped into a gentle decline. He held the air of a man who intended to enjoy the time he had left. He passed his days at Lord Beaverbrook's villa on the Riviera, or at the elegant La Pausa, Coco Chanel's former perch above the Mediterranean shore. He spent weeks cruising aboard *Christina*, a floating palace owned by Aristotle Onassis, where hours dissolved into a haze of fine food and finer company.

Adrift or ashore, he painted when the mood struck. Sometimes he wrote to old friends, and he was always content to lose himself in a good book when conversation slackened and his muses slept. A record of books ordered for Winston for one Onassis cruise included twenty-three volumes, mostly novels, ranging from Jack London's *Call of the Wild* to Balzac's *Beatrix*.[1]

There was no urgency now, no rush, no old man in a hurry. He let the world pass him by.

In April 1959, another stroke reminded him that life still had its cruel side. But by now, strokes were hit-or-miss affairs. Some mattered, some didn't. This one turned out to be a rumble, not a thunderclap, and a month later, Winston felt well enough to see his old friend.[2]

At the National Press Club earlier that year, John Horner of the *Washington Evening Star* asked the president his impressions of his World War II colleagues.

Horner's question was prompted by the release of Bernard Montgomery's memoirs. The field marshal claimed Ike, not a great soldier in the true sense of the word, had bungled the war with his "broad front" strategy. Monty could have won it by Christmas 1944, had Ike only listened to him.

In front of cameras or microphones, Ike subscribed to the adage "If you can't say something nice, say nothing at all." Responding to Horner, he said nothing about Monty—or de Gaulle, who had been elected president of France the previous month. He briefly mentioned Bradley and Marshall and Sir Charles Portal, but he lingered on his English friend:

> I think Mr. Churchill is one of those men that I have known that clearly deserves the title of great. I think this is the title that can be applied accurately to only a few men, because no matter how much we respect the capabilities of any individual, we never can use that title or that adjective, as I see it, until the man has been proven in a position of great responsibility.
>
> He can be great in certain qualities; but great in the carrying of responsibility, like Mr. Churchill, is a very unusual qualification and one that entitles him, I think, overall to that designation. And this in spite of the fact that I probably had more differences of opinion, more quite warm arguments with Mr. Churchill than I suppose did any other person, certainly in the allied forces, because I happened to be of a nationality that he could not shut up if he wanted to. . . .
>
> He was really not only to my mind a great man; he is certainly one of my greatest friends that is not of my nationality.[3]

With one year left in his presidency, Ike looked forward to hosting the great man. The two would relax at the White House, visit Ike's farm at Gettysburg, and reminisce about the years when giants walked the earth. "For several days you and I should have some fun in making a final decision as to the identity of the General, Admiral or Air Marshal who really did win the war!" he wrote Winston.[4]

"I cannot tell you how eagerly I am looking forward to seeing him," he wrote to Pug Ismay. "I asserted that he was one of the few men that I knew that, in my opinion, was entitled to be considered one of the 'greats' of our time; and that my friendship with him would never be shaken."[5]

Ike's family saw his mood brighten as the calendar advanced. "I was with my Dad several times when Churchill was going to be there, and he always acted like a teenager getting ready for the heaviest date he'd ever had in his life," recalled John, who was working in the White House as his father's military aide. "I think it became real affection that my Dad had for Churchill."[6]

"History will be kind to me, for I intend to write it," Winston once quipped. America was kind to him, too. This was no state visit, and Sir Winston was no longer the face of Her Majesty's Government. But he was the heart of Britain, an Englishman loved and respected in his mother's homeland.

At Washington National Airport, Ike waited on the tarmac as *Columbine*'s ramp dropped. Out stepped a beaming Winston Churchill, homburg up top, gold-headed cane at his side. He looked chipper and confident as he held out his hand to a beaming Ike.

"Well, my friend, you're back again," said Ike.

Winston's eyes shone. "I am indeed glad to see you," he said.

Smiling, the two men stepped to a small platform. Taking Winston by the elbow, Ike spoke for the newsreels: "Sir Winston, this is a great honor indeed to welcome you once more to the United States. I do so not only as my dear friend of wartime days, but as one who is, after all, half American himself."

"I always love coming to America," Winston replied. "But," he added with an impish grin, "I shall not say—as most people travelling nowadays about the world seem to do—everything I think."

An appreciative laugh rippled through the crowd. The quip was directed at Montgomery, and everyone caught the reference. Ike couldn't help but chuckle.[7]

Winston's mind came alive with memories as Ike showed him around the White House. They walked the old, familiar halls. Ike and Mamie offered him his usual suite, the Rose Room—now called the Queen's Room, after her stay there in 1957.

Winston's sixth stay at the White House was quiet, stripped of pomp and pageantry. It lacked the "Action This Day" pace of the Roosevelt years or the conspiratorial urgency of his two earlier visits. Gone were the generals, admirals, air marshals, and aides; they were replaced by a private secretary, Anthony Montague Browne; Winston's sole bodyguard; and a nurse.

Longtimers at the White House knew Winston's habits, but age and stamina required a few updates to the "Winston Method." Montague Browne spelled out the old man's limits: He would make friendly remarks on arrival, but no prepared addresses. The press must not hound him, and there would be no dinner or luncheon speeches—though "of course, Sir Winston is almost certain to get up at the end of the meal and say a few sentences of thanks to his hosts."[8]

His personal needs were no longer the stuff of legend. He cut down on walking, sparing trips up the stairs. His appetite had softened, but he would not be handcuffed to any diet, and "he still likes white wine at lunch, champagne with dinner." During private meals, Mamie recalled, "His equerry, whose name I think was Browne, would come in and fix his little napkin on him and it was fastened with two gold safety pins—like we used to fasten our children's bibs with, only his were solid gold. And he'd sit there like a little cherub and eat his lunch."[9]

Gold pins couldn't deflect signs of decline. Winston lived in a cocoon of near deafness, and his refusal to wear a hearing aid frustrated Ike. The tip of one finger had become gangrenous, and his gait was a painful shuffle. John recalled, "It was something of a shock to witness the difficulty with which he made his way down the long hallway from the Queen's Room."[10]

As Ike watched his friend's struggle, he felt a pang of sadness. Standing next to Winston, he told his daughter-in-law, Barbara, "I wish you could have met him in his prime."

Hearing nothing, Winston just smiled.[11]

The next afternoon, the pair made their way to Walter Reed Hospital, where they called on Winston's old nemesis, John Foster Dulles. The cancer that had taken root in his colon around the time of Suez had metastasized to his spine and was sapping what was left of his life. Shortly before the visit, doctors removed fluid from his abdomen and implanted radioactive gold, giving him just enough strength to sit up and see visitors in his suite's sitting room.

For a few minutes, Ike, Dulles, and Winston chatted, the animus of yesterdays falling away like a dried leaf. In wheelchair and blue silk pajamas, Dulles was a shadow of the lectern thumper who had foiled Winston's dreams of a peace summit. He had no more battles to fight: not for country, not for ideals—not even for his life. All that was left for him was the quiet pain of waiting, his final weeks measured in morphine shots and goodbyes.

With some pride, Ike pointed out an oil portrait of Churchill over the sitting room fireplace. "There is the picture I painted of you, the one I wrote about," he said with a smile. Dulles asked an orderly to take down the painting for Winston's inspection.

Winston took a close look. It was a bit clunky, but a recognizable likeness. Respectable, even. Winston shied from portraits and faces, and his brush style, like his statecraft, was more sweeping than Ike's. But he admired Ike's willingness to tackle portraiture and complimented the execution.

"It's very good—very good," he said.[12]

They moved on to Ward 8, occupied by a sleeping George C. Marshall. The man Winston had dubbed the "Organizer of Victory" had been felled by a massive stroke at his Virginia home. Now he lay, hovering between life and death, awaiting the angel that would come for him in a few months. As Winston stood in the doorway of Marshall's room, his eyes glossed over with tears. He and Ike quietly moved on, leaving Marshall to his vigil.[13]

The spring weather offered a reprieve from the shadows of Walter Reed, and Winston and Ike spent other moments fishing in waters of the past. They also ranged into recent frustrations. Ike "went on to speak unfavourably of the French in general, and General de Gaulle in particular," Montague Browne told his diary. "He clearly has a paternal feeling for the NATO military machinery, dating no doubt from his tenure at SHAPE, and thought that the French might well wreck it."[14]

Talk turned to Monty. The field marshal who claimed Ike prolonged the war had recently written to Ike suggesting they catch up when Monty visited America that spring. Perhaps, he suggested, he could stay as Ike's guest at the White House.

The month before, Monty had given a CBS television interview to Edward R. Murrow criticizing American Cold War leadership. The

United States suffered from a "lack of decision at the top level," he said, in part because Eisenhower and his secretary of state "aren't very well, very fit." He suggested that soldiers do not make good politicians and should stay out of politics—the day before flying to Moscow to be wined and dined by Nikita Khrushchev. For good measure, Monty dredged up his old criticisms of the broad front, Berlin, Prague, and Vienna.[15]

Ike remarked "how wounded he had been by Monty's interview," Montague Browne remembered. "Monty gives interviews saying that I was not a competent commander in the field, only a professional good chap," Ike griped. "In his writing he slates me again and again. And then he has the gall to suggest coming to stay with me!"

"Sir Winston succeeded to a great extent, I think, in smoothing the ruffled feathers," Montague Browne noted. "But it was surprisingly evident how affected the President is by personal criticisms leveled at him from abroad. . . . For someone in his position [he] seemed surprisingly thin-skinned."[16*]

"Washington gets quite blasé about their own politicians, and most other heads of state too," recalled John Eisenhower. When Churchill came to town, it was different. "We thought we were seeing a real piece of history."[17]

At a black-tie White House dinner for Winston, Ike rose for remarks about his guest of honor. As he spoke, he found himself drifting back to his days as an unknown War Department assistant, a time when the obscure one-star met the man who would change his life.

"For me, there is a certain coincidence between this meeting and the circumstance that initiated my friendship with Sir Winston," he told

* Winston did note that Monty's picture, which Ike kept in the second-floor family quarters, occupied the same place as the last time he had visited, in 1954. Winston, seeing this, concluded that there was a limit to how far Ike would hold a grudge.

dinner guests. "I met him in this house—and this was something for a newly-commissioned brigadier—in the same room that he is now occupying when I met him. I had seen him from some distance at a December 1941 conference in the War Department; but as I said, I was a brigadier, and in that meeting I didn't get close to the head of the table."

He smiled. "Throughout this friendship, beginning in early 1942," he said, "I have had a great privilege which has come to only a few men: to be exposed to a great mind, to a great leader, to hear an eloquent tongue, to know him as a leader, a statesman, a political leader, a politician. And also to know him as an American."

After his reverie wound down, he sat and Winston rose to respond. Steadying himself, he rendered his ancient refrain with the grace of a retired actor reciting his favorite lines from *Henry V.*

"I feel most strongly that our whole effort should be to work together," he said. To America, Britain could never be just another country. "I think that it is in close and increasing fellowship, the brotherhood of English-speaking peoples, that we must work. . . . It is in a close and increasing fellowship with you, our American friends and brothers, that our brilliant future rests."[18]

"The brotherhood of English-speaking peoples." At 84, Winston's swan song would be no quiet coda. It was a fortissimo chord—a melody repeated, augmented, and amplified to bring out notes he had played for thirty years. Come dictators, come strokes, come ravages of time, nothing would separate the theme from the man who composed it. It would be his signature piece until the end of his days.

"Of all the prominent men Ike ever dealt with, I am confident that Churchill was his favorite," John Eisenhower wrote years later. "Never once did I ever hear Ike say a derogatory word about him. Naturally, he loved to tell stories of Churchill's foibles, but he did so affectionately."[19]

Ike knew those foibles better than any other American, but loved him anyway. When he learned that Field Marshal Brooke had published diary entries, written in moments of frustration, scathingly critical of Winston's judgment, he told Pug Ismay he was shocked.

"I could not imagine myself as being guilty of writing anything, ten years after the war was over, that could be construed as disparaging the accomplishments of the wartime Prime Minister," he wrote. "All of us got impatient, at times, with some of the mannerisms, the idiosyncrasies, and even the demands of Winston. But I had supposed that all of us felt that these were of no consequence as compared to his great contributions to the war effort and, for myself, I never lost an unbounded admiration and personal liking for him."[20]

The son reflected his father's admiration. "We knew he was a canny, wily devil," John told an interviewer. "We knew about his faults, but he, there was still something about him, what he had stood for, that touched us."[21]

That something seeped down through the generational branches. Before John left for work during Winston's visit, his 8-year-old daughter, Susan, asked him to give Mr. Churchill a watercolor of a horse she was learning to ride. John passed it to Montague Browne for delivery, and a few days later, a letter from Winston arrived, addressed to Miss Susan Eisenhower. He thanked the young girl for her painting and encouraged her to continue. He said he hoped it would give her as much enjoyment as it gave him. In shaky handwriting, he signed it, "Winston S. Churchill."[22]

From the White House, Ike whisked Winston by helicopter to his Gettysburg farm. As they flew over the Pennsylvania countryside, an aide asked Winston, "Beautiful country, isn't it?"

He nodded, plucking the cigar from his mouth. "Yes. Just like England."[23]

At the famous battle site, Winston surprised his hosts by accurately picking out the hallowed ground of the Round Tops and Pickett's

Charge. War had a way of firing his interest, and his voice quickened as he described the battle's pivotal second and third days.[24]

The next morning found the two men sitting on a couch in the farmhouse's glass-walled porch. When conversation began to flag, Ike suggested, "Perhaps we ought to have a Coca-Cola or something to drink."

"Or something." Winston concurred with something. "Yes, I'd like a little whisky," he said.

Ike savored his Coke in the cool morning air as Winston sipped his highball. "President Eisenhower was a very abstemious drinker," remembered Arthur Nevins, the farm's caretaker. "That was a little early for drinking, except for Winston Churchill, apparently."[25]

The two men climbed into an electric golf cart, Winston wearing a white ten-gallon hat, holding a cigar in one hand, and gripping the cart rail with the other. Ike took the wheel and drove Winston on a tour of his farm. At the White House, Ann Whitman couldn't suppress a giggle when she saw a news photograph of the two men captioned, "Sir Winston hanging on for dear life as the President took him across bumpy terrain in a golf cart."[26]

After inspecting Ike's livestock, they went back to the helicopter and flew to Washington for Winston's departure. Flanked by Ike and Mamie, Winston shuffled out the portico door one last time and rode to the British embassy for a farewell dinner.

That evening, a curious embassy staffer asked Winston about the animals he saw on the Eisenhower farm. To everyone's surprise, Winston was "able to say precisely how many of each had been shown to him. Except for the pigs." Winston said he had not been allowed to see any pigs.[27]

In November 1960, as the world watched John F. Kennedy edge out Richard Nixon to become America's thirty-fifth president, Winston slipped and broke a small bone in his back. News traveled fast, and a lame-duck Eisenhower cabled from the White House, "All the people in America are distressed to hear of your accident, none more so than I."[28]

Winston replied two weeks later, touching on a subject he had some experience with. "As the time approaches for you to lay down your great and burdensome Office, I would like to convey to you the warmth of my personal feelings for you and the sincerity of my hope for your happy and peaceful future," he wrote. "My memories of our friendship and association are constant and good. We worked together for many years, and I do not think that I need to tell you of the high regard and affection in which I hold you."[29]

Through his long sunset, Winston's commitment to the Anglo-American brotherhood never flagged. But commitment carried burdens, even this late in the day. It meant guarding Britain's raw feelings in the wake of Suez, so when Ike wrote to ask permission to quote some of Winston's letters discussing Egypt and the Canal in his White House memoirs, Winston demurred.

Wary of reopening old wounds, Winston hoped Ike would bury that memory in the backyard and let someone else inscribe its tombstone. "I think that on the whole it might be best to leave these issues, which are of quite recent date and still alive, to lie unpublished for some time to come," he advised.[30]

"Churchill was fond of Dad. Dad, I think, was even more fond of Churchill," John Eisenhower concluded. Though warm as ever, Winston didn't fully mirror the admiration Ike felt for him. When they were the free world's leaders, Winston had pursued Ike, begging for meetings to arrange peace talks with the Russians. At the time, Ike had kept him at arm's length, only grudgingly deigning to official meetings on two occasions. For their only proper summit, Ike had even insisted that the French attend, so the world would know his and Winston's wasn't an exclusive relationship. "No ganging up," and all that.

In retirement, their roles shifted. Winston was a man of the world—the western world, anyway—and demands of state no longer required him to court Ike the way he once had. He enjoyed spending time with Ike on occasion and flew from the Riviera to London to attend a reunion dinner with Ike, Monty, Brooke, and the rest at the American ambassador's residence. But he did not gush about Ike to his friends or offer public paeans the way Ike did for him.

Their friendship had warped in the heat of Suez, a contest Ike had won and Winston's beloved Empire had lost. Now, after a quarter century of Winston wooing and pursuing three U.S. presidents, it was a retired Ike who was the suitor.[31]

Winston soldiered on through 1961, commencing a season of lasts. In the spring he visited New York, his sixteenth and final trip to his mother's homeland. In November, he uttered his last words in Parliament—a simple thank-you to the opposition leader for birthday wishes. The next year, he painted his last oil study, *The Goldfish Pool at Chartwell*.[32]

His closest friends were mostly gone. Lord Beaverbrook, Lord Cherwell, Jan Smuts, all gone. Brendan Bracken, gone. His firstborn, Diana, gone by her own hand. With no official burdens to bear, Chartwell had become his Avalon. He walked the grounds and took in its gardens. He found solace in the company of butterflies and goldfish. He kept a steady correspondence with Ike, who, also in retirement, inquired after his health, asked after Clemmie, and sent expressions of friendship.[33]

In June 1962, Winston suffered his last major accident in Monte Carlo, breaking his hip in a fall while stepping out of bed at the Hôtel de Paris. With his lower body encased in a cast, Winston was seized with a sense of inevitability. As doctors stabilized him, he expressed a simple, profound wish: "I want to die in England." Montague Browne relayed the request to No. 10 Downing, and Harold Macmillan dispatched a RAF Comet to fly him home.[34]

Winston was ready for Death, but Death was not ready for Winston. Doctors set a pin in the fractured hip, and before long he was sitting up in his private room.

"When I arrived," one doctor wrote, "the coffee, brandy and cigars appeared. Sir Winston poured the coffee himself and always asked whether I preferred white or brown sugar. Then the brandy . . . The big ceremonial was choosing the cigar. About four boxes were placed on his bed tray. Each was opened and he pawed through the cigars to find the one that was exactly right; he sniffed them, he rolled them between his fingers and listened to them. What that did defeated me, because he was deafer than me."[35]

In August, Winston received a welcome distraction. While Ike and Mamie were vacationing in Europe with their grandchildren, Ike made a point of stopping by Middlesex Hospital to see his old friend.

"He was quite weak . . . his mind going back feebly to incidents of the war days," Ike recalled. "Though it was sad to see him helpless, he managed at times to smile and even asked his aide, Montague-Brown, for a whiskey and soda—which he didn't touch." A thespian to the end, Winston hung on to his props.

To the outside world, Ike kept a cheerful face. "He looks like the same old Winston to me," he told reporters when he emerged. "It was a wonderful thing to see him. We talked about personal things—about when we had last seen each other and when we hoped to meet again."

He paused, serious for a moment. "I think the world of him," he said, his words coming from deep within. "He is a man I think the whole nation can be very proud of. I just had the feeling again I was seeing a very great man."

Winston, too, perked up briefly after Ike's visit. "The general was in good heart," he reported.

The bitterness of Suez had faded into the tapestry. It was now consigned to the backstory, a closet in which hung the other arguments. Not forgotten, of course—but left to history.

What remained, distilled through the years, was a bond of two friends who would meet with a smile and leave with a glow.[36]

Sixteen years younger than Winston, Ike fared better in retirement. Now "General Eisenhower"—Congress had given Ike his stars back through a special law—he spent summers in Gettysburg and winters near Palm Springs, California. He kept busy with correspondence with old friends, reminiscing over their years in Normandy and North Africa and Italy and Germany.

His admiration for Winston grew with separation of time and space. "He's a great thinker and he's a great patriot, and he thinks not only just in terms of those little islands or even only of the British Empire," Ike told an interviewer. "He's talking about Western Civilization."[37]

Ike wrote the great thinker regularly, congratulating him on birthdays, wedding anniversaries, and, in 1963, on his honorary citizenship, bestowed by Congress at the urging of President Kennedy.

"I often find myself wishing that several of us could get together for a whole week of 'chin and chatter,'" he wrote in the spring of '63. "If we could have such people as Al Gruenther, Ken Strong, Peter Portal, Omar Bradley, Bert Harris and others, we could really have a lot of fun. . . . Maybe we could go to Culzean in Scotland or to the George Cinq in Paris. . . .

"Of course, so many are gone," he continued. "Good old Bedell, Admiral Ramsay, and Leigh-Mallory. Others are out of circulation because of health, among these one I miss is Arthur Tedder."[38]

Inside, he felt a pang of sorrow as he contemplated his friend's shortening horizon. "I am distressed about Winston's decline," he wrote Pug in 1964, the year Winston gave up his parliamentary seat. "It seems a rather sad end for such a gallant old warrior."

Time would drape their old differences in nostalgia. Two years later, Ike would write, "Through the first three years of my Presidency Prime Minister Churchill and I remained virtual partners in matters of an international character. Our common experiences of World War II helped to sustain a spirit of comradeship, which always seems to exist among veterans of any campaign."

Ike saw Winston again in August that year, recovering from another stroke, and kept abreast of his condition through mutual friends. But their brief meeting that summer was another of Winston's lasts.[39]

"Thank Heaven he is beyond the reach of agony—though not of boredom," wrote Winston's oldest living friend, Violet Bonham Carter.[40]

He watched the world from Chartwell through languid eyes. South Vietnam boiled, the Beatles climbed the pop charts, Martin Luther King Jr. won the Nobel Peace Prize, and Lyndon Johnson raised the banner of a murdered JFK. The Empire, even the pretense of empire, was a faded dream from a long-ago night.

But by late 1964, the 90-year-old hull that had carried Winston from the Hindu Kush to New York, to Moscow and points between, took on water and began to sink, leaving his mind adrift on an empty sea.

"How much longer do you think I shall have to wait?" he asked during a lucid moment. In London, in his Hyde Park Gate home over lunch, he turned to his former daughter-in-law, Pamela Harriman, and pouted, "I have done my bit. I should be allowed to depart in peace."[41]

What would that peace look like? Unlike Ike, who firmly believed in the Christian afterlife, Winston didn't see himself on streets of gold with saintly choirs singing, world without end, Amen. Having spent one life flying through hurricanes, he didn't want another tour. He wanted stillness. The absolute tranquility of a billion years' sleep.

"Do you believe in the afterlife?" his son once asked him.

"No, I believe in a beautiful black abyss," Winston said.

But he added, with a smile, "I may be wrong. I may wake up and find I am a coolie in China. That would be very unfair. I would lodge a complaint."[42]

"Action This Day" had been Winston's standing order as prime minister. For nine decades under the sun, he had dictated his long speech and penciled in what corrections he could. Now it was for the audience to decide what to make of the manuscript. Life should have packed its typewriter and quietly slipped out the door.

But his soul tarried, notepad in hand, as if waiting to record one last triumph, one last speech, one last cigar, one final toast to Queen and Country.

Or one final blow. The stroke hit on January 12, 1965, leaving him bedridden, mostly unconscious, barely able to mumble. As the shadows lengthened, his son-in-law Christopher Soames recorded his last coherent words: "I'm so bored with it all."[43]

Twelve days later, on the seventieth anniversary of his father's death, Winston wandered off into his beautiful black abyss.

When he heard Winston was on his deathbed, Ike began thinking of what he would say about the man he met in the shadow of Pearl Harbor.

"The one thing I could do that probably all the others couldn't—they could use all the purple words and they can find all the adjectives, lovely adjectives, and all the rest, but I knew this man in a peculiar way," he remembered. "I was in an Allied Force and in his country, where he was half of my boss, and therefore we got very, very close."[44]

For three days, Ike ignored his golf clubs to focus on what Winston Churchill meant to him. Memories came flooding back: The evil they had faced. The world they worked to protect. Hitler and Stalin, tobacco and cocktails, hydrogen bombs and NATO, the Mid East, Indochina, and the Iron Curtain.

The transatlantic partnership they built during the war, then rebuilt in peace.

He picked up a yellow pad and began to write. Words came fast and fluid. When he finished, he read his draft to Mamie.

She smiled at him.

"Ike, this is wonderful. Don't you change a word, and don't you get anyone to change it."[45]*

Years before, the Queen had ordered the Duke of Norfolk to undertake Churchill's funeral celebration "on a scale befitting his position in history." The result, "Operation Hope Not," was a 415-page battle plan laying out the most elaborate nonroyal funeral since the death of the Duke of Wellington: Three days lying in state in Westminster Hall. Nine martial bands. A procession of eighteen military units, a 90-gun salute from St. James's Park, and the appearances of 320,000 mourners marked a farewell to England's greatest son.[46]

The Churchill family issued a dozen private invitations to Winston's American friends, with Ike topping the list. He wouldn't have missed the send-off for the world. A late January day found him standing silently at attention beside Winston's funeral bier in Westminster Hall, reflecting on the passing of a giant. That evening, he met for drinks and

* It wasn't Ike's first run at Winston's eulogy. While president, he had drafted a tribute in case Winston died before January 20, 1961, Ike's last day in office. The White House version was statesmanlike, coming from a national leader, not the beating heart of an old friend. "The world has lost one of the truly great men of our time," the draft began. "Sir Winston—in time of war and in time of peace—captured the imagination of all Americans. His indomitable courage and his indestructible belief in the society of free nations and in the dignity of free men became a symbol of our way of life."

memories with old friends like Alex, Pug, Tedder—brothers from the war's darkest days.[47]

On the morning of January 30, Big Ben fell silent. In St. James's Park, howitzers boomed ninety times in slow succession, marking each year of Winston's life. Then the ceremony began.

Winston's coffin was borne from Westminster to St. Paul's Cathedral on a horse-drawn gun carriage, the Union Flag draped over the casket. From the cathedral's stone steps, Anthony Eden, Clement Attlee, and Harold Macmillan, Winston's honorary pallbearers, escorted the coffin down the aisle.

Taking his place next to French President Charles de Gaulle, Queen Juliana of the Netherlands, Supreme Court Chief Justice Earl Warren, and Vice President Hubert Humphrey, Ike sat through the order of service. Readings from I and II Corinthians. The Archbishop's prayer. Choral music and Winston's favorite hymns—among them "Battle Hymn of the Republic," a nod to his kinship with America.

Then the National Anthem. The cavalry's bugle call, "Last Post," followed, after two minutes of silence, by "Reveille."[48]

Ike watched his mentor's coffin as it was carried out of the church to a motor launch on the Thames River.

As the casket faded from view, Ike walked quietly to the Registrar's Office across from St. Paul's, where the BBC had set up a makeshift broadcast studio. There he would deliver his eulogy.

In the clear, firm voice he had found in wartime London, Ike summed up his twenty-three-year friendship with Winston Leonard Spencer Churchill:

> I was privileged to meet, to talk, to plan and to work with him for common goals. Out of that association, an abiding—and to me precious—friendship was forged. It withstood the trials and fric-

tions inescapable among men of strong convictions, living in an atmosphere of war.

The war ended, our friendship flowered in the later and more subtle tests imposed by international politics. Then, each of us, holding high official post in his own nation, strove together so to concert the strength of our two peoples that liberty might be preserved among men and the security of the free world wholly sustained. . . .

May God grant that we—and the generations who will remember him—heed the lessons he taught us: in his deeds, in his words, in his life.

May we carry on his work until no nation lies in captivity, no man is denied opportunity for fulfillment.

There was no tremor; there was no break. Ike's voice, stripped of ornamentation, held the firm, upbeat cadence of a man who had walked through history at Churchill's side:

"And now to you, Sir Winston—my old friend—farewell."[49]

ACKNOWLEDGMENTS

The foregoing take on an extraordinary friendship would not have been possible without the help of two gifted polymaths. Allegra Jordan graciously poured her background in writing, business management, Cicero, history, poetry, literature, and ethics into a preliminary review that sanded down rough edges, blocked cringeworthy metaphors, and put flabby chapters on a much-needed diet. Hal Elrod—my best-read friend, hiking pal, and past master of matters technological, theological, and literary—added invaluable insights that let the story be the story and deleted errors before they could take flight. To them, and their dear companions, Ted and Jennifer, I owe more than I can express.

This book would not have seen light of day without the work of my editor, David Howe, and the advocacy of Folio's Jeff Kleinman and Will Murphy. Emily Walden added lyrical insights, while Rachel Johnston and Austin Jordan supported my work and pushed me to find better ways of expressing the book's ideas. The helpful staffs of the Library of Congress, the Roosevelt Library, Cambridge's Churchill Archives, the Columbia Oral History Project, the U.S. Army Heritage and Educational Center, and, of course, the Eisenhower Library were crucial in supplying the studs and sheetrock needed to build the house. I would also be remiss in failing to thank my mentor, Arthur Steinberg, for his encouragement of my writing during breaks from courtroom drama—and for the stellar example he set as a wise lawyer and good man.

Naturally, my most constant source of personal encouragement over five years writing this book came from my wife, Galina. She brought warmth, love of history, and irrepressible joy to a world tangled by Covid, courtrooms, canines, and the challenges life throws at us all. *Сегда и навсегда*—"always and forever."

SELECT BIBLIOGRAPHY

PRIMARY SOURCES

Archival Collections

Churchill College, Cambridge University (CAC)
Columbia University, Columbia Oral History Project (COHP)
Dwight D. Eisenhower Presidential Library (EL)
Franklin Delano Roosevelt Presidential Library
Harry S. Truman Presidential Library (HSTL)
Johns Hopkins University
    The Papers of Dwight D. Eisenhower (EP)
Library of Congress
National Archives and Records Administration (NARA)
National Museum of Health and Medicine
    Otis Historical Archives
National Security Archive, George Washington University (online)
New York Times Archive
North Atlantic Treaty Organization Archives
Seely G. Mudd Library, Princeton University
    John Foster Dulles Oral History Collection (JFDC)
The Times (London) Archive
United States Army Heritage and Education Center (AHEC)
U.S. Department of State, *Foreign Relations of the United States*
Yale University Library, Yale University
    Henry L. Stimson Collection

Oral Histories

Abel, Elie (COHP)
Achilles, Theodore (JFDC)
Adams, Sherman (COHP, EL, JFDC)
Aiken, George (JFDC)
Aldrich, Winthrop (COHP, JFDC)
Allen, George V. (COHP, JFDC)
Alsop, Joseph (JFDC)
Anderson, Dillon (COHP, JFDC)
Armstrong, W. Park (JFDC)
Asbjornson, Mildred (JFDC)
Aurand, Evan (COHP)
Barker, Ray (COHP, EL)
Barnes, Roswell (JFDC)
Beale, Sir Howard (JFDC)
Benedict, Stephen (COHP)
Bennett, Charles I. (EL)
Berg, Harold (EL)
Betts, Thomas (EL)
Bird, John (EL)
Bissell, Richard (COHP, JFDC, EL)
Black, Eugene (JFDC)
Bohlen, Charles (COHP, JFDC)
Bonesteel, Charles (AHEC)
Bowie, Robert (CAC, JFDC, COHP)
Bradley, Omar (COHP)
Brainard, C. L. (COHP)
Briggs, Ellis (COHP)
Broshous, Charles (EL)

Brown, Lillian (EL)
Brownell, Herbert (COHP, JFDC, EL)
Brownell, Samuel (COHP)
Bruce, David (JFDC)
Burgess, Carter (COHP)
Burgess, Randolph (JFDC, EL)
Burke, Arleigh (JFDC)
Byrnes, James (JFDC)
Cabell, Charles (JFDC)
Cannon, Craig (EL)
Chiang Kai-shek and Madame (JFDC)
Childs, Marquis (JFDC)
Churchill, Winston (grandson) (CAC)
Clark, Mark (JFDC)
Clay, Lucius (COHP, JFDC)
Cochran, Jacqueline (COHP, EL)
Collins, J. Lawton (JFDC, AHEC)
Couve de Murville, Maurice (JFDC)
Dean, Arthur (JFDC)
Devers, Jacob (EL)
Dewey, Thomas (JFDC)
Donovan, Robert (COHP, JFDC)
Douglas, Lewis (COHP)
Drezmal, Alene (EL)
Drummond, Roscoe (JFDC)
Dulles, Allen (JFDC)
Dulles, Avery (JFDC)
Dulles, Eleanor (COHP, JFDC)
Eban, Abba (JFDC)
Eisenhower, Barbara (EL)
Eisenhower, Dwight (JFDC, EL)
Eisenhower, John S. D. (CAC, COHP, EL)
Eisenhower, Mamie (EL)
Eisenhower, Milton (COHP, JFDC, EL)
Eisenhower Staff (EL)
Elsey, George (CAC)
Ennis, William (AHEC)
Evans, Luther (COHP)
Ewald, William (EL)
Flanders, Ralph (COHP)
Folliard, Edward (COHP)
Foster, William (JFDC)
Franks, Sir Oliver (JFDC)
Freers, Edward (JFDC)
Goodpaster, Andrew (CAC, COHP, JFDC, EL)
Gray, Gordon (COHP, JFDC, EL)
Gruenther, Alfred (COHP)
Hacker, Louis (COHP)
Hagerty, James (COHP, JFDC, EL)
Hall, Leonard (JFDC)
Hamblin, Grace (CAC)
Handy, Thomas (EL)
Harlow, Bryce (COHP, JFDC, EL)
Harr, Karl (COHP, JFDC)
Harriman, Averell (JFDC)
Harriman, Kathleen (CAC)
Harriman, Pamela (CAC)
Heaton, Leonard (JFDC, EL)
Heilbronn, Kurt (EL)
Herwarth, Hans von (COHP)
Howard, Katherine (COHP)
Houghton, Amory (JFDC)
Hughes, Emmet (JFDC)
Hughes, John (JFDC)
Humphrey, George, and Herbert Hoover Jr. (JFDC)
Irwin, John (JFDC)
Jefferson, Louis (JFDC)
Jehl, Sue (EL)
Kennan, George (JFDC)
Kieve, Robert (EL)
King, Helen (COHP, EL)
Kinna, Patrick (CAC)
Kirk, Grayson (COHP)
Krock, Arthur (JFDC)
Lambert, Gerard (JFDC)
Lee, William (COHP, EL)
LeMay, Curtis (JFDC)
Lemnitzer, Lyman (COHP)
Lodge, Henry Cabot (JFDC)
Luce, Clare Boothe (COHP)
Luce, Henry (JFDC, EL)
MacArthur, Douglas, II (EL, JFDC)
Macomber, Phyllis (JFDC)
Macomber, William (JFDC)
Makins, Roger (CAC, JFDC)
Mann, Thomas (EL)
Mayer, René (JFDC)
Mazo, Earl (COHP)
McAdam, Charles (COHP)
McCaffrey, William (AHEC)
McCann, Kevin (COHP, EL)
McCarty, Nancy (COHP, EL)
McCloy, John (COHP, JFDC)
McCrum, Marie (EL)
McIlvaine, Robinson (EL)
McKay, Lawrence (EL)
Mendès France, Pierre (JFDC)

Merchant, Livingston (JFDC)
Minnich, Arthur (EL)
Moaney, John (COHP, EL)
Montague Browne, Anthony (CAC)
Morgan, Gerald (JFDC)
Murphy, Robert (COHP)
Murray, Edmund (CAC)
Nel, Elizabeth (CAC)
Nevins, Arthur (EL, COHP)
Nixon, Richard (JFDC)
Norstad, Lauris (JFDC, EL)
Patterson, Bradley (COHP)
Peckham, Arthur (JFDC)
Persons, Wilton (COHP)
Pineau, Christian (JFDC)
Pinette, Mattie (EL)
Portal, Charles (EL)
Prochnow, Herbert (JFDC)
Pyle, Howard (COHP)
Quesada, Elwood (COHP, EL)
Rabb, Maxwell (COHP, JFDC, EL)
Radford, Arthur (JFDC)
Ramsey, Lloyd (AHEC)
Reston, James (JFDC)
Ridgway, Matthew (JFDC)
Rob, Charles (CAC)
Roberts, Chalmers (COHP)
Robertson, Walter (COHP)
Roosevelt, Curtis (CAC)
Salisbury, Harrison (COHP)
Scherer, Raymond (COHP)
Schoenberg, Irving (EL)
Schulz, Robert (EL)
Schwartz, Doris (JFDC)
Scott, Inez (EL)
Shanley, Bernard (COHP, JFDC)
Shepley, James (COHP, JFDC)
Sherrod, Robert (COHP)
Simpson, William (EL)
Slater, Ellis (COHP)
Smith, Howard K. (COHP)
Snider, Dwight (EL)
Snider, Orin (COHP)
Soames, Mary Churchill (CAC)
Spaak, Paul-Henri (JFDC)
Sprague, Robert (JFDC)
Stassen, Harold (JFDC)
Steelman, John (HSTL)
Stephens, Thomas (COHP, JFDC)
Swan, D. Walter (COHP, EL)
Taylor, Maxwell (JFDC)
Thayer, Robert (COHP, JFDC)
Thompson, Richard (AHEC)
Twining, Nathan (JFDC)
Wainhouse, David (COHP)
Walters, Vernon (EL)
Wheaton, Anne (COHP)
Whitman, Ann (EL)
Wilcox, Francis (COHP)
Woods, George (JFDC)
Woodward, Jack (EL)
Wriston, Henry (COHP)
Yates, Charles (COHP)

Photographic Collections

AHEC
Churchill Archives
Eisenhower Library
NARA

Books

Adams, Sherman, *Firsthand Report* (Harper & Bros. 1961)

Alanbrooke, Lord, *War Diaries 1939–1945* (Alex Danchev and Daniel Todman, eds.) (U. California Press 2001)

Allen, George E., *Presidents Who Have Known Me* (Simon & Schuster 1950)

Bowie, Robert, and Richard Immerman, *Waging Peace: How Eisenhower Shaped an Enduring Cold War Strategy* (Oxford U. Press 1998; Oxford U. Press 2000 ed.)

Boyle, Peter, ed., *The Churchill-Eisenhower Correspondence 1953–1955* (U. of North Carolina Press 1990)

Bradley, Omar, *A Soldier's Story* (Henry Holt 1951; Modern Library 1999 ed.)

———, and Clay Blair, *A General's Life* (Simon & Schuster 1983)
Butcher, Harry, *My Three Years with Eisenhower* (Simon & Schuster 1946)
Byrnes, James, *All in One Lifetime* (Harper & Bros. 1958)
Channon, Henry, *The Diaries 1938–43* (Simon Heffer, ed.) (Hutchinson 2021)
Churchill, Winston, *Great Contemporaries* (Butterworth 1937; ISI Books 2012 ed.)
———, *The Second World War* (6 vols., Houghton Mifflin 1948–1953)
———, *The Irrepressible Churchill* (Kay Halle, ed.) (Robson Books 1987; Butler & Tanner 2000 ed.)
———, *The Churchill War Papers* (Martin Gilbert, ed.) (3 vols., W. W. Norton 1993–2001)
———, *The Churchill Documents* (Martin Gilbert and Larry P. Arnn, eds.) (23 vols., Hillsdale College Press 2006–2019)
———, *Churchill by Himself* (Richard M. Langworth, ed.) (PublicAffairs 2008)
———, *Churchill in His Own Words* (Richard M. Langworth, ed.) (Edbury Press 2008, 2012 ed.)
Clark, Mark, *Calculated Risk* (Harper & Bros. 1950)
Clark, William, *From Three Worlds* (Sidgwick & Jackson 1986)
Colville, John, *The Fringes of Power: 10 Downing Street Diaries 1939–1955* (W. W. Norton 1985)
Cox, Vivian, *Seven Christmases* (Nick Thorne, ed.) (Nikkay Associates 2010)
Cutler, Robert, *No Time for Rest* (Little, Brown 1965)
Eden, Anthony, *Full Circle: The Memoirs of the Rt. Hon. Sir Anthony Eden* (Cassell 1960)
Eisenhower, Dwight D., *Crusade in Europe* (Doubleday 1948, 1952 ed.)
———, *Mandate for Change: The White House Years, 1953–1956* (Doubleday 1963)
———, *Waging Peace: The White House Years, 1956–1961* (Doubleday 1965)
———, *At Ease: Stories I Tell to Friends* (Doubleday 1967)
———, *General Eisenhower on the Military Churchill* (James Nelson, ed.) (W. W. Norton 1970)
———, *The Papers of Dwight D. Eisenhower* (Alfred D. Chandler et al., eds.) (21 vols., Johns Hopkins 1970–2001)
———, *Letters to Mamie* (John S. D. Eisenhower, ed.) (Doubleday 1977)
———, *The Eisenhower Diaries* (Robert Ferrell, ed.) (W. W. Norton 1981)
Eisenhower, John S. D., *Strictly Personal: A Memoir* (Doubleday 1974)
———, *General Ike: A Personal Reminiscence* (Free Press 2003)
Graebner, Walter, *My Dear Mister Churchill* (Michael Joseph 1965)
Hagerty, James, *The Diary of James C. Hagerty: Eisenhower in Mid-Course, 1954–1955* (Robert H. Ferrell, ed.) (Indiana U. Press 1983)
Hassett, William, *Off the Record with FDR 1942–1945* (Rutgers U. Press 1958)
Hughes, Emmet, *The Ordeal of Power: A Political Memoir of the Eisenhower Years* (Atheneum 1963)
Ingersoll, Ralph, *Top Secret* (Harcourt Brace 1946)
Ismay, Hastings, *The Memoirs of General Lord Ismay* (Viking 1960)
Kennedy, John, *The Business of War: The War Narrative of Major-General Sir John Kennedy* (Bernard Fergusson, ed.) (Hutchinson 1957)
Leahy, William D., *I Was There* (Victor Gollancz 1950)
Lloyd, Selwyn, *Suez 1956* (Jonathan Cape 1978, Coronet 1980 ed.)
Macmillan, Harold, *Macmillan Diaries: The Cabinet Years 1950–1957* (Peter Catterall, ed.) (Macmillan 2003; Pan Books 2004 ed.)
Maisky, Ivan, *The Maisky Diaries* (Gabriel Gorodesky, ed.) (Yale U. Press 2015)
McKeogh, Michael J., and Richard Lockridge, *Sgt. Mickey and General Ike* (G. P. Putnam's Sons 1946)
Montague Browne, Anthony, *Long Sunset: Memoirs of Winston Churchill's Last Private Secretary* (Cassell 1995; Podkin Press 2009 ed.)
Montgomery, Bernard, *Memoirs of Field-Marshal Montgomery* (Signet Books 1959)
Moran, Lord (Charles Wilson), *Churchill: The Struggle for Survival 1940–1965* (Houghton Mifflin 1966)

Murphy, Robert, *Diplomat Among Warriors* (Doubleday 1964)
Nixon, Richard, *Six Crises* (Doubleday 1962, Pyramid Books 1968 ed.)
———, *Leaders* (Warner 1982)
Nutting, Anthony, *No End of a Lesson* (Constable 1967)
Patton, George, *The Patton Papers* (Martin Blumenson, ed.) (2 vols., Houghton Mifflin 1974)
Pawle, Gerald, *The War and Colonel Warden* (Corgi 1963)
Reilly, Michael, *Reilly of the White House* (Simon & Schuster 1947)
Roosevelt, Elliott, *As He Saw It* (Duell, Sloan & Pearce 1946)
Roosevelt, Franklin, *FDR: His Personal Letters* (Elliott Roosevelt, ed.) (Duell, Sloan & Pearce 1950)
Sherwood, Robert, *Roosevelt and Hopkins* (Harper & Bros. 1948)
Shuckburgh, Evelyn, *Descent to Suez* (W. W. Norton 1986)
Slater, Ellis, *The Ike I Knew* (Ellis D. Slater Trust 1980)
Smith, Walter Bedell, *Eisenhower's Six Great Decisions* (Longmans, Green 1956)
Snyder, Marty, *My Friend Ike* (Frederick Fell 1956)
Soames, Mary, ed., *Speaking for Themselves* (Doubleday 1998)
Stagg, J. M., *Forecast for Overlord* (W. W. Norton 1971)
Stalin, Josef, *The Kremlin Letters* (David Reynolds and Vladimir Pechatnov, eds.) (Yale U. Press 2018)
Strong, Kenneth, *Intelligence at the Top* (Doubleday 1968)
Summersby, Kay, *Eisenhower Was My Boss* (Prentice-Hall 1948)
———, *Past Forgetting* (Simon & Schuster 1975)
Tedder, Arthur, *With Prejudice* (Little, Brown 1966)
Thompson, Walter, *Assignment: Churchill* (Farrar, Straus and Young 1955)
Truman, Harry, *Memoirs* (2 vols., Doubleday 1955–1956)

Other Primary Sources

Aldrich, Winthrop, "The Suez Crisis," *Foreign Affairs* (April 1967)
CBS Reports, "D-Day Plus 20 Years—Eisenhower Returns to Normandy," https://www.youtube.com/watch?v=vNaxTXfjfXk
Center for Naval Analysis, "Suez Crisis, 1956" (April 1974), https://nsarchive.gwu.edu/sites/default/files/documents/20515408/doc-5-cna-suez-1956.pdf
Eisenhower, John S. D., "General Ike," PCNTV podcast, https://www.youtube.com/watch?v=NJPNA7wGuXA
Luce, Clare Boothe, "Sunday Painters: Churchill, Eisenhower and Kennedy," *McCall's* (January 1967)
National Security Council, "Basic National Security Policy" (NSC 162/2)
Peck, John H. "The Work Day," *Atlantic Monthly* (March 1965)
Pickett, William B., ed., "George F. Kennan and the Origins of Eisenhower's New Look" (interview of Andrew Goodpaster, Robert Bowie, and George Kennan), Princeton Institute Monograph Series (2004)
Roosevelt, Eleanor, "Churchill and the White House," *Atlantic Monthly* (March 1965)

SECONDARY SOURCES

Books

Ambrose, Stephen E., *Eisenhower and Berlin 1945* (W. W. Norton 1967, 2000 ed.)
———, *Supreme Commander* (Doubleday 1970; U. Miss. Press. 1999 ed.)
Atkinson, Rick, *An Army at Dawn* (Henry Holt 2002)
———, *The Day of Battle* (Henry Holt 2007)
———, *The Guns at Last Light* (Henry Holt 2013)
Barr, Niall, *Eisenhower's Armies* (Pegasus 2015)

Beschloss, Michael, *The Conquerors* (Simon & Schuster 2002, 2007 ed.)
Blumenson, Martin, *Breakout and Pursuit* (U.S. Army, Chief of Military History 1993)
Brandon, Dorothy, *Mamie Doud Eisenhower* (Charles Scribner's Sons 1954)
Brugioni, Dino, *Eyes in the Sky* (Naval Institute Press 2010)
Caddick-Adams, Peter, *Winston Churchill* (Swift Press 2024)
Carr, Jack, and James M. Scott, *Targeted: Beirut* (Atria 2024)
Catherwood, Christopher, *Churchill, Eisenhower, and the Making of the Modern World* (Lyons Press 2023)
Charlwood, David, *Churchill and Eden* (Pen and Sword 2020)
Conquest, Robert, *Stalin: Breaker of Nations* (Penguin 1992)
Crosswell, D. K. R., *Beetle* (U. Kentucky Press 2010)
Dannatt, Richard, and Allen Packwood, *Churchill's D-Day* (Diversion 2024)
Deaile, Melvin, *Always at War* (Naval Institute Press 2018)
Dementi, Brian, *Churchill & Eisenhower Together Again* (Dementi 2015)
D'Este, Carlo, *Eisenhower* (Henry Holt 2002; Owl Books 2003 ed.)
Donovan, Robert, *Eisenhower: The Inside Story* (Harper & Bros. 1956)
———, *Confidential Secretary* (Dutton 1988)
Doran, Michael, *Ike's Gamble* (Free Press 2016)
Eisenhower, David, *Eisenhower: At War 1943–1945* (Wings Books 1986)
Eisenhower, John S. D., *Allies: Pearl Harbor to D-Day* (Doubleday 1982; Da Capo 2000 ed.)
———, *The Bitter Woods* (Da Capo 1995)
Eisenhower, Susan, *Mrs. Ike* (Farrar, Straus and Giroux 1996)
———, *How Ike Led* (Thomas Dunne 2020)
Frank, Jeffrey, *Ike & Dick* (Simon & Schuster 2013)
Gaddis, John, et al., eds., *Cold War Statesmen Confront the Bomb* (Oxford U. Press 1999)
Gilbert, Martin, *Winston Churchill* (8 vols., Houghton Mifflin 1966–1988)
———, *Churchill: A Life* (Henry Holt 1991)
———, *Winston Churchill's War Leadership* (Vintage 2004)
Goodwin, Doris Kearns, *No Ordinary Time* (Simon & Schuster 1995)
Hamilton, Nigel, *Commander in Chief* (Houghton Mifflin Harcourt 2016)
Harrison, Gordon, *Cross-Channel Attack* (U.S. Army, Chief of Military History 1951)
Hermiston, Roger, *Two Minutes to Midnight* (Biteback 2023)
Hitchcock, William L., *The Age of Eisenhower* (Simon & Schuster 2018, 2019 ed.)
Hogan, David W., Jr., *A Command Post at War: First Army Headquarters in Europe, 1943–1945* (Center of Military History 2000)
Holloway, David, *Stalin and the Bomb* (Yale U. Press 2008)
Holzer, Harold, *The Presidents vs. The Press* (Dutton 2020)
Horne, Alistair, *Harold Macmillan, Volume I: 1894–1956* (Macmillan 1988; Viking 1991 ed.)
Howe, George, *Northwest Africa* (U.S. Army, Chief of Military History 1957)
Humes, James, *Eisenhower and Churchill* (Forum 2001)
Isaacson, Walter, and Evan Thomas, *The Wise Men* (Simon & Schuster 1986, 2013 ed.)
Jacobs, Travis Beal, *Eisenhower at Columbia* (Routledge 2000)
Janeway, Eliot, *The Struggle for Survival* (Yale U. Press 1951)
Jenkins, Roy, *Churchill* (Farrar, Straus and Giroux 2000; Plume 2001 ed.)
Johnson, Paul, *Eisenhower: A Life* (Viking 2014)
Jordan, Jonathan W., *Brothers, Rivals, Victors* (NAL/Caliber 2011)
———, *American Warlords* (NAL/Caliber 2015)
Kimball, Warren, *The Juggler* (Princeton U. Press 1991, 1994 ed.)
Korda, Michael, *Ike* (HarperCollins 2007; Harper Perennial 2008 ed.)
Kotkin, Stephen, *Stalin: Waiting for Hitler* (Penguin 2017, 2018 ed.)

Kunz, Diane, *The Economic Diplomacy of the Suez Crisis* (U. of North Carolina Press 1991)
Kyle, Keith, *Suez* (St. Martin's Press 1991)
Larson, Arthur, *Eisenhower: The President Nobody Knew* (Charles Scribner's Sons 1968)
Larson, Erik, *The Splendid and the Vile* (Crown 2020)
Leaming, Barbara, *Churchill Defiant* (HarperCollins 2010)
Leebaert, Derek, *The World After the War* (OneWorld 2018)
Louis, William Roger, and Ross Owen, eds., *Suez 1956* (Clarendon Press 1989)
Lucas, W. Scott, *Divided We Stand* (Hodder and Stoughton 1991, 1996 ed.)
MacDonald, Charles, *The Last Offensive* (U.S. Army, Chief of Military History 1973)
Major, Norma, *Chequers* (Cross River Press 1991)
Maloney, Sean, *Emergency War Plan* (Potomac Books 2021)
Manchester, William, and Paul Reid, *The Last Lion* (Little, Brown 2012)
Matloff, Maurice, and Edwin Snell, *Strategic Planning for Coalition Warfare* (2 vols., U.S. Army, Chief of Military History 1953–1959)
McCullough, David, *Truman* (Simon & Schuster 1992)
Meacham, Jon, *Franklin and Winston* (Random House 2003)
Miller, Merle, *Ike the Soldier* (G. P. Putnam's Sons 1987)
Montefiore, Simon Sebag, *Stalin: Court of the Red Tsar* (Knopf 2003)
Newton, Jim, *Eisenhower: The White House Years* (Doubleday 2011)
Nichols, David, *Eisenhower 1956* (Simon & Schuster 2011, 2012 ed.)
Nong Van Dan, *Churchill, Eden and Indo-China* (Anthem 2011)
O'Brien, Phillips Payson, *The Strategists* (Dutton 2024)
Olson, Lynne, *Citizens of London* (Random House 2010)
Paradis, Michel, *The Light of Battle* (Mariner 2024)
Pearson, Jonathan, *Sir Anthony Eden and the Suez Crisis* (Palgrave Macmillan 2002, 2003 ed.)
Petraeus, David, and Andrew Roberts, *Conflict* (HarperCollins 2023)
Pitt, Barrie, *Churchill and the Generals* (Sidgwick & Jackson 1981; Pen and Sword 2004 ed.)
Pogue, Forrest, *The Supreme Command* (U.S. Army, Chief of Military History 1954)
Potter, John, *Pim and Churchill's Map Room* (Northern Ireland War Memorial 2014)
Reynolds, David, *In Command of History* (Random House 2005; Basic Books 2007 ed.)
Rhodes, Richard, *Dark Sun* (Simon & Schuster 1995, 2005 ed.)
Roberts, Andrew, *Masters and Commanders* (HarperCollins 2009)
———, *The Storm of War* (HarperCollins 2011)
———, *Churchill: Walking with Destiny* (Viking 2018)
Ruane, Kevin, *Churchill and the Bomb in War and Cold War* (Bloomsbury Academic 2016, 2018 ed.)
———, and Matthew Jones, *Anthony Eden, Anglo-American Relations and the 1954 Indochina Crisis* (Bloomsbury Academic 2019, 2021 ed.)
Schlesinger, Stephen, and Stephen Kinzer, *Bitter Fruit* (Harvard U. Press 1982, 2005 ed.)
Schmuhl, Robert, *Mr. Churchill in the White House* (Liveright 2024)
Schneer, Jonathan, *Ministers at War* (Basic Books 2014)
Sherwin, Martin, *Gambling with Armageddon* (Knopf 2020)
Shinkle, Peter, *Ike's Mystery Man* (Steerforth 2018)
Smith, Jean Edward, *Eisenhower in War and Peace* (Random House 2012)
Stoler, Mark, *Allies and Adversaries* (U. of North Carolina Press 2000)
Thomas, Evan, *Ike's Bluff* (Little, Brown 2012; Back Bay 2013 ed.)
Tucker-Jones, Anthony, *Churchill Cold War Warrior* (Frontline 2024)
Tunzelmann, Alex von, *Blood and Sand* (HarperCollins 2016)
Vale, Allister, and John Scadding, *Winston Churchill's Illnesses, 1886–1965* (Frontline 2020)
Watry, David M., *Diplomacy at the Brink* (Louisiana State U. Press 2014)

Weigley, Russell, *Eisenhower's Lieutenants* (Indiana U. Press 1981, 1990 ed.)
Weintraub, Stanley, *Final Victory* (Da Capo 2012)
Williamson, Daniel, *Separate Agendas* (Lexington Books 2006, 2007 ed.)
Wilmot, Chester, *Struggle for Europe* (Collins 1952; Konecky & Konecky 2005 ed.)
Young, John, *Winston Churchill's Last Campaign* (Clarendon Press 1996)

Other Secondary Sources

Bourque, Stephen, "Rouen: La Semaine Rouge," *Journal of Military and Strategic Studies* (2012)
Brattestad, Ingvild, "This Bloody Place Guatemala," master's thesis, Norwegian U. of Science and Technology (2015)
Broughton, James M., "Northwest of Suez: The 1956 Crisis and the IMF," *IMF Staff Papers* (Fall 2001)
Bucknam, Mark A., "The Eisenhower Administration and the Suez Crisis: Spying on Allies and Friends," monograph, National War College (2000)
CIA, "Battle for Iran" (May 1954; August 2019 declassification), https://www.cia.gov/readingroom/document/01384460
Cullather, Nicholas, *Operation PB Success* (Central Intelligence Agency, History Staff 1994)
De Tingo, Geoffrey C., "Eisenhower's Pursuit of Strategy," monograph, U.S. Army Command and General Staff College (2013)
Dodd, Lindsey, and Andrew Knapp, "How Many Frenchmen Did You Kill?" *French History* (2008)
Gerth, Matthew, "The Stress of Her Disregard: Britannia's Suez Fiasco in Consideration of Anglo-American Diplomacy," master's thesis, Eastern Kentucky U. (2016)
Gray, Peter William, "The Strategic Leadership and Direction of the Royal Air Force," doctoral thesis, U. of Birmingham (2009)
Hamilton, Eamon, "Sir Anthony Eden and the Suez Crisis of 1956," master's thesis, U. of Birmingham (2016)
Hanania, Richard, "Tracing the Development of the Nuclear Taboo: The Eisenhower Administration and Four Crises in East Asia," *Journal of Cold War Studies* (Spring 2017)
Hayes, Grace Person, *History of the Joint Chiefs of Staff in World War II: The War Against Japan* (U.S. Joint Chiefs of Staff, Historical Section)
Koch, Scott, "Zendebad, Shah!" (CIA June 1998; November 2017 declassification), National Security Archives online
Meers, Sharon I., "The British Connection: How the United States Covered Its Tracks in the 1954 Coup in Guatemala," *Diplomatic History* (July 1992)
National Security Agency, "The Soviet Land-Based Ballistic Missile Program 1945–1972," https://www.archives.gov/files/declassification/iscap/pdf/2010-005-doc2.pdf
National Security Agency / Central Security Service, "The Suez Crisis: A Brief COMINT History (Office of Archives and History 1988), https://www.nsa.gov/portals/75/documents/news-features/declassified-documents/cryptologic-histories/Suez_Crisis.pdf
Owen, Lord, "The Effect of Prime Minister Anthony Eden's Illness on His Decision-Making During the Suez Crisis," *QJM: An International Journal of Medicine* (June 2005)
Santucci, Joe, "The Lens of Power," doctoral dissertation, Air U. (2013)
Skaggs, Thomas M. S., "The Czech-Egyptian Arms Deal of 1955," master's thesis, U. of Louisville (2015)
Taafe-McMenamy, Margaret, "Operation Ajax: A Case Study on Analyst–Policy Maker Tensions and the Challenges of Estimative Intelligence," monograph, U.S. Army Command and General Staff College (2015)
Wilber, Donald, "Overthrow of Premier Mossadeq of Iran" (Clandestine Service March 1954), https://nsarchive2.gwu.edu/NSAEBB/NSAEBB28/
Young, John W., "Great Britain's Latin American Dilemma," *International History Review* (November 1986)

NOTES

ABBREVIATIONS

ACW Ann C. Whitman
AHEC United States Army Heritage and Education Center
BCOS British Chiefs of Staff
BLM Bernard L. Montgomery
BNA British National Archives
CAC Churchill Archives, Churchill College, Cambridge University
CCOS Combined Chiefs of Staff (U.S.-British)
CD *The Churchill Documents* (23 vols.)
COHP Columbia Oral History Project, Columbia University
DDE Dwight D. Eisenhower
DOS Department of State
EL Dwight D. Eisenhower Presidential Library
EP *The Papers of Dwight D. Eisenhower* (21 vols.)
FDR Franklin D. Roosevelt
FDRL Franklin D. Roosevelt Presidential Library
FRUS *Foreign Relations of the United States*
GCM George C. Marshall
Gilbert Martin Gilbert, *Winston S. Churchill* (8 vols.)
HST Harry S. Truman
HSTL Harry S. Truman Presidential Library
IWM Imperial War Museum
JCS Joint Chiefs of Staff (U.S.)
JFD John Foster Dulles
JFDC John Foster Dulles Oral History Collection, Princeton University
JSM British Joint Service Mission (Washington)
JSDE John Eisenhower
LC Library of Congress
LT *The Times* (London)
MP *Papers of George Catlett Marshall* (7 vols.)
NARA National Archives and Records Administration II
NSC National Security Council
NYT *The New York Times*
PP *The Patton Papers* (2 vols.)
PP-LC George S. Patton Papers, Library of Congress
SP Henry L. Stimson Collection, Yale University
USAMHI U.S. Army Military History Institute
WP *The Churchill War Papers* (3 vols.)
WBS Walter Bedell Smith
WSC Winston Spencer Churchill

Names with dates lacking corresponding descriptions are diary entries.

PROLOGUE: FORTY THOUSAND DEAD FRENCHMEN

1. WSC-DDE, 4/29/44, CD 19:2600; Tedder 534 ("hundred trains"); Dodd and Knapp 481; Bourque 81; Butcher 507, 509, 520 ("fifty-one divisions"); meeting notes, 5/2/44, CD 20:25; Gray, "Strategic Leadership," 238–41; Brooke, 4/5/44, CD 19:2310; Joint Intelligence Committee, 5/20/44, Gilbert 7:775; DDE, memorandum, 3/22/44, EP 3:1782–85. 2. War Cabinet, minutes, 4/3/44, CD 19:2291–93; Butcher 516 (4/14/44); Dannatt and Packwood 209; Reynolds 378; DDE, *Crusade*, 232. 3. War Cabinet, minutes, 4/3/44, CD 19:2291–93. 4. WSC-DDE, 4/3/44, CD 19:2293 ("severity"); Tedder 522–23. 5. DDE, 3/22/44, EP 3:1785 ("relieved"); Defence Committee, minutes, 4/13/44, CD 19:2405, 4/19/44, CD 19:2491, and 4/26/44, CD 19:2566; War Cabinet, minutes, 4/27/44, CD 19:2572; Brooke, 4/19/44, CD 19:2495; Butcher 518 (4/13/44), 530 (4/28/44), 533 (5/1/44); Private Office, 4/28/44, CD 19:2578; WSC-DDE, 4/29/44, CD 19:2599; WSC-Cherwell, 5/2/44, CD 20:30; DDE-WSC, 5/2/44, EP 3:1842–44. 6. DDE-WSC, 4/5/44, EP 3:1809 ("Prime"). 7. Tedder 522–23; Brooke, 4/13/44, CD 19:2393; War Cabinet, minutes, 4/11/44, CD 19:2372–73; Defence Committee, minutes, 4/13/44, CD 19:2393, 2405; WSC-Portal, 4/12/44, CD 19:2387; Butcher 533 (4/28/44); War Cabinet, minutes, 5/2/44, BNA ("General"). 8. Defence Committee, minutes, 5/3/44, CD 20:54; WSC-FDR, 5/7/44, CD 20:103–04.

PART ONE: FORGED IN FIRE

1. WSC-Clementine, 4/6/45, CD 21:872–73; DDE, press conference, 5/15/57, www.youtube.com /watch?v=mOrtOlU8f9Y.

ONE: WINSTON HOURS

1. DDE, interview, 8/5/65, 16, 1965 Principal File (box 2), EL; DDE-Barnes, 1/17/42, EP 1:62; GCM, Pogue, Hughes 242–46; McKeogh and Lockridge 3, 14; D'Este 283. 2. DDE, 1/4/42, Pre-Pres. Papers, Misc. File, EL. 3. WSC photograph, 12/13/41, IWM. 4. Moran, 12/22/41, WP 3:1668; WSC-Halifax, 12/17/41, WP 3:1638; White House itinerary, 12/22/41, WP 3:1667; Walter Thompson 248; Harland-Gilbert, 12/7/81, CD 20:1109; Moran, 12/22/41, WP 3:1669; Roberts 700, 737; Cox 113–16; Sherwood 442; WSC, *Grand Alliance*, 663; WSC, press conference, 12/23/41, WP 3:1669–73; Gilbert 7:23. 5. Clare Luce–C. D. Jackson, 9/29/54, Jackson-Luce, 4/3/44, C. D. Jackson Papers (box 104), EL; Walter Thompson 252; Eleanor Roosevelt 77; Roberts 700. 6. Hassett 169 ("fish"); Reilly 125 ("ate"). 7. Kinna, interview, CAC, 691; Nel, interview, 9/9/94, CAC, 1–2; Peck 71; Gilbert, *War Leadership*, 9–11; Graebner 48–49. 8. Kinna-Gilbert, 10/10/84, WP 3:1676. 9. Nel, interview, 9/9/94, CAC, 2–3; "Grace Hamblin on Churchill," CAC, 7; Peck 74; Grabner 55; Gilbert 7:117–18. 10. Gilbert, *War Leadership*, 14–15. 11. Walter Thompson 178–89; Montague Browne, interview, CAC, 476; Graebner 34, 66–68, 74; Hamblin, interview, CAC, 1316 ("terrifying"); Nel, interview, 9/9/94, CAC, 5; Charles Wilson, 12/27/41, WP 3:1692; Roberts 702; Gilbert 7:30–31. 12. Goodwin 311 ("wonderful"); Elsey, interview, CAC, 1147; Schmuhl 237. 13. WSC-Attlee, 1/3/42, CD 17:14; Curtis Roosevelt, interview, CAC, 1350; WSC, *Grand Alliance*, 605; Halifax, 1/1/42, CD 17:6 ("nude"); Walter Thompson 248; Schmuhl 36–42. 14. Summersby, *Forgetting*, 73–74. 15. Stimson, 12/24/41, Yale Library. 16. Stimson, 12/24/41, Yale Library. 17. DDE, *Ease*, 147, JSDE, *Ike*, 180–81. 18. DDE, "Marshall and Churchill," 11/17/66, EL ("boys"). 19. Stimson, 12/25/41 and 1/16/42, Yale Library; WSC-Auchinleck, 12/25/41, and WSC-Curtin, 12/25/41, Gilbert 7:28–29. 20. WP 1/14-15/42, CD 18:85. 21. George VI, 1/19/42, Roberts 709 ("married"); Roberts 707; Brooke 209 ("harem"); War Cabinet, minutes, 1/17/42, CD 17:94.

TWO: LONDON'S BEST FRIEND

1. WSC, speech, 3/26/42, CD 17:444 ("unbroken"). 2. Roberts 723; Gilbert, *War Leadership*, 29 ("KBO"). 3. U.S. ABC 4/6, 1/13/42 and ABC-4/CS-1, at jcs.mil Arcadia documents; DDE-GCM, 3/25/42, EP 1:206–07 n. 1; Matloff and Snell 104, 113–14, 181–87, 383. 4. BCOS, memorandum, 4/9/42, Gilbert 7:87; War Cabinet, minutes, 6/11/42, Gilbert 7:121. 5. WSC-FDR, 6/1, 13, 20/42,

Gilbert 7:116, 122, 128. 6. White House logs, 6/22/42, http://www.fdrlibrary.marist.edu/daybyday/daylog/june-22nd-1942/; DDE, 6/22/42, EL; Butcher 24; Schmuhl 81. 7. DDE, 5/5/42, EP 1:292; DDE-GCM, 5/11–12/42, EP 1:293–95. 8. DDE, *Crusade*, 56 ("executes"); DDE, 6/8/42, 6/11/42, EP 1:333, 337 ("guy"). 9. Butcher 3–4, 6; Lemnitzer, interview, 11/21/72, COHP 5; Summersby, *Forgetting*, 44 ("whorehouse"); DDE-GCM, 6/24/42, EP 1:359. 10. Paradis 127–38. 11. DDE, press release, 7/14/42, EP 1:383; DDE-GCM, 6/30/42, EP 1:367; Butcher 42; DDE-Hartle, 7/19/42, EP 1:396. 12. DDE, *Crusade*, 76 ("tomcat"); Ingersoll 77; Bonesteel, interview, AHEC, 128 ("murmurs"). 13. Ismay 258–59; D'Este 327 ("son-of-a-bitch"). 14. DDE, 5/27/42, EP 1:319; Summersby, *Forgetting*, 24–25 ("worms"). 15. DDE-Mamie, 8/26/42, *Letters* 38 ("mountebank"). 16. Summersby, *Forgetting*, 37–39, 45 ("deeaah"). 17. Summersby, *Forgetting*, 47 ("wrinkles"); DDE, "Marshall and Churchill," 11/17/66, EL 15. 18. Whitman, interview, OH-511 6; McKeogh and Lockridge 51; Thomas 27 ("Bang"); Hughes 149 ("adrenaline"); Donovan, *Confidential*, 43; Jehl, interview, OH-517 39 ("swear"); Ewald, interview, 12/16/77, EL, 40 ("vulgarity"). 19. Shanley, interview, COHP 116 ("lousy"); DDE, interview, 12/1/53, ACW Diary Series (box 1), EL; Susan Eisenhower 48. 20. Butcher 5; Summersby, *Forgetting*, 39 ("dog"). 21. Butcher 3; Jehl, interview, OH-517 4; Mattie Pinette, 6/4/44, George Hall Papers (box 1), EL 8. 22. McKeogh and Lockridge 25, 39, 166; Butcher 6; Summersby, *Boss*, 18; Summersby, *Forgetting*, 41; Heilbronn, interview, 3/9/93, EL 23; "Marty," NYT, 7/2/74. 23. Butcher 3–5; Summersby, *Boss*, 23–24, 31–32. 24. Major 10, 26–28; Pim, 4/7/44, CD 19:2317. 25. DDE, 7/5/42, *Eisenhower Diaries* 70–71 ("dumps"); DDE, "Marshall and Churchill," 11/17/66, EL; Walter Thompson 178; Sherwood 582; Paradis 18–19. 26. DDE, *Military Churchill*, 23; DDE, 7/5/42, *Eisenhower Diaries* 71 ("averse"). 27. McKeogh and Lockridge 44. 28. Butcher 9. 29. DDE-GCM, 7/17/42, EP 1:390; Butcher 22–23. 30. Kennedy 257; BCOS, 8/4/42, Gilbert 7:163 ("arguments"); DDE-Somervell, 7/27/42, EP 1:424; Butcher 28. 31. Maisky 510; Roberts 762 ("Commander"). 32. DDE-GCM, 7/17/42, EP 1:389. 33. Butcher 29 ("blackest"); DDE-GCM, 7/23/42, EP 1:412. 34. WSC-FDR, 7/31/42, Gilbert 7:158. 35. Butcher 40; DDE-GCM, 8/15/42, EP 1:468; FDR-WSC, 8/6/42, EP 1:479 n. 1; DDE, *Letters*, 22. 36. DDE, *Crusade*, 61, 84 ("Tuesdays," "slang").

THREE: THE OGRE'S DEN

1. WSC-Wavell, 8/16/42, CD 17:1088 (poem). 2. Gilbert 7:164; Soames 466 ("Ogre"); Ismay 338. 3. Walter Thompson 268 ("match"). 4. Roberts 754 ("lathe"). 5. Jacob, notes, Gilbert 7:185; Roberts 753–55; Jenkins 700. 6. WSC–War Cabinet and FDR, 8/16/42, CD 17:1088 ("duty"). 7. Summersby, *Boss*, 30 ("picturesque"); DDE-Mamie, 9/13/42, *Letters*, 40 ("god-send"). 8. Butcher 76, 140; Summersby, *Boss*, 30–32; McKeogh and Lockridge 40; Moaney, interview, OH-328 6, 14–16 ("saluting"). 9. Summersby, *Boss*, 32; Woodward, interview, OH-512 6; McKeogh and Lockridge 54–55 ("Jerkers"); Moaney, interview, OH-328 13–15. 10. Stephens, interview, OH-161, EL 60; Summersby, *Forgetting*, 27, 183; DDE-Gruenther, 2/26/43, EP 2:995; Moaney, interview, OH-328 15; McKeogh and Lockridge 34–35; Snyder 26, 35–36, 59; Woodward, interview, OH-512 5; McKeogh and Lockridge 34; "News of Food," NYT, 7/29/52; Summersby, *Boss*, 33. 11. DDE-Mamie, 10/13/42, *Letters*, 46 ("talk"); DDE-JSDE, 10/13/42, EP 1:617; Butcher 140; Summersby, *Boss*, 36; Summersby, *Forgetting*, 66; McKeogh and Lockridge 41–42. 12. Summersby, *Boss*, 32. 13. Butcher 90. 14. Summersby, *Boss*, 52 ("S.O.B." "S.S."); Nevins, interview, OH-380 23–24 ("mean"); JSDE, interview, 8/25/82, COHP 5. 15. DDE-Gailey, 9/19/42, EP 1:568 ("fishing-rod"). 16. Butcher 97; Kennedy 262. 17. DDE, *Military Churchill*, 18 ("pathos"). 18. Butcher 96; Roberts 753 ("bullfrog"). 19. Butcher 74–75 (8/25/42); Walter Thompson 179, 251. 20. Graebner 62. 21. Butcher 75 ("gurglings"); Summersby, *Forgetting*, 147. 22. DDE, *Military Churchill*, 22 ("mediocre"). 23. DDE-Ismay, 10/7/42, EP 1:601 n. 1. 24. WSC, *Hinge*, 487 ("sixty"); Butcher 95; DDE, "Churchill and Marshall," 11/17/66, EL 28. 25. Staff conference notes, 9/21/42, Gilbert 7:233–34; Butcher 494. 26. Butcher 97. 27. Butcher 118; DDE-GCM, 9/21/42, EP 1:570 ("astonished"). 28. Butcher 161–62; Summersby, *Boss*, 41–42 ("nun"). 29. McKeogh 85 ("luck"). 30. Butcher 166 ("monkeys"). 31. DDE-GCM, 11/7/42, EP 2:667 ("brickbats") and 669 n. 8.

FOUR: "A DAMNED GOOD ASSASSIN"

1. Smith-DDE, 11/6/42, EP 1:653 n. 1; DDE-GCM, 11/7/42, EP 2:666–67; Butcher 162, 168; Summersby, *Boss*, 40; McKeogh and Lockridge 46. 2. Murphy 102 ("attention"). 3. EP 1:625 n. 2; Butcher 178a ("Kiss"); DDE-GCM, 10/17/42, EP 1:626. 4. DDE-Butcher (9/2/42), EP 1:527; Butcher 106. 5. DDE-GCM, 11/7/42, EP 2:668; Butcher 171 ("declined"). 6. Butcher 174, 179; Jean Edward Smith, *Eisenhower* (hereinafter "JES"), 221. 7. Clark, *Risk*, 103–07; Butcher 178a ("headache"). 8. Murphy 139–40; Clark, *Risk*, 106, 121–23; Butcher 192; DDE-Smith, 11/13/42, EP 2:706; Howe 265. 9. Butcher 192 ("skunk"); "Liberal Tribute," London *Times*, 11/18/42; Clark, *Risk*, 111–14. 10. DDE-Smith, 11/14/42, EP 2:713 ("devil!"); Butcher 8; Kennedy 251; DDE-Smith, 11/17/42, EP 2:734; DDE-Smith, 11/18/42, EP 2:736 ("pants"). 11. Darlan-DDE, 11/21/42, Butcher 206–07 ("lemon"); McKeogh and Lockridge 49. 12. DDE-Hodgson, 12/4/42, EP 2:795 ("soapy"). 13. DDE-JSDE, 12/20/42, EP 2:855 ("bum"). 14. EP 2:738 n. 4; WSC, speech, 12/10/42, Gilbert 7:275 ("hamper"); Roberts 765. 15. WSC-FDR, 12/11-12/42, Gilbert 7:276–78 ("Kentucky"); Makins, interview, CAC, 262; WSC-DDE, 12/10/42, EP 2:827 n. 1; "Macmillan," NYT, 4/8/55; EP 2:886 n. 1; Colville, 5/19/45, CD 21:1482. 16. Butcher 229. 17. Butcher, 12/17/43, 12/20/43, Pre-Pres. Papers, (box 166), EL ("Ch-ee-r-i-s-t"); Butcher 200, 214, 218, 230–32. 18. WSC-Alexander, 12/28/42, CD 17:1553 ("happy"). 19. WSC-DDE, 12/16/42, CD 17:1528 ("animal"). 20. WSC-DDE, 12/31/42, CD 17:1567 ("deeply"); DDE-WSC, 1/1/43, EP 2:882–83 ("assure").

FIVE: NECK IN A NOOSE

1. John Martin, 1/13/43, and WSC-Attlee, 1/13/43, Gilbert 7:293 ("agreeable"). 2. Patton, 1/9/43, 1/17/43, PP 2:154–55. 3. Patton, 1/18/43, PP-LC (box 1) ("cunning"). 4. BCOS, draft memorandum, 1/5/43, Gilbert 7:285. 5. Wedemeyer 192 ("We came"). 6. Patton, 1/15/43, PP-LC (box 1); Butcher 237. 7. DDE, *Crusade*, 135. 8. DDE, *Crusade*, 137. 9. Patton, 1/15/43, PP-LC (box 1) ("thread"). 10. Butcher 243 ("noose"). 11. Brooke 365 ("rarefied"); WSC-Clementine, Roberts 767 ("direction"); DDE-GCM, 2/8/43, EP 2:942. 12. Kennedy 289 ("expression").

SIX: "TAPS"

1. WSC-DDE, 2/2/43, CD 18:321 ("breakfast"); DDE-Brooke, 1/30/43, EP 2:932; Butcher 255. 2. WSC-GCM, 2/21/43, EP 2:970 ("mental"). 3. Brooke, 2/5/43. 4. Jacob, 2/5–6/43, CD 18:348–51; Elizabeth Layton, letter, Gilbert 7:278 ("worse"); Butcher 255. 5. DDE-GCM, 2/8/43, EP 2:942 ("concrete"); WSC, *Hinge*, 647–48, CD 18:353. 6. DDE-GCM, 1/27/43, EP 2:925; WSC, *Hinge*, 647–48, CD 18:353; Butcher 255 ("ceiling"). 7. Butcher 255 ("target"). 8. Butcher 255–56 ("soul"). 9. Jacob, 2/6/43, CD 18:359. 10. Howe 402–03, 414–16; DDE-GCM, 2/15/43, EP 2:956; DDE-CCOS, 2/21/43, EP 2:973; Butcher 263–64 ("walloping"); Summersby, *Boss*, 61 ("funeral"); McKeogh and Lockridge 73 ("lower"). 11. DDE-JSDE, 2/19/43, EP 2:965 ("pawns"). 12. WSC-DDE, 2/25/43, Gilbert 7:353 ("Kasserine"); Butcher 265–66. 13. King-WSC, 2/22/43, CD 18:491 ("US"); Alexander-WSC, 2/27/43, Gilbert 7:360 ("shocked"). 14. WSC–King, 2/22/43, CD 18:493–94 ("blaspheme"). 15. WSC, speech, 2/11/43, EP 2:961 n. 1; Gilbert 7:338; DDE-CCOS, 2/11/43, Gilbert 7:338; DDE-WSC, 2/17/43, EP 2:959. 16. WSC-DDE, 2/13/43, Principal File (box 23), EL ("disaster"); WSC-Hopkins, 2/13/43, Gilbert 7:338 ("awful"). 17. DDE-CCS, 4/7/43, CD 18:933–34; DDE, *Crusade*, 162–63; EP 2:1086 n. 1. 18. WSC-BCOS, 4/8/43, CD 18:937–28 ("Stalin"); Tedder 429–30; EP 2:1086 n. 1. 19. Butcher 308–09. 20. DDE-WSC, 5/10/43, EP 2:1121 ("greatest").

SEVEN: FINITO BENITO

1. Kennedy 273 ("difficult"). 2. Roberts 772 ("Champagne"). 3. WSC-Smuts, 7/16/43, Gilbert 7:414. 4. CCOS, Trident minutes, 5/25/43, 11:30 a.m., Gilbert 7:414; WSC, *Hinge*, 811; DDE, "Churchill and Marshall," 11/17/66, EL 30. 5. Brooke, 5/28/43, CD 18:1460; Butcher 315–16. 6. DDE-Ismay, 12/3/60, Name Series (box 19), EL; DDE, *Military Churchill*, 33. 7. Butcher 317 ("Christmas"). 8. DDE, *Ease*, 265; EP 2:1053; Gilbert 7:430. 9. Roberts 620; DDE, *Crusade*, 166.

10. WSC-DDE, 6/11/43, CD 18:1572; DDE, memo, 7/1/43, EP 2:1232, 1233 n. 8; Butcher 343 ("11,121"). 11. C. R. Thompson–DDE, 6/24/43, Principal File (box 80), EL; DDE, *Ease*, 265 ("$1.60"); DDE-WSC, 7/3/43, EP 1:1236 ("brandy"). 12. WSC-DDE, 7/21/43, Principal File (box 23), EL; DDE-WSC, 7/21/43, EP 2:1271 and nn. 1–2 ("aerodrome"). 13. Butcher 337. 14. Eden, *Reckoning*, 332–33 ("cowpat"); Roberts 764. 15. "Eisenhower," NYT, 11/11/43. 16. Clay, interview, 2/20/67, COHP 40–41 ("smile"). 17. Patton, 7/12/43, *Patton Papers*, 2:283; Butcher, 7/13/43, EL ("stepped"); Jordan, *Brothers*, 201–02 ("hell"). 18. FDR-WSC, 7/26/43, EP 2:1288 n. 1. 19. Butcher 372 ("ships"). 20. WSC-Hopkins, 8/2/43, CD 18:2143 ("fighting"); DDE, *Ease*, 276. 21. Butcher 382 ("bellyaches"). 22. Butcher 382 ("ping-pong"); DDE-GCM, 8/4/43, EP 2:1315. 23. DDE-GCM, 8/4/43, EP 2:1315–16 ("rock"). 24. WSC-DDE, 8/16/43, Principal File (box 23), EL ("unceremonious"). 25. WSC-DDE, 9/21/43, CD 19:216; JES 302. 26. Roberts 779 ("treat").

EIGHT: LAND OF THE CYCLOPS

1. WSC-DDE, 10/7/43, CD 19:397–98 ("Dodecanese"); Cadogan, 10/7/43, CD 19:409; WSC-FDR, 10/7–8/43, CD 19:399, 423; War Cabinet, minutes, 10/6–7/43, CD 19:376, 395–96; DDE-CCOS, 10/5/43, EP 3:1488; DDE-Tedder, 10/5/43, EP 3:1487. 2. Kennedy 275 ("toy"). 3. Reynolds 379 ("owed"). 4. WSC-Ismay, 10/2/51, EP 12:589–90 ("judgment"). 5. DDE, *Crusade*, 191 ("sympathy"); JSDE, *Ike*, 194. 6. DDE-CCOS, 10/9/43, EP 3:1497, CD 19:450 ("Rhodes"). 7. War Cabinet, minutes, 10/6–7/43, CD 19:378, 396; FDR-WSC, 10/8–9/43, CD 19:422, 438. 8. Marian Holmes, 10/7/43, Gilbert 7:524 ("fools"); WSC, *Closing*, 223 ("acute"). 9. DDE-WSC, 10/9/43, EP 3:1495 ("distressing"). 10. WSC-Eden, 10/9/43, CD 19:446; WSC-Cunningham, 10/10/43, CD 19:451; WSC, *Closing*, 203–25; WSC-DDE, 7/1/48, CD 22:1098 ("unhappy").

NINE: "THE DEVIL IS ON MY SIDE"

1. BCOS, minutes, 11/18/43, CD 19:914; Brooke, 11/18/43; DDE, "Churchill and Marshall," 11/17/66, EL 42; Paradis 158. 2. DDE, *Crusade*, 194 ("colored"). 3. King, 4/6/43 ("USA"). 4. Brooke, 11/18–19/43, 472–74 ("spite"). 5. DDE, "Churchill and Marshall," 11/17/66, EL 43 ("embarrassing"). 6. DDE, unpublished manuscript, 8/24/67, JSDE, *Allies*, 389 ("happy"). 7. Butcher, 12/5/43, EL ("Arlington"); Butcher 453. 8. Butcher 440. 9. Cadogan, 1/28/43, CD 19:983; Ismay 337–38, CD 19:978; WSC, *Closing*, 302–06, CD 19:979; Eureka, minutes, 11/28/43, CD 19:985–94; Gilbert 7:572–73. 10. Cadogan, 12/1/43, CD 19:1045 ("donkey"); Colville 2/24/45, CD 21:533. 11. JSDE, interview, CAC, 996 ("tragic"). 12. Soames, interview, CAC, 89 ("hurt"). 13. Eden, *Reckoning*, 426–27, CD 19:997 ("Devil"). 14. Ingersoll 48 ("stand"); Makins, interview, CAC, 265; Eureka, minutes, 11/30/43, CD 19:1031, 1043. 15. Moran, 11/29/43, CD 19:1016. 16. Ismay 337–38, CD 19:978; Moran, 11/29/43, in Moran 136–41 and CD 19:1015.

TEN: EISENHOWERPLATZ AND 10 DOWNING

1. Elliott Roosevelt 209; JES 317; Summersby, *Forgetting*, 146 ("boy"). 2. DDE, "Churchill and Marshall," 11/17/66, EL 31; Pogue, Marshall, 3:306–7 ("muskets"). 3. Elliott Roosevelt 209 ("argued"). 4. WSC, *Closing*, 369–70, CD 19:1108 ("warmest"); Ingersoll 78. 5. Brooke, 12/10–11/43; WSC, *Closing*, 373; WSC-FDR, 12/21/43, Gilbert 7:606; James Grigg–Brooke, 12/15/43, CD 19:1152; War Cabinet, minutes, 12/15/43, CD 19:1150; WSC-FDR, 12/18–21/43, CD 19:1168, 1184; WSC-Hopkins, 12/22/43, CD 19:1188; Vale and Scadding 91–96; Roberts 808. 6. Walter Thompson 285–86; Gilbert 7:619–20; Macmillan, 12/25/43, CD 19:1230; Hollis–War Cabinet Office, "Conference," 12/25/43, CD 19:1224–25; Butcher 462; Macmillan, 12/25/43 ("ballet"); Martin-wife, 12/25/43, CD 19:1232 ("unable"); DDE, "Churchill and Marshall," 11/17/66, EL 51–52. 7. Butcher 468; DDE-GCM, 1/17/43, EP 3:1661; Cannon, interview, 10/69, EL 6. 8. DDE, *Crusade*, 60 ("Eisenhowerplatz"); DDE, *Ease*, 269. 9. Reynolds 288; WSC-Attlee, 12/14/43, Gilbert 7:605–06; DDE-Ismay, 12/3/60, Post-Pres. Papers, Name Series (box 19), EL; Jehl, interview, OH-517 6. 10. DDE, *Crusade*, 225; Pogue, *Supreme Command*, 97. 11. Jehl, interview, OH-517 7; Paradis 247. 12. Butcher 525 (coffee-tea); Jehl, interview, OH-517 21.

13. Snyder 35–45; DDE-GCM, 1/28/44, EP 3:1693; Butcher 474, 477; McKeogh and Lockridge 101, 105–06, 109. 14. McKeogh and Lockridge 105; Butcher 458; Summersby, *Forgetting*, 175–76. 15. Butcher 480; McKeogh and Lockridge 106–07, 111 (Telek). 16. Summersby, *Forgetting*, 146–47 ("deplored"); Jenkins 730. 17. DDE, interview, 8/5/65, 24, 1965 Principal File (box 2), EL ("9:30"). 18. Summersby, *Forgetting*, 182 ("stinks"). 19. DDE, *Crusade*, 61 ("swing"). 20. WSC, speech, 2/22/44, CD 19:1824–25; EP 3:1748 n. 1; DDE-WSC, 2/23/44, EP 3:1748; Butcher 494–95; Jackson-Luce, 4/3/44, C. D. Jackson Papers (box 70), EL ("unsteadily"); Paradis 213, 344. 21. WSC-Attlee, 3/12/44, Gilbert 7:708 ("extortion"). 22. WSC-Eden, 2/27/44, CD 19:1900 ("screw"). 23. DDE-WSC, 5/20/44, EP 3:1877; DDE-GCM, 5/23/44, EP 3:1885; Butcher 548, 553; Paradis 344–45. 24. DDE-WSC, 5/29/44, 6/1/44, EP 3:1893, 1900 ("indicate"); WSC-DDE, 5/31/44, CD 20:340 ("inconvenience"); Paradis 346–47. 25. DDE, "Churchill and Marshall," 11/17/66, EL 65–67. 26. Summersby, *Boss*, 8 ("godlike"), 24. 27. Summersby, *Boss*, 24 ("impulse"). 28. DDE, *Ease*, 272; Butcher 535; Snyder 54 ("delicacy"). 29. WSC-Eden, 3/4/44, CD 19:1966 ("telegrams"); Schmuhl 186–90. 30. WSC–Jumbo Wilson, 3/7/44, CD 19:1988; Summersby, *Boss*, 24. 31. DDE, 2/7/44, EP 3:1710–11. 32. Butcher 475; Paradis 202–03. 33. DDE-BLM, 1/13/44, EP 3:1654; DDE-Smith, 1/13/44, EP 3:1655–56; DDE-GCM, 1/18/44, EP 3:1662; Gilbert 7:678; Butcher 472, 493 ("shoulders"). 34. DDE-GCM, 2/6/44, EP 3:1707; Butcher 493–94. 35. DDE, 2/7/44, EP 3:1712; DDE-GCM, 2/8/44, EP 3:1714; BCOS, minutes, 3/22/44, Gilbert 7:715–16. 36. Butcher 524 ("wrangling"). 37. JSDE, *Ike*, 199; Paradis 203–09. 38. DDE, interview, 7/31/68, 1968 Principal Series (box 40), EL 12; Butcher 478; Gilbert 7:716.

ELEVEN: "ARE WE BEASTS?"

1. Casey, 6/27/43, CD 18:1728 ("beasts?"). 2. Tedder 508–12; Butcher 476–98; EP 3:1756; Kennedy 310. 3. Butcher 498; Patton, 3/8/44, PP-LC (box 2) ("children"). 4. DDE-Tedder, 2/29/44, EP 3:1755 ("feet"); DDE-GCM, 3/1/44, EP 3:1758; WSC-BCOS, 1/9/44, CD 19:1377; Paradis 240–41. 5. WSC–Portal/Ismay, 2/29/44, CD 19:1929 ("lobe"); Brooke, 2/29/44, CD 19:1933; DDE-Tedder, 2/29/44, EP 3:1755; DDE-Tedder, 3/9/44, EP 3:1765; Butcher 498–99; Paradis 242. 6. Butcher 502, 520. 7. Butcher 509; Kennedy 324; Paradis 264. 8. War Cabinet, minutes, 4/3/44, CD 19:2291–93; Tedder 521. 9. WSC-DDE, 4/3/44, CD 19:2293 ("severity"); DDE-GCM, 4/3/44, EP 3:1804; Butcher 512. 10. Tedder 523–26; DDE-WSC, 4/5/44, EP 3:1809; Brooke, 4/5/44, CD 19:2310 ("awful"). 11. War Cabinet, minutes, 4/13/44, CD 19:2402–03; Tedder 523–25; WSC-Portal, 4/12/44, CD 19:2387. 12. WSC, 4/5/44, Dannatt and Packwood 210 ("unhealable"); Brooke, 4/13/44, CD 19:2393; War Cabinet, minutes, 4/13/44, CD 19:2402–04; Tedder 526. 13. DDE, 4/12/44, EP 3:1820–21; Butcher 525; Paradis 258–59. 14. War Cabinet, minutes, 4/19/44, CD 19:2487–88, 2491; Brooke, 4/19/44, CD 19:2495; Butcher 521–22; Tedder 526. 15. War Cabinet, minutes, 3/27/44, CD 19:2573. 16. Private Office diary, 4/28/44, CD 19:2578; WSC-DDE, 4/29,44, CD 19:2599–2600; Tedder 528–29; Defence Committee, minutes, 5/3/44, CD 20:49; Dannatt and Packwood 208. 17. DDE-WSC, 5/2/44, EP 3:1843–44; Tedder 529. 18. Butcher 530, 533, 535. 19. WSC-Cherwell, 5/2/44, CD 20:30. 20. War Cabinet, minutes, 5/2/44, CD 20:33; Tedder 529. 21. Defence Committee, 5/3/44, CD 20:48 ("spoil"); Tedder 530–31. 22. WSC-FDR, 5/7/44, CD 20:103 ("hate"). 23. FDR-WSC, 5/11/44, CD 20:149 ("prepared"). 24. WSC-DDE, 5/16/44, CD 20:174; WSC-Tedder, 5/21, 5/29, 5/30/44, and WSC-Eden, 5/28/44 ("Terrible"), CD 20:230, 311, 318, 328–29; Tedder 534; Butcher 543.

TWELVE: "WE WILL GO DOWN TOGETHER"

1. WSC–James Grigg, 4/18/44, CD 19:2466–67 ("girdeth"); WSC-Morrison, 2/22/44, CD 19:184; WSC-Lascelles, 3/4/44, CD 19:1968. 2. Collins, interview, AHEC 155. 3. WSC-FDR, 4/12/44, CD 19:2383; Brooke, 4/7/44, CD 19:2318 ("weepy"); Kennedy 328 ("fire"); Bradley, *Soldier's Story*, 242. 4. DDE, interview, 8/11/65, 74, 1965 Principal File (box 2), EL ("choked"); DDE-Ismay, 12/3/60, Name Series (box 19), EL; Nevins, interview, 4/23/70, COHP 27–28. 5. CBS Reports, "D-Day Plus 20 Years" ("Passchendaele"). 6. Butcher 535 (5/9/44) ("thing"). 7. Colville, *Fringes*, 485 ("fun"). 8. DDE, *Crusade*, 166. 9. Ramsay-WSC, 5/16/44, Gilbert 7:772–73 ("mention"). 10. DDE, *Military Churchill*, 38–40 ("burden"); Butcher 556; Roberts 819. 11. King-WSC,

5/31/44, CD 20:339; Pim, 6/1/44, CD 20:343; King-WSC, 6/2/44, CD 20:357; WSC-King, 6/3/44, CD 20:363; King-WSC, 6/4/44, Jenkins 744; JSDE, *Ike,* 178. 12. Mattie Pinette, 6/2/44, George Hall Papers (box 1), EL; CBS Reports, "D-Day Plus 20 Years"; Paradis 337, 354; David Keys, "Concrete Traces Reveal Eisenhower's D-Day HQ," *Independent,* 5/13/94. 13. Butcher 559. 14. Butcher 559–60 ("moisten"). 15. Stagg 112–19; CBS Reports, "D-Day Plus 20 Years" ("OK"); WBS 55; D'Este 526–27; Tim Rives, "OK, We'll Go," *Prologue Magazine* (Spring 2014), www.archives.gov/publications/prologue/2014/spring/d-day-ok-well-go. 16. Pyle, interview, COHP 95 ("Xerxes"). 17. DDE-JSDE, 4/16/44, EP 3:1821 ("point"). 18. Mattie Pinette, 6/5/44, George Hall Papers (box 1), EL 11; DDE, interview, 8/5/65, 25, 1965 Principal File (box 2), EL ("news"). 19. Butcher 610 ("blame"). 20. CBS Reports, "D-Day Plus 20 Years" ("oblivion"). 21. Cunningham, 6/5/44, CD 20:378 ("incorrigible"); Brooke, 6/5/44, CD 20:376 ("damp"); Dannatt and Packwood 239. 22. Pawle 302, CD 20:377 ("twenty thousand"); Thompson, 6/5/44, CD 20:377.

THIRTEEN: MONTY'S BICYCLE

1. McKeogh and Lockridge 116–17; Paradis 382. 2. Mattie Pinette, 6/6/44, George Hall Papers (box 1), EL; McKeogh and Lockridge 117 ("soberest"). 3. Butcher 569–70; Paradis 386–87. 4. Summersby, *Forgetting,* 195 ("supercritical"); JSDE, *Personal,* 63 ("rank"); Paradis 140. 5. JSDE, *Ike,* 180, *Personal,* 67 ("weather"). 6. WBS, memo, Subject File, EL, EP 3:1969 n. 1; Butcher 603, 608; DDE-Ismay, 1/14/59, Name Series (box 19), EL; DDE-BLM, 7/10/44, EP 3:1990 n. 1. 7. BLM-DDE, 7/12/44, EP 3:2002 n. 1, 2029 n. 1 ("flames") 8. DDE-BLM, 7/14/44, EP 3:2003. 9. Butcher 7/20/44, EL; EP 3:2020 n. 2; Blumenson, *Breakout,* 194. 10. EP 3:2020 n. 2 ("position"); WSC-BLM and reply, 7/27/44, CD 20:896, 897. 11. Butcher 7/20–22/44, EL ("indigo"). 12. Butcher 7/20/44, EL ("Teddy"). 13. Brooke, 7/26/44, CD 20:893; Butcher 625; Sherwood 811 ("bicycle"); EP 3:2020 n. 2; JES 377–78. 14. Butcher, 7/25/44, EL ("scalp," "subject"). 15. Butcher 630, 631–32.

FOURTEEN: RIND OF AN ORANGE

1. David Eisenhower 317. 2. WSC-FDR, draft dated 6/30/44, CD 20:661 ("ruined"). 3. WSC-FDR, 7/1/44, CD 20:668 ("talons"). 4. WSC-Ismay, 7/6/44, CD 20:727 ("smirchings"); WSC-Smuts, 7/5/44, CD 20:702. 5. DDE-GCM, 8/11/44, EP 4:2066–67 ("stirred"); DDE, *Military Churchill,* 18; Butcher 639 ("mantle"). 6. DDE, interview, 7/31/68, 1968 Principal Series (box 40), EL 12–14 ("pathos"). 7. Brooke, 8/4/44, CD 20:958; WSC-FDR, 8/4/44, CD 20:969; BCOS-JSM, 8/5/44, CD 20:982; DDE, *Crusade,* 282. 8. WSC-DDE, 8/4/44, CD 20:968 ("latch key"). 9. WSC–Jumbo Wilson, 8/4/44, CD 20:961 ("switch"); WSC-BLM, 8/4/44, CD 20:968. 10. WSC-Cunningham, 8/4/44, CD 20:970–71 ("busy"). 11. Kennedy 334. 12. DDE-GCM, 8/5/44, CD 20:973 ("wavered"). 13. Mattie Pinette, 8/5/44, George Hall Papers (box 1), EL ("kitten"); Pogue, *Supreme Command,* 275–76. 14. DDE, interview, *Military Churchill,* 17 ("compliance"). 15. Butcher 634 ("no"); Handy, interview, 5/22/73, EL 195. 16. Cunningham, 8/5/44, CD 20:981 ("bounced"). 17. JSM-BCOS, 8/6/44, CD 20:986–87, 7:880. 18. BCOS, minutes, 8/7/44, CD 20:998; BCOS-JSM, 8/7/44, CD 20:1003 ("favoured"); WSC-Hopkins, 8/6/44, CD 20:989; Hopkins-WSC, 8/7/44, CD 20:1006; DDE-CCOS, 8/8/44, CD 20:1012–13. 19. Butcher 638 ("pouty"). 20. DDE, *Crusade,* 283–84 ("Balkans"); JSDE, "General Ike," PCNTV podcast, https://www.youtube.com/watch?v=NJPNA7wGuXA&t=3363s 21. Butcher 644 ("adorable"). 22. DDE-WSC, 8/11/44, EP 4:2065. 23. WSC-GCM, 8/11/44, EP 4:2066 ("despondent"). 24. JSDE, interview, CAC, 992 ("irreplaceable"). 25. "Sergeant Murray on Churchill," CAC ("cheat"). 26. Charles Thompson, 8/12/44, CD 20:1055; WSC, *Triumph,* 84, CD 20:1055 ("sailing"). 27. WSC-Clementine, 8/17/44, CD 20:1101 ("Patch"); Thompson, 4/15/44, CD 20:1089; WSC-King, 8/16/44, CD 20:1094. 28. Colville, 9/1/44, CD 20:1234 ("bull-fight"); Jumbo Wilson–WSC, 9/2/44, CD 20:1252–53. 29. WSC-DDE, 8/17/44, CD 20:1105. 30. DDE-WSC (through Jumbo Wilson), 8/24/44, EP 4:2095 ("fat"). 31. DDE-GCM, 8/24/44, EP 4:2094 ("laugh").

FIFTEEN: "HE'S AFTER MY JOB"

1. "Allied," London *Times,* 8/30/44; Brooke, 8/30/44, CD 20:1211; Thompson, 8/30/44, CD 20:1210; Lord Camrose, 8/31/44, CD 20:1220; Colville, 8/31/44, CD 20:1221; DDE-WSC, 9/1/44, CD

20:1246; Butcher 647–51. 2. Butcher 652. 3. WSC-DDE, 8/31/44, 9/2/44, CD 20:1228, 1251. 4. DDE-WSC, 9/1/44, EP 4:2110 ("promotion"). 5. Colville, 9/1/44, CD 20:1234. 6. BLM, 9/9/44, Gilbert 7:953 ("holding"). 7. BLM-DDE, 9/4/44, EP 4:2120 n. 1; DDE-BLM, 9/5/44, EP 4:2120; Butcher 642 ("Berlin"), 673; DDE, interview, 7/31/68, 1968 Principal Series (box 40), EL 13 ("damn"); DDE-Ismay, 12/3/60, EP 21:2182 ("hair-brained"). 8. DDE-Ramsay et al., 9/4/44, EP 4:2116. 9. Jordan, *Brothers*, 399–401. 10. Patton, 8/23/44, 9/15/44, PP-LC (box 1) ("sir," "madder"); Ingersoll 219 ("sympathetic"). 11. Hemingway, *Dangerous Summer*, 169 ("bullfighter"). 12. BLM 245–46; EP 4:2224 n. 2. 13. Ira Eaker–DDE, "Montgomery Strikes Out," 1964 Principal File (box 33), EL ("sire"). 14. Butcher 675; Jehl, interview, OH-517 38; DDE-BLM, 10/13/44, EP 4:2222 ("drastic"); DDE, "Marshall and Churchill," 11/17/66, EL.

SIXTEEN: URSA MAJOR

1. WSC-Eden, 5/2/44, CD 20:29 ("crocodiles"). 2. FDR-WSC, 6/11/44, CD 20:458. 3. WSC-FDR, 6/11/44, CD 20:459. 4. Macmillan, 10/8/44, CD 20:1586. 5. WSC-Eden, 8/14/44, CD 20:1086; Dixon, 8/16/44, CD 20:1095; War Cabinet, minutes, 9/4/44, CD 20:1266; WSC-FDR, 9/4/44, CD 20:1269. 6. Moran, 8/21/44, CD 20:1132 ("cancer"); Ruane 90. 7. WSC-King, 10/7/44, CD 20:1583–84; Colville, 10/8/44, CD 20:1592. 8. WSC-Smuts, 10/9/44, CD 20:1594 ("Ursus"); Stalin-WSC, 9/30/44, CD 20:1508; Christopher H. Sterling, "Getting There: Churchill's Wartime Journeys," *Finest Hour* (Autumn 2010); Colville, 10/7/44; John Martin, 10/7/44, CD 20:1577; Brooke, 10/8/44, CD 20:1585; Harvey, 10/8/44, CD 20:1590 9. Arthur Birse, minutes, 10/9/44, CD 20:1602 ("cocks"); Harriman, *Envoy*, 558–59, CD 20:1640–41. 10. WSC, *Triumph*, 198–99, CD 20:1596 ("cynical"); Jacob, note, 10/26/44, and Bridges, note, 11/8/44, Gilbert 7:992. 11. WSC-Clementine, 10/13/44, CD 20:1648 ("Bear"); Roberts 843. 12. Stalin-WSC, 10/19/44, CD 20:1733 ("Hunter"). 13. WSC-Eden, 11/4/44, CD 20:1870 ("interest"). 14. WSC-Eden, 11/7/44 and 12/11/44, CD 20:1891 ("price) and 20:2189 ("percentages").

SEVENTEEN: UNDESIRABLE GOSSIP

1. WSC-DDE, 11/3/44, CD 20:1856; DDE-WSC, 11/4/44, CD 20:1865; Brooke, 11/14/44 and 11/24/44 ("chauffeur"); Reynolds 388 ("horrible"); Butcher 716; JES 407; Roberts 848. 2. BLM 274; BLM-DDE, 11/30/44, Pogue 312–13 ("*fail*"); Butcher 718; BLM-Brooke, 11/28/44, EP 4:2325 n. 2. 3. DDE-GCM, 1/10/45, EP 4:2143. 4. DDE-BLM, 12/1/44, EP 4:2324–25 ("beg"). 5. Brooke, 11/28/44 ("madness"). 6. Brooke, 12/4/44 ("amenable"). 7. WSC-Smuts, 12/3/44, CD 20:2082 ("reverse"). 8. WSC-FDR, 12/6/44, CD 20:2115–17. 9. JSDE, *General Ike*, 20 ("irked"). 10. FDR-WSC, 12/10/44, CD 20:2173.

EIGHTEEN: CLEANSING THE TEMPLE

1. DDE, *Crusade*, 338; David Eisenhower 570. 2. Hogan 211–12; David Eisenhower 569 ("repeat"). 3. DDE-GCM, 2/16/44, EP 3:1731 ("impossible"). 4. Butcher 730; Hogan 213–15. 5. Bradley and Blair, *General's Life*, 363. 6. Bradley, *Soldier's Story*, 476 ("object"); Strong 225–27. 7. DDE–Bradley/BLM/Devers, 12/20/44, EP 4:2363–65; Butcher 733–34; David Eisenhower 571. 8. Strong 226 ("Brad"). 9. Wilmot 59 ("temple"); David Eisenhower 576. 10. David Eisenhower 589–90. 11. Butcher, 12/27/44, EL; DDE, *Crusade*, 360–61; David Eisenhower 592–94 ("failure"). 12. Cunningham, 12/19/44, CD 20:2283. 13. BCOS, minutes, 12/19/44, CD 20:2285; WSC-DDE, 12/22/44, CD 20:2319 ("confidence"); War Cabinet, minutes, 12/20/44, CD 20:2301; Colville, 12/22/44, CD 20:2319–20; DDE-WSC, 12/23/44, CD 20:2323; London *Times*, 12/23/44, CD 20:2329; Butcher 734. 14. WSC-Smuts, 12/21/44, CD 20:2308 ("Gough's"); Colville, 12/22/44, CD 20:2320. 15. WSC-Clementine, 12/28/44, CD 20:2394; Gibert, *War Leadership*, 69. 16. BLM-Brooke, 12/24–27/44, Gilbert 7:1120, 1126, 1133. 17. Bradley and Blair, *General's Life*, 361 ("sharks"). 18. David Eisenhower 589. 19. BLM-DDE, 12/29/44, EL ("failure"). 20. BLM-DDE, 12/31/44, EL ("devoted"); BLM-DDE, 1/2/45, EP 4:2388 n. 3.

NINETEEN: "A WISE AND PROPER THING"

1. Pogue 398; David Eisenhower 593; EP 4:2357 n. 3. 2. DDE-CCOS, 12/31/44, EP 4:2386; DDE-GCM, 1/5/45, EP 4:2397–98; David Eisenhower 602. 3. De Gaulle, *Salvation*, 169, EP 4:2397 n. 1; De Gaulle–DDE, 1/1/45, EP 4:2392 nn. 1–2; David Eisenhower 602–03. 4. David Eisenhower 603. 5. Colville, 1/3/45, Gilbert 7:1129; Thompson, 1/3/45, CD 21:36; Staff Conference, minutes, 1/2/45, Gilbert 7:1142. 6. DDE-WBS, 8/22/44, EP 4:2089–90 n. 1; GCM-DDE, 1/7/45, EP 4:2401 n. 1; DDE-GCM, 1/5/45, EP 4:2397; Pogue 400; David Eisenhower 604–05; Cooper-WSC, 1/2/45, CD 21:24–25; Thompson, 1/3/45, CD 21:36; Brooke, 1/3/45, CD 21:34; DDE-WSC, 11/9/45, EP 6:531; WSC, *Second World War*, 6:245, Gilbert 7:1140; DDE, *Crusade*, 363 ("wise"); "Savior," NYT, 8/16/49; DDE, "Marshall and Churchill," 11/17/66, EL ("soda"). 7. DDE-GCM, 1/5/45, EP 4:2397–98 ("justified"); Butcher 738.

TWENTY: APPLAUSE AND APPLESAUCE

1. Butcher 737; Weigley 505 ("fancy"). 2. BLM-WSC, 1/6/45, CD 21:59 ("friendship"); BLM 278–82; WSC-BLM, CD 21:59 n. 5 ("invaluable"); WSC-FDR, 1/6/45, CD 21:61. 3. BLM 278–82, CD 21:66 ("overboard"). 4. JSDE, *Bitter*, 389 ("FORESAW"). 5. BLM 278–82, CD 21:63; Joseph Quinn, "How Nazi 'Fake News' Split Allied Commanders in 1945," https://blog.nationalarchives.gov.uk/how-nazi-fake-news-split-allied-commanders-in-1945/. 6. JSDE, *Bitter*, 390 ("SLUR"). 7. DDE, *Crusade*, 356 ("incident"). 8. DDE-GCM, 2/9/45, EP ("rankling"); DDE-Brooke, 2/12/45, EP; Butcher 743. 9. Moran 254–55 ("cock-a-doodle"). 10. WSC–Ismay/BCOS, 1/10/45, CD 21:97. 11. WSC, speech, 1/18/45, CD 21:172–73 ("proud"); War Cabinet, minutes, 1/11/45, CD 21:112; Colville, 1/9/45, CD 21:87; WSC-DDE, 1/9/45, CD 21:87.

TWENTY-ONE: THE RIVIERA OF HADES

1. WSC-FDR, 1/1/45, CD 20:4 ("Malta"); WSC-DDE, 1/9/45, EP 4:2412 n. 1; Sarah Churchill–Clementine Churchill, CD 21:391 ("Riviera"); Hopkins-FDR, 1/24/45, Gilbert 7:1159. 2. WSC-Eden, 1/25/45, Gilbert 7:1170 ("quarrel"). 3. C. R. Thompson, 2/3/45, CD 21:312; Charles Murphy, recollection, 4/16/46, 63, C. D. Jackson Papers (box 41), EL. 4. Cadogan–Lady Cadogan, 2/8/45, CD 21:410. 5. War Cabinet, memorandum, 2/18/45, speech of 2/8/45 ("Marshal"). 6. Argonaut, statement, 2/11/45, CD 21:456–61. 7. WSC-Eden, 4/11/45, CD 21:392; Nel, interview, 9/9/94, CAC, 25 ("curtain"). 8. War Cabinet/Attlee–WSC, 2/12/45, Gilbert 7:1215; Colville, 2/15/45, Gilbert 7:1216; Bracken-WSC, 2/13/45, CD 21:472; Beaverbrook-WSC, 2/14/45, CD 21:479. 9. WSC, speech, 2/26/45, CD 21:551 ("repudiate"); Eden–James Stuart, 2/17/45, Gilbert 7:1224; War Cabinet, minutes, 2/19/45, Gilbert 7:1228. 10. Colville, 2/28/45, CD 21:569 ("cheated"). 11. War Cabinet, minutes, 3/6/45, Gilbert 7:1242, Gilbert 7:1244–45; FDR-WSC, 3/11/45, Gilbert 7:1249–50; WSC-FDR, 3/18/45, Gilbert 7:1254 ("rock").

TWENTY-TWO: LOVERS' QUARRELS

1. Bradley, "Ifs of History," Blair Collection (box 49), USAMHI ("100,000"); Bradley, *Soldier's Story*, 535. 2. DDE, interview, 8/11/65, 66, 1965 Principal File (box 2), EL; DDE, interview, *Military Churchill*, 54–57; Bradley, *Soldier's Story*, 533; Butcher 509, 788, 798–800, EP 4:2559 n. 1; WSC-Ismay, 3/17/45, CD 21:693. 3. DDE-Stalin, 3/28/45, EP 4:2551 ("hands"). 4. DDE-BLM, 3/28/45, EP 4:2552, and 3/31/45, EP 4:2568. 5. WSC-FDR, 3/29/45, CD 20:790–91. 6. DDE-WSC, DDE-GCM, 3/30/45, EP 4:2560, 2562–63. 7. WSC-FDR, 3/27/45, CD 20:772; WSC-Eden, 3/25/45, CD 20:762. 8. WSC-DDE, 3/31/45, CD 21:806 ("relegation"). 9. Stalin-DDE, 4/1/45, EP 4:2584 n. 1; DDE, interview, 8/11/65, 63–66, 1965 Principal File (box 2), EL; DDE-GCM, 3/30/45, EP 4:2559. 10. Summersby, 4/30/45, EP 4:2564 n. 2; Donovan, *Confidential*, 46; DDE-WSC, 4/1/45, EP 4:2572–73, CD 20:820 ("disturbed"). 11. Brooke, 4/1/45, CD 21:810; WSC-BCOS, 3/31/45, CD 20:804–05; Ambrose, *Berlin*, 54–55. 12. JCS-BCOS, 3/30/45, Pogue 442. 13. WSC-FDR, 4/1/45, CD 21:817. 14. WSC-DDE, 4/2/45, CD 21:825, EP 4:2579 n. 1 ("Poland"). 15. DDE-WSC, 4/2/45, EP 4:2597 ("sense"). 16. BLM-DDE, 4/6/45, EP 4:2494–95; DDE-BLM,

4/8/45, EP; DDE, interview, 8/11/65, 60–62, 1965 Principal File (box 2), EL. 17. FDR-WSC, 4/5/45, CD 21:858–59; WSC-FDR, 4/5/45, CD 21:859 ("*amantium*"); Marian Holmes, 4/5/45, Gilbert 7:1276. 18. WSC-Clementine, 4/6/45, CD 21:872–73 ("quarrel"). 19. Graebner 121 ("Berlin"). 20. DDE-GCM, 4/23/45, EP 4:2640–41 ("intermingle"); Butcher 804. 21. DDE, interview, 9/13/66, 4, 1966 Principal File (box 1), EL ("personal"). 22. Arthur Larson 33 ("boss").

TWENTY-THREE: KATTEGAT & BOHEMIA

1. Harriman 362, CD 20:1677 ("Holy"). 2. WSC-Stalin, 4/1/45, Gilbert 7:1277; Raczynski-Eden, 4/1/45, Gilbert 7:1277; WSC-Eden, 4/19/45, CD 21:1037. 3. Halifax-WSC, 12/24/44, CD 20:2343; War Cabinet, minutes, 4/3/45, Gilbert 7:1278; WSC-Ismay, 4/7/45, and WSC-BCOS, 4/7/45, CD 21:888 ("hurry"). 4. WSC, answers, 4/12/45, CD 21:927–28; Thompson, 4/12/45, CD 21:926. 5. Colville, 4/12/45, CD 21:933. 6. Walter Thompson 303 ("agony"). 7. Nicolson, 4/13/45, CD 21:938 ("blow"). 8. Pim, recollection, 4/12/45, CD 21:934; Nel, interview, 9/9/94, CAC, 37 ("crumpled"); WSC-HST, 4/13/45, CD 21:943; WSC–Eleanor Roosevelt, 4/13/45, CD 21:941. 9. Summersby, 5/4/45, Wyden Papers, EL ("Denmark"). 10. WSC-Eden, 4/18/45, Gilbert 7:1302. 11. DDE-BLM, 3/31 and 4/6/45, EP 4:2568, 2594; DDE-Brooke, 4/27/45, EP 4:2650; DDE-GCM, 4/27/45, EP 4:2652 ("waking"). 12. Cunningham, 5/3/45, CD 21:1266. 13. WSC-HST, 4/27/45, Principal File (box 22), EL; WSC-HST, 4/30/45, CD 21:1218 ("liberation"); Colville, 4/23/45, CD 21:1094; WSC–Foreign Office, 4/16/45, CD 21:991–92; Orme Sargent–WSC, 5/1/45, CD 21:1242; WSC-Eden, 4/26/45, CD 21:1164. 14. HST-WSC, 5/1/45, CD 21:1248 ("unwise"). 15. WSC-DDE, 5/7/45, CD 21:1318 ("tie"). 16. WSC–James Byrnes, 8/31/48, Gilbert 8: 428 ("utmost"). 17. Nixon, *Leaders*, 33 ("MacArthur"). 18. Colville, 5/1/45, CD 21:141 ("breath"); Roberts 873. 19. Butcher 827; DDE-CCS, 5/4/45, EP 4:2682; Brooke, 5/4/45, CD 21:1276; BLM-WSC, 5/3/45, CD 21:1267; "Telephone Conversations," 5/4/45, CD 21:1287–88. 20. WSC-Eden, 5/4/45, CD 21:1277 ("terrible"). 21. WSC-Clementine, 5/4/45, Gilbert 7:1333 ("death"). 22. Ismay 394–95 ("Pug"). 23. DDE-CCOS, 5/7/45, EP 4:2696 ("fulfilled"); Pim, memoirs, Gilbert 7:1336 ("redeemed").

TWENTY-FOUR: "I AM NOW A LONDONER"

1. DDE-Hodgson, 9/30/43, EP 3:1473 ("hole"). 2. "Eisenhower," NYT, 5/16/45 ("friends"); Summersby, *Boss*, 255–56 ("relaxed"); Summersby, *Forgetting*, 225. 3. DDE-WSC, 5/19/45, EP 6:69–70. 4. London *Times*, 6/12/45; Butcher 852–53; Paradis 253 ("stranger"). 5. London *Times*, 6/12/45; "London Welcomes Her Newest Citizen," NYT, 6/13/45, British Movietone News, www.youtube.com/watch?v=wQHM9oqufv0; DDE, *Ease*, 299. 6. DDE, speech, 6/12/45, www.eisenhowerlibrary.gov/eisenhowers/speeches ("preserve"). 7. Summersby, *Forgetting*, 228 ("tears"); Summersby, *Boss*, 259 ("soliloquy"). 8. "Eisenhower Wins Acclaim," "London Welcomes Her Newest Citizen," NYT, 6/13/45 ("Londoner myself"). 9. WSC, speech, 6/12/45, CD 21:1677–78 ("Ike"); "Londoner," "Freeman," London *Times*, 6/13/45.

TWENTY-FIVE: ORDER OF THE BOOT

1. WSC-FDR, 3/18/45, CD 21:699 ("pygmies"). 2. WSC-Eden, 5/8/44, Gilbert 7:761 ("drunk"). 3. Montague Browne, interview, CAC, 499 ("Demons"). 4. WSC, *Triumph*, 399–400, CD 21:935 ("bond"). 5. WSC-HST, 5/12/45, Gilbert 8:7 ("curtain"). 6. Byrnes 290. 7. Roberts 932 ("ethics"); HST, speech, 12/24/45, trumanlibraryinstitute.org/holiday-addresses-harry-s-truman/ ("Sermon"). 8. Ruane 129 ("puny"). 9. Roberts 883 ("Second"); Ruane 91–92, 119–20. 10. Moran, 7/23/45, 301; Brooke, 7/23/45 ("blot"). 11. Gilbert 8:92. 12. Roberts 882; Jackson-Luce, 7/29/45, C. D. Jackson Papers (box 104), EL; Nicolson, 2/7/44, CD 19:1672. 13. Gaddis 173–75. 14. Attlee-WSC, 5/21/45, CD; Colville, 5/21/45; Gilbert 8:20–23; WSC-FDR, 11/8/44, CD 20:1894 ("pilot"). 15. Byrnes 296. 16. Marian Holmes, 7/26/45, 26; Roberts 885. 17. Roberts 884 ("humour"); Potter 66; Roberts 885. 18. Moran 310 ("aeroplane"). 19. King, 7/26/45, Roberts 885 ("sad"); WSC, *Words*, 41; Roberts 885 ("Boot"). 20. Soames, interview, CAC, 105 ("FINIS").

INTERREGNUM: THE RISING SON

TWENTY-SIX: RETURN OF THE NATIVE

1. "Spare," NYT, 6/18/45; "Paper," NYT, 6/21/45; "Timetable," NYT, 6/19/45; NYC Department of Records, "New York City Receptions," 7/7/2023, https://www.archives.nyc/blog/2023/7/5/dnbh65uwd3fx6br445c90udmpwixrz. 2. "Eisenhower's No," NYT, 1/25/48; "Capital to Greet," NYT, 6/18/45; Jehl, interview, OH-517 15. 3. McCullough 429–30 ("whale"); DDE, *Crusade*, 444 ("definitely"); DDE, interview, 1/3/67, 16, Newton 55. 4. DDE-CCOS, 5/12/45, EP 6:31, 6:32 n. 2. 5. Butcher 858, 860–61, 933. 6. Butcher 933 ("cooperation"). 7. "Rally," "Stalin," NYT, 8/13/45; JSDE, interview, OH-291, EL 34; DDE, *Crusade*, 428. 8. "Amity," NYT, 8/14/45 ("benign"); "Freedom," NYT, 8/15/45; EP 6:286; JES 451–52. 9. Murphy, interview, 2/3/71, COHP 3. 10. DDE-Patton, 9/29/45, EP 6:394–95; Summersby, *Boss*, 276 ("wink"); Jordan, *Brothers*, 539, 542 ("taste"); Patton–Beatrice Patton, 10/15/45, PP-LC (box 19). 11. DDE-Mamie, 9/3/45, *Letters*, 270; *Daily Mail*, 5/16/45. 12. Summersby, *Forgetting*, 176; Korda 443. 13. DDE-WBS, DDE-Clay, DDE-Summersby, 11/22/45, EP 6:542–46; JES 440–44; DDE-Summersby, 3/11/46, EP 7:647, and 6/1/48, EP 10:78, Drezmal, interview, George Hall Papers (box 1), EL 29–30; Steelman, interview, HSTL 203–05; Susan Eisenhower, *Mrs. Ike*, 240 ("overestimated"); Susan Wittig Albert, *The General's Women*, "Bibliographic Epilogue," at https://susanalbert.com/wp-content/uploads/2019/04/Biographical-Afterword-TGW.pdf.

TWENTY-SEVEN: THE MISSOURI WILDERNESS

1. Nel, interview, 9/9/94, CAC, 31 ("warmonger"). 2. DDE-WSC, 8/27/45, EP 6:310–12 ("admiration"). 3. DDE-WSC, 12/18/45, EP 7:651 ("separated"). 4. DDE–Jumbo Wilson, 12/17/45, EP 7:646; Susan Eisenhower, *Mrs. Ike*, 237. 5. DDE-Butcher, 12/26/45, EP 7:684 ("circle"); DDE-Gault, 12/17/45, EP 7:647; DDE-Ismay, 1/29/45, EP 7:805; Paradis 150. 6. DDE-WSC, 12/18/45, Principal File (box 124), EL. 7. EP 7:685 n. 2 ("*gurglings*"). 8. Butcher 75 ("soup"). 9. WSC-DDE, 1/26/46, CD 22:189 ("late"). 10. DDE-WSC, 1/30/46, EP 7:809 ("'Diary'"). 11. WSC–Attlee and Bevin, 3/7/46, CD 22:241 ("admirable"); Elsey, interview, CAC, 1162, 1168; Clark Clifford, recollection, CD 22:223–24; Byrnes 349; Ruane 149. 12. WSC, speech, 3/5/46, CD 22:232–35 ("curtain"). 13. "Scored," NYT, 3/7/46 ("catastrophe"); *Chicago Sun*, 3/6/46, CD 22:238 ("domination"); Roberts 896; Ruane 152. 14. Warbey Motion, 3/11/46, CD 22:252; "Stirred," NYT, 3/7/46; "Speech," London *Times*, 3/6/46; Roberts 896 ("polemics"). 15. *Pravda*, 3/14/46, CD 22:255; Ruane 151. 16. Leebaert 377. 17. WSC, speech, 3/8/46, CD 22:246 ("pious"); "Text," NYT, 3/9/46. 18. DDE, "Churchill and Marshall," 11/17/66, EL ("colossal"); EP 7:810 ("cigar"); Charles Murphy, recollection, 3/14/46, C. D. Jackson Papers (box 41), EL ("animal"); "Coach," NYT, 3/9/46. 19. DDE, introduction, 3/9/46, CD 22:248 ("happy"); Schulz, interview, OH-150 at 37–38. 20. WSC, speech, 3/5/46, Principal File (box 22), EL ("bridge"). 21. Charles Murphy, recollection, 3/14/46, C. D. Jackson Papers (box 41), EL ("stimulants").

TWENTY-EIGHT: POPULARITY: "ENORMOUS"

1. "The Gang," NYT, 11/15/14; DDE-Gosden, 7/9/51, EP 12:409; McAdam, interview, 5/28/76, COHP 7. 2. Snyder 87–92; Susan Eisenhower, *How Ike Led*, 105. 3. "Decision by Eisenhower," NYT, 1/25/48; JSDE, interview, OH-291, EL 13, 37; "Eisenhower's No," NYT, 1/25/48 ("enormous"). 4. "Decision by Eisenhower," NYT, 1/25/48. 5. DDE-WSC, 6/12/48, Principal File (box 23), EL ("struggle"). 6. WSC-DDE, 7/27/48, Principal File (box 23), EL ("intervene"). 7. Jehl, interview, OH-517 40; Douglas Black, memo, 4/1/48, Newton 51; Cannon, interview, 10/69, EL 13–14; DDE, *Ease*, 327; ACW, interview, OH-511 8; JES 469; Kieve, interview, OH-411, EL 10–11 ("noble"). 8. DDE-WSC, 6/6/48, Principal File (box 22), EL ("great"); DDE, *Crusade*, 239; Arthur Larson 5 ("MacArthur"). 9. JES 469; Newton 51. 10. Cannon, interview, 4/5/75, EL 64; JES 15; Newton 52. 11. "Test," NYT, 5/4/48; "Eisenhower," NYT, 5/3/48.

TWENTY-NINE: RED DAWN

1. Henry Luce, notes, 4/14–17/55, C. D. Jackson Papers (box 41), EL. 2. Colville, 8/21/44, CD 20:1134–35. 3. WSC, speech, 10/9/48, CD 22:1184–86 ("perpetrated") 4. Douglas-Lovett, 4/17/48,

FRUS 3:90 ("raze"). 5. WSC, speech, 10/9/48, CD 22:1184–86 ("bloodshed"). 6. Gilbert 8:399–400; WSC, speech, Roberts 912 ("moral"). 7. WSC-Ismay, 7/6/44, CD 20:726 ("psalm-singing"). 8. WSC-Shaw, 8/18/46, CD 22:435 ("panda"). 9. WSC, speech, 2/14/50, Roberts 915 ("summit"). 10. WSC, speech, 12/14/50, Roberts 918 ("Appeasement"). 11. Roberts 915–16. 12. WSC, speech, 3/6/47 CD 22:645 ("grief").

THIRTY: TAKING THE BLACK

1. DDE-Earl Eisenhower, 5/3/48, EP 10:56 ("lost"). 2. King, interview, OH-365 4. 3. Kirk, interview, OH-364 12–13 ("approach"). 4. JES 485–86. 5. Cannon, interview, 4/5/75, EL 53-54 ("stack"). 6. DDE, 3/19/49, EP 10:545–46; DDE, *Ease*, 354–55 ("days"); DDE, interview, 9/13/66, 1966 Principal File (box 1), EL 1; JES 487, 548. 7. DDE-WSC, n.d., and WSC-DDE, 1/31/49, Principal File (box 22), EL ("frank"). 8. EP 10:547 n. 7. 9. DDE, *Ease*, 355. 10. Clare Luce Booth, interview, 1/11/68, COHP 10 ("order"). 11. Butcher 546, 550; Schulz, interview, 1/6/68, COHP 103; Cannon, interview, 4/5/75, EL 69–70; "Wife," NYT, 7/13/52; DDE, *Ease*, 340; Newton 53. 12. DDE-WSC, 9/21/50, EP 11:1130 ("canvas"). 13. Luce 92 ("golf"); Susan Eisenhower, *How Ike Led*, 225. 14. SHAPE, *SHAPE History*, vol. 1, 12/9/53, 9, NATO Archives; Gilbert 8:467.

THIRTY-ONE: SUPREME COMMANDER (AGAIN)

1. "Pact," NYT, 9/28/50; Cannon, interview, 4/5/75, EL 77; Gruenther, interview, 4/20/67, COHP, 30. 2. WSC-DDE, 9/14/50, Gilbert 8:557; Pownall-Ismay, 1/3/51, Gilbert 8:582. 3. DDE-WSC, 12/6/50, EP 11:1461–62; EP 11:1462 n. 1. 4. "Atlantic Leaders," NYT, 12/13/50; North Atlantic Council, "Sixth Session, Brussels, December 1950," NATO Archives, https://archives.nato.int/uploads/r/nato-archives-online/3/d/6/3d6b36537e8505523d74617f9cfb252056292f45cef89abc8ff62ca7aa149a7d/C_6-VR_1_ENG_NHQL743343.pdf ("mountain"); "Resolution," 12/19/50, Doc. C6-D/8, NATO Archives, https://archives.nato.int/resolution-sur-la-nomination-dun-commandant-supreme; Leebaert 281; C. H. Donnelly, "Official Title of Supreme Allied Commander Europe and of his Headquarters," 1/3/51, NATO Archives, https://archives.nato.int/uploads/r/null/1/1/119507/SGM-0004-51_ENG_PDP.pdf. 5. Susan Eisenhower, *Mrs. Ike*, 256–57. 6. Footage at https://www.youtube.com/watch?v=kPtrPR9Y3cA. 7. DDE, 2/13/53, EP 14:43; JSDE, interview, OH-291, EL 37, 45; Mamie Eisenhower, interview, OH-12 134–37; Cannon, interview, 4/5/75, EL 89; JES 499; Susan Eisenhower, *Mrs. Ike*, 257–58. 8. JSDE, interview, OH-291, EL 45 ("paper"). 9. DDE, 6/11/51, EP 12:340 ("Norway"); DDE-WSC, 12/6/50, EP 11:1461; SACEUR, "Periodic Report to the Standing Group," 3/13/51, NATO Archives, https://archives.nato.int/uploads/r/null/1/1/113023/SG_120_ENG_PDP.pdf; North Atlantic Military Committee, "Record of Meeting of the Standing Group," 12/29/50, NATO Archives, https://archives.nato.int/uploads/r/null/1/0/108150/RECORD-SG-044-50_ENG_PDP.pdf; Cannon, interview, 10/69, EL 26, 31–32, 35; "Eisenhower Aide," NYT, 11/22/52; Gruenther, interview, 4/20/67, COHP, 28–29. 10. Gruenther, interview, 4/20/67, COHP, 29, 31 ("Billy"); MacArthur, interview, OH-538 20–21. 11. *Time*, 1/7/51 ("history"). 12. DDE, speech, 7/3/51, CD 22:2104–06 ("wise"); EP 12:400 n. 2. 13. JSDE, *General Ike*, 211. 14. WSC-Woolton, 7/5/51, CD 22:2109 ("speeches"). 15. WSC-DDE, 7/5/51, CD 22:2109 ("servants"). 16. DDE, *Ease*, 376 ("heady"); DDE-WSC, 7/11/51, EP 12:414–15 ("timorous"). 17. JSDE, *General Ike*, 212 ("statesman"). 18. DDE-Ismay, 10/2/51, EP 12:589; Reynolds 379–80 ("obdurate"). 19. Macmillan, *Diaries*, 102. 20. Attlee-WSC, 9/20/51, Gilbert 8:638 ("Election").

THIRTY-TWO: PRIME MINISTER (AGAIN)

1. Leebaert 298; Kunz 6, 11. 2. Roberts 916, 919; Gilbert 8:512; Leebaert 325. 3. Macmillan, 6/14/51, Gilbert 8:615; Roberts 924 ("breakfast"). 4. Roberts 920 ("rifle"); Gilbert 8:648 ("finger"). 5. WSC, speech, 10/6/51, CD 22:2176 ("trigger"); WSC, broadcast, 10/8/51, CD 22:2180 ("parley"); Roberts 922. 6. *Manchester Guardian*, 10/27/51; Leebaert 329. 7. Brown, *Sunset*, 437; Roberts 923; Watry 6; Gilbert 8:676; WSC, speech, 12/6/51, Gilbert 8:667; Leebaert 287, 331. 8. WSC, speech, 11/10/52, CD 23:724; Leebaert 316. 9. Leebaert 325–26 ("bastard"). 10. Leebaert 309, 317, 320–21. 11. "Eisenhower," NYT, 12/18/51. 12. Hermiston 101 ("Commonwealth"). 13. Hermiston 317. 14. Montague Browne, interview, CAC, 487; Leebaert

361. 15. Leebaert 362–63; Montague Browne, interview, CAC, 487 ("E"); Eden, CD 20:1622 ("bearable"). 16. Bracken-Beaverbrook, 10/16/46, CD 22:493 ("Heaven"); Lucas 53; Harvey, 3/28/44, CD 19:2223; Gilbert 8:227, 633; Shuckburgh 62, 66; Roberts 925; Colville, 4/8/52, *Fringes*, 644–45. 17. DDE-WSC, 12/14/51, EP 12:790–91; Goodpaster, interview, CAC, 1060–61. 18. Goodpaster, interview, CAC, 1077 ("grand"). 19. DDE, 12/21/51, EP 12:810 ("glory"). 20. DDE-Lovett, 1/28/52, EP 13:925 ("boom"). 21. "Eisenhower," NYT, 12/18/51 ("history"). 22. Moran 381 ("raped").

THIRTY-THREE: THE SEDUCTION OF A SOLDIER

1. Slater, interview, COHP 3–4. 2. JES 479; Stephens, interview, OH-161, EL 58 ("dovetail"); Macmillan, *Diaries*, 485, 489 ("sympathy"); Paradis 130–31. 3. Achilles, interview, JFDC 11 ("*McCall's*"). 4. "Eisenhower Sees," NYT, 11/6/51; "Truman Offers," NYT, 11/8/51; "Truman Denies," NYT, 11/9/51; Susan Eisenhower, *How Ike Led*, 111–12; JES 505–06; DDE, 10/29/51, EP 12:667–68 ("transcendent"). 5. Bowie and Immerman 70–71; Snyder 104. 6. "Eisenhower Tells," NYT, 4/11/52; Snyder 106 ("transcend"). 7. "Serenade," NYT, 2/9/52; Snyder 109–13. 8. "Eisenhower Vote," NYT, 3/19/52; Snyder 130, 132. 9. "General," NYT, 3/21/52 ("re-examine"). 10. "Eisenhower," NYT, 3/20/52; "General," NYT, 3/21/52; Clay, interview, 2/20/67, COHP 10; Clay, interview, JFDC 7; Brownell, interview, 2/24/77, EL 4–5; Eleanor Dulles, interview, 6/18/62, COHP 523. 11. Brownell, interview, 1/25/67, COHP 39 ("gee"). 12. Brownell, interview, 1/25/67, COHP 19, 40 (head start, "distinct"); Clay, interview, 2/20/67, COHP 7–8; Brownell, interview, 2/24/77, EL 4. 13. NYT, 4/13/52.

THIRTY-FOUR: A GENERAL ON CAMPAIGN

1. Colville-DDE, 4/28/52, Principal File (box 22), EL; DDE-Gault, 4/28/52, Principal File (box 22), EL; NYT, 5/16/52. 2. Colville, 5/15/52, CD 23:440–41 ("cordial"). 3. DDE-WSC, 5/22/52, CD 23:460 ("wish"). 4. Brownell, interview, 2/24/77, COHP 16; Slater, interview, COHP 4. 5. Luce, interview, JFDC 21 ("slogan"); DDE, speech, NYT, 8/26/52 (attack). 6. "Week's Korea," NYT, 11/6/52; "Eisenhower's," NYT, 11/6/52; "Official," NYT, 11/6/52 ("Heartbreak"). 7. Bowie and Immerman 78–79; Newton 75. 8. Graebner 65–66; "Churchill," NYT, 7/6/52 ("unshirted"). 9. Abel, interview, 12/10/70, COHP 43 ("syntax"); JSDE, interview, OH-15 101; Benedict, interview, 9/13/68, COHP 38–39; Holzer 194–95. 10. Kieve, interview, OH-411, EL 14 ("backyard"). 11. "Churchill Hopeful," NYT, 11/21/52; Colville, *Fringes*, 676; Roberts 933 ("arrow"). 12. Thomas 23 ("destroy"). 13. WSC-Clementine, 7/11/52, Gilbert 743–44 ("headway"); "Churchill," NYT, 7/12/52. 14. Roberts 933; Reynolds 379–80. 15. "Bevan," NYT, 11/13/52; WSC-DDE, 11/12/52, CD 23:729. 16. Defence Committee, minutes, 11/11/52, CD 23:771; "Churchill," NYT, 11/21/52; Graebner 120; Colville, 6/13–15/52, *Fringes*, 650–51 ("Eisenhower"). 17. Colville, 1/1/53, *Fringes*, 658, Gilbert 8:788. 18. Colville, 8/22–25/52, *Fringes*, 654–54, Gilbert 8:756. 19. Colville, 11/9/52, CD 23:721 ("disturbed").

PART TWO: RED LIGHTNING

1. Colville, 12/6/53, CD 23:1329 ("smiled"). 2. Makins, interview, CAC, 278.

THIRTY-FIVE: DINNER AT BERNIE'S

1. Eleanor Dulles, interview, JFDC 137; Briggs, interview, 6/19/70, COHP 26; JSDE, interview, 8/25/82, COHP 11. 2. Allen, interview, 3/7/67, COHP 35–36; Hughes 70–71 ("flourishes"); Lucas 20–21. 3. Lucas 20–21. 4. DDE, interview, 7/28/64, JFDC 40; DDE, *Mandate*, 142; Thomas 50; Macmillan, *Storm*, 321; Young 111. 5. Aldrich, interview, JFDC 40 ("mistrusted"); Lucas 81. 6. "Hope," NYT, 11/15/52; "Churchill," NYT, 11/25/52 ("congratulations"); Cabinet, minutes, 12/4/52, CD 23:750; Alsop, interview, JFDC 3; DDE, interview, 7/28/64, JFDC 40 ("cat"). 7. Aldrich, interview, 10/16/72, COHP 4. 8. Aldrich, interview, 7/15/64, JFDC 1. 9. "Eisenhower Selects," NYT, 12/1/52; Dewey, interview, JFDC 23. 10. DDE, 2/13/53, EP 14:45. 11. "Churchill," NYT, 12/27/52; Colville, 1/1/53, CAC, CD 23:793; Roberts 932. 12. Makins, interview, CAC, 276; WSC-DDE, 12/18–20/52, International Series (box 18), EL; Note, Gilbert 8:761; DDE-WSC, 12/17/52, EP 13:1450

("easels"); Graebner 120; Young 114. 13. "Churchill," NYT, 12/27/52; WSC-Eden, 11/13/52, CD 23:721; DDE-Baruch, 12/18/52, EP 13 1452 ("'unplanned'"). 14. WSC, remarks, 1/5/53, C. D. Jackson Papers (box 110), EL ("extraordinary"); Colville, 1/5/53, CD 23:796; "Churchill," NYT, 1/6/53. 15. "Churchill," NYT, 1/6/53; Schulz, interview, 1/6/68, COHP 105; Gilbert 8:789; Leebaert 375. 16. Colville, 1/5/53, CD 23:796; "Churchill," NYT, 1/6/53 ("better"); Leebaert 376. 17. Colville, 1/5/53, CD 23:796 ("protoplasm"). 18. DDE, 1/6/53, *Diaries*, 223. 19. WSC-Eden, 1/6/53, CD 23:798–99 ("supply"). 20. WSC–Eden and Butler, 1/8/53, CD 803–04 ("speech"); Shuckburgh, 1/16/53, CD 23:812 ("hurry"); Young 121. 21. Colville, 1/7/53, CD 23:801. 22. DDE-WSC, 3/16/53, International Series (box 17), EL. 23. DDE, 1/6/53, EP 13:1481–82, 2/12/53, EP 14:42–44 ("retire"); DDE, "Marshall and Churchill," 11/17/66, EL 99 ("service"). 24. Makins, interview, CAC, 278 ("distinction"). 25. Colville, 1/7/53, CD 23:801; Gilbert 8:792; Roberts 935–36; WSC, *Words*, 32; Roberts 944; WSC-Eden, 3/30/53, CD 23:927; Moran 580 ("unimaginative"). 26. Colville, 1/12/53, CD 23:809 ("stature"); Ruane 220; Young 120.

THIRTY-SIX: 75 PERCENT COLD-BLOODED

1. JSDE, interview, 8/25/82, COHP 11 ("players"). 2. Leebaert 381–82. 3. DDE, 5/14/53, *Diaries*, 237; Newton 87 ("good"); JSDE, interview, OH-15 17; Hughes 74, 77. 4. Donovan, *Confidential*, 40; Ewald, interview, 12/16/77, EL 50. 5. DDE-McNarney, 9/16/43, EP 2:1430 ("memoirs"); Crosswell 45. 6. JSDE, interview, 8/25/82, COHP 6; Allen, interview, 3/7/67, COHP 4; Crosswell 45, 47–48. 7. Haldeman, 6/29/71, Haldeman Diaries, Nixon Library ("prat"); Nixon, *Leaders*, 335; Crosswell 105. 8. Thomas 13 ("cold-blooded"). 9. Snyder–Meier, 4/3/53, DDE Personal File (box 8), EL; Donovan, *Confidential*, 44 ("minutes"); Mattie Pinette, 6/3/44, George Hall Papers (box 1), EL ("Elegy"); JSDE, interview, OH-291, EL 50–51; Murphy, interview, 10/12/72, COHP 25 ("spoiled"). 10. Donovan, *Confidential*, 45–47. 11. Slater 39 ("lose"). 12. Thomas 243; Allen 116–17. 13. Slater 36 ("robust"). 14. Mamie Eisenhower, interview, 7/20/72, EL ("eight"); Donovan, *Confidential*, 15–16.

THIRTY-SEVEN: SPARKS JUMPING AROUND A FUSE

1. NSC minutes, 2/11/53, FRUS 15:770; Clark-JCS, 2/9/53, FRUS 15:758; Newton 99; JES 558–59. 2. DDE-Calhoun, 10/1/51, EP 12:586 ("Bankruptcy"). 3. Lemnitzer, interview, 11/21/72, COHP 7–8; Gray, interview, 6/25/75, EL 16. 4. Abel, interview, 12/10/70, COHP 2–3; NSC, minutes, 5/13/53, FRUS 15:1017; Newton 94; Leebaert 383. 5. NSC, minutes, 2/11, 3/31 and 5/13/53, FRUS 15:770, 826, 1014–15 ("taboo"). 6. "Eisenhower," NYT, 1/30/53. 7. "Perturbed," NYT, 2/1/53; "Formosa," NYT, 2/9/53. 8. "French," NYT, 2/1/53. 9. DDE-WSC, 2/2/53, EP 14:18–19 ("dupes"). 10. WSC-DDE, 2/7/53, CD 23:836 ("correspondence"). 11. Young 128 ("Marshal"). 12. "Moscow," 3/7/53, *Guardian* ("died").

THIRTY-EIGHT: "IT WOULD BE A PITY IF A SUDDEN FROST NIPPED SPRING IN THE BUD"

1. WSC-DDE, 4/6/53, International Series (box 18), EL; WSC, speech, 4/17/53, CD 23:958; Moran, 3/7/53, 112; Gilbert 8:805; Soames, interview, CAC, 126–27. 2. WSC-DDE, 3/11/53, CD 22:905 ("Bernie's"). 3. "Text," NYT, 3/17/53 ("question"). 4. WSC-DDE, 4/6/53, International Series (box 18), EL ("purpose"). 5. Cutler 322–23; Bowie and Immerman 110; Hermiston 86. 6. NSC, minutes, 3/11/53, FRUS 8:1117–19; Editorial Note, FRUS 8:1098; Hughes 101 ("yapping"); Thomas 81 ("criminal"); Debevoise-Jackson, 9/16/55, C. D. Jackson Papers (box 110), EL; Hagerty, interview, OH-91, EL 336; "Program of Psychological Preparation for Stalin's Passing from Power," 11/1/52, FRUS 8:1060 ("die"). 7. Hall, interview, JFDC 17 ("God"); Call notes, 3/4/53, JFD Papers, Telephone Conversations (box 10), EL; Ruane 224–25; Young 140. 8. Hagerty, interview, JFDC 19 ("hell"). 9. DDE, interview, 7/28/64, JFDC 42; Jebb-Eden, 11/12/53, CD 23:906; NSC, minutes, 3/4/53, FRUS 8:1091–93. 10. DDE-WSC, 3/11/53, EP 14:92–93 ("mill"); Call notes, 3/11/53, JFD Papers, Telephone Conversations (box 10), EL. 11. Cutler 321; Bowie and Immerman 110–14. 12. Hagerty, 1/5/54, Hagerty Papers (box 1a), EL ("bottle"); Gaddis 94, 98. 13. DDE-Baruch, 3/10/53, ACW Diary Series

(box 3), EL; Lubell-Baruch, 3/7/53, JFD Papers, White House Memoranda Series (box 1); Eisenhower Staff, interview, OH-508, EL; Bowie and Immerman 113. 14. Kieve, interview, OH-411, EL 6 ("hospitals"). 15. NSC, meeting minutes, 3/11/53, FRUS 8:117–20; Bowie, interview, CAC, 1176. 16. Hughes 103 ("like"); Thomas 60–61. 17. Hughes 107, 112 ("Dammit"). 18. Bowie and Immerman 118–19. 19. Thomas 61 ("pew"); Hughes 105. 20. "Purger," NYT, 4/19/53; "Britain's," NYT, 4/16/53; Hughes 111; WSC-DDE, 4/11/53, CD 23:938–39. 21. Bowie and Immerman 46–47; Hughes 111. 22. DDE-WSC, 4/11/53, CD 23:943 ("sympathy"). 23. WSC-DDE, 4/12/53, CD 23:944 ("frost"). 24. DDE-WSC, 4/13/53, EP 14:168 ("tenor"); Macmillan, *Diaries*, 223. 25. "5-Point," "Eisenhower," NYT, 4/17/53; Newton 130. 26. Adams 102–03; Cutler 322; Thomas 64. 27. DDE, speech, 4/16/53, NYT, 4/17/53 ("pay"); Newton 132. 28. Cutler 322, Thomas 64.

THIRTY-NINE: WINSTON STRIKES BACK

1. WSC-DDE, 4/22/53, CD 23:963; Gilbert 8:811. 2. DDE-WSC, 4/25/53, EP 14:181–82 ("concrete"); DOS, Intelligence Estimate, 3/4/53, FRUS 8:1086; Bohlen, interview, JFDC 24–25; CIA, Special Estimate 39, "Consequences," 3/10/53, EL online; "First Step," NYT, 4/26/53. 3. "Text," NYT, 4/19/53; "Russia," NYT, 4/17/53; "Soviet," NYT, 4/25/53; "Soviets," NYT, 4/19/53; "Agreement," NYT, 4/26/53; "Washington," NYT, 4/28/53. 4. "Churchill," NYT, 4/23/53; WSC-DDE, 5/4/53, CD 23:986 ("intercourse"); Cabinet, minutes, 4/28/53, CD 23:975; Hermiston 178. 5. EP 14:208 n. 2 ("foresee"). 6. DDE-WSC, 5/5/53, CD 23:986–87 ("astonishment"). 7. WSC-DDE, 5/7/53, CD 23:990–91 ("negation"); Nixon, *Leaders*, 38. 8. Aldrich, interview, 10/16/72, COHP 18, 28–29, 36–37; EP 14:19 n. 2; Ruane 226 ("fool"). 9. Eden, *Circle*, 51–52, 54; Ruane 225; Owen 388. 10. WSC, speech, 5/11/53, CD 23:1003, 1007–09 ("piecemeal"); Hermiston 185. 11. Hermiston 186 ("pacific"); Aldrich-DOS, 5/12/53, FRUS 6:984 ("misgivings"); Williamson 21. 12. DDE, press conference, 5/14/53 ("earnest"); Ruane 225–26. 13. Macmillan, 5/12/53 ("ignorant"), and 6/1–7/53.

FORTY: BORROWED TIME

1. DDE-Smith, 5/20/53, EP 14:239; Young 167. 2. Cutler 316 ("sharp"); C. D. Jackson, 5/20/53, C. D. Jackson Papers (box 68), EL; NSC, minutes, 5/20/53, FRUS 15:1067; Leaming 199; Young 167–68; Donovan, *Inside*, 201–02. 3. NSC, minutes, 5/13/53, FRUS 15:1016 (worse). 4. DDE-WSC, 5/20–21/53, CD 23:1032, EP 14:239–40. 5. WSC-DDE, 5/24/53, International Series (box 20), EL, and CD 23:1042 ("golf"). 6. DDE-WSC, 5/26/53, CD 23:1043; Telephone calls, 5/28/53, ACW Diary Series (box 4), EL; Smith-DDE, 5/25/53, International Series (box 20), EL ("battleship"). 7. WSC-DDE, 5/28/53, CD 23:1047 ("'Golf'"). 8. WSC-DDE, 6/12/53, CD 23:1110 ("recurring"); DDE-WSC, 6/13/53, EP 14:292, and 6/19/53, CD 23:1118; Moran, 6/16/53. 9. Vale and Scadding 210–12; Moran 435 ("spasm"); Roberts 938. 10. Colville, 6/5–8/65; Gilbert 8:848, 856; Montague Browne, interview, CAC, 534; Colville-Butler, 6/25/53, CD 23:1130; Macmillan, *Diaries*, 241; Roberts 938–39; Leaming 207; Hermiston 234. 11. Ruane 227 ("oak"); Moran, 6/25/53, 119 ("bear"). 12. Macmillan, 7/2/53, *Tides*, 525, Gilbert 8:859; WSC-Salisbury, 7/6/53, CD 23:1156; Colville, 7/19/53. 13. WSC-DDE, 6/26/53, International Series (box 20), EL ("medical"). 14. DDE-WSC, 6/26/53, CD 23:1137 ("distressed"). 15. WSC-DDE, 7/1/53, CD 23:1140 ("goat"). 16. Gilbert 8:859. 17. Macmillan, *Diaries*, 241; Macmillan, *Tides*, 516, CD 23:1146 ("gaiety"). 18. WSC-DDE, 4/9/53, International Series (box 18), EL. 19. Moran 128 ("anger"); Reynolds 453. 20. Itinerary, Personal File (box 942), EL; Colville, *Fringes*, 674–75; Reynolds 453; Roberts 943. 21. Moran 125. 22. Montefiore, 506–07. 23. Moran, 7/10/53, 140 ("halfway"). 24. Moran, 7/12/53, 143 ("fools"). 25. Moran, 7/14/53, 443–46 ("bitched"). 26. Henry Luce, notes, 4/14–17/55, C. D. Jackson Papers (box 41), EL. 27. WSC-DDE, 7/17/53, Gilbert 864–65 ("Malenkov"). 28. Moran 466 ("king"). 29. Moran 466–67 ("lied"). 30. Moran 161 ("Stevenson"). 31. Colville, 7/24/53, CD 23:1174 ("stupid"); Moran, 7/24/53. 32. Moran 473, 480, 482. 33. JSDE, interview, CAC, 1008 (summits); Bowie, interview, CAC, 1196; Goodpaster, interview, CAC, 1067; Wilcox, interview, 4/3/72, COHP 48–49; Hagerty, interview, OH-91, EL 183. 34. Ridgway-Bradley,

6/26/53, JFD-Herter (box 1), EL ("hand"). 35. Pyle, interview, COHP 95–96; Hughes 151 ("shirt"). 36. DDE-WSC, in Moran, 7/21/53, 447–48. 37. Montague Browne, interview, CAC, 483 ("thrilled").

FORTY-ONE: THE PEACOCK THRONE

1. Roberts 920. 2. Minutes, 3/6/53, FRUS 10:480–81; Koch 7–8; Lucas 24; Newton 103; Taafe-McMenamy 17; Shinkle 161. 3. Allen Dulles–DDE, 3/1/53, and Minutes, 3/4/53, 3/6/53, FRUS 10:469–72, 480–81, 915–16; JES 622–23; Office of National Estimates, "Probable Developments of Iran Through 1953," National Intelligence Estimate 75 (11/13/52), President's Secretary Files, HSTL online; Taafe-McMenamy 23; Eden-WSC, 3/5/53, CD 23:879. 4. WSC-DDE, 6/20/53, 6/23–24/53, International Series (box 20), EL. 5. Hughes 136 ("Mosaddeq"). 6. Makins-WSC, 6/21/53, CD 23:1123 ("puppet"). 7. CIA, "Battle for Iran," 31, 41; Note, FRUS 10:737–38, 16:602, 611, 637; Taafe-McMenamy 24, 26; Wilber 18. 8. JFD–Allen Dulles, 7/24/53, FRUS 10:738; CIA, "Battle," 53; Hermiston 298–303. 9. CIA, National Intelligence Estimates (draft), 8/12/53, FRUS 10:657. 10. WBS-DDE, 8/18/53, FRUS 10:748 ("failed"). 11. DDE, *Mandate*, 164, 166 ("pajamas"); "CIA Confirms Role in 1953 Iran Coup," https://nsarchive2.gwu.edu/NSAEBB/NSAEBB435/; Newton 109, 119. 12. DDE, 10/8/53, Taafe-McMenamy 8 ("embarrassed"); Henderson-DOS, 8/21/53, FRUS 10:759 ("blamed"). 13. Hermiston 308, quoting Kermit Roosevelt, *Countercoup*, 206 ("Young"). 14. Gilbert 8:878; Leebaert 393.

FORTY-TWO: COUNTING CARDS

1. Holloway 306–07 ("whip"). 2. Holloway 303–07, 316–17 ("birds"). 3. DDE, 7/16/53, ACW File, DDE Diary, Dec. 1952–July 1953 (box 3), EL; Newton 127; NSC, minutes, 9/24/53, FRUS 2:469; NSA, "Soviet Land-Based," 52–54; Holloway 322–24; Maloney 95–96. 4. Chester Hansen, 3/6/45, AHEC ("glass"); Roberts 911. 5. DDE-Clay, 2/9/52, EP 13:963–64. 6. DDE–Charles Wilson, 10/20/51, EP 12:659–60 ("solvency"); Bowie and Immerman 44. 7. DDE-Allen Dulles, 9/8/53, FRUS 2:461 ("dictatorial"); NSC, minutes, 2/11/53, 3/31/53, FRUS 2:236, 264; JSDE, interview, 8/25/82, COHP 14; Bowie and Immerman 22, 39; Hughes 75. 8. DDE, *Mandate*, 449; NSC 162/2, 10/30/53; Robert Bowie, interview, in Pickett 30–31; Cutler 308–09; Cutler, minutes, 7/16/53, FRUS 2:397–99; Cutler, memorandum, 5/9/53, FRUS 2:323–25; Pickett 3–4, 22–25; ACW-Goodpaster interview, OH-308, EL 2; Bowie and Immerman 124–26; Shinkle 123–25; Lay-NSC, 7/22/53, FRUS 2:400–410; Directing Panel, "Project Solarium," 6/1/53, FRUS 2:360–65; Newton 128; Kennan-Byrnes, 2/22/46, HST Administration File, HSTL. 9. JSDE, interviews, OH-15 9 and OH-291, EL 87.

FORTY-THREE: A GOAT, A SIX-SHOOTER, AND ATOM BOMBS

1. WSC-DDE, 11/5/53, International Series (box 20), EL ("deadlock"). 2. Robert Bowie, interview, in Pickett 35; NSC 162/2, 10/30/52; Young 215; Ruane 232; Hermiston 378. 3. WSC, speech, 10/10/53, Hermiston 336; Roberts 941. 4. London *Times*, 10/12/53 ("triumph"); Notes, 11/6/53, ACW Diary Series (box 5), EL. 5. DDE-WSC, 11/7/53, CD 23:1280; USSR Foreign Ministry–Embassy, 11/3/53, FRUS 8:658. 6. Moran 529; WSC-DDE, 11/8/53, Gilbert 8:910. 7. Schmuhl 226, 322 n. 30 ("Tragedy"); Montague Browne 154 ("pity"); Roberts 942; Reynolds 436, 447. 8. "Churchill," NYT, 12/4/53; "Sidelights," NYT, 12/9/53; Roberts 942 ("Goat"). 9. "The Day the World Watched," *Royal Gazette*, 11/5/03; Brian Meade, "How I Looked After Churchill and Eisenhower," *Living Magazines Cardiff*, 8/27/2014; Moran 536 ("disabilities"). 10. "Sidelights," NYT, 12/9/53. 11. Shuckburgh, 12/4/53, 113 ("royal"). 12. Bowie, interview, CAC, 1193 ("friendship"), and 8/11/67, 33-34 COHP ("cards"). 13. Hagerty, interview, OH-91, EL 192 ("Sir"). 14. Jackson-Cutler, 5/11/53, C. D. Jackson Papers (box 37), EL, Lucas 19 ("apex"). 15. Hermiston 378 ("crowning"). 16. Itinerary, 12/4/53, ACW Diary Series (box 1), EL; Memo, 12/4/53, International Meetings (box 1), EL; JFD, memo, 12/4/53, FRUS 5:1739–40; Colville, 12/4/53, *Fringes*, 682–84; DDE, *Mandate*, 249 ("deafness"). 17. Minutes, 12/4/53, FRUS 5:1739–40. 18. Minutes, 12/4/53, FRUS 5:1739–40; DDE, *Mandate*, 250. 19. Colville, 12/4/53, CD 23:1317 ("Canute"); "Sergeant Murray

on Churchill," CAC. 20. Colville, 12/4/53, CD 23:1317. 21. Colville, *Fringes*, 682–83 (fuse, "smoke"). 22. Minutes, 12/4/53, FRUS 5:1751–53. 23. Eden, *Circle*, 54; Minutes, 12/4/53, FRUS 5:1758; Hagerty notes, 12/4/56, International Meetings (box 1), EL. 24. Minutes, 12/4/53, FRUS 5:1754–61 ("girl"); Minutes, 12/4/53, CD 23:1323–24; Hagerty notes, 12/4/56, International Meetings (box 1), EL; Colville, *Fringes*, 683 ("violent," "pained," "whiskey"); Shuckburgh, 12/4/53, 113 ("bricks"). 25. Ruane 230–31. 26. DDE, 12/10/53, EP 15:742–43; DDE, *Mandate*, 248; Colville, *Fringes*, 685 n. 1; Roberts 943; Ruane and Jones 74; Ruane 249. 27. Minutes, 12/5/53, 11:30 a.m., FRUS 5:1767–69; Itinerary, 12/5/53, ACW Diary Series (box 1), EL; Colville, 12/6/53, CD 23:1325; Minutes, 12/5/53, EL, www.eisenhowerlibrary.gov/sites/default/files/file/atoms_Binder5.pdf; Ruane 237. 28. Memo, 12/6/53, FRUS 5:1787; British minutes, n.d., International Meetings (box 3), EL; DDE, 12/6/53, EP 15:733 ("fatuous"); Colville, 12/6/53 ("distinction"). 29. DDE, 12/10/53, EP 15:744 ("mixture"). 30. DDE-Hazlett, 12/24/53, Name Series (box 18), EL ("distasteful"). 31. Moran 539 ("trusts"). 32. Stephens, interview, OH-161, EL 54 ("finish"). 33. DDE-WSC, 12/8/53, CD 23:1351 ("Clemmie"); Donovan, *Confidential*, 50–51. 34. WSC-DDE, 12/8/53, DDE-WSC, 12/9/53, CD 23:1352 ("Goat"); WSC-DDE, 12/9/53, AWD International Series (box 19), EL (slightly different wording). 35. Montague Browne, interview, CAC, 491; Moran 540–41 ("bastard").

FORTY-FOUR: TWILIGHT'S LAST GLEAMING

1. "Urban-Industrial Target List," in https://nsarchive2.gwu.edu/nukevault/ebb538-Cold-War-Nuclear-Target-List-Declassified-First-Ever/; Rhodes 563–64; Maloney 66–68, 79, 127–30 ("Moscow"). 2. DDE-Simon, 4/4/45, Gaddis 107; DDE, speech, 11/1/56, www.presidency.ucsb.edu/documents/address-convention-hall-philadelphia-pennsylvania ("preposterous"). 3. Hagerty, interview, 3/2/67, COHP, 526 (spaghetti). 4. DDE, 12/10/53, EP 15:748 ("catastrophe"). 5. DDE-WSC, 2/9/54, CD 23:1431. 6. Clementine-WSC, 2/13/54, CD 23:1442. 7. Eden-WSC, 3/2/54, CD 23:1467 ("armaments"). 8. DDE-WSC, 3/2/54, CD 23:1468 ("friendly"). 9. WSC-DDE, 3/8/54, CD 23:1469–70 ("monster") 10. DDE-WSC, 3/19/54, EP 15:965 ("appalling"); DDE, press conference, 3/10/54. 11. "Preconditions," NYT, 12/9/53. 12. Richard Lovell, letter, *BMJ* 310 (June 10, 1995): 1537–38; Moran 241; Shuckburgh 156–57, Gilbert 8:964; *Daily Mirror*, 4/1/54, Gilbert 8:964 ("Decay"); Ruane 249–51. 13. Moran, 4/8/54, 258–59 ("relinquish"); DDE, press conference, 3/10/54; Ruane 245–47.

FORTY-FIVE: GOOD FOR THE GANDER

1. Cabinet, minutes, 2/3/54, Gilbert 8:946; "Controversy," NYT, 3/28/54. 2. MacArthur, interview, OH-538 21; Colville, 12/8/53, CD 23:1349; Watry 6. 3. DDE-Harriman, 10/20/51, Leebaert 326 ("exploiting"); DDE, 10/8/53, EL (online). 4. DDE, 12/10/53, EP 15:744 ("'ganging'"). 5. WSC-DDE, 12/19/53, CD 23.1367 ("acute"). 6. DDE-WSC, 12/21/53, CD 23:1370–71 ("Arab"); Allen W. Dulles, 12/21/53, AWD Series (box 5), EL. 7. WSC-DDE, 12/22/53, CD 23:1372 ("petty"). 8. Ruane and Jones 67. 9. DDE-Hazlett, 4/27/54, Newton 158. 10. NYT, 3/25/54; DDE, press conference, 4/7/54 ("dominos"); MacArthur, interview, OH-528 37; Nong 129. 11. Hagerty, 4/1/54, FRUS 13:1205; MacArthur, interview, OH-538 28–29 ("tail"). 12. DDE-Gruenther, 4/26/54, EP 15:1034 ("paternalism"): Robertson, interview, COHP 74. 13. JSDE, interview, 8/25/82, COHP 35 ("'white'"); Hagerty, 4/7/54, Hagerty Papers (box 1a), EL; Abel, interview, 12/10/70, COHP, 40. 14. DDE-JFD, telephone conversation, 4/3/54, FRUS 13:1231; Abel, interview, 12/10/70, COHP 14, 17; Adams, interview, JFDC 21; NSC, memorandum, 4/9/54, and NSC, memorandum, 4/6/54, Leebaert 414; Ruane and Jones 104. 15. DDE-WSC, 4/5/54, CD 23:1515 ("Thailand"). 16. WSC, broadcast, 1/20/40. 17. Moran, 4/28/54, 431 ("Cambodia"); Nixon, *Leaders*, 9; Nong 93. 18. WSC-DDE, 4/7/54, CD 20:1356 ("Indo-China"); JFD–State, 4/13/54, FRUS 13:1319-20; Leebaert 409; Dan 128, 130; Ruane and Jones 99–101; Ruane 255–58. 19. Radford-JFD, 4/27/54, FRUS 6:1030–31; WSC-Radford, minutes, 4/26/54, CD 23:1549–50 ("Anglia"); Ruane and Jones 74, 107–08, 116, 147–48; Ruane 251. 20. DDE-Hazlett, 4/27/54, EP 15:1044 ("morbid"); Leebaert 413. 21. Hagerty, 4/29/54, FRUS 13:1429; DDE-JFD, 4/23/54, EP 15:1030; Robertson, interview, COHP 76–77. 22. NSC, minutes, 4/29/54, FRUS 13:1440–41 ("veto"); Cutler-Smith, 4/30/54, FRUS 13:1446–47; Cutler,

memo, 5/3/54, FRUS 13:1462. 23. Shuckburgh, 5/2/54, 187 ("run"); DDE-WSC, 5/12/54, EP 1:1068–69 n. 3; WSC-DDE, 6/10/54, CD 23:1601; Ruane and Jones 127 ("feelings"); WSC-Eden, 5/28/54, CD 23:1588 ("friendship").

FORTY-SIX: FAMILY MATTERS

1. Hagerty, 6/22/54, Hagerty Papers (box 1), EL; Hagerty, 6/14/54 ("old"); DDE-WSC (4/26/54 draft), ACW Diary Series (box 4), EL; WSC-DDE, 4/22/54, CD 23:1546–47; DDE-WSC, 4/23/54, EP 15:1031; WSC-DDE, 6/10/54, CD 23:1602. 2. DDE, press conference, 6/16/54 ("friend"). 3. Young 266; Hagerty, 6/24/54 ("colonialism"). 4. Memo, 6/24/54, President's Personal File (box 960), EL. 5. NYT, 6/25/54 ("stooped"). 6. Colville, 6/25/54, CD 23:1625. 7. WSC, speech, CD 23:1624; NYT, 6/26/54 ("family"). 8. Colville, 6/25/54, *Fringes*, 691–92; Moran 278; Ruane 247; Young 266. 9. President's Appointments, 6/25/54, EL; NYT, 6/26/54. 10. Hagerty, 6/25/54, Hagerty Papers (box 1), EL; NYT, 6/26/54; JSDE, *Personal*, 232. 11. Note, 6/25/54, ACW Diary Series (box 2), EL; FRUS 6:1076, 1077; NYT, 6/26/54. 12. "Memorandum," 6/25/54, FRUS 6:1080–84. 13. Memorandum, 6/25/54, FRUS 6:1078; Itinerary, 6/25/54, Hagerty Papers (box 5), EL; NYT, 6/26/54 ("get up"). 14. Notes, 6/25/54, International Series (box 20), EL; Memorandum, 6/25/54, FRUS 6:1077–78; Lodge, memo, 6/26/54, FRUS 6:1107–09 ("'cottage'"). 15. Memorandum, 6/25/54, FRUS 6:1085–86 ("doom"); Schmuhl 234; Ruane 256. 16. Hagerty 6/26/54; Colville, 6/26/54, CD 23:1625–26 ("raging"). 17. Donovan, *Confidential*, 73. 18. ACW, 6/26/54, ACW Diary Series (box 2), EL and FRUS 6:1097–99 ("face"); Roberts 944. 19. Moran 599; Colville, 6/24/54; Ruane 268; Roberts 944. 20. Hagerty, 6/27/54, Hagerty Papers (box 1), EL ("conversation"). 21. President's Appointments, 6/27/54, ACW Diary Series (box 2), EL; JFD, memo, 6/27/54, International Series (box 20), EL, and FRUS 6:1111–12. 22. Hagerty, 6/27/54, FRUS 6:1111 ("obsessed"). 23. Hagerty 6/26/54 ("shouting"). 24. Hagerty, 6/28/54 ("10:30"); Colville, 6/28/54, CD 23:1631; Hagerty, interview, OH-91, EL 221–22. 25. Hagerty, 6/29/54, FRUS 6:1124. 26. Colville, 6/29/54, CD 23:1633 ("'Ike'"); Donovan, *Inside*, 74. 27. WSC-MDE, 6/30/54, CD 23:1640 ("pleasantest"); WSC-MDE, 7/9/54, CD 23:1670; Note, ACW Diary Series (box 2), EL. 28. C. D. Jackson, 5/20/53, C. D. Jackson Papers (box 68), EL ("kid"). 29. WSC, *Churchill by Himself*, 339 ("bull").

FORTY-SEVEN: GRASS UNDERFOOT

1. Colville, 7/2/54, CD 23:1641–43 ("Americanised"); Gilbert 8:1010. 2. Moran 610 ("gulf"). 3. WSC-Molotov (draft), 7/2/54, CD 23:1645 ("opinion"); Colville, 7/2/54, *Fringes*, 697–98. 4. Macmillan, 7/6/54 ("folly"); Colville, 7/2–4/54, CD 23:1643–44, 1649 ("unscrupulous"); WSC-DDE, 7/7/54, CD 23:1650. 5. Graebner 40; Moran, 7/5/54, 296. 6. WSC-DDE, 7/7/54, CD 23:1650. 7. DDE-WSC, 7/7/54, CD 23:1651 ("grass"). 8. EP 15:1167 nn. 5–6; Telephone call, 7/7/54, JFD Papers (box 10), EL ("stroke"). 9. WSC-DDE, 7/8/54, CD 23:1665 ("vexed"). 10. DDE-WSC, 7/8/54, CD 23:1667 ("vexed"). 11. WSC-DDE, 7/9/54, CD 23:1671 ("moonshine"). 12. DDE-WSC, 7/22/54, EP 15:1207–09 ("milestone"); EP 15:1210 n. 5. 13. Cabinet minutes, 7/26/54, CD 23:1711–12; WSC-Molotov, 7/26/54, CD 23:1713; Ruane 280–81; Young 284. 14. WSC-DDE, 8/8/54, CD 23:1724–25 ("parlay").

FORTY-EIGHT: WET WORK

1. WSC-DDE, 8/8/54, CD 23:1724–25 ("sceptical"). 2. Pawle 272 ("Indians"). 3. DDE-Gruenther, 11/30/54, EP 15:1413–14. 4. DDE, 12/20/53, EP 15:743 ("Philosophically"); Arthur Larson 101 ("canoe"). 5. CIA, "Guatemalan Procurement of Arms," 6/23/54, https://www.cia.gov/readingroom/docs/DOC_0000921353.pdf; Schlesinger and Kinzer 10–11, 148–52, 160–63; Leebaert 419–20. 6. Lucien Vandenbroucke, "'Confessions' of Allen Dulles," *Diplomatic History* 8, no. 4 (Fall 1984): 372–73 ("flag"); Schlesinger and Kinzer 170. 7. Hagerty, 6/18/54, Hagerty Papers (box 1), EL; Schlesinger and Kinzer 21–22, 172, 168–73, 177; Cullather 102–03. 8. Goodpaster, interview, 8/2/67, COHP 45 ("violence"); Schlesinger and Kinzer 177–78. 9. Brattestad 2–3. 10. Hagerty, 6/24/54, EL, Lucas 36 ("nose"); Schlesinger and Kinzer 181. 11. Dixon-F.O., 6/24/54, Brattestad 1,

40 ("independent"). 12. Ruane 263 ("Foster"); Moran 602 ("killed"). 13. Makins, interview, Lucas 23 ("intuitive"). 14. Robertson, interview, COHP 78 ("cards"). 15. Brattestad 44. 16. Hagerty, 6/26–28/54, Hagerty Papers (box 1a), EL ("turkey"); Eden, *Full Circle*, 136; Leebaert 423; Brattestad 39; Memorandum, 6/29 meeting, International Series (box 20), EL. 17. Colville, *Fringes*, 694 ("foolish"); Hagerty, FRUS 6:1100. 18. Moran 603 ("Guatemala"); Brattestad 48 ("pebble"); Lodge-JFD, 6/26/54, JFD Papers, Subject Series (box 11), EL; Colville, *Fringes*, 694; Kunz 47; Leebaert 424. 19. Eden, *Circle*, 138; Leebaert 424–25. 20. "Arbenz," NYT, 6/28/54. 21. Schlesinger and Kinzer 183 ("*sulfatos*"). 22. Schlesinger and Kinzer 184–85.

FORTY-NINE: ATOMIC BULLETS

1. Cabinet minutes, 7/7/54, CD 23:1655–56 ("weapons"); Macmillan, Diaries, 328. 2. Eden-WSC, 3/9/53, CD 23:903; Cutler, "Notes on Conference," 12/22/53, EL (online); Hughes 163. 3. "Chinese," NYT, 9/4/54; Williamson 110. 4. NSC, minutes, 9/9/54, FRUS 14:584; Radford–Charles Wilson, 9/11/54, FRUS 14:604; DDE-WSC, 3/29/55, EP 16:1640 ("doom"); "Formosa," NYT, 9/8/54; Gaddis 103. 5. EP 15:1301 n. 1; NSC, minutes, 9/12/54, FRUS 14:614–23; Lemnitzer, interview, 11/21/72, COHP 8–9; Leebaert 436. 6. WSC-Eden, 10/10/54, CD 23:1803; WSC-DDE, 12/7/54, CD 23:1848; DDE-WSC, 12/14/54, EP 15:1444; WSC-DDE, 2/15/55, CD 23:1907–09 ("step"); Cabinet, minutes, 2/15/55, CD 23:1905–06; Williamson 110–11. 7. DDE-WSC, 2/18/55, EP 16:1574–76 ("distresses"). 8. DDE, press conference, 3/16/55, American Presidency Project, CD 23:903 ("bullet," "hysterical"); JSDE, interview, 8/25/82, COHP 15. 9. DDE-WSC, 3/29/55, EP 16:1640–42 ("1930"). 10. WSC-Eden, 2/19/55, CD 23:1920 ("tiger").

FIFTY: "NEVER BE SEPARATED FROM THE AMERICANS"

1. Graebner 18–19 ("patter"). 2. Gilbert 8:1036; "Britain," NYT, 10/31/56; Kunz 35; Waterhouse, speech, 7/20/54, CD 23:1715; "Churchill," NYT, 7/30/54; Moran 303; Doran 62; Kunz 46; Roberts 945 ("defended"). 3. Eden-WSC, 8/10/54, CD 23:1728; Shuckburgh, 3/11/54, 4/21/54, 167, Gilbert 8:971, CD 23:1472; Colville, 3/29/55, *Fringes*, 704; WSC-Baruch, 8/29/54, CD 23:1768. 4. "Lag," NYT, 7/11/54; Ruane 285. 5. Moran 591 ("tired"). 6. WSC, speech, 11/30/54, CD 23:1827; London *Times*, 6/15/54 (coalition); Colville, *Fringes*, 705; Roberts 946; Hermiston 334. 7. WSC-DDE, 11/28/54, CD 23:1824; WSC-DDE, 11/19/54, Boyle, 178–79 ("privilege"). 8. DDE-Hazlett, 12/7/54, EP 15:1437 ("greatness"); JSDE, *Personal*, 314–15. 9. Luce 91 ("canvas"). 10. DDE-WSC, 12/14/54, EP 15:1445; DDE-WSC, 1/25/55, International Series (box 18), EL. 11. WSC-DDE, 1/11/55, CD 23:1866, and 2/5–7/55, EP 16:1525 n. 10 ("results"). 12. Eden, 1/6/55, CD 23:1865; Macmillan, 2/17/55, Gilbert 8:1095. 13. Roberts 947. 14. Moran 673 ("'royal'"). 15. Ismay-DDE, 6/8/59, Name Series (box 19), EL. 16. Macmillan, 2/25/55 and 2/26/55, Gilbert 8:1097. 17. Makins-Eden, 3/10/54, CD 23:1939 ("plans"); Colville, 3/29/55, *Fringes*, 705–06; DDE-Coty, 3/11/55 EP 16:1613, JFD Papers, White House Memoranda Series (box 3), EL; EP 16:1614 n. 6. 18. Colville, 3/29/55, *Fringes*, 704–07, Gilbert 8:1103 ("bets"). 19. WSC-Eden, 3/12/55, CD 23:1944 ("time-tables"). 20. Macmillan, 3/12/55, *Diaries*, 404 ("Dorneywood"). 21. Macmillan, 3/16/55, *Diaries*, 407 ("disappointment"); WSC-Clementine, 3/15/55, Gilbert 8:1110; Roberts 949; Young 311–12. 22. WSC-DDE, ACW Diary Series (box 10), EL ("would be"), and 3/18/55, CD 23:1960 ("portrait"). 23. DDE-WSC, 3/22/55, EP 16:1626–28 ("'zipper'"). 24. WSC-DDE, dated April 1955, CD 23:1959 ("resign"). 25. Colville, 4/5/55, CD 23:1982 ("Puddle-duck"). 26. Colville, recollection, CD 23:1979. 27. Colville, *Fringes*, 708, ("believe"); Colville, recollection, CD 23:1980; Montague Browne, interview, CAC, 488. 28. Gilbert 8:1123, Roberts 949 ("separated"). 29. "Churchill," NYT, 4/7/55.

PART THREE: WATERLOO SUNSET

1. DDE, remarks, 1/14/59, presidency.ucsb.edu ("great"). 2. Makins, interview, CAC, 278 ("distinction").

FIFTY-ONE: RELIEF AND DENUDATION

1. Macmillan, 4/6/55, *Diaries*, 426 ("Englishman"). 2. Eden-DDE, 5/6/55, FRUS 5:164; EP 16:1698 n. 1; Macmillan, 5/5/55 ("top"). 3. WSC-Eden, 5/31/55, CD 23:2012 ("Krushev"). 4. Henry Luce, notes, 4/14–17/55, C. D. Jackson Papers (box 41), EL ("molecules"); EP 16:1706 n. 1. 5. Hughes 167–68 ("gape"). 6. ACW-DDE, 7/14/55, Donovan, *Confidential*, 85 ("'boy'"). 7. DDE, *Mandate*, 530 ("disappointment"); DDE-WSC, 7/15/55, EP 16:1782. 8. WSC-DDE, 7/18/55, International Series (box 20), EL ("formidable"). 9. Goodpaster, interview, 9/8/67, COHP, 125–26, 130–31. 10. "Four-Power," *Le Figaro*, 7/25/55 ("Nothing"). 11. Roberts 953 ("exercise"). 12. Bradley-DDE, 9/19/55, DDE Pres. Papers, Confidential File (box 104), EL; Roberts 953. 13. DDE-WSC, 3/29/56, EP 16:2099–2100 ("miss"). 14. WSC-DDE, 4/16/55, International Series (box 20), EL ("friendship"). 15. DDE-WSC, 4/27/56, EP 16:2138–29.

FIFTY-TWO: "WE DON'T NEED THE AMERICANS FOR THIS"

1. Lucas 56. 2. Aldrich, interview, 7/15/64, JFDC 3; Lucas 54; Owen 393; Kunz 62–63. 3. Bowie, interview, JFDC, 24; Robertson, "JFD and the Far East," JFDC Oral History Collection, 73 ("busboy"). 4. Call notes, 8/31/54, JFD Papers, Telephone Conversations (box 2), EL; Lucas 35 ("sunlamp"); WSC-Clementine, 8/10/55, Soames 595. 5. Aldrich, interview, 7/15/64, JFDC 6. 6. Robertson, interview, COHP 78. 7. Kunz 40; Humphrey, interview, JFDC 23; "Egypt," NYT, 7/18/56. 8. Black, interview, JFDC, 2–5, 10; Humphrey and Hoover, interview, JFDC, 23–24, 35; Makins, interview, JFDC, 5–6; Armstrong, interview, 9/10/65, JFDC, 15–16; Skaggs 45–46; NYT, 9/28/55; Goodpaster, interview, 8/2/67, COHP 80; DDE, 8/8/56, EP 17:2239–40; Eleanor Dulles, interview, 6/18/62, COHP 725; Hoover, memo, 7/19/56, FRUS 15:861–62; Bowie, interview, JFDC, 30–31; DDE, 2/8/56, EP 16:2008–09; DOS, memorandum, 1/31/56, FRUS 15:110; Kunz 39, 44–45, 59, 68; Doran 106; Leebaert 449; Press conference, 5/23/56 ("divorce"). 9. JFD-DDE, 3/28/56, FRUS 15:420–21 and NARA (declassified); Doran 159–60; Lucas 111, 113. 10. Black, interview, JFDC 14–15; Allen Dulles, interview, JFDC 16, 64–65, 70; "Text," NYT, 7/20/56; Humphrey and Hoover, interview, JFDC 33 (Hoover); Rountree, memo, 7/19/56, FRUS 15:867–72; Kunz 71; Lucas 135. 11. Black, interview, JFDC 15 ("paper"); NSA, "Suez Crisis: A Brief Comint History (1988)," 8; DDE, 8/8/56, EP 17:2239–40; Eleanor Dulles, interview, 4/5/78, COHP 82; Goodpaster, interview, 8/2/67, COHP 79. 12. Childs, interview, JFDC, 30 ("kick"). 13. "Egypt Takes," NYT, 7/27/56 ("120,000"); Lucas 139. 14. "Nasser's Revenge," *Time*, 8/8/56; "Egypt," NYT, 7/28/56; U.S. consul–DOS, 7/26/56, Lucas 139 ("Savior"). 15. Aldrich, interview, JFDC 17; Aldrich-JFD, 7/27/56, FRUS 16:3–5; Lucas 142–43; Horne 403, 405 ("Mussolini"). 16. Horne 403; Kunz 79. 17. Bowie, interview, JFDC, 23–24, 27–28; Montague Browne 209. 18. Nutting, BBC Radio interview, 10/28/06 ("murdered"); Nutting 34, ("destroyed"); Watry 112–13. 19. Montague Browne 209. 20. WSC-Clementine, 7/30/56, CD 23:2119–20 ("vigour"). 21. Roberts 956 ("hardest-hearted"). 22. Moran, 8/1/56, 702 ("swine"); Roberts 955. 23. Macmillan, 8/5/56, *Diaries*, 584; Horne 405; Montague Browne 209; WSC-Eden, 8/6/56, CD 23:2122–23. 24. Montague Browne 209 ("perch"); Macmillan, 8/7/56, *Diaries*, 585; Bohlen, interview, JFDC 271; Moran, 8/16/56, 703–05; Gilbert 8:1208. 25. Eden-WSC, 8/17/56, CD 23:2128 ("firmly"); WSC-Reeves, 9/4/56, CD 23:2129; Lucas 188–89. 26. "Nasser's Revenge," *Time*, 8/8/56; JFD, memorandum, 8/30/56, FRUS 16 328–39; Goodpaster, interview, 8/2/67, COHP 81. 27. Goodpaster, interview, 8/2/67, COHP 82. 28. Murphy, memo, 8/1/56, FRUS 16:95–96 ("disgorge"). 29. Makins, interview, JFDC, 3 ("listen"); Aldrich, interview, JFDC 18. 30. Bowie, interview, JFDC 34 ("cat"). 31. DDE-Eden, 9/2/56, EP 17:2263–64 ("force"). 32. Eden-DDE, 9/6/56, FRUS 16:401–02 ("mercy"). 33. Memorandum of call, 9/7/56, FRUS 16:403; Notes, 9/7/56, ACW Diary Series (box 8), EL. 34. Goodpaster, interview, 8/2/67, COHP 81; Lucas 154–55, 166; Murphy, interview, JFDC 41. 35. Eden-WSC, 9/21/56, CD 23:2130. 36. Makins, interview, CAC, 284. 37. DDE, broadcast, 10/12/56, American Presidency

Project; Thomas 216 ("thanksgiving"). 38. DDE, "Memorandum," 10/15/56, ACW Diary Series (box 8), EL; Brugioni 174; NARA, "CIA U-2 Missions Flown—1956–66—Chronological," 4/1/69, in "History of the Office of Special Activities from Inception to 1969"; Radford, interview, JFDC 62; Santucci 167, 186; NSA, "Suez," 17; DDE, *Waging*, 56, 73 ("uneasy"). 39. JFD, memo, 10/21/56, FRUS 16:764–65; Doran 190. 40. Louis and Owen 119–20; Note, FRUS 16:776–77; Nichols 190; Lucas 244–45. 41. Armstrong-JFD, 12/5/56, FRUS 16:1265; Lucas 196, 254. 42. DDE, "Memorandum," 10/15/56, ACW Diary Series (box 8), EL; CIA, memo, 10/26/56, FRUS 16:787–88 (unconfirmed); Radford, interview, JFDC 63; Nichols 192. 43. JFD-Aldrich, 10/26/56, FRUS 16:788 ("disturbed"); William Macomber, interview, JFDC 73; Murphy, interview, JFDC 39; DDE, *Waging*, 75 ("dark"). 44. NARA, "CIA U-2 Missions Flown—1956–66," 4/1/69, in "History of the Office of Special Activities from Inception to 1969"; Santucci 175–79; Bissell, interview, 9/7/66, JFDC 26; Brugioni 182. 45. NSA, "Suez," 19 ("taped"). 46. Armstrong, interview, 9/10/65, JFDC, 18–19, 22–23 ("wheel"). 47. Notes, 10/28/56, ACW Diary Series (box 8), EL ("conscience"). 48. Nichols 193; Hughes 212 ("egging"). 49. DDE, interview, 7/28/64, JFDC 38. 50. Aldrich-DOS, 10/29/56, FRUS 16:818 ("unwilling"). 51. Hughes 212–13 ("stupid"); Nichols 198 ("490"). 52. Norman Brook–WSC, 10/4/56, Gilbert 8:1213; Montague Browne 211.

FIFTY-THREE: DEATH OR GLORY

1. DDE, *Waging*, 72 ("knifed"); Bucknam 2–3. 2. Bissell, interview, 9/7/66, JFDC 24; Goodpaster, interview, 1/16/78, EL 110; NARA, "CIA U-2 Missions Flown—1956–66—Chronological," 4/1/69, in "History of the Office of Special Activities from Inception to 1969"; Notes, 10/30/56, ACW Diary Series (box 8), EL. 3. Goodpaster, memorandum, 10/29/56, 7:15 p.m., FRUS 16:833–35; Nichols 203. 4. Goodpaster, interview, 9/8/67, COHP, 136 ("commitment"); Bucknam 4; DDE, *Waging*, 73. 5. "Pact," London *Times*, 11/3/54. 6. Goodpaster, memorandum, 10/29/56, 7:15 p.m., FRUS 16:833-35; Wilcox, interview, 4/3/72, COHP 38; Lucas 258 ("throw"). 7. JCS-commanders, 10/29/56, FRUS 16:845; Goodpaster, memorandum, 10/29/56, 8:15 p.m., FRUS 16:839–40; DDE, *Waging*, 73 (doors); "President's," London *Times*, 10/30/56. 8. "Two Powers," NYT, 10/31/56. 9. JFD, memorandum of phone conversation, 10/29/56, EL (JFD Papers, General Telephone Conversations), and Editorial Note, FRUS 16:840–41 ("snarling"). 10. DDE-Eden, 10/30/56, EP 17:2340–41 ("friend"). 11. Goodpaster, memorandum, 10/30/56, FRUS 16:851–52 ("mid-Victorian"). 12. Eden-DDE, 10/30/56, FRUS 16:856–57 ("destruction"). 13. Radford, interview, JFDC 65. 14. DDE-Eden, 10/30/56 (draft), FRUS 16:874–75 and nn. 1–2; DDE-Eden, draft, Ann Whitman Series, Dulles-Herter box 5, October 1956 (1), EL, in Lucas 265–66 ("pray"). 15. "Grave," London *Times*, 10/31/56; "Eden's," NYT, 10/31/56 ("compliance"); Aldrich, interview, JFDC 22–23. 16. Aldrich, "Suez Crisis." 17. White House, memorandum, 10/30/56, 2:17 p.m., FRUS 16:863 ("crude"); Adams, interview, 8/15/64, JFDC 29. 18. JSDE, interview, 8/25/82, COHP 43; Hughes 136–37 ("stupidity"). 19. DDE–Eden and Mollet, 10/30/56, FRUS 16:867 and n. 2; White House memo, 10/30/56, 4:25 p.m., FRUS 16:873–74; Aldrich, interview, JFDC, 23; Nichols 221. 20. Ministry of Defence Information Room Record, 11/1–2/56, 0200, CAC. 21. "Britain, France Move," NYT, 10/31/56; "R.A.F. and Navy," NYT, 11/1/56; Bucknam 3. 22. Radford, interview, JFDC 66 ("help"); Louis and Owen 119–21. 23. DDE, speech, 10/31/56, American Presidency Project online ("error"); "Speech," NYT, 11/1/56; Hughes, interview, JFDC 32; Notes, 10/31/56, ACW Diary Series (box 8), EL; DDE-Hazlett, 11/2/56, FRUS 16:944–45; Hughes, *Ordeal*, 220–21. 24. NSC, minutes, 11/1/56, FRUS 16:905–15 ("slipped"). 25. DDE, interview, 7/28/64, OH-14, EL, Lucas 270 ("twenty-four"); Goodpaster, interview, Lucas 270 ("waiting"). 26. DDE–Henry Miller, 5/5/44, EP 3:1848–49; Butcher 539; Jordan, *Brothers*, 540; DDE-GCM, 9/6/43. 27. Nichols 211 ("citizenship"). 28. Memorandum, FRUS 16:932–33; "Text," NYT, 11/2/56; "Remarks," NYT, 11/2/56; Luce, interview, JFDC 14–15; "U.S. Move," NYT, 11/2/56; "Eden Defies," NYT, 11/3/56; Leebaert 475; U.N. Resolution 1000, 11/5/56. 29. Burke, interview, JFDC, 14; "Britons," NYT, 11/1/56; Nutting 128–29 ("deplorable"). 30. "Britons," NYT, 11/2/56; "'Eden Must Go,'" *News Chronicle*, 11/5/56; "Throng," NYT, 11/5/56. 31. "Resignation," London *Times*, 11/5/56; "Nutting," NYT, 11/4/56; Lucas 267. 32. Moran 412. 33. "Churchill's," NYT, 10/14/56; Montague Browne, interview, WCHL Collection, CAC, 5; Soames, interview, CAC, 72. "Churchills," NYT, 11/29/56; "Eden," NYT, 11/1/56; Montague

Browne 211–12; "Text," NYT, 11/4/56 ("flickered"); "Churchill," NYT, 11/4/56. 34. Eden-WSC, 11/5/56, CD 23:2144 ("thank"); WSC-Eden, 11/5/56, Gilbert 8:1221 ("glad"). 35. "Summary of Developments," 11/1/56, DDE Pres. Papers International Series (box 47), EL; NYT, 11/3/56; Nutting 133; Brugioni 187. 36. DOS, memorandum, 11/4/56, FRUS 16:974–75; "Airfields," NYT, 11/2/56; "Mideast Oil," NYT, 11/4/56. 37. "Paratroopers," NYT, 11/6/56; "Crackling Hell," NYT, 11/7/56; Kyle 444–45. 38. Kyle 449–50; Tunzelmann 391–92. 39. Tunzelmann 392 ("perfectly"); Kyle 452. 40. "Paratroopers," NYT, 11/6/56; "Landing," NYT, 11/6/56; "Invaders," NYT, 11/7/56; Tunzelmann 395; Kyle 455. 41. "Cease-Fire," London *Times*, 11/7/56 ("*coup*"). 42. "Moscow," NYT, 11/6/56. 43. "Texts," NYT, 11/6/56 ("rocket"); "Moscow," NYT 11/6/56. 44. Nichols 225, 239. 45. Bohlen-DOS, 11/5/56, FRUS 16:995; Goodpaster, memo, 11/5/56, FRUS 16:1000–1001 ("Hitler's"). 46. Hughes 223 ("bucket"). 47. Dillon-DOS, 11/1/56, FRUS 16:901, 919–21; Brugioni 187 ("stupid"). 48. DOS, memo, 11/6/56, FRUS 16:1023–24; Goodpaster, memo, 11/6/56, FRUS 16:1001, 1015 ("alert," "war"); "Gruenther," NYT, 11/14/56; JSDE, interview, 8/25/82, COHP 34; NARA, "CIA U-2 Missions Flown"; Goodpaster, interview, 1/16/78, EL 112; Prochnow, interview, JFDC 33–34. 49. JCS, memorandum, 11/6/56, FRUS 16:1036–37. 50. Eden-DDE, 11/5/56, FRUS, 16:985–86 ("vision"). 51. Gwendolyn Carter, "Expanding Commonwealth," *Foreign Affairs* (October 1956); Kunz 13–14. 52. NYT, 11/26/56; "100," NYT, 11/28/56; Prochnow, interview, JFDC 42; Kunz 136–37; Tunzelmann 407. 53. Goodpaster, "Telephone Conversation," 11/7/56, 10:27 a.m., FRUS 16:1045–46; Memo, 11/7/56, FRUS 16:1051–52; DDE-Eden, 11/7/56, FRUS 16:1055; Kunz 137. 54. Eden, *Full Circle*, 556; Lloyd, *Suez*, 210–11; Kunz 131–33. 55. White House, news release, 11/5/56, FRUS 16:1007–08; Owen 400; Eamon Hamilton 16. 56. Lucas 280 ("Churchill"). 57. Shuckburgh 362 ("A.E."); William Clark, 11/4/56 ("mad").

FIFTY-FOUR: THE OLD MAN AND THE SEA

1. Court Jeweler, "State Opening of Parliament Tiaras: 1950s and 1960s," thecourtjeweller.com/2020/10/state-opening-of-parliament-tiaras.html; *Daily Express*, "A Retrospect of the State Opening of Parliament," 7/2/16, express.co.uk/pictures/royal/6197/The-Queen-State-Opening-of-Parliament-pictures; Hansard 11/6/56 columns 1–4 ("grave"). 2. "Eden Backs," NYT, 11/7/56 ("Horse Guards"). 3. Aldrich-Hoover, 11/6/56, FRUS 16:1015; Aldrich, interview, JFDC 29; "Eden," NYT, 11/7/56; "Keightley," NYT, 6/19/74; "Acclaims," NYT, 11/7/56. 4. "Eden," NYT, 11/7/56 ("think"); Tunzelmann 915. 5. Telephone transcript, 11/6/56, FRUS 16:1025–27 ("damn"); DDE-Eden, 11/6/56, FRUS 16:1028; ACW Notes, 11/7/56, ACW Diary Series (box 8), EL. 6. Notes, 11/7/56, ACW Diary Series (box 8), EL; Eden-DDE, 11/7/56, FRUS 16:1041. 7. NSC minutes, 11/15/56, FRUS 16:1127–28. 8. NSC minutes, 11/8/56, 11/15/56, FRUS 16:1071, 1128; DOS-Wadsworth, 11/18–26/56, FRUS 16:1148–1202; Kunz 141. 9. Aldrich-Hoover, 11/19/56, FRUS 16:1150–51 ("prestige"). 10. Kunz 145. 11. Aldrich-Hoover, 11/19/56, FRUS 16:1150–51; "Eden, Looking Pale," NYT 11/25/56. 12. Charlwood 233; NYT, 12/9/56, 12/16/56.

FIFTY-FIVE: "DESPICABLE CONDUCT"

1. Telephone call, 11/20/56, International Series (box 17), EL; "Eden's Exit," NYT, 12/5/56; "Eden Retirement," NYT, 12/8/56; Charlwood 233; Eden-WSC, 1/9/57, CD 23:2151; Gilbert 8:1227. 2. Kunz 156. 3. DDE-Aldrich, telephone transcript, 11/20/56, International Series (box 17), EL; Minutes, 11/20/56, FRUS 16:1166–67; Notes, 11/20/56, ACW Diary Series (box 8), EL; Kunz 151–52; Radford, interview, JFDC 68; Nichols 273. 4. Kunz 159 (vacuum). 5. JFD, memo, 12/12/56, FRUS 27:677 ("felt"). 6. "Britain," NYT, 12/9/56 ("fiasco"); Aldrich, interview, JFDC 50–51 ("Frenchman"). 7. Tunzelmann 424 ("tail"). 8. JFD, memo, 11/27/56, FRUS 16:1202–03; Hoover-DDE, 11/26/56, Name Series (box 19), EL; "Landlord," NYT, 12/12/56; Aldrich-State, 12/8/56, FRUS 27:673. 9. Lucas 314 ("anti-American"); "100," NYT, 11/28/56 ("anti-Americanism"); "Anti-American," NYT, 12/2/56; Aldrich-DOS, 12/8/56, FRUS 27:676; Hoover-DDE, 11/26/56, Name Series (box 19), EL; London *Times*, 11/27/56 and 11/29/56. 10. JFD, memo, 11/27/56, FRUS 16:1202 ("deserted"). 11. Bissell, interview, 9/7/66, JFDC 26–27; Murphy, interview, JFDC 44. 12. Burke, interview, JFDC 20 ("hell"). 13. Lucas 307 ("mistake").

FIFTY-SIX: OIL ON CANVAS

1. "Churchill," NYT, 1/10/57. 2. Montague Browne 213. 3. Moran, 11/26/56, 416; Montague Browne, interview, CAC, 504; Montague Browne 213. 4. Colville, 11/29/56, *Fringes*, 721 ("ill-conceived"); Cunningham, 9/21/44, CD 20:1431; Montague Browne, interview, 7/17/81, CAC, 502 ("squaring"). 5. Moran, 12/6/56, 416, 710; Montague Browne, interview, CAC, 504; Montague Browne 213. 6. Aldrich, interview, 10/16/72, COHP 18 ("running"). 7. Montague Browne, interview, CAC, 490 ("disappointed"). 8. Montague Browne 213. 9. Clementine–Moran, 2/15/65, Gilbert 8:1225 ("fences"); London *Times*, 1/10/57. 10. Colville, "Reminiscences," 6/8/65, Gilbert 8:1222 ("enemy"); Montague Browne 213; WSC-DDE, 11/23/56, CD 23:2144–45 ("Anglo-American"); Gilbert 8:1222. 11. DDE-WSC, 11/27/56, EP 17:2412–24 ("saddens"). 12. Montague Browne 214 ("vexed"); Queen Elizabeth–WSC, 11/30/56, Gilbert 8:1223 ("speedily"). 13. James Lees-Milne, 9/15/57, Gilbert 8:1250–51 and Roberts 955 ("Almighty"). 14. DDE, interview, 7/31/68, 1968 Principal File (box 10), EL. 15. DDE-WSC, EP 18:112; DDE-Hall, 3/25/57, EP 18:111–12 and PPF (box 960), EL ("feels"). 16. DDE-Redmond, 10/30/57, EP 18:525 n. 1, 526; DDE-Rockefeller, 10/31/57, EP 18:531. 17. WSC-DDE, 12/16/57, CD 23:2194; WSC-Beaverbrook, 12/16/57, CD 23:2195; WSC–Franklin Murphy, 1/22/58, International Series (box 20), EL; DDE-WSC, 12/18/57, EP 18:621 ("paintings"). 18. EP 18:558 n. 2; DDE-WSC, 11/9/57, EP 18:557–58. 19. DDE-WSC, 1/23/58, 2/5/58, 2/21/58, 3/28/58, International Series (box 20), EL; Gilbert 8:1260–61. 20. WSC-DDE, 3/58, CD 23:2209 ("setback"); DDE-WSC, 3/28/58, International Series (box 40), EL. 21. WSC, notes, undated, Gilbert 8:1271–72 ("foolish"). 22. WSC-Macmillan, 7/15/58, Gilbert 8:1272 ("worth").

FIFTY-SEVEN: "AFTER A BRIEF SILENCE, REVEILLE"

1. CD 23:2281. 2. Roberts 956–58. 3. DDE, remarks, 1/14/59, presidency.ucsb.edu ("great"). 4. DDE-WSC, 1/23/58, 2/5/58, 3/28/59, 1/20/59, International Series (box 20), EL ("fun"). 5. DDE-Ismay, 1/14/59, Name Series (box 19), EL ("'greats'"). 6. JSDE, interview, CAC, 1005–06 ("teenager"). 7. Secret Service Report, 5/11/59, International Series (box 20), EL; Memo to ACW, 9/15/55, Personal File (box 942), EL; Montague Browne 261; Appointments, 5/4/59, ACW Diary Series (box 41), EL; "Briton," NYT, 5/5/59 ("friend"). 8. Aurand, interview, 5/1/67, COHP, 62; Schmuhl 250; WSC-Baruch, 4/23/59, CD 23:2245; Brown-Gordon-Lennox, 4/23/59, Gilbert 8:1292. 9. "Information," 4/25/59, International Series (box 20), EL ("champagne"); Mamie Eisenhower, interview, OH-12 171 ("gold"). 10. JSDE, *Personal*, 232 ("shock"); "Professor Robb on Churchill," CAC; Roberts 958; Schmuhl 253. 11. Barbara Eisenhower, interview, OH-492, EL 115 ("prime"); JSDE, interview, CAC, 1009; JSDE, *Ike*, 214; Montague Browne 263. 12. Telephone Notes, and President's Appointments, both 5/5/59, ACW Diary Series (box 41), EL; Heaton, interview, JFDC 11; "Churchill," NYT, 5/6/59 ("painted"). 13. Secret Service Report, 5/11/59, International Series (box 20), EL; John R. Pierce, ed., *Walter Reed Army Medical Center Centennial* (Borden Institute 2009), 105 (Ward 8). 14. Montague Browne–Caccia, 5/21/59, CD 23:2249 ("SHAPE"). 15. "Montgomery," NYT, 4/29/59 ("fit"); "Air," London *Times*, 4/29/59; Gilbert 8:1294. 16. Montague Browne–Caccia, 5/21/59, CD 23:2249; Montague Browne, interview, CAC, 504–05 ("thin-skinned"); DDE-Guingand, 6/29/59, EP 20:1548. 17. JSDE, interview, CAC, 1010–11. 18. President's Appointments, 5/6/59, ACW Diary Series (box 41), EL; DDE/WSC, remarks, 5/6/59, International Series (box 40), EL ("brigadier"). 19. JSDE, *Ike*, 179 ("foibles"). 20. DDE-Ismay, 1/25/58, EP 18:689 ("idiosyncrasies"). 21. JSDE, interview, CAC, 1011 ("canny"). 22. JSDE, *Personal*, 233. 23. Aurand, interview, 5/1/67, COHP 62–63 ("Beautiful"); DDE, "Churchill and Marshall," 11/17/66, EL 101. 24. Montague Browne 263. 25. Nevins, interview, 4/23/70, COHP 37–38 ("abstemious"). 26. EP 20:1495 n. 1 ("life"); "Eisenhower and Churchill," NYT, 5/7/59. 27. Secret Service Report, 5/11/59, International Series (box 40), EL; DDE-WSC, 5/26/59, International Series (box 20), EL; Gilbert 8:1296 ("pigs"). 28. DDE-WSC, 11/17/60, Gilbert 8:1316 ("accident"). 29. WSC-DDE, 12/2/60, International Series (box 20), EL ("burdensome"). 30. DDE-WSC, 6/6/62 and WSC-DDE, 6/23/62, 1962 Principal File (box 1), EL ("unpublished"). 31. JSDE, interview, "General Ike," youtube.com/watch?v=NJPNA7wGuXA&t=3363s ("fond"); "President," NYT, 9/2/59. 32. Montague Browne, interview, 7/14/87, Gilbert 8:1322; Hansard, 11/30/61, 650:608–09; Roberts 958–59. 33. Gilbert 8:1318.

34. Roberts 960; Gilbert 8:1335; Jenkins 911. 35. Seddon, "Personal Note," Gilbert 8:1336 ("pawed"). 36. "Eisenhower," London *Times*, 8/11/62, 8/16/62; DDE, "Marshall and Churchill," 11/17/66, EL 103 ("helpless"); "Eisenhower," NYT, 8/11/62 ("Winston"); Macmillan, 7/20/62, Gilbert 8:1337. 37. "Excerpts," NYT, 2/16/62 ("Civilization"). 38. DDE-WSC, 4/15/63, 1963 Principal File (box 40), EL; DDE-Ismay, 6/25/64, 1964 Principal File (box 40), EL; DDE–J.F. Kennedy, 4/6/63, 1963 Principal File (box 40). 39. DDE-Ismay, 6/25/64, 1964 Principal File (box 40), EL ("gallant"); DDE, "Marshall and Churchill," 11/17/66, EL 99 ("partners"); Manchester and Reid 1051. 40. Bonham Carter–Gilbert, 2/28/63. 41. Ismay-DDE, 6/18/64, 1964 Principal File (box 40), EL; Pamela Harriman, interview, CAC, 1432 ("depart"). 42. Pamela Harriman, interview, CAC, 1432 ("coolie"). 43. Roberts 961 ("bored"); Vale and Scadding 428. 44. Schmuhl 247. 45. DDE, interview, 8/5/65, 1965 Principal File (box 2), EL ("wonderful"). 46. Roberts 962–63; Reynolds 528. 47. Itinerary, 1965 Principal File (box 16), EL; "Oppose," NYT, 1/26/65; Humes 5–6. 48. "Basil King," *Marlborough News*, 2/3/2015 (online). 49. "Text," NYT, 3/31/65 ("flowered").

INDEX

Note: Italicized page numbers indicate material in photographs or illustrations.

ABOUT THE AUTHOR

Jonathan W. Jordan is a historian and an award-winning author of five books, including the *New York Times* bestseller *Brothers, Rivals, Victors: Eisenhower, Patton, Bradley, and the Partnership That Drove the Allied Conquest in Europe*. He is a regular book critic for *The Wall Street Journal* and the author of nearly two dozen articles appearing in *MHQ: The Quarterly Journal of Military History*, *World War II* magazine, *Military History*, and *World War II History* magazine. He has made numerous live, televised, podcast, and radio appearances. Jon lives with his family in the Atlanta area.